A Comprehensive
Manchu-English Dictionary

Harvard-Yenching Institute Monograph Series 85

A Comprehensive
Manchu-English Dictionary

Jerry Norman

with the assistance of Keith Dede and David Prager Branner

Published by the Harvard University Asia Center

and distributed by Harvard University Press

Cambridge (Massachusetts) and London, 2013

Printed in the United States of America

The Harvard-Yenching Institute, founded in 1928 and headquartered at Harvard University, is a foundation dedicated to the advancement of higher education in the humanities and social sciences in East and Southeast Asia. The Institute supports advanced research at Harvard by faculty members of certain Asian universities and doctoral studies at Harvard and other universities by junior faculty at the same universities. It also supports East Asian studies at Harvard through contributions to the Harvard-Yenching Library and publication of the *Harvard Journal of Asiatic Studies* and books on premodern East Asian history and literature.

Library of Congress Cataloging-in-Publication Data

Norman, Jerry, 1936–2012.

A comprehensive Manchu-English dictionary / Jerry Norman ; with the assistance of Keith Dede and David Prager Branner.

p. cm. — (Harvard-Yenching Institute Monograph Series; 85)

ISBN 978-0-674-07213-8 (alk. paper)

1. Manchu language–Dictionaries–English. I. Dede, Keith. II. Branner, David Prager. III. Title.

PL477.N65 2013

494'.1–dc23

2012028386

∞ Printed on acid-free paper

Last figure below indicates year of this printing

23 22 21 20 19 18 17 16 15 14 13

Contents

Foreword

It is a distinct privilege for the Harvard University Asia Center to issue Jerry Norman's *Comprehensive Manchu-English Dictionary*, a revision of the author's *A Concise Manchu-English Lexicon*, originally published by the University of Washington Press in 1978. Its appearance, the result of years of patient effort, is a major event in the field of Manjuristics and will be welcomed by the growing number of scholars and students pursuing Manchu studies. I am pleased to be able to herald its arrival.

For over thirty years, the Norman *Lexicon* has been the standard reference work for all English-speaking scholars and students, an invaluable guide for anyone seeking to unlock the secrets held in the documents written in the Manchu language. While it is primarily based on previous Qing-era dictionaries, the *Lexicon* is distinguished by the contributions of Mr. Guang Lu, a speaker of Sibe who played the role of native informant when Professor Norman prepared the first Taiwan edition of the dictionary in the 1960s. Those contributions are present also in this revised *Dictionary*, along with a substantial number of new and expanded entries — about one-third more than the *Lexicon* — based on extensive reading of original materials of all sorts by the author. His inclusion of detailed notes on Manchu script and pronunciation is another significant enhancement of the older work.

From the very beginning of my studies with our common teacher, James Bosson, I was alerted to the fact that Professor Norman was preparing a revised version of the *Lexicon*. Anyone who had the pleasure of a personal acquaintance with the author knows that, possessing the qualities of a true *junzi*, he warmly welcomed all contributions and suggestions for improvement. Now, at last, that revision is complete, and will take its place alongside the original on bookshelves in studies and libraries around the world.

It fills me with sadness to have to note that Professor Norman passed away as this dictionary was going to press, and he did not live to see the final result of his painstaking labor, a new "Norman." For, like other lexicographical classics — "Larousse," "Liddell and Scott," "Nelson," "Mathews," and "Redhouse" — in this case, too, the author's surname stands, immortally, for the work.

erei jalin gingguleme arahangge

Mark C. Elliott
Harvard University

Editor's Preface

Jerry Lee Norman (1936–2012) was born to Okies — Depression-era refugees from the Dust Bowl of Oklahoma, who settled down as farm workers in California. He was fascinated with language from childhood. Denied permission to study Latin in school, he taught himself using an old textbook, and soon knew so much that his school asked him to teach other students. After a stint studying Chinese in the Army Language school, and a year preparing for the priesthood in a Benedictine priory (one recently transplanted to the United States from China), he finally decided his calling was to study Chinese language and so matriculated as an undergraduate at the University of California at Berkeley. At Berkeley he studied linguistic field methods, Chinese, and Mongolian, continuing into the doctoral program. He also attained a high level of fluency in Russian during those years. Norman was the principal American student of Yuen Ren Chao 趙元任 (1892–1982) in descriptive and historical Chinese linguistics. He spent almost his whole teaching career at the University of Washington, Seattle.

The two years of his Fulbright grant in Taiwan, from 1965–67, were spent largely on Manchu, even though he completed all the work for a ground-breaking dissertation on Mǐn dialects of Chinese at the same time. He told me the story in an interview in 2006:

> When I got to Taiwan, they had in the office there a copy of the book by Tulišen 圖理琛 (1667–1741), who was a Manchu official sent by the Kāngxī Emperor to Russia in something like 1725. And he wrote an account of his journey, which is really for intelligence purposes and so forth, and very interesting — very repetitious but very interesting … .

> I was working on that and I constantly was coming up against this problem that there's no Manchu dictionary in English. So I would use the Japanese *Manwa jiten* 滿和辭典 (which also has Chinese glosses in it, so that was quite usable). And I also had Erich Hauer's *Handwörterbuch der Mandschusprache*. But at least half the time I'd look the Manchu up and then I had to go and look up the German words. So at some point I just decided, well, why not — I have all this time, you know — maybe I should compile my own dictionary.

> So the first thing I did was cut up the Manchu-Japanese dictionary. Since I had research funds, I had a blueprint copy made of it, printed only on one side. I hired an assistant to cut all the entries out and paste them on cards. At that time in Taiwan you couldn't buy cards; you couldn't go to the stationery store and say "I want four-by-five cards," or any size — you had to have them made. So we had a whole bunch of cards made and pasted all the cut-outs onto the cards. And then we had a great big file cabinet made, with

drawers, and so we put all the cards in there — it was in alphabetical order already. I would go into the office, early in the morning, maybe beginning at 6:30 or 7:00, and I just went through the whole thing and translated it. I had a Japanese gloss and a Chinese gloss probably from the *Wǔtǐ Qīng wénjiàn* 五體清文件 or something like that. The Japanese was relatively simple; I could deal with most of that, with a dictionary. And I had Hauer, and Hauer had more entries, so I sometimes added entries that were in Hauer but weren't in the Japanese material. And in working that way I finished the thing in about seven months — went through all the cards in seven months.

Then I got another assistant who typed it up as a manuscript and went through, corrected things, and so forth, and then I made another copy and had it printed in Taiwan — just purely privately; I paid for it.

This was all done on a Fulbright to study Chinese! He added:

But I had so much *time*, you know. I'd never in my life had a period when nobody told me to do anything.

What he produced in Taiwan was only the foundation of the present book. He spent the next forty-five years refining and expanding it by reading Manchu documents and consulting other materials, including recordings and transcriptions of living Sibe 錫伯 that he made in Taiwan. (He described his teacher in Taiwan, [Kongur] Kuang Lu [孔古爾] 廣祿, 1900–73, as a gifted extempore storyteller in the Sibe tradition.) An initial edition of the dictionary was published in 1978, but the present volume is considerably expanded from that, and also includes a guide to pronunciation as Norman learned it.

In later years, he had much help on this project from the members of a Manchu study group based in Portland, Oregon, whom he names in his own preface. In 2005, he asked me to begin helping him put it in order for publication, which I have done using LaTeX (including the "multicol" package, with gratitude to Frank Mittelbach). I am glad to acknowledge the help of my mother, Shirley Branner — even though she knows no Manchu or Chinese, she patiently read through the entire manuscript twice for sense and correct order of entries. Most of the editing and typesetting work was done in 2011 and 2012, with the very last corrections made to the text on 28 June, 2012. Five days later, Prof. Norman entered the hospital, and a few days after that he was gone.

Jerry Norman was a scholar of rare erudition, though retiring by temperament. His memory for words and expressions, even in tongues he did not know, left people floored. And few linguists I have known possessed his true instinct for the workings of language. Beyond those gifts, he was also a sincere and gentle person, whose willingness to share what he knew touched many people far beyond his rather small circle of students.

Norman's Manchu name was Elbihe, 'raccoon dog'.

David Prager Branner
City College of New York
and Columbia University
16 July, 2012

Author's Preface

The present work is a large-scale revision and enlargement of my 1978 *Concise Manchu-English Lexicon*, now long out of print. Much of the revision has grown out of my reading of Manchu texts and discussions with colleagues and students over the course of many years.

Manchu was the dynastic language of the Qing dynasty (1644–1911). As such it was employed in all sorts of official writing down to the end of the dynasty; in addition, it was the vehicle of an enormous translation literature, mostly from Chinese, encompassing virtually every genre — classics, histories, literary anthologies, and novels as well as scientific and religious works.

As a spoken language, Manchu was already in serious decline in most of the Qing empire by the beginning of the nineteenth century. In Manchuria it continued to be spoken in some remote areas well into the twentieth century; there it is now moribund with only a few elderly speakers remaining. Spoken Manchu lives on, however, in Sibe, a closely related language now spoken in the Ili 伊犁 region of Xinjiang. Written Sibe is especially close to the literary Manchu of the Qing dynasty. The present dictionary is based exclusively on Qing dynasty sources.

Manchu is a Tungusic language; in many respects it is an atypical member of this family. Together with the extinct Jurchen language, it forms a southern branch of the aforesaid family. Whether Manchu descends from Jurchen is hard to say due to our imperfect knowledge of the latter. It is probably more realistic to view both Jurchen and Manchu as members of a dialect continuum; if so it is possible that the two languages were based on two different regional forms of a single Jurcheno-Manchu language which had somewhat different dialectal bases. Manchu itself, although in general very uniform, ex-hibits a certain amount of dialect mixture which is especially evident in early (seventeeth century) texts where one can from time to time find variant forms of the same word. Some such variants are included in the present dictionary.

In addition to being a valuable tool for anyone seriously studying the last imperial dynasty of China, Manchu has also played an important role in the comparative study of the Altaic languages. Even for those who have doubts about the validity of an Altaic language family, the links among the Turkic, Mongolic, and Tungusic languages are so numerous and evident that it is difficult to see how one could study the language of one of these groups without some reference to the others. Manchu clearly has undergone deep influence from Mongolic languages; the earliest stratum of Mongolic loanwords probably goes back to Khitan, of which we unfortunately have only a sketchy knowledge. In addition to lexical influence one may detect considerable Mongolic syntactic influence. Chinese influence on

Manchu is often exaggerated; such influence is mostly reflected in loanwords, some of which appear to be very old and may have been inherited indirectly from Khitan and Jurchen.

The influence of Manchu on the study of Classical Chinese texts should also be mentioned. Many early sinologists knew Manchu and used Manchu translations of early Chinese texts in their works. The noted German sinologist and manchurologist, Erich Hauer, expressed a widely held view in 1930:

> Manchu is for beginning and for advanced sinologues an aid of the first order. A knowledge of this language gives one the possibility of consulting the Chinese-Manchu parallel texts of the classics and well-known historical works produced by scholarly commissions at the order of the emperors of the eighteenth century and to gain an understanding of the grammar and syntax of this monosyllabic, isolating language which lacks any sort of inflexion. At present in Leipzig and Berlin where Manchu is taught all students specializing in the Chinese language are advised to take Manchu as a subsidiary subject.

Whether this is still the case is certainly debatable, but the influence of Manchu translations on the early period of European sinology is hardly open to question.

The present dictionary employs the Möllendorf system of romanization with all entries in alphabetic order. There are three letters with diacritics: **š**, **ū**, and **ž**; **š** follows **s** and **ū** follows **u**; **ž** appears after **y**. Of these, **ž** is used only to transcribe foreign words; the same is true of four other letters: **dz**, **g'**, **k'**, and **ts**; **dz** and **ts** have been put in separate sections but **g'** and **k'** have been added to the end of the **g** and **k** sections respectively.

Official titles follow Brunnert and Hagelstrom's 1912 *Present Day Political Organization of China*. The translations of titles in this work tend to be functional rather than literal; moreover, the Manchu terms do not always represent a direct translation of their Chinese equivalents. Brunnert and Hagelstrom's translations are followed by the abbreviation *BH* and the relevant section of their book. Translations of titles and institutions without the notation *BH* are my own. The Chinese equivalents of Manchu titles are given in parentheses. Certain other unusual terms like the names of Chinese constellations and varieties of Chinese calligraphy are also supplied with Chinese characters.

Verbs are cited in their **-mbi** forms; in this I merely follow the practice of Qing dynasty dictionaries. Irregular verb forms are given where relevant. Verbal roots containing the neutral vowels **i** and **u** can take either **-ha** or **-he** in their perfect participial forms; these variants have been given where possible; for some verbs of this type I have been unable to find actual textual examples. Moreover, one finds a certain amount of variation, sometimes even within the same text. For example, the perfect participial form of **bujumbi** can be found both as **bujuha** and **bujuhe** in various texts. In general, forms in **-ha** are more common with such verbal roots. Derived forms like the passive, causative, frequentive, and reciprocal have been given separate entries.

The present dictionary is intended to be a basic reference tool for students and scholars of Manchu, be they historians, students of Chinese literature, or linguists. In general geographical and personal names are not included, nor are names of various rare mythological beasts and minor Chinese deities.

Acknowledgments

Much gratitude is owed to James Bosson, my first Manchu teacher and constant supporter in all my Manchu endeavors. I must also acknowledge my great debt to Kuang Lu 廣祿, my second Manchu teacher and a living link to both spoken and written Manchu. Over the long period during which I have worked on this dictionary many others, both colleagues and students, have made important contributions to my work. I would especially like to mention Stephen Durrant, Margery Lang, Felicia Hecker, Hanson Chase, and the late Elian Chuaqui who at various stages offered valuable assistance. More recently I have profited much from input of the members of the Portland Manchu Study Group: Stephen Wadley, Keith Dede, Thomas Larsen, and Brian Tawney. Finally, I gratefully thank my wife, Stella Chen Norman, for her patience and assistance with matters Chinese. More recently I am much in debt to David Prager Branner who has prepared the manuscript for publication; without his help I doubt that the dictionary would ever have attained its present form.

Everyone understands, I am sure, that final responsibility for any errors or infelicities lies with the author alone.

Selected Bibliography

Allen, Grover M. 1938–40. *The Mammals of China and Mongolia*. 1 vol. in 2. New York: American Museum of Natural History.

An Shuangcheng, ed. 1993. 安雙成主編. *Man-Han dacidian* 滿漢大辭典. Shenyang: Liaoning Minzu Chubanshe 遼寧民族出版社.

Baily, L. H. 1949. *Manual of Cultivated Plants Commonly Grown in the United States and Canada*. New York: Macmillan.

Brunnert, H. S. and Hagelstrom, V. V. 1912. *Present Day Political Organization of China*. Shanghai: Kelly and Walsh, Limited.

Chao, Yuen Ren. 1953. "Popular Chinese Plant Words: a Descriptive Study." *Language* 29: 379–414.

Han i araha manju gisun I buleku bithe. 1708. Beging [Beijing]: Wuying Dian 武英殿, Daicing gurun i elhe taifin i dehi nadaci aniya 清康熙四十七年.

Haneda Tōru 羽田亨. 1937. *Manwa jiten* 滿和辭典. Kyoto: Kyōto Teikoku Daigaku Man-Mō Chōsakai 京都帝國大學滿蒙調查會.

Hauer, Erich. 1952–55. *Handwörterbuch der Mandschusprache*. Wiesbaden: Otto Harrassowitz.

Hu Zengyi 胡增益, ed. 1994. *Xin Man-Han dacidian* 新滿漢大詞典. Urumqi: Xinjiang Renmin Chubanshe 新疆人民出版社.

Jiangsu Xin Yixueyuan 江蘇新醫學院. 1977. *Zhongyao dacidian* 中藥大辭典. Shanghai: Kexue Jishu Chubanshe 科學出版社.

Kungang 崑岡. 1899. *Da Qing huidiantu* 大清彙典圖. Reprint, Taipei: Qiwen Chubanshe 啟文出版社, 1965.

Möllendorf, O.F. von. 1877. "The Vertebrata of the Province of Chih-li with Notes on Chinese Zoological Nomenclature." *Journal of the North China Branch of the Royal Asiatic Society* (n.s.), 11 (1877): 41–111.

Qingwen zonghui 清文總彙. 1897. Beijing: [n.p.]

Shaw Tsen-huang [Shou Zhenhuang] 壽振黃. 1936. *The Birds of Hopei Province*. Peiping: Fan Memorial Institute of Biology.

Shou Zhenhuang 壽振黃. 1964. *Zhongguo jingji dongwu zhi: shou lei* 中國經濟動物誌: 獸類 [The economic animals of China: wild animals]. Beijing: Kexue Chubanshe 科學出版社.

Sowerby, Arthur de Carle. 1916. "Recent Research upon the Mammalia of North China." *Journal of the North China Branch of the Royal Asiatic Society* 47: 53–82.

Sowerby, Arthur de Carle. 1922–30. *The Naturalist in Manchuria*. 5 vols in 3. Tientsin: Tientsin Press.

Tong Yuquan 佟玉泉 et al. 1987. *Sibe Manju gisun i buleku bithe*. Urumqi: Xinjiang Renmin Chubanshe 新疆人民出版社.

Yuzhi wuti Qingwen jian 御製五體清文鑒. 1957. Reprint. Beijing: Minzu Chubanshe 民族出版社.

Zaxarov, Ivan. 1875. *Polnyj Man'čžursko-Russkij slovar'*. Sankt Peterburg: Akademii Nauk, Reprint, Peipeing, 1939.

Zheng Zuoxin 鄭作新, ed. 1963. *Zhongguo jingji dongwu zhi, niao lei* 中國經濟動物誌: 鳥類 [The economic animals of China: birds]. Beijing: Kexue Chubanshe 科學出版社.

Guide to Manchu Pronunciation, Romanization, and Traditional Script

The only living tradition of reading Manchu aloud is found among the Sibe minority in Xīnjiāng. What follows here is based on the pronunciation of my late Manchu teacher, Professor Kuang Lu 廣祿 (1900–1973) of National Taiwan University; he was born and received his early education in Cabcal where the bulk of the Sibe minority reside. His pronunciation of Written Manchu represents how Manchu texts were read aloud or chanted in the early twentieth century among the Sibe. I studied Manchu with Professor Kuang for the better part of two years in the mid-1960s in Taipei. He was a native speaker of Sibe, a vernacular form of Manchu which is still widely spoken in the Cabcal region of the Ili Valley in Xīnjiāng. When read aloud, all the vowels of Written Manchu were pronounced with their full value, whereas in Professor Kuang's vernacular, vowel reduction is pervasive. Here the Möllendorff transcription is used as a starting point for a discussion of how Manchu should be pronounced.

Single Letters

a   *Pronunciation*: [ɑ]. This letter is pronounced as a low unrounded vowel. Its value varies somewhat depending on what consonant precedes it; after uvulars it has a low back articulation: **gala** [ɢɑlɑ] 'hand', **hala** [χɑlɑ] 'clan, surname'. Elsewhere the articulation is more fronted: **baba** 'everywhere' [b̥aba], **sasa** 'together' [sasa].

　　　　Traditional script: In isolation, **ᠯ**; in initial position, **�**; in medial position, **ᠠ**; in final position, **ᠯ** and **ᠵ**. *Note*: The final form **ᠵ** appears only in ligature with the letters **b** and **p**.

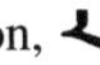

b   *Pronunciation*: [b̥]~[b]. Manchu **b** when it is initial in a word, is pronounced as a bilabial unaspirated stop which somewhat resembles the *b* of English, but without the usual voicing. A much closer sound would be the *b* in the Chinese word *bái* [b̥ai] 'white'. Between voiced segments (vowels and sonorants) it is voiced. At the end of a word **b** is voiceless, unaspirated, and generally unreleased; before another consonant it is voiced before **d** or **g**, but voiceless and aspirated before an aspirated consonant: **abdaha** 'leaf' [abdaχa], **debkembi** 'bring up again' [d̥əpkʰəmbi].

Traditional script: In isolation, none; in initial position, 𐒻 ; in medial position, 𐒻 ; in final position, 𐒻. *Note*: The bottom curving stroke becomes the first stroke of the next letter. For example: **ba** 𐒻; **be** 𐒻; **bi** 𐒻; **bo** 𐒻 ; **bu** 𐒻; **bk** 𐒻. With word-final **a** and **e**, written **ba** 𐒻; **be** 𐒻.

c *Pronunciation*: [tsʰ]~[tɕʰ]. This letter represents an aspirated affricate similar to the *ch* of English *chair*. Before the high front vowel **i** it had a more palatal variant: **cimari** [tɕʰimɑri] 'morning'; before other vowels it was retroflexed: **calu** [tsʰɑlʊ] 'granary'.

Traditional script: In isolation, none; in initial position, 𐒻; in medial position, 𐒻; in final position, none.

d *Pronunciation*: [d̥]~[d]. The letter **d** when it occurs initially is an alveolar unaspirated stop similar to the *d* in Chinese *duō* [d̥uo] 'many'. Between voiced segments it was fully voiced: **mederi** [mədəri] 'sea'.

Traditional script: In isolation, none; in initial position, 𐒻 and 𐒻; in medial position, 𐒻 and 𐒻; in final position, none. *Note*: The letters 𐒻 and 𐒻 are used before *e* and *u*.

e *Pronunciation*: [ə]. Manchu **e** is a central unrounded vowel. It sounds somewhat like the vowel in English *shut*, or the weakened vowel in the second syllable of *sofa*. It is not pronounced as far back as Chinese *e* as in *dé* [d̥ɤ]. It should not be pronounced like the vowel in English *met* [mɛt].

Traditional script: In isolation, 𐒻; in initial position, 𐒻; in medial position, 𐒻 and 𐒻; in final position, 𐒻, 𐒻, 𐒻, and 𐒻. *Note*: The medial form 𐒻 is used after **t**, **d**, **k**, **g**, and **h**. The final form 𐒻 is used after **t** and **d**, and the final form 𐒻 is used after **k**, **g**, and **h**. The final form 𐒻 appears only in ligature with the letters **b** and **p**.

f *Pronunciation*: [f]. Like the English *f*, the Manchu sound is a voiceless labiodental fricative.

Traditional script: In isolation, none; in initial position, 𐒻 and 𐒻; in medial position, 𐒻 and 𐒻; in final position, none. *Note*: Before **a** and **e**, Manchu **f** is written 𐒻 or 𐒻; before the other vowels it is written 𐒻 or 𐒻.

g *Pronunciation*: [g̊]~[g], [ɢ̥]~[ɢ]. Before the vowels **i**, **e**, and **u** Manchu **g** is a voiceless, unaspirated velar stop when it occurs initially: [g̊]; between voiced segments it is voiced: [g]. Before the vowels **a**, **o**, and **ū** it has a uvular articulation, voiceless initially and voiced between voiced segments: [ɢ̥]~[ɢ]. It is likely that the voiced variants described here were pronounced as fricatives, [ɣ], before **i**, **e**, and **u** and [ʁ] before **a**, **o**, and **ū**.

Traditional script: In Manchu script **g** is written with two different letters. When it represents a velar (before **i**, **e**, and **u**), it is written with the front **g**: In isolation, none; in initial position, ﻧ; in medial position, ﻧ; in final position, none. The bottom curving stroke of the front **g** becomes the first stroke of the next letter, creating a ligature. For example: **ge** ﻧ; **gi** ﻧ; **gu** ﻧ. When it represents a uvular (before **a**, **o**, or **ū**), it is written with the back **g**: In isolation, none; in initial position, ﻧ; in medial position, ﻧ; in final position, none. Unlike the front **g**, the final stroke of the back **g** does not serve as the first stroke of the next letter.

h   *Pronunciation*: [x]~[χ]. Before **i**, **e**, and **u**, **h** is a voiceless velar fricative: [x]. Before **a**, **o**, and **ū**, it is pronounced as a voiceless uvular fricative: [χ]. Between voiced segments it was most likely voiced: [ɣ]~[ʁ].

Traditional script: In Manchu script **h** is written with two different letters. When it represents a velar (before **i**, **e**, or **u**) it is written with the front **h**: In isolation, none; in initial position, ﻧ; in medial position, ﻧ; in final position, none. The bottom curving stroke of the front **h** becomes the first stroke of the next letter, creating a ligature. For example: **he** ﻧ; **hi** ﻧ; **hu** ﻧ. When it represents a uvular (before **a**, **o**, or **ū**) it is written with the back **h**: In isolation, none; in initial position, ﻧ; in medial position, ﻧ; in final position, none. Unlike the front **h**, the final stroke of the back **h** does not serve as the first stroke of the next letter.

i   *Pronunciation*: [i]. This vowel is similar to the *i* of Spanish or French, a high, front unrounded vowel.

Traditional script: In isolation, ﻧ and ﻧ; in initial position, ﻧ; in medial position, ﻧ and ﻧ; in final position, ﻧ. *Note*: this vowel is written ﻧ when it represents the isolated genitive postposition; it is written ﻧ when it is the second half of an ascending diphthong such as **ai** or **oi** and followed by a consonant.

j   *Pronunciation*: [d̥ʐ̥]~[dʐ̥, d̥ʑ̥]~[dʑ̥]. when initial in a word, Manchu **j** represents a voiceless, unaspirated affricate similar to the *j* in English *judge*; before the high, front vowel **i** it has a more palatal pronunciation: [d̥ʑ̥]~[dʑ̥], whereas before other vowels it is retroflexed [d̥ʐ̥]~[dʐ̥]. In word-initial position it has a voiceless onset but is voiced between voiced segments.

Traditional script: In isolation, none; in initial position, ﻧ; in medial position, ﻧ; in final position, none.

k   *Pronunciation*: [kʰ]~[qʰ]. Manchu **k** is a voiceless, aspirated velar stop before the vowels **i**, **e**, and **u** and a voiceless, aspirated uvular stop before the vowels **a**, **o**, and **ū**. At the end of a word, depending on the preceding vowel, it may have either a velar or uvular pronunciation, depending on the vowel: **lak** [lɑq] 'just right', **fik** [fik] 'densely'. In final position it was voiceless and probably unreleased. Before another consonant in the middle of a word, **k** will be voiceless before another voiceless consonant, but voiced before **b** and **d**; **akta** [aqʰa], **akdan** 'trust' [ɑɢdan].

Traditional script: *Note*: In Manchu script **k** is written with two different letters. When it represents a velar (before **i**, **e**, and **u**) it is written with the the front **k**: In isolation, none; in initial position, ʔ; in medial position, ʔ; in final position, Ꝫ. The bottom curving stroke becomes the first stroke of the next letter, creating a ligature. For example: **ke** ʔ, **ki** ʔ, **ku** ꝗ. When it represents a uvular (before **a**, **o**, or **ū**) it is written with the back **k**: In isolation, none; in initial position ʔ; in medial position before a vowel, ɟ; in medial position before a consonant, "ɟ; in final position, "ꝰ. Unlike the form before **i**, **e**, and **o** the final stroke of the back **k** does not serve as the first stroke of the next letter.

l   *Pronunciation*: [l]. This consonant is very similar to English *l*. It probably had a lighter (non-velarized) articulation before **i** but was somewhat velarized before other vowels: [ɫ].

Traditional script: In isolation, none; in initial position, ᴊ; in medial position, ᴊ; in final position, ᴊ.

m   *Pronunciation*: [m]. English *m* and Manchu **m** are for all practical purposes identical.

Traditional script: In isolation, none; in initial position, ᴎ; in medial position, ᴎ; in final position, ᴎ.

n   *Pronunciation*: [n]. Very similar to English *n* [n]. Before **i** it is palatalized: [ɲ]. Finally, **n** is very weakly articulated, in some cases merely realized as a nasalization of the preceding vowel: **morin** [mɔrin]~[mɔrĩ].

Traditional script: In isolation, none; in initial position, ˌɟ; in medial position, ˌɟ and ɟ; in final position, ꝲ and ˌꝲ. *Note*: In medial position before a vowel, the letter **n** is written ˌɟ, otherwise it is written ɟ. In native Manchu words, the word-final **n** is always written ꝲ, but in Chinese words it is sometimes written ˌꝲ.

ng   *Pronunciation*: At the end of a word, **ng** is a velar nasal like the *ng* in English *sing*: **wang** 'Prince' [waŋ]. See below for the combination **ngg**.

Traditional script: In isolation, none; in initial position, none; in medial position, ʔ; in final position, ʒ.

ngg   *Pronunciation*: This combination occurs only between vowels in the middle of a word. Sibe speakers pronounce it as a velar (or uvular) nasal: [ŋ~N]. This contrast is probably purely phonetic, since there are no minimal pairs involving [ŋ] and [N]. In early Manchu it seems possible that **ngg** may have been pronounced [ŋg~NG], at least in some dialects.

    Traditional script: The written representation of **ngg** is a composition of **ng** and **g**.

o   *Pronunciation*: [ɔ]. A lower mid, back, unrounded vowel similar to the vowel in English *law* [łɔ].

    Traditional script: In isolation, ᡆ; in initial position, ᡆ; in medial position, ᠣ; in final position, ᠣ᠋.

p   *Pronunciation*: [pʰ]. A voiceless, aspirated stop like the *p* in the English word *pail* [pʰeil].

    Traditional script: In isolation, none; in initial position, ᡦ; in medial position, ᡦ; in final position, none. *Note*: The bottom curving stroke becomes the first stroke of the next letter. For example: **pa** ᡦ; **pe** ᡦᠠ; **pi** ᡦ; **po** ᡦ; **pu** ᡦᠣ. With word-final **a** and **e**, written **pa** ᡦᠠ; **pe** ᡦᠠ.

r   *Pronunciation*: [ɾ]. A voiced alveolar flap, rather similar to the *r* of Japanese. Note that *r* very rarely occurs initially, and then only in loanwords.

    Traditional script: In isolation, none; in initial position, ᠷ; in medial position, ᠷ; in final position, ᠷ᠋.

s   *Pronunciation*: [s]~[ɕ]. Before **i** Manchu **s** is palatalized: [ɕ], a sound similar to the initial sound in Chinese *xī* [ɕi] 'west'. Before other vowels it is like the *s* in English *saw* [sɔ].

    Traditional script: In isolation, none; in initial position, ᠰ; in medial position, ᠰ; in final position, ᠰ᠋.

š   *Pronunciation*: [ʂ]. This Manchu sound is similar to English **sh** but without any lip-rounding except when it occurs before a rounded vowel. It is most similar to the Běijīng pronunciation of *sh*: **šan** 'ear' [ʂan]. For the combination **ši**, see below.

    Traditional script: In isolation, none; in initial position, ᡧ; in medial position, ᡧ; in final position, none.

t   *Pronunciation*: [tʰ]. A voiceless, aspirated alveolar stop like the *t* in English *tea* [tʰiː]. When **t** occurs, as it rarely does, at the end of a native Manchu word it is voiceless and unaspirated. Before a voiceless consonant internally in a word, **t** is voiceless and unaspirated: **bithe** 'book' [b̥itxə]; before a voiced consonant it was probably voiced but there are very few examples: **batmaga** 'ruby' [b̥admɑɢɑ].

Traditional script: In isolation, none; in initial position, 𝑝 and 𝑏; in medial position, 𝖺, 𝖺, and 𝑞; in final position, 𝑞 . *Note*: 𝑝 or 𝖺 before **e** and **u**. 𝑞 before a consonant.

u   *Pronunciation*: [u]. This vowel is like the *u* of Spanish or Italian or similar to the vowel in English *do* [du:].

Traditional script: In isolation, 𝖽'; in initial position, 𝖽'; in medial position, 𝖽 and 𝖽; in final position, 𝖽 and 𝖽. *Note*: The medial and final forms do not have a dot when they follow **t**, **d**, **k**, **g**, and **h**.

ū   *Pronunciation*: [ʊ]. The vowels **u** and **ū** are not phonemically distinct; by far the most common function of the two vowels is to distinguish velars from uvulars before the vowel /u/: **ku** [kʰu], **kū** [qʰʊ], **gu** [g̊u], **gū** [ɢʊ], **hu** [xu], **hū** [χʊ]. After **y**, **ū** is used to represent a high, front, rounded vowel in Chinese loanwords: **giyūn** [g̊ijyn]~[g̊jyn] 'thirty catties'. In a small number of cases **ū** is a carryover from the early, unreformed script: **tūmbi** 'to hit a wooden clapper' was most likely pronounced [dumbi].

Traditional script: In isolation, 𝖽 ; in initial position, 𝖽 ; in medial position, 𝖽; in final position, 𝖽.

w   *Pronunciation*: [w]~[v]. In early Manchu **w** was most likely a bilabial approximant like English *w* [w]. In modern vernacular forms of Manchu (including Sibe) it is pronounced as a labiodental fricative: [v].

Traditional script: In isolation, none; in initial position, 𝖺; in medial position, 𝖺; in final position, none. *Note*: Only occurs before the vowels **a** and **e**. Before other vowels, this represents the letter **f**.

y   *Pronunciation*: [j]. The letter **y** is pronounced like the *y* of English: [j], a palatal voiced approximant.

Traditional script: In isolation, none; in initial position, 𝖺; in medial position, 𝖺; in final position, none.

ž   *Pronunciation*: [ɻ] A voiced, retroflex approximant like the *r* in Chinese *rén* 人 'person'. It occurs only in loanwords. See also **ži**, described below.

Traditional script: In isolation, none; in initial position, 𝖳; in medial position, +; in final position, none. *Note*: Used to represent the initial sound in Chinese *ri* 日 .

Letters Related to Chinese Loanwords

In addition to the letters above, another set of letters and digraphs is used in loanwords from Chinese and occasionally loans from other languages.

cy   *Pronunciation*: [tʂʰ ʅ]. **Cy** is used for the Chinese syllable *chǐ* 尺 'foot measure': **cy** [tʂʰ ʅ]. 'foot measure'.

    Traditional script: In isolation, ⅄; in initial position, ⅄; in medial position, ⅄; in final position, ⅄. *Note*: Used to represent the sound of Chinese *chī* 吃.

dz   *Pronunciation*: [dz̥ʅ]. This combination is used for the Chinese syllable *zi* [dz̥ʅ] or the initial sound of a word like *zū* [dz̥u]: **dz** [dz̥ʅ] 'viscount', **dzungdu** [dz̥uŋdu] 'governor general'.

    Traditional script: In isolation, none; in initial position, ⅄; in medial position, ⅄; in final position, none. *Note*: Used to represent the initial sound in Chinese *zǐ* 子.

g'   *Pronunciation*: [g̊]. This letter is used to transcribe [g̊] when it occurs before the back vowels **a** and **o**: **g'an** [gan] 'steel'; cf. **ganggan** [ɢaŋɑn] 'hard'.

    Traditional script: In isolation, none; in initial position, ⅄; in medial position, ⅄; in final position, none. *Note*: Used to represent the initial sound in Chinese *gāng* 剛 when it comes before **a** or **o**.

h'   *Pronunciation*: [x]. Rarely used. When found it is to indicate that an **h** before **a** and **o** is pronounced as a velar and not as a uvular: **h'an** [xan].

    Traditional script: In isolation, none; in initial position, ⅄; in medial position, ⅄; in final position, none.

jy   *Pronunciation*: [dz̥ʐʅ]. This digraph transcribes the Chinese syllable *zhi* [dz̥ʐʅ]: **jyfu** [dz̥ʐʅfu] 'prefect'.

    Traditional script: In isolation, ⅄; in initial position, ⅄; in medial position, ⅄; in final position, ⅄. *Note*: Used to represent the sound of Chinese *zhǐ* 只.

k'   *Pronunciation*: [kʰ]. This letter is used to transcribe velars before the vowel **a** or **o**: **k'a** [kʰa], **k'o** [kʰɔ]. Note that the apostrophe after **g'**, **h'**, and **k'** does not indicate aspiration as some have claimed in the past.

Traditional script: In isolation, none; in initial position, ⟨◌⟩; in medial position, ⟨◌⟩; in final position, none. *Note*: Used to represent the initial sound in Chinese *kāng* 康 when it comes before **a** or **o**.

sy   *Pronunciation*: [sɿ]. Used for the Chinese syllable *si* [sɿ]: **sy** [sɿ] 'temple'.

Traditional script: In isolation, ⟨◌⟩; in initial position, ⟨◌⟩; in medial position, ⟨◌⟩; in final position, ⟨◌⟩. *Note*: Used to represent the sound of Chinese *sì* 四.

ši   *Pronunciation*: [ʂʅ]. Used for the Chinese syllable *shi* [ʂʅ]: **šicing** [ʂʅ tɕʰiŋ] 'celadonite'.

Traditional script: **Ši** is spelled as a composition of **š** and **i**.

ts   *Pronunciation*: [tshɿ]. Used for the Chinese syllable *ci* [tsʰɿ] or for the initial consonant in *cū* 粗 'coarse' [tsʰu]: **tsang** [tsʰɑŋ] 'granary'.

Traditional script: In isolation, none; in initial position, ⟨◌⟩; in medial position, ⟨◌⟩; in final position, none. *Note*: Used to represent the initial sound in Chinese *cè* 册. The Chinese syllable *cǐ* 此 is written ⟨◌⟩.

ži   *Pronunciation*: [ɻʅ]. Used for the Chinese syllable *ri*, as in *rìběn* 'Japan'.

Traditional script: The written representation of **ži** is a composition of **ž** and **i**.

Vowels in Combination

Manchu has numerous diphthongs and triphthongs. Some are written with combinations of vowels, but others take the form of **i** before **y** and a vowel (**iya**, **iye**) or **u** before **w** plus a vowel (**uwa**, **uwe**).

The traditional script represents diphthongs and triphthongs simply as combinations of other vowels, so those forms are not detailed here.

ai   *Pronunciation*: [ai̯]. This digraph sounds like the English word *eye* [ai̯] or the *ai* in Chinese *lái* [lai] 'come'.

au   *Pronunciation*: [ɑu̯]. This combination is sometimes encountered in the transcription of Chinese names or words; this sound is more commonly represented by **oo** (see below).

ei   *Pronunciation*: [əi̯]. It is also permissible to pronounce this diphthong as [ei̯], as in English *day* [dei̯].

eu *Pronunciation*: [əṷ]. It is permissible to pronounce this diphthong as [oṷ] as in the English word *go* [goṷ].

io *Pronunciation*: [i̯ɔ]~[i̯u]. In Manchu orthography [i̯ɔ] and [i̯u] were both written **io**. One can usually determine which is meant by the other vowels in a word. **Niohe** 'wolf' is pronounced [ɲi̯uxə] whereas **niohon** 'green' is pronounced [ɲi̯ɔχɔn]. In the first word [i̯ɔ] is not compatible with the **e** of the second syllable whereas in the second word [i̯u] is not compatible with the **o** of the following syllable.

ioi *Pronunciation*: [y]. This combination of vowels is used to transcribe the Chinese vowel sound [y]: **gioi dz** [g̊y d̥z̩] 'tangerine'.

iya *Pronunciation*: [i̯ɑ]. It is important to note that **iya, iye, uwa,** and **uwe** all represent single syllables: **kiyakū** [kʰi̯ɑqʰʊ] 'river perch', **tuwa** [tʰṷɑ] 'fire'.

iyai *Pronunciation*: [i̯ai]. This combination occurs only in a few Chinese loans: **giyai** [g̊i̯ai] 'street'.

iye *Pronunciation*: [i̯ə]. **Niyere** [ɲi̯ərə] 'weak'.

iyo *Pronunciation*: [i̯ɔ]. This combination seems to have had the same value as **io** and in some cases they are interchangeable. **niyolmon~niolmon** [ɲi̯ɔlmɔn] 'moss'.

iyoo *Pronunciation*: [i̯aṷ]. **Fiyoo** [fi̯aṷ] 'dustpan'. Used to transcribe Chinese *iao* [i̯aṷ] in loanwords: **piyoo** [pʰi̯aṷ] 'credential, ticket'.

iyu *Pronunciation*: Rare but probably pronounced [i̯u]: **niyaniyun** 'betel nut' [ɲi̯aɲi̯un].

iyū *Pronunciation*: [i̯y]. Used only to transcribe Chinese words: **siyūn fu** [çi̯yn fu] 'provincial governor'.

oi *Pronunciation*: [ɔi̯]. Manchu **oi** sounds like the diphthong in English *boy* [bɔi̯].

oo *Pronunciation*: [aṷ]~[ɔṷ]. When reading Manchu aloud, the Sibe pronounce this diphthong like the *ao* in Chinese *báo* [b̥aṷ] 'thin'. It may have originally had the value [ɔṷ], as it still does in some of the vernacular Manchu dialects spoken in Manchuria.

ui *Pronunciation*: [ui̯]. This combination is similar to the diphthong in English *buoy* [bui̯].

ūi *Pronunciation*: [ʊi̯]. This diphthong occurs exclusively after uvular consonants: **hūise** 'Moslem' [χʊi̯sə].

uwa *Pronunciation*: [ṷɑ]. The *ua* in the first syllable of English *qualify* [kʰṷɑləfai̯].

uwai   *Pronunciation*: [u̯ai̯]. Like the *uai* of Chinese *kuài* [kʰu̯ai̯] or the first syllable of English *quinine* [kʰu̯ai̯nai̯n]: **kuai šeo** 'bailiff' [kʰu̯ai̯ ʂəu].

ūwa   *Pronunciation*: [u̯ɑ]. This diphthong occurs exclusively after uvular consonants: **hūwa** [χu̯ɑ] 'courtyard'.

ūwai   *Pronunciation*: [u̯ɑi̯]. Like **ūwa**, this combination occurs only after uvulars: **hūwaise** [χu̯ɑi̯sə] 'pagoda tree'.

uwe   *Pronunciation*: [u̯ə]. This diphthong sounds similar to the first syllable of English *wonder* [wʌndɚ]: **huwesi** 'knife' [χu̯əçi].

Stress

In Professor Kuang's pronunciation of Written Manchu stress generally fell on the final syllable: **bira** [b̥irá] 'river', **arambi** [ɑrɑmbí] 'do, make', **sile** [çilə́] 'soup', **fulgiyan** [fulg̊i̯án] 'red', **tuwaha** [tʰu̯ɑχá] 'looked'. Traditionally among the Sibe written texts were chanted; this stress pattern may be due to the rhythm employed in this chanting style.

Conventions and Symbols

item	meaning
boldfaced words	Manchu
italicized words	words in languages other than Manchu (including Sibe) or English
$\longrightarrow$	*see* or *see under*
—	introduces an explanation
single quotes (' ')	sometimes used to give a literal translation of the Manchu, or where an example of usage is supplied after a definition

The order of the dictionary is basically alphabetical, with three important exceptions:

1. Any letter with a diacritic (**ū š ž**) always appears after the same letter without a diacritic; the two are treated as entirely different symbols.

2. Those consonants marked with a following apostrophe (**g'**, **k'**, **h'**) are treated as distinct from their unapostrophized forms. So **begu** precedes **beg'o**, and so forth.

3. Indentation is used to set off compound expressions. In the case of verbs, those with simple grammatical suffixes are considered to belong to the same headword, but words with derivational morphology (including the causative and passive) are felt to be different and so are placed under different entries.

So **acambi** 'to meet' (etc.) and its causative **acabumbi** are separate headwords, as are the derived noun **acabun** 'union' and adjective **acabungga** 'united'; a number of derived expressions beginning with **aca-** and **acabu-** are presented under their respective head verbs, and compound expressions beginning with **acabun** and **acabungga** are similarly placed under those headwords.

In original Manchu documents, certain suffixes may or may not have a space between them and the preceding word. This ambiguity, which affects the alphabetization of entries, principally affects the genitive and instrumental **-i** but also dative/locative **-de** and to a lesser extent accusative **-be**. The entries in this dictionary are taken from original sources and have not been fully regularized with respect to the presence or absence of this space. It is simply the luck of attestation that accounts for the difference between the two, and the reader must remember to look for both forms. For example, among the compounds of **boo** are both **booi oyo** 'roof of a house' and **boo i hošo** 'the northwest corner of a house'. Both could have been written either **boo i** . . . or **booi** . . . .

But for the convenience of the reader, every attempt has been made to cross-reference entries that appear subordinated to some headword whose spelling is different.

Parts of speech are not marked. Word classes in Manchu are largely clear by inspection (unlike in Chinese): verbs have verbal morphology and nouns can take case particles. English-language definitions generally make clear any ambiguous cases.

Place names and personal names are omitted unless they are attested in actual words or phrases. After Kāngxī times, Chinese toponyms were spelled out in the current Guānhuà (Mandarin) pronunciation using the special letters used for transliterations.

Important suffixes appear in parentheses for some Manchu forms, for example,

> **durumbi**: (**-ha**)
> **fosorombi**: (**-ko**)

Arabic numerals are used in two situations:

1. in parentheses, to distinguish words that are different even though they appear to be identical, for instance

    > **acimbi**: (**1**) (**-ka**) to move slightly
    > **acimbi**: (**2**) (**-ha**) to load

2. followed by a period, to distinguish substantially different meanings of the same word:

    > **gidambi**: **1**. to press, to crush, to roll flat; **2**. to stamp (a seal); **3**. to force, to press (to do something); **4**. to quell, to crush, to defeat; **5**. to raid, to plunder; **6**. to suppress, to hold back (laughter); **7**. to close, to shut, to turn off; **8**. to hide, to deceive, to put on; **9**. to preserve (with salt, brine, honey, etc.), to pickle; **10**. to brood, to hatch; **11**. to build (granaries)

A Comprehensive
Manchu-English Dictionary

A ᠠ ᠠ

a: **1**. the male or positive principle, yang; **2**. convex, raised; **3**. interjection of response; **4**. interjection of fear; **5**. (vocative particle); **6**. a 'tooth' (barb-like projection to one side) in the Manchu script

a a: an interjection of casual response

a i bukdan: the outside edge of a piece of folded paper

a i jalan: the human world (as opposed to the underworld)

a jijun i acangga: a bronze identification token with raised characters used to gain admittance to a city at night

a jilgan: a yang tone in music

a fa sere onggolo: ⟶ **afanggala**

a si: a sound used for driving chickens or birds

a ta: (onomatopoetic) the sound of a commotion

aba: **1**. hunt, battue; **2**. where?

aba bargiyambi: to call in a hunt, to call in a battue

aba saha: hunting

aba sarambi: to spread out a battue line

aba sindambi: to form up a battue

aba tucimbi: to depart on a hunt or battue

abalabumbi: (causative of **abalambi**)

abalambi: to participate in a battue, to hunt

abalanambi: to go to participate in a battue, to go to hunt

abalandumbi: to hunt together, to participate in a battue together; also **abalanumbi**

abalanjimbi: to come to participate in a battue

abalanumbi: to hunt together, to participate in a battue together; also **abalandumbi**

abdaha: leaf

abdaha aisin: gold leaf

abdaha efen: **1**. a kind of steamed pastry made using leaves as wrappings; **2**. a small cake shaped like a leaf

abdaha i fesin: leafstalk

abdahanambi: to produce leaves

abdahaname banjimbi: to produce leaves, to become leafy

abdalambi: ⟶ **abtalambi**

abdangga: **1**. having leaves, leafy; **2**. folded accordion fashion

abdangga afaha: **1**. a paper folded accordion fashion; **2**. an album of painting or calligraphy

abdangga bithe: **1**. a document folded accordion fashion; **2**. document of enfeoffment

abdangga fungnehen: an Imperial document on yellow or gold paper

abdangga moo: the Chinese fan palm

abdari: a kind of small oak tree

abgari: idle, without occupation, retired official

abgari banjimbi: to be idle, to live in retirement

abici: from where, whence; cf. **aibici**

abida: Amida Buddha

abide: ⟶ **aibide**

abimbi: to swell; cf. **aibimbi**

abishūn: ⟶ **aibishūn**

abišaha dabišaha: distantly related, not genuinely related

abka: **1**. sky, heaven; **2**. weather; **3**. Emperor; **4**. god, deity; **5**. (as an exclamation) O Heavens!

    abka be ginggulere yamun: (欽天監) Imperial Board of Astronomy, *BH* 223

    abka be ginggulere yamun i aliha hafan: (欽天監監正) Director of the Imperial Board of Astronomy, *BH* 223

    abka be ginggulere yamun i ilhi hafan: (欽天監監副) Vice-Director of the Imperial Board of Astronomy, *BH* 223

    abka gereke: it has dawned

    abka heyenehebi: there are a few clouds in the sky

    abka na: heaven and earth, the universe

    abka saru: **1**. by heaven!, heaven knows!; **2**. (an oath) cursed by heaven

    abka šu na i giyan: astronomy and geography

    abka tusihiyen oho: the sky has become overcast with mist and clouds

abkai: by nature, naturally, natural

    abkai ari: a demon of the sky, a scoundrel, a thoroughly mischievous person

    abkai banjibungga enduri: (天后神) the name of the sea goddess

    abkai buhūngge kiru: a banner bearing the symbol of the 'heavenly deer'

    abkai buten: the horizon

    abkai cira: the Emperor's countenance

    abkai cooha: 'heavenly troops' — an honorific title for the Imperial forces

    abkai dailan: an Imperial punitive expedition

    abkai dengjan: a lantern hung on a pole

    abkai duka be neire mudan: (啟天門之章) the music used in rites honoring a new Metropolitan Graduate

    abkai durungga tetun: (天體儀) a model of the heavenly bodies

    abkai ejen: God (a Christian term)

    abkai ejen i tanggin: Christian church, Catholic church

    abkai fejergi: all under heaven — the world, the universe

    abkai fulingga: the Tianming (天命) reign period, 1616–26

    abkai han: the heavenly sovereign — God on high

    abkai han i deyen: the throne room in the Temple of Heaven in Beijing

    abkai han i ordo: the circular altar to Heaven

    abkai horgikū: (天之樞) the first star of the Great Bear

    abkai imiyangga goloi bolgobure fiyenten: (奉天清吏司) a section of the Bureau of Justice in Mukden

    abkai jui: the Son of Heaven, the Emperor

    abkai morin: a mythical beast — like a horse but with fleshy wings

    abkai moringga kiru: a banner bearing the symbol of the 'heavenly horse'

    abkai sihiyakū: 'the axis of heaven' — the same as **abkai horgikū**

    abkai sukdun: weather, air

    abkai sure: the Tiancong (天聰) reign period, 1627–35

    abkai šu: astronomy

    abkai šu i hontoho: (天文科) Astronomical Section, *BH* 230

    abkai šurdejen usiha: the seven stars of the Big Dipper

    abkai tan: the altar of heaven

    abkai ten i usiha: the North Star

    abkai tsang: an Imperial grain depository

    abkai warangge: 'killed by Heaven' — cursed, damned

    abkai wehiyehe: the Qianlong (乾隆) reign period, 1736–96

    abkai yang: the sun

abkambi: an old form of **agambi** 'to rain'

abkana: heaven and earth — a great deal, very much (in children's speech)

abkawaru: cursed by heaven — an oath

absa: **1**. a fishing implement — a board at the end of a boat to which a net was attached; **2**. a birchbark container

absabumbi: (causative of **absambi**)

absalan: **1**. the upper front leg bone of a pig or other domestic animal; **2**. upper arm bone, humerus

absambi: (**-ka**) to become dry and shriveled, to become skin and bones, to become sickly or emaciated

absi: **1**. how?; **2**. where to?, whither?; **3**. what a … !, how … !; **4**. how very … , very, extremely

    absi casi akū: perturbed, flustered

    absi feciki: how wonderful!, how strange!

    absi gamara: what is to be done?

    absi hairaka: what a shame

    absi hihanakū: how worthless

    absi hojo: very good, excellent

    absi ocibe: no matter what

    absi oho: what happened?

    absi ojoro: what can one do?, what for?

    absi ojoro be sarkū: not knowing how it happened

    absi serengge: what are you saying?, nothing of the sort

    absi yabsi: **1**. really very … ; **2**. what kind of?

absimbi: ⟶ **absambi**

abtajambi: **1**. to fall off, to come apart; **2**. to fall off (said of feathers)

abtalabumbi: (causative of **abtalambi**)

abtalambi: to break off (branches), to prune

abtarambi: to yell, to scream, to cause a commotion

abtukūlambi: to miss hitting an animal in a mortal spot (in hunting)

abu: almost, nearly

    abu abu oho: almost happened

abuci ilha: *Lycoris radiata*: red spider lily

abuha: *Caprella bursa*: shepherd's purse (a kind of wild vegetable)

    abuha hūlha: accomplice

    abuha ilha: hollyhock

abulimbi: (-**ka**) to become exhausted

abuna: *Draba nemorosa*: woodland draba

aburambi: **1**. to fight wildly or blindly; **2**. to pounce

    aburame tantambi: to hit and fight wildly

aburanambi: **1**. to come to blows, to grapple with; **2**. to pounce on

aburi: wicked, vicious, brutal, ferocious, envious, ruthless, cruel

    aburi ehe: **1**. evil, the myriad evils; **2**. ruthless, brutal, (said of women) violently jealous

acabubumbi: (causative of **acabumbi**)

acabufi: ⟶ **acabumbi** (subheading)

acabuki: flatterer, sycophant

acabukū: flatterer, an obsequious person

acabumbi: **1**. (causative of **acambi**); **2**. to join, to put (back) together, to connect; **3**. to bring together, to introduce, to recommend; **4**. to present (to an audience); **5**. to tune a stringed instrument; **6**. to mix, to mingle; **7**. to come together, to have (sexual) relations, to mate, to couple; **8**. to adapt to, to make fit, to attune, to adjust, to match, to harmonize; **9**. to wait on, to attend; **10**. to be obsequious, to flatter; **11**. to collate, to proofread; **12**. to graft (trees); **13**. to be efficacious, to be suitable

acabufi bodombi: to calculate together, to do accounts

acabufi bodoro fiyenten: (會計司) Department of Accounting; cf. *BH* 829B

acabufi wecere wecen: a sacrifice to the Imperial ancestors performed in the palace on New Year's Eve

acabuha jakdan i šugi: resin, gum

acabume arara hafan: (纂修官) official proofreader, revisor; cf. *BH* 94, 139, 177

acabume banjibukū: (編修官) Compiler of the Second Class, *BH* 200B

acabume bodombi: to do accounts

acabume bodoro hafan: (司會) finance officer

acabume bumbi: to supply, to provide

acabume bure hafan: (供給官) supply officer

acabume hūlara falgangga: (對讀所) examination reading office

acabume hūlara hafan: (對讀官) examination reader

acabume tuwara bithe: a tally consisting of two fitting parts

acabume tuwara bithei kunggeri: (勘合科) office in the Board of War for issuing tallies

acabure niyalma: middleman

acabun: summary, union, harmony, adaptation, efficacy, effect

acabun akū: lacking efficacy, inefficacious

acabun i fulhun: (應鍾) one of the six minor pipes in music

acabun wecen: offering made on a hill to the earth god

acabungga: **1**. united, harmonized, adapted; **2**. appropriate, commensurate, corresponding

acabungga boji: contract

acabungga fukjingga hergen: (墳書) an ancient style calligraphy

acabungga inenggi: a day on which the yin and yang elements harmonize

acabungga jungken: chimes

acabure: ⟶ **acabumbi** (subheading)

acalambi: **1**. to act together, to act mutually; **2**. to have dealings with

acalame simnembi: to assemble all the candidates in the capital for the Imperial Examination, to go for the Imperial Examination

acambi: **1**. to meet, to get together, to come together, to combine; **2**. to visit (the home of the deceased after a funeral); **3**. to be in agreement, to be in harmony, to be on friendly terms, to make up after a quarrel; **4**. to engage in sexual intercourse, to copulate, to mate; **5**. to correspond to, to match, to fit, to be equal to; **6**. to be fitting, to be appropriate; **7**. (after the conditional converb) should, ought, must

acara be tuwame: in accordance with what is appropriate

acarakū: inappropriate, unfitting

acamjabumbi: **1**. (causative of **acamjambi**); **2**. to put together, to assemble

acamjambi: to come together in one place, to pool together (money)

acamjangga: composite, composed of smaller components

acamjangga besergen: a large bed composed of a number of individual beds put together

acamjangga mulan: a large bench composed of several individual smaller benches

acan: **1**. harmony, concord, union, meeting, juncture, convergence; **2**. joined, jointly, together; **3**. domino piece

acan alban i usin: public field

acan beidesi: (通判) Second Class Subprefect, *BH* 849A

acan giranggi: collarbone

acanambi: **1**. to go to meet; **2**. to fit, to suit, to be to the point, to be correct

acanaha sere hergen i temgetu: a tally consisting of two halves with characters written across it

acandumbi: to meet together; also **acanumbi**

acangga: **1**. harmonious, fitting, matching; **2**. a tally, an identification token

acangga inenggi: a day that the heaven's stems, earth's branches, and the five elements all coincide favorably

acanjimbi: (imperative: **acanju**) to come to meet, to come for an audience

acanjime isanjire tulergi gurun i bithe ubaliyambure kuren: (會同四夷譯館) Residence for Envoys of the Four Tributary States, *BH* 392

acanju: (imperative of **acanjimbi**)

acanumbi: to meet together; also **acandumbi**

acara: ⟶ **acambi** (subheading)

acarakū: ⟶ **acambi** (subheading)

acibumbi: (causative of **acimbi**)

aciha: load, burden, baggage

aciha dasatambi: to pack one's luggage for a trip

aciha fulmiyen: baggage, freight

acihi: stake, share

acihi jafambi: to hold a stake or share in a game of chance

acihilabumbi: (causative of **acihilambi**)

acihilambi: **1**. to divide equally; **2**. to form in pairs, to perform in pairs

acilambi: in wrestling, to throw by grabbing the neck

acimbi: **(1)** **(-ka)** to move slightly

acimbi: **(2)** **(-ha)** to load

acire kiyoo: a baggage litter

acire morin: packhorse

acin: load, burden

acin temen: pack camel

acindumbi: to load together

acinggiyabumbi: **1**. (causative of **acinggiyambi**); **2**. to be moved, to be affected emotionally

acinggiyambi: **1**. to touch, to move slightly; **2**. to move emotionally, to affect; **3**. to employ, to draw on (funds)

acire: ⟶ **acimbi** (subheading)

acu: ouch! (said when burned by something hot)

acu acu: coming apart, disintegrating

acu facu: with loving tenderness

acu facu seme: in pain

acu facu seme mujimbi: to groan in pain

acuhiyadabumbi: (causative or passive of **acuhiyadambi**)

acuhiyadambi: to defame, to slander, to calumniate, to incite dissension, to sow discord

acuhiyan: slander

    acuhiyan koimali: sycophantic and devious

acuhūn: harmonious, peaceful, well, on good terms

    acuhūn akū: **1**. unharmonious, at enmity; **2**. out of sorts, not well

acun: confused

    acun cacun i: **1**. confused, erratic; **2**. at odds, having differing views of something

    acun de cacun: at odds, in disagreement

ada: **1**. plank, board; **2**. raft

    ada ficakū: musical pipes consisting of sixteen sections

adabumbi: **1**. (causative of **adambi**); **2**. to attach (troops to someone), to send along with; **3**. to aid, to give assistance

    adabufi wesimbure bithe: a copy of a memorial presented to the throne

    adabuha amban: an accompanying official

    adabuha wesimbure bithei kunggeri: (副本科) archives section

    adabume wecembi: to make an offering in the ancestral temple when the tablet of a newly deceased person is placed among the ancestral tablets

adada: Brrr! — an exclamation used when it is very cold

    adada ebebe: **1**. an exclamation of surprise; **2**. clicking the tongue in amazement

    adada edede: (onomatopoetic) the sound of teeth chattering with cold

adafi: ⟶ **adambi** (subheading)

adage: exclamation of affection used when patting an old person or a child on the back

adaha: **1**. a chest or trunk on a wagon

adaha: **2**. ⟶ **adambi** (subheading)

adaki: **1**. neighbor; **2**. neighboring, adjacent

    adaki boo: neighboring house or family

adakū: assistant

adali: like, same

    adali akū: different, varying, uneven

adalikan: somewhat like, rather similar

adaliliyan: somewhat like

adalingga: similar

adališambi: to resemble, to be like (used with **de**)

adambi: **1**. to accompany, to stand by; **2**. to be attached to, to be close to, to be next to; **3**. to form the encirclement at a battue; **4**. to stitch together; **5**. to line up together

adafi kadalara amban: (宗人) Director of the Imperial Clan Court, *BH* 60

adafi simnere hafan: (副考官) assistant examiner

adaha baicara dooli hafan: (僉使道) assistant intendant

adaha bithei da: (侍讀學士) Reader of the Academy, *BH* 194

adaha giyangnara bithei da: (侍講學士) Expositor of the Academy, *BH* 195

adaha giyangnara hafan: (侍講) Subexpositor, *BH* 197

adaha hafan: (輕車都尉) a hereditary title of the sixth grade, *BH* 944

adaha hūlara bithei da: (侍讀學士) Reader of the Academy, *BH* 194

adaha hūlara hafan: (侍讀) Subreader of the Academy, *BH* 196

adaha kadalara da: (參將) Lieutenant-Colonel, *BH* 752A, 800

adaha tukiyesi: (副榜) a degree candidate entered on the secondary list, *BH* 629B

adame morilambi: to ride side by side

adame tembi: to sit next to, to live as neighbors

adanambi: **1**. to go to be near, to go to attend; **2**. to go to form the encirclement at a battue

adanjimbi: to come to accompany, to come to be attached

adanumbi: to form the encirclement at a battue together

adarame: how?, why?, how so?, what is to be done?

    adarame gamambi: how should one handle the matter?, what is to be done?

    adarame jempi: how can one bear to … ?

    adarame ohode: in which way?, under what circumstances?

    adarame ohode sain: how should one do it?

    adarame ohoni: how was it?

    adarame seci: how might … ?

adasun: lapel

adasungga: having lapels

adislambi: to bless, to pronounce a benediction

    adislame dobombi: to read a portion of scriptures at the beginning of a fasting period, to fast

adistit: blessing

adu: garment; cf. **etuku adu**

aduci: herder

aduhi: leather trousers

adulabumbi: (causative of **adulambi**)

adulambi: to herd

adulasi: herdsman

adun: **1.** herd; **2.** swarm

    adun be kadalara yamun: (太僕寺) Court of the Imperial Stud, *BH* 936B

    adun i amban: (上駟院卿) Director of the Palace Stud, *BH* 88

    adun i da: the head of a herd

    adun i hiya: (上駟院侍衛) Guard of the Palace Stud, cf. *BH* 88

    adun umiyaha: a swarming insect that attacks new grain shoots

adunggiyabumbi: (causative or passive of **adunggiyambi**)

adunggiyambi: to mistreat, to be cruel to, to torment

adurambi: to appear again after healing (said of a sore or boil), to become worse after a period of healing

afabubumbi: (causative of **afabumbi**)

afabumbi: **1.** (causative of **afambi**); **2.** to hand over to, to entrust to; **3.** to commission, to order, to bid

    afabume unggire bithe: a document from a higher organ to one of its subordinates

afaha: **1.** list, chapter, page, sheet (said of paper)

afaha: **2.** ⟶ **afambi** (subheading)

afahanambi: to form a congealed layer (at the top of a liquid)

afahari: a strip of paper, a tally, a label

    afahari dahabure ba: (僉票處) Letter Office of the Grand Secretariat

afahasi: an agricultural official appointed in ancient times by the Emperor

afakiyambi: to run about rapidly, to stumble about, to fall headlong

afakū: valiant fighter, hero

afambi: **1.** to attack, to fight, to do battle, to lay siege to; **2.** to cause trouble, to be contentious; **3.** to be restive, to kick off the hobbles, to paw the ground restively (said of horses); **4.** to encounter, to run into; **5.** to have charge of, to be charged with, to be assigned to (a post); **6.** to trip over something and fall, to stumble, to stagger

    afaha ba: position of responsibility

afara ba: battlefield

afara cuwan: ⟶ **afara jahūdai**

afara jahūdai: warship

afara morin: a horse used in battle

afara wan: a siege ladder

afan: fight, battle, clash

    afan amba: quarrelsome

afanambi: to go to attack, to strike

afandumbi: to attack together, to fight together; also **afanumbi**

afanggala: **1.** beforehand, prematurely; **2.** before one realizes it

    afanggala jabdumbi: to shoot before everyone else on a battue

afanjimbi: to come to fight or attack

afanumbi: to attack together, to fight together; also **afandumbi**

afara: ⟶ **afambi** (subheading)

afaralame: fighting retreat

afatambi: **1.** to attack, to fight (said of a group); **2.** to stumble

afin: the hem of a fur jacket's lining; cf. **naimisun**

afini: ⟶ **aifini**

afiun: opium

afiya: grass and bean plants cut together while still green

    afiya tura: a small pillar over rafters

aga: rain

    aga baire dorolon: a sacrifice offered for rain

    aga baire mukdehun: the altar for rain sacrifices

    aga dambi: to rain

    aga de hanggabumbi: to get caught in the rain

    aga galaka: the rain has cleared up

    aga jelaha: the rain has stopped

    aga labsan: raindrop

    aga muke: one of the twenty-four solar divisions of the year falling on February 19 or 20

agada: the rain deity

    agada moo: one of the names of the tamarisk (so called because the fluttering of its leaves foretells rain)

agambi: to rain

    agahai nakarakū: to rain incessantly

agangga: pertaining to rain

    agangga sara: an umbrella

age: **1**. (皇子) Prince, son of an Emperor, *BH* 13; **2**. a polite term of address, master, sir, lord; **3**. ouch!, ow!; cf. **ake**

ageli: a swelling found on the larch (*Larix leptolepis*) that is used as a medicine

agengge: pertaining to a superior — your, yours

agese: (plural of **age**)

agu: a respectful term of address for men, sir, master

agusa: (plural of **agu**)

aguse: (plural of **agu**)

agūlambi: to treat another person as senior or leader; cf. **ahūlambi**

agūra: **1**. vessel, implement, tool, weapon; **2**. a spear with a panther's tail attached; **3**. penis

agūra enduri: deity of a banner

agūra hajun: weapons

agūrai hiya: an Imperial bodyguard who carried a spear with a panther's tail attached

ag'aja: ether

aha: **1**. slave; **2**. ⟶ **aga**

aha nehū: serving boys and maids

aha sengse: lazy slave-girl! (a deprecation addressed to a lazy woman)

ahada: a slave overseer, slave master

ahada gurjen: katydid

ahada šusiha: a whip carried by the Emperor as he entered the throne room

ahadan: an old badger; cf. **dorgon**

ahalakci: (Mongolian) chief, head

ahambi: cf. **agambi**

ahandumbi: cf. **ahantumbi**

ahantumbi: to serve as a slave

ahasi: (plural of **aha**)

ahita: a flared slit at the edge of a waist-length jacket

ahūcilabumbi: (causative of **ahūcilambi**)

ahūcilambi: to treat as one's senior, to be older than

ahūlabumbi: (causative of **ahūlambi**)

ahūlambi: to act as an elder brother

ahūn: **1**. elder brother; **2**. older (said of a male)

ahūn deo: brothers (collectively)

ahūn deo arambi: to become bosom friends

ahūn i bodome: according to the difference of age

ahūngga: eldest, of the first rank, eldest son

ahūngga ahūn: eldest brother

ahūngga enen: children of the chief wife

ahūngga jui: eldest son

ahūra: ⟶ **agūra**

ahūrambi: to frighten a reclining animal

ahūri hūyari: sound used to frighten reclining animals

ahūšambi: to honor as one's senior, to treat as an elder brother

ahūta: (plural of **ahūn**)

ai: **1**. what?, which?; **2**. exclamation of regret or admiration

ai ai: all kinds, various kinds

ai ai jaka: all sorts of things

ai akū banjimbi: to live without lacking any necessity

ai amtangga: How is it interesting?

ai aniya: In what cyclical year were you born?

ai baingge: From where?, Whence?

ai baita: What (matter)?, For what reason?, What use is it?

ai bi: What difference is there?, What use is there?

ai boljon: What certainty is there?, Perhaps

ai dabumbi: Why care about … ?

ai dalji: Of what concern is it?, Of what benefit is it?

ai demun: What manner?

ai derei: How can I have the face to … ?, How dare I … ?

ai erinde: When?

ai ganaha: Why should one?, Of what use it?, **si tede ai ganaha** 'What do you want from him?'

ai gelerakū: ⟶ **ai gelhun akū**

ai gelhun akū: How dare … ?, does not dare …

ai geli: How dare I … ?, How dare you!, You're welcome

ai gūnin: What is the meaning?

ai hala: **1**. What's the point of doing it? (said of frightening things); **2**. What is (your) surname?

ai haran: For what reason?

ai hendume gaimbi: How could (I) accept it?

ai hendure: all the more … , not to mention …

ai hihan: What is so unusual about that?

ai jalin: For what reason?

ai jempi: How can one bear to … ?

ai joboro: What is there to worry about?, What is bothering you?

ai jojin: For what reason, From what motive?

ai kani: Of what relevance is it?

ai koro: Why worry?

ai maka: an expression of surprise

ai maktahai: ⟶ **ai jojin**

ai ocibe: in any case

ai ombini: What can be done?, What is wrong?

ai onggolo: How is that … ?

ai secibe: For some reason or other

ai seme: Why?, For what reason?

ai sere: says what?

ai sui: Why go to the trouble?, Why bother to?

ai šolo: when?, at what point?

ai turgun: why?, for what reason?

ai turgun de: why?, for what reason?

ai tusa: What benefit is it?

ai uttu ger seme wajirakū: What endless prattling!

ai wei seme: this way and that, in an indefinite way

ai yadara: ⟶ **ai joboro**

ai yokto: **1**. How could (you)?, How could (you) have the nerve to … ?; **2**. to what good purpose?, for what?, How could I be so bold to … ?

aiba: ⟶ **aibi**

aibaci: Whence?, From where?

aibade: Where?

aibi: **1**. used in rhetorical questions after the imperfect converb: what difference does it make?; **2**. how can it be?, how can … ?

aibi haibi akū: lacking in confidence, despondent; cf. **ebi habi aku**

aibici: Whence?, From where?

aibide: Where?

aibideri: From where?

aibimbi: to swell

aibingge: From where?

aibishūn: slightly swollen

aici: which (said of several things)?, what sort of … ?

aici jergi: what sort of?

aidagan: **1**. a four-year-old wild boar; **2**. shoulder

aidagan i kalka: wild boar meat cooked with the skin on

aidahan: ⟶ **aidagan**

aidahan i sencehe: (壁) the name of a star

aidahan sika: short bristles on a horse's tail

aidahašambi: **1**. to act like a boar; **2**. to be stubborn or obstinate, to use force

aide: where?, whither?, why?, how?

aide bahafi: for what reason?

aide bi: what official position does he hold?

aide uttu oho: how can it be like this?

aifini: a long time before, much earlier, already

aifinici: for a long time already

aifumbi: (-ka) to break one's word, to back away from a promise, to renege

aigan: archery target

aigeli: what more? (same as **ai geli**)

aiha: glazed ware, colored glaze

aiha deijire kūwaran: a factory for making glazed products

aiha sirgei dengjan: a lamp or lantern made of glass fiber mounted on a wooden stand

aiha šušu: corn (maize)

aihadambi: to leap, to be restive (said of horses or cattle)

aihadašambi: to tyrannize, to ride roughshod over

aihaji: material used for making glazed ware

aihana: glaze

aihanambi: **1**. to glaze; **2**. to form soot inside an oven bed

aihū: female sable; cf. **seke**

aihūma: **1**. (soft-shelled) turtle, *Trionyx*; **2**. cuckold

aihūme: bellows made of leather

aijirgan: (金燕) *Hirundo dauurica*: red-rumped swallow

aika: **1**. if, whether; **2**. any; **3**. something; **4**. can it be that … ?, I surmise that … , (used with **gese**), seemingly: **aika gisureki gese** 'he seems to want to speak', **aika amtanggao** 'is there anything interesting?'

aika ohode: every time, always, frequently

aika uttu aika tuttu: whether like this or like that

aikabade: if, in the case that

aikan: a precious object

aikan faikan: ⟶ **aikan**

aikanambi: **1**. if it is this way, if one does thus; **2**. if something happens

aikanaha: if it is like that (what will we do?), like **tuttu ohode ainambi**

aikanarahū: lest it be like that, I fear it will be like that

aikte: *Prunus japonica*: Korean cherry

aili: village, hamlet

ailimbi: to avoid the main road, to detour

ailime genehe: went by a detour

ailinambi: to go a roundabout way

ailungga: elegant, charming, graceful, refined, smart-looking

aimaka: probably, seemingly

aiman: tribe, minority group

  aiman hoki: tribe, tribal grouping

  aiman i adaha jorisi: (土司指揮僉事); *BH* 861A

  aiman i ahūcilaha hafan: (土司長官); *BH* 861A

  aiman i elbire dahabure hafan: (土司招討使); *BH* 861A

  aiman i elbire hafan: (土司招討使); *BH* 861A

  aiman i hafan: (土司) chieftain of a native tribe; cf. *BH* 861A

  aiman i hafan i kunggeri: (土官科) section on native administrators; cf. *BH* 861A

  aiman i minggada: (土司千戶) chieftain of one thousand, *BH* 861A

  aiman i selgiyere bilure hafan: (土司宣撫使); *BH* 861A

  aiman i selgiyere tohorombure hafan: (土司宣慰使); *BH* 861A

  aiman i tanggūda: (土司百戶) chieftain of one hundred; cf. *BH* 861A

  aiman i toktobure bilure hafan: (土司安撫使); *BH* 861A

aimika cecike: a name for the wren

aimin taimin: refractory, contrary to what is proper or natural

ainaci: ⟶ **ainambi** (subheading)

ainaha: ⟶ **ainambi** (subheading)

ainambahambi: How to obtain?, How can?

ainambi: to do what?, how?, how is (are) … ?, what's up?, why?

  ainaci ainakini: so be it

  ainaci ojoro: What can one do (so that it turns out well)?

  ainaha: **1**. What sort of?, Which?; **2**. What happened?

  ainaha seme: surely, without fail, categorically

  ainahabi: What has happened?, What's wrong?

  ainahai: **1**. how, how can?; **2**. not necessarily

  ainahai ombini: how can it be?

  ainahai uttu ni: How can it be like this?, What an outrage!

ainahani: what happened?

ainambihe: how did it come to be?

ainame: **1**. how?; **2**. expediently, tentatively, casually, in a dilatory manner

ainame acabumbi: to agree without giving serious thought, to have a casual sexual liaison

ainame ainame: for the time being, negligently, carelessly, in a dilatory manner, as one pleases

ainame gamambi: to perform perfunctorily

ainara: **1**. What sort of?; **2**. What is one to do?; **3**. (used at the beginning of a request or expression of hope): I hope that … , Will you please … ?

ainarahū: lest something happen, I fear something will happen

ainarangge: What is done?; **sini ere ainarangge**?: 'What is this that you have done?'

ainci: perhaps, probably, apparently, presumably, approximately

aini: (the instrumental form of **ai**) wherewith?, whereby?

ainu: How?, Why?, How is it that. . .?

aise: (sentence particle) perhaps, probably, presumably

aisembi: say what?, is called what?

  aisehe: what did (he) say?

  aiseme: **1**. why?; **2**. ⟶ **ai seme**

aiserengge: what sort of speech?, **sini ere aiserengge** 'what is this you say?'

aisha: *Chloris sinica*: Chinese gold-wing

  aisha cecike: ⟶ **aisha**

aisi: interest, benefit, profit

  aisi nemšembi: to put profit first

  aisi obumbi: to bring benefit to

  aisi tembi: to earn interest

aisilabukū: **1**. helper; **2**. prime minister

aisilabumbi: (causative of **aisilambi**)

aisilakū: **1**. helper; **2**. prime minister

  aisilakū hafan: (員外郎) Assistant Department Director, *BH* 291

aisilambi: to help, to aid, to reinforce, to provide

  aisilame baicara dooli hafan: (副使道) Assistant Superintendent; cf. *BH* 185E, 835A

aisilame benembi: to dispatch funds for assistance

aisilame benere menggun: funds dispatched for assistance

aisilame bure menggun: grant money

aisilame dasara dooli hafan: (參政道) intendant for governmental affairs

aisilame icihiyara dooli hafan: (參議道) assistant intendant

aisilame jafaha silgasi: (捐貢) a person who obtained a licentiate degree by purchasing it

aisilame jafaha tacimsi: (捐監) an official of the Imperial Academy

aisilame jafara baita be icihiyara boo: (捐納房) a section of the Board of Revenue concerned with the purchase of official titles

aisilame kadalara da: (副將) Colonel, *BH* 752

aisilame tacibure hafan: (助教) Assistant Teacher, *BH* 638

aisilame tuwara hafan: (副總裁官) assistant director

aisilan: help, aid, assistance

aisilandumbi: to help together, to help one another; also **aisilanumbi**

aisilangga: (副將) colonel of a brigade; cf. *BH* 752, 656D

aisilanjimbi: to come to help

aisilanumbi: to help together, to help one another; also **aisilandumbi**

aisilatambi: to help often

aisimbi: to bless, to uphold, to give support to

aisimu ilha: *Tulipa edulis*

aisin: gold

aisin argacan: a golden broadax carried in processions

aisin badiri ilha: a kind of red flower whose petals overlap one another like alms bowls

aisin cangga: a golden signal bell

aisin cecike ilha: *Cytisus scoparius*: scotch broom

aisin ceri ilha: *Vaccaria vulgaris*: cowherb

aisin cifeleku: a golden spittoon

aisin dengjan ilha: ⟶ **aisimu ilha**

aisin dere obokū: a golden basin used for face washing

aisin dosimbure faksi: goldsmith

aisin gioro: the surname of the Qing royal family

aisin hiyan i hoseri: a golden incense vessel

aisin hoošan: gold paper, gold leaf

aisin hūntahan ilha: a kind of calendula

aisin i dalgan: gold nugget

aisin i sese: golden thread

aisin ijuha: gold plated

aisin ilhangga sukū: leather decorated with golden flowers

aisin inggali: **1**. golden wagtail; **2**. a kind of yellow flower

aisin jalasu: golden token or emblem carried in processions

aisin jofohori: kumquat

aisin kanggiri: a small golden bell worn on hats by officials

aisin lakiyangga hiyan dabukū: a golden warming pan held in the hands

aisin lashangga ose loho: a gilded Japanese sword

aisin lujen: an Imperial chariot with golden squares on the top (drawn by elephants)

aisin malu: a golden wine container carried in processions

aisin muduri poo: (金龍砲) a kind of large bronze cannon

aisin mulan: a square gilded stool carried in processions

aisin nenden ilha: the Chinese trollius, a kind of flower

aisin nikekungge mulan: a stool with carved golden dragon decorations

aisin niyanjan: a chariot with golden decorations

aisin sese noho suje: silk woven with intertwined golden threads

aisin šu ilha: nasturtium

aisin šugin i iletu kiyoo: a gilded sedan chair

aisin ujima: another name for the chicken

aisin ujungga garu: a golden-headed swan

aisin ujungga yengguhe: a yellow-headed parrot

aisin usiha: the planet Venus

aisin usihangga kiru: a banner of the Imperial Escort with the planet Venus depicted on it

aisingga: profitable, helpful

aisirgan: canary

aisiri toro ilha: Chinese *Hypericum*

aisuri: a bird resembling a lark, with a short tail, white neck, and golden eyes

aitububumbi: (causative of **aitubumbi**)

aitubumbi: **1**. (causative of **aitumbi**); **2**. to save, to revive, to cure

aitubun: salvation, revival

aitumbi: to come to, to recover

aituri: a kind of wild kumquat

aiyongga ilha: golden sandflower

aja: mother

ajabumbi: **1**. (causative or passive of **ajambi**); **2**. to begin a story

    ajabume gisurembi: to tell from the beginning

ajaja: interjection of surprise

ajambi: to make a small cut, to mar by cutting

aji: first-born

    aji muyari: *Nephelium longana*: dragon's-eye

ajida: small, a small bit

    ajida jofohori: trifoliate orange

ajigalambi: to treat as a child

ajigan: young, small; cf. **ajige**

    ajigan tacin: elementary instruction

ajige: small, little, young

    ajige ajige: a bit, a little

    ajige bileri: a small *suǒnà* 唢呐 flute

    ajige bukdari: a small folded book used for notices and memorials

    ajige buren: a small brass horn

    ajige ceng: Hinayana

    ajige giyalakū moo: a small piece of wood attached to the front of a ship's mast

    ajige halhūn: one of the twenty-four solar divisions of the year — the seventh or eighth of August

    ajige hefeli: the lower belly

    ajige hiya silmen: *Accipiter virgatus*: sparrow hawk

    ajige hošo: the outside corner of the eye

    ajige hūwašan: a novice Buddhist monk

    ajige jalu: one of the twenty-four solar divisions of the year — the twenty-first or twenty-second of May

    ajige konggoro niongniyaha: a small yellow wild goose

    ajige kūrcan: a small gray crane

    ajige mama: the measles

    ajige mujilen: care, careful

ajige nimanggi: one of the twenty-four solar divisions of the year — the twenty-second or twenty-third of November

ajige ningge eršembi: to get the measles

ajige niyo coko: *Vanellus vanellus*: a small peewit

ajige suri: a kind of silk

ajige suseri: *Peucedanum graveolens*: dill

ajige šahūrun: one of the twenty-four solar divisions of the year — the sixth or seventh of January

ajige šošobun: (小结) small summary — one part of a formal essay

ajige tacikū: elementary school

ajige yangsimu niyehe: small sheldrake (a kind of duck)

ajigen: **1**. youth, young; **2**. small; cf. **ajige**

ajigesi: rather small, a bit smaller

ajilabumbi: (causative of **ajilambi**)

ajilambi: **1**. to remove the chaff; **2**. to tan (hides)

ajin: *Huso dauricus*: great sturgeon, kaluga

ajirgalambi: to cover (as a mare by a stallion)

ajirgan: a male horse, donkey, camel, or dog

    ajirgan sogi: an edible wild grass with prickles on its leaves, thistle

ajirhalambi: ⟶ **ajirgalambi**

ajirhan: ⟶ **ajirgan**

ajirka: did not recognize, confused (an acquaintance)

ajisi: a fruit that tastes like a persimmon and is the shape and size of the little finger

ak: exclamation of fear or sudden surprise

aka niyehe: loon, dabchick, birds of the genus *Gavia*

akabumbi: **1**. (causative of **akambi**); **2**. to sadden, to bring grief to, to make suffer

akaburu: an oath: may grief come upon you!

akacuka: sad, pitiful, grievous

akacun: sadness, grief

akambi: (**-ka**) to be sad, to grieve

    akame gecehe: the ice has frozen all the way to the bottom; cf. **akiyame gecehe**

akdabumbi: (causative of **akdambi**)

akdacuka: dependable, trustworthy, believable

akdacun: **1**. trust, trustworthiness, credibility; **2**. what one depends on, livelihood

    akdacun akū: not dependable, doubtful

akdambi: to depend on, to trust, to believe

akdan: trust

akdandumbi: to trust or depend on one another

akdukan: rather dependable, reliable, firm

akdulabumbi: (causative of **akdulambi**)

akdulambi: **1**. to protect, to guarantee, to defend, to fortify, to insure; **2**. to promise; **3**. to recommend

> **akdulame uhumbi**: to wrap securely

> **akdulara bithe**: a letter of guarantee

> **akdulara niyalma**: guarantor

akdulandumbi: to fortify or defend together, to promise together, to recommend together; also **akdulanumbi**

akdulanumbi: to fortify or defend together, to promise together, to recommend together; also **akdulandumbi**

akdulara: ⟶ **akdulambi** (subheading)

akdun: **1**. firm, strong, dependable, solid, sturdy; **2**. trust (for **akdan**)

> **akdun acangga**: a pass consisting of two matching pieces used for admittance to a city at night

> **akdun girdan**: a silken pennant on which the word **akdun** was embroidered

> **akdun jurgangga sargan jui**: a woman who does not marry after the death of her betrothed

> **akdun akū**: undependable

> **akdun sargan jui**: a woman who does not marry after the death of her betrothed

> **akdun temgetu**: credentials used by an Imperial envoy

akdungga: **1**. firm, solid, enduring; **2**. having creditability, credible

> **akdungga furdan**: solid gateway

ake: **1**. interjection used when touching something hot; **2**. expression of disgust

akiya: river perch; cf. **kiyakū**

akiyabumbi: **1**. (causative of **akiyambi**); **2**. to dry, to smoke

akiyambi: to dry up

> **akiyame gecehe**: frozen to the bottom

akiyan nimaha: a fish frozen into the ice

akjaba: *Veratrum nigrum*: false hellebore

akjambi: (-**ka**) to thunder

akjambulu: flying squirrel

akjan: thunder

> **akjan darimbi**: thunder roars, to thunder

> **akjan i adali durgimbi**: to roar like thunder

akjandambi: to thunder continuously

akjuhiyan: **1**. brittle, crisp; **2**. easy to anger

aksabumbi: **1**. (causative of **aksambi**); **2**. to frighten (off)

aksalambi: to be startled

aksambi: (-**ka**) to be shy, to be retiring, to hide because of fear, to be spooked

> **aksara sirga**: 'a shy deer' — metaphor for someone who is shy

aksambumbi: ⟶ **aksabumbi**

aksara: ⟶ **aksambi** (subheading)

aksargan: a belt on which a quiver is fixed

akšambi: (-**ka**) to become rancid, to spoil

akšan: water plants left hanging on trees after a flood recedes, branches and plants floating on the surface of water, flotsam, decayed matter

> **akšan taha gese**: like left-behind flotsam

akšantambi: to smell of decaying matter

akšulabumbi: (causative or passive of **akšulambi**)

akšulambi: to slander, to revile

akšun: **1**. harsh, unkind, mean, sarcastic; **2**. rancid, spoiled

> **akšun be**: an oath used to revile a person

> **akšun da**: gullet, throat

> **akšun gisun**: **1**. slanderous words, slander; **2**. harsh words, irony, sarcasm

akta: gelding

> **akta morin**: gelding

> **akta uše**: girth (saddle belly-strap)

aktalabumbi: (causative of **aktalambi**)

aktalakū moo: a horizontal wooden support over a door or window, a lintel

aktalambi: **1**. to straddle, to span; **2**. to castrate

aktaliyan: a rectangular cloth container with a slit in the middle so that both ends can be used as bags

akū: particle of negation: there is not, there are not, does not exist, is not here (there)

> **akū ci**: otherwise; cf. **akūci**

> **akū oho**: died

> **akū ojorode**: at the point of death

> **akūi ten**: ⟶ **amba ten**: the great ultimate — the ultimate principle of the universe

akūci: otherwise

akūhangge: dead person

akūmbi: to die

akūmbumbi: to endeavor, to exert to the utmost, to do one's best, to fulfill, to exhaust, to use up

akūmi: clothes made of fish skin

akūn: akū plus the interrogative particle **-n**

akūnambi: to reach (the opposite shore), to go to the end

> **akūname**: everywhere, all over, all around

> **akūnarakū ba akū**: utterly complete, there is nothing that is not reached or completed

akūngge: that which is not, that which does not exist

akūnjimbi: to arrive at this shore, to come to this side

akūtala: until nothing is left

ala: **1**. a hill with a level top; **2**. ⟶ **alan**

> **ala gasha**: a name for the pheasant

> **ala ulhūma**: ⟶ **ala gasha**

ala šala: tenderly, affectionately

alabumbi: (causative of **alambi**)

alajan: collarbone, clavicle

alakdaha: for **alakdahan**

> **alakdaha asu**: a net for catching the jerboa

alakdahan: *Allactaga sibirica*: five-toed jerboa

alambi: **1**. to tell, to report; **2**. to wrap with birch bark; **3**. to incise birch bark

alimbumbi: (causative of **alamimbi**)

alamimbi: to carry across one's back

alan: **1**. birch bark; **2**. the shoulder and breast parts of armor

> **alan erembi**: to peel off birch bark

> **alan weihu**: birchbark canoe

alanambi: to go to report

alandumbi: to report together; also **alanumbi**

alanggibumbi: (causative of **alanggimbi**)

alanggimbi: to send to report

alanjimbi: (imperative: **alanju**) to come to report

alanju: (imperative of **alanjimbi**)

alanumbi: to report together; also **alandumbi**

alarame: **1**. along a low hill; **2**. forming small hills

alari ilha: *Ixora chinensis*: mountain vermilion

alašan: **1**. inferior horse, a nag; **2**. a person who uses his strength to no avail

> **alašan morin**: inferior horse, nag

albabun: tribute, tribute products

> **albabun jafambi**: to present tribute

albalambi: to awe, to intimidate, to coerce

alban: **1**. public service, official business; **2**. official, public, fiscal; **3**. corvée, forced labor; **4**. tax, duty, tribute

alban booi turigen i namun: (官房租庫) Office for Collecting Rent of Confiscated Property, *BH* 82

alban cagan: **1**. official commission, official document; **2**. public service, corvée

alban de dosimbumbi: to press into corvée labor

alban de kambi: ⟶ **alban kambi**

alban de yabumbi: to go to an official post

alban diyan: government hostel

alban gaimbi: to collect tax or duty

alban halan akū: unfortunately

alban i bumbi: to provide at public expense

alban i hūda: official price (as set by the government)

alban i hūsun: corvée laborer

alban i usin i bolgobure fiyenten: (屯田清吏司) a section in the Board of Works concerned with military colonists

alban jafambi: to present tribute

alban jafanjimbi: to bring tribute

alban kambi: to go out on an official errand

alban šulehen: duties and taxes

alban tacikū: (官學) School of the Imperial Household, *BH* 87

alban tacikūi juse: students of the above school

alban weilembi: to do official work

albani cece: silken gauze offered as tribute

albani lamun hoošan: a kind of blue paper used for making borders

albani suje: silk offered as tribute

albasi: **1**. functionary, the person on duty; **2**. corvée laborer

albatu: **1**. rough, coarse, common, ordinary; **2**. subject people

albatukan: rather coarse

albatulambi: to act or speak coarsely

alcu: the concave side of a **gacuha**

alda: a half-grown pig

aldahi ahūn deo: second cousins

aldaka: bark of a kind of wild peach tree

aldakū: a wall placed on an archery field behind the targets

aldangga: distant (in relationship)

> **aldangga dalan**: a dike built far from shore

> **aldangga mukūn**: distant clan

> **aldanggai**: distantly, from a distance

aldanggakan: rather distant

aldarambi: (**-ka**) to die young

aldarkan: death before the age nineteen, a premature death

aldasi: halfway, midway, short-lived, cut off midway, premature (death)

aldasi ohobi: died young

aldasi wajimbi: to die young

aldasilambi: to turn back or stop halfway, to be incomplete, to die young

aldungga: strange, queer, uncommon, uncanny, ghostly

alga: ⟶ **alha**

algan: a net for catching quail

algidambi: to praise, to extol

algimbi: (**-ka**) to be famous, to become known

algimbumbi: **1**. (causative of **algimbi**); **2**. to make known, to propagate

algin: **1**. fame; **2**. the male otter; cf. **hailan**

algindambi: to praise, to laud

algingga: famous, well-known

algingga jubengge: given to spreading rumors, given to talking loosely

algintu: famous person, celebrity

algišambi: **1**. to be respected, to be well known; **2**. to boast, to put on airs; **3**. to advertise, to make known

algiyabumbi: (causative of **algiyambi**)

algiyambi: to skim the fat from the top of soup

alha: **1**. many colored, variegated, mottled; **2**. satin in which the woof and the warp are of different colors; **3**. a horse of more than one color; **4**. ⟶ **elhe alhai**

alha bulha: many colored, splendid

alha uihe beri: a bow made from spotted buffalo horn

alhabumbi: **1**. (causative of **alhambi**); **2**. at a shamanistic performance, to gather a crowd around so that by their shouting a trance may be induced in the shaman

alhacan: mottled

alhacan niyehe: *Eunetta falcata*: falcated teal

alhacan ulhūma: the small ring-necked pheasant

alhambi: to go into a trance (said of a shaman)

alhangga: spotted, speckled

alhangga anahūn moo: spotted *nánmù* 楠木 wood

alhari: spotted, variegated

alhari coko: a kind of variegated Fukienese pheasant

alhari niyehe: a kind of white spotted duck

alhata: scattered, dispersed, mixed, variegated

alhata suwaliyata: mixed, variegated

alhata yali: pork in which strips of lean and fat alternate

alhatanambi: to become spotted or mottled

alhatu: spotted, variegated

alhuru dudu: a dove with a yellow spotted back

alhūdabumbi: (causative of **alhūdambi**)

alhūdambi: to imitate, to pattern after

alhūdan: pattern, model

alhūdangga: pertaining to a pattern or model

alhūdanjimbi: to come to imitate

alhūdanumbi: to imitate one another

alhūji mama: an ugly old lady spirit

alhūwa: membrane (particularly the membrane on the heart or liver), the cornea of the eye, bamboo membrane

alhūwa burimbi: to form a cataract on the eye

alhūwa yali: diaphragm

alibumbi: **1**. (causative of **alimbi**); **2**. to present (a document to a superior), to offer

alibume wesimbure bithe: a congratulatory letter presented to the throne

alibure bithe icihiyara kunggeri: (都書科) section concerned with handling officials' leave permits and other petitions

alibure bukdan: a kind of name card used by lower officials and students

alibun: a petition

alibunjimbi: to come to present

alibure: ⟶ **alibumbi** (subheading)

alifi: ⟶ **alimbi** (subheading)

aligan: support, retainer, base, pedestal

aliha: ⟶ **alimbi** (subheading)

alihan: a strip of lining along the hem of an unlined garment

alikiyari: a kind of small green parrot

alikū: a tray, the tray used for weighing on a scale, the lower millstone

alikūlambi: to put on a scale, to put on a millstone

alimbahambi: to become accustomed to, to tolerate

alimbaharakū: **1**. intolerable, insupportable; **2**. greatly, exceedingly, very much

alimbi: **1**. to receive, to accept, to undertake, to enjoy; **2**. to endure; **3**. to oppose, to withstand; **4.** to support, to hold up; **5.** to take a falcon on the hand

alifi baicara amban: (左都御史) Senior President of the Censorate, *BH* 207A

alifi bošoro falgangga: (督催所) Office of Incitement, *BH* 493-4

alifi dasara hafan: (令尹) District Magistrate, *BH* 856

alifi hafumbure hafan: (通政使) Commissioner of the Transmission Office, *BH* 928

alifi kadalara amban: (宗令) Presiding Controller of the Imperial Clan Court, *BH* 57

alifi simnere hafan: (正考官) Examiner, *BH* 629B

alifi tacibure hafan: (學正) Departmental Director of Schools, *BH* 851A-6

aliha amban: (尚書) President of a Board, *BH* 276

aliha bithei da: (大學士) Grand Secretary, *BH* 131

aliha cooha: a Manchu or Mongol cavalryman

aliha da: (大學士) an abbreviation of **aliha bithei da**

aliha hafan: (正卿) Director; cf. *BH* 933, 934

aliha niyalma: steward, manager

aliha tacibure hafan: (祭酒) Libationer, *BH* 421A-l

alime gaimbi: to accept, to receive

alin: mountain

alin bira giyalabumbi: to be separated by mountains and rivers

alin cecike: *Passer rutilans*: russet sparrow

alin cibirgan: mountain swallow

alin efimbi: for a mirage to appear on a mountain

alin i bethe: the foot of a mountain

alin i boso: the shady or north side of a mountain

alin i cai ilha: *Camellia sasanqua*: sasanqua

alin i cecike: mountain sparrow (probably *Passer rutilans*)

alin i ebci: mountain slope

alin i hisy: steep area on a mountain

alin i jukidun: *Urocissa erythroryncha*: Chinese blue magpie

alin i mudan: mountain curves, a winding mountain road

alin i oforo: mountain ridge

alin i saiha: slope under the peak of a mountain

alin i saksaha: *Cyanopolius cyaneus*: Asiatic blue magpie

alin i ulhūma: Reeve's pheasant; cf. **nikan ulhūma**

alin i wai: a hidden spot among the curves and turns of a mountain

alin jakaraha: the mountains have become distinct at dawn

alin jakarambi: for mountains to become visible just before dawn

alin jalgangga moo: *Ailanthus glandulosa*: tree of heaven

alin ulejembi: there is a landslide

alin yadali cecike: *Garrulax davidi*: thrush

alinjimbi: to come to accept

alioi: the yang tones of the major scale

alioi hūwaliyasi: (協律郎) Chief Musician, *BH* 389-1

alirame: along a mountain

alisun: grain that has sprouted from lost or abandoned seeds

ališabumbi: (causative of **ališambi**)

ališacuka: depressed, sad, morose

ališambi: (-ka) to be listless, to be bored, to be unhappy, to worry

ališame kenehunjembi: to tarry, to be uncertain, to be undecided

ališatambi: to be deeply depressed

alitun: a small table for offerings

aliyabumbi: (causative of **aliyambi**)

aliyacun: **1.** regret, repentance, remorse; **2.** waiting

aliyakiyambi: to linger, to pace back and forth while waiting, to slow down to allow someone to catch up

aliyambi: **1.** to wait; **2.** to regret, to repent, to feel remorse

aliyasungga: patient, long-suffering

aljabumbi: **1.** (causative of **aljambi**); **2.** to banish, to make leave, to exorcise

aljambi: **1.** to leave, to part from someone; **2.** to lose (color); **3.** ⟶ **angga aljambi**

alkūn: pace, step, gait

alkūn amba: wide-gaited

alkūn be sindambi: to hasten one's pace

almin indahūn: a dog with a long muzzle

altahana: **1**. pea tree; **2**. *Caragana leucophloea* (a plant)

altan harhana: ⟶ **altahana**

alun indahūn: a dog with a short muzzle

ama: father, head of the household

    ama aja: mother and father, parents

amaga: afterward, later, future

    amaga baita: funeral affairs

    amaga enen: descendant

    amaga inenggi: in the future

    amaga jalan: later generation, posterity

amagangge: that which is later

amaha: ⟶ **amaga**

amaka: husband's father

amala: **1**. behind; **2**. after, later

    amala fiyanjilambi: to form a rear guard, to cover the rear

    amala obumbi: to set aside

    amala tutambi: to leave behind

amargi: **1**. back, behind; **2**. north

    amargi colhon i kiru: (北嶽旗) a banner with Mt. Heng (恆山) depicted on it

    amargi falgangga: (後所) Fifth Subdepartment of the Imperial Equipage Department, *BH* 122

    amargi fisembuhe boo: a building behind the main house

    amargi fiyentehe: (後股) the last section of a formal essay

    amargi juwere jekui kunggeri: (北漕科) a bureau of the Board of Revenue concerned with transporting grain from the south (Yunnan) to the north

    amargi nahan: the *kàng* on the north side of the room

amargingge: **1**. that which comes after; **2**. afterbirth; **3**. pertaining to the north

amari: after, afterward

amarilambi: to fall behind, to fall short

amarimbi: to fall behind

amasi: **1**. backward, to the back, toward the back, northward; **2**. after, henceforth

    amasi bumbi: to sacrifice to the Big Dipper

    amasi dushumbi: to draw the right hand back forcefully (in archery)

    amasi julesi: backward and forward

amasikan: a little bit behind

amata: (plural of **ama**)

amba: big, great, vast, important

    amba ajige: large and small (size)

    amba bayara: (護軍營) guard division; cf. *BH* 734

    amba beikuwen: one of the twenty-four solar divisions of the year falling on January twentieth or twenty-first

    amba ceng: Mahayana

    amba doro: Imperial rule

    amba dulin: a majority

    amba duwalinaha: (大簇) one of the six tones of the major scale

    amba elhe niyanjan: (大安輦) an Imperial chariot drawn by six men

    amba elioi: (大呂) one of the six tones of the minor scale

    amba erdemungge gurun: Germany

    amba garma: a large yellow mosquito; cf. **galman**

    amba halhūn: one of the twenty-four divisions of the solar year falling on August twenty-third or twenty-fourth

    amba hiyoošun: the filial piety of the Emperor

    amba hiyoošungga: supremely filial — an epithet of the Emperor

    amba holbonggo hoošan: paper used for making money that is burned as a sacrifice

    amba hošo: the inner corner of the eye

    amba hūwaliyambure deyen: (太和殿) the main throne hall in the Beijing palace

    amba ija: horsefly

    amba koolingga hafan: (太史) Compiler of the Second Class, *BH* 200B

    amba kumun: music played when the Emperor retired to his private chambers after a banquet

    amba lampa: great chaos

    amba muke: a flood

    amba muru: **1**. probably, generally, in outline, approximately; **2**. sketch, outline

    amba nimanggi: one of the twenty-four divisions of the solar year falling on the seventh or eighth of December

    amba sargan: the first or chief wife

    amba suri: a kind of rough silk

amba šahūrun: one of the twenty-four divisions of the solar year falling on the twentieth or twenty-first of January

amba šoge: a fifty-ounce silver ingot

amba šošobun: (大結) great summary — the last part of a formal essay

amba tacin: Mahayana (Buddhism)

amba ten: (太極) the great ultimate — the ultimate principle of the universe

amba toosengge abka: mighty heaven

amba yabungga: (title for a deceased Emperor)

amba yali: meat offered and eaten at a sacrifice

amba yolonggo jahūdai: a kind of fast war junk

ambakaliyan: rather large, somewhat big

ambakan: rather big, a person who is rather large

ambakasi: rather large

ambaki: haughty, proud, pompous

ambakilambi: to act haughtily

ambalinggū: **1**. big and tall, stalwart, imposing, grand, great; **2**. dignified

ambalinggū alin i alban tacikū: (景山官學) School at the Red Hill, *BH* 87B

ambalinggū munggan: (景陵) the mausoleum of the Kangxi Emperor

amban: **1**. high official, minister; **2**. subject, vassal; **3**. your servant (used by officials when addressing the Emperor); **4**. ⟶ **amba**

amban i manambi: **1**. to be carried out carelessly; **2**. (the month) has thirty days

ambarambi: to do on a large scale, to do in a big way

ambarame: greatly, very much

ambarame giyangnara hafan: (經筵講官) an official charged with explaining the classics to the Emperor

ambarame simnembi: to hold the tri-yearly examination in the capital

ambarame wecere wecen: the sacrifice offered by the Emperor to all the Imperial ancestors every five years

ambasa: **1**. (plural of **amban**); **2**. rather large

ambasa saisa: (君子) a worthy, wise man, a true gentleman

ambu: aunt: mother's elder sister

ambuhai ambuhai: unintentionally

ambula: **1**. very, exceedingly; **2**. wide, extensive; **3**. many

ambula asarara fiyenten: (廣儲司) Department of the Privy Purse, *BH* 77

ambula beikuwen: extremely cold

ambula iktambure namun: (廣積庫) the name of an armory under the Board of Works

ambulakan: rather greatly, rather much

ambuma: uncle: mother's elder sister's husband

ambumbi: to overtake and catch

ambuta: (plural of **ambu**)

amcabumbi: (causative or passive of **amcambi**)

amcadambi: **1**. to make friends or claim kinship with someone of a higher social station, to play up to; **2**. to strive to overtake; **3**. to speak before someone else has a chance

amcakūšambi: **1**. to follow, to pursue; **2**. to interrogate, to question; **3**. to investigate

amcambi: **1**. to pursue, to chase, to catch up to; **2**. to hurry, to rush; **3**. to act in retrospect, to act posthumously; **4**. to review (a case); **5**. **dobori be amcame**: under cover of darkness; **6**. to take advantage of; **7**. to make up for gambling losses; **8**. to recover something lost

amcame fungnembi: to enfeoff posthumously

amcame gebu bumbi: to give a name posthumously

amcame gūnimbi: to think back in retrospect

amcarakū: cannot make it on time, unable to meet a deadline

amcanambi: to go to pursue, to rush (over)

amcangga: pertaining to pursuit

amcangga jahūdai: the name of a kind of large warship

amcanjimbi: to come to pursue, to come pursuing, to catch up with

amcarakū: ⟶ **amcambi** (subheading)

amcatambi: ⟶ **amcadambi**

amda musihi: **1**. unsociable, aloof; **2**. in confusion

amda musihi akū: cold, indifferent

amdulabumbi: (causative of **amdulambi**)

amdulambi: to paste, to glue

amdun: glue, paste, birdlime

amdun bilcambi: to spread glue

amga: ⟶ **amaga**

amgabumbi: **1**. (causative of **amgambi**); **2**. to put to bed

amgacambi: to sleep together

amgambi: to sleep

amganambi: to go to sleep

amha: wife's father

amhabumbi: ⟶ **amgabumbi**

amhacambi: ⟶ **amgacambi**

amhambi: ⟶ **amgambi**

amhan: ⟶ **amha**

amhanambi: ⟶ **amganambi**

amhūlan: a whistle used by hunters

amida: small-leaf poplar, aspen

> **amida nimalan**: sallow

amihūn: realgar

amila: the male of fowl

> **amila coko**: rooster, cock

amilambi: **1**. to anoint a Buddhist icon's eyes with blood and thereby impart life to it; **2**. to grasp the cantle of a saddle

> **amilame cashūn fiyelembi**: to vault backward grasping the cantle of a saddle

amin: cantle

amji: uncle: father's elder brother

amjita: (plural of **amji**)

amsu: food presented to the Emperor

> **amsu i da**: (尚膳正) Chief Trencher-Knight, *BH* 91

> **amsu ibebumbi**: to set food before the Emperor

amsulambi: to dine (used for the Emperor)

amsun: offerings of wine and food to a deity

> **amsun dagilara boo**: (神廚) the place where offerings of wine and food were prepared

> **amsun i da**: (司胙長) official in charge of preparing offerings of food and wine

> **amsun i janggin**: (司胙官) an official concerned with the preparation of offerings of food and wine

> **amsun i yali**: meat used as an offering to a deity

> **amsun jafambi**: to prepare an offering of food or wine

amtalambi: **1**. to try, to test food, to take a test; **2**. to try out a bow

amtan: **1**. taste, smell; **2**. interest, delight

> **amtan acabumbi**: to flavor, to add seasoning

> **amtan akū**: **1**. tasteless; **2**. boring, uninteresting

> **amtan bahambi**: to acquire a taste

> **amtan dosimbi**: to be satisfied with, to be pleased with

> **amtan gaimbi**: to take a taste

> **amtan simten**: taste, flavor

amtan simten akū: listless, bored

amtan tuhembi: to have one's fun spoiled, to have a damper thrown on things, to become discouraged

amtangga: **1**. tasty, delicious; **2**. enjoyable, interesting, fun, interested in

> **amtanggai**: pleasurably

amtašambi: to taste continually or often

amtun: (俎) a kind of ancient sacrificial vessel

amu: **1**. aunt: father's elder brother's wife, mother's sister; **2**. sleep; **3**. pancreas

> **amu gaimbi**: to take a nap

> **amu getembi**: to awake from sleep

> **amu isinjimbi**: to fall asleep

> **amu jimbi**: for sleep to come, to fall asleep

> **amu mangga**: very sleepy

> **amu sektu**: sleeping lightly

> **amu sureke**: wide awake after waking up

> **amu suwaliyame**: half asleep, having a sleepy aspect

> **amu šaburambi**: to become sleepy

amuran: fond of, intent on, good at, assiduous

amurangga: devotee, one who is fond of something, that which one is fond of

amurgan: a kind of fine-grained yellow wood used to make arrow shafts

amurtu sarla: a swift gray horse

amušabumbi: to fall asleep; cf. **amu šaburambi**

amuta: (plural of **amu** [**1**])

an: **1**. usual, ordinary, common; **2**. order, discipline

> **an akū**: irregular, unusual

> **an be tuwakiyambi**: to follow what is customary

> **an ciktan i tanggin**: a hall where the Emperor gave instruction or lectured

> **an i**: as usual, as customary

> **an i baita**: an everyday matter

> **an i buda**: everyday, ordinary food

> **an i gisun**: saying, proverb

> **an i gu**: ordinary jade

> **an i jergi**: ordinary, usual

> **an i niyalma**: layman (as opposed to a monk or nun), secular person

> **an i ucuri**: usually, ordinarily

> **an i wesimbure bithe**: a memorial dealing with a private matter but lacking an official seal

> **an jergi**: ⟶ **an i jergi**

> **an kemun**: rule, common practice, custom

an kooli: custom, usage

an wehe: whetstone

anabumbi: 1. (causative or passive of **anambi**); 2. to yield to, to be defeated

anabure etere: victory and defeat, loss and gain

anafu: garrison, border garrison

anafu cooha: garrison troops

anafu tembi: to be on garrison duty, to be stationed at a garrison

anafulabumbi: (causative of **anafulambi**)

anafulambi: to garrison, to guard a frontier

anagan: 1. excuse, pretext; 2. intercalary

anagan arambi: to make an excuse or pretext

anagan i biya: the intercalary month

anahūn moo: *Machilus nanmu*: *nánmù* 楠木 tree

anahūngga gurung: an Emperor's coffin

anahūnjambi: to be yielding, to be humble, to be modest, to yield to, to give up voluntarily

anahūnjan: modesty, reticence

anahūnjangga: modest, humble, reticent

anakū: 1. key; 2. pretext

anakū arambi: to make an excuse, to use a pretext

anakū fa: a sliding window

anakū jui: posthumous child: a child born after its father has died

anakū sejen: a one-wheeled pushcart

anakūi da: (司鑰長) Keeper of Palace Keys, *BH* 108

anambi: 1. to push; 2. to urge, to prompt; 3. to extend (a deadline), to delay; 4. to appoint; 5. to make excuses, to blame others; 6. to push wider (a battue); 7. to forsake, to reject

aname: 1. even: **ama (ci) aname** 'even farther'; … **ci aname** … **de isitala** 'from … to…'; 2. in order, in sequence, one after another, one by one; 3. according to; 4. perfunctorily, carelessly, making do with; cf. **ainame**

aname arambi: to write in order

anameliyan: with the chest protruding

anami: a grown Manchurian moose; cf. **kandahan**

anan: 1. an Imperial carriage; 2. pushing, urging; 3. sequence

anan i: in turn, successively

anan i silgasi: (挨貢) a graduate promoted to a position that became vacant yearly

anan šukin: obsequious, timid, lacking in self-confidence

anangga: 1. a pretext; 2. having a pretext

anashūn: flexible, yielding, modest, unassuming

anatambi: 1. to push together or repeatedly; 2. to put off (until another time), to procrastinate; 3. to shift blame to someone else, to shirk responsibility

ancu hiyan: a kind of fragrant grass burned at sacrifices

anculan giyahūn: hawk

anculan gūwara: ⟶ **ancun gūwara**

ancun: earring, ear pendant

ancun gūwara: probably *Bubo bubo*: the North China eagle owl

ancun i bohori: decorations of gold, coral, or some other precious material attached to ear pendants

ancun ilha: a kind of jasmine

ancun umiyaha: cockroach

ancurahi: gilded leather; cf. **gina**

anda: 1. a sworn brother, bosom friend, friend from childhood; 2. how truly

anda jafambi: to swear an oath of brotherhood

anda sadun: friends and in-laws

anda saikan: really good, very good

andahalambi: to be ashamed, to become ashamed

andahašambi: to turn red from embarrassment

andala: on the way, midway, halfway

andala giyamun: a post-station along the route

andan: an instant, a moment

andande: suddenly, in an instant, at once

andarambi: to be shy of strangers (said of children)

andargi: along the way

andarki: ⟶ **andargi**

andasi: halfway, half of the way

andubumbi: 1. to dispel worries, to take it easy; 2. to pause for a rest

anduhūri: indifferent, coldhearted, unfriendly

anduhūrilambi: to treat (a person) coldly

anfu: a garrison, a border post; cf. **anafu**

anfulambi: ⟶ **anafulambi**

ang: the sound made by camels and donkeys, a scream used in battle

ang seme: the sound of moaning

ang seme afambi: to attack while shrieking war whoops

ang seme nidumbi: to moan, to groan in pain

angga: 1. mouth, mouthful; 2. opening, hole; 3. pass, gate

angga acambi: 1. to testify in court; 2. to kiss

angga aifumbi: to break one's word

angga akšun: abusive, slanderous

angga alimbi: to be promised in marriage

angga aljambi: to promise, to agree to

angga arambi: to acknowledge orally

angga bahambi: to obtain a confession

angga baibi miosiri miosirilambi: to have a slight smile on one's face

angga baimbi: to interrogate (a criminal)

angga be jusimbi: to jabber, to engage in idle talk

angga cakcahūn: tight-mouthed, hard to control (said of horses)

angga cira: 1. tight-mouthed (said of horses); 2. tight-lipped, secretive

angga cukcuhun: lips protruded — an expression of annoyance

angga dambi: to interrupt, to speak up, to interfere

angga de gamaha ba akū: (liquor) has never touched his lips

angga de gamambi: to touch the lips (said of liquor)

angga duyen: weak-mouthed (said of horses)

angga ehe: sarcastic, caustic

angga faksi: clever in speech, glib

angga fecuhun: without appetite

angga fodorombi: to protrude the lips in annoyance

angga gahūšambi: to be at a loss for words

angga gaimbi: to kiss

angga gakahūn: with the mouth agape

angga gejenggi: garrulous, talkative

angga hetumbi: to earn a living, to scrape along, to get by

angga hetumbumbi: to earn a living, to get by

angga hotohon: having lips that protrude upward

angga hūdun: loose-tongued

angga i anakū: a pretext for scandal or gossip

angga i hošo: the corner of the mouth

angga ici: not thinking before speaking, fluently, effortlessly (said of speech)

angga isi: please try some (said when offering food to a guest)

angga isibumbi: to make or let taste first

angga isimbi: to taste first

angga jafambi: 1. to close the mouth; 2. to catch a prisoner of war who is to be used as an informer

angga johimbi: the opening (of a boil) shrinks and heals

angga labdahūn: having lips that hang down

angga mangga: stubborn, reluctant

angga mentuhun: without feeling in the mouth (said of horses)

angga mimimbi: to close the mouth

angga ojombi: to kiss

angga sonjombi: to have a craving for odd foods when one is pregnant, to be picky about eating

angga sula: loose-mouthed (said of horses)

angga sulfambi: to migrate to another place because of a lack of food, to eke out an existence, to keep body and soul together

angga šoforombi: to purse the lips

angga tucimbi: to come to a head (said of a boil)

anggai anakū: pretext for gossip

anggai dambi: to blow, to puff, to butt in, to interrupt

anggai fakjin: mnemonic formula

anggai ici: ⟶ **angga ici**

anggai jasimbi: to transmit by word of mouth, to deliver a verbal communication

anggala: 1. population, persons; 2. (postposition) in place of, instead of, rather than, not only

anggalai bele: military rice allotment

anggalambi: to request, to demand

anggalinggū: fluent, glib

anggara: a large jar, a container for water

anggari janggari: all mixed up, in disarray

anggasi: widow

anggasi hehe: widow

anggasibumbi: (causative of **anggasimbi**)

anggasilambi: to be a widow, to preserve widowhood

anggasimbi: to taste, to try

anggatu: muzzle for domestic animals

anggi: (Mongolian) group, part

anggir niyehe: *Cascara ferruginea*: the ruddy sheldrake

anggiyan: thornback (a kind of sea fish)

anggūta: **1**. muzzle; **2**. a piece of iron attached to the end of a sword's hilt

aniya: year

    aniya aliha gūsai siden yamun: (值年旗衙門) General Headquarters of the Banners, *BH* 718

    aniya arambi: to celebrate the New Year

    aniya biya: the first lunar month

    aniya goidaha: old

    aniya hūsime: for an entire year, a whole year

    aniya i fe inenggi: the last day of the year

    aniya inenggi: New Year's day

    aniya nurhūme: for years running, for years on end

    aniya tome: every year

aniyadari: every year

aniyaingge: pertaining to a (certain) year

aniyalame: for an entire year, a whole year

aniyangga: **1**. pertaining to a certain year in the twelve-year cycle; **2**. aged

    aniyangga nimeku: a chronic illness

    aniyangga sakda: an aged man

anja: plow

anji: adze

anjibumbi: to use an adze (causative of **anjimbi**)

anjikū: small adze

anjimbi: to hack, to chop with an adze

anju: meat and fish, animal products, food forbidden to Buddhists

    anju belhere ba: (葷局) a place in the banqueting-court where food was prepared for state occasions

anta: for **antaka**

antaha: guest, stranger

    antaha be boigojilara bolgobure fiyenten: (主客清吏司) Reception Department, *BH* 376A

    antaha be tuwašatara bolgobure fiyenten: (賓客清吏司) Department for the Reception of Foreign Guests

    antaha i kuren: hostel for foreign envoys

    antahai boo: room for receiving guests

antahalambi: to entertain, to be a guest

antaharambi: to be a guest, to act as a guest, to stand on ceremony

antahasa: (plural of **antaha**)

antahasi: aide to a high official or general, private advisor

antahašambi: to act as a guest, to be polite

antai: ⟶ **antaka**

antaka: How is it?, What is it like?, What about … ?, How about … ?

antarhan cecike: one of the names of the sparrow; cf. **fiyasha cecike**

antu: the south side of a mountain, the sunny side of a mountain

antuhūri: cold, indifferent

anwan: sea perch

ao: an interjection expressing doubt

ar: the sound of calling or shouting

    ar seme: shouting loudly

ara: **1**. chaff, husks of grain; **2**. interjection of pain or surprise

    ara fara: an interjection of pain, the sound of expectorating

    ara fara sembi: to wail, to cry loudly

    ara uyan buda: gruel made from chaff

arabumbi: (causative of **arambi**)

araha: ⟶ **arambi** (subheading)

arajan: strong distilled liquor made from milk; cf. **arjan**

arake: ⟶ **ara** (as an interjection)

arambi: **1**. to do, to make; **2**. to write; **3**. to feign, to pretend; **4**. to celebrate; **5**. to appoint to a vacant post temporarily; **6**. to recognize as an adopted relation; **7**. to serve as, to act as, to use as

    araha: adopted, appointed

    araha bayarai jalan i janggin: (委護軍參領) an appointed Colonel of the Guards Division, *BH* 734

arandumbi: to do, write (etc.) together; also **aranumbi**

aranjimbi: to come to do, write, etc.

aranumbi: to do, write, etc., together; also **arandumbi**

arašan: propitious, refreshing

    arašan aga: a seasonable rain, a propitious rain

    arašan agangga kiru: a gray banner with the symbol of a dragon sewn on it

arbun: **1**. form, shape, image, appearance; **2**. situation, circumstances; **3**. scene, scenery

    arbun be tuwame: in view of the circumstances, depending upon circumstances

    arbun de: in appearance

arbun dursun: form, appearance, situation
arbun fiyan: appearance, countenance
arbun giru: appearance
arbun i angga: juncture of two rivers
arbun i ba: a strategic point
arbun muru: situation
arbun tacihiyan: Buddhism
arbungga: **1**. possessing form, having good form, pertaining to images; **2**. scenic, presentable
arbungga tacihiyan: Buddhism
arbušambi: to move, to behave
arbutai: in appearance only, for appearance's sake
arca burga: *Salix urbaniana*: large-leaf willow; cf. **aršan burga**
arcambi: to block, to block the way
arcan: cream, milk thickened with wine and sugar
arcilan burga: ⟶ **arca burga**
arda: untried, new, a greenhorn
ardashūn: delicate, fragile
are: an interjection of pain
arfa: barley, grain
arfa dib: (Sanskrit Yavadvīpa 'Isle of Grain') Java
arfukū: fly swatter, fly whisk
arga: **1**. plan, method; **2**. plot, scheme; **3**. fang; cf. **argan**
arga akū: there is nothing one can do about it
arga baimbi: to look for a way
arga de dosimbi: to fall into a trap, to fall for a plot
arga de tuhembi: to fall into a trap, to be a victim of deceit
arga deribumbi: to think up a plan
arga jali: plot, deceit
argai wambi: to murder
argabumbi: (causative of **argambi**)
argabuha dalan: a dike built in the shape of a crescent moon
argacan: a large ax, halberd, battle ax
argadabumbi: (causative of **argadambi**)
argadambi: to use artifice or cunning (against), to outwit
argai: ⟶ **arga** (subheading)
argali: female of Darwin's sheep; cf. **uhūlja**
argambi: to hunt animals in the mountains using a sickle-shaped battue line, to form a crescent or sickle shape

argan: **1**. sprout; **2**. crescent; **3**. fang, tooth of a saw; **4**. a 'tooth' in the Manchu script
argan mudun: a fine file
argan ošoho: fangs and claws
arganacambi: to sprout continually
arganambi: **1**. to form a crescent; **2**. to germinate, to sprout
arganaha: formed a crescent moon
argangga: crafty, cunning
argat: ⟶ **arhat**
argat moo: *Podocarpus macrophyllus*: yew, plum pine (Chinese *luóhàn sōng* 羅漢松)
argatu: male roe, roebuck; cf. **sirga**
argatu sirga: ⟶ **argatu**
argiyabumbi: (causative or passive of **argiyambi**)
argiyambi: **1**. to peel off, to shave off, to scrape off, to strip away, to remove; **2**. to remove from an official post; **3**. to prune, to take branches away from a tree; **4**. to quell, to wipe out
argūma sarla: an isabella horse
arhan: ⟶ **argan**
arhat: an arhat
ari: **1**. an evil spirit; **2**. a good-for-nothing, a thoroughly mischievous person; **3**. what a ghost becomes after its death
ari yakca: (a Buddhist term) devil, evil-spirit
arjan: distilled liquor made from milk; cf. **arajan**
arkan: scarcely, barely, just
arkan arkan: barely, by the skin of one's teeth
arkan karkan: barely, scarcely
arkan seme: scarcely, barely, just, reluctantly
arke: interjection of pain used when bumping into something
arki: distilled liquor, strong liquor
arsalan: lion
arsalangga: pertaining to the lion, lion-like, leonine
arsarakū: strange, out of the ordinary
arsari: ordinary, common, everyday, commonplace
arsari banjimbi: to lead an average life
arsari šanyan bele: medium quality rice
arsari šaraka: half-white, impure white
arsari tuwabungga hoošan: medium-size paper used for announcements
arsaringge: an average person
arsubumbi: (causative of **arsumbi**)
arsumbi: (-ka) to sprout, to germinate
arsun: bud, sprout
arsun i cai: tea made of the buds of tea leaves

aršan burga: *Salix urbaniana*: large leaf willow

aršu: one of the names of the quail; cf. **mušu**

artabumbi: (passive of **artambi**)

artambi: to delay, to hold up

artu: a three-year-old horse

aru: (Mongolian) north

arun durun: trace

    arun durun akū: without a trace

arun furun: news

    arun furun akū: without news

asaha fasaha: hurried, rushed, busy

asanggi: 100 quadrillion, countless, infinite

asarabumbi: (causative of **asarambi**)

asarambi: **1**. to put away for safekeeping, to store; **2**. to harbor in one's heart; **3**. to imprison, to put in custody; **4**. to detain

asaran: storage; cf. **namun asaran**

asari: tower, throne room, archive

    asari i baita be alifi kadalara amban: (領閣事) Assistant Director of the Library, *BH* 104B

    asari i baita be dame kadalara amban: (提舉閣事) Director of the Library, *BH* 104B

    asari i baita be sirame kadalara hafan: (直閣事) Officials on duty at the Library, *BH* 104B

asha: **1**. wing; **2**. anything worn hanging from the belt; **3**. a piece of iron placed on the back of armor under a shoulder piece

    asha sarambi: to spread the wings

ashabukū: a leather clasp for a belt

ashabumbi: (causative of **ashambi**)

ashambi: **1**. to wear hanging from the belt, to wear hanging from a button on the lapel, to wear hanging out the side; **2**. to wear a hat

    ashara fungku: a kerchief carried from the belt

    ashara šusihe: a wooden plaque worn on the belt that served as identification for an official who wished to enter a walled city after dark

ashan: **1**. side; **2**. appendage; **3**. peripheral, subordinate

    ashan da: (內閣學士) Sub-Chancellor of the Grand Secretariat, *BH* 133

    ashan i amban: (侍郎) Vice-President of a Board, *BH* 279

    ashan i baicara amban: (副都御史) Vice-President of the Censorate, *BH* 207B, 208

    ashan i bithei da: (學士) Sub-Chancellor of the Grand Secretariat, *BH* 133

    ashan i boo: wing of a building

    ashan i duka: a side entrance to the palace

    ashan i hafan: (男) baron

ashanambi: **1**. to develop wings; **2**. to become distended on two sides

ashangga: winged

    ashangga mahala: an old style hat with long black wings on two sides

    ashangga singgeri: bat

    ashangga yerhuwe: a winged ant, flying ant

ashara: ⟶ **ashambi** (subheading)

ashargan: a pendant for the belt

ashūbumbi: (passive of **ashūmbi**)

ashūlambi: ⟶ **ashūmbi**

ashūmbi: **1**. to reject, to refuse; **2**. to draw the right hand back to shoot an arrow or throw a spear; **3**. to fend off, to chase off; **4**. to give up, to abandon

    ashūme sindambi: to shoot an arrow by drawing the right hand back

asi: very

asigan: ⟶ **asihan**

asiha: young, small

asihaki: having a youthful appearance in spite of one's age

asihan: young, youth

    asihan aisin hūntahan ilha: *Adonis davurica*: pheasant's eye

    asihan sargan: concubine

asihasa: (plural of **asihan**); cf. **asihata**

asihata: **1**. (plural of **asihan**); **2**. youth (often used as a singular)

asihiyabumbi: (causative of **asihiyambi**)

asihiyambi: to trim off, to pare off, to prune

asikaliyan: somewhat small

asikan: somewhat small

asikasi: someone or something rather small

aska faska: busy, bustling

asu: a net (for catching game or fish)

    asu uksin: net armor

    asu wešen: net for deer and rabbits

asuci: a hunter who uses a net for catching game

asuki: a small noise

asuki akū: noiseless

asuki wei akū: without the slightest noise

asukilabumbi: (causative of **asukilambi**)

 asukilabure fu: a wall that causes echoes to rebound

asukilambi: to make a small noise

asukingga: noisy, boisterous

asumbi: to lift up a garment that is too long

asuri: Asura, a demigod who fights with devas in the air

asuršambi: to threaten one another, to provoke one another

asuru: very, exceedingly

 asuru encu ba akū: not too different

aša: aunt: elder brother's wife

ašašambi: ⟶ **aššambi**

ašata: (plural of **aša**)

aššabumbi: (causative of **aššambi**)

aššalambi: to move slightly, to squirm

aššambi: to move, to shake, to vibrate

 aššara arbušara: movement

aššan: **1**. movement, vibration; **2**. behavior; **3**. one of the eight trigrams of the *Yijing* (symbolizing thunder)

aššandumbi: to move together

ašumbi: (-ka) to hold in the mouth

ašumbumbi: **1**. (causative of **ašumbi**); **2**. to stick in the mouth

 ašumbuha fadu jan: a 'duckbill' whistling arrow

atan: the point of a fish hook

atanggi: when?

 atanggi bicibe: no matter when

 atanggi ocibe: before long, soon

atarambi: to make a commotion, to cause a row; cf. **abtarambi**

atmula: one of the names for the *Canarium album*: Chinese sweet olive

atu: a female fish

atuha: a male fish

 atuha dafaha: a male chum salmon

atuhūn: dowry

 atuhūn fudembi: to bring a dowry to the groom's house

aya: **1**. interjection of praise or surprise; **2**. ⟶ **ai**

ayalambi: **1**. to wax, to cover with a wax coating; **2**. to form a vesicle (during smallpox)

ayalaha ilhangga hoošan: a kind of flowered paper covered with a layer of wax

ayambi: to flutter, to struggle (like a fish that has taken the hook)

ayambumbi: to captivate, to entice; cf. **gisurehei ayambumbi**

ayan: **1**. large, great; **2**. wax, candle; **3**. *Cervus elaphus*: Manchurian wapiti, elk

 ayan buhū: *Cervus elaphus*: Manchurian wapiti, elk

 ayan dengjan: candle

 ayan dobokū: candlestick

 ayan edun: storm winds, windstorm

 ayan fodoho: *Salix purpurea*: purple osier

 ayan gaha: a kind of large crow with a white neck

 ayan gintehe: a tree with green bark, small leaves, and fine wood — good for bows and knife handles

 ayan gurjen: black tree cricket

 ayan harsa: beech marten

 ayan hiyan: the name of grass burned at sacrifices — rue

 ayan i calu: (蠟倉) wax storehouse of the Imperial household

 ayan i fithengge: snuff — the part of the candle wick that is already burned

 ayan i hafirakū: a candle snuffer

 ayan i niyaman: wick (of a candle)

 ayan i niyaman tebuku: a container for burned wick ends

 ayan jelken: a species of weasel

 ayan malanggū: sesame

 ayan silmen: the male of the sparrow hawk

 ayan suwayan: truly precious, honorable

 ayan šugiri hiyan: incense made from Indian resin

 ayan toktokū: a lantern with a candle in it

 ayan wehe: a shiny smooth stone

ayantumbi: to soar upward (said of hawks and eagles)

ayao: ⟶ **ayoo**

ayara: sour milk, buttermilk, koumiss

ayari: wax-like

 ayari ilha: *Chimonanthus praecox*: wintersweet

ayoo: a final particle denoting fear or doubt

B ꦏ

ba: **1**. place, location; **2**. land; **3**. *lǐ*: a Chinese mile (= 0.5 kilometers); **4**. circumstances, occasion; **5**. wager, stake (at gambling); **6**. hegemon, overlord

ba anabumbi: to yield one's place

ba aname: everywhere, all over

ba arambi: to make a place, to get out of the way

ba ba: everywhere, every place

ba baimbi: to act as a go-between

ba bumbi: to give a place to, to give a portion to

ba dzung: (把總) Sublieutenant, *BH* 752F

ba i gisun: dialect, local language

ba i tacin: local custom

ba i ten: foundation, base

ba jiyoo: plantain, banana

ba na: territory, land, local

ba na i nirugan: map

ba na i nirugan nirure boo: (輿圖房) Department of Cartography in the Workshop of the Imperial Household

ba na tuwara niyalma: a geomancer

ba siyan dere: (八仙桌) a large square dining table

ba sulabumbi: to leave a vacant place

ba wang: hegemon-king

ba wang asu: a kind of net for catching fish

babaci: from everywhere

babade: everywhere

babi: **1**. without recompense; **2**. for no reason, gratuitously; **3**. unoccupied, unemployed; **4**. simply, merely; **5**. ordinary, commonplace, average; cf. **baibi**

babuhan: a five-fingered leather glove for holding falcons

babun: **1**. handle on a bucket or basket; **2**. crupper

babungga: having a handle

baci: ⟶ **ba ci**

bacihi: **1**. husband and wife of a first marriage, married for the first time; **2**. married while still a child

bacihi haha: newly married man

bacihi sargan: newly married woman

bacihilambi: to be betrothed as a child

bada: dissipation, waste

badalambi: to squander, to dissipate, to waste

badan: dish, tray

badar: a monk's alms bowl; cf. **badiri**

badar seme: speaking without due deliberation, speaking wildly

badaraka: abundant, rich

badarambi: (-ka) to become wide, to expand, to become larger, to become prosperous

badarambumbi: **1**. (causative or passive of **badarambi**); **2**. to enlarge, expand, to propagate

badarambungga: magnifying, enlarging

badarambungga buleku: magnifying glass

badaran: enlargement, widening, growth

badarangga doro: the Guangxu (光緒) reign period, 1875–1908

bade: (postposition) even in the case that, if even …

badiri: a monk's alms bowl

badun: a weight measure — ten pecks, a bushel

badun jahūdai: a ship whose stern had the shape of a bushel measure

badzung: (把總) Sublieutenant, *BH* 752F

bagiyambi: to hold a small child's legs while he or she urinates or defecates

baha: (perfect participle of **bahambi**)

baha bahai: **1**. unintentionally, unexpectedly; **2**. promptly, immediately

bahabukū: ⟶ **mujilen bahabukū**

bahabumbi: **1**. (causative or passive of **bahambi**); **2**. to dream; **3**. to become tipsy, to get intoxicated; **4**. to cause to comprehend; **5**. to be felt, to be perceived, to be affected by; **6.** to be able

bahaci: ⟶ **bahambi** (subheading)

bahafi: ⟶ **bahambi** (subheading)

bahai balai: irresponsibly, recklessly

bahambi: (perfect participle: **baha**) **1.** to get, to obtain; **2.** to be able

  bahaci: I hope that …

  bahaci tuttu: if only it were so!

  bahafi: (used before another verb) manage to, succeed in

  bahara songko: tracks that show that the prey has been wounded.

  baharakū songko: tracks that show that the prey has escaped

bahana: the central pole of a Mongolian yurt

bahanambi: **1.** to go to get; **2.** to be able, to know how to do something; **3.** to experience; **4.** to understand

bahanasi: connoisseur, expert

bahanjimbi: to come to get

bahara: ⟶ **bahambi** (subheading)

baharakū: ⟶ **bahambi** (subheading)

bahiya: pine cone

bai: **1.** plain, simple; **2.** for nothing, free, in vain; **3.** at leisure, unemployed; **4.** only; **5.** particle of finality

  bai irgen: common people

  bai niyalma: **1.** layman; **2.** a man without work or position

  bai tembi: to live in leisure, to live in retirement

bai tiyei bithe: visiting card

baibi: **1.** plain, ordinary; **2.** for nothing, with no purpose, vainly, simply, merely

  baibi ainu: why should … ?, why?

baibingge: ordinary person, useless person

baibula: *Tersiphone paradisi*: the paradise flycatcher

baibulan: ⟶ **baibula**

baibumbi: **1.** (causative of **baimbi**); **2.** to require, to need, to use

baibungga: **1.** necessary, essential, necessity; **2.** expense, provision

baicabumbi: (causative of **baicambi**)

  baicabure temgetu: a certificate of inspection

baicambi: to inspect, to examine, to investigate, to survey

  baicame acabumbi: to verify, to check

baicame beidere hafan: (按察使) Provincial Judge, *BH* 830

baicame fonjimbi: to enquire about, to seek information

baicame icihiyambi: to investigate and deal with accordingly

baicame tuwara hafan: (監察御使) Censor, *BH* 213

baicame wakalara kunggeri: (糾參科) a section of the Court of State Ceremonial that was in charge of fixing punishments for officials who failed to pay a courtesy visit to the court after receiving an Imperial favor

baicara be ufarambi: to neglect one's supervisory duties

baican: inspection, examination

  baican i ejeku: (都事) Official of the Censorate Chancery, *BH* 211

baicanabumbi: (causative of **baicanambi**)

baicanambi: to go to inspect

baicandumbi: to inspect together; also **baicanumbi**

baicanjimbi: to come to inspect

baicanumbi: to inspect together; also **baicandumbi**

baicara: ⟶ **baicambi** (subheading)

baicasi: (檢校) Prefectural Police Inspector, *BH* 850

baidalambi: **1.** to punish; **2.** to deceive

baihanabumbi: (causative of **baihanambi**)

baihanambi: to go to seek, to go to request

baihanjimbi: to come to seek, to come to visit

baikū: lewd woman, wanton woman, hussy

baili: kindness, mercy, tenderness

  baili isibumbi: **1.** to repay a kindness; **2.** to bestow a favor

  baili jafambi: to repay a kindness

bailingga: merciful, kind

  bailingga ejen: benefactor

  bailingga niyalma: benefactor

bailisi: **1.** beneficiary; **2.** 'one who seeks happiness,' i.e., a Buddhist, Daoist, or shaman

baimbi: (imperative: **baisu**) to seek, to look for, to wish, to ask for

  baime: (used as a postposition) toward

  baime dahanjimbi: to come to surrender, to switch loyalty to

  baime suimbi: to search high and low

baindumbi: **1.** to seek together, to discuss; **2.** to seek one another; also **bainumbi**

baingge: of a certain place

bainjimbi: to come to seek, request, ask for

bainumbi: **1**. to seek together, to discuss; **2**. to seek one another; also **baindumbi**

baise: Chinese cabbage, napa cabbage

> **baise sogi**: Chinese cabbage

baisin: without an official position, at leisure

baising: settlement, village

baisu: (imperative of **baimbi**)

baita: matter, affair, business, event

> **baita akū**: free, not busy, it does not matter, it is no use, useless

> **baita alimbi**: to take up an office

> **baita be aliha hafan**: (府丞) Vice-Governor of Peking, *BH* 793

> **baita be dara fiyenten**: (經歷司) Registry Office of the Imperial Clan Court, *BH* 63

> **baita be kadalara hafan**: (提調官) Proctor, *BH* 94, 139, 144, etc.

> **baita belheku**: (孔目) Junior Archivist, *BH* 202

> **baita dambi**: to take care of affairs

> **baita de afaha hafan**: (供事官) Clerk, *BH* 190, 267

> **baita de amuran**: meddlesome, officious

> **baita de dara hafan**: (經歷) Commissary of Records, *BH* 826

> **baita de hamirakū**: not in conformity with the matter, does not correspond to the matter at hand

> **baita dekdebumbi**: to make trouble, to raise a disturbance

> **baita efulembi**: **1**. to stir up trouble; **2**. to dismiss a case

> **baita ejere boo**: (掛號房) registration office — the police station of the Peking Gendarmerie

> **baita ejere hafan**: (校理) a Secretary of the Wenyuange (文淵閣)

> **baita faššan**: deed, achievement, exploit

> **baita hacin**: item, business, affairs, case (at law)

> **baita hacin i boo**: (案房) Business Office of the Board of Finance

> **baita i sekiyen**: a quotation from the statutes

> **baita icihiyambi**: to manage affairs, to handle business

> **baita jafame**: in accordance with the circumstances

> **baita obumbi**: to make something an item of business, to make something one's cause

> **baita oburakū**: does not treat as a matter of consequence

> **baita sartabumbi**: to bungle some matter

> **baita sita**: matters and affairs

> **baita turgun**: circumstances

> **baita tušaha niyalma**: a person involved in a matter, injured party

> **baita tušara niyalma**: someone involved in a matter

> **baita ufarambi**: for a mistake to occur, for something to go wrong

> **baita wesimbure ba**: (奏事處) Chancery of Memorials to the Emperor, *BH* 105

> **baita yabun**: affairs, business

> **baitai icihiyasi**: (經歷) Registrar, *BH* 64, 117, 212, etc., cf. **baita de dara hafan**

> **baitai sarasi**: (知事) Archivist, *BH* 830A, etc.; cf. *BH* 506

> **baitai turgun**: the cause of an event

baitakū: ⟶ **baita akū**; useless

> **baitakū gisun**: nonsense, rubbish

> **baitakū ucuri**: ordinary times

baitalabumbi: **1**. (causative or passive of **baitalambi**); **2**. to be employed as an official

> **baitalabure hafan**: (騎都尉) a hereditary rank of the seventh grade, *BH* 944

baitalambi: to use, to employ

> **baitalara de isimbi**: to be sufficient for use

baitalan: **1**. use, utilization; **2**. expenditure, expense; **3**. implement, something in daily use

> **baitalan de acabure namun**: (供用庫) a storehouse for wax and incense

baitalara: ⟶ **baitalambi** (subheading)

baitangga: **1**. usable, applicable, useful; **2**. errand boy, handyman, underling

baitasi: (都事) official of a chancery, *BH* 211, 212B

baižin: ⟶ **baisin**

bajar seme: **1**. filled with sundry things; **2**. thriving, luxuriant

bajargi: the far shore, the opposite shore

baji: a little bit (more), a while

> **baji nonggimbi**: to add a little bit more

> **baji ome**: in a short while

bajikan: just a tiny bit (more)

bajila: on the opposite shore

bajima: a little while more

bajimashūn: a while thereafter

baju: **1**. the dregs from **arki**; **2**. base and useless thing

bakalaji: ⟶ **bakalji**

bakalji: a bone above the hoof of a horse or cow, pastern

bakcambi: ⟶ **bakjambi**

bakcilabumbi: **1**. (causative or passive of **bakcilambi**); **2**. to put in opposition, to make oppose

bakcilambi: to oppose, to be opposite, to sit or stand opposite

  bakcilaha ekcin: the opposite shore

  bakcilame: opposite, facing

bakcin: the opposite side, opponent, opposite number

  bakcin akū: without match, peerless

  bakcin waka: is no match (for)

bakja bakjalame ilimbi: to rear up and stop (said of horses)

bakjabumbi: (causative of **bakjambi**)

bakjakan: viscous, thick (said of a liquid), concentrated

bakjalambi: to rear (said of horses), to come to a sudden stop

  bakjalame ilimbi: to come to a sudden stop (said of a galloping horse)

bakjambi: (**-ka**) to congeal, to coagulate, to curdle, to condense

baksalabumbi: (causative of **baksalambi**)

baksalambi: **1**. to tie into bundles; **2**. to divide (troops) into squads

baksan: **1**. a bundle; **2**. a clump of grass; **3**. rank, detachment, squad

  baksan arambi: to form into a detachment

  baksan meyen: the ranks, line (of soldiers)

baksanda: squad leader

baksangga: **1**. an ancient Chinese grain measure equaling eight bushels; **2**. pertaining to a bundle or squad

  baksangga ficakū: a *shēng* 笙, a classical Chinese wind instrument

baksatu: (把總) Sublieutenant, *BH* 752F

baksi: a scholar, a learned man, gentleman

bakta: the placenta of cattle

baktaka: ⟶ **baktambi** (subheading)

baktakū: the internal organs

  baktakū singgeku: internal organs, viscera

baktambi: (**-ka, -ndara**) **1**. to contain, to encompass; **2**. to bear, to endure

  baktaka gisun: fable, parable, allegory

baktambumbi: **1**. to be indulgent (toward), to forgive; **2**. to accept, to put up with, to suffer (misfortune); **3**. to encompass, to contain

  baktambume gamambi: to forgive, to excuse

  baktambume giljambi: to forgive

  baktambume kūwarambi: to excuse, to pardon

baktambun: **1**. forgiveness; **2**. contents

baktan: capacity, contents

baktandambi: to contain, to hold

  baktandarakū: does not fit, will not go in, unforgivable

  baktandarakū arahabi: put on great airs, posed as something great

  baktandarakū bayan: extremely rich

baktangga: **1**. containing, encompassing; **2**. reserved, restrained

  baktangga buleku: compass (for determining direction)

  baktangga iktangga: implication, hidden meaning

balai: blindly, vainly, carelessly, indiscriminately, falsely, unreasonably

  balai baitalambi: to misuse, to use indiscriminately

  balai cihai: at will, doing as one pleases

  balai daišambi: to run wild, to make trouble

  balai derakū: shameless

  balai doksirambi: to act ruthlessly, to act brutally

  balai erembi: to have vain hopes

  balai facuhūrambi: to behave wildly, to act in an unrestrained manner

  balai febgiyembi: to speak heedlessly

  balai femen: vain talk, useless prattling

  balai gisurembi: to speak nonsense

  balai ici sindambi: to put something down carelessly, to put just any old place

  balai ondombi: to move blindly, to act but to no purpose

balakta: clots of blood on an afterbirth

balama: **1**. mad, crazy; **2**. (sentence particle) only, just, however, but

balamadambi: to rave, to act crazily

balamdambi: ⟶ **balamadambi**

balba: having poor eyesight

balcitambi: to vouch for

balda: white on the chest of an animal, a pig with white feet; cf. **balta**

baldargan: probably *Cerchneis naumanni*: the lesser kestrel

baldarhan: ⟶ **baldargan**

baldasitambi: to slip, to skid

balhambi: to redeem a vow made to avoid smallpox

balingga: ⟶ **bailingga**

baliya: **1**. interjection used when laughing at someone's ineptitude; **2**. an interjection of pity

baljun: ghost, apparition, goblin

  baljun i tuwa: ghostly fire, *ignis fatuus*, phosphorescent light

balta: a dog whose nose ridge is white, white hair on an animal's chest, a pig with white feet

baltaha: the hair under the chin of a sable

balu: blind; ⟶ also **dogo**

bambi: (**-ngka, -ndara**) **1**. to be tired, to be lazy, to feel too lazy to do something; **2**. to gnaw a hole

ban: **1**. a troop; **2**. half

  ban ši guwan hafan: (辦事官) attendant in various governmental offices

banaje tebumbi: to have evil spirits driven out by a shaman

banaji: the earth god

banasi: myrtle

bancan duha: the rectum of horses, donkeys, and mules

bancuka: tired, lazy, unwilling

banda hara: *Polygonum aviculare*: knotweed

banda mafa: the god of hunters

bandajin: **1**. idler; **2**. things collected by rodents

bandambi: to tire, to become fatigued

bandan: bench, stool

  bandan asu: a large fish net attached to a pole and carried by two men

bandi: learned man, pundit

bando: the shrub *Pentapetes phoenicea*, scarlet mallow

bang: bulletin, notice

  bang yan: number two in the palace examination

bangguhe: myna bird

bangnambi: to accuse someone of doing something wrong

bangse: night watchman's clapper

bangtu: **1**. bracket, support for a rafter; **2**. a cloud-shaped stirrup

baniha: thanks, gratitude, thank you!

  baniha arambi: to thank

  baniha bumbi: to thank

banihalambi: to thank

banihūn: seriously wounded and sure to be brought down (said of game)

banihūnjambi: to treat kindly

banilji: wart on a horse's leg

banimbi: ⟶ **banjimbi**

banin: **1**. form, appearance, shape; **2**. nature, essence; **3**. temper, temperament, disposition

  banin buyenin: disposition, temperament

  banin doksin: impatient, short-tempered

  banin ehe: ugly in appearance

  banin giru: appearance

  banin hahi: impatient, short-tempered

  banin i cihai: willfully, indiscriminately

  banin mafa: paternal grandfather

  banin mama: paternal grandmother

  banin sain: having a good appearance, good-looking

  banin salgabun: natural disposition

  banin wen: appearance, aspect, looks

baninambi: ⟶ **banjinambi**

baninarakū: indefatigable

baningga: **1**. natural, essential, having form; **2**. matter, material; **3**. scarcely enough, just sufficient

banirke eniye: stepmother

banitai: **1**. by nature, inborn; **2**. (as a noun) nature, essence

banitaingge: that which has a nature, being alike by nature

banji: a game that uses twenty-four black and white pieces on a chessboard

  banji efimbi: to play the game of **banji**

banjibukū: compiler; cf. **acabume banjibukū**

banjibumbi: **1**. (causative of **banjimbi**); **2**. to give birth to, to quicken; **3**. to compile, to compose, to make up, to organize, to form (e.g., a military unit)

banjibume arara hafan: (纂修官) Proofreader, *BH* 94, 139

banjibume dasakū: (修撰) Compiler of the First Class, *BH* 200A

banjibun: a compendium, a creation, a product

banjibungga: productive, creative

banjicuka: ⟶ **jili banjicuka**

banjiha: ⟶ **banjimbi** (subheading)

banjimbi: **1.** to live, to be born, to give birth to; **2.** to form, to come into existence, to become

banjiha ahūn: consanguineous elder brother

banjiha ama: natural father

banjiha ba: female sexual organ

banjiha deo: consanguineous younger brother

banjiha eniye: natural mother

banjiha inenggi: birthday

banjire hethe: means of livelihood, family property

banjire muru: way of life

banjire sain: get along well together, on good terms with

banjire urse: people of means

banjire were: life, livelihood

banjime: ⟶ **banji**

banjin: **1.** appearance; **2.** livelihood; **3.** life; **4.** ⟶ **banin**

banjin bucen: life and death

banjin fiyan: appearance

banjin wen: livelihood, way of life

banjinambi: **1.** to go to a place to live; **2.** to appear, to come into the world, to be born, to appear externally, to appear spontaneously; **3.** can, to be able

banjinarakū: inappropriate (as), unbecoming, to be unable

banjinarakū baita: an improbable or impossible thing

banjinjimbi: **1.** to come to live (in a new place), to come to seek a livelihood; **2.** to be born

banjire: ⟶ **banjimbi** (subheading)

banjirke: step- (as in stepmother, stepfather, etc.)

banjishūn: having sufficient money or goods to lead a comfortable life

banjitai: by nature, inborn, naturally; cf. **banitai**

banjitai dalangga: a natural dike

banuhū: ⟶ **banuhūn**

banuhūn: lazy

banuhūšambi: to be lazy, to be indolent

bar bar seme: many people talking together

bar bir seme: in profusion, in great quantity, many people talking

barabumbi: **1.** (causative of **barambi**); **2.** to mix, to mix among, to mingle together

barabume tecembi: to sit together in one place

barag'alanda: the Sanskrit name for the mandarin duck

barambi: to mix together, to soak one's rice with soup, to pour soup on rice

barambumbi: ⟶ **barabumbi**

baramida: jackfruit

baramit: pāramitā: the means leading to nirvana

baran: **1.** quantity (of troops); **2.** military strength, disposition of troops; **3.** circumstances, situation; **4.** form, appearance, outline

baran akū: without any ado, simply, without ceremony

baran karambi: to watch at a distance

barandza: *prajñā*: transcendental knowledge

barbehe: a name for the myna

bardanggi: **1.** boastful, arrogant; **2.** braggart

bardanggi akū: it would be boastful to say …

bardanggilambi: to brag, to boast

bargin: ⟶ **burgin**

bargiyabumbi: (causative of **bargiyambi**)

bargiyafi: ⟶ **bargiyambi** (subheading)

bargiyaha: ⟶ **bargiyambi** (subheading)

bargiyakū: functionary charged with collecting taxes, tax collector

bargiyambi: **1.** to store, to preserve, to protect; **2.** to take in, to receive, to harvest, to gather, to collect; **3.** to shave both ends of an arrow shaft

bargiyafi afabure kunggeri: (收發科) Registry, *BH* 251

bargiyaha temgetu: a confirmation of receipt, a receipt

bargiyara asarara falgangga: (收掌所) Section of Archives, *BH* 535

bargiyara asarara hafan: (收掌官) Collector, *BH* 652F

bargiyan: collecting, harvest

bargiyanambi: to go to collect

bargiyara: ⟶ **bargiyambi** (subheading)

bargiyaralambi: ⟶ **bargiyatambi**

bargiyashūn: narrowing toward the mouth

bargiyatambi: **1**. to protect, to take care of; **2**. to bring together in one place; **3**. to straighten up, to fix up, to put in order; **4**. to hold back, to dam up

>**bargiyatara dalangga**: a dam

barin: female of a beast of prey

barkiyambi: to understand, to grasp, to perceive, to notice

>**barkiyame gūnihakū**: without attention, heedlessly, carelessly

>**barkiyarakū**: without paying attention, carelessly

bartanambi: to become stained by sweat

baru: (postposition) toward

barun: **1**. a full year or month; **2**. surroundings

>**barun se**: one full year of life

basa: salary, emolument, recompense

>**basa bumbi**: to pay a salary to, to give recompense to

>**basa wecembi**: to make a thanksgiving offering for rain

>**basa werimbi**: to leave a small offering along the road or in the mountains for the gods in thanks for a safe passing

basagiyambi: ⟶ **basunggiyambi**

basan: **1**. a girth: the belly-strap for a horse's saddle; **2**. a wickerwork of willow placed on the roof

basilambi: to box, to engage in the sport of boxing

basubumbi: (causative or passive of **basumbi**)

basucun: cause for joking or derision, mockery

basugiyambi: ⟶ **basunggiyambi**

basumbi: to make fun of, to deride, to mock, to ridicule

basunggiyambi: to talk in one's sleep

>**basunggiyara mangga**: often talks in his sleep

basunumbi: to deride together

baša: wife's younger sister

bašakū: a (fly-) whisk

bašambi: **1**. to chase away, to drive off; **2**. to urge, to press; **3**. to push (a cart), to drive (a vehicle)

bašilambi: **1**. to engage in Chinese boxing; **2**. to do skilled work

bata: enemy, opponent

>**bata be alimbi**: to meet the enemy

>**bata gaimbi**: to take revenge

batak seme: (onomatopoetic) the sound of something metallic striking the ground

batalabumbi: (causative of **batalambi**)

batalambi: to be an enemy, to oppose

batangga: hostile, inimical

batkalambi: to deceive, to cheat, to swindle

batmaga: ruby

batun: incompletely thawed — thawed on the surface but still frozen underneath

baturu: **1**. brave; **2**. hero

>**baturu fafuri**: brave, courageous

>**baturu horonggo**: valiant

>**baturu kiyangkiyan**: hero, heroic, brave

baturulambi: to be brave, to act bravely

baturungga: endowed with courage, brave

bayabumbi: (causative of **bayambi**)

bayalambi: to be happy, to be glad

bayambi: (**-ka**) to be rich, to become rich

bayambumbi: **1**. (causative of **bayambi**); **2**. to enrich

bayan: **1**. rich, rich man; **2**. having many pocks (from smallpox)

>**bayan aniya**: a bountiful year

>**bayan wesihun**: wealth and honor, wealthy and respected

bayara: guard, troops on guard duty

>**bayarai jalan i janggin**: (護軍參領) Colonel, *BH* 734

>**bayarai juwan i da**: (護軍校) Lieutenant, *BH* 734

>**bayarai kūwaran**: barracks of the banner guard northwest of Beijing

>**bayarai tui janggin**: (護軍統領) Captain-General, *BH* 734

bayasa: (plural of **bayan**)

be: **1**. we (exclusive); **2**. accusative particle; **3**. (伯) count, earl (the title); **4**. a wooden crossbar in front of a wagon shaft; **5**. food for birds, bird feed, chicken feed

be hiyan: silver pheasant; cf. **šunggin gasha**

bebeliyembi: (**-ke**) to grow stiff from the cold

beberembi: (**-ke**) to grow stiff from the cold

bebu: sounds used to lull a baby to sleep, lullaby

bebušembi: to sing lullabies to, to lull to sleep

becebumbi: (causative or passive of **becembi**)

becembi: to scold, to reproach, to reprimand

becen: reprimand, rebuke

>**becen acambi**: to quarrel

>**becen daišan**: quarreling and fighting

>**becen jaman**: quarrels and arguments

becun: quarrel, squabble

    becun coko: fighting cock

    becun ulhūma: a fighting pheasant

becunubumbi: (causative of **becunumbi**)

becunumbi: to fight, to quarrel

bederceku: **1**. shrinking, cringing; **2**. a timid, shrinking person

bedercebumbi: **1**. (causative of **bedercembi**); **2**. to withdraw, to give up

bedercembi: to retreat, to withdraw

bederebumbi: **1**. (causative of **bederembi**); **2**. to send back, to withdraw (transitive verb), to refuse, to return a courtesy or gift

bederembi: **1**. to return; **2**. to withdraw, to retreat; **3**. to withdraw (at court or at a ceremony); **4**. to pass away, to die

    bedereme katarambi: to go slowly (said of a horse)

bederi: stripes or spots on animals or birds

    bederi cecike: a black bird with white spots and a long beak

    bederi moo: the tiger-stripe tree of Hainan

bederineme banjimbi: to form stripes or spots

bederingge: having spots or stripes

bedu: a name for the tiger; cf. **tasha**

bedun: sturdy, solidly made

beging: Beijing

begu: pubic area; cf. **beku**

beg'o: the ginkgo

behe: ink, ink stick

    behe i hūcin: a kind of spring (so called because it issues from stones resembling ink sticks)

    behe suimbi: to grind an ink stick

    behei foloro falga: (墨刻作) a section of the Imperial Library concerned with carving wooden blocks for printing

    behei namu: a large round ink vessel

    behei tehe: an ink stick holder

behelebumbi: (causative of **behelembi**)

behelembi: to grind an ink stick to make ink

bei: an inscribed memorial stone, stele

    bei wehe: stele, inscribed stone

bei ye: *Betula utilis*: patra, a kind of tree

beibun i efen: sacrificial cakes

beidebumbi: (causative or passive of **beidembi**)

beidembi: to examine (a case), to try (a case), to judge

    beideme fonjimbi: to interrogate

beidere boo: (刑房) tribunal of the Court of Colonial Affairs

beidere jurgan: (刑部) Board of Justice, *BH* 438

beidere jurgan i kungge yamun: (刑科) Department of Criminal Cases, *BH* 218A

beidere jurgan i toktoho gisun: set phrases used by the Board of Justice, legal terms

beiden: examination, trial

    beiden be aliha amban: (司寇) minister of justice in antiquity

    beiden be tuwancihiyara yamun: (大理司) Court of Judicature and Revision, *BH* 215

beidere: ⟶ **beidembi** (subheading)

beidesi: judge

beiduri: sapphire

beiguwan: a military title

beiguwe: root of the mustard plant

beiguwen: **1**. frost, cold; **2**. ⟶ **beikuwen**

beiguwerembi: **1**. to freeze, to frost; **2**. ⟶ **beikuwerembi**

beihe: an edible seaweed, kelp; cf. **kanin**

beihuwe: a straw figure, scarecrow

beikuwen: cold, frigid

beikuwerembi: (**-ke**) to be cold, to frost

beile: *beile*, ruler, Prince of the third rank

    beile i faidan i da: (司儀長) Major-Domo of a Prince's Palace, *BH* 44

    beile i fujin: wife of a **beile**

    beile i jui doroi gege: daughter of a **beile**

    beile i sargan doroi fujin: wife of a **beile**

beileci: a short-haired autumn pelt

beilecilembi: **1**. to molt, to shed fur; **2**. to act haughtily

beilecinembi: to form an autumn coat of short hair (on animals)

beise: *beise*, Prince, a Prince of the fourth rank

    beise i fujin: the wife of a **beise**

beje: the back of an oven-bed

beji: a winning combination in the game of **gacuha**

bejihiyebumbi: (causative of **bejihiyembi**)

bejihiyembi: to console, to comfort, to soothe

bejilembi: to make a hidden allusion

    bejilere gisun: riddle

bekde bakda: ⟶ **bekte bakta**

bekdun: debt, loan

    bekdun arambi: to owe a debt

    bekdun be edelembi: to owe a debt

bekdun bošombi: to call in a debt

bekdun edelembi: to owe a debt

bekdun gakdun: debts, heavily in debt

bekdun i ejen: creditor

bekdun juwen gaimbi: to take out a loan, to take on debt

bekdun sindambi: to make a loan, to lend money at interest

bekdun šumin: deeply in debt

beki: firm, strong

bekiken: rather firm, somewhat firm

bekilebumbi: (causative of **bekilembi**)

bekilembi: to make fast, to make firm, to strengthen

bekin: confidence, trust

bekitu: **1**. strong, burly; **2**. stable, dependable

bekte bakta: flustered, alarmed, panic-stricken, in a flurry

bektelembi: to cut off the feet as a punishment

bekterembi: (**-ke**) to be frozen in one's tracks, to be dumfounded by fear, to be terrified

bekto: fritillary (an herbal medicine)

beku: pubis of a woman, *mons veneris*

belci: madman, deranged

    belci nimeku: madness, insanity, mental illness

belcidembi: to act like a madman, to act insane, to lose one's mind

    belcideme daišambi: to rave, to raise a great commotion

bele: hulled rice, an edible grain

    bele be hašambi: to store rice

    bele buda: cooked rice

    bele nemembi: to hull rice

    belei sihabukū: a funnel for rice

belebumbi: (causative or passive of **belembi**)

belek seme: happily, joyfully

beleke: (Mongolian) gift

belembi: **1**. to harm an innocent person through a false accusation, to calumniate, to frame someone, to slander; **2**. to murder treacherously — especially one's Prince

belemimbi: to hull rice; cf. **niyelembi**

belen: **1**. false accusation; **2**. a treacherous murder

belendumbi: to accuse one another

beleni: ready-made, already prepared, finished

    beleniališambi: to be free, to be unoccupied

beleningge: something ready-made, that which is already prepared

belge: a grain of rice, the core of fruit

belgembi: to tie things to a saddle

belgenembi: to form into grains

belgeri ilha: the opium poppy

belhebuku: (祇候) an official in charge of the needs of foreign emissaries

belhebumbi: (causative of **belhembi**)

belhembi: to prepare

    belhere cooha: reserves (troops)

    belhere hafan: (供奉官) the same as **belhebuku**

belhen: preparation

belhendumbi: to prepare together; also **belhenumbi**

belhenembi: to go to prepare

belhenjimbi: to come to prepare

belhenumbi: to prepare together; also **belhendumbi**

belhesi: (鋪排) preparer — one who prepares everything for a service in a temple

belhetu: (儲將) an official in charge of military supplies

beli: dolt, fool

beliyedembi: to act foolishly, to do in a foolish way

beliyeken: somewhat foolish

beliyembi: ⟶ **beliyedembi**

beliyen: slow-witted, silly, foolish, idiotic

    beliyen nimeku: mental retardation

    beliyen yokto: dolt, moron, simpleton

bemberembi: (**-ke**) to repeat oneself or talk foolishly due to senility

ben: **1**. talent, capability; **2**. a pad or book of paper

    ben faksi: skill, technique

bencan: capital (money)

benciyan: ⟶ **bencan**

benebumbi: (causative of **benembi**)

    benebume simnembi: to take a preliminary examination for the degree of Metropolitan Graduate

benembi: to send (away from the speaker), to deliver, to give as a gift

benesi: messenger; cf. **wesimbure bithei benesi**

bengnebumbi: (causative of **bengnembi**)

bengneli: suddenly, hastily, flustered

bengnembi: to be in haste, to hasten

bengsen: talent, capability

    bengsen akū: incompetent

bengsengge: talented (person)

benjimbi: (imperative: **benju**) to send (hither), to deliver (hither)

benjihe bithe bargiyara boo: (來文房) registry for incoming correspondence in the Workshop of the Imperial Household

benju: (imperative of **benjimbi**)

beo: the accusative particle joined to the interrogative particle

berebumbi: (causative of **berembi**)

berembi: (-**ke**) to be dumfounded by fright or anger, to be confused about how to handle some matter

beren: a door or window frame

berge: a latch or toggle, a small piece of wood or metal to which a rope is attached

bergelembi: to attach to a latch or toggle

bergu: ⟶ **berhu**

berhe: **1**. the bridge of a stringed instrument; **2**. a small horizontal piece of wood attached to a tiger spear; **3**. eye discharge caused by the wind

berhelembi: **1**. to attach a bridge to a stringed instrument; **2**. ⟶ **bergelembi**

berhu: sister-in-law: term of address used by a wife to her husband's younger sister, or by an elder sister to her younger brother's wife

beri: a bow

beri arambi: to draw a bow full length (at mounted archery)

beri belhere ba: (備弓處) the place where the Emperor's bows were prepared and kept

beri cambi: to draw a bow

beri cira: the bow has a hard pull, the bow is taut

beri darambi: to draw a bow

beri darimbi: ⟶ **beri darambi**

beri dobton: a bow case

beri faksi: **1**. a bowmaker; **2**. a water strider (insect)

beri fitheku: a crossbow

beri giru: the shaft of a bow

beri ja: the bow has a light pull

beri jafakū: the grip of a bow

beri nu: a crossbow

beri sirdan: bow and arrow

beri tabumbi: to string a bow

beri tatambi: to draw a bow

beri uhuken: the bow has a weak pull

beri uli: bowstring

beri beri: each one, severally, one after another, helter-skelter

beri beri son son i: in groups, all together, in every direction, helter-skelter

berileku: a drill

beringga usiha: the constellation *hú* (弧)

beringge: **1**. archer, bowman; **2**. pertaining to archery

beringge cooha: archers

bertebumbi: (causative or passive of **bertembi**)

bertembi: to dirty, to soil

berten: dirt, grime, blemish

berten akū: without blemish, flawless

bertenembi: to get dirty, to get blemished

beserei: a mongrel mixture of a **taiha** hunting dog and the common house dog

besergen: bed

besergen de tafambi: to get into bed

beserhen: ⟶ **besergen**

beseri: ⟶ **beserei**

bešehun: stupefied, besotted, dazzled, led astray

bešembi: (-**ke**) **1**. to be saturated, to be swamped; **2**. to do to excess, to drink to excess

bešeme agambi: to rain enough to saturate the ground

bešembumbi: (causative of **bešembi**)

bešerhun: ⟶ **bešehun**

bete: inadequate, useless, ineffective

beten: earthworm, bait

bethe: foot, (lower) leg

bethe budurimbi: to trip and fall

bethe bukdambi: **1**. to bend the knee, to kneel on one knee; **2**. to draw a tally stick

bethe demniyeme cashūn fiyelembi: to do trick riding with the legs swinging backward

bethe dubeheri: standing on tiptoes

bethe endebumbi: to lose one's footing

bethe fahambi: to stomp

bethe fatan: sole of the foot

bethe gocime fiyelembi: to do trick riding with the legs drawn in

bethe hiyahambi: to cross one's legs

bethe i fatan: the sole of the foot

bethe i fatan i hergen: plantar lines

bethe i hūsun: porter, bearer

bethe nenggelembi: to stand on tiptoes

bethe niohušulembi: to go barefoot

bethe niohušun: barefooted

bethe tambi: to get the feet entangled, to trip

bethe tukiyehei fiyelembi: to do trick riding with the feet lifted in the air

bethei fileku: a foot warmer

betheleku: a trap for entangling the feet of birds

bethelembi: **1**. to sleep with the legs together; **2**. to arrange grain in small piles to allow it to dry; **3**. to entangle a bird's feet in a snare

betheleme amgambi: to sleep with the feet and legs together, to lie with legs touching, to sleep together

betheleme dedumbi: to lie with one's feet touching those of another person

bethengge: having legs or feet

beye: **1**. body, self; **2**. capital

beye acambi: to have sexual intercourse

beye akdambi: to rely on oneself

beye be arambi: to commit suicide

beye be dasambi: **1**. euphemism for to castrate; **2**. to cultivate oneself

beye be felembi: to lay down one's life, to defy death

beye be sumbi: to confess, to reveal the truth about oneself.

beye beye: each one, individually

beye cihakū: **1**. unwell, indisposed; **2**. impatient; **3**. against one's will

beye de bimbi: to become pregnant

beye de gocimbi: to place near oneself

beye de ombi: to become pregnant

beye de singgebumbi: to enrich oneself at someone else's expense

beye dekdereleme kurbume fiyelembi: to ride balancing oneself on the hands

beye dursun: the body

beye elembi: to be pleased with oneself

beye fasimbi: to hang oneself

beye forgošombi: to turn around, to face about

beye forombi: to turn around

beye fulahūn: naked

beye gaibumbi: to lose one's life, to perish, to die

beye gercilembi: to turn oneself in, to surrender voluntarily

beye halambi: to repent

beye hetumbumbi: to support oneself, to be self-sufficient

beye hūwalabumbi: to lose one's virginity, to be deflowered

beye iletulembi: to become incarnate, to appear in bodily form

beye isihimbi: **1**. to go into labor; **2**. to deliver (a baby)

beye jabumbi: to confess

beye jursu: pregnant

beye madagan: capital and interest, principal and interest

beye mehumbi: to bow

beye nikebumbi: to act in person, to do personally

beye niohušun: naked

beye osohon: small in stature

beye sahangge: intimate friend, soul mate

beye salimbi: to act on one's own, to decide for oneself, to take initiative, to control oneself, to act arbitrarily, to be one's own master

beye sisambi: to exert oneself

beye teksin: well built (figure)

beye tomsombi: to control oneself

beyebe tuwancihiyambi: to cultivate oneself

beye ufarambi: to be killed

beye wajimbi: to perish, to be killed

beyebumbi: (causative of **beyembi**)

beyei: by oneself, independently

beyeingge: one's own

beyembi: to freeze, to be cold

beyen: freezing, cold

beyese: (plural of **beye**)

bi: **1**. I, me; **2**. there is, there are, has, have

bi sini meifen be: 'I am going to cut off your head!' — an oath

bibumbi: **1**. (causative of **bimbi**); **2**. to detain, to retain, to keep back, to leave behind

bidarum: coral

bidere: bi + dere

biduri: lapis lazuli

bigan: wilderness, an uncultivated area, wild

bigan i cai: wild tea

bigan i ciyanliyang: tax on uncultivated land

bigan i coko: pheasant, ring-necked pheasant

bigan i gintala: wild celery

bigan i hukšen: a hawk that has escaped from captivity

bigan i hutu: a ghost or spirit that dwells in the wilderness

bigan i ibagan: a malevolent spirit dwelling in the wilderness

bigan i mucu: *Vitis Thunbergii*: wild grape

bigan i niongniyaha: the wild goose

bigan i singgeri: field mouse, vole

bigan i ulgiyan: wild pig; cf. **aidagan**

bigan i weceku: the shamanistic god of the wilderness

bigan tala: the steppe, the wilds, wilderness

bigan tatanambi: to camp, to bivouac

bigan urangga moo: *Calophyllum inophyllum*: the wild tung tree

bigarambi: to be in the wilderness, to wander in the wilderness

bigarame: across the wilderness, through the wilds

bigarara mahatun: a cap used for distant journeys

bigatu: wild

bigatu niyehe: wild duck, mallard

bigatu uniyehe: wild duck, mallard

biha: crumb, small piece, chip

bihan: ⟶ **bigan**

bihe bihei: for a long time, gradually

bijabumbi: (causative of **bijambi**)

bijambi: to break, to snap (intransitive verb)

bikcu: Buddhist monk

bikcuni: Buddhist nun

bikita: (璧) a constellation, the 14th of the lunar mansions, made up of γ in Pegasus and α in Andromeda

bikita tokdonggo kiru: a banner with the constellation **bikita** depicted on it

bila ilha: an exotic white flower that blooms in autumn

bilabumbi: (causative or passive of **bilambi**)

bilagan: period, term, deadline

bilagan i temgetu: a paper on which a term or deadline is recorded

bilambi: **1**. to break; **2**. to dull; **3**. to set a date, to fix a term, to limit

bilame gaimbi: to subtract, to take away

bilan: ⟶ **bilagan**

bilasi: singer

bilca: cake made from bean and millet flour

bilcambi: to smear, to spread a sticky substance on something

bilci: ⟶ **bulji**

bilembi: to lay eggs, to give birth to pigs and dogs

bilerhen: lark

bileri: a wind instrument with eight holes and a metal mouthpiece — a *suǒnà* 嗩呐

bilesi: a player of the *suǒnà* 嗩呐, a trumpeter

bilga: ⟶ **bilha**

bilgacungga: ⟶ **bilhacungga**

bilgešembi: to brim, to be too full (pertaining to liquids)

bilha: **1**. throat; **2**. a very narrow passage; **3**. a smoke hole

bilha dasambi: to clear the throat

bilha hahūrambi: to choke

bilha ilenggu i gese amban: (元老大臣) respectful title for members of the State Council

bilha sibuhabi: became all choked up

bilhacungga: gluttonous

biljambi: (**-ka**) to be soaked, to be drenched, to be soaked with blood

biltembi: (**-ke**) **1**. to overflow, to flood (said of a river); **2**. to be arrogant

biltembumbi: (causative of **biltembi**)

bilten: large lake, large marsh, large expanse of shallow water

bilubumbi: (causative of **bilumbi**)

bilukan: on the sly, secretly

bilukū: one who deceives by using sweet talk, a confidence man

bilumbi: (**-ha**) **1**. to stroke, to rub, to nourish, to caress, to fondle; **2**. to cut meat into small pieces; **3**. to pacify (a region)

bilun: pacification

bilungga: pacified

bilurjambi: to swindle by pretending to be honest

bilušambi: to be affectionate toward, to act affectionately

bimbi: (imperfect participle **bisire**, imperative: **bisu**) **1**. to exist, to be, to be alive; **2**. to stay, to remain

bihe fonde: while still alive

bimšu: female quail

bin dz: betel nut; cf. **merseri**

bing biyan: camphor

bing biyang: (onomatopoetic) sound made by the *suǒnà* 嗩呐 or flute

binggiya: water chestnut

bingha: (畢) a constellation, the 19th of the lunar mansions, made up of eight stars in Taurus

bingha toktonggo kiru: a banner depicting the constellation **bingha**

bingse: steelyard

bingselembi: to weigh on a steelyard

bingsiku: autumn cicada

binse: ⟶ **bin dz**

bir biyar seme: hanging to the floor (said of clothing)

bir seme: hanging loose

bira: river

bira be kadalara tinggin: (河廳) Office of River Management

birai angga: mouth of a river

birai cargi: the other side of the river

birai dalin i falgangga: unloading area on a riverbank

birai dengjan: a paper lantern in the form of a lotus (used to light the way on a river excursion)

birai ebergi: the close bank of the river

birai hūya: an edible river snail

birai jugūn be uheri kadalara amban: (河道 總督) Director-General of River Conservation, *BH* 820D

birai onggolo: tributary

birai onggon: river cove

birai seremšen i kunggeri: (河防科) section for river control in the Board of Works

birai weilen i falga: (河工甲) Bureau of River Works in the Board of Civil Appointments

biraman: Brahman

birangga: having or pertaining to a river

birangga kiru: (河旗) a banner decorated with the design of a flowing river

birca hiyan moo: the name of an exotic tree whose wood is used for making scroll rods

birebumbi: **1**. (causative or passive of **birembi**); **2**. to be washed away

biregen: a willow palisade built along a frontier

biregen jase: boundary planted with willows

birehen: ⟶ **biregen**

bireku: roller, rolling pin

bireku moo: a wooden roller for rolling seed

birembi: **1**. to rush, to charge; **2**. to wash away (in a flood), to flush, to wash up; **3**. to breach (a

levee); **4**. to roll out (dough), to crush seeds with a roller

bireme: completely, thoroughly, universally, without exception

bireme hereme: totally and completely

bireme yabubure bithe icihiyara ba: (通行書 籍處) an office of the Printing Office and Bookbindery charged with the distribution of books

biren: tigress, female leopard

biren i hūya: an edible river snail

biren tasha: tigress

biren yarha: female leopard

birendumbi: to collide, to run into one another

birenembi: to go to run into

biretei: totally, universally, completely, widespread

birga: ⟶ **birgan**

birgan: creek, brook, rivulet, small waterway

birgešembi: **1**. to overeat; **2**. to hang loosely, to dangle, to sway

birhešembi: ⟶ **birgešembi**

birku: ⟶ **bireku**

bisambi: (**-ka, -ra/-ndara**) to overflow, to flood

bisan: **1**. flood, inundation; **2**. excessive water in a field

bisarambi: (**-ka,-pi**) to overflow, to pour out everywhere

bisari ilha: an exotic white flower that grows along rivers

bisi: crab louse, tick

bisimbi: ⟶ **bišumbi**

bisin: **1**. a flat iron clasp, a decorative rivet or tack found on knives, cruppers, bridles, etc.; **2**. smooth, unblemished; cf. **bišun**

bisin durdun: smooth crêpe

bisin eldengge loho: a sword with a smooth pommel

bisin ilhangge kofon suje: a smooth patterned Soochow silk

bisire: (imperfect participle of **bimbi**)

bisire ebsihe: one's whole life

bisirelengge: all that exists

bisireltu: worthy of adoration

bisirengge: having, existing, that which exists

bisu: (imperative of **bimbi**)

bisurembi: to crawl, to creep

bišubumbi: (causative of **bišumbi**)

bišukan: **1**. somewhat smooth; **2**. temperate in eating

bišumbi: (**-ha**) to smooth, to rub, to stroke, to pet, to grope, to feel

bišun: **1**. having a flat surface, level, flat, plane; **2**. lacking forked branches; **3**. temperate in eating, not ravenous

bišuri moo: coconut palm

bišušambi: to keep rubbing, to caress repeatedly

bita: river island, sand bar, eyot

bithe: **1**. book; **2**. letter; **3**. written symbol; **4**. civil (as opposed to military)

   bithe boo: a study

   bithe dere: writing desk

   bithe foloro faksi: engraver, one who carves wooden boards for printing

   bithe fucihi doose: Confucianism, Buddhism, and Daoism

   bithe hūlambi: to study

   bithe hūlara hafan: (讀祝官) Reciter of Prayers, *BH* 79, 382B

   bithe noho suje: silk with writing woven into the pattern

   bithe sabsimbi: to tattoo characters on a criminal's face (a form of punishment)

   bithe sarambi: to leaf through a book

   bithe šuwaselara falga: (刷書作) the court printing office

   bithe uncara puseli: bookstore

   bithe yabubure boo: (咨文房) Office of the Palace Apothecary

   bithei amban: (文大臣) a high civil dignitary

   bithei boo: study, studio

   bithei deretu: writing desk

   bithei hafan: (文官) a civil official

   bithei hafan i fungnehen i kunggeri: (文誥科) office in charge of posthumous honors

   bithei hafan i temgetu: a document sent to a **bithei hafan**

   bithei hafan sindara bolgobure fiyenten: (文選清吏司) Department for the Selection of Civil Officials; cf. *BH* 335

   bithei jafašakū: (掌書) Librarian, *BH* 639

   bithei joringga: table of contents

   bithei kuren: library

   bithei niyalma: scholar, civil official

   bithei šungsi: (翰林) Member of the National Academy, *BH* 191

   bithei šusai: (文秀才) a baccalaureate of the civil examinations

   bithei tacikū: (儒學) a provincial school for preparing civil and military candidates for the examinations

   bithei tacin: Confucianism

   bithei tacin coohai erdemu: scholarship and military strategy

   bithei yamun: (翰林院) the National Academy, *BH* 191 ff.

bithelembi: to notify in writing, to send a letter to

bithesi: (筆貼式) scribe, secretary, clerk, *BH* 293

   bithesi i kunggeri: (筆貼式科) section of clerks in the Board of Civil Appointments; cf. *BH* 293

bitubumbi: (**-ha**) **1**. (causative of **bitumbi**); **2**. to see in a dream

bituhan: border, edging

bitumbi: (**-ha**) to edge, to border, to go along the border, to adorn, to decorate

   bitume gamara: ambiguous, vague

biturame: along a mountain, via a mountain, along the edge

biwanggirit: (Sanskrit vyākaraṇa) exposition, explanation, grammar

biya: moon, month

   biya aliha ba: (當月處) Record Office, *BH* 497

   biya aliha fiyenten: (當月司) Record and Registry Office, *BH* 455

   biya amba: the month has thirty days

   biya be bodome: monthly

   biya fekuhe: overdue (said of a pregnant woman)

   biya halan: menstruation

   biya jalumbi: to be full, of the moon

   biya i kiru: moon banner

   biya i manashūn: the end of the month, after the 20th of the month

   biya jembi: there is an eclipse of the moon

   biya kūwaraha: the moon has a halo

   biya manara isika: the moon has almost disappeared

   biya osohon: the month has twenty-nine days

   biyai dašuran usiha: comet

   biyai hafan ilgara boo: (月官房) a department of the Imperial household charged with the monthly rotation of officials

   biyai halan: menstruation

biyai icereme: at the beginning of the month

biyai kūwaran: halo around the moon

biyai manashūn: after the 20th of the month

biyabiyahūn: pale, wan

biyabiyashūn: ⟶ **biyabiyahūn**

biyadar seme: speaking recklessly

biyadari: every month

biyahūn: pale, wan

biyai: ⟶ **biya** (subheading)

biyaingge: of a certain month

biyalame: months long, lasting for months, for an entire month

biyalanggi: blabbermouth, gossiper

biyalari ilha: *Rosa indica*: the monthly blooming rose

biyaldasitambi: to fluctuate greatly

biyalumbi: **1**. to slip away, to flee; **2**. to act furtively, to act stealthily

 biyalume yabumbi: to flee, to escape

biyan: inscribed tablet above a door

biyan sio: (編修) Compiler of the Second Class, *BH* 200B; cf. **acabume banjibukū**

biyancihiyan: pale, wan

biyandu: hyacinth bean, kidney bean

biyangga: moon-like, lunar, round

 biyangga efen: small round cakes filled with sweetened bean paste eaten at the moon festival, moon cakes

 biyangga fa: a window shaped like a full moon

 biyangga inenggi: the 15th of the eighth month — the moon festival

 biyangga longkon: a round gong

 biyangga tungken: a hand drum in the form of the moon

biyanggidei: a name for the golden pheasant; cf. **junggiri coko**

biyangsikū: cicada

biyangsiri ilha: an exotic flower — 'cicada's blossom'

biyantaha: a scar on the head, a spot on the head where one's hair is sparse

biyantu: cudgel

biyar seme: brimming (full of water), flooding

biyara: a kind of swallow found in Manchuria and Mongolia

biyarambi: to become pale, to shine with a white light

biyargiyan: faint, pale

biyargiyašambi: to be gray, colorless (said of the weather), to be pale, to be subdued

biyarimbi: to glare, to hurt the eyes (because of brightness)

biyarišambi: to blind (said of a strong light in the eye)

biyashūmbi: ⟶ **biyalumbi**

biyatar seme: **1**. ⟶ **biyadar seme**; **2**. roaring (of thunder)

biyohalambi: to get away, to escape

biyolokošombi: to tell yarns, to talk idly

biyolumbi: to shave smooth, to level off

biyombi: to smooth off a surface

biyoo: **1**. a memorial to the throne, manifesto; **2**. ⟶ **biyooha**

 biyoo bithe: a memorial to the throne

 biyoo bithe wesimbumbi: to present a memorial

 biyoo umiyaha: silkworm

biyooha: **1**. cocoon; **2**. a horse with a white spot on the end of its nose

 biyooha suje: satin made from wild cocoons

 biyooha suri: silk made from wild cocoons

biyoohari ilha: an exotic white flower that grows in mountain areas — its bloom resembles a cocoon

biyoolambi: ⟶ **biyolumbi**

biyor seme: trickling, slowly, lazily, dragging (clothes), slack, limp

 biyor seme etumbi: to wear clothes that are too long or too large

 biyor seme eyembi: to flow in a trickle

 biyor seme uyan: dangling and soft

biyoran: a cliff of red earth

biyorong seme: slowly, languidly

bo ho: mint

bo ioi: a monk's eating bowl

bo sy: Persia

boboršombi: to cherish, to dote on, to be unable to part with

bocehe: ⟶ **bocihe**

boceri ilha: *Lychnis senno*: campion, catchfly (a kind of flower)

bocihe: ugly

bocihi: ⟶ **bocihe**

 bocihi tuwabumbi: to make a fool of oneself, to disgrace oneself

boco: **1**. color, complexion; **2**. sex, lust

boco de dosimbi: to be lustful, to be lecherous

boco de narambi: to be a womanizer

boco hacin: dyestuff

boco hacin i namun: (顏料庫) a storehouse for iron, bronze, incense, wax, paper, etc., belonging to the Board of Revenue

boco i silhi: boldness in sexual adventures

boconggo: colored, brightly colored, colorful

boconggo arsalangga kiru: (彩獅旗) a banner bearing the likeness of a lion

boconggo nisiha: goldfish

boconggo šugin i iletu kiyoo: (彩漆亮轎) a ceremonial sedan chair painted many colors

boconggo ulhūmangga kiru: (華蟲旗) a banner bearing the likeness of a pheasant

bodi: bodhi: enlightenment; **2**. a volume or chapter of a Buddhist sutra

bodisatu: bodhisattva

bodise: the hard red fruit of the Indian Bodhidharma tree out of which rosaries are made

bodisu: ⟶ **bodise**

bodobumbi: (causative or passive of **bodombi**)

bodofi: ⟶ **bodombi** (subheading)

bodogon: plan, plot, scheme, strategy

bodogon i bithei kuren: (方略館) Military Archives Office, *BH* 139

bodohon: **1**. a small pendant of precious stones worn by officials at court; **2**. ⟶ **bodogon**

bodohonggo: good at strategy, full of plans and ideas

bodokū: abacus

bodombi: **1**. to think, to consider, to take into account; **2**. to plan, to make plans; **3**. to calculate, to reckon; **4**. to drive wild animals to a predetermined place so they can be killed

bodofi bure kunggeri: (支科) the name of a section in the Board of Revenue

bodoro ba akū: regardless of, it does not matter which

bodoro boo: (算科) Office of Calculations in the Board of Works

bodoro tacikū: (算學) school of mathematics

bodomimbi: to talk to oneself

bodon: calculation, plan, policy, strategy

bodon yohibun: military strategy

bodonggiyambi: ⟶ **bodomimbi**

bodonggo: concerning planning, containing plans

bodonombi: to go to reckon or plan

bodonumbi: to plan or scheme together

bodor seme: mumbling (through the teeth)

bodori: the handle of a plow

bodoro: ⟶ **bodombi** (subheading)

bofulabumbi: (causative of **bofulambi**)

bofulambi: to wrap

bofun: a wrapper, a wrapping cloth, a bundle

bohibumbi: (causative of **bohimbi**)

bohikū: wrapping for women's feet

bohimbi: to bind the feet

bohokon: somewhat muddy, opaque

bohomi: **1**. a winnowing fan for gaoliang (sorghum) and sesame; **2**. hulls of gaoliang and sesame seed

bohon: muddy, opaque, dull, clouded over (the pupil)

bohori: **1**. pea; **2**. a covering for lanterns

bohori debse: deep-fried pea cakes

bohoto: a camel's hump

boifuka: a clay flute with six holes

boigocilambi: to come from the earth, to glean from the earth

boigoji: **1**. host, master; **2**. polite word for someone's wife; **3**. owner

boigojilambi: to act as host or master

boigon: **1**. family, household; **2**. property

boigon anggala: members of a household, family

boigon anggalai dangse: population register

boigon banjimbi: to live, to get along, to manage a household

boigon i boo: (戶房) an office in the Court of Colonial Affairs

boigon i jurgan: (戶部) Board of Revenue, *BH* 349

boigon i jurgan i toktoho gisun: phrases used by the Board of Revenue

boigon nahan: household

boigon nahan jafambi: to take care of the household

boigon salimbi: to inherit property

boihocilambi: ⟶ **boigocilambi**

boihoji: ⟶ **boigoji**

boihoju: the god of the earth, the shrine of the earth god

boiholombi: to get free, to get loose (from a trap)

boihon: **1**. earth, ground, soil; **2**. ⟶ **boigon**

boihon dalan: an earthen dam

boihon hašambi: to bank up with earth (around the roots of a plant)

boihon i buktan: an earthen mound used as a landmark

boihon i dalgan: clod

boihon i hoton: an earthen wall

boihon i karman: an earthen fortress

boihon i kemneku: an earthen mound used like a sundial

boihon i mutun: an earthen mound one foot high and ten feet square at the base

boihon i ūren: clay image

boihon moo i weilen: building, construction

boihon usiha: Saturn

boihon usihangga kiru: a yellow banner embroidered with a picture of Saturn

boihon yaha: coal

boihojilambi: ⟶ **boigojilambi**

boingge: ⟶ **booingge**

boisile: amber

boisiri ilha: 'amber flower' — the name of an exotic flower

boje: an accounting book

boji: **1**. go-between in a business deal, witness to a contract; **2**. contract, deed

boji bithe: written contract

boji ilimbi: to make up an agreement or contract

boji sekiyen: a preliminary contract or deed

boji uncehen: a final contract or deed

bojilambi: to pawn, to mortgage

bojina keire: a splendid brown horse

bojiri ilha: chrysanthemum

bokda: (Mongolian) holy, divine, saint, holy man

bokida: fringe, tassel (often made of precious stones)

bokida ilha: an exotic, pale yellow flower that droops like the weeping willow

bokidangga: having a tassel or fringe

bokirshūn: stiff, unable to move the limbs normally

bokita: an unperforated blunt arrow

bokori gaimbi: to kick playfully in the rear

bokson: **1**. threshold; **2**. the curved part of the ends of a bow

bokšokon: graceful, elegant

bokšolombi: to be graceful, to be elegant, to dress elegantly

bokšon: the breastbone

bokto: hunchback

bolabumbi: (causative of **bolambi**)

bolambi: **1**. to roast, to broil, to bake (in a pan), to cook dry; **2**. ⟶ **boolambi**

bolanjimbi: to come to report; cf. **boolanjimbi**

bolbonombi: to concentrate in one place, to be concentrated together; cf. **bombonombi**

bolgo: **1**. clean, clear; **2**. honest, sincere; **3**. incorrupt, pure, serene

bolgo be jembi: to eat only vegetarian food

bolgo jeku: vegetarian fare

bolgo duingge hoošan: a kind of paper made from the bark of a tree

bolgo hican: a person who eats little

bolgo tob: honest, incorrupt

bolgobumbi: (causative of **bolgombi**)

bolgobure obohon: (姑洗) the name of a classical musical note corresponding in function to E

bolgokon: somewhat clean, somewhat clear

bolgombi: (-ko) **1**. to become clean; **2**. to determine victory or defeat, to have a test of strength, to measure one's strength with someone

bolgome afambi: to engage in a decisive battle

bolgomimbi: to abstain, to fast, to abstain from meat products

bolgomi targa: 'fast and abstain' — inscription on a tablet posted on fast days

bolgon: clean, cleanliness

bolgonggo: **1**. elegant, refined; **2**. clear, pure

bolgosaka: clean

bolgosu: ⟶ **bolhosu**

bolho: ⟶ **bolgo**

bolhombi: ⟶ **bolgombi**

bolhosu: a slave of the third generation

boli: glass

bolibumbi: (causative of **bolimbi**)

bolikū: **1**. bait; **2**. flag-sign on a shop

bolilambi: to embroider dragons on satin

bolimbi: to lure with bait, to entice

bolin: **1**. lure, enticement, bait; **2**. a dragon embroidered on satin

bolin gecuheri: brocade with writhing dragons depicted on it

boljobumbi: (causative of **boljombi**)

boljoci: ⟶ **boljombi** (subheading)

boljohon: agreement, covenant

boljohon be cashūlambi: to go back on an agreement

boljombi: to agree on, to promise, to fix (a date), to decide to

boljoci ojorakū: cannot be determined, unpredictable, cannot be foreseen, perhaps

boljon: 1. wave; 2. ⟶ **boljohon**

boljon akū: unexpected, unforeseen

boljon colkon: waves

boljon gidakū: bow of a wooden canoe

boljon weren: waves and ripples

boljonggo: conventional, determined by custom, customary

bolmin: incorrupt, sincere

bolokon: somewhat clean

bolombi: (**-ko**) to be exhausted, used up, to be empty

bolori: autumn, fall

bolori be bodoro hafan: (秋官正) an official of the observatory

bolori beidere baita: autumn assizes — the time when executions took place

bolori beidere baita be uheri icihiyara ba: (總辦秋審處) central office for the autumn assizes

bolori dulin: the autumnal equinox

bolori forgon i muke: autumn floods

bolori fulana ilha: begonia

bolori mudan ilha: Japanese anemone

bolorikten: autumn sacrifice to the ancestors

bolosu: glass

bolosu deijire kūwaran: Imperial glass factory

bombi: (**-ngko, -ndoro**) to pierce, to bore, to make a hole with an awl or pick

bombokon: out of humor, annoyed, bored, embarrassed

bombon: a pile, a wad, a cluster, a bunch

bombonombi: to pile up (said of clouds), to form into layers, to swarm (said of bees), to form a large group

bombornombi: to dodder, for one's head to shake (said of old people)

bon: ice pick, tool for making holes in ice

bon i bombi: to break up with a pick

boncihiyan: shrill (like the sound of a broken cymbal)

bongcilihi: a fish from the Eastern Sea whose flesh and bones resemble those of the roe deer

bonggibumbi: (causative of **bonggimbi**)

bonggimbi: to send (away from the speaker)

bonggo: 1. point, apex; 2. first

bonggo de genembi: to go first, to go at the head

bonggo dosikasi: (會元) number one in the examination for Metropolitan Graduate

bonggo morin: outrider, lead horse

bonggo sonjosi: (狀元) number one in the palace examination

bonggo šusai: (案首) number one in the baccalaureate examination

bonggo tukiyesi: (解元) number one in the provincial examination

bongjonggi: 1. coarse, vulgar; 2. a coarse, vulgar person, a lout

bongko: 1. bud of a flower; 2. a wooden cap placed over the point of an arrow

bongko dalangga: a weir built at a fork in a river

bongko sukiyara duka: an ornamental gate in which sections of decorated wood are suspended

bongkon: yellow side ornaments that hang down on both sides of an official's hat

bongkonombi: to form a bud

bongsimu niyehe: one of the names of the wild duck

bonio: 1. monkey; 2. the ninth earth's branch (申)

bonio biya: the seventh month

bonio erin: period of the day from 3 PM to 5 PM, late afternoon

bonionggo: pertaining to the monkey

bonionggo aniya: year of the monkey

bonme: (imperfect converb of **bombi**) downward

bonme gabtambi: to shoot an arrow downward

bonme wasimbi: to descend from a high place

bono: hail

bono foribumbi: to be hailed upon

bonombi: to hail

bontoho: bareback, horse without a saddle

bontoho morin yalumbi: to ride a horse bareback

bontoholobumbi: (causative of **bontoholombi**)

bontoholombi: to be empty, to be bare, to be deprived, to come to nothing

bontu: an adze, chisel

boo: 1. house, room; 2. family, home

boo aname: every house or household

boo be fambumbi: to go astray

boo boigon: household, household affairs

boo ciowan jihai kūwaran: (寶泉局) Coinage Office, *BH* 366

boo dekjibumbi: to establish one's own family

boo giya: (保甲) constable

boo giyalan: room

boo guwan: (保官) guarantor

boo i encehen: family property

boo i hošo: the northwest corner of a house

boo nahan: household

boo nahan ilibumbi: to establish a family

boo nimaha: whale

boo yuwan jihai kūwaran: (寶源局) Coinage Office, *BH* 460A

booci tucike temgetu: an official certificate allowing a person to become a Buddhist monk

booci tucimbi: to leave one's household, to become a Buddhist monk or nun

booi amban: (內務府總管) Department Director of the Imperial Household

booi da: (管領) officials of the fifth and sixth rank in the Imperial Household

booi durugan: a family genealogy

booi hafan: the person in charge of the family affairs of a high official

booi hehe: housemaid

booi ilan gūsa: (內府三旗) the three banners of the Imperial Household, *BH* 97

booi ilan gūsai aliha coohai kūwaran: (內府三旗驍騎營) office in charge of the affairs of the three banners of the Imperial Household; cf. *BH* 97

booi ilan gūsai bayara kūwaran: (內府三旗護軍營) Imperial Guards, *BH* 97A

booi niru: head of a banner in the household of a Prince or in the Imperial Household

booi nirui bayara: (包衣擺牙剌) bond-servant guard in the household of a Prince or in the Imperial Household

booi niyalma: member of a household

booi oyo: roof of a house

boobai: **1**. treasure; **2**. the state seal

boobai soorin: throne of the Emperor

boobai suburgan: pagoda

boobai wehe: precious stone, gem

booci: ⟶ **boo** (subheading)

boodz: **1**. mistress of a brothel; **2**. ⟶ **boose**

boofulambi: ⟶ **bofulambi**

boofun: ⟶ **bofun**

booha: side dish, a dish served with liquor

booha belhere falgari: (珍饈署) department in the Court of Banqueting charged with the preparation of side dishes

boohalabumbi: (causative of **boohalambi**)

boohalambi: **1**. to eat side dishes; **2**. to offer side dishes to the dead on the eighth day after burial

booi: ⟶ **boo** (subheading)

booinge: member of the family, belonging or pertaining to a household or family

boolabumbi: (causative of **boolambi**)

boolambi: **1**. to report; **2**. ⟶ **bolambi**

boolan: report

boolan hoošan: newspaper

boolanabumbi: (causative of **boolanambi**)

boolanambi: to go to report

boolanjimbi: to come to report

boongga jahūdai: houseboat

boose: package, bundle

booselambi: to wrap, to make a package

booši: ⟶ **boobai wehe**

bor seme: gushing forth

borbo: Achilles tendon

borboki niyehe: *Nettion crecca*: the common teal

borcilaha: dried beef and mutton cut into squares and used to make soup

borcilambi: to hang up to dry

borcilaha yali: ⟶ **borcilaha**

bordobumbi: (causative of **bordombi**)

bordokū: food used for fattening livestock

bordombi: to fatten (livestock)

borgo: ⟶ **borhon**

borgombi: ⟶ **borhombi**

borhombi: **1**. to pile up, to amass; **2**. to gather around, to circle, to surround

borhoho nimaha: fish that come together in a great mass

borhome tecembi: to sit in a circle

borhon: conglomeration, heap, swarm, pile

borhon borhon: in piles, in heaps, in swarms

borhonombi: to form a heap or swarm

borhoto: *Caryopteris mongolica*: blue spirea

borimbi: to lull a baby to sleep

borinambi: **1**. to freeze gradually at the headwaters of a stream; **2**. to get stopped up, to stick to something; **3**. to harden (said of nasal mucus)

borjin dobi: gray fox

borjin niyehe: *Anas platyrhynchos*: mallard

boro: **1**. gray; **2**. summer hat

   boro fulan: gray horse

   boro seberi: black horse with white left hooves

borombi: (**-ko**) to turn (dark) gray

   boroko mucu: ripe grapes

borton: dirty (especially the face)

bortonombi: to have a dirty face

bos gurun: Persia

bose: package, bundle; cf. **boose**

boselambi: to bundle, to wrap

bosho: kidney, waist

bosholobumbi: (causative of **bosholombi**)

bosholombi: to be narrow at the middle

boshonggo: having a waist, narrow at the middle, kidney-shaped

boso: **1**. the north side of a mountain; **2**. cloth

   boso aigan: an archery target made of cloth

bosongge: made of cloth

bosoro: *Phoenix dactylifera*: date palm

boši: (博士) ⟶ **taciha hafan**

bošobumbi: (causative or passive of **bošombi**)

bošohon: a bright yellow dye

bošokū: **1**. a driver, a pusher; **2**. (領催) corporal, *BH* 746

bošombi: **1**. to urge, to press, to drive, to exhort; **2**. to expel, to put out; **3**. to rush, to hurry

bošondumbi: to urge or expel together; also **bošonumbi**

bošonjimbi: to come to urge or expel

bošonombi: to go to urge or expel

bošonumbi: to urge or expel together; also **bošondumbi**

bu: town surrounded by a mud wall, village

bubu baba: mumbling

bubumbi: (causative of **bumbi**)

buburšembi: to delay, to tarry

bubuyen: **1**. grown stiff from the cold; **2**. unable to get one's words out

buca: ewe

bucebumbi: (causative of **bucembi**)

bucehe: ⟶ **bucembi** (subheading)

bucehengge: dead person or thing — an oath

buceli: the spirit of a dead person, a ghost, apparition

   buceli benembi: to exorcise a ghost that is causing an illness

   buceli dosika: the spirit of a dead person has entered another person (and speaks through him)

bucembi: to die

   bucehe aha: dead slave — an oath

   buceme susame: dying and perishing (used to describe an enemy in disarray)

   bucere weile: a capital crime

bucen: death; cf. **banjin bucen**

bucere: ⟶ **bucembi** (subheading)

buceshūn: deathly pale

bucetei: until death, scorning death, to the last, desperately

   bucetei afambi: to fight to the last

buceten: despair, desperation

bucilebumbi: (causative of **bucilembi**)

bucileku: a kind of crownless hat with earlaps worn by women

bucilembi: to put down the earlaps on a hat

buculimbi: ⟶ **bucilembi**

buda: cooked cereal, cooked rice, food

   buda arambi: to cook

   buda belhere ba: (飯局) the palace kitchen

   buda jembi: to eat (in general)

   buda muke waliyambi: to pour off excess water after boiling rice or other cereal

   buda nimeku: jaundice

   budai boo: kitchen

   budai faksi: cook

   budai muke: rice broth

budalambi: to eat cooked cereal or cooked rice

budembi: to die

buduhu: *Saurogobio dabryi*: loach

   buduhu moo: *Acer ginnala*: the Amur maple, a tree whose leaves and branches are used to make black dye: cf. **wence**

budukan: somewhat useless or inadequate

budulimbi: ⟶ **buldurimbi**

budun: **1**. commonplace, mediocre, second-rate; **2**. weak, incompetent; **3**. jar, jug, crock; cf. **butūn**

   budun daifu: incompetent doctor

   budun eberi: weak, deficient

   budun ehelinggu: weak, inferior

budun niyalma: mediocre person

budun oliha: cowardly

budurhūna: *Suaeda prostrata*: Mongolian seepweed, a kind of grass that grows on alkaline soil and is eaten by camels

bufaliyambi: to correct oneself, to modify one's previous remarks

bufuyen: unclear (said of speech)

buge: 1. gristle; 2. ⟶ **buhe**

   buge giranggi: cartilage

   buge monggon: windpipe

   buge muke: a solution used for dying grass linen, indigo dye; cf. **buhe**

   buge yasa: an eye disease of cattle and horses

bugū: ⟶ **buhū**

buha: wild buffalo

   buha gurgu: wild buffalo

   buha singgeri: mole

   buha uihe beri: a bow made of wild buffalo horn

buhatu: yak

buhe: indigo

   buhe muke: ⟶ **buge muke**

buheliyebumbi: (causative of **buheliyembi**)

buheliyembi: to cover

buheliyen: 1. cover, covering; 2. seed-bearing hemp

buhere: *Alcedo atthis*: little kingfisher

buhi: 1. inner surface of the thigh; 2. knee; 3. deerskin, buckskin

   buhi adame: knee to knee

   buhi arambi: to sit with one leg toward the rear

   buhi gūlha: boots made of buckskin

buhiyebumbi: (causative of **buhiyembi**)

buhiyecuke: suspicious, suspect

buhiyecun: suspicion, distrust

buhiyembi: to suspect, to surmise, to guess

buhiyembumbi: (causative of **buhiyembi**)

buhiyen: a guess, a surmise

   buhiyen efin i kūwaran: gambling establishment

   buhiyen i efin: a game of chance played with red and black pieces

buhiyendumbi: to suspect one another; also **buhiyenumbi**

buhiyenumbi: to suspect one another; also **buhiyendumbi**

buhū: deer

buhūngge: deer-like, pertaining to deer

bujabumbi: (causative of **bujambi**)

bujambi: (**-ka**) to awake from apparent death, to come back to life

bujan: forest, woods

bujantu ulhūma: one name for a pheasant

bujengsy: (布政司) ⟶ **dasan be hafumbure yamun**

bujihilambi: to be annoyed, to get mad

buju baja: innumerable, uncountable

bujubumbi: (causative of **bujumbi**)

bujumbi: (**-ha**) to boil, to cook

bujun: 100,000

buka: a ram

bukdabumbi: 1. (causative or passive of **bukdambi**); 2. to surrender, to give in, to yield

bukdalambi: to bend, to crease

bukdambi: 1. to fold, to bend, to curve; 2. to string a bow by using the knees; 3. to lose (money); 4. to bow to superior force, to submit

bukdambumbi: (causative or passive of **bukdambi**)

bukdan: a bend, a fold

bukdangga: folded, bent

   bukdangga dengjan: lantern made of folded paper or cloth

bukdari: a memorial or other paper folded accordion fashion

   bukdari acabure falga: (摺配作) a section of the Printing Office concerned with memorials

   bukdari arara kunggeri: (本科) a section of the Court of Colonial Affairs concerned with memorials

   bukdari icihiyakū: (待詔) Compiler, *BH* 203

   bukdari icihiyakū i tinggin: (待詔廳) Office for Compilation of Edicts, *BH* 203

   bukdari icihiyasi: (書寫) clerk of the Court Chancery

bukdarun: a folded examination paper

   bukdarun bargiyara hafan: (收卷官) officer in charge of collecting examination papers

   bukdarun de doron gidara hafan: (印卷官) officer who stamped examination papers

   bukdarun i jumanggi: a bag in which examinations were kept

   bukdarun i talgari: the outside of a folded examination paper

bukdashūn: bent, crumpled

bukdašambi: to press down, to hold down, to force a horse to obey by using the reins

bukdu bakda: dragging one's foot, stiff-legged

bukduhun: elevation, rise

bukdun: ⟶ **bekdun**

buksa: an area of ponds and dry land interspersed, a partially cleared field, a field in which some spots have been burned off

    buksa buksa: interspersed, criss-crossing

buksibumbi: (causative of **buksimbi**)

buksimbi: (**-ha**) to ambush, to lie in wait for

    buksiha cooha: troops lying in ambush

buksin: ambush

buksinambi: to go to ambush

buksindumbi: to ambush at several places simultaneously; also **buksinumbi**

buksinumbi: to ambush at several places simultaneously; also **buksindumbi**

buksu: the lumbar region, the loins, the buttocks

buksuri: **1**. hesitant in speech; **2**. ambiguous, vague, equivocal

buksurilambi: to act or do in an unclear or muddled way

buktalimbi: to pile up (grain)

    buktalime wambi: to kill in piles

buktambi: (**-ka**) to get a stiff neck, to get a crick in the neck

buktan: mound, pile

    buktan buktan: in piles, in mounds

buktu: a hunchback, deformed

buktulin: sack made of cloth or leather for carrying clothes or bedding

buku: wrestler

bukulembi: to put down the earlaps of a cap

bukūn: (spelled with a front **k**) *Naemorhedus goral*: goral

bula: thorn, burr

    bula hailan: a kind of zelkova tree

    bula ilha: thistle (a kind of flower)

    bula moo: thorn bush

    bula sogi: spinach

    bula u hederebuhe: was stuck by prickles and thorns

    bula urangga moo: *Erythrina indica*: coral tree

bulambi: ⟶ **bolambi**

bulangga: having thorns, thorny

bulangga sogi: a kind of wild vegetable with prickled leaves

bulari moo: a kind of thorny bush that grows in Sichuan

bulca yali: the sinewy flesh from the arms and legs

bulcakū: a person who dislikes and avoids work

bulcakūšambi: to shun work habitually

bulcambi: to shun work, to evade, to shirk

bulcandumbi: to shun work together

bulcatambi: to shun work continually

bulcin: ⟶ **bulji**

buldu: small male pig

bulduri: a kind of roe deer that wanders in an area along the coast of North Asia (said to arrive in great herds at certain times and can be killed with clubs)

buldurimbi: to stumble, to trip (said of horses and cows)

bulehen: *Grus japonensis*: crane

bulehengge: crane-like, pertaining to the crane

    bulehengge kiru: (仙鶴旗) a banner bearing an embroidered image of a crane

buleke: (Mongolian) gift; cf. **beleke**

    buleke jaka: ⟶ **buleke**

buleku: **1**. mirror, lens; **2**. a round piece of metal used to protect the heart in combat

    buleku bithe: dictionary

    buleku dobton: case for a mirror

    buleku obumbi: to draw lessons from, to use as a reference

bulekušebumbi: (causative of **bulekušembi**)

bulekušembi: **1**. to look in a mirror, to reflect; **2**. to examine, to scrutinize, to use for reference; **3**. to have a thorough understanding of, to know clearly, to judge clearly

bulen: ⟶ **bulun**

buleri: horn, trumpet

bulga: ⟶ **bulha**

bulgari: suddenly, abruptly

bulgiyambi: to gild, to plate with gold

bulha: many-colored, polychrome

    bulha orho: *Spiranthes sinensis*: Chinese spiranthes

bulhacan niyehe: falcated teal; cf. **alhacan niyehe**

bulhacan ulhūma: one name for a pheasant

bulhari: smoked cowhide

bulhūmbi: to bubble up, to swell up, to gush forth, to surge

buli butu: unclear, muddled

bulimbi: to catch food or bait on the surface of the water (said of fish)

buling seme: **1**. startled, dumb-struck; **2**. sparkling, bright (said of the eyes)

bulinjambi: **1**. to be startled, to be dumb-struck; **2**. to be lazy

buliyambi: to swallow

buljan: growth on the skin, bump, swelling

buljanambi: to form a growth on the skin, to scar over, to heal, to develop a bump

bulji: ⟶ **buljin**

buljin: of one color, monochrome, pure (unadulterated)

    buljin yacin: completely black

bultahūn: **1**. prominent, obvious, bulging, out in the open; **2**. exposed, brought to light

    bultahun tucinjimbi: to come to the surface, to become prominent

bultahūri: bulging out (especially the eyes)

bultari: sticking out, swollen, protruding suddenly

bultarilambi: to protrude suddenly

bulturimbi: ⟶ **buldurimbi**

bulukan: warm

    bulukan šeri: a warm spring

bulumbi: to stack hay in piles

bulun: **1**. a cock (of hay), haystack; **2**. the hub of a wheel

    bulun jafambi: to stack in piles

buluntumbi: to copulate (said of snakes and similar creatures)

bumbi: (**-he**) to give

bumbuku: a leaf bud

bumbulcambi: to swell, to distend

bumbuli: a cake made with oil and wheat flour

bunai: 100,000

buncuhūn: warm, neither too hot nor too cold, pale (said of the sun's color)

bung bung: the sound of a horn, the sound made by blowing into a conch shell

bunggimbi: to give as a present

bungjan: a hunchback, a person with protruding shoulders

bungjanambi: to hump the shoulders, to have a hump

bungnambi: to oppress unjustly, to accuse falsely

bunjiha: a kind of sparrow with large head and eyes

bur bar seme: in profusion, in great quantity

bur bur seme: gurgling forth, swelling up (said of a water spring)

bur seme: pouring forth, gushing out

burabumbi: (causative of **burambi**)

buraki: dust

    buraki jalan: the mortal life, this world

    buraki toron: dust

burakišambi: to throw up dust (said of the wind)

burambi: **1**. to splash with water, to pour over; **2**. to distill

buran taran: in disarray

buranggiyambi: to cook meat quickly in boiling water, to parboil

burašambi: to blow up snow

burdebumbi: (causative of **burdembi**)

burdembi: to blow on a conch, to sound an advance or retreat on a conch

burdenumbi: to blow the conch together

buren: conch horn, brass horn, trumpet

    buren umiyaha: a snail

burenembi: to peel off (intransitive verb), to peel and crack (e.g., the surface of a dry lake bed)

burga: **1**. willow branch; **2**. willow tree

burgambumbi: to billow up (said of incense)

burgasu notho: willow bark

burgašambi: to hang over, to float (smoke or mist)

    burgašame niyamniyambi: to have an archery contest to see who can shoot best at wild game from horseback

burgibumbi: (causative of **burgimbi**)

burgimbi: (**-ha**) to be in disarray, to be flurried, to be alarmed and confused

burgin: **1**. opportunity, favorable situation; **2**. a spell, an interval, a sudden burst (of rain); **3**. disarray, disorder; **4**. pommel; cf. **burgiyen**

    burgin bargin: **1**. confused, chaotic, in disarray, tumultuous; **2**. in gusts

    burgin burgin i: in sudden bursts, in disarray

burgindumbi: to be in disarray together; also **burginumbi**

burginumbi: to be in disarray together; also **burgindumbi**

burgišambi: to be in frequent or constant disarray

burgiyelembi: to grasp the pommel, to use the pommel

burgiyen: **1**. the outside surface; **2**. pommel; **3**. stingy, miserly

burhambi: to be reduced to poverty and ruin

burhimbi: ⟶ **burgimbi**

burhišembi: ⟶ **burgišambi**

buribumbi: **1.** (causative or passive of **burimbi**); **2.** to sink

burimbi: (**-ha**) **1.** to cover, to stretch over a surface; **2.** to attach the outer surface of a garment

burkimbi: to bury, to inter

burlambi: ⟶ **burulambi**

burtei: widespread, common; cf. **biretei**

buru bara: dim, unclear, hazy, hidden

   buru bara ba: the netherworld

burubumbi: **1.** to disappear without a trace; **2.** to die (said of a Prince)

buruhun: dim, only partially visible, clouded

burulabumbi: (causative of **burulambi**)

burulambi: to flee, to take to flight

burulandumbi: to flee together; also **burulanumbi**

burulanumbi: to flee together; also **burulandumbi**

burulu: a horse having mixed red and white hair

burumbi: (**-ha**) to cover up, to hide

burut: subordinate, troops under one's command

busajambi: to be blind due to an injury

busalambi: to blind

busanggiyambi: to search urgently for something lost

buse: a fortified location

buse da: lily root that can be boiled and eaten

busehe ilha: lily

buserebumbi: (causative or passive of **buserembi**)

busereku: **1.** an uncouth person; **2.** pederast, sodomite

buserembi: **1.** to act uncouthly; **2.** to commit pederasty or sodomy

   buserere baita: pederasty, sodomy

bushe: blister from a burn

bushenembi: to get a blister from being burned

busu busu agambi: to rain a fine rain

busubumbi: (**-ke**) to suffer a relapse

busumda: lily

buša: more

bušakan: a little more

bušuhūn: stingy, cheap

bušuku: a harmful spirit that bewitches children and animals, a fox-sprite

   bušuku dondon: moth

   bušuku yemji: animal-sprites and ghosts

bušukudembi: to be possessed by a fox-sprite

bušukulembi: to practice ghostly arts, to appear as an animal-sprite

butabumbi: (causative of **butambi**)

butalin: a clasp for an arrowhead

butambi: **1.** to fish (with a net), to hunt; **2.** to earn (money)

butan: game (at hunting)

butan halan: an expression of regret

   butan halan akū: what a shame!

butanambi: to go to catch, to go to hunt or fish

butemji: **1.** cunning, deceitful; **2.** insidious, sinister

buten: **1.** the foot of a mountain; **2.** the hem of a garment; **3.** boundary, horizon; cf. **abkai buten**

buterembi: **1.** to go along the foot of a mountain; **2.** to hem

   butereme: along the mountain's foot

butha: hunting and fishing

   buthai niyalma: hunter, fisherman, sportsman

   buthai yamun: a section of the Imperial Household in charge of procuring fish and wild game

buthambi: to hunt, to fish; cf. **buthašambi**

buthasi: **1.** hunter, fisherman; **2.** (虞人) an official of ancient times in charge of hunting grounds

buthašabumbi: (causative of **buthašambi**)

buthašambi: **1.** to hunt, to fish; **2.** to earn (money); **3.** to gather, to collect

   buthašara be kadalara fiyenten: (都虞司) Department of the Household Guard and the Imperial Hunt, *BH* 80

   buthašara niyalma: hunter

butu: dark, dim, hidden, secret, pertaining to the underworld

   butu arga: plot intrigue, ruse

   butu buruhun: dim, gloomy

   butu duha: caecum, blind gut

   butu dushun: dim, gloomy

   butu haksan: dark and dangerous

   butu halhūn: sultry, hot and humid, close

   butu hūlha: thief

   butu hūlhi niyalma: a stupid person who makes no reply when spoken to

   butu sabirgi noho suje: satin cloth woven without golden threads

   butu sejen: a closed vehicle used for the transport of criminals

butu wambi: to assassinate

butui: secretly

butui bejilere gisun: riddle

butui hebe: conspiracy

butui jalan: the underworld

butuha: ⟶ **butumbi** (subheading)

butuken: rather dim, rather secret

butulebumbi: (causative of **butulembi**)

butulembi: **1**. to cover, to cover up, to stop up; **2**. to act secretly

    butuleme wambi: to assassinate

butumbi: (-ha) to hibernate

    butuha cibin: a kind of hibernating swallow

butun: hibernation

butur seme: weeping without cease

buturi: heat rash, acne, pimples

buturinambi: to develop heat rash or acne

butūn: crock, large jar; cf. **budun**

buya: **1**. small, tiny; **2**. low, insignificant; **3**. lowly, base, inferior

    buya fujin: Imperial concubine

    buya fusihūn: lowly, mean, humble

    buya hafan: petty official

    buya irgen: people of lowly estate

    buya julen: novel, romance

    buya juse: a child (under ten years of age)

    buya niyalma: ordinary person, a mean person (as opposed to a gentleman), a self-deprecatory term used in referring to oneself

    buya subsi: trifling, insignificant

    buya tušan i hafan: (小京官) officials of the seventh and eighth ranks attached to the Councils and Secretarial Offices, *BH* 299

    buya yabun: trifle, small matter

buyakasi: small, minute, of little consequence

buyarambi: to be petty, to act in a petty way, to be small scale

buyarame: **1**. of small import, insignificant; **2**. miscellaneous

    buyarame baita icihiyara boo: (火房) an office concerned with miscellaneous small dealings

    buyarame ejembi: to make miscellaneous jottings, to take notes

    buyarame hacin i kunggeri: (雜科) section in the Board of Works for miscellaneous business

    buyarame hafan: officials of the lower ranks

    buyarame jaka: miscellaneous small things

    buyarame jujurame: timidly, narrow-mindedly, pettily

buyasi: small, petty, tiny, insignificant

buyebumbi: (causative of **buyembi**)

buyecuke: desirable, precious, enchanting, amiable, cute

buyecun: desire, longing, love

buyembi: to desire, to long for, to admire, to like, to love, to yearn for, to do gladly, to be passionate about

buyen: desire

    buyen ciha: longing and desire, personal desire, greed

    buyen cisui: in one's own personal interest, according to one's personal desires

    buyen i tuwa: fire of lust

buyendumbi: to desire together, to like one another; also **buyenumbi**

buyenin: **1**. feeling, desire, emotion; **2**. sexual desire, lust

buyenumbi: to desire together, to like one another; also **buyendumbi**

buyeršembi: to admire, to envy

būrtu kara: a fine black horse

C ᠴ

ca: tendon, sinew

    ca mangga: stubborn, not easy to deal with, difficult

ca yuwan yamun: (察院) Bureau of Inspection

cab seme: blindly, recklessly

cabdara: a brown horse with white mane and tail

cabdari: ⟶ cabdara

cabgan suru: a pure white horse

cabi: the hair on the breast and stomach (of a horse)

cabihan: a float on a fish line

cabsimbi: to protect

cabumbi: (causative of cambi)

cacarakū: a gray grasshopper

cacari: a tent

    cacari boo: a square tent with cloth sides

cacihiyambi: to drip, to run (said of the nose)

cacubumbi: (causative of cacumbi)

cacumbi: to sprinkle, to spill, to pour a libation, to drip

cacun: ⟶ acun cacun

cacurambi: to make a racket, to kick up a row

cadabumbi: (causative of cadambi)

cadambi: to wind, to coil around

cadari: (Sanskrit kṣatriya) the warrior caste in India

cafur cifur seme: smooth and slippery (said of tasty food)

cagaci: (供事) Clerk, BH 190, 267

cagan: 1. books, documents, papers; 2. koumiss; cf. cahan

cagan han: (Mongolian) the Russian Czar

cagatu ulhūma: *Gennaeus nycthemerus*: the silver pheasant

cahan: koumiss

cahara: a vessel carried on one's person for drinking water

caharnambi: 1. to clear the throat and nostrils (said of a horse); 2. to have a clear discharge from the nose (said of cattle)

cahi: hasty, hurried

cahimbi: to divide, to partition

cahin: 1. well crib — sometimes used simply in the sense of 'well'; 2. compartment for storing grain, bin, crib

    cahin i usin: a well field (a kind of field allotment in ancient times)

cahū: 1. a virago, termagant; 2. teapot

cahūdambi: ⟶ cahūšambi

cahūšambi: to brawl, to speak sharply, to squabble, to be vituperative (said of women)

cai: tea

    cai abdaha: tea leaves

    cai abdaha i kunggeri: (茅茶科) a section of the Board of Rites concerned with matters relating to tea

    cai fuifumbi: to brew tea

    cai i boo: teahouse

    cai i da: (尚茶正) Chief Cup-bearer, BH 91

    cai morin be kadalara yamun: (茶馬司) Office of Tea and Horse Revenue; cf. BH 844A

    cai nenden ilha: *Camellia sasanqua*: a camellia

    cai taili: a tea tray

caida: tea essence — strong tea to be diluted with water before drinking

caidu: a kind of bean eaten while drinking tea

caise: 1. hairpin; 2. a cake made of fried vermicelli

caisi: ⟶ caise

cak seme: 1. neatly; 2. tightly, firmly; 3. solidly (freezing); 4. suddenly

    cak sere beikuwen: freezing cold

cakcahūn: inflexible, unbendable, hard to draw (said of a bow)

cakcin: ten billion

cakilgatu kuluk: a fine horse with whorls of hair on both hind legs

cakiri: 1. half-cooked, half-done; 2. sable or fox pelts speckled with white hair

    cakiri damin: a white-speckled eagle

cakiri šongkon: a white-speckled falcon

cakjambi: (-ka) to become crusted over (said of snow)

cakjame gecembi: to freeze hard

caksaha: *Pica pica*: magpie; cf. **saksaha**

caksambi: ⟶ **caksimbi**

caksikū: a small cymbal

caksikū ucun amba kumun: music accompanied by cymbals and singing performed for the Emperor when traveling, when prisoners of war were presented, and when troops were inspected

caksikū ucun narhūn kumun: music played at banquets given in honor of victorious generals

caksimbi: **1**. to rattle, to vibrate, to beat a cymbal, to make an uproar; **2**. to make a strike with the **gacuha**; **3**. to praise; **4**. to ache (said of the bones and joints); **5**. to cry (said of magpies)

caksime jembi: to make smacking sounds while eating

cakū: white-necked

cakūha: a white-necked magpie

cakūlu: having white spots or markings

cakūlu cecike: probably *Oenanthe oenanthe*: the white chat

cakūlu honggon cecike: a small bird with a light-yellow head and a white speckled neck

cakūlu kiongguhe: the Fujian myna

cakūlu kurehu: a white-headed woodpecker

cakūlun: jackdaw or crow with a white ringed neck

cakūlutu cecike: *Pycnonotus sinensis*: Chinese bulbul

cakūran: *Santalum album*: sandalwood

cakūri hiyan: sandalwood incense

cala: **1**. over there, on the other side; **2**. previously, before; **3**. besides, in addition to

calabumbi: **1**. (causative of **calambi**); **2**. to differ

calabure ba akū: there is no difference, almost the same

calabun: **1**. mistake, error; **2**. difference

calabure: ⟶ **calabumbi** (subheading)

calambi: **1**. to err, to miss; **2**. to be different

calanambi: to go to miss, to go to make an error

calcin: water that flows on top of ice in the springtime

calfa: incompletely dried birchbark — also called **fulgiyan alan**

calgabun: contrariness, perverseness, disloyalty

calgari: impractical, pedantic, clinging to outmoded ideas, inexperienced, not business-like

calgari leolen: impractical view

calgari mudaliyan: high-sounding and impractical

calgibumbi: to form waves (as when the wind blows up the water in a river), to overflow, to surge

calgimbi: to beat, to lap (said of waves), to splash, to overflow (the banks of a river)

calgin: wave, surge, overflowing

calhari: ⟶ **calgari**

calihūn: *Acanthis linaria*: the mealy redpoll

calimbi: **1**. to collapse from fatigue; **2**. to cling, to hold on; **3**. to have trouble breathing; **4**. to grab by the hair; cf. **ciyalimbi**

caliyan: **1**. pay and provisions (military); **2**. tax, levy

caliyan i boo: (錢糧房) Pay Office of the Printing Office and Bookbindery

caliyan i fiyenten: (經會司) Pay Office of the Board of Revenue in Mukden

caliyan i kunggeri: (金科) an office of the Board of Revenue

caliyangga šusai: (廩生) Stipendiary, *BH* 577C, 629A, 631

caliyasi: tax collector

calu: a granary

calu cahin: granaries

calu cahin i baita be uheri kadalara yamun: (總督倉場衙門) Head Office of Government Granaries at the Capital

calu i kunggeri: (倉科) section on granaries in the Board of Revenue

calungga: **1**. pertaining to a granary; **2**. a grain measure equaling sixteen bushels

calungga bele: rice from a granary

camangga: stubborn; ⟶ **ca mangga**

camanggadambi: to be stubborn, to put on airs

cambi: (-ngka/-ha) **1**. to stretch, to pitch (a tent or yurt), to draw (a bow), to build (a bridge); **2**. to run away (said of a horse)

came gecehe: frozen solid all of a sudden

camci: slip (garment worn under a woman's gown), long padded jacket

camda: **1**. a leather case; **2**. haze, mist

came: ⟶ **cambi** (subheading)

camgan: ⟶ **camhan**

camgan bithe: horizontal inscribed board

camhan: a temporary arch or structure (over a street) that carries slogans or holiday greetings

camhari: inscribed stone, boundary stone

camhata: piebald, speckled

camnambi: to catch after an initial miss (said of falcons), to seize prey on a second try

camsi: a tent erector

camtumbi: (of clouds) to spread densely

can: **1.** a small cymbal; **2.** a bowl with a narrow bottom; **3.** meditation, dhyāna; **4.** ⟶ **can nimaha**

can nimaha: *Lota lota:* burbot

can tembi: to sit in meditation

can tere boo: meditation hall

cananggi: day before yesterday, previously

cang: **1.** the autumnal sacrifice; **2.** sacrificial wine

cang cang: (onomatopoetic) the sound of bells

cang cing: ⟶ **cang cang**

cang seme: **1.** hard, fast; **2.** (onomatopoetic) the sound made by a bowstring when it is released

cang seme gecembi: to freeze solid

cang seme mangga: very hard

cangga: a small gong

canggali: impatient, easily exhausted

canggalimbi: to be exhausted, to get tired, to tire

canggi: only, nothing but, just

canjurabumbi: (causative of **canjurambi**)

canjurambi: to greet by holding joined hands up at face level and bowing slightly

cangka: **1.** perfect participle of **cambi**; **2.** a white horse with red eyes, nose, and lips

cangkai: only, just, simply

cangkambi: to kill small fish in shallow water with stones

cankir niongniyaha: the speckled goose of Qinghai

cao seme: immediately, straightaway

car cir: (onomatopoetic) the sound of meat sizzling (used to describe a painful wound)

car seme: **1.** painful (said of a burn); **2.** at a breath, at a stroke

cara: **1.** a tall wine vessel made of gold, silver, or pewter; **2.** a horse with red around its eyes, nose, and lips; **3.** ⟶ **cara aniya**

cara aniya: the year before last

cara ihan: a striped cow

caranambi: to have white spots or flecks

carcan seme: shrieking, screaming

carcinambi: **1.** to congeal, to begin to freeze, to ice up; **2.** to develop a blister

cargi: **1.** there, over there, that side, beyond; **2.** formerly, ago: **ilan aniya i cargi** 'three years ago'

cargi aniya: the year before last

cargi biya: the month before last

cargi dalin: the opposite shore

cargi jalan: the other world, the world of the dead

cargilakū: firecracker, fireworks

cargimbi: to explode

carki: a wooden clapper

carki tūmbi: to hit a wooden clapper

carkidambi: to beat time with a clapper

carkimbi: **1.** to rattle together (as belt pendants), to create a dissonance, to tinkle; **2.** to sound hoarse

carnambi: ⟶ **caranambi**

carubumbi: (causative of **carumbi**)

carumbi: to fry, to deep-fry

carure boo: pastry kitchen, place where pastries were prepared

carur seme: in an oily manner, smoothly

carure: ⟶ **carumbi** (subheading)

cas seme: **1.** vaguely, in a fragmentary way; **2.** suddenly, unexpectedly

cas seme donjimbi: to hear only bits and pieces

cashūlabumbi: (causative or passive of **cashūlambi**)

cashūlambi: **1.** to turn one's back on, to stand or sit with one's back to; **2.** to break (an agreement), to go back on (one's word), to betray; **3.** to be ungrateful

cashūlame tembi: to sit back to back

cashūn: **1.** backward, facing backward, with one's back toward someone; **2.** opposite, contrary

cashūn edun: tail wind, a wind at one's back

cashūn forombi: to turn backward

cashūn gisun: irony

cashūn tembi: to sit with one's back to

casi: in that direction, thither, to there

casi akū ebsi akū: neither here nor there, without direction, neither coming nor going

casi forombi: to turn in that direction

casiba ilha: a white flower found in Mongolia

casikan: a little in that direction

cata: a quadrillion

ce: **1**. they; **2**. an Imperial document on yellow or gold paper; **3**. a written answer to a question

cebke: flat side of the **gacuha**

cebke cabka: finicky, picky (about food)

cece: silk gauze

    cece dardan: a kind of silk gauze

    cece gecuheri: silk gauze decorated with dragon patterns; cf. **gecuheri**

    cece undurakū: silk gauze with dragon patterns on it; cf. **undurakū**

cecen: distention (of the belly)

cecercuke: annoying, vexing, infuriating, detestable

cecerembi: **1**. to press tightly, to embrace tightly; **2**. to be taut and hard to draw (said of a bowstring)

ceceri: a kind of loose-textured silk, lustring

    ceceri šošontu: an ancient crown-shaped head covering

ceceršembi: **1**. to exert a great amount of effort, to quiver from exertion; **2**. to hold tightly, to embrace tightly

    ceceršeme cincilambi: to examine closely

    ceceršeme hajilambi: to make love

    ceceršeme jafambi: to grasp tightly

    ceceršeme yabumbi: to have sex, to act in an indecent manner

cecike: a small bird; cf. **gasha**

    cecike be fulgiyere sihan: a blowpipe for shooting birds

    cecike be latubure darhūwan: a glued pole for catching small birds

    cecike fulgiyeku: a blowpipe for shooting small birds

    cecike mimi: a wild vegetable, the leaves of which can be eaten raw

    cecike tatara asu: a net for catching small birds

cecikelembi: to notch an arrow holding it between the thumb and forefinger

cehun: distended, flatulent, overly full (said of the belly)

cejehen: a piece of wood on the end of a tow rope

cejeleku: a detachable collar used with a Manchu garment

cejen: the upper part of the chest

cejen anambi: to expand the chest (as a gesture of pride)

cejen telebumbi: to have a pain in the chest

cekceri: a shallow brass cooking vessel

cekcihiyan: a small tripod

ceke: **1**. a short jacket made of wild animal pelts; **2**. the side of a **gacuha**

cekemu: Japanese satin, velveteen

cekjehun: having a protruding chest, pigeon-chested

ceku: a swing

cekudembi: to swing in a swing

cekulembi: ⟶ **cekudembi**

celebumbi: (causative of **celembi**)

celehe: ⟶ **celembi** (subheading)

celehen: a courtyard paved with bricks

    celehen i amba kumun: music played while the Emperor returned to the palace from a banquet and while officials were thanking him for favors received

    celehen i bolgonggo kumun: music played during Imperial banquets

    celehen i hūwa: a courtyard in front of the throne hall

celeheri: terrace, platform; cf. **celheri**

celeku: a ruler, measuring stick

    celeku dangse: resident register

celembi: **1**. to measure (with a ruler); **2**. to tire after a long journey; **3**. to pave with bricks or stone

    celehe jugūn: a brick-paved path through the palace

celheri: a paved platform before an official building, a terrace, a platform; cf. **celeheri**

celin: a band on the bootleg that is attached to the trousers to hold the boot tight

celmen: nap or pile on cloth

celmeri: thin, slender, well-proportioned (said of a person's figure)

celmerjembi: **1**. to hang down; **2**. to be well-proportioned

cembe: (accusative of **ce**: them)

cen: one one-hundred-millionth

cen hiyang: *Aquilaria agallocha*: agalloch, eaglewood

cenci: (ablative of **ce**): from them, than them

cencilembi: to examine carefully

    cencileme tuwambi: to take a careful look at

cende: (dative of **ce**): to them, for them

cendebumbi: (causative of **cendembi**)

cendeku: an instrument used for testing

> **cendeku sihan**: a pointed pipe used for extracting samples from grain sacks

cendekušembi: **1**. to probe, to put to the test, to try out; **2**. to try to verify a fact by feigning ignorance; **3**. to tempt

cendembi: to check, to verify, to try out, to put to the test

cendendumbi: to test or verify together; also **cendenumbi**

cendenumbi: to test or verify together; also **cendendumbi**

cendz tubihe: an orange

cene: a peony

cengme: coarse Tibetan wool

cengmu: ⟶ **cengme**

cengsiyang: prime minister

ceni: (genitive of **ce**): of them, their

ceningge: theirs

cense: ⟶ **cendz tubihe**

cerguwe: roe, fish eggs

> **cerguwe waliyambi**: to lay eggs (said of fish)

cerhuwe: ⟶ **cerguwe**

cerhuwenembi: **1**. to get a boil or abscess on the finger, to develop a whitlow; **2**. to become pregnant (said of fish)

ceri: gauze, netting (of silk)

> **ceri suje**: a satin that resembles gauze

ceringge ilha: a red flower from South China

cese: register, official record

> **cese i namun**: (冊庫) storage room for registers in the Board of Rites

ci: **1**. (ablative particle): from, by way of, than; **2**. rank, military formation; **3**. paint, lacquer; **4**. space, interval

> **ci akū**: uninterruptedly, constantly

> **ci sindambi**: to line up

cib cab: quiet, still

cib cib seme: very quietly

cib gukubun: silence and extinction, nirvana

cib seme: **1**. quietly; **2**. swiftly (said of an arrow)

cibahanci: a lamaist nun

cibiha: a white-necked crow that flies in flocks

cibin: *Hirundo rustica*: swallow

> **cibin cecike**: ⟶ **cibin**

cibingga kiongguhe: a kind of myna that resembles a swallow

cibirgan: a small bird resembling a swallow with reddish head and back

cibiri ilha: a yellow flower that grows on a vine and blooms in late spring

cibsembi: to be quiet, to be silent

cibsen: quietness, stillness

cibsidambi: to lament incessantly

cibsimbi: to lament, to deplore, to sigh over, to regret

cibsin: **1**. a lament; **2**. a funeral notice

cibsindumbi: to lament together; also **cibsinumbi**

cibsinumbi: to lament together; also **cibsindumbi**

cibsonggo: **1**. harmony, harmonious; **2**. the right side of an ancestral temple

cibsu hiyan: incense used at sacrifices

cibtui: repeatedly, intently, intensively, exclusively

cibumbi: to be squeezed (into a narrow space), to be blocked off, to be crowded

cici goci: timidly, fearfully, full of doubt, hesitant

cidahūn: pelt of a snow rabbit

> **cidahūn kurume**: coat made from a snow-rabbit pelt

cifabumbi: (causative of **cifambi**)

cifahan: viscous mud, mud used as plaster

cifahangga aisin: gold paint

cifambi: to smear on, to plaster

cifeleku: a spittoon

cifelembi: to spit

cifenggu: spit, saliva

cifun: tax, duty

> **cifun arambi**: to impose a tax

> **cifun gaimbi**: to collect tax or duty

> **cifun i bithe**: tax receipt

> **cifun i bithei menggun**: property deeds tax

> **cifun i menggun**: tax money

cifuri niyehe: a name for the common teal

cige: ⟶ **cihe**

cigu niru: (旗鼓) Captain of the Banner Drum — a Chinese official of the palace

ciha: desire, wish

> **cihai**: as one wishes, according to one's desires

> **cihai balai**: arbitrarily, willfully

> **cihai cihai**: with great willingness

> **cihai sindambi**: to act in a wanton fashion, to act in a self-willed way, to act capriciously

> **cihai yabumbi**: to behave arbitrarily

cihakū: **1**. unwilling; **2**. uncomfortable, ill, not feeling well

cihalahai: as one likes, according to one's desire

cihalambi: **1**. to like, to be fond of, to want, to be willing; **2**. to look for shortcomings, to look for others' errors

cihalan: **1**. desire, wish; **2**. fondness, hobby

cihalšambi: **1**. to desire ardently; **2**. always to be looking for others' shortcomings

cihan: desire

cihan buyen akū: without desire or interest

cihangga: **1**. willing, eager; **2**. fond of, keen on

cihangga waka: unwilling

cihanggai: willing, eager, willingly, eagerly

cihanggai ergen toodambi: to be willing to pay with one's life

cihe: louse

cihetei: *Equus hemionus*: wild ass

cihin: granary, place for storing rice; cf. **cahin**

cik: a circle written in texts as a form of punctuation

cik sindambi: to add a circle as a sign of punctuation

cik tongkimbi: ⟶ **cik sindambi**

cik cak seme: rustling, making a small noise

cik cik: suddenly (to think of something)

cik cik seme: sadly, morosely, anxiously

cik cik seme gūnimbi: to think of constantly, to come to mind suddenly and often, to be anxious about something

cik seme: suddenly

cik seme gūnimbi: to think of suddenly

cikeku: **1**. bamboo strips or reeds from which mats are made; **2**. stalk of a rice plant, stubble; **3**. inner bark, bast

cikešembi: to be a little lame (said of horses or cows)

cikimbi: (**-ha**) to insert or attach snugly, to fit exactly, to fit or attach tightly (as a tenon in a mortise)

cikirakū: not fitting snugly

cikin: **1**. edge, border; **2**. the bank of a river

cikingge fu: a boundary wall

cikirambi: to go along the edge, border, or bank

cikirame: along the edge, border, or riverbank

cikiri: **1**. wood shavings; **2**. a dog or horse with white or light blue eyes; **3**. white hairs or small areas of white on a pelt

cikiri dobihi: a black fox pelt speckled with white hairs

cikiri niyehe: a wild duck dappled with white around the eyes and bill

cikiringge: reed-colored, catkin-colored

cikiršambi: to be shy, to be bashful, to be embarrassed

cikjalambi: to form a sprout within the ground

ciksimbi (1): (**-ka**) to mature, to grow up, to become tough (said of the muscles)

ciksika boigon: well-to-do household

ciksika haha: adult male

ciksimbi (2): (**-ha**) **1**. to chirp; **2**. to ache (said of the bones)

ciksin: adult, grown-up, mature, able-bodied

ciktambi: to take root, to grow up

ciktan: relationship, natural law, principle

ciktarambi: (**-ka**) **1**. to mature, to become established in life; **2**. to be in readiness; **3**. to flourish, to spread out

cikten: **1**. trunk, stem, shaft (of an arrow); **2**. one of the ten heaven's stems

cikten gargan: heavenly stems and earthly branches (*tiāngān dìzhī* 天干地支)

ciktenembi: to go along the trunk or stem, to form a stem

cikteneme: along the trunk or stem

cilba: having the same given name; cf. **silba**

cilbambi: to give the given name

cilburi: a guide rope fastened to a bridle ring to lead beasts of burden, a tether

cilcimbi: (**-ka**) to swell (as a wave), to come in (for high tide)

cilcin: **1**. swelling, bump, tumor; **2**. not smooth, lacking fluency, rough and bumpy

cilcin akū: clear-cut, straightforward, smooth (said of speaking or writing)

cilcin madambi: to vent one's anger

cilcinambi: to form a boil, swelling, or bump on the skin

cilebumbi: (causative of **cilembi**)

cilembi: **1**. to apply lacquer, to paint; **2**. to make a sound by plucking a taut cord

cilikū: choking, difficulty in swallowing

cilikū nimeku: dysphagia

cilimbi: (**-ha**) to choke, to swallow with difficulty

cilime hagame songgombi: to sob

cilin: **1**. ⟶ **celin**; **2**. unicorn; cf. **sabintu**

cilme: ⟶ **celmen**

cimaha: **1**. tomorrow; **2**. morning

cimaha inenggi: tomorrow, the next day
cimari: **1**. tomorrow; **2**. morning; **3**. a measure equivalent to six *mǔ* 畝
  cimari erde: tomorrow morning, early in the morning
cimaridari: every morning
cimarilame: early in the morning
cimci: shirt
cime: *Concorhynchus nerka*: sockeye salmon, nerka
cimeke giranggi: **1**. the foot bones of an animal; **2**. all the small bones in a pig's foot below the anklebone (used by small girls as toys)
cimikū: a pacifier: a nipple-shaped object for babies to suck on
cimilan: a whistle that makes sound when air is sucked through it rather than being blown
cimkišambi: to be without appetite, to find food tasteless
cin: **1**. chief, principal, main; **2**. straight, straightforward; **3**. the south side; **4**. a small white heron
  cin i boo: main room, principal room
  cin i diyan: principal palace
  cin i duka: the main gate
  cin i ergi: place of honor
  cin i gamambi: to handle in a straightforward and honest way
  cin i tembi: to sit in the place of honor (at a meal)
  cin i wasimbi: to come straight down
  cin wang: Prince, *BH* 13
cincilabumbi: (causative of **cincilambi**)
cincilambi: to look at carefully, to observe, to examine, to scrutinize
cincilan: an implement used for observation
cindahan: *Lepus timidus*: snow rabbit, varying hare
  cindahan cabi: the fur on the underside of a snow rabbit
cing cang: the sound of chipping ice, the sound of pounding earth
cing k'o muji: highland barley (grown in Tibet and Qinghai)
cing seme: **1**. flaming, flashing; **2**. in a throng, crowding; **3**. prosperously; **4**. straight upward
  cing seme banjimbi: to live prosperously
  cing seme dambi: to flame
cinggambi: ⟶ **cingkambi**

cinggilakū: a small bell used by Buddhist monks
cinggin: a three-year-old pig
cinggir seme: sound of a bell ringing
cinggiri ilha: a purple, bell-shaped exotic flower
cinggiya: **1**. superficial, limited in scope, having narrow views; **2**. short (said of time); **3**. short (of stature); **4**. not far
cinggiyakan: somewhat narrow
cinggiyan: ⟶ **cinggiya**
cingiri: *Gracula religiosa*: myna bird
cingkabumbi: **1**. (causative or passive of **cingkambi**); **2**. to gorge oneself, to be stuffed, to be puffed up, to be inflated
cingkai: **1**. very, greatly, by far; **2**. by all means, feel free to, at will; **3**. willfully, arbitrarily, wantonly
  cingkai amgambi: to oversleep
  cingkai colgoroko: preeminent, surpassing, outstanding
  cingkai encu: vastly different, completely different
cingkambi: **1**. to be filled, to be stuffed full; **2**. to do something to the utmost, to be to an extreme degree
  cingkame: fully, to the full extent
  cingkame fargambi: to pursue to the end
  cingkame jembi: to eat to satiety, to eat one's fill
  cingkame yabumbi: to walk without stopping
cingkašambi: to stuff full
cingnembi: to glue an arrowhead to the shaft
cingnur: spy, sentry
cinjiri: myna bird; cf. **cingiri**
cinuhūlambi: to smear red with cinnabar, to write with red ink
cinuhūn: **1**. cinnabar; **2**. bright red
  cinuhūn i araha bukdarun: copy of an examination written in red ink
  cinuhūn i menggun: funds for official use
cinurgan: a small sparrow-like bird with a black back and vermilion plumage
cir seme: gushing out, hurrying
  cir seme hūdun: bouncing along quickly
cira: **1**. strict, stern; **2**. hard, solid; **3**. face, complexion
  cira aljaha: the expression (on his face) changed
  cira elheken oho: his face has an angry look

cira fafulambi: to forbid strictly

cira gūwaliyambi: to turn pale

cira morin: powerful horse

cira nirugan: portrait

cira sindaha: his face has a happy look

cira takambi: to practice physiognomy

cira takara niyalma: physiognomist

ciralabumbi: (causative of **ciralambi**)

ciralambi: to be strict, to act strictly

ciran: solemnity, seriousness

cirangga: colored, having color

cirashūn: ⟶ **cirgashūn**

circan: a bright yellow pigment

circinambi: to freeze on the surface

cirgabukū miyoocan: air rifle

cirgabumbi: **1**. to stop up, to block up, to hold back; **2**. to be stopped up, to be blocked up; **3**. to swash, to surge (said of waves)

cirgashūn: impeded, blocked, stiff

    cirgashūn dedumbi: to lie stiffly, to lie without moving

cirgebumbi: (causative of **cirgembi**)

cirgeku: a wooden implement used to pound earth, a ramrod

cirgembi: **1**. to ram, to pound (earth); **2**. to loosen a bowstring; **3**. to unhitch

cirgešembi: to pound steadily

cirhashūn: ⟶ **cirgashūn**

cirhembi: ⟶ **cirgembi**

cirhūbumbi: (causative of **cirhūmbi**)

cirhūmbi: to take back, to let a bow go lax, to lower a sword after having brandished it

    cirhūme gūnimbi: to change one's mind

cirku: pillow

    cirku hengke: *Cucumis melo*: winter melon

    cirku moo: wooden posts on both sides of a threshold

    cirku ninggu i baita: sexual intercourse

    cirku wehe: stone pillars or supports on both sides of a threshold

cirubumbi: (causative of **cirumbi**)

ciruku: ⟶ **cirku**

cirumbi: (**-he**) to support, to pillow, to use as a pillow

cise: vegetable or flower garden

cistan: a thin strip of paper placed on official documents to show places where corrections were to be made

cisu: **1**. private, private interest or profit; **2**. selfish

    cisu akū: unselfish

    cisu baita: private matter

    cisu be yabumbi: to seek private gain

    cisui: in one's own interest, on one's own initiative, naturally (see also **ini cisui**), private

    cisui boji: a private contract or deed (without an official seal)

    cisui bucembi: to die by suicide

    cisui doore urse: smugglers

    cisui gamambi: to handle on one's own, to handle without authorization

    cisui hungkerehe jiha: illegal coins

cisudembi: to act for one's private interest

cisui: ⟶ **cisu** (subheading)

cisulembi: to act in one's own interest, to do privately, to keep for one's own private use

citu morin: a famous swift horse

ciyalibumbi: (causative or passive of **ciyalimbi**)

ciyalimbi: to grab by the hair (in a fight)

ciyalindumbi: to grab one another's hair when fighting

ciyan dzung: (千總) ⟶ **minggatu, ciyandzung**

ciyan hū: (千戶) chief of one thousand families in a military district

ciyan ši: (僉事) Secretary

ciyandzung: (千總) Lieutenant, *BH* 752E

ciyang wei: primrose

ciyanliyang: provisions — the same as **caliyan**

ciyanši: (僉事) Secretary

cob seme: appearing suddenly, standing out from the crowd

cobalabumbi: (causative of **cobalambi**)

cobalambi: to pry up, to lift with a lever, to prize open

coban: **1**. a lever, a bar for prying; **2**. a medical quack

cobangga gin: a scale for weighing heavy objects

cobašambi: to pry up, to prize open

cobdaha: bamboo leaf

    cobdaha šungkeri ilha: *Bletilla striata*: a kind of terrestrial orchid

cobolan: an owl — the same as **yabulan**

cobto: **1**. rags, shreds; **2**. to shreds; **3**. cloth remnant

    cobto cobto: in rags, ragged, tattered

    cobto cobto hūwajaha: tore into shreds

cobtojombi: to have a piece torn from one's clothing

cocarambi: **1**. to act heedlessly or carelessly; **2**. to make trouble, to create a disturbance

cocarame afambi: to attack without waiting for orders, to make a premature attack

cocari: the common snipe; cf. **karka cecike**

cocirambi: ⟶ **cocarambi**

coco: penis

coco i da: glans of the penis

coco i sen: opening of the urethra

codoli: **1**. clever but arrogant, conceited; **2**. high-spirited, hard to handle (said of livestock)

cohombi: **1**. to advance to regular status a person holding temporary office, to make a special selection from candidates for a vacancy; **2**. to do especially; cf. **cohome**

cohome: **1**. especially, on purpose, exclusively; **2**. merely, only, directly

cohonggo: special

cohonggo kingken: (特磬) a Chinese musical instrument

cohoro: piebald, dappled

cohoto: copper or tin forks used in playing with a **gacuha**

cohotoi: special, exclusive, especially, exclusively

cok cak: (onomatopoetic) the sound of kissing

cok cak sembi: to snap, to click

cokcihiyan: **1**. peak, ridge; **2**. towering, precipitous

cokcohon: jutting up, vertical

cokcohon godohon: towering (height)

cokcohori: ⟶ **cokcohon**

cokcorombi: to rise up vertically, to be high

coki: having a prominent forehead

coki uju: a jutting forehead

cokimbi: to stick in the ground (arrows and like objects)

coko: **1**. chicken; **2**. the tenth of the earth's branches (酉)

coko biya: the eighth month

coko erin: period of the day from 5 PM to 7 PM

coko ilha: *Stachys aspera*: betony, woundwart

coko megu: a mushroom that grows in rich soil — it has a white top and is black inside

coko nakambi: to roost

coko sence: ⟶ **coko megu**

coko umgan i toholiyo: a pastry made of chicken eggs, honey, sugar, walnuts, and glutinous rice

cokonggo: pertaining to the cyclical sign **coko**

cokonggo aniya: year of the chicken

cokto: arrogant, conceited, self-important

coktolombi: to be proud, to flaunt, to act arrogantly

cokūlu: ⟶ **cukūlu**

colabumbi: (causative of **colambi**)

colambi: to stir-fry

colgambi: to chatter, to clamor; cf. **curgimbi**

colgogan fulan: a breed of black horses raised by the Ainugan tribe

colgon: ⟶ **colhon**

colgoroko: **1**. towering, lofty; **2**. prominent, surpassing, excelling

colgorombi: (-ko) to surpass, to excel

colgoropi: prominent, imposing

colho: towering

colho moo: *Catalpa kaempieri*: Chinese catalpa

colhon: peak, high promontory

colhorombi: ⟶ **colgorombi**

colhoron: a commanding peak

colibumbi: (causative of **colimbi**)

colikū: an engraving knife

colimbi: to engrave, to carve

colire faksi: engraver

colkon: a wave

colkon cecike: a small, long-beaked black-backed bird that eats pine cones

colo: courtesy name, nickname, title

colo bumbi: to grant a title

colo tukiyembi: to enfeoff, to grant a title

coman: goblet, large cup for wine

comari ilha: *Gardenia jasminoides*: gardenia

comboli: mid-section, area below the ribs, waist

comcok: bunch, cluster

comcok erihe: one style of rosary

comgombi: to stamp, to tread on

comko morin: dapple-gray horse

comlimbi: to cut designs from folded paper

comnombi: **1**. to peck at food; **2**. to pound rice; **3**. to hobble the front legs of a horse

como: ⟶ **coman**

conggai: *Ceryle lugubris*: spotted kingfisher; cf. **cunggai**

conggalabumbi: ⟶ **congkibumbi**

conggimbi: ⟶ **congkimbi**

conggiri: a kind of cymbal

conggišambi: ⟶ **congkišambi**

conggošombi: to collide; cf. **cunggūšambi**

congkibumbi: (causative of **congkimbi**)

congkimbi: **1.** to peck; **2.** to fight (said of quails); **3.** to pound grain to remove the husk

congkiri gūwasihiya: a name for the eastern egret; cf. **gūwasihiya**

congkišakū: a pestle

congkišambi: **1.** to peck constantly; **2.** to husk rice using a mortar and pestle

contoho: a hole or gap in a wall or dike

contohojombi: to form a hole or gap

coo: a spade

coo bithe: paper money

coocarambi: ⟶ **cocarambi**

coociyanli: *Calandrella rufescens*: sand lark

cooga: ⟩ **cooha**

coogan: *Egretta garzetta*: the little egret

cooha: **1.** army, troops; **2.** soldier; **3.** military, martial

cooha baitalambi: to use military force

cooha bargiyambi: to reassemble troops

cooha be aliha amban: (司馬) Minister of War (in antiquity)

cooha be kadalara tinggin: (清軍廳) Bureau of Military Affairs — an organ for dealing with military offenses in each province

cooha bederembi: troops return (victoriously)

cooha dain: troops, armies

cooha gocimbi: to withdraw troops

cooha huwekiyebure temgetu: a silver placard given to a soldier as a commendation

cooha ilimbi: to raise troops

cooha kambi: to serve in the military

cooha moringga fiyenten: office of a military commander

cooha niyalma: soldier, military man

cooha obume banjibure kunggeri: (編軍科) section in the Board of War in charge of military banishment

cooha obure weile: an offense punished with military banishment

cooha simnembi: to muster troops

cooha urebure tinggin: (演武廳) bureau concerned with drilling troops

coohai agūra: weapon

coohai agūra i kunggeri i baita alire boo: (軍器科值房) Arsenal of the Weapons Office in the Board of Works

coohai agūra i kunggeri i baita hacin i boo: (軍器科案房) Chancery of the Weapons Office in the Board of Works

coohai agūra i kunggeri i bodoro boo: (軍器科算房) Accounting Office of the Weapons Office of the Board of Works

coohai amban: (武大臣) a high military dignitary

coohai baitai kunggeri: (軍務科) Military Affairs Bureau in the Board of War

coohai baitalan i kūwaran: (軍需局) Military Supplies Depot

coohai baitalan i namun: (軍需庫) Commissary Warehouse; cf. *BH* 656A

coohai baran: military strength, disposition of troops

coohai belhen i bolgobure fiyenten: (武庫清吏司): a department in the Board of War; cf. *BH* 415A

coohai boo: **1.** (兵房) War Office of the Bureau of Colonial Affairs; **2.** barracks

coohai caliyan: military pay

coohai cuwan: military boat

coohai dasan i simnembi: to take an examination in the military arts

coohai erdemungge i kunggeri: (將材科) a section of the Board of War concerned with the promotion of officers

coohai fa: the art of war

coohai fafun: martial law

coohai fiyan: the disposition of an army

coohai fiyan be nonggibure mudan: music played while the Emperor inspected the troops

coohai fiyenten: (兵司) the Military Bureau in Mukden

coohai hafan: a military officer

coohai hafan i fungnehen i kunggeri: (武誥科) a section concerned with posthumous enfeoffment of military officers

coohai hafan i temgetu: credentials of a military officer

coohai hafan sindara bolgobure fiyenten: (武選清吏司) Department of Selection, *BH* 415A

coohai jahūdai: warship

coohai jurgan: (兵部) Board of War, *BH* 415

coohai jurgan i kungge yamun: (兵科) war section of the Grand Secretariat

coohai kooli: the art of war, warcraft

coohai kūwaran: military camp

coohai moringga fiyenten: (兵馬司) police office; cf. *BH* 796

coohai mudan: military strength

coohai nashūn: important military matters

coohai nashūn i amban: (軍機大臣) Grand Councillor, *BH* 129

coohai nashūn i ba: (軍機處) Council of State, *BH* 128

coohai niyalma: soldier, warrior

coohai tusangga inenggi: favorable days for military undertakings

coohai urse: soldiers, troops

coohalambi: to go to war, to send troops

coohalaha morin: war horses

coohalame genembi: to go on a military expedition

coohan: ⟶ **coogan**

coohiyan: Korea; cf. **solho**

coolambi: ⟶ **colambi**

coolan gaha: a red-beaked bird resembling a raven

coolgon: ⟶ **colgon**

cooman: ⟶ **coman**

cor seme: gushing forth uninterruptedly

corboho: ⟶ **corbombi** (subheading)

corbokū: a device used to hold open the mouth of a horse (or other domestic animal)

corbombi: to pry the mouth open (said of domestic animals)

corboho tura: a post or stump to which animals are tied while given medicine

cordombi: to play (Mongolian instruments such as the **coron** and **mekeni**)

corho: **1**. an iron tube for holding a tassel on a helmet; **2**. a wooden tube used in the brewing of liquor; **3**. spout (on a teapot or kettle)

corhon: another name for the woodpecker; cf. **fiyorhon**

coro: the day after tomorrow

corodai: a name for the phoenix; cf. **garudai**

coron: **1**. a four-holed wooden flute; **2**. a temporary wooden shelter; cf. **coron boo**

coron boo: a temporary shelter built of wood

coron gocika: the belly has fallen (said of horses and cattle)

coron tatan: a small temporary structure that is made of wood and tent-shaped

cos: (onomatopoetic) the sound of ricocheting or rebounding

cosho: **1**. a pointed piece of metal attached to the end of a weapon's grip; **2**. a nail on a horse's harness for attaching the crupper

cotho: eggshell

cotoli: ⟶ **codoli**

cu: **1**. interjection used to set a dog on someone or something; **2**. Get out!

cu ca: the sound of whispering or murmuring

cu niru: a fire arrow, rocket

cuba: a woman's sleeveless court garment decorated with dragon patterns

cuba sijigiyan: a woman's court garment — a cape decorated with dragon patterns

cubdaha: ⟶ **cobdaha**

cubumbi: to be squeezed into a narrow space; cf. **cibumbi**

cubume tembi: to sit tightly together

cucu caca: (onomatopoetic) the sound of whispering or talking in a low voice

cudu: one ten billionth

cuiken: golden plover

cuikengge mahatun: a hat worn in ancient times by astrologers

cuk cak seme: bitterly, viciously (said of fighting)

cukcambi: to protrude

cukcaha weihe: bucktooth

cukcuhun: **1**. protruding forward (said of an animal's ears); **2**. pouting (with the lips protruding)

cukcurembi: to face forward, to protrude

cuku: **1**. a kind of dessert made from glutinous rice and eaten from a bowl; **2**. an interjection used when someone sits on another person's clothing

cukubumbi: (causative of **cukumbi**)

cukulembi: to stir up, to incite, to set a dog on prey

cukumbi: **1**. to become tired, to be spent; **2**. to lift the buttocks slightly, to rise slightly from one's seat

cukūlu: **1**. nearsighted; **2**. a horse that goes about hanging its head

cukūmbi: to hang down (the head), to look down, to bow down, to lie prostrate

cukūršembi: to bow down profoundly

cukūšambi: to rush about blindly

culasun moo: a kind of cedar with bamboo-like leaves

culgambi: 1. to inspect troops, to hold an inspection; 2. to hold an assembly

culgan: 1. inspection of troops (especially by the Emperor); 2. an assembly, a league, an alliance

    culgan acambi: 1. to inspect troops; 2. to hold an assembly

    culgan i da: leader of an alliance

culhan: ⟶ **culgan**

culin cecike: a name for the oriole; cf. **gūlin cecike**

culuk seme: coming and going all the time, suddenly coming and going

cumbuli: ⟶ **comboli**

cumcumbi: to squat holding one's arms about the knees

cumcurambi: 1. to pass quickly with the body bowed in front of a superior; 2. to dart away, to disappear (said of animals frightened by the approach of an enemy)

cun cun i: gradually, by degrees

cunceo: a fine silk

cung cung seme: going forward with the head bowed

cung seme: ⟶ **cung cung seme**

cung yang inenggi: the ninth day of the ninth month — a festival

cunggai: *Ceryle lugubris*: spotted kingfisher; cf. **conggai**

cunggur niyehe: *Podiceps ruficollis*: Chinese little grebe

cungguru: 1. navel; 2. stem, footstalk of fruit

cunggūšambi: to butt, to beat the head on something, to collide with, to shove

cunu gasha: *Halcyon pileata*: black-capped kingfisher

cur car seme: (onomatopoetic) the sound of firecrackers and rockets, the sound of boiling water

cur seme: 1. (onomatopoetic) the sound of a rocket flying; 2. slipping, sneaking

    cur seme genehe: slipped out, swept past, slid past

curbi gasha: *Halcyon smyrnensis*: turquoise kingfisher

curgimbi: (**-he**) to chatter, to make lots of noise, to make an uproar, to clamor

curgin: chattering, noise, commotion

curgindumbi: to make a commotion (said of a group), to prattle, to prate

curhū: the young of the pike

curhūmbi: to go a distance (said of road)

curhūn: distance a bird can fly with one flap of its wings

curun: a measure of length equal to thirty Chinese feet

cus seme: ⟶ **cur seme**

cuse: 1. bamboo; 2. silk; 3. a cook

    cuse moo: bamboo

    cuse moo i arsun: bamboo shoots

    cuse moo i fuldun: bamboo grove

    cuse moo i itu: *Bambusicola thoracica*: bamboo partridge

    cuse moo i undehen: a bamboo stave used for whipping

    cuse singgeri: a small cat-like animal that eats bamboo roots

cuseingge hoošan: paper made of bamboo fiber

cusengge nicuhe: a pearl-like product growing on bamboo

cuseri: made of bamboo, pertaining to bamboo, bamboo-like

    cuseri cecike: a small gray-bodied bird with red feet

    cuseri duingge hoošan: a paper made from bamboo

    cuseri hoošan: a white paper made from bamboo

    cuseri toro ilha: oleander

cusile: crystal

cuwan: boat, ship; cf. **jahūdai**

    cuwan fekumbi: to board a boat (in a battle)

    cuwan i ejen: commander of a ship

    cuwan tembi: to take a boat

cuwangnambi: 1. to seize by force, to pillage, to rob; 2. to rush

    cuwangname dosimbi: to rush into, to go rushing in

cūn moo: *Toona sinensis*: Chinese toon tree

cūn ša: a flowered light silk used for making summer clothing

cy: **1**. a five-holed flute; **2**. a Chinese foot (measure, about one third of a meter); **3**. a bamboo rod used for flogging
cylebumbi: (causative or passive of **cylembi**)

cylembi: to flog with a bamboo rod
cyming: an Imperial order of posthumous enfeoffment

D ᠊ᡩ ᡩ

For words beginning with **dz**, see the section beginning on page 87.

da: **1**. root, stock, base, foundation, source; **2.** leader, chief; **3**. a fathom, the length of the outstretched arms — about eight Chinese feet; **4**. trunk of a tree; **5**. a measure word for various elongated things

da an i: as usual, as always, as before

da arambi: to lay a foundation

da banin: nature, inherent character

da be onggombi: to forget one's origins

da beye bahambi: to recuperate

da beye kokirabumbi: to lose one's capital

da beye menggun: capital, principal

da ci: ⟶ **daci**

da dube: stock and branches, beginning and end

da fujuri: *curriculum vitae*

da fulehe: foundation, base

da futa: the main rope attached to a net used for trapping; cf. **dangdali**

da gašan: one's native place, hometown

da gin dz: sister-in-law: a wife of wife's elder brother

da gio: brother-in-law: elder brother of one's wife

da jiha: matrix for copper coins

da jokson: the starting line for mounted archers

da mafa: original ancestor, great-great-grandfather

da mama: great-great-grandmother

da muru: in broad outline, in general

da sargan: the chief wife, first wife

da sekiyen: background, one's personal history

da sekiyen mafa: progenitor

da songkoi: as before

da sunto: the model for the dry measure **sunto**

da susu: native place

da šu: uncle: father's younger brother

da tolombi: to count the hits at archery

da turgun: personal record

da ujui usiha: the brightest star in the constellation Draco

da unggu mafa: great-great-grandfather

da unggu mama: great-great-grandmother

da uše: a line from the reins that passes through the bit of a bridle

dababumbi: **1**. (causative of **dabambi**); **2**. to go too far, to overstep, to go across; **3**. to do or act excessively; **4**. to boast, to exaggerate

dababurakū: thrifty

dabagan: a mountain pass

dabaha: ⟶ **dabambi** (subheading)

dabakū: wedges of wood on both sides of a gate, allowing wheeled vehicles to enter

dabala: **1**. (sentence particle) only, merely; **2**. (postposition) besides

dabali: **1**. excessively, exceeding, too; **2**. (postposition) beyond, across, through; **3**. surpassing, superior

dabali duleke: passed beyond

dabali fekuhe: jumped across

dabali fiyelembi: to jump across (equestrian trick)

dabali uše: a strap on the wagon-saddle that is attached to the shaft of the cart

dabali wesike: rose beyond

dabalikan: somewhat excessive

dabambi: to cross, to surpass, to go beyond, to climb over

dabaha nimeku: consumption, tuberculosis

dabara oloro: crossing and fording

daban: excess

dabanambi: to surpass, to cross over, to go to cross, to be excessive, to increase, to become even greater

dabara: ⟶ **dabambi** (subheading)

dabargan: a long rectangular bag with a hole in the middle allowing each end to be used as a pocket (often carried on the shoulder or from the belt)

dabašakū: **1**. excessive, not content with one's lot; **2**. a person who tries to live beyond his means or station

dabašambi: to act without restraint, to act in a dissipated way, to overstep one's authority, to act presumptuously

dabatala: excessively, presumptuously

dabci: having one's eyes askew, suffering exotropia

dabcikū: a double-edged sword

   dabcikū antaha: swordsman

dabcilakū: a small hunting knife, a dagger

dabcilambi: to go askew, to run crooked

dabdali: uncontrollable, unmanageable (said of horses)

dabduri: quick-tempered, excitable, irritable, irascible, impetuous, testy

dabduršambi: to be short-tempered, to be irritable, to get excited, to flare up

dabgibumbi: (causative of **dabgimbi**)

dabgimbi: to weed, to pull weeds with the hands

dabgiyambi: ⟶ **dabkimbi**

dabkabumbi: (causative or passive of **dabkambi**)

dabkambi: to haunt, to torment, to bring harm to (said of ghosts), to bewitch

dabkibumbi: (causative or passive of **dabkimbi**)

dabkimbi: **1**. to repair with glue or plaster; **2**. to whip on (a horse)

dabkūri: double, having layers, storied (building)

   dabkūri dalan: a doubled dike or dam

   dabkūri dorgi hoton: the Forbidden City

   dabkūri duka: a double gate

   dabkūri kotoli: a double sail

   dabkūri leose: a storied building

   dabkūri omolo: great-grandchild

   dabkūri taili: a double blossom

dabkūrilambi: to double, to overlap

   dabkūrilame banjimbi: to be double (said of flowers)

dabsi: upper arm

dabsimbi: to incline, to wane (said of the sun or moon)

   dabsiha biya: waning moon

dabsitambi: to try to get the first word in

   dabsitame faksidambi: to argue skillfully

dabsulabumbi: (causative of **dabsulambi**)

dabsulambi: to preserve in brine, to salt, to pickle

dabsun: salt

   dabsun be giyarire yamun: (巡鹽司) Department of Salt Control; cf. *BH* 835B

   dabsun be yabubure bithe be pilere baicara falgangga: (批驗鹽引所) Office of the Salt Examiner; cf. *BH* 835A

   dabsun cifun i menggun: salt gabelle, salt tax

   dabsun ebubure ba: wharf where salt was unloaded

   dabsun fuifure haha: salt worker

   dabsun fuifure kūwaran: salt works, saltern

   dabsun gidambi: to salt (fish)

   dabsun hūdai niyalma: salt merchant

   dabsun i baita be baicara hafan: (鹽政) Controller of Salt Affairs; cf. *BH* 369, 369A

   dabsun i cifun: salt tax

   dabsun i kūwaran: salt factory, salt works

   dabsun i urse: salt smugglers

   dabsun juwere baita be kadalara hafan: (鹽運使) Salt Controller, *BH* 835

   dabsun juwere beidesi: (運判) Sub-Assistant Salt Controller, *BH* 835A

   dabsun juwere ilhici: (運副) Deputy Assistant Salt Controller, *BH* 835A

   dabsun juwere kadalasi: (提舉) Salt Inspector, *BH* 835A

   dabsun juwere uheci: (運同) Assistant Salt Controller, *BH* 835A

   dabsun tucire ba: an area where salt is produced, a salt mine

   dabsun tuyeku yonggan: ammonium chloride

dabta: a pot in which fish glue is made

dabtabumbi: (causative of **dabtambi**)

dabtambi: to do repeatedly, to do over a long period of time; **2**. to pile up (intransitive verb); **3**. to repeat over and over in order to instill, to din into; **4**. to beat metal thin

   dabtara folho: a hammer for beating metal

dabtan: again, repeatedly; ⟶ **dahūn dabtan i**

dabubumbi: (causative of **dabumbi**)

dabukū: brazier, small oil lamp

dabumbi: **1**. (causative of **dambi**); **2**. to light (a fire or lamp); **3**. to figure in with, to take into account, to include, to consider; **4**. to be injured

   dabume: including, comprising, consisting of

   daburakū: not included, not taken into account

dabunambi: to go to burn

dabunjimbi: to come to burn

daburakū: ⟶ **dabumbi** (subheading)

dacakū: a wide hair ornament worn in the chignon of Sibe women

daci: **1**. from the beginning, once upon a time, formerly, hitherto; **2**. by itself, by nature

daci dubede isitala: from beginning to end

dacilabumbi: (causative of **dacilambi**)

dacilambi: to inquire, to seek information, to find out

dacilanjimbi: to come to inquire

dacukan: rather sharp

dacun: **1**. sharp (as a knife); **2**. shrewd, decisive, resolute; **3**. crack (said of troops)

dacun jeyengge amba jangkū: a very sharp large sword

dacun silin: crack (said of troops)

dacun sukdun: high spirits, high morale (especially of troops)

dacungga: sharp, crack (said of troops)

dadage: interjection of affection used when patting an old person or a child on the back

dadarambi: (-ka) to open (the mouth), to open wide, to expand

dadari: a trap for weasels and marmots

dade: **1**. originally, at first, in the beginning; **2**. (postposition) in addition to, not only … but …

dadu moo: gangplank

dadun: **1**. lame; **2**. without hands or feet

dafaha: *Oncorhynchus keta*: chum salmon

dafun: an arrow wound

dafun ehe: the arrow wound is too shallow (not deep enough to kill)

dafun sain: the arrow wound is deep (deep enough to kill)

dagilabumbi: (causative of **dagilambi**)

dagilambi: **1**. to prepare, to make ready; **2**. to set out (food or drink)

dahabumbi: **1**. (causative of **dahambi**); **2**. to subdue, to subjugate; **3**. to take along, to cause to follow; **4**. to recommend a person possessing a special talent or merit for a high post without the official examination; **5**. to paint, to decorate with

dahabure afaha: receipt, bill, list of merchandise

dahabure afahari: a note containing an order of the Emperor inserted into a memorial to the throne

dahabure gisun tucibumbi: to give a grade on the official examination

dahacambi: **1**. to follow together; **2**. to receive, to meet; **3**. to obey

dahalabumbi: (causative of **dahalambi**)

dahalambi: **1**. to follow, to pursue, to run down; **2**. to bring a countersuit against

dahalame: in accordance with

dahalanjimbi: to come following

dahalasi: follower, servant

dahali: **1**. second, next, subsidiary; **2**. in playing with the **gacuha**, the second bone throw

dahali sonjosi: (榜眼) number two in the Imperial examination, *BH* 629C

dahalji: footman, attendant, manservant under a lifetime contract

dahaltu: orderly, manservant

dahambi: (perfect participle **daha**) **1**. to follow; **2**. to submit, to surrender; **3**. to obey

dahame: (postposition) because, since

dahan: a horse between two and five years old, a young horse

dahancambi: to follow together, to obey together

dahanduhai: **1**. before long, in a while, shortly, subsequently, presently, soon; **2**. one after another, in succession

dahandumbi: to follow after one another; also **dahanumbi**

dahanjimbi: to come following, to come to surrender

dahanumbi: to follow after one another; also **dahandumbi**

daharalame: following, attending

dahashūn: **1**. obedient, compliant; **2**. posthumous title for the wife of an official of the seventh order

dahasi: a granary attendant

dahasu: obedient, docile

dahasun: one of the eight trigrams of the *Yijing* (symbolizing earth)

dahata: a leather bag to hold arrowheads, affixed inside a quiver

dahibumbi: (causative of **dahimbi**)

dahimbi: to repeat, to do again

dahime: again, same as **dahin**, **dahūme**

dahin: again

    dahin dabtan: again and again

    dahin dahin: repeatedly, again and again

dahū: a fur coat worn with the fur outside

dahūbumbi: **1.** (causative of **dahūmbi**); **2.** to recover, to win back

dahūlambi: to wear a **dahū**

dahūmbi: **1.** to repeat, to do again; **2.** to repair a torn mat; **3.** to keep one's word

    dahūme: again

    dahūme banjimbi: to come back to life, to revive

    dahūme beidembi: to retry a case, to re-examine

    dahūme gaimbi: to retake, to regain

    dahūme kimcimbi: to re-examine

    dahūme simnembi: to retake an examination

    dahūme weilembi: to rebuild, to restore

dahūn: again, repeatedly

    dahūn dabtan i: repeatedly

    dahūn dahūn i: repeatedly, time after time

dahūngga: recovered, restored

dai joo: (待詔) clerk of the Court Chancery

dai li sy yamun: (大理寺) Court of Judicature and Revision, *BH* 215

dai mei: tortoise shell

dai šeng: the hoopoe; cf. **indahūn cecike**

dai tung doohan i tuwame kadalara hafan i yamun: (大通橋監督衙門) the Office of the Grain Transport Inspector at Datong Bridge

daibihan: **1.** frame, casement; **2.** border or edging on quivers and bags

daicilambi: to run at an angle, to run askew

daicing: the Manchu dynasty, the Qing dynasty

daidan doholon: a kind of sour-tasting wild vegetable with willow-like leaves

daifaha: a fence made of reeds and willow branches

daifan: (大夫) a high official in ancient times

daifasa: (plural of **daifan**)

daifu: **1.** medical doctor; **2.** a senior official in ancient China

    daifu hafan: senior official

    daifu i doro: medicine (the study of)

daifulambi: ⟶ **daifurambi**

daifurabumbi: (causative of **daifurambi**)

daifurambi: to treat, to practice medicine

    daifurame dasambi: to treat medically, to heal

    daifurame yabumbi: to practice medicine

    daifurara bithe: medical text

daifusa: (plural of **daifu**)

daihan: a fish weir

dailabumbi: (causative or passive of **dailambi**)

dailambi: **1.** to make war against, to undertake a punitive expedition against; **2.** to be mad, to be possessed; cf. **daišambi**

    dailaha indahūn: a mad dog

    dailaha nimeku: insanity

dailan: a military campaign, a punitive expedition

dailanabumbi: (causative of **dailanambi**)

dailanambi: to go to make war against, to go to make a punitive expedition against

dailandumbi: to make war against one another; also **dailanumbi**

dailanjimbi: to come on a punitive expedition against

dailanumbi: to make war against one another; also **dailandumbi**

dain: **1.** troops, army; **2.** war, battle; **3.** enemy

    dain cooha: troops, army

    dain dekdebumbi: to start a battle, to start a war

    dain i agūra: military weapon

    dain i gurun: enemy country

    dain i haha: a warrior, a soldier

    dain i sejen: chariot

daipun: a mythical great bird, the roc

daise: substitute

daiselabumbi: (causative of **daiselambi**)

daiselambi: to substitute for someone, to take over a post temporarily

daisiyoolambi: to sell on commission

daišambi: to act like a madman, to rave, to rage

dakda dakda: in great leaps

dakda dikdi: ⟶ **dakda dakda**

dakdahūn: **1.** curled upward, suspended upward; **2.** too short (said of clothes that have curled upward)

dakdarambi: to be exposed

dakdari: suddenly, unexpectedly, first

dakdaršambi: **1.** to jump (up on); **2.** to act in an aggressive manner; **3.** to be exposed constantly

daksa: a misdeed, a fault

daksin: ⟶ **daksa**

dakū: ⟶ **uhe dakū**

dakūla: the skin on the belly of a fish or animal

dalabumbi: (causative of **dalambi**)

dalaci: foreman, leader

dalambi: 1. to be the leader, to be at the head; 2. to measure in fathoms

dalan: 1. withers; 2. dam, dike

dalangga: dam, dike, pertaining to a dam or dike

dalba: side

  dalbai ahūn: older half brother

  dalbai boo: side wings of a house

  dalbai hehe: concubine

  dalbai jui: illegitimate child

  dalbai moo: running boards on the outside of a ship's railing

  dalbai niyalma: bystander

dalbaki: on the side, located at the side(s)

  dalbakici: from the side, laterally

dalbarame: along the side

dalbashūn: on the side, lying on its side

  dalbashūn dedumbi: to lie on the side

dalda: 1. secluded, hidden spot; 2. hidden, concealed

daldabumbi: (causative of **daldambi**)

daldahan: 1. leather covering for the hole in a ball (**mumuhu**); 2. the flat bone of a falcon to which a bell is hung

daldakū: 1. a screen, a veil; 2. a curtain hung over the entrances of houses when the Emperor passed

daldambi: 1. to hide from view, to screen, to cover; 2. to taboo

daldangga: a protective wall erected behind a door

daldashūn: covered, hidden

dalgan: piece, lump, clod, fragment

  dalgan boihon: clod of earth

  dalgan dalgan i: piece by piece, in pieces

dalganambi: to form a lump, to form pieces

dalgiyambi: to adorn, to embellish

dalgiyan wehe: red ocher

dalhan: ⟶ **dalgan**

dalhi: repetitious, annoying, tedious

dalhidambi: 1. to be repetitious, to be tedious; 2. to be persistent

dalhūdambi: to prattle on and on, to chatter, to nag

dalhūkan: rather sticky, bothersome, annoying

dalhūn: 1. sticky; 2. annoying, bothersome, too talkative

  dalhūn cifenggu: sputum, phlegm

dalhūwan: a sticky pole used for catching birds

dalibumbi: 1. (causative of **dalimbi**); 2. to cover over

dalibun: 1. shelter, refuge; 2. obstacle

dalihanambi: to become crumbly, to harden (said of fat)

dalikū: screen, covering, a protective screen at a doorway, a protective covering, a shelter

  dalikū uce: a storm door

dalimbi: 1. to block off, to obstruct, to screen off, to seal, to cover up, to conceal, to protect, to deceive; 2. to force an animal back into a battue; 3. to drive (livestock or a wagon)

  dalime tosombi: to guard against

dalin: shore, riverbank, limit

  dalin akū: limitless

dalirame: along the shore, along a riverbank

dalitambi: to block off, to screen off, to cover

dalitungga mahatun: a hat worn in ancient times by military officials

daliyan: a long rectangular bag with an opening in the middle so that both ends serve as bags — usually hung over the shoulder or from the belt

daljakū: unconnected with, unrelated, of no importance

dalji: relation, bearing, connection

  dalji akū: unconnected, unrelated; cf. **daljakū**

daljingga: related to, concerned with

dalukan: bothersome, annoying, persistent

dalumbi: to adhere tightly — as bark to a tree or hair to the skin of a scalded slaughtered animal

dambagu: tobacco

  dambagu gocikū: a pipe (for smoking)

  dambagu gocimbi: to smoke (tobacco)

  dambagu jembi: to smoke tobacco

  dambagu omimbi: ⟶ **dambagu gocimbi**

  dambagu tebumbi: to put tobacco (in a pipe)

dambi: 1. to burn (intransitive verb); 2. to blow (said of the wind), to rain, to snow; 3. to take care of, to care about; 4. to mind someone else's business, to interfere; 5. to operate, to work (intransitive verb); 6. to help, to assist; 7. to join forces with

  dame afambi: to assist in battle

  dara cooha: reinforcements, relief troops

dambumbi: **1**. (causative of **dambi**); **2**. to interfere, to meddle; **3**. to add, to mix; **4**. to apply (medicine)

damdan: a trillion

dame: ⟶ **dambi** (subheading)

damin: eagle, vulture

damjalabumbi: (causative of **damjalambi**)

damjalambi: **1**. to carry on a pole; **2**. to pierce through with an arrow

damjan: a carrying pole, a carrying-pole load

    damjan sebsehe: an insect with a fat body and long wings, resembling a grasshopper

    damjan sele: a window or door latch

damjatala: clear through, clean through (said of an arrow)

damnambi: to sift, to strain

damtulabumbi: (causative of **damtulambi**)

damtulambi: to pawn

    damtulara puseli: pawnshop

    damtulara puseli i cifun: pawnbroker's tax

damtun: an article for pawning, a hostage

    damtun werimbi: to leave behind as a hostage

damu: only, but

dan: a snare for wild fowl, wolves, and foxes

dan dabumbi: to notice, to pay attention to

    dan daburakū: without noticing someone, to pay no attention (to other people)

dan bi amba kumun: musical compositions played while foreign dignitaries and emissaries ascended the steps to the throne room

dan mu: sandalwood; cf. **cakūran**

dan tiyan: pubic region, area below the navel

danahūn cecike: a name for the hoopoe; cf. **indahūn cecike**

danambi: to go to take care of, to go to aid, to be concerned with

    danara cooha: reinforcements

    danara hafan: (都司) First Captain, *BH* 752C

dancalambi: for a bride to visit her parents' home for the first time after her marriage

dancan: the wife's family

    dancan i boo: the wife's family

    dancan i ergi: wife's side of the family, in-laws

dancarambi: ⟶ **dancalambi**

dang: only, just

    dang seme: only

dangdaka: stretched out, with legs extended, comfortable

dangdali: a dragnet used for catching fish

dangdalilambi: to use a **dangdali** in fishing

dangdambi: to stretch out (the legs), to extend

dangga: elder, belonging to the older generation

danggasa: (plural of **dangga**)

danggi: at least, a little bit

danggiri: a small brass gong hung from a crook (used by Buddhist monks)

dangkan: a hereditary house slave

dangnabumbi: (causative of **dangnambi**)

dangnaci: ⟶ **dangnambi** (subheading)

dangnahan: leather insole (said of a boot)

dangnambi: **1**. to substitute, to replace; **2**. to oppose, to pit against

    dangnaci ojorakū: irreplaceable

dangniyabumbi: (causative of **dangniyambi**)

dangniyambi: to kick a football (**mumuhu**)

dangpuli: a pawnshop

dangsaha: an open-topped birchbark basket

dangse: records, document, register, archive, the census register

    dangse asarara kunggeri: (櫃科) Archives Office of the Board of Works

    dangse baitai boo: (檔案房) Office of Documentary Affairs

    dangse bargiyara hafan: (典籍) Sub-Archivist, *BH* 412A, 413A

    dangse bargiyara tinggin: (典籍廳) Archives Office, Records Office

    dangse ci hūwakiyambi: to expunge from the banner roll

    dangse de dedubumbi: to keep in the archives, to store in the archives

    dangse efulere ba: (註銷處) section for the disposal of records

    dangse ejere hafan: (典簿) Archivist, *BH* 412A, 413A

    dangse ejere tinggin: (典簿廳) Record Office, *BH* 202, etc.

    dangse faksalambi: to remove from the family register, to expunge from the census register

    dangse jafašakū: (主簿) Registrar, *BH* 220, etc.

    dangse jafašara hafan: (主簿) Registrar, *BH* 220, etc.

    dangse jafašara kunggeri: (司案科) Registry Section of the Office of the Gendarmerie

dangse jafašara tinggin: (主簿廳) Registry Office

dangsibumbi: (causative of **dangsimbi**)

dangsimbi: to reprove, to censure, to rebuke, to reprimand

dangšan: **1**. end of a thread, small piece of thread; **2**. end or remnant of a blade of grass (left after cattle have eaten)

daniyalabumbi: (causative of **daniyalambi**)

    daniyalabuha wai i ba: a curve or recess offering protection

daniyalambi: to seek cover from, to go to for protection, to hide

daniyambi: ⟶ **daniyalambi**

daniyan: cover, refuge, safe place, protection

    daniyan i ba: refuge, solitary place, retreat

danjimbi: to come to take care of, to come to aid

danosg'a ilha: *Achyranthes aspera*: prickly chaff-flower

danumbi: to care for one another, to aid one another

dar seme: shivering

    dar seme šahūrun: shivering cold

    dar seme šurgembi: to shake with cold or fright

dara: **1**. waist, lower back

    dara goloho: sprained one's back

    dara golombi: to have an ache in the lower back

    dara niyaniyarilambi: to sprain one's back

    dara singgiyambi: to have a sore back

dara: **2**. ⟶ **dambi** (subheading)

darabubumbi: (causative of **darabumbi**)

darabumbi: to invite to drink, to offer a toast, to serve (wine)

darama: waist, midsection

    darama ergi: small of the back, lumbar region

darambi: (-ka) **1**. to draw a bow taut; **2**. to be tamed, to be domesticated; **3**. to pick a quarrel with someone, to tease, to provoke; **4**. to be accustomed to

darambumbi: to train (falcons, dogs, etc.), to tame

daranambi: to go to draw a bow

darang seme: long and straight, outstretched

    darang seme dedumbi: to lie stretched out full length

daranumbi: to invite one another to drink, to toast one another

darasu: an undistilled Mongolian liquor

darašambi: to stretch a bow fully taut

darbahūn: lying straight on the back

darbalji: *Accipiter nisus*: sparrow hawk

dardaha: ephemerid

dardan: satin interwoven with golden threads

dardan seme: trembling

    dardan seme šurgembi: to shiver with cold

dargalabumbi: **1**. (causative or passive of **dargalambi**; **2**. to dismiss, to force into retirement)

dargalambi: to retire (from an official post), to leave office, to resign

    dargalaha amban: a dignitary who has retired with full pay

dargimbi: to shake, to tremble

dargiya: jugular veins

dargiyambi: to hold ready for combat, to wield

dargūwan: a wooden hoe

    dargūwan yangsambi: to hoe with a wooden hoe

darha cecike: *Troglodytes troglodytes*: North China wren

darhūwa: reed

    darhūwa cecike: ⟶ **darha cecike**

darhūwalambi: to hitch up a horse

darhūwan: **1**. pole, staff; **2**. plowing stick; **3**. the beam of a balance; **4**. ⟶ **dargūwan**

dari: (postposition) each, every

daribumbi: **1**. (causative of **darimbi**); **2**. to touch lightly, to graze (said of an arrow); **3**. to be related, to have ties of kinship; **4**. ⟶ **niyaman daribumbi**

darimbi: (-ka/-ha) **1**. to scrape against, to rub a sore (said of horses); **2**. to pass through, to drop by, to perform an errand or other action on one's way somewhere else or while doing something else; **3**. to make fun of, to mock; **4**. to roar (said of thunder)

    darime ijumbi: to ridicule, to satirize

darimbumbi: to develop a sore by rubbing; cf. **darubumbi**

darin: a sore caused by rubbing, a saddle sore

darinambi: to drop in on, to pay a casual visit

daringga: having a saddle sore

darka cecike: snipe; cf. **karka cecike**

darmalame: along the back

darsu: ⟶ **darasu**

dartai: **1**. in an instant, suddenly, unexpectedly; **2**. temporarily

    dartai andande: suddenly, in a moment

dartai de: suddenly

dartai siden: for the time being, temporarily

darubumbi: **1**. (causative of **darumbi**); **2**. to be obligated; **3**. to develop friction sores; **4**. to be prone to frequent illnesses

darudai: a name for the phoenix; cf. **garudai**

daruga: (Mongolian) chief, commander

darugan: ⟶ **darhūwan**

daruha: ⟶ **darumbi** (subheading)

daruhai: **1**. often, continually, regularly; **2**. long-term, regular

   daruhai hūsun: a person engaged for long-term labor

darumbi: **1**. to buy on credit; **2**. to recognize someone mistakenly, to mistake someone for someone else

   daruha urun: a daughter-in-law taken into the home as a child

darun: **1**. wharf, dock; **2**. a watering spot for livestock; **3**. place on a stream for drawing water

dasa: (plural of **da**)

dasabumbi: (causative of **dasambi**)

dasakū: corrector, one thing used to repair something else

dasambi: **1**. to rule; **2**. to correct; **3**. to cure; **4**. to repair; **5**. to cultivate (virtue)

   dasaha jugūn: a road prepared for the Emperor

dasame: again

   dasame eigen gaimbi: to remarry, to take a second husband

   dasame waselambi: to retile

dasan: rule, government, control

   dasan be hafumbure yamun: (通政使司) Transmission Office, *BH* 928

   dasan be selgiyere hafan: (布政使) Lieutenant-Governor or Financial Commissioner, *BH* 825, etc.

   dasan i baita: government business, political affairs

dasangga: keeping order, having talent for government

dasargan: a prescription, a formula

dasarhan: ⟶ **dasargan**.

dasartungga: pertaining to a reformer

dasatambi: to put in order, to arrange, to repair

dashūwan: **1**. a bow case; **2**. left, east (only in certain fixed expressions)

dashūwan dube: (五甲喇) the fifth **jalan**

dashūwan gala: (東四旗) the four left banners

dashūwan i muheren: a ring on a bow case

dashūwan meiren: (四家喇) the fourth **jalan**

dashūwatu: (左軍) adjutant of the left battalion

dasibumbi: (causative or passive of **dasimbi**)

dasihi: dust, dirt

dasihikū: ferocious

   dasihikū gasha: a bird of prey

dasihimbi: **1**. to swoop down and seize (said of birds of prey); **2**. to go on a punitive expedition, to send troops to quell (an uprising); **3**. to immolate

   dasihire hafan: (遊擊) Major, *BH* 752B

dasihiyabumbi: (causative of **dasihiyambi**)

dasihiyakū: a feather duster

dasihiyambi: to dust with a feather duster

dasikū: a cover, a top

dasimbi: to cover, to shut

dasin: **1**. handle, grip, stalk; **2**. measure word for objects with handles

dasitambi: to conceal, to gloss over

dasu: children

   dasu maktambi: to use felled trees as a defense against enemy arrows

dasukū: fish hawk, osprey; cf. **suksuhu**

dašose: boy, lad, servant boy

dašurambi: to harm, to damage, to endanger, to jeopardize

dašuran: damage, harm, endangerment, jeopardy

data: (plural of **da**)

datsai faksi: one who decorated houses on festivals

datsailambi: to decorate houses during a festival

dayabumbi: **1**. (causative or passive of **dayambi**); **2**. to execute, to put to death; **3**. to eliminate

dayacambi: to depend on together

dayambi: **1**. to depend on, to rely on (someone else's power or influence); **2**. to stand by the side of, to get near; **3**. to catch fire, to burn

dayanambi: to go to depend on

dayancambi: to shake the head (said of horses)

dayandumbi: to depend on one another; also **dayanumbi**

dayanjimbi: to come to rely on

dayanumbi: to depend on one another; also **dayandumbi**

de: (the dative-locative particle)

deb seme: everywhere

debderembi: to beat, to flap (wings)

debderšembi: to beat the wings vigorously

debe daba: swarming (said of insects), crawling (like maggots)

debembi: (**-ke, -ndere**) to overflow, to run over, to flood

> **debere be gidara jahūdai**: a boat used at flood time

deben: **1**. overflowing, flooding; **2**. ocean tide, flood tide

debenjimbi: to come flowing in, to come flooding in

debere: ⟶ **debembi** (subheading)

deberen: the young of animals

> **deberen gūlin cecike**: a small Chinese oriole; cf. **gūlin cecike**

> **deberen honin**: lamb

debeye orho: straw used for making mats, a kind of grass that grows in sunless areas of forests

debkebumbi: (causative of **debkembi**)

debkejembi: to come unraveled, to come undone

debkelebumbi: (causative of **debkelembi**)

debkelembi: to untwist, to unravel

debkembi: (**-ke**) to bring up again, to take up some old business once again, to renege, to back out

debse: **1**. a cake or candy made of fruit; **2**. a ceremonial arrow used by shamans

debsehun: drooping (eyelids), sleepy-looking

debserembi: to droop (said of the eyelids)

debsibuku: cloth of a flag or banner; cf. **wadan**

debsiku: **1**. fan (made of feathers); **2**. a cloth pennant hung from a pole in ancient times

debsilembi: to tower above, to go before

debsimbi: to fan, to flap, to flutter

> **debsire garunggū kiru**: a banner depicting a soaring phoenix

debsin: fanning, flapping

debsitembi: to fan continually, to flutter continually, to flap continually

debšembi: ⟶ **debsimbi**

debtelebumbi: (causative of **debtelembi**)

debtelembi: to untangle, to unravel

debtelin: a volume (of an old-style book), a book, a notebook

> **debtelin i burgiyen**: cover of a book

debumbi: (causative of **dembi**)

> **debume sindambi**: to fill a vacancy

dede dada: **1**. frivolous, flippant, flighty; **2**. shaking, shivering

dedenggi: frivolous, loose in behavior (said of women)

dedubumbi: **1**. (causative of **dedumbi**); **2**. to let lie, to put to rest; **3**. to put to bed; **4**. to rise (said of dough), to leaven; **5**. to put in the archives

deducembi: to lie down together, to sleep together

dedumbi: **1**. to lie down, to lie; **2**. to spend the night (with); **3**. (transitive verb) to bed, to take to bed (a woman)

> **dedure biya**: month of confinement after childbirth

> **dedure boo**: bedroom

dedun: **1**. an overnight stopping place, a post station; **2**. one day of a journey

> **dedun i hūsun**: servant at a post station

> **dedun i morin**: post horses

dedunebumbi: (causative of **dedunembi**)

dedunembi: to go to spend the night

dedungge hengketu: an insignia on wood of a reclining melon (used by the Imperial guard)

dedure: ⟶ **dedumbi** (subheading)

defe: **1**. a measure for cloth, a bolt (of cloth); **2**. border, hem; **3**. the width of cloth, a breadth of cloth

defelinggu: bolt (of cloth)

defeliyembi: (**-ke**) to lie in strips

defere: *Dryopteris crassirhizoma*: thick-stemmed wood fern

defu: bean curd; cf. **turi miyehu**

dehe: fishhook

dehebumbi: (causative of **dehembi**)

dehehe: ⟶ **dehembi** (subheading)

dehele: a short sleeveless jacket, a fur riding jacket

dehelembi: to hook, to catch with a hook

dehelen: a short sleeveless jacket; cf. **dehele**

deheli sonjosi: (探花) third in the court examination

dehema: uncle: husband of mother's sister

dehemata: (plural of **dehema**)

dehembi: **1**. to refine, to smelt, to temper; **2**. to cure (tobacco)

> **dehehe aisin**: refined gold

deheme: aunt: mother's younger sister

dehemete: (plural of **deheme**)

dehen: **1**. refining, smelting, curing; **2**. boundary of a field, low bank of earth between fields; cf. **usin dehen**

dehengge šurukū: a boat hook

deherembi: to stir up, to rouse

dehi: forty

dehici: fortieth

dehimbi: ⟶ **dehembi**

dehinggeri: forty times

dehite: forty each

dehurembi: to search everywhere

dehureme baimbi: to search everywhere

deide: black buckwheat flour, whole buckwheat flour

deijibumbi: (causative or passive of **deijimbi**)

deijiku: firewood, wood for fuel

deijiku be kemnere kūwaran: (惜薪廠) storage place for fuel in the Board of Works

deijimbi: to burn (transitive verb)

deijin: burning

deijin i hija: a vessel used for burning offerings (e.g., paper money)

deijin i ukdun: a kiln for tile and bricks

deisun: waistband (of skirts and trousers)

deji: **1**. choicest (part), the cream, the best part; **2**. the first portion offered as a sacrifice to the deities or to the guest of honor

deji bumbi: to offer the choicest part to one's elders or superiors

deji jafambi: to take the best or choice part

dejimbi: ⟶ **deijimbi**

dek seme: furiously, severely

dek seme becembi: to scold severely

dekde dakda: up and down, uneven

dekdebumbi: **1**. (causative of **dekdembi**); **2**. to reappear, to rise again

dekdehun: **1**. somewhat high, rather high; **2**. upward

dekdeku: a float on a fishing pole, a float for an oil lamp

dekdeku doohan: a pontoon bridge, a floating bridge

dekdelembi: to get up, to spring up

dekdeljembi: to start (from fright while sleeping)

dekdembi: (**-ke**) to float, to rise

dekden: floating, rising

dekden i gisun: **1**. everyday saying; **2**. baseless talk, gossip

dekden i henduhengge: as the saying goes …

dekdengge: exalted

dekdenggi: the fat that floats to the surface of water in which meat is boiled

dekdeni gisun: ⟶ **dekden i gisun**

dekderelambi: to float on the surface

dekderhūn: a name for the seagull; cf. **kilahūn**

dekderilembi: to rise high

dekderšembi: **1**. to have vain hopes, to engage in wishful thinking; **2**. to go beyond what is proper, to have lascivious thoughts

deke: ⟶ **deken**

deken: **1**. rather high; **2**. a *mǔ* 畝: approximately one sixth of an acre; **3**. a rise, a high place

dekjibumbi: (causative of **dekjimbi**)

dekjimbi: (**-ke**) **1**. to develop, to improve, to prosper; **2**. to burn

dekjire jalungga namun: (將盈庫) Depository for the Salt and Post administration

dekjin: developing, prospering

dekjin tuwa: prairie fire, forest fire, wild fire

dekjingge: prosperous, flourishing, thriving, outstanding, excelling

dekjire: ⟶ **dekjimbi** (subheading)

deksitembi: to be uneasy, to be anxious

delbin: brim of a hat

dele: **1**. top, on top, on top of, in addition to; **2**. the Emperor

dele acambi: to have an audience with the Emperor

dele hargašambi: to have an audience with the Emperor

dele tembi: to occupy the place of honor (at a banquet)

dele wala akū: lacking knowledge of decorum

delebumbi: to hold up, to support

delejen: a courtyard without walls or moats

deleken: rather high or superior, somewhat over

delembi: to catch in a noose

delennge: pertaining to the top, exalted

delen: udder, teat

delerembi: (**-ke**) to come apart at the joints (said of wooden objects)

deleri: **1**. top, surface; **2**. superficial, careless; **3**. uppermost

delesi akū: supreme, the best

delferi: careless, frivolous, casual

delfin: ⟶ **delfiyen**

delfiyen: too wide, loose, baggy (said of clothes and hats)

delge: ⟶ **delhe**

delhe: a land area equal to 100 *mǔ* 畝 or 6.7 hectares, or 16.5 acres, one *qǐng* (頃)

delhebumbi: **1**. (causative of **delhembi**); **2**. to cut up (a slaughtered animal)

delhembi: **1**. to part, to separate (intransitive verb); **2**. to get divorced

delheme tembi: to live apart

delhen: **1**. ⟶ **delhe**; **2**. dividing, separation

delhendumbi: ⟶ **delhentumbi**

delhentumbi: to make one's last will and testament, to say a final farewell

delhentuhe gisun: will, testament

delhetu niru: ⟶ **booi niru**

dell wehe: a large stone, a boulder in a stream

delihun: spleen

delihun madambi: to swell (said of a horse's belly)

delišembi: **1**. to gust (said of the wind), to be carried along by a current or the wind; **2**. to billow, to surge

deliyehun: ⟶ **delihun**

deliyembi: to burn (intransitive verb)

delmecembi: to warn

delulembi: to grab the mane of a horse

deluleme fiyelembi: to trick ride while grabbing the mane

delun: mane, hair on the neck of a horse or pig, bristles

delun gidame fiyelembi: to trick ride while pressing down on the horse's mane

dembei: greatly, to a high degree, exceedingly

dembi: **1**. to calculate, to reckon; **2**. to take one's turn at duty

demci: **1**. (Tibetan) manager, majordomo (in a lamaist monastery); **2**. a lama healer, doctor

demesi: an arrogant or conceited person

demesilembi: to swagger, to act boastfully, to act in a conceited way

demnembi: ⟶ **demniyembi**

demnecembi: ⟶ **demniyecembi**

demniyebumbi: (causative of **demniyembi**)

demniyecembi: **1**. to shake, to rock, to sway; **2**. to consider, to assess, to estimate

demniyelembi: to stretch oneself

demniyembi: to estimate the weight of an object by weighing it in the hand

demsi: ⟶ **demesi**

demtu: (斗) a constellation, the 8th of the lunar mansions, made up of six stars in Sagittarius

demtu tokdonggo kiru: (斗宿旗) a banner depicting the third of the lunar mansions

demulembi: to be strange, to act strangely

demun: **1**. trick, crafty idea, underhanded device; **2**. unorthodox idea or doctrine

demun deribumbi: to play a trick, to employ an underhanded device

demungge: **1**. strange, tricky, peculiar, heretical; **2**. monster, odd creature

demungge feksin: trick riding

den: **1**. high, tall; **2**. loud

den bojiri ilha: sunflower

den jilgan i: in a loud voice

den i ici: upward

den tu: direction pennant

dendebumbi: (causative of **dendembi**)

dendecembi: to divide between one another, to share with one another

dendembi: to divide, to share

dendeme kadalara yamun: (分司) a suboffice of a larger unit

dendeme tacibure hafan: (學錄) Sub-Registrar, *BH* 412A

denden dandan: step by step

dendenumbi: to share together

deng: lamp, lantern

deng lung: lantern

deng tsoo: wick

deng deng seme: gagging, choking

deng seme: **1**. at a loss for words, unable to answer; **2**. restrained, blocked

deng seme ilimbi: to stop from exhaustion (said of horses)

deng seme oho: at a loss for words, at wit's end

dengge: **1**. glorious; **2**. distant, far away

denggebumbi: (causative of **denggembi**)

denggeljembi: to shake, to reel

denggembi: to throw far, to fling, to send flying, to throw (in wrestling)

dengjan: lamp, light

dengjan dabumbi: to light a lamp, to turn on a light

dengjan i sindakū: a lampstand

dengjangga: pertaining to lamps or lights

dengji orho: bulrush

denglu: lantern; cf. **deng**, **deng lung**

denglung: ⟶ **denglu**

dengnebumbi: (causative of **dengnembi**)

dengnehen: the leg of a boot

dengneku: a small steelyard

dengnekulembi: to weigh on a small steelyard

dengnembi: to weigh on a small steelyard, to balance, to compete with

dengniyembi: **1**. to play with a football (**mumuhu**); **2**. to toss a ball to and fro

dengse: a small steelyard

   dengse i ilga: a steelyard weight

dengselebumbi: (causative of **dengselembi**)

dengselembi: to weigh on a small steelyard; cf. **dengnembi**

dengsibumbi: (causative of **dengsimbi**)

dengsimbi: to rattle, to vibrate, to bump along (said of a carriage)

dengsitembi: to tremble (from fright), to shake, to vibrate up and down

dengtsoo: wick

deo: **1**. younger brother; **2**. younger (said of males)

deocilebumbi: (causative of **deocilembi**)

deocilembi: to perform the duties proper to a younger brother, to show fraternal deference

deocin: duty of a younger brother, fraternal deference

deocingge: one who is assiduous in performing the duties of a younger brother

deocy: fermented bean paste

deodenjembi: to move

deone: a four-year-old bovine

deote: (plural of **deo**)

deotelembi: to behave like a younger brother

der dar seme: **1**. many, very; **2**. beautifully arrayed; **3**. charming and gentle

der der seme: snow-white

der seme: **1**. in profusion, many; **2**. snow-white

derakū: without shame, without face, shameless, undignified

derakūlambi: to act shamelessly, to insult

derakūngge: shameless

derbebumbi: (causative of **derbembi**)

derbehun: damp, moist

   derbehun sukdun: damp air

derbembi: to be damp, to become damp

derbembumbi: to become wet or damp

dercilembi: to lay out a corpse, to prepare a corpse for burial

derden dardan: shaking, vibrating

   derden dardan aššambi: to shake, to vibrate

derden seme: shaking, trembling, shivering with cold

derdu: a bib worn next to the skin over the breasts

   derdu cecike: a small bird resembling a thrush

derduhi: camphor

dere: **1**. face; **2**. 'face' (Chinese *miànzi* 面子), reputation, honor; **3**. table; **4**. surface; **5**. direction, area; **6**. a measure word for flat objects; **7**. (sentence particle) probably, likely

dere acambi: to meet

dere arambi: to do someone a favor

dere banimbi: ⟶ **dere banjimbi**

dere banjimbi: to take 'face' (Chinese *miànzi* 面子) into account, to have a regard for personal friendship, to act from personal motives

dere de eterakū: to be too embarrassed to say something, to be unable to do something for fear of giving offense

dere de tacibumbi: to instruct personally

dere efulembi: to have a falling out with, to quarrel with a friend

dere fan dasambi: to set out a table (said of food or delicacies)

dere felembi: to disregard 'face' (Chinese *miànzi* 面子), to act without shame

dere funceburakū: to have no way to save face

dere fusimbi: to shave (the whiskers)

dere gaimbi: to act for motives of honor, to stand up for one's honor

dere jileršembi: to blush with shame, to feel deeply embarrassed

dere mahūlambi: to embarrass someone, to make things very difficult for someone

dere mangga: shameless, bold

dere silemin: thick-skinned, shameless

dere šehun: thick-skinned, impervious to embarrassment

dere šehun girurakū: ⟶ **dere mangga**

dere šufa: facial wrinkles

dere tokome: in the presence of, facing, in person, personally, face to face

dere waliyabumbi: to lose face

dere waliyatambi: to lose face, to form a grudge against

dere yasa: face and eyes, appearance, visage

derei: (genitive or instrumental of **dere**);
⟶ **emu derei**, **ai derei**

derei bangtu: ornaments on the corners of a table

derei bethe: a table leg

derei hašahan: tablecloth, table cover

derei sidehun: table support

derei talgari: table top

derecuke: ⟶ **derencuke**

derencuke: decorous, proper

derencumbi: to treat with partiality because of a personal relationship, to show favoritism

dereng darang: sanctimonious, feigning propriety, barely able to behave properly;
⟶ **derengge darangga**

derengge: decorous, proper, noble (in one's actions), honored

derengge darangga: illustrious, eminent, celebrated, majestic

derengge jan: a square hunting arrow having a hole on each of its four sides

derengtu: portrait

deresu: *Lasiagrostis splendens*: feather grass, broom grass

deretu: long table, long desk

derge: erect, straight

derge simhun: the index finger

dergi: **1.** top, above, over; **2.** upper; **3.** east, eastern; **4.** Emperor; **5.** the best, superior; **6.** pertaining to the Imperial Palace

dergi abka: heaven above

dergi adun i jurgan: (上駟院) the Palace Stud, *BH* 88

dergi amba fukjingga hergen: (上方大篆) a kind of seal script

dergi amsu cai i boo be uheri kadalara ba: (總管御膳房茶房處) Office in Charge of the Imperial Buttery; cf. *BH* 91

dergi arga: the best plan

dergi asari: eastern tower, another name for the **Dorgi Yamun**

dergi ashan boo: the eastern side room

dergi bithe foloro ba: (御書處) the Imperial Library, *BH* 94A

dergi bithei boo: (尚書房) study room for the young Princes (the Emperor's sons)

dergi bithei taktu: (御書樓) Imperial Library

dergi buthai hacin belhere ba: (上虞備用處): the Imperial Hunting Department, *BH* 733

dergi colhon i kiru: (東嶽處) a blue banner depicting the form of a mountain

dergi ejen: Emperor

dergi ergi: the east, eastern direction

dergi ergi munggan i baita be alifi icihiyara yamun: (東陵承辦事務衙門) Administration of the Eastern Tombs

dergi ergi munggan i booi amban i yamun: (東陵內務府總管衙門) Office of the Superintendent of the Eastern Tombs

dergi ergi munggan i weilere jurgan: (東陵工部) Board of Works of the Eastern Tombs

dergi ergi simnere bithei kūwaran: name of a small gatehouse to the left of the Mingyuan tower in the Examination Hall

dergi femen: the upper lip

dergi fiyenten: (東司) Eastern Section of the Imperial Equipage Department, *BH* 122

dergi gurung ni baita be aliha yamun: (詹事府) Supervisorate of Imperial Instruction, *BH* 929

dergi gurung ni baita be aliha yamun i aliha hafan: (詹事府詹事) Chief Supervisor of Instruction, *BH* 929

dergi gurung ni baita be aliha yamun i ilhi hafan: (詹事府少詹事) Supervisor of Instruction, *BH* 929

dergi hese: Imperial edict

dergi hese be gingguleme dahara baita hacin be kimcime baicara ba: (稽察欽奉上諭事件處) Chancery for the Publication of Imperial Edicts, *BH* 105A

dergi horon be badarambure mudan: a musical piece played after the Emperor had inspected the troops

dergi hošo: the east

dergi nahan: the *kàng* (oven-bed) located against the west wall of a house — this was considered the *kàng* of honor

dergi oktoi boo: (御藥房) the Imperial Dispensary, *BH* 92

dergi šongge inenggi: the first day of the month

dergiken: somewhat upper, superior, or high

dergingge: eastern, upper

dergišembi: ⟶ **derkišembi**

derguwe: ⟶ **derhuwe**

derhi: a straw or rush mat

>   **derhi orho**: grass used for making mats

derhuwe: a fly, housefly

>   **derhuwe bašakū**: fly whisk, fly swatter

>   **derhuwe ija**: horse fly

deri: (ablative particle) from, than, via, by way of

deribumbi: **1**. (causative of **derimbi**); **2**. to begin, to let begin; **3**. to conjure up, to think up (a plan); **4**. to play (music); **5**. to initiate

>   **deribume ilibure kunggeri**: (開設科) bureau concerned with promotions and discharges in the Board of Civil Appointments

>   **deribure fiyentehe**: (起股) the section following the introduction in a formal essay

>   **deribure giyangnan**: (起講) the third part of a formal essay

deribun: **1**. beginning; **2**. cause

>   **deribun duben**: beginning and end

>   **deribun giyangnan**: the second section of an eight-legged essay

>   **deribun šanggan**: cause and effect, karma

deribunggilembi: to make a beginning

deribure: ⟶ **deribumbi** (subheading)

deribušembi: to begin, to originate

derimbi: (-ke) **1**. to have a change of heart, to be disloyal; **2**. to have blurred vision, for the eyes to dim

derishun: **1**. changed (in heart), rebellious; **2**. cruel

derkimbi: to soar high, to hover over

derkišembi: to flutter in the wind

dersen: pure, genuine, unmixed

>   **dersen gabsihiyari**: a kind of swift dog

>   **dersen hooša n**: a kind of pure white paper — 'white crane paper'

dertu cecike: a small bird resembling a starling; named **dertu** from its song

desereke: overflowing, expansive

deserembi: (-ke, -pi) to overflow (in great quantity)

deserepi: overflowing, superabundant

desi: **1**. upward; **2**. eastward

>   **desi wasi**: up and down, all around

desihi: a kind of trap attached to a tree over a stream, used to catch sable and various other small animals

desihimbi: to throw down with both hands (at wrestling)

desiku: a shamanistic arrow with a tuft of *Abutilon avicennae* (flowering maple) tied to it

desunggilembi: to emphasize, to stress; **2**. to appeal, to call on

desunggiyembi: **1**. to scream in a loud voice; **2**. to stir up dust

dethe: **1**. pinion feathers, wing feathers, tail feather (of a pheasant); **2**. arrow feathers

>   **dethe idumbi**: to glue on arrow feathers

>   **dethei fusheku**: fan made of feathers

dethengge kiltan: (羽葆幢) a pennant having five red tassels

detu: marsh, swamp

>   **detu dambi**: the swampland is being burned off (in preparation for cultivation)

deyebuku: kite (a flying toy)

deyebumbi: (causative of **deyembi**)

deyembi: to fly

>   **deyere cuwan**: an airplane

>   **deyere dobi**: **1**. genus *Sciuropterus*: flying squirrel; **2**. a bat

>   **deyere gese**: quickly, swiftly, as if flying

>   **deyere gūwasihiyangga kiru**: (振鷺旗) a banner embroidered with the image of a heron

>   **deyere singgeri**: a flying squirrel (genus *Sciuropterus*)

>   **deyere šanyangga fukjingga hergen**: (飛白書) a style of calligraphy

deyen: palace, great hall, throne room

>   **deyen boo**: main hall of a temple

>   **deyen de simnembi**: to take the palace examination

>   **deyen de tembi**: to take one's place in the throne room (for an audience)

deyengge: flying, airborne

deyenggu: **1**. a kite (a kind of toy); **2**. choral singing

deyenggulembi: to sing in unison

deyere: ⟶ **deyembi** (subheading)

di: (帝) god

diba: (Tibetan) governor, regent

digi: false hair encased in a net, worn by Chinese women; cf. **šošokū**

dilbihe: (氐) a constellation, the 3rd of the lunar mansions, made up of four stars (α, ι, γ, and β) in Libra

dilbihe tokdonggo kiru: (氏宿旗) an escort's banner having the constellation **dilbihe** depicted on it

ding hiyang: *Syringa vulgaris*: lilac; cf. **imeten ilha**

dingse orho: a grass that grows in clumps, has narrow leaves and yellow blossoms; flour made from its dried roots mixed with wheat flour and egg white serves as a foot salve

dise: draft (of a document or essay)

diselambi: to make a draft

diyalambi: ⟶ **diyanlambi**

diyan: **1**. palace, throne room, great hall; **2**. hostel, inn

    diyan de tembi: to take one's place in the throne room (for an audience)

diyandz: **1**. the spots on dice or dominoes; **2**. ornament of filigree animals

diyanlambi: **1**. to mortgage; **2**. to take a trick at cards

diyanši: (典史) Prison Warder, *BH* 766A

do: **1**. the internal organs; **2**. the filling of pastries, **giyose**, and so forth; **3**. round-bottomed wicker basket

dobi: fox

    dobi ibagan: fox spirit

    dobi yasha: a net for catching fox

dobihi: a fox pelt

dobiri: an animal resembling a fox that can climb trees

dobke: a name for the screech owl; cf. **hūšahū**

dobokū: ⟶ **ilhai dobokū**

dobombi: to offer (in a ceremony)

dobon: **1**. offering; **2**. night

    dobon dulin: midnight

    dobon i šu ilha: a gilded wooden lotus flower

dobonio: all night

dobonombi: to go to offer

dobori: night

    dobori abkai tampin: the second vessel of a water clock

    dobori be amcame: under the cover of darkness

    dobori dulime: that very night, under the cover of night, the whole night through

    dobori dulime jimbi: to come (unexpectedly) at night

    dobori dulin: midnight

    dobori indembi: to spend the night

    dobori inenggi akū: day and night

dobori jetere giyahūn: a name for the horned owl; cf. **fu gūwara**

dobori nukcime: that same night, that very night

dobtokū: a sheath, a covering (for objects)

dobtolobumbi: (causative of **dobtolombi**)

dobtolokū: a sheath or covering for large things

dobtolombi: to sheathe, to cover

dobtolon: doubled sack for a corpse

dobton: **1**. a small sheath, a small bag (for a seal), a container for tallies; **2**. a cover, a cover for Chinese style books; **3**. scabbard

dobtonggū: pertaining to a cover or sheath

dobukū: a falcon's perch

dobumbi: **1**. (causative of **dombi**); **2**. to place a falcon on its perch; **3**. ⟶ **doombi**

dodangga: **1**. a monster; **2**. a sorcerer; **3**. a blind man

dodo: fetus, embryo

dodobumbi: **1**. (causative of **dodombi**); **2**. to force into a squat (at wrestling); **3**. to crouch

dodombi: to squat

dodori: a hat with a wide brim

dogo: blind

    dogo ija: a gadfly with a colored head

dogon: a ford, a ferry (place where people are ferried across streams)

    dogon angga: a ford, a ferry (a place where people are ferried across streams)

    dogon jafaha: the ford has frozen — the river is frozen hard enough to cross

doha: a tick

doho: **1**. lime (the mineral); **2**. blind; cf. **dogo**

    doho hafirambi: to fill in the crevices of brickwork with mortar

    doho muke hungkerembi: to pour mortar (a mixture of lime, sand, and water) into the crevices of brickwork

dohodombi: to hop on one foot

doholobumbi: (causative of **doholombi**)

doholombi: **1**. to cover with lime; **2**. to hold between the legs (at wrestling)

doholon: lame

    doholon yoo: a sore on a horse's hoof

dohon: ⟶ **dogon**

dohošombi: to limp, to be lame

doidon: lame, a cripple

doigomšolombi: to go before, to precede

doigomšombi: to prepare beforehand, to make precautions, to do in advance

doigon: beforehand, previously

    doigonde: beforehand, previously, in advance

doingge leke: a flat cake with a jujube filling

dojihiyan: a name for the black bear; cf. **mojihiyan**

dok seme: fiery, raging (said of a flame)

dokdo dakda: by leaps and bounds, to and fro

dokdohon: upward, rising abruptly, springing up

    dokdohon furgi: a breakwater jutting out diagonally from a dike

dokdohori: in rows on a high place

dokdolambi: to start (from fright), to spring up

dokdolombi: to protrude upward

dokdori: standing up suddenly

    dokdori iliha: sprang up, stood up suddenly

dokdorilambi: ⟶ **dokdolambi**

dokdorjambi: to act unsettled, to be erratic, to jump about

dokdoršombi: ⟶ **dokdorjambi**

dokdoslambi: to be startled

dokita: a wild boar; cf. **kitari**

dokjihiyan: the high spots on both sides of the skull, the two extremities of the forehead

    dokjihiyan niru: a small arrow with a flattened head

doko: **1**. material used for lining clothes, lining; **2**. path, short cut

    doko jugūn: path, short cut

    doko yenju: path

dokolombi: **1**. to look on in a favorable light, to show favor to, to dote on, to show partiality; **2**. to wrap both legs around the opponent's legs (in wrestling); **3**. to take a short cut

dokomimbi: to line (a garment)

doksidambi: to be cruel, to act violently

doksin: cruel, violent, fierce, wild, bad-tempered (said of livestock)

    doksin ehe urse: hoodlums, thugs

    doksin fudasi: ruthless, tyrannical, savage, pitiless

    doksin furu: cruel, ruthless

    doksin hatan: violent, fierce

    doksin nimeku: acute illness

    doksin oshon: brutal, savage

doksintu enduri: god of the wind

doksirambi: to act cruelly, to act violently, to mistreat

doksoho: ⟶ **doksombi** (subheading)

doksohon: protruding, sticking out

doksombi: to jut out, to protrude

    doksoho weihe: protruding tooth

dola: barren land

dolbi niru: a kind of arrow somewhat smaller than a **keifu**

dolcin: **1**. ford; **2**. waves

dolgin: wave

doli: **1**. the pulp of fruit, flesh of a melon; **2**. unsteady pace (said of a horse)

dolmobumbi: (causative of **dolmombi**)

dolmombi: to add more liquor to a cup already containing some, to fill a cup with liquor, to top off

dolo: **1**. inside, the inside, inner; **2**. on the inside, interiorly, secretly

    dolo akambi: to grieve, to be sorrowful

    dolo gosimbi: to be very hungry

    dolo ilimbi: not to yield easily (said of a bowstring)

    dolo ping sembi: to eat to satiety

    dolo tatabumbi: to be worried, to be concerned

    dolo tatašambi: to be anxious, to show concern for

    dolo tokobumbi: to have sharp pains in the belly

dolori: **1**. inside, inner; **2**. secretly

dombi: to alight (said of birds and insects)

domnobumbi: (causative of **domnombi**)

domnombi: **1**. to pay respects in the Manchu manner (said of women); **2**. to play on the water (said of dragonflies)

domnon: obeisance made by Manchu women

    domnon singgeri: **1**. field mouse; **2**. ground squirrel

domo: **1**. female undergarment; **2**. teapot

    domo etuku: female undergarment

don: fluttering of birds from one place to another, alighting (said of birds)

    don hadambi: to be caught in a net stretched across a river (said of fish swimming upstream)

donambi: to alight in a swarm

dondoba: wasp

dondon: a small butterfly, a moth

dongjihiyan: lower jaw of a sheep

dongmo: a round pot for holding milked tea

dongniyorombi: to raise the head high (said of horses)

donjibumbi: **1.** (causative of **donjimbi**); **2.** to notify

donjimbi: to listen, to hear

donjici: have heard that …

donjin: what has been heard, hearsay

donjinambi: **1.** to go to hear; **2.** to be generally known

donjindumbi: to listen together; also **donjinumbi**

donjinjimbi: to come to listen

donjinumbi: to listen together; also **donjindumbi**

dono: ⟶ **tono**

doobumbi: (causative of **doombi**)

doobure cuwan: ferryboat

doobure hūsun: a ferryboat man

doobungga: pertaining to a ferry

doobungga jahūdai: ferryboat

doocan: a Buddhist or Daoist rite offered for a dead soul

doocang: ⟶ **doocan**

doocang arambi: to perform a religious ceremony, especially one for the dead

doodz: a bully, a rowdy

doogan: ⟶ **doohan**

doohan: bridge

doohan jugūn i kunggeri: (橋道科) Office of Bridges and Roads in the Board of Works

doohanjimbi: to cross a bridge

doolabumbi: (causative of **doolambi**)

doolambi: **1.** to pour; **2.** to make a clean copy

doolame arambi: to make a clean copy

dooli: (道) Circuit, *BH* 213

dooli hafan: (道) Intendant, *BH* 838

dooli yamun: (道) Office of the Provincial Censor, *BH* 213

doombi: to cross (a river)

doonambi: to go to cross (a river)

doonjimbi: to come to cross (a river)

doorambi: to imitate

dooran: **1.** unexploited land, virgin land; **2.** land spared from a prairie fire; **3.** a person spared from smallpox; **4.** old grass remaining in new grass

doorin: gangplank, a plank used to board and to disembark from a vessel

doorin i hūsun: caretaker of a gangplank

doose: a Daoist priest

doose be kadalara fiyenten: (道錄司) Bureau for Daoist Affairs

dooseda: a Daoist abbot, an official in charge of Daoist affairs

doosi: greedy, covetous, corrupt

doosi nantuhūn: corrupt, venal

doosidambi: to covet, to be covetous, to be greedy

doosidaha weile araha ulin i namun: (贓罰庫) Treasury (where fines were deposited), *BH* 456

dorakū: **1.** impolite, rude; **2.** immoral; **3.** unreasonable

dorakūlambi: to be unreasonable, to act wrongly, to be impolite to

doran: **1.** a row of armored scales (on a suit of armor); **2.** ⟶ **dooran**

dordon dardan seme: shivering, shaking

dorgi: inside, inner, the inner part; **2.** Imperial, the court; **3.** secret

dorgi amban: (內大臣) Senior Assistant Chamberlain of the Imperial Bodyguard, *BH* 98

dorgi amsu i boo: (內膳房) the palace pantry

dorgi ba: **1.** inland area; **2.** the palace

dorgi bade bolgomimbi: to observe the major fast in the palace

dorgi baita be uheri kadalara yamun: (總管內務府) the Imperial Household, *BH* 75

dorgi belhere yamun: (奉宸苑) Bureau of Imperial Gardens and Hunting Parks, *BH* 90

dorgi bithe ubaliyambure boo: (內繙書房) Manchu-Chinese Translation Office, *BH* 140

dorgi bithesi: (中書) Secretary of the Grand Secretariat, *BH* 137

dorgi bodogon: strategy, military planning

dorgi boo: inner chamber, bedroom, women's quarters

dorgi calu: (內倉) Imperial Granaries, *BH* 567

dorgi calu be kadalara yamun: (內倉監督衙門) Office of the Inspector of Imperial Granaries, *BH* 567

dorgi efen i boo: (內餑餑房) the palace bakery

dorgi faidan be kadalara yamun: (鑾儀衛) the Imperial Equipage, *BH* 109

dorgi faidan sindara namun: (內駕庫) storage place for the Imperial Escort

dorgi hanciki hafan: court officials

dorgi hobo: an inner coffin

dorgi hoton: the Imperial city

dorgi kadalan i yamun: (內關防衙門) Chancery of the Imperial Household, *BH* 85

dorgi koolingga hafan: (內史) Secretary of the Grand Secretariat, *BH* 137

dorgi oktosi: (御醫) Imperial Physician, *BH* 238

dorgi simnengge kunggeri: (內考科) office concerned with examinations and civil appointments in the capital

dorgi suri: a kind of silk thinner and coarser than satin

dorgi tanggingge boo: (內堂房) the name of an office in the Board of Civil Appointments

dorgi turgun: internal cause or factor

dorgi yamun: (內閣) Grand Secretariat, *BH* 130

dorgici: (ablative of **dorgi**): from inside

dorgici goholombi: at wrestling, to catch the inside of an opponent's thigh with one's foot

dorgici halgimbi: to wrap one's legs around an opponent's thigh while holding his head

dorgideri: **1**. from inside; **2**. in private, secretly

dorgolombi: to be stunted, to shrivel up

dorgon: *Meles meles*: badger

dorgon i uncehen: 'badger's tail' — the inflorescence of the sorrel

dorgori: a name for the wild boar; cf. **kitari**

dorhon: ⟶ **dorohon**

dorimbi: to rise up on the hind legs, to rear (said of livestock), to jump (said of rabbits)

doro: **1**. doctrine, precept, morality, Dao, way, rule, rite, ritual; **2**. gift

doro arambi: to salute, to greet, to perform a ritual

doro be aljambi: to act contrary to proper behavior

doro be dasara tanggin: (修道堂) the name of the first hall of the west wing of the Imperial Academy

doro be songkoloro mudan: music performed at court during a wine-drinking ceremony

doro benembi: to give a gift

doro de aisilaha amban: (光祿大夫) honorary title of the first rank class one, *BH* 945

doro de hūsun akūmbuha amban: (通議大夫) honorary title of the third rank class one, *BH* 945

doro de hūsun buhe amban: (中議大夫) honorary title of the third rank class two, *BH* 945

doro de tusa araha amban: (資政大夫) honorary title of the second rank class one, *BH* 945

doro de tusa obuha amban: (通奉大夫) honorary title of the second rank class two, *BH* 945

doro de wehiyehe amban: (榮祿大夫) honorary title of the first rank class two, *BH* 945

doro eldengge: the Daoguang (道光) reign period, 1821–50

doro erdemu: morality, morals

doro jafambi: to be in power, to hold the reins of government

doro jorire yamun: (鴻臚寺) Court of Banqueting, *BH* 934

doro šajin: the administration and the law

doro yangse: **1**. veining, grain (of wood); **2**. form, proper form

doro yoso: rites and customs, propriety, norm of behavior

doroi amba kiyoo: a large golden Imperial sedan chair carried by sixteen men

doroi beile: (多羅貝勒) Prince of the Blood of the third degree, *BH* 18

doroi beile i efu: (郡君儀賓) the son-in-law of a **doroi beile**

doroi dengjan: lanterns hung on both sides of the palace gate during important ceremonies

doroi efu: (縣主儀賓) son-in-law of a Prince of the second degree

doroi etuku: court dress, ceremonial garments

doroi faidan: vehicular procession of a noble personage

doroi faidan i kiyoo: an Imperial sedan chair carried by sixteen men

doroi fujin: (郡主福晉) wife of a Prince of the Blood of the second degree (**doroi giyūn wang**)

doroi gebu: a monk's religious name

doroi gege: (縣主) daughter of a Prince of the Blood of the second degree, *BH* 31

doroi giyūn wang: (郡王) Prince of the Blood of the second degree, *BH* 17

doroi jaka: gift

doroi mahatun: a hat worn during the Shang dynasty

doroi sara i fiyenten: (擎蓋司) Umbrella Section (of the Equipage Department), *BH* 119

doroi suhen girdangga: (儀鍠氅) an emblem used on the banner of the Imperial Guards

doroi umiyesun: a belt for a court dress or ceremonial garment

doroi yoro: a ceremonial arrow

dorohon: small in stature (said of children)

dorokūlambi: ⟩ **dorakūlambi**

dorolobumbi: (causative of **dorolombi**)

dorolombi: **1**. to salute, to greet with the hands joined in front of the face, to pay one's respects; **2**. to perform a rite

doroloro sektefun: a kneeling cushion

doroloro temgetu: a placard showing where one should kneel during a ceremony

dorolon: **1**. rite, ceremony; **2**. propriety

dorolon amba faidan: a procession in which the Empress took part

dorolon be jorire šusai: master of ceremonies

dorolon be kadalara fiyenten: (掌儀司) Department of Ceremonial, *BH* 79

dorolon faidan: a procession in which the Imperial concubines took part

dorolon i amba kiyoo: a golden sedan chair employed by the Empress and carried by sixteen men

dorolon i boo: (禮房) Office of Rites in the Court of Colonial Affairs

dorolon i ejehen: rules for the performance of ceremonies

dorolon i jurgan: (禮部) Board of Rites, *BH* 376

dorolon i jurgan i kungge yamun: (禮科) Section of Ceremonies, *BH* 822

dorolon i jurgan i toktoho gisun: phrases used by the Board of Rites

dorolon i tetun i bithei kuren: (禮器館) depository for ritual books and paraphernalia

dorolon kooli i kunggeri: (禮儀科) section concerned with ritual in the Court of Banqueting

dorolon kumun gabtan jafan bithe ton: the six arts — rites, music, archery, chariot driving, writing, and mathematics

dorolonjimbi: to come to salute

dorolonombi: to go to salute

doron: a seal, a stamp

doron be dara ba: (印管處) Office of the Seal in the Board of Civil Appointments

doron be tuwakiyara kunggeri: (知印科) Office of the Seal in the Court of Colonial Affairs

doron be tuwašara ba: (監印處) Office of the Seal in the Board of Finance

doron gaimbi: to confiscate an official's seal

doron gidaha boji: a contract or bill of sale with an official seal on it

doron gidambi: to put one's seal on

doron hungkerere kūwaran: (鑄印局) seal-casting section of the Board of Rites

doron i boco: a seal stamp pad

doron i boo: (印房) the Office of the Seal in a government bank; cf. *BH* 549

doron i hoošan: plain paper stamped with a seal

doron i tuwakiyasi: (知印) keeper of the seal

doron i uncehen: the last stroke of a Chinese character or the last flourish in a Manchu or Mongolian word

doron i wesimbure bithe: a memorial dealing with official business and stamped with a seal

doron suihe: a seal with its silk ribbon

doron temgetu i kunggeri: (印信科) Office of the Seal in the Board of Rites

doronggo: **1**. moral, honest, possessing proper principles; **2**. Daoist-like; **3**. gentle (said of horses)

dosholobumbi: (causative or passive of **dosholombi**)

dosholombi: to love, to favor, to dote on

dosholome gosimbi: to dote on, to show a special liking for

doshon: **1**. favor, love; **2**. favorite, favored person

doshon haha: homosexual friend

doshon haha jui: catamite

doshon hehe: paramour, mistress

doshon niyalma: ⟶ **doshon haha**

dosi: **1**. to the inside, into; **2**. (with **de**) addicted to; **3**. ⟶ **doosi**

dosi gocimbi: to inhale

dosi gocime guwembumbi: to make a sound while inhaling

dosi tulesi: inward and outward

dosidambi: ⟶ **doosidambi**

dosikan: a little inward, a little bit into

dosikasi: (進士) Metropolitan Graduate — a holder of the highest degree in the Imperial examination system, *BH* 629C

dosila: a garment's narrow lapel underneath a larger lapel

dosimbi: (-ka) **1**. to enter, to advance; **2**. to succeed in an examination, to pass an examination; **3**. to become addicted to; **4**. to join (an organization)

dosire de ilibure kiru: (入蹕旗) a yellow banner used to signal courtiers to rise as the Emperor returned to his palace

dosimbumbi: **1**. (causative of **dosimbi**); **2**. to put into, to insert, to inlay, to admit a guest

dosin: one of the eight trigrams of the *Yijing* (representing fire)

dosinambi: to go in, to go to enter, to accede, to go forward, to advance

dosinan: (a Buddhist term) destiny, form of appearance in the rebirth cycle (Sanskrit gati)

dosindumbi: to enter together; also **dosinumbi**

dosinjimbi: to come in, to come to enter

dosinumbi: to enter together; also **dosindumbi**

dosire: ⟶ **dosimbi** (subheading)

dosobumbi: (causative of **dosombi**)

dosombi: to bear, to tolerate, to be patient

dosorakū: unbearable

dosombumbi: (causative of **dosombi**)

dotori: inner excellence, hidden talent

dotori akū: lacking inner excellence

doyoljombi: to get sprained (said of a horse's or mule's hind leg)

doyonggo: satin with brocaded dragons

du: **1**. hip, hipbone, upper part of the thigh bone; **2**. capital city

du de gaimbi: to grab by the hip (in wrestling)

du ergi: a side flap on a Chinese garment

du giranggi: hipbone, upper part of the thigh bone

du sele: iron objects worn on both thighs for hanging bow cases and quivers

du giowan ilha: azalea; cf. **senggiri ilha**

dube: **1**. end, extremity; **2**. point, sharp point

dube akū: endless, limitless

dube bele: sprouted grain

dube da: circumstances, beginning and end, outcome, main threads

dube tucike: has come to an end

dubei forgon: final period, end period

dubei jecen: outer limit, farthest boundary

dubei sukū: the foreskin

dubei toldohon: a clasp at the end of a scabbard

dubede: at the end, at last, finally

dubegeri: ⟶ **dubeheri**

dubeheri: **1**. at the end, at last, finally; cf. **dubede**; **2**. scarcely; **3**. ⟶ **bethe dubeheri**

dubei: ⟶ **dube** (subheading)

dubeingge: the end one, the last one

dubembi: to terminate, to end, to die

dubembumbi: (causative of **dubembi**)

duben: end, termination

duben deribun: the beginning and end

dubengge: pointed, sharp

dubentele: up until the end, lifelong

duberi: toward the end, just before the end

dubesilembi: to terminate, to be at an end

dubesitele: until the end

dubi: bean flour, crushed beans

dubibumbi: (causative of **dubimbi**)

dubimbi: (-ke/-he) to get accustomed, to become domesticated, to get acquainted with

dubihe tacin: custom, convention

dubise: a cake made from bean flour

dubise efen: ⟶ **dubise**

dubumbi: ⟶ **tūbumbi**

dudu: **1**. *Streptopelia orientalis*: eastern turtledove; **2**. (都督) a military governor; **3**. ⟶ **dutu**

dudu niyehe: the teal; cf. **borboki**

dudu dada: the sound children make when first learning to speak

dudungge cecike: a name for the myna

duduri: the crown of a hat

dufe: dissolute, lascivious, indecent, lacking restraint, lewd

dufe buyen: sexual desire, sexual passion

dufe gūnin: indecent thoughts

dufe hayan: obscene, lewd

dufedembi: to act dissolutely, to carouse, to indulge in sexual excesses

dugūi: a narrow bridge, a plank

dugūi cohoro: a horse with zebra-like stripes

duha: intestine, gut

duha do: innards, inner organs

duhan: ⟶ **duha**

duhan singgeri: a small black rat-like animal that has a gut-like growth on its stomach

duhembi: (**-ke**) to be finished, to be completed, to die

duheke beye: corpse

duhembumbi: (causative of **duhembi**)

duhembume ujimbi: to take care of a relative, to care for one's parents until they die

duhen: scrotum

duhentele: until the end

duibulebumbi: (causative of **duibulembi**)

duibulembi: to compare, to give as an example

duibulen: comparison, example, metaphor

duibumbi: to arrange, to put into order

duici: fourth

duidz: a pair, a couplet; ⟶ **duise**

duilebumbi: (causative of **duilembi**)

duilembi: **1**. to judge, to try, to examine, to determine the truth; **2**. to proofread

duilen: judicial hearing, interrogation

duilen i ejeku: (評事) Assistant Secretary of the Court of Judicature and Revision, *BH* 216

duilesi: judge, arbiter

duin: four

duin arbun: the four forms of man: youth, old age, masculine, feminine

duin bilten: the Yangtze, the Yellow River, the Huai River, the Ji River

duin biya: the fourth month of the lunar calendar

duin dere: the four directions

duin durbejen i monggo boo: a four-sided Mongolian yurt

duin ergi: the four corners of the world, the four directions

duin ergi aiman i kunggeri: (四夷科) Office of the Peoples of the Four Directions in the Board of Rites

duin erin: the four seasons

duin erin i ilhangga tumin lamun sara: a dark blue processional umbrella embroidered with the flowers of the four seasons

duin forgon: the four seasons

duin gargan: the four limbs, hands and feet

duin hošo: the four directions, the four oblique directions: SE, NE, SW, NW

duin ici: in the four directions

duin irungge mahatun: a hat with four tufts on top, worn by officials in antiquity

duina: one hundred-sextillionths, an infinitesimal amount

duingge: folded in four, in fours, four times

duingge hoošan: a sheet of paper four times larger than an ordinary sheet

duinggeri: four times

duise: an antithetical couplet

duite: four each

duka: gate

duka be kadalara hafan: (監門官) Gatekeeper at the examination hall

duka hūlambi: to shout outside a gate, to knock at a gate

duka jafambi: to guard a gate

duka sumbi: to open a gate

dukai bakcin: across from one's gate

dukai bongko: an adornment over a gate

dukai enduri: god of the gate

dukai enduri namun: (門神庫) a depository in the Board of Works where images of the gate god were stored

dukai girin: facing the gate, at the gate

dukai kiru: (門旗) a red banner embroidered with the word for gate

dukai senggele: board placed on each side of a gate

dukduhun: raised, elevated, piled up, protruding, arched

dukdurembi: (**-ke**) to rise up, to swell

dukdurhun: unlevel, lumpy, raised

dukdurhun boihon: unlevel ground, bumpy ground

dukduršembi: to rise up, to form a lump

dukjimbi: to talk loudly

dukjime durgimbi: to talk loudly

duksembi: (**-ke**) to blush, to turn red

duksi: *Rhamus davurica*: Manchurian buckthorn

duksumbi: ⟶ **duksembi**

duksursehun: rough (said of terrain)

dulan nimaha: **1**. name of a small sea fish with a small mouth and rough scaleless skin; **2**. shark

dulba: inexperienced, foolish (because of a lack of experience), muddled, ignorant, stupid

dulbadambi: to act carelessly or foolishly

dulbakan: rather careless, somewhat inexperienced or foolish

dulduri: a pilgrim's staff with nine rings around it

dule: really, in fact, when you come right down to it, actually

dulebumbi: ⟶ **dulembumbi**

dulefun: degree of an angle

    dulefun sandalabure durungga tetun: (距度儀) a sextant of the Beijing observatory

dulembi: (**-ke, -re/-ndere**) **1**. to pass, to go by; **2**. to burn

    duleke aniya: last year

    duleke biya: last month

dulembumbi: **1**. (causative of **dulembi**); **2**. to endure, to pass through, to experience; **3**. to set on fire; **4**. to cure; **5**. to let off, to let slip by, to indulge

    dulembume gamarakū: not impetuous, not overly hasty

dulemšeku: negligent, careless, rough, sketchy

dulemšembi: **1**. to neglect, to act negligently, to act carelessly; **2**. to forgive, to excuse

dulendumbi: to pass together; also **dulenumbi**

dulenumbi: to pass together; also **dulendumbi**

dulga: half, half-filled

    dulga julge: medieval times

dulgakan: a little less than half (filled)

dulibumbi: (causative of **dulimbi**)

dulimba: middle, center

    dulimba be aliha usiha: the stars λ and μ in the Big Dipper

    dulimba be bodoro hafan: (中官正) Astronomer for the Mid-year, *BH* 229

    dulimba hūwaliyasun bolgonggo kumun: music played while food was brought in for a palace banquet

    dulimba hūwaliyasun sirabungga kumun: music played while the Emperor returned to the palace from a congratulatory ceremony

    dulimba hūwaliyasun šoo kumun: music played while the Emperor returned to the palace from a congratulatory ceremony

    dulimba hūwaliyasun šunggiya kumun: music played during the offerings at the altars of heaven, earth, and millet, as well as at the Ancestral Temple and the Temple of Confucius

    dulimba hūwaliyasun ya kumun: music played during the offerings at the altars of heaven, earth, and millet, as well as at the Ancestral Temple and the Temple of Confucius

    dulimba i gurun: China

    dulimba i tu: a banner carried in the center of a battle line

    dulimba jugūn: the path leading from the main part of a residence to the main gate

    dulimba sele: a metal clasp in the middle of a quiver or bow case

dulimbade: in the midst of

dulimbai elioi: (仲呂) one of the six minor pipes

dulimbai falgangga: (中所) Central Office of the Imperial Equipage Department; cf. *BH* 109

dulimbai fiyentehe: the central section of a classical essay

dulimbai fulhun: (黃鍾) one of the six major pipes

dulimbai gurun: China

dulimbai hecen i baicara yamun: (中城察院) Censorate Office of the Middle City (Beijing)

dulimbai hecen i cooha moringga fiyenten: (中城兵馬司) Police Office of the Central City

dulimbai irgen gurun: the Chinese Republic

dulimbai simhun: the middle finger

dulimbaingge: the middle one

dulimbangge: ⟶ **dulimbaingge**

dulimbi: (**-ha**) to stay up all night, to watch, to keep a vigil

dulin: half, middle

dumbi: (for **tūmbi**) to hit, to strike, to forge (a sword) dumin cecike: a cuckoo nestling

duna: chalcedony

duncihiya: ⟶ dunjihiyana

dundabumbi: (causative of dundambi)

dundambi: to feed pigs, to raise pigs

dundan: pig food, swill

dunen: a four-year-old ox

dung: a cave

dung guwa: ⟶ dungga

dungga: watermelon

dungga use: watermelon seed

dunggami: of the same age

dunggu: cave, grotto

dungki: weak in judgment, fatuous, silly

dungsun: one hundred million

dunjihiyana: former, earlier

dur dar seme: shaking, trembling

dur seme: the sound of many people talking or laughing, the sound of drums, with a commotion, as a group

dur seme injembi: to burst out laughing, to laugh uproariously

durahūn: staring, fixed (said of the eyes)

durambi: to stare

duranggi: 1. muddy, murky; 2. given to excessive drinking

duranggilambi: 1. to soil, to make muddy; 2. to drink excessively

durbe: a dog with two spots on its forehead

durbejen: 1. square, four-cornered; 2. corner, angle

durbejen dere: a square table at which eight people can sit

durbejen simelen: a square pond at the Altar of Earth

durbejengge: square, having corners

durbejengge šufatu: a square turban used in antiquity

durbejitu: carpenter's square

durbembi: to be frightened (said of a group of people), to shake from fright

durdun: crêpe

durdun ša: crêpe

durgebumbi: (causative or passive of durgembi)

durgecembi: to shake violently, to be convulsed

durgembi: to shake, to tremble

durgeme akjambi: thunder rolls

durgeme gelembi: to be overawed

durgešembi: ⟶ durgecembi

durgimbi: to coo, to warble

durgire dutu: a person who, through deafness, makes silly or irrelevant remarks

durgiya: the morning star

durgiya usiha: the morning star

durha: four short wooden teeth attached to a flail

durhun: ⟶ durahūn

duri: a swinging cradle

duri de dedubumbi: to place a baby in a cradle

duribumbi: (causative or passive of durimbi)

duribuhe ejen: a dispossessed owner

durilembi: to rock in a cradle

durimbi: (-he) 1. to seize, to rob; 2. to sleep in a cradle; 3. to place in a cradle

durindumbi: to seize together; also durinumbi

durinumbi: to seize together; also durindumbi

durma: (Tibetan) dough molded in various shapes, used in lamaist ceremonies

dursuki: similar, looking alike

dursuki akū: mischievous, unpresentable, irregular, of irregular behavior, unworthy, unseemly, undesirable, roguish, good-for-nothing

dursukilebumbi: (causative of dursukilembi)

dursukilembi: to make alike, to use as a model, to copy

dursulebukū: an interpreter in ancient South China

dursulembi: to imitate, to copy, to use as a model

dursulen: essential or core principle

dursulen i wecen: a sacrifice made to the Jade Emperor during times of war

dursun: likeness, form, shape, model, pattern, appearance

dursungga: having form, material

durugan: list, chart, register, diagram

durugan fisen: genealogical register

durujun: a name for the stork; cf. weijun

durulambi: to provide a model

durulembi: to form, to model

durumbi: (-ha) to become old and weak, to become decrepit

durun: 1. form, shape, figure; 2. model, mold; 3. rule, norm; 4. plan, blueprint

durun arambi: to pretend, to put on airs

durun hiyan: incense pressed into blocks

durun i efen: molded cakes

durun i hiyan: cake of incense

durun i matan: candies molded in various shapes

durun i yaha: charcoal bricks

durun kemun: rule, regulation, practice, custom

durun muru: shape, form

durun nirumbi: to draw up a building plan

durun sindambi: to pretend, to feign

durun tuwakū: model, example

durungga: **1**. exemplary, model; **2**. having form, representational

durungga dobtolon: an animal or devil mask worn over the head during certain games

durungga tetun: instrument — especially an astronomical instrument

durungge: exemplary

durusga moo: *Corypha umbraculifera*: Indian palm — a plant whose leaves were used for paper

dushubumbi: (causative of **dushumbi**)

dushumbi: **1**. to sling, to hurl; **2**. to yank, to pull hard at, to do with a violent motion; **3**. to emboss

dushure faksi: silversmith

dushun: dark in color, dull, slow-witted, muddled

dushutembi: to fling around

dusihi: **1**. a two-piece man's skirt, a mail skirt; **2**. a front lapel

dusihilebumbi: (causative of **dusihilembi**)

dusihilembi: to hold (as in a sack or pocket), to hold in an upturned garment

dusihiyen: **1**. unclear, misty, blurred; **2**. muddle-headed, stupid

dusy: (都司) captain; cf. **danara hafan**

dute: on the inside, inner

dute talu: a short cut

dute yali: meat adhering to skin

dutelembi: to go by a short cut

duteleme yabumbi: to go by a short cut

duthe: **1**. the vertical wooden support of a window lattice; **2**. name of a fish with red-spotted scales

duthengge: having a grate or lattice work

dutu: deaf, a deaf person

dutung: (都統) Lieutenant General; cf. **gūsai ejen**

duturembi: to feign deafness

duwali: **1**. category, kind, type, party, clique; **2**. confederate, accomplice

duwali acabumbi: to match up

duwalibun: a book arranged according to categories, an encyclopedia

duwalinambi: to categorize

duwalingga: of the same type or category

duwalingge: a person belonging to the same party or clique

duwan: **1**. satin; **2**. weeds; **3**. a pock still not broken out

duwanse: satin

duwara: mayfish, sweetfish

duwargiya: ⟶ **durgiya**

duwargiyan: bright, brilliant

duwargiyan usiha: Venus, Orion

duyembi: to act coldly or indifferently

duyembumbi: to attack an unprepared enemy, to make a surprise attack

duyen: **1**. cold, indifferent, distant (said of people); **2**. stubborn, restive (of horses)

duyun cecike: one of the names of the goatsucker; cf. **simari cecike**

DZ ᠵ

For words beginning with **d**, see the section beginning on page 63.

dz: (子) viscount

dz ming jung: chime clock

dzai siyang: (宰相) prime minister

dzambag'a: *Michelia champaca*: the champac tree

dzandan: sandalwood; cf. **cakūran**, **dan mu**

dzandz: ⟶ **dzanse**

dzang: **1**. (Western) Tibet; **2**. Buddhist or Daoist scripture

dzanse: a finger presser, a torture device used in interrogating women

dzanselabumbi: (causative of **dzanselambi**)

dzanselambi: to apply the finger presser

dze er ma ni ye: Germany

dzengse: an orange

dzoguwan: workshop foreman

dzooli: (皂隸) petty attendant in a *yámen*, lictor

dzun hūwa majan: (遵化長披箭) a long slender arrow

dzung bing guwan: (總兵官) the commander of Chinese troops in a province

dzung giya: (總甲) Superintendent of Block Wardens

dzung ni duka: a religious sect

dzung sika: palm fronds

dzung žin fu: (宗人府) the Imperial Clan Court; cf. **uksun be kadalara yamun**

dzungdu: (總都) Governor General; cf. **uheri kadalara amban**

dzungse: glutinous rice filled with meat or sweet bean paste and wrapped in bamboo leaves

E ᠪ

e: **1**. *yīn*, the female or negative principle; **2**. an exclamation used to call someone's attention, an exclamation of surprise or exasperation; **3**. an expression of affirmation

e i bukdan: the inside of a crease or fold

e i jalan: the underworld

e jijun i acangga: an identification token cast in bronze with indented characters used to gain entrance to a city at night after the gates have been closed

ebci: **1**. rib; **2**. framing timbers (of a ship); **3**. (steep) side of a hill

ebcileme: along the (steep) side of a hill

ebdereku: **1**. destroyer; **2**. destructive, harmful

ebdereku hūlha: someone who brings harm and destruction

ebderembi: to harm, to destroy, to ruin

ebderen: destruction, havoc, harm

ebderen i deribun: (夷則) a classical musical pitch corresponding in function to G sharp

ebebe: interjection of surprise

ebebumbi: (causative of **ebembi**)

ebeci: ⟶ **ebci**

ebegei: **1**. if only, oh that … ; **2**. interjection of fear

ebele: this side

ebembi: (**-ke**) to become soaked through, to become soggy

ebenembi: ⟶ **ebeniyembi**

ebeniyebumbi: (causative of **ebeniyembi**)

ebeniyembi: to soak, to steep (tea)

eberegi: ⟶ **ebergi**

eberehun: ⟶ **eberhun**

eberembi: (**-ke**) to diminish, to decrease, to decline, to subside

eberembumbi: (causative of **eberembi**)

ebergi: **1**. this side, this place; **2**. after

eberhuken: rather weak

eberhun: weak

eberi: weak, deficient, inadequate, inferior, less

eberi oktosi: incompetent doctor, quack

eberiken: somewhat deficient

eberingge: not up to par, inferior

ebetuhun: hollow, empty

ebetuhun holo: empty, lacking substance, false

ebi habi: **1**. discouraged, dejected; **2**. abashed, embarrassed

ebi habi akū: not feeling well, without energy, listless, in bad humor

ebibumbi: (causative of **ebimbi**)

ebilun: delicate, sickly (said of a child)

ebimbi: to be full (after eating), to be sated

ebišebumbi: (causative of **ebišembi**)

ebišembi: to bathe, to swim; cf. **elbišembi**

ebišere oton: bathtub

ebišenembi: to go to bathe or swim

ebišenumbi: to bathe or swim together or in a group

ebišere: ⟶ **ebišembi** (subheading)

ebken tebken: indifferent, standoffish

ebsi: hither, up until now, since

ebsi casi akū: hither and yon, back and forth

ebsi casi de: back and forth, hesitant

ebsi forombi: to turn and face in this direction

ebsi jio: come here

ebsi oso: like this!

ebsihe: (postposition) exhausting, exerting, up to the last, to the extent of: **mutere ebsihe** 'to the best of one's ability'

ebsihei: ⟶ **ebsihe**

ebsihiyan: hither, up until now

ebsiken: a little in this direction

ebsingge: what has been up until now, existing until now, long-lasting

ebšembi: to hurry, to hasten, to be busy

ebšu: a newly hatched quail

ebte: **1**. small bird, fledgling; **2**. a young hawk taken from the nest and raised at home

ebubumbi: **1**. (causative of **ebumbi**); **2**. to dismantle a tent, to unpack, to unload; **3**. to marry off (a daughter)

> **ebubure ba i cifun**: a duty imposed at the place of unloading

> **ebubure camhari**: a notice ordering riders to dismount at the gates of the palace

ebubun: **1**. stopover on a journey; **2**. provisions for traveling officials

> **ebubun i kunggeri**: (下程科) office in charge of caring for emissaries to the court

ebubure: ⟶ **ebubumbi** (subheading)

ebuhu: quick, urgent

> **ebuhu medege**: urgent news

> **ebuhu sabuhū**: in a rush, in a flurry, agitated, hurried

ebumbi: to dismount, to get off a vehicle, to stop (at an inn), to get down

ebundumbi: to stop or stay (said of a group), to get off (said of a group); also **ebunumbi**

ebunembi: to go to stop, to go to dismount

ebunjimbi: **1**. to come to stop or stay, to come to dismount; **2**. to descend (said of a deity)

ebunumbi: to stop or stay (said of a group), to get off (said of a group); also **ebundumbi**

eburgi: the confluence of two rivers

eci: surely, indeed, really

> **eci ai**: of course, certainly

> **eci ainara**: what else is one to do? — of course

ecike: uncle: father's younger brother; cf. **eshen**

ecikese: (plural of **ecike**)

ecimari: this morning

ecine: secretly, behind one's back

ede: (dative or locative of **ere**): to this, here, then, and then, in this (matter)

> **ede aibi**: what difference does this make?

> **ede ainambi**: what is one to do in this matter?

edede: ⟶ **ededei**

ededei: brrr! — the sound of teeth chattering with cold

edekirakū: an incorrigible person, a good-for-nothing

edelembi: to be lacking, to be deficient, not to be enough, to owe a debt

> **edelehe nimeku**: deformity, disability

edembi: (-ke) to go bad (said of food and milk)

eden: **1**. lack, deficiency; **2**. lacking, deficient, blemished; **3**. a scrap of cloth

eden dadan: a deficiency, a lack, incomplete

> **eden dadun**: ⟶ **eden dadan**

edeng: *Pristis pectinatus*: a sawfish

ederi: this time, this way, by here, from here

> **ederi tederi**: here and there, this way and that

> **ederi tederi bulcatambi**: to look for ways to avoid things

edulebumbi: (causative of **edulembi**)

edulembi: to be paralyzed, to suffer a stroke

> **edulehe nimeku**: paralysis, stroke

edumbi: to blow (said of the wind)

edun: **1**. wind; **2**. a cold

> **edun be seferembi**: to grab at shadows

> **edun biyai baita**: sexual intercourse

> **edun buraki niyalma**: prostitute

> **edun dambi**: the wind blows

> **edun dasihikū**: the two largest pinions on birds of prey

> **edun de funtumbi**: to brave the wind

> **edun de šasihalabumbi**: to be toppled by the wind

> **edun dekdeke**: **1**. a wind has arisen; **2**. has caught cold

> **edun faitakū**: a board nailed upright on a rafter

> **edun faitambi**: to sail crosswind

> **edun faitame yabure jahūdai**: one type of large seagoing warship

> **edun febumbi**: to be stopped by a headwind

> **edun fur sembi**: the wind blows softly (said of the south wind in the summer)

> **edun goimbi**: to catch cold, to get the flu

> **edun i temgetu**: a flag that shows the direction of the wind, wind pennant

> **edun i wala**: downwind

> **edun kituhan**: organ, harmonium

> **edun nakambi**: the wind ceases

> **edun nesuken oho**: the wind has calmed

> **edun nesuken šun genggiyen i mudan**: a musical composition played at the banquet after the plowing ceremony

> **edun nimeku**: a cold, rheumatism

> **edun su akū**: not the least bit of wind

> **edun tugi**: sexual intercourse

> **edun tuwambi**: to relieve oneself, to go to the toilet

edungge: pertaining to the wind

> **edungge gasha**: a kind of sparrow hawk

> **edungge hiyebele**: a kind of buzzard

edungge šungkeri ilha: *Angraecum falcatum*: wind orchid

edunggiyebumbi: (causative of **edunggiyembi**)

edunggiyembi: to winnow, to throw up into the wind

efebumbi: to lose one's sight, to blind

efehen: large adze

efembi: to be blind

efen: bread, pastry, cake, any kind of bread-like product made from flour

efen belhere ba: (點心局) kitchen where pastries were prepared for the palace

efibumbi: (causative of **efimbi**)

eficembi: to play together

efiku: toy, game, fun

efiku injeku: fun and laughter, a good time

efiku injesi: joker, a person who likes to play tricks, trickster

efimbi: to play, to enjoy oneself, to act (in a drama)

efime ondombi: to play around, to fool around

efire hehe: actress

efire jaka: toy, plaything

efire urse: actors

efin: game, play

efin de dosimbi: to be addicted to play

efire: ⟶ **efimbi** (subheading)

efisi: buffoon, clown, jester

efisi injesi: clowns and merrymakers

efiyecembi: ⟶ **eficembi**

efiyembi: ⟶ **efimbi**

efiyen: ⟶ **efin**

efu: **1**. the husband of one's elder sister; **2**. brother-in-law: wife's elder brother; **3**. the husband of wife's elder sister; **4**. the husband of an Imperial Princess

efujebumbi: **1**. (causative of **efujembi**); **2**. to ruin, to destroy, to overthrow

efujembi: **1**. to be ruined, to be spoiled, to be defeated, to cease to function; **2**. to be dismissed from a position

efujen: destruction, ruin, downfall

efulebumbi: (causative of **efulembi**)

efulembi: **1**. to destroy, to ruin, to break; **2**. to defeat, to crush; **3**. to remove from office, to dismiss

efulehe dabsun: denatured salt

efulehe hafan: an official who has been dismissed

efulen: destruction, ruin

efute: (plural of **efu**)

egipet: Egypt

eguletu alha: a horse with cloud-like markings

ehe: bad, evil, inauspicious

ehe acabun: bad omen, bad sign

ehe algin: infamy

ehe ba: destiny, fate

ehe be deribumbi: to do evil

ehe boco menggun: poor quality silver (containing impurities)

ehe dosinan: **1**. vulgar taste; **2**. evil incarnation

ehe efin: dirty trick

ehe gūnimbi: to take something amiss

ehe gūnin: evil intent

ehe hafan: an evil official

ehe horon: rank poison, deadly poison

ehe inenggi: an inauspicious day, a day on which there is bad weather

ehe sain: of no consequence, trifling

ehe sui: sin

ehe sukdun: miasma, evil vapors

ehe tacin: bad habit

ehe urse: bandits

ehe wa: a bad smell, a stink

ehe weilengge niyalma: criminal charged with homicide

ehecubumbi: (causative or passive of **ehecumbi**)

ehecumbi: to slander, to defame, to accuse falsely

ehecure gisun: slander

ehecun: animosity, grudge

ehelinggu: **1**. inferior, low-grade, mediocre; **2**. incompetent

eheliyan: stupid, simple

eheliyanggū: ⟶ **ehelinggu**

eheliyenggu: ⟶ **ehelinggu**

ehembi: ⟶ **eherembi**

eherebumbi: (causative of **eherembi**)

eherembi: **1**. to become evil or fierce, to act fiercely; **2**. to have a falling out with, to be on bad terms with someone; **3**. to turn bad (said of the weather)

eherendumbi: **1**. to become evil (said of a number of people); **2**. to be on bad terms with each other

ehurhen: a lark with a yellow beak, black head, yellow eyes, red back, and spotted wings

ei: **1**. an interjection for calling attention; **2**. an interjection of derision

ei ei: **1**. the sound of crying; **2**. the sound of derisive laughter

eibi haibi akū: ⟶ **ebi habi aku**

eici: **1**. or; **2**. perhaps

    eici ainara: can do nothing about it

    eici … eici … : now … now … , either … or …

eicibe: no matter, be it as it may, in any case

eifu: grave

    eifu falan: graveyard

    eifu fetembi: to dig a grave

    eifu kūwaran: cemetery

    eifu musen: graves

    eifu temgetu: grave marker, headstone, funerary inscription

    eifu waliyambi: to visit a grave to honor the dead, to make an offering at a grave

eifun: **1**. rash, sores, scabies; **2**. leprosy

eifunembi: to develop a boil or a swelling, to get goose flesh

eigen: husband

    eigen gaijambi: to take a husband, to marry (said of a woman)

    eigen gaimbi: to take a husband, to get married (said of a woman)

    eigen sargan: husband and wife

eigete: (plural of **eigen**)

eihen: **1**. donkey, ass; **2**. brown

    eihen boco: brown

    eihen cuse: brown silk

eiheri: **1**. brown; **2**. the name of a fabulous rat-like beast

eihesi: person riding or driving a donkey

eihume: the hard-shelled turtle

    eihume usiha: the name of a star in the Milky Way

eihumengge fukjingga hergen: (龜書) a style of calligraphy

eihumengge usiha: ⟶ **eihume usiha**

eihun: stupid, foolish, ignorant, benighted, lacking understanding

eihutu: ignoramus, fool, dummy

eikte: *Ribes mandschuricum*: Manchurian red currant

eimebumbi: (passive of **eimembi**)

eimeburu: you hateful thing!

eimecuke: hateful, loathsome, repugnant

eimecun: repugnance, antipathy

eimede: **1**. repugnant (person); **2**. smart, lovable (said of children)

eimedembi: to feel aversion or repugnance

    eimedere jaka: a repulsive thing

eimedese: (plural of **eimede**)

eimembi: (**-ke, -re/-ndere**) **1**. to abhor, to detest, to find unpleasant; **2**. to be bored, to be tired of

eimembumbi: (causative or passive of **eimembi**)

eimemburu: ⟶ **eimeburu**

eimercuke: abominable, detestable; cf. **eimecuke**

eimerecuke: ⟶ **eimercuke**

eimpe: the name of a wild vegetable with large, long leaves, used to make soup; cf. **empi**

eisi: ⟶ **esi**

eite: halter, bridle

eiten: all (in attributive position), every

    eiten baita: everything, every matter

    eiten ergengge: all living creatures

    eiten jaka: everything, every object

eiterebumbi: (causative of **eiterembi**)

eitereci: ⟶ **eiterembi** (subheading)

eiterecibe: ⟶ **eiterembi** (subheading)

eitereku: **1**. swindler, imposter; **2**. deceptive, fraudulent, cunning

eiterembi: **1**. to deceive, to cheat, to defraud; **2**. to do repeatedly

    eitereci: in general, for the most part, thoroughly

    eiterecibe: in any case, all in all, on the whole

    eitereme: **1**. even though, even if; **2**. repeatedly, again and again; **3**. approximately

    eitereme yabumbi: to act deceitfully

eiteršembi: to cheat on the sly

eje: a castrated bovine, an ox

ejebukū: annalist, chronicler

ejebumbi: (causative of **ejembi**)

ejebun: record, notes

ejehe: **1**. an Imperial rescript, edict, decree; **2**. in older texts used for **eje**, 'ox, cattle'

ejehen: commentary, gloss, note

ejeke: industrious, assiduous, diligent

ejeku: **1**. Secretary; **2**. (侍讀) Reader, *BH* 135, 196

    ejeku hafan: (主事) Second Class Secretary of a Board, *BH* 292

    ejeku i tinggin: (都事廳) Chancery of the Censorate, *BH* 211

ejelebumbi: (causative of **ejelembi**)

ejelembi: to be master of, to rule, to occupy by force, to establish control over

ejeleme salimbi: to monopolize, to take exclusive control of

ejelendumbi: to occupy together, to occupy (said of a group); also **ejelenumbi**

ejelenumbi: to occupy together, to occupy (said of a group); also **ejelendumbi**

ejelesi: owner, possessor, occupier

ejeltu: owner, one possessing authority

ejembi: to remember, to take account of, to record, to note down

ejen: **1**. master, host, owner; **2**. ruler, lord, Emperor

ejen ilimbi: to be one's guide, to be leader, to be master

ejergen: governance

ejesi: recorder

ejesu: memory

ejete: (plural of **ejen**)

ejetun: record, description, gazetteer

ejetun bithei kuren: (志書館) Office for the Compilation of Dynastic Records

ejetungge: pertaining to records

ejihe: dried milk products, cheese

ejilembi: ⟶ **ejelembi**

ek sembi: to be tired of, to be annoyed with

ek tak seme: irately, reprovingly, overbearingly, arrogantly

ek tak seme esukiyembi: to reprove arrogantly

ekcin: **1**. bank (of a river); **2**. an evil spirit

ekcin jolo: ugly, hideous, monstrous, savage

ekcumbi: to slander someone behind his or her back

eke: **1**. (a pause particle used when one cannot think of what to say next); **2**. you there!

eke eke sembi: to stutter, to stammer

eke ya: who was it now? (said when one cannot think of a person's name)

eke yaka seme: speaking of everything under the sun

ekehe: ⟶ **eke**

ekembi: to ache, to be painful

ekidun cecike: another name for the crow tit; cf. **kidun cecike**

ekimbi: ⟶ **ekiyembi**

ekisaka: still, quiet, calm

ekiyehun: **1**. deficient, lacking, insufficient; **2**. vacant, unoccupied

ekiyehun oron: vacant official position

ekiyembi: **1**. to diminish, to be deficient, to be too little, to be lacking; **2**. to be vacant, to be unoccupied; **3**. to go away (a boil or swelling); **4**. to subside (flood waters)

ekiyembumbi: (causative of **ekiyembi**)

ekiyembure dalangga: a dam used to regulate the flow of water in a river

ekiyen: lacking, decrease, vacancy

ekiyendembi: ⟶ **ekiyembi**

ekiyendere gucu: a false friend, a dangerous friend

ekiyendere jalin i menggun: meltage fee: value of the metal lost in the coin-minting process (Chinese *huǒhào* 火耗)

ekiyendere ton: loss (of some commodity)

ekiyeniyebumbi: (causative of **ekiyeniyembi**)

ekiyeniyembi: to lessen, to diminish

ekiyeniyere nonggire cese: population register

ekšembi: to hurry, to hasten, to be busy

ekšeme gardambi: to rush, to hasten

ekšeme saksime: rushing, hurrying, in a rush

ekšendumbi: to hurry (said of a group); also **ekšenumbi**

ekšenumbi: to hurry (said of a group); also **ekšendumbi**

ekšun: **1**. bothersome, troublesome (said of a person); **2**. the dregs of yellow rice wine

ekšun baju: dregs, dross

ektembi: to stamp the front hoof on the ground, to paw the ground

ekteršembi: **1**. to distinguish oneself, to excel; **2**. to act with enthusiasm or vigor, to be agitated, to be high-spirited

elbebumbi: (causative of **elbembi**)

elbefembi: to talk carelessly, not giving sufficient heed to what one is saying

elbeku: a cover, a shelter put up as a protection against the sun

elbembi: **1**. to cover; **2**. to thatch; **3**. to watch over, to protect

elben: **1**. grasses used to make thatch, speargrass; **2**. cover; **3**. grass or reeds used in thatching

elben fembi: to cut thatch with a sickle

elben gūwara: a kind of owl

elben i boo: a thatched house, a humble cottage

elben i jeofi: a thatched hut with a round roof

elbenfembi: to speak nonsense

elbengge: pertaining to cover

elbengge gu: a covering for offerings in ancient times

elbesu: a person rash in speech and actions

elbetu: **1**. coarse (said of workmanship); **2**. a sacrificial hat worn during the Shang dynasty

elbibumbi: (causative of **elbimbi**)

elbihe: *Nyctereutes procyonoides*: raccoon-dog

elbihengge: pertaining to the raccoon-dog

elbimbi: to summon, to call together, to invite, to win over to one's own side, to muster, to recruit (troops)

elbindumbi: to bring over to one's own side (said of a group); also **elbinumbi**

elbinembi: to go to summon

elbinumbi: to bring over to one's own side (said of a group); also **elbindumbi**

elbišebumbi: (causative of **elbišembi**)

elbišembi: to bathe, to swim; cf. **ebišembi**

elbišenembi: to go to take a bath in a river

elbišenumbi: to bathe together in a river

elcin: emissary, messenger

elcin cecike: one of the names of the **mejin cecike**

eldedei: a name for the lark; cf. **wenderhen**

eldehen: one of the eight trigrams of the *Yijing* (symbolizing wind)

eldembi: (**-ke, -pi**) **1**. to shine, to glow; **2**. to shine forth, to be well known; **3**. (honorific) to be born

eldeke inenggi: birthday of an exalted person

eldembumbi: **1**. (causative of **eldembi**); **2**. to glorify, to extol

eldembume enggelenembi: to go to, to visit (honorific)

elden: light, glory, resplendence

eldenembi: to go to shine, to shine there

eldengge: shining, glowing, resplendent, glorious

eldengge ambalinggū: glorious and grand

eldengge saracan usiha: (華蓋) the name of a constellation

eldengge wehe: a (funerary) inscription, stele

eldenjimbi: to come to shine, to grace a place with one's presence

eldepi: bright, brilliant, glorious, splendid

elderhen: a name for the lark; cf. **wenderhen**

elderi moo: legendary mulberry tree of the Eastern Sea

elderi usiha: the seventh star of the Great Dipper

eldešembi: to shine incessantly

ele: **1**. (used after a participle) all; **2**. still more, especially

ele ... ele ... : the more ... the more ...

ele elei: **1**. still more, to an even greater degree; **2**. continuous

ele mila: free and easy, casual, at ease

ele tala akū: similar, comparable

elebumbi: (causative of **elembi**)

elecun: contentment, satisfaction

elecun akū: unsatisfied, covetous

elecun sambi: to be content, to be satisfied

elehudembi: to be satisfied, to be content

elehun: content, calm, satisfied with one's lot, tolerant, content in adversity, at ease, relaxed, composed, unperturbed

elehun sijirhun: frank, candid

elehun sula: free and easy, unrestrained, content

elei: **1**. still more, more; **2**. almost

elei elei: still more, much more, more and more

elei elekei: almost, hardly

elekei: almost, hardly, scarcely

elemangga: **1**. on the other hand, on the contrary, in spite of that; **2**. still more, especially

elembi: to suffice, to be enough

elere ebsihei: to the best of one's ability

elemimbi: to tow (a boat)

elen: **1**. sufficiency; **2**. a goal

elen de: sufficiently

elen de isimbi: to reach a sufficient level, to be enough

elen de isinambi: to reach a goal

elen ombi: to be sufficient

elen telen akū: matched in strength, evenly matched

elengge: everything

elenggi: slovenly, lazy (said of women), indolent

elere: ⟶ **elembi** (subheading)

elerembi: (**-ke**) **1**. to bare the chest; **2**. to become exhausted from running, to be out of breath

eleri: **1**. sufficient, self-satisfied; **2**. disorderly (said of clothing)

eletele: until (it is) enough, in sufficient quantity

eletele bumbi: to give in sufficient quantity

eletembi: to do the utmost

elgebumbi: (causative of **elgembi**)

elgembi: to lead an animal by the reins

elgin: ⟶ **elgiyen**

elgiyeken: somewhat rich, somewhat prosperous

elgiyen: prosperous, rich, plentiful, abundant

> **elgiyen aniya**: a good year (said of a harvest)
>
> **elgiyen i fusembure fiyenten**: (慶豐司) Pasturage Department, *BH* 83
>
> **elgiyen ice calu**: a granary in the city of Beijing
>
> **elgiyen jalungga calu**: a granary located in Zhili
>
> **elgiyen tesuhe namun**: a silver depository in Shanxi
>
> **elgiyen tumin**: rich and abundant
>
> **elgiyen tumin calu**: a granary just outside Beijing
>
> **elgiyen tusangga calu**: a granary by Anhe bridge

elgiyengge: richly endowed, lavish

elhe: **1**. peace, calm, well-being; **2**. peaceful, healthy; **3**. slow, easy

> **elhe akū**: not well, not feeling well
>
> **elhe alhai**: slowly, easily, calmly, easygoing
>
> **elhe be baimbi**: to ask after a person's health
>
> **elhe be fonjimbi**: to inquire after a person's health
>
> **elhe nelhe**: safe and sound, free from danger
>
> **elhe nuhan**: at ease, not rushed, casual
>
> **elhe sain**: well, in good health
>
> **elhe sebjen feye**: cozy nest
>
> **elhe taifin**: **1**. peace; **2**. the Kangxi (康熙) reign period, 1662–1722
>
> **elhei**: slowly

elhebumbi: to calm, to let rest

> **elhebure hiyan**: benzoin resin, gum resin
>
> **elhebure hiyan moo**: the tree *Styrax benzoin* from which gum benzoin is obtained

elhei: ⟶ **elhe** (subheading)

elheken: rather well, gentle, rather slow, nice and slow

elhekū: (contraction of **elhe akū**)

elhembi: **1**. to be calm; **2**. to do slowly, to act slowly

elhengge: peaceful, pacific

elheo: how are you?

elherhen: a name for the lark; cf. **wenderhen**

elhešebumbi: (causative of **elhešembi**)

elhešembi: to take it easy, to act leisurely, to do slowly

> **elhešeme iselembi**: to show stiff opposition

> **elhešeme jibgešeme**: hesitating to go forward, holding back

eli: one thousandth of a Chinese foot

elin: storeroom under the roof, loft

elintu: *Cynopithecus*: a large black ape

elintumbi: to observe from afar

elioi: the six lower pipes of the ancient Chinese music scale

elje: jawbone of a whale

> **elje beri**: a bow made from the jawbone of a whale

eljembi: to oppose, to resist, to defy

eljendumbi: to oppose one another; also **eljenumbi**

eljenjimbi: to come to oppose

eljenumbi: to oppose one another; also **eljendumbi**

elkei: ⟶ **elekei**

elkibumbi: (causative of **elkimbi**)

elkimbi: **1**. to summon by waving the hand, to signal to, to greet; **2**. to brandish a sword in preparation for entering combat

elkindumbi: **1**. to wave (said of a group); **2**. to brandish (said of a group); also **elkinumbi**

elkinumbi: **1**. to wave (said of a group); **2**. to brandish (said of a group); also **elkindumbi**

elmin: an unbroken horse

elmiyen: ⟶ **elmin**

elu: onion, scallion

eluri: prodigy, prodigious

embici: **1**. or; **2**. perhaps; **3**. in the first place

emci: (Mongolian) doctor, healer

> **emci lama**: lamaist healer or doctor

emde: together

emderi: ⟶ **emu derei**

emdubei: continually, persistently, steadily, frequently, earnestly, keep on …

eme: mother

emeke: husband's mother — mother-in-law

emekei: how frightful!

emembihede: sometimes, now and then, at times

ememu: some

> **ememu bihede**: at times
>
> **ememu erinde**: sometimes
>
> **ememu fonde**: sometimes, at certain times
>
> **ememu urse**: some people

ememungge: some (as a substantive)

emete: (plural of **eme**)

emgei: ⟶ **emgeri**

emgeri: **1**. once; **2**. already

emgi: together

    emgi simnere hafan: assistant to the examination proctor

emgilembi: to act together, to act mutually, to unite

emhe: wife's mother — mother-in-law (in some early texts it may also refer to a husband's mother)

emhulembi: **1**. to monopolize; **2**. to take for oneself, to take for one's own use

emhun: alone, sole, lonely, by oneself

    emhun beye: alone, all on one's own

    emhun canggi: all alone

    emhun simeli: lone, solitary

    emhun tembi: to live in solitude

emile: female (frequently used with bird and animal names), woman

emilebumbi: (causative of **emilembi**)

emilembi: to cover, to screen off, to block out

emke: one (as a substantive)

    emke emken i: one by one, little by little, one another

emkeci: once, point by point, in detail

    emkeci akū: totally

emken: ⟶ **emke**

empi: the name of a number of low herbs of the *Artemisia* or *Chenopodium* families, sweet wormwood; cf. **eremu**

empirembi: to talk nonsense, to talk foolishly

emte: one each

emtelembi: to receive one each

emteli: alone, sole, single, independent

    emteli beye: unmarried man

    emteli haha: commoner

    emteli ilimbi: to stand alone, to be isolated

emtenggeri: once each

emtun: ⟶ **amtun**

emtungge jodon: plain hemp cloth, sackcloth

emu: one

    emu adali: the same

    emu akū: not the same

    emu anan: one after another, in turn

    emu andande: in case, if by any chance

    emu angga: one mouthful

    emu bade: together, in one place

    emu bade obume sindambi: to stake all on a single bet

    emu biha: a small bit, a small segment

    emu bokto: one hump, dromedary

emu bukdan: one sheet of folded paper

emu burgin: one spell of confusion

emu cimari: the amount of land that can be plowed in a single day — approximately six *mǔ* 畝

emu da dambagu: one cigarette

emu de oci: in the first instance

emu dedume: the distance between two post stations

emu derei … emu derei … : on the one hand … on the other hand …

emu dobonio: the whole night

emu ergen i: in one breath, in one swallow, in one burst of effort

emu erguwen: one period of twelve years

emu erin: one (meal) time

emu erinde: for a moment

emu falan: a little while, a while

emu fehun: one pace (five Chinese feet)

emu fiyen: one set of feathers on an arrow

emu futa: **1**. one *shēng* (180 Chinese feet); **2**. one string of cash

emu futa jiha: one string of cash

emu gala: one arm's length, half a fathom

emu gargan: one brigade of soldiers

emu girin: one area, one region

emu girin i ba: one district, one region

emu gūnin i: intently, wholeheartedly, with singleness of mind

emu haha: one man's measure (thirty *mǔ* 畝)

emu hungken jiha: 5662 strings of cash and 369 pieces

emu hūfan: a joint business venture, partnership

emu i ginggulere ordo: a pavilion housing inscribed stone tablets

emu i hafure: consistently

emu ici: consistent, hitherto, up to now

emu ikiri: in succession, in a row

emu indeme: one stage of a journey, the distance between two post stations

emu jemin i okto: one dose of medicine

emu jergi: a while, a period of time

emu jukte: one large slice (of meat)

emu julehen i: with one's whole attention, with singleness of purpose, directly

emu juwe giyan: one or two items

emu kiya: one cell of a honeycomb

emu mangga: at one go, in a single action

emu mari: once, one time

emu marin yabuha: made a round trip

emu mukūn: one clan

emu oci: at first, in the first place

emu okson: one pace

emu sefere: one handful

emu siran i: in a row, successively

emu suihen i banjimbi: to live keeping one's mind on what is truly important

emu šuru saliyan i cikten: a stick or rod exactly one span long

emu talgan: one surface, one flat object

emu temuhen: one round or cylindrical object, a spool

emu udu: several, a series of, successively

emu udunggeri: several times

emu ufuhi sulabumbi: to leave an extra portion of cloth in a seam to be used for letting out garments when they are outgrown

emu uhun: one parcel, one bundle

emu yabun emu aššan: every action and motion

emu yohi: one complete set (of a book)

emuci: first

emude: in the first place

emursu: having one layer, simple, unlined

emursu etuku: an unlined garment, an unpadded garment

emuse: one year old

en: yes — interjection used to answer affirmatively

en en seme: saying yes, yes …

en je seme: ⟶ **en en seme**

en jen: ready, finished, complete

en jen i belhembi: to make ready

encebumbi: (causative of **encembi**)

encehedembi: ⟶ **encehešembi**

encehen: talent, ability, capability, resourcefulness

encehen akū: lacking the ability to do something, not adept, lacking talent

encehengge: **1**. a capable person, an adept one; **2**. capable, talented; **3**. adept at currying favor

encehešembi: **1**. to curry favor with someone in authority; **2**. to ask someone to intercede in some matter

encehun: ⟶ **encehen**

encembi: to apportion food and drink to guests at a meal

encina: suddenly, all at once

encu: **1**. different, other, strange; **2**. (as an adverb) separately, differently

encu demun: heterodoxy

encu facu: doting (on a child)

encu falan: country estate; cf. **encu falga**

encu falga: country estate

encu hacin i: extraordinarily

encu inenggi: another day

encu tacihiyan: heterodox teachings

encu tembi: to live separately

encuhen: ⟶ **encehen**

enculebumbi: (causative of **enculembi**)

enculembi: to be different, to do differently, to go one's separate ways

enculeme: separately, in addition

enculeme tuwambi: to view differently

encumbi: ⟶ **encembi**

encungge: that which is different

endebufi: ⟶ **endebumbi** (subheading)

endebuku: error, mistake, accident

endebuku be mishalara tinggin: (繩愆廳) the name of a section of the Imperial Academy

endebuku ufaracun: errors and mistakes

endebumbi: **1**. (causative of **endembi**); **2**. to go astray, to err, to lose one's grip, to do by accident; **3**. to be killed; **4**. to be choked, to be stifled

endebufi wambi: to kill by accident

endebume: by accident, accidently

endembi: **1**. to err, to be mistaken about; **2**. euphemism for 'to die'

endereo: am I not right?

enderi senderi: uneven, battered, in bad shape, broken, incomplete

endeslambi: to make a small error

enduhen: a name for the crane; cf. **bulehen**

enduri: spirit, god, deity

enduri cecikengge loho: a sword with the image of a divine bird on its blade

enduri fayangga: soul, divine spirit

enduri gege: divine maiden

enduri girdan: a banner hung before holy images

enduri hutu: spirits and ghosts

enduri namun: a storehouse for religious vessels and paraphernalia

enduri nikebun: painted icon of a god, a plaque with a god's name written on it

enduri niyalma: an immortal, a Daoist deity

enduri sukdun: spirit

enduri urgunjebure kumun: a piece of music played at minor sacrifices

enduri weceku: spirits and gods

endurin: a Daoist immortal, celestial being, supernatural being

enduringge: **1**. divine, holy, sacred; **2**. referring to the Emperor, Imperial

enduringge ejen: the divine lord — the Emperor

enduringge erdemu ambula selgiyere mudan: a musical piece played at banquets given in honor of meritorious generals and officials

enduringge hese: Imperial order

enduringge niyalma: a holy man, a sage, a saint

endurise: (plural of **enduri**)

enen: descendants, progeny

enenggi: today

enenggi cimari: this morning

enese: (plural of **enen**)

eneshuken: somewhat sloping

eneshun: gently sloping

eneshun meifehe: a gentle slope

eneshun tafukū: steps in front of the platform in a temple

enethe: India; cf. **enetkek**

enetkek: India, the valley of the Ganges, Indian, Sanskrit

enetkek hergengge loho: a sword with Sanskrit written on the blade

eng: **1**. interjection of pain; **2**. interjection of disapproval

eng seme: drawling (an answer), groaning

engge: a bird's beak

engge fulgiyan itu: *Alectoris graeca*: Chinese Chukar partridge

enggeci: ⟶ **enggici**

enggelcembi: to act in an excessive way

enggele senggele akū: unaffectionate, indifferent (to relatives or friends)

enggelebumbi: (causative of **enggelembi**)

enggeleku: a ledge or projection on a cliff, an overhang

enggelembi: **1**. to jut out, to project; **2**. to rise (said of prices); **3**. to lean forward (to look); **4**. to border on, to overlook, to command a view of

enggeleme tuwambi: to lean out to look

enggelenembi: to go to watch, to approach, to pay a visit (honorific), to go (honorific)

enggelenjimbi: to come near, to come to pay a visit (honorific), to come (honorific)

enggelenjire be yarure girdan: (降引幡) a banner used by the Imperial Escort

enggeleshun: projecting outward

enggeljembi: ⟶ **enggelcembi**

enggemu: saddle

enggemu faksi: a saddler

enggemu gaimbi: to unsaddle

enggemu hūwaitambi: to put on a saddle

enggemu tohombi: to put on a saddle, to saddle

enggerhen: a towering projection

enggete moo: a tree overhanging a stream

enggetu cecike: *Phylloscopus fuscatus*: brown bush warbler

enggici: secret, secretly, privately

enggici bade: secretly, privately

enggici de: secretly, in private

enggici gisun: talk behind someone's back

enggule: *Allium victorialis*: a kind of onion that grows in sandy soil

engki congki: just enough

enihen: bitch: female dog

enihun: loosely wound (said of fibers)

enirhen: wisteria

eniye: mother

eniyehen: ⟶ **enihen**

eniyehun: ⟶ **enihun**

eniyeingge: pertaining to motherhood, maternal

eniyen: female moose (*Alces alces*)

eniyen buhū: doe

eniyeniye: hibernation (of snakes)

enji: vegetable dishes, vegetarian

enji belhere ba: (素局) kitchen for the preparation of vegetarian dishes for the Emperor

enteheme: **1**. eternally, always; **2**. (as an adjective) eternal, everlasting

enteheme asarara calu: a granary located in Heilongjiang

enteheme banjimbi: to live forever

enteheme elgiyen calu: a granary in Ilan Hala

enteheme elgiyengge calu: a granary in Shandong

enteheme elhe calu: a granary in Guangdong

enteheme fakcambi: to pass away, to die

enteheme ginggun calu: granaries in the provinces

enteheme goidame: perpetually, forever

enteheme iktambure calu: a granary in Heilongjiang

enteheme jalungga namun: a silver depository in Jiangsu

enteheme julge: high antiquity

enteheme taifin calu: a granary in Jilin

enteheme tusa arara namun: the treasury of Dongling

enteheme tusangga calu: emergency granaries

entehen: regular, fixed, long-term

entehen hethe: fixed property, real property

entehen mujilen: perseverance, constancy

entehetei: forever

enteke: this sort of, this kind of

entekengge: one like this, such a one

eo: lotus root

eo hi: puppet show

eoke: ⟶ **oke**

erde: early, early in the morning

erde baicara dangse: *yámen* employee's attendance record

erde buda: breakfast

erde goidara de: sooner or later

erdedari: every morning

erdeken: rather early, nice and early

erdelembi: to be early, to do early

erdemu: **1**. virtue, moral conduct; **2**. talent, skill; **3**. military art, martial skill

erdemu be neileku: (諭德) an official one step lower in rank than **tuwancihiyakū** in the Supervisorate of Imperial Instruction

erdemu etehe poo: (德勝礮) the name of a large cannon

erdemu gasha: a name for the chicken

erdemu gebu: talent and fame

erdemu gūnigan: (literary or artistic) talent

erdemu muten: talent, capability

erdemungge: virtuous, moral, talented

ere: this

ere ai demun: what is this all about?

ere aniya: this year

ere be tuwahade: from this it can be seen that …

ere biya: this month

ere cimari: this morning

ere dade: in addition, moreover

ere durun i: in this fashion

ere foni: this time; cf. **ere fonji**

ere fonci: recently, of late

ere fonji: this time

ere mini nimeku: this is my weakness

ere niyalma de dotori bi: this man has hidden talents

ere niyalma fisikan: this man just gets by

ere tere seme: making no distinction between one's own and other's

ere ucuri: of late, recently

ere uju be tongki: cut off this head! — an expression of abuse

ere yamji: tonight, this evening

erebe ainambi: how should (we) handle this?

ereci: hereafter, after this

ereci amasi: henceforth

erei jalin: because of this, for this reason

erei turgunde: for this reason

erebumbi: (causative of **erembi**)

ereci: ⟶ **ere** (subheading)

erecuke: hopeful, expectant

erecun: hope, expectation

erecun akū: hopeless

erehunjebumbi: (causative of **erehunjembi**)

erehunjembi: to hope constantly, to hope earnestly

erei: ⟶ **ere** (subheading)

ereingge: this person's

erembi: **1**. to hope; **2**. to peel birch bark off a tree

eremu: *Artemisia annua*: yellow artemisia, sweet wormwood

erendumbi: to hope together

ereni: by this, through this, from this, therefore

eretele: up until now, up to this point

ergece niyehe: the mandarin duck; cf. **ijifun niyehe**

ergecembi: to rest often, to rest (said of a group)

ergecun: rest, leisure, repose

ergelebumbi: (causative or passive of **ergelembi**)

ergelembi: **1**. to force, to coerce; **2**. to torment; **3**. to carry (one's arm) in a sling

ergeleme dahabumbi: to force a surrender

ergeleme gaimbi: to take by force

ergelen: force, coercion

ergeletei: by force, obligatory

ergembi: to rest, to pause

    ergerakū: indefatigable

ergembumbi: (causative of **ergembi**)

ergen: **1**. breath, life; **2**. penis

    ergen beye: body and life

    ergen da: end of the penis

    ergen dambi: to breathe

    ergen de isibumbi: to cause to die, to lead to death

    ergen den: breathing is difficult

    ergen fulimburakū: gasping for words, short of breath

    ergen gaijambi: to take a breath

    ergen gaimbi: to breathe

    ergen guwembi: to save one's life, to escape death

    ergen hetumbi: to manage to get by

    ergen hetumbumbi: to make one's livelihood

    ergen i sen: the opening of the urethra

    ergen jaka: penis

    ergen jocimbi: to be murdered, to perish

    ergen sumbi: breathing stops, to stop breathing

    ergen susambi: to get killed, to give up one's life

    ergen šelembi: to stake one's life, to be desperate

    ergen tambi: life hangs on a thread

    ergen temšembi: to struggle to live (said of an ill person), to gasp for breath

    ergen tucimbi: to breathe

    ergen yadambi: to stop breathing, to die

ergendembi: to rest

    ergenderakū: never rests, without rest

ergendumbi: to rest (said of a group); also **ergenumbi**

ergengge: **1**. living, living creature; **2**. (Buddhist term) sentient being

    ergengge jaka: living creature

    ergengge wambi: to kill living things (forbidden in Buddhism)

ergenumbi: to rest (said of a group); also **ergendumbi**

ergerakū: ⟶ **ergembi** (subheading)

ergešembi: to breathe hard from fatigue or overeating, to pant

ergi: **1**. direction, side; **2**. this side

ergingge: pertaining to direction

ergule: self-willed

    ergule oho: departed from the pattern, lost shape, did not act properly

ergume: court dress

erguwe: ⟶ **erhuwe**

erguwejitu: compasses

erguwembi: to go around, to circle around, to form a circle (said of the moon)

    erguwere garunggū fukjingga hergen: a style of calligraphy

erguwen: **1**. perimeter, circumference; **2**. a period of twelve years, a cycle

    erguwen aniya: the cyclical year of one's birth

    erguwen de torhombi: to go around in a circle

erguwere: ⟶ **erguwembi** (subheading)

erhe: **1**. a green frog; **2**. ⟶ **erihe**

erhembi: ⟶ **ergembi**

erhuwe: a piece of red felt used to cover the hole on the top of a yurt

erhuweku: a small niche or shrine for religious objects or images

erhuwembi: ⟶ **erguwembi**

eri: Isn't it like this?, Isn't it here?

eribumbi: (causative of **erimbi**)

eridari: ⟶ **erindari**

erihe: a Buddhist rosary (with 108 beads)

    erihe be tolombi: to recite the rosary

eriku: broom

    eriku šušu: broom straw

    eriku usiha: comet

erilembi: to act at the right time, to keep the proper time, to do often

    erileme: at the right time, on time, from time to time

    erileme guwendere jungken: a chiming clock

    erilere niongniyaha: a name for the wild goose; cf. **bigan i niongniyaha**

erimbi: to sweep

erimbu: a gem, a precious stone

    erimbu ilha: a bright red exotic flower

    erimbu wehe: a precious stone, a gem, a jewel

erin: **1**. time, season; **2**. one of the two-hour divisions of the day

    erin akū: often

    erin be amcame: punctually

    erin de acabume: on time, at the proper time

    erin dobori akū: both day and night

    erin fonjire jungken: alarm clock

erin forgon: propitious time, the right moment, time

erin forgon i ton i bithe: a calendar book

erin forgon i ton i bithe de afaha hafan: (司書) Compiler in the Calendar Section, *BH* 229

erin forgon i ton i bithe kunggeri: (時憲科) a section of the Board of Rites concerned with calendrical matters

erin forgon i ton i bithe weilere tinggin: (司書廳) a bureau in the Imperial Board of Astronomy concerned with the compilation of the calendar

erin forgon i ton i hontoho: (時憲科) Calendar Section in the Imperial Board of Astronomy, *BH* 229

erin hūda: current price

erin i kemneku: a small sundial

erin i kemun: clock, watch

erin jafafi: on time, punctually

erin ke seme: at every moment

erin nimaha: shad

erin sonjoro tacikū: a school at which astronomy was taught

erin sonjosi: geomancer

erin tulimbi: to be overdue

erin tutambi: to exceed a deadline

erin tuwara hafan: (司晨) Assistant Keeper of the Clepsydra, *BH* 231

erin tuwara hontoho: (漏刻科) Section of the Clepsydra, *BH* 231

erindari: **1**. often, regularly; **2**. every time, on every occasion

eringge: pertaining to time

eringge gasha: a name for the chicken

eringge niongniyaha: a name for the wild goose; cf. **bigan i niongniyaha**

eritun: soapberry, plants in the genus *Sapindus*

erke: powerful, strong, bold

erken terken: this way and that, in various ways, faltering, stalling

erki: **1**. willful, self-willed, despotic; **2**. leaning on a parent in order to walk (said of a child)

erkilembi: to use force, to act despotically, to be self-willed

erku: ⟶ **eriku**

erpe: a growth on the lip, cold sore, herpes

erpenembi: to form a growth on the lip

erse: (plural of **ere**); cf. **ese**

erselen: a lion; cf. **arsalan**

ersulen: a kind of willow whose branches were used to make cages

ersun: ugly, repulsive

ersun jilgan: harsh voice

erše mama: midwife

eršebumbi: (causative of **eršembi**)

eršeku: an attendant in a local official office

eršembi: **1**. to serve, to wait on, to attend; **2**. to take care of (children); **3**. to get smallpox

ertele: up until now

ertumbi: to depend on, to rely on

ertun: dependence, reliance

eru: fearless, intrepid, brave, robust

eruken: rather fearless, rather intrepid

erulebumbi: (causative of **erulembi**)

eruleci: torturer, executioner

erulembi: to torture, to punish

erumbi: ⟶ **erulembi**

erumci: executioner

erun: torture, punishment

erun be getukelere tacihiyan de aisilara temgetun: (明刑弼教旌) an inscribed banner of the Imperial Escort

erun be ginggulere fiyenten: (慎刑司) Judicial Department (of the Imperial Household), *BH* 81

erun koro: torture and punishment, penalty

erun nikebumbi: to apply torture, to inflict punishment

erun sui: **1**. torment; **2**. torture and crime! (a term of abuse)

eruwedebumbi: (causative of **eruwedembi**)

eruwedembi: to drill (a hole), to make a hole with an auger

eruwen: drill, auger

ese: (plural of **ere**: these people, these)

eseingge: these people's

eshen: uncle: father's younger brother

eshete: (plural of **eshen**)

eshuken: somewhat raw

eshun: **1**. raw; **2**. untried, untamed, unfamiliar, strange

eshun ceceri: raw silk of one color

eshun fandz: aborigine

eshun giowanse: ⟶ **eshun ceceri**

eshun gurgu: wild animal, untamed animal

eshun juken: unskilled, out of practice
eshun lingse: fine-figured raw silk
eshun niyalma: stranger
eshun sele: raw iron, pig iron
eshun suberi: white raw silk
eshungge: raw, strange, unfamiliar
eshurebumbi: (causative of **eshurembi**)
eshurembi: **1**. to change suddenly for the worse; **2**. to go wild (said of a trained bird)
eshurumbi: ⟶ **eshurembi**
esi: certainly, of course (usually followed by the conditional converb)
    esi oci: naturally, of course, certainly
    esi seci ojorakū: **1**. having no alternative, having no way out; **2**. involuntarily
esihe: scale (of a fish)
esihengge: scaled, having scales
esike: (interjection) I am full, I have had enough to eat
esukiyebumbi: (causative of **esukiyembi**)
esukiyembi: to scream, to screech, to shout, to rail at, to reprove, to bawl out, to give a dressing-down
esunggiyembi: to shout, to yell (angrily)
eše: brother-in-law: husband's younger brother
ešebumbi: (causative of **ešembi**)
ešembi: **1**. to scale (a fish); **2**. to be slanting or oblique
    ešeme acabuha hergen: (切音字) a device for recording the pronunciation of Chinese characters by using two other characters
ešemeliyan: somewhat slanting
ešen: slanting, oblique
    ešen i boo: a side hall in the palace
ešengge: slanting, oblique, diagonal
    ešengge fu: a diagonal wall
    ešengge moo: a ship's diagonal planking outboard
    ešengge mudan: oblique tones
ešenju boo: an obliquely built house
ešenju jugūn: a diagonal road
ešerge moo: a deep-grained tree that grows in the mountains
ešete: (plural of **eše**)
etefi: ⟶ **etembi** (subheading)
etehen: victory
etembi: **1**. to overcome, to win, to be victorious; **2**. to be hard on one end (a bow); **3**. to be able

etefi marimbi: to return victoriously
eteme halambi: to surmount, to make a change for the better
eteme kadalambi: to take mandatory measures
eterakū: having no alternative, acting against one's will
etere be toktobure poo: (制勝礮) the name of a large bronze cannon
eten: **1**. force, resistance; **2**. victory
etenggi: strong, powerful, tough, despotic
etenggilebumbi: (causative of **etenggilembi**)
etenggilembi: to use force, to resort to force
    etenggileme: forcibly
eterakū: ⟶ **etembi** (subheading)
etere: ⟶ **etembi** (subheading)
eteri ilha: the name of a dark red exotic flower
etubumbi: (causative of **etumbi**)
etuhuken: rather strong, rather powerful
etuhun: **1**. strong, powerful, vigorous; **2**. dowry; cf. **atuhūn**
    etuhun dahabumbi: to accompany the bride to the house of the bridegroom
etuhušebumbi: (causative of **etuhušembi**)
etuhušembi: to act unreasonably, to act tyrannically, to act despotically, to parade one's might, to try to overcome others, to act violently
etuku: clothing, garment
    etuku adu: clothing
    etuku belhesi: an official in ancient times who was in charge of ritual clothing for the king and nobility
    etuku dusihi: clothes
    etuku halambi: euphemism for 'to menstruate'
    etuku lakiyara golbon: clothes rack
    etukui ifin: seam in a garment
etukulembi: to dress
    etukulere buleku: a dressing mirror
etukungge: pertaining to clothing
etumbi: to put on (clothing), to wear
eu: lotus root; cf. **eo**
eu jeu: Europe
eye: **1**. pit for storing grain, vegetables, etc.; **2**. pit of a grave; **3**. pitfall; **4**. dungeon; **5**. pit used as a dwelling
eyebuku: ⟶ **mukei eyebuku**
    eyebuku asu: a fish net used to catch fish swimming close to the surface

eyebumbi: (causative of **eyembi**)

eyembi: **1**. to flow; **2**. to sink (said of a steelyard)

    eyefi sekiyefi: laggard, dallying, lazy

    eyehe sohin: a moving ice floe

    eyere jobolon: baneful influence, harmful effect

    eyere usiha: meteor, falling star

eyemeliyan: a bit sinking (said of a steelyard)

eyempe: ⟶ **eimpe**

eyen: flow, current

    eyen i demun: lascivious, lewd

    eyen seyen akū: indifferent, unaffected

eyenembi: to flow in that direction

eyer hayar: natural and unrestrained, gracefully, free and easy, floating easily

eyere: ⟶ **eyembi** (subheading)

eyeri hayari: ⟶ **eyer hayar**

eyerjembi: to have a fresh appearance, to look nice and fresh

eyeršebumbi: (causative or passive of **eyeršembi**)

eyeršecuke: despicable, hateful, disgusting

eyeršembi: **1**. to feel sick to the stomach; **2**. to be disgusted

eyun: **1**. elder sister; **2**. elder (said of females)

eyungge: elder (said of girls)

eyute: (plural of **eyun**)

F ᡳ ᡤ

fa: **1**. window; **2**. magic; **3**. dharma; **4**. technique, skill, method

fa be fekumbi: to jump out of the window

fa cikin: window sill

fa i gebu: religious name

fa i orolokū: window screen

fa i sangga: an opening in the latticework of a window

fa ulhūma: *Lyrurus tetrix*: black grouse

fa ši: senior Buddhist monk, honorific term for a Buddhist or Daoist monk

fabumbi: **1**. (causative of **fambi**); **2**. to cause to dry up, to dam up (a river); **3**. to chase down (a defeated opponent)

facabumbi: (causative of **facambi**)

facambi: **1**. to disperse, to scatter; **2**. to fall into disarray; **3**. to be perturbed; **4**. to unravel, to come apart

facame susumbi: to be scattered

facihin: ⟶ **facuhūn**

facihiyambi: to bustle about, to dash about

facihiyašabumbi: (causative of **facihiyašambi**)

facihiyašambi: **1**. to worry, to be upset; **2**. to be assiduous, to make an effort

facihiyašandumbi: to worry (said of a group); also **facihiyašanumbi**

facihiyašanumbi: to worry (said of a group); also **facihiyašandumbi**

facimbi: ⟶ **facambi**

facuhūlambi: ⟶ **facuhūrambi**

facuhūn: **1**. confused, in disarray, confusion; **2**. rebellion, disorder; **3**. dissolute, lewd

facuhūn dekdebumbi: to cause trouble, to rebel

facuhūn i ba: diaphragm, midriff

facuhūn i da: cause of trouble, cause of ruin

facuhūngga: confused, messy, disorderly

facuhūrabumbi: (causative of **facuhūrambi**)

facuhūrambi: **1**. to be in disorder, to rebel; **2**. to feel confused and disoriented (said of a sick person)

fadabumbi: (causative or passive of **fadambi**); **2**. to be harmed through magic

fadagan: magic

fadagan deribumbi: to perform magic

fadaku: a kind of mythical venomous worm used to make poison

fadaku okto: venom, toxin

fadambi: to employ magic (in order to harm someone)

fadame bušukulembi: to bewitch, to deceive through superstition

fadame eiterembi: to deceive, to make a fool of

fadarhūn: a name for the woodpecker; cf. **fiyorhon**

fadu: a bag or pouch (hung at the waist)

fadu jan: a whistling arrow with a square head

fadulabumbi: (causative of **fadulambi**)

fadulambi: to pack in a bag

fafaha: a kind of wild sour cherry

fafulabumbi: (causative of **fafulambi**)

fafulambi: **1**. to prohibit; **2**. to issue a decree, to fix by law; **3**. to restrain; **4**. to direct, to rule

fafun: law, decree, prohibition

fafun be miosihodombi: to pervert the law

fafun be necimbi: to transgress the law

fafun i bithe: the code of law

fafun i gamambi: to handle by law — to put to death

fafun jafaha hafan: judge

fafun kooli: laws and statutes

fafun kooli bithei kuren: (律例館) Commission of Laws, *BH* 439

fafun selgiyen: decree, promulgation of a law

fafun šajin: regulations and prohibitions

fafungga: **1**. having legal force, legal; **2**. worthy of respect; **3**. stern, strict

fafungga ama: a stern father

fafungga baibula: paradise flycatcher; cf. **baibula**

fafungga cira: strict, severe

fafungga inenggi: holiday, festival

fafuri: **1**. energetic, diligent; **2**. brave, courageous; **3**. irascible, irritable, fierce

fafuringga: **1**. assiduous, industrious, energetic; **2**. irritable, testy, hot-tempered; **3**. courageous, intrepid

fafuršambi: to make an effort, to summon up one's courage, to act energetically

fafushūlambi: **1**. to make an oath, to swear; **2**. to make an appeal to troops before battle

fafushūn: **1**. oath, vow; **2**. a declaration or oath made to troops before battle

faha: **1**. kernel, grain, seed, the pit of a fruit; **2**. eyeball

faha sindambi: to mature (said of grain or fruit)

fahabumbi: (causative or passive of **fahambi**)

fahala: **1**. opaque, cloudy, containing suspended particles; **2**. dark purple

fahala nure: heavy, opaque liquor

fahala suran: slops, water left over from cooking or washing rice

fahambi: **1**. to throw, to throw down (at wrestling); **2**. to stamp (one's foot)

fahame gisurembi: to attack someone verbally

fahame injembi: to be convulsed with laughter

fahame tembi: to throw oneself into a chair from fatigue

fahanambi: to form fruit or grain

faharambi: to remove the seeds from hazel and pine nuts

fahatambi: to stamp (one's foot)

fahi: inner thigh, perineum

fahūn: **1**. liver; **2**. courage; **3**. rim of a wheel

fahūn ajige: timid, fearful

fahūn akū: without courage

fahūn amba: brave, daring

fahūn i alhūwa: **1**. diaphragm; **2**. membrane that grows on the liver of animals

fahūn mangga: intrepid, valiant

fahūn nišargan: a growth in the throat

fahūn silhi: **1**. courage, heroic spirit; **2**. close friend

faidabumbi: (causative of **faidambi**)

faidambi: to line up, to arrange in order, to display, to rank

faidame ilimbi: to stand in a row, to stand in line

faidame sindambi: to display, to set out neatly

faidan: **1**. row, rank, formation, file; **2**. escort; **3**. procession; **4**. military formation

faidan be dasara hafan: (治儀正): Assistant Section Chief (of the Equipage Department), *BH* 123, 125

faidan be jorire hafan: (雲麾使) Assistant Marshal, *BH* 125

faidan be kadalara hafan: (冠軍使) various officials of the Equipage Department; cf. *BH* 115, 123

faidan be tuwancihiyara hafan: (整儀尉) Controller of the Sixth Class, *BH* 125

faidan be tuwara hafan: (鑾儀使) Commissioner of the Imperial Equipage Department, *BH* 111

faidan i da: (王府長史) Commandant of a Prince's Palace, *BH* 43

faidan i dabcikū i fiyenten: (班劍司) Sword Section (of the Imperial Equipage Department), *BH* 122

faidan i etuku: clothing worn by the Imperial Escort

faidan i hafan: (典儀) Assistant Major-Domo of a Prince's Palace, *BH* 46

faidan i janggin: general term for officials in the Imperial Equipage Department

faidan i kiyoo: a sedan chair that was used by the Empress in processions and carried by eight porters

faidan i niyalma: porters and insignia bearers of the Imperial Escort

faidan i sejen: a carriage used by the Empress

faidan i tungken: a large drum used by the Imperial Escort

faidan i yamun: (鑾儀衛) Imperial Equipage Department, *BH* 109

faidandumbi: to line up (said of a group); also **faidanumbi**

faidangga: **1**. ordered, ranked; **2**. articles for show, displays; **3**. decorations, furnishings

faidangga dengjan: a pair of lamps placed on the altar at state sacrifices

faidangga ulabun: biography (in one of the official Chinese histories) faidanumbi: to line up (said of a group); also **faidandumbi**

faidasi: (席班) Usher (in the Board of Rites), *BH* 382B

    faidasi mahatun: a hat worn by officials in ancient times

faifan: clapping

faifuhalambi: to dye blue with indigo

faihacambi: **1.** to worry, to fret; **2.** to pant, to be short of breath

faijima: ⟶ **faijuma**

faijuma: **1.** strange, odd; **2.** inappropriate, amiss, unfavorable; **3.** taking a turn for the worse (said of an illness), serious (said of an illness)

faisha: palisade, fence

faishalabumbi: (causative of **faishalambi**)

faishalambi: to build a palisade

faishan: ⟶ **faisha**

faitabumbi: (causative or passive of **faitambi**)

faitaburu: May you be cut to pieces! (an expletive)

faitaha: ⟶ **faitambi** (subheading)

faitakū: a small saw (used to cut bones)

faitalambi: to cut off

faitambi: **1.** to cut, to slice; **2.** to cut off, to shorten; **3.** to cut out clothing; **4.** to follow someone's tracks

    faitaha yali: sliced meat

    faitara baita: surgical operation

faitan: **1.** eyebrow; **2.** a cut

    faitan feherembi: to knit the brow

faitanumbi: to cut together

faitara: ⟶ **faitambi** (subheading)

faitarabumbi: (causative of **faitarambi**)

faitarambi: to cut into pieces, to mince

    faitarame wambi: to kill by cutting to pieces — an extreme form of capital punishment

    faitarame wara weile: a crime punishable by delimbing and execution

fajambi: **1.** to defecate (said of birds and animals); **2.** to fade (said of stars)

fajan: feces (of animals and birds), dung

    fajan fuhešembi: to roll dung into balls

    fajan jafambi: to be constipated

    fajan onggombi: to become constipated (said of animals)

fajiran: a wall, a partition

faju: **1.** fork of a tree; **2.** the part of the hand between the thumb and the index finger

fajuhū: ⟶ **fajukū**

fajuhūrambi: to perform anal coitus, to engage in sodomy

fajukū: anus

    fajukū sangga: anal opening

fak fak: anxious, impatient

fak fik: (onomatopoetic) the sound of fruit falling

fak seme: **1.** sturdily, vigorously; **2.** with a plump, with a thud

    fak seme banjimbi: to grow up to be sturdy

    fak seme faraka: fell into a faint

    fak seme tehe: sat down with a plump

    fak seme tuheke: fell with a thud

faka: a wooden pole with a fork at one end

fakaca: short in stature

fakadambi: to hit a ball with a stick (a kind of game), to bat a ball

fakari: short-legged

fakašambi: ⟶ **fakadambi**

fakcabumbi: (causative of **fakcambi**)

fakcambi: **1.** to come apart, to divide (intransitive verb), to split, to separate; **2.** to part, to leave

    fakcame aljambi: to part, to leave

    fakcame samsimbi: to disperse

    fakcara doro be arambi: to take one's leave

fakcan: splitting, separation

fakcangga: distinct, separated

fakcashūn: estranged, alienated, divisive

fakdangga cecike: a name for the myna; cf. **kūbulin ilenggu cecike, guwendehen**

fakiri gasha: a name for the chicken

fakjilambi: **1.** to support oneself, to hang on to, to cling to, to insist; **2.** to cling to one another without yielding (at wrestling); **3.** to defend oneself, to plead innocence

    fakjilame: persistently, insistently

    fakjilame gisurembi: to disagree, to argue, to hold fast to one's views

    fakjilame marambi: to refuse stubbornly

    fakjilame tuwakiyambi: to hold fast, to defend vigorously

fakjin: **1.** support, purchase; **2.** one's own judgment, self confidence; **3.** spur on a male fowl

    fakjin akū: without support, having nothing to hold on to, lacking something to rely on

fakjin baharakū: lacking self mastery, unable to decide for oneself, unable to act on one's own

fakjin nikeku: dependence, support and reliance

faksa: **1**. straight into, deep into; **2**. violently (angry), wholeheartedly, greatly

faksa bayambi: to become rich suddenly, to strike it rich

faksa bayan: fabulously rich

faksa jili banjimbi: to fly into a rage, to become enraged

faksabun: ⟶ **joringga i faksabun**

faksalabumbi: **1**. (causative of **faksalambi**); **2**. to separate, to remove

faksalambi: **1**. to divide, to separate; **2**. to distinguish, to analyze

faksalame banjimbi: to live apart

faksalame hokombi: to get divorced

faksalame ilgambi: to distinguish, to differentiate

faksalan: **1**. judgment, decision; **2**. separation, division

faksi: **1**. craftsman, workman, artisan; **2**. skilled; **3**. clever, shrewd

faksi bošoro da: (司匠) Overseer, Inspector of Works, Clerk of Works, Overseer of Works, *BH* 77, 82, 96, 460A

faksi cecike: a name for the wren; cf. **darha cecike**

faksi da: chief artisan

faksi gisun: sweet words, luring speech

faksi jurgan: (武備院) Imperial Armory, *BH* 89

faksi mangga: exquisite, skilled

faksidambi: to act shrewdly, to act cleverly, to argue cleverly

faksikan: rather clever, shrewd, or skilled

faksikan i forgošome fiyelembi: to do a skillful turn at trick riding

faksikan i gamambi: to handle cleverly

faksingga: endowed with skill, skillful

faksisa: (plural of **faksi**)

faksisai kunggeri: (匠科) a section of the Board of Works concerned with artisans

fakū: a stone dam in a river (used for catching fish)

fakūri: pants, trousers

fakūri ferge: the seam in the seat of trousers

falabumbi: **1**. to exile, to banish, to expel; **2**. to get lost; **3**. ⟶ **gūnin falabumbi**

falabure weile: crime punished by exile

falabure weile tuhebumbi: to sentence to banishment

falabun: exile, banishment

falan: **1**. floor; **2**. threshing floor; **3**. quarter of a town, neighborhood, residential area; **4**. sacrificial site; **5**. a while, a short period

falan falan i: in gusts

falan sombi: to offer bread on the threshing floor after the autumn harvest

falangga: pertaining to the floor or earth

falangga dengjan: a lantern hung on a pole that is stuck in the earth

falangga nahan: an earthen floor with a passage under it through which hot air from an outside fire passes — a kind of central heating

falanggū: the palm of the hand

falanggū dumbi: to clap the hands

falanggū faifan: applause

falanggū forimbi: to clap the hands

falanggū usiha: a sweet fruit that comes from Yunnan and shaped like a man's palm

falasu: enamel, enamelware

falga: **1**. clan, tribe; **2**. all the people living on one street, quarter of a town; **3**. office, bureau; **4**. group, clump, grove; **5**. measure word for buildings; **6**. gust (of wind)

falga falga: in clumps, in groves, in gusts

falga i da: person in charge of a part of town

falgai boo: **1**. house of a rich family, mansion, domicile; **2**. house with a courtyard

falgangga: **1**. office, subsection; **2**. Second Class Transport Station on the Grand Canal (所), *BH* 834

falgari: bureau, office

falgari i aisilakū: (置丞) Director of an Office, *BH* 389, 391

falgari i icihiyakū: (置正) Assistant Director of an Office

falha: ⟶ **falga**

fali: **1**. measure word for solid objects, a lump, a piece; **2**. a unit of money

falibumbi: (causative of **falimbi**)

falimbi: **1**. to tie a knot, to bind; **2**. to be firm or fast, like something bound together; **3**. to befriend, to form an alliance with, to associate with; **4.** to become sworn brothers or sisters; **5.** to conclude (a treaty or agreement)

faliha gucu: bosom friend, intimate friend

falime ejembi: to keep firmly in mind

falime guculembi: to make friends, to form a friendship

falin: **1.** association, alliance; **2.** tying, binding

falindumbi: to be bound to one another

falingga: having connection, connected, bound, associated

falintambi: to stagger, to walk unsteadily

falintu monio: a name for the monkey

falishūn: intermittent

falmahūn: (房) a constellation, the 4th of the lunar mansions, made up of four stars in Scorpio

falu: *Megalobrama terminalis*: Manchurian bream

famambi: ⟶ **fambumbi**

fambi: **1.** to dry up, to become very thirsty; **2.** to become tired

fambumbi: to get lost, to lose one's way

famha: **1.** a stick or board for winding thread or yarn; **2.** a roll of raw silk fiber

fan: **1.** pan, dish, tray; **2.** barbarian, foreign; **3.** Sanskrit

    fan dasafi tukiyembi: to put assorted delicacies on a tray and offer them to guests

    fan fere: a small gulch or canyon, the course of a creek or a spring

    fan suwan: mango

    fan šu: sweet potato

fancabumbi: **1.** (causative or passive of **fancambi**); **2.** to cut off someone's breathing, to choke, to stifle; **3.** to lock the gates of the Forbidden City; **4.** to cook slowly over low heat

fancacuka: vexing, annoying, stifling, causing despair

fancacun: anger, displeasure

fancaha: ⟶ **fancambi** (subheading)

fancakū nimeku: epilepsy

fancambi: **1.** to get angry; **2.** to be stifled, to smother, to feel suffocated; **3.** to be stuffy, to be oppressive (said of the weather)

    fancaha niyalma: someone suffering from a heat stroke

    fancame halhūn: stifling hot

    fancame injembi: to be convulsed with laughter

fancarambi: to ridicule, to deride

fandi: a wooden grip on an oar or on a mast

fandz: **1.** foreigner, (western) barbarian; **2.** aborigine, tribal people; **3.** ⟶ **fanse**

    fandz i ba: tribal area, border region (inhabited by Mongols, Tibetans, etc.)

fang: square (as in 'square feet')

fang jang: **1.** Buddhist abbot; **2.** an abbot's quarters

fang seme: solidly, immovably

fangdz: prescription, recipe

fangga: magic, possessed of magic powers

    fangga bithe: amulet, fetish, charm

    fangga niyalma: necromancer

fangkabumbi: **1.** (causative of **fangkambi**); **2.** to repay a debt with an object of equivalent value, to make restitution, to compensate for

    fangkabume salibumbi: to compensate

fangkakū: an earth packer — usually a large flat stone

fangkala: low, short

fangkambi: to throw down, to drive, to beat

    fangkame tembi: to sit in a rigid, unnatural manner, to sit erect

fangnai: firmly, with determination, resolutely, stubbornly

    fangnai burakū: refuses to give

    fangnai ojorakū: **1.** resolutely refuses; **2.** unsure, irresolute

fangnambi: to deny, to go back on what one has said, to disavow, to renege

    fangname faksalambi: to indulge in sophistry, to argue in an implausible manner

    fangname laidambi: to deny what one has said

fangse: **1.** pongee, a light raw silk; cf. **sirgeri**; **2.** banner; **3.** prescription

fangsikū: racks used for drying noodles on both sides of a stove

fangšakū: **1.** a device used for smoking fox, rabbits, badgers, etc. from their holes; **2.** censer, vessel for burning incense

fangšambi: **1.** to smoke (transitive verb), to fumigate, to smoke out, to cense; **2.** to deny, to lie, to prevaricate

fangšangga tubi: a rack for smoking meat and fish

fanihiyan: a chopping board

faniyahiyan: ⟶ **fanihiyan**

faniyan: ⟶ **fanihiyan**

fanse: **1**. bailiff, policeman; **2**. trader, peddler

far far seme: weak, lacking energy

far seme: in profusion, in large quantity

fara: **1**. an ox-drawn sleigh used for carrying hay or wood; **2**. horn strips on both sides of a grip; **3**. shafts of a wagon

faradambi: to get stuck in the mire (said of wheels)

farambi: **(1)** (-ka) to faint, to lose consciousness

farambi: **(2)** (-ha) to spread out freshly harvested grain to dry

farambumbi: (causative of **farambi** [2])

farang seme: solidly, immovably

    farang seme tembi: to sit immovably

farangga: having shafts

    farangga duka: the outer door of an official office

    farangga dukai takūrsi: bailiff of the outer door

farfabumbi: **1**. (causative of **farfambi**); **2**. to be confused; **3**. to get lost

farfambi: **1**. to be in disarray, to be confused, to be unclear; **2**. to throw swiftly (at the game of **gacuha**)

fargabumbi: (causative or passive of **fargambi**)

fargambi: to pursue

    fargara cooha: pursuit troops

farganambi: to go to pursue

fargi: a perch for chickens

farha cecike: a name for the wren; cf. **darha cecike**

farhūdambi: **1**. to darken; **2**. to act in a foolish or muddled way, to become confused; **3**. to do something in the dark

farhūkan: rather dark

farhūn: dark, obscure, unclear, confused, muddled

    farhūn dobori: in the depths of night

    farhūn gerhen: dusk

    farhūn suwaliyame: in the period just before dawn

farhūšambi: to act blindly

fari: ⟶ **geri fari**

farilambi: **1**. to become dark; **2**. to be upset, to be worried

faringgiyambi: to cut with a sickle and lay out to dry

farsa: **1**. mint; **2**. a very small freshwater fish of little value

farsa giranggi: lower bones of the rib cage, asternal or floating ribs

farsi: **1**. piece, strip; **2**. a unit of currency

    farsi farsi: in pieces, in strips

farsilabumbi: (causative of **farsilambi**)

farsilambi: to cut or make in pieces

    farsilaha cinuhūn: cinnabar in pieces

    farsilaha hiyan: incense in pieces

    farsilaha okto: medicinal pellets or pills

    farsilame faitambi: to cut into pieces, to slice

farsinambi: to be in pieces

faršambi: to risk one's life, to act carelessly, to brave (rain, snow)

faršatai: fearlessly, recklessly, without heed for life

    faršatai yabure niyalma: knight-errant

fartahūn: **1**. having large nostrils; **2**. shaped at one end like a horn; **3**. protruding, thick at the end

farudai: the phoenix of the east

fasak seme: the sound made by a beast or bird emerging suddenly from a thicket

fasan: fish weir

    fasan fekumbi: **1**. to become disloyal, to rebel; **2**. to jump out of a weir (said of fish)

    fasan iren: fish weir

fasar seme: **1**. in many pieces, scattered, in great numbers; **2**. not cooked done (said of rice)

    fasar seme genehe: crumbled, became undone

    fasar seme hūwajaha: broke into many pieces

    fasar seme labdu: in great quantity

fase: **1**. raft; **2**. the weights used on a scale or steelyard

fasibumbi: **1**. (causative of **fasimbi**); **2**. to hang, to execute by hanging

fasilan: **1**. fork, forking; **2**. disturbance, interference, obstacle, trouble, discord

    fasilan be deribumbi: to raise obstacles, to complicate (an issue)

    fasilan gisun: ambiguous speech, equivocal words

    fasilan niru: a forked arrow

    fasilan salja: a road with a three-way forking

fasilangga: forked

fasimbi: **1**. to hang (oneself); **2**. to cling to, to climb

    fasime bucembi: to die by hanging

faššabumbi: (causative of **faššambi**)

fassambi: to exert effort, to go to a lot of trouble, to take pains, to bestir oneself, to act vigorously

fassan: effort, zeal, merit, achievement, feat, exploit

    fassan be baicara bolgobure fiyenten: (稽動 清吏司) a section of the Board of Civil Appointments; cf. *BH* 337

fassandumbi: to exert effort together; also **fassanumbi**

fassangga: expending effort, meritorious, industrious

fassanumbi: to exert effort together; also **fassandumbi**

fasu: a name for the quail; cf. **musu**

fatabumbi: (causative of **fatambi**)

fatak: (onomatopoetic) the sound of falling objects

fatakū: the name of a dark red flower

fatambi: to pinch, to pick (fruit)

    fatame bodombi: to count on one's fingers

fatan: **1**. the sole of the foot or a shoe — also used as a term of contempt; **2**. a comb-like tool used for working silk on a loom, weaver's reed

fatanambi: to go to pinch or pick

fatanjimbi: to come to pinch or pick

fatanumbi: to pick together

fatar seme: **1**. to the best of one's ability, with all one's might; **2**. busying oneself with serving a guest, affably

    fatar seme assambi: to wiggle with all its might (a fish)

fatarambi: **1**. to pinch repeatedly; **2**. to use things sparingly

    fatarame bodombi: to count on the fingers

fatari ilha: a flower resembling the gardenia, with small leaves

fatarsabumbi: (causative of **fatarsambi**)

fatarsambi: **1**. to pinch repeatedly; **2**. to be in the habit of using things sparingly

fatha: hoof, foot (of fowl), claw

    fatha beri: a bow with cow's hooves mounted on it

    fatha weihuken: feeling weak in the legs because of fear

fathacambi: ⟶ **fathasambi**

fathasambi: **1**. to be discouraged, to be dejected, to be despondent; **2**. to be anxious, to be fretful, to be agitated

fayabumbi: (causative of **fayambi**)

fayabun: expense, consumption

fayambi: **1**. to spend, to squander, to consume; **2**. to sell

fayangga: soul, the yang soul

    fayangga akū golombi: to be scared to death

    fayangga gaimbi: to call the soul (said of shamans)

    fayangga hūlambi: ⟶ **fayangga gaimbi**

    fayangga oron: the yang soul and the yin soul

    fayangga tucimbi: the soul departs from the body

    fayangga tuhembi: **1**. to be terrified, to be scared out of one's wits, to be panic stricken; **2**. to feel despondent, to lose heart

fe: old, not new, worn out

    fe amba calu: a granary in Beijing

    fe an i: in the old, customary way

    fe baita: an old case (at law)

    fe demun: old trick

    fe durun: old-fashioned

    fe gucu: old friend

    fe inenggi: the old days, formerly

    fe kooli: old regulations

    fe susu: one's native place

    fe yamji: the last day of the old year

febgiyembi: to talk while in a delirium, to talk in one's sleep

febhi: ⟶ **febigi**

febigi: larvae of the scarab

febsehe: a locust-like insect

febumbi: to be stopped by a head wind

fecehun: ⟶ **fecuhun**

feciki: strange, odd, wonderful

fecikilembi: to do in a wondrous manner

fecitembi: to see through

fecuhun: low, base, devious, unfaithful (said of a wife)

fede: Advance!, Work hard!

fefe: vulva, female sexual organs

fehe: ⟶ **fembi** (subheading)

feherembi: (-ke) **1**. to calm down, to become placated; **2**. ⟶ **faitan feherembi**

feheren: the area between the eyebrows

fehi: **1**. brain, brains; **2**. memory

    fehi akū: without memory

fehubumbi: (causative or passive of **fehumbi**)

fehuhen: a footrest, a foot rail

fehulembi: to tread on

fehumbi: to step on, to tread on, to trample

fehun: a pace

fehunembi: to go to tread on, to trespass

fehunjimbi: to come to tread on

fehutembi: to trample, to trod (said of several persons)

fehutenumbi: to trample together, to trample (said of a group)

fei: (妃) an Imperial Concubine (of the third rank), *BH* 8

fei dz: nut of the tree *Torreya nucifera*, torreya nut; cf. **fisha**

fei dzoo: soap

fei gin: gold leaf

feibihe: ⟶ **febigi**

feidz: ⟶ **fei dz**

feifumbi: to boil, to brew; ⟶ **fuifumbi**

feigin: ⟶ **fei gin**

feihe: ⟶ **fehi**

feingge: an old thing

feise: brick, tile

    feise kūwaran: brick factory

    feise mooi kunggeri: (磚木刻) a section of the Board of Works

    feise wehe: brick

    feisei duka: the name of the lcft or right gates before the main gate of the examination hall

fejergi: under, underneath

    fejergi beye: lower parts of the body

    fejergi cooha: troops of the Green Banner

    fejergi femen: the lower lip

    fejergi ing: Green Banner, Chinese troops

fejergingge: that which is below

fejile: under, underneath

    fejile baha: became pregnant

    fejile bi: is pregnant

fejilebumbi: (causative of **fejilembi**)

fejilembi: to catch with a **fejilen**

fejilen: a noose made of hair from a horse's tail (used for catching wild fowl)

fejiri: under, underneath

fejun: base, vile

fekcehun: ⟶ **fekcuhun**

fekceku: a drug used for poisoning fish — it is made from the leaves and bark of a tree resembling the walnut

fekcembi: 1. to jump, to hop; 2. to beat, to pulse

fekcuhuken: somewhat astringent

fekcuhun: astringent, puckery (like the taste of an unripe persimmon)

fekcuri: the name of a sweet but astringent fruit

feksibumbi: 1. (causative of **feksimbi**); 2. to gallop (a horse); 3. to set dogs on game at night

feksiku: a many-hooked pole placed at the bottom of a body of water to catch carp

feksimbi: to run, to gallop

feksimbumbi: (causative of **feksimbi**)

feksin: gallop

feksindumbi: to run together; also **feksinumbi**

feksinumbi: to run together; also **feksindumbi**

fekšembi: to kick

fekšulembi: to treat with alum

    fekšulehe duingge hoošan: paper treated with alum (to be used for painting)

fekšun: 1. alum; 2. puckery, astringent

fekubumbi: (causative of **fekumbi**)

fekucembi: to leap up, to jump (rope), to hop, to skip

fekucenumbi: to leap up in a group

fekumbi: 1. to jump, to leap; 2. to wrinkle up (said of cloth that has been wet)

fekumbumbi: 1. (causative of **fekumbi**); 2. to make horses go at a fast gallop

fekun: a leap, a jump, the length of one jump

    fekun waliyabumbi: to have a fright, to be terrified

fekunembi: to jump across (away from the speaker), to jump to the other side

fekunjimbi: to jump across (toward the speaker)

fekuri: horizontal supports on the shafts of wagons and sledges

fekuteme: intermittently

felebumbi: (causative of **felembi**)

felefi: ⟶ **felembi** (subheading)

felehudembi: 1. to affront, to offend, to vex; 2. to be brash, to be presumptuous, to act rashly, to act in an offensive manner

    felehudeme necimbi: to affront, to offend

felehun: 1. brash, brazen, offensive; 2. brashly, recklessly, accidentally

feleku: tassel or ornament on a bridle

felembi: 1. to act recklessly; 2. to assassinate; 3. to roll one's hair into a chignon, to bind up one's hair

    felefi yabumbi: to act recklessly

    felere antaha: assassin

felheri ilha: *Rubus rosaefolius*: roseleaf raspberry
feliyebumbi: (causative of **feliyembi**)
feliyembi: **1**. to walk, to take steps; **2**. to frequent (a place); **3**. to discuss marriage
    feliyeme yabumbi: to go for a walk
feliyen: walking
fembi: **1**. to lay out new-mown hay or other grass to dry; **2**. to talk heedlessly
    fehe gisun: careless talk
    feme gisurembi: to talk nonsense, to speak heedlessly
femen: **1**. lip; **2**. seam
    femen acabumbi: to sew together
    femen kamnimbi: to close the lips tightly
fempi: **1**. a paper seal used on envelopes and on doors; **2**. measure word for letters; **3**. envelope
    fempi de tebumbi: to insert into an envelope
    fempi dobton i kunggeri: (封筒科) a section in the Court of Colonial Affairs
fempilebumbi: (causative of **fempilembi**)
fempilembi: to seal
    fempilehe dobton: a sealed paper pouch for official reports
    fempilehe dobtonoho bithe: a document sealed in a pouch
fen: a square piece, a slice
fen eli: tiny bit, small amount
fendz: portion, share, contribution
fenehe: tinder, kindling
    fenehe cecike: *Phylloscopus inornatus*: pseudo goldcrest
fenehin: ⟶ **fenehe**
fenembi: to go to lay out new-mown hay
feng: bee, wasp
fengse: pan, jug
    fengse i tuwabun: an artificial landscape or scene placed in a bowl
fengseku: a small porcelain pan or bowl
fengsi: a practitioner of geomancy
fengšen: prosperity, good fortune
    fengšen be aliha usiha: two of the stars in the Great Dipper
fengšengge: prosperous, fortunate
fengšun: ⟶ **fungšun**
fenihe: swarm, flock
    fenihe ulhūma: a kind of pheasant that flies in flocks

fenihiyen: a small table for burning incense
feningge: something old
feniyeku: one member of a swarm or flock
    feniyeku weijun: a name for the stork; cf. **weijun**
feniyelembi: to form a flock, to swarm, to flock
feniyen: flock, swarm, drove, herd, crowd
    feniyen acambi: to gather in a flock
    feniyen duwali: confederate
    feniyen feniyen i: in flocks, in swarms
    feniyen ijilambi: to gather in a herd
feniyengge: forming flocks, swarming
feo io: ephemerid
fepi: cutting board for fodder
fer far seme: weakly, fluttering slowly like a butterfly in flight
fer fer: (onomatopoetic) the sound of yelping dogs
fer seme: fluttering, floating, wafting
fere: **1**. bottom, base, floor; **2**. the central banner in a battue; **3**. the back felt wall of a yurt
    fere de: after all, at base, actually
    fere gūsa: the Bordered Yellow Banner
    fere heceme: completely, exhaustively
    fere jalan: the first **jalan** of a banner
    fere sele: a piece of iron in the bottom of a quiver
    ferei bele: rice on the floor of a granary
    ferei boo: the building behind the main house
    ferei moo: crosspiece between the legs of a table or bed
ferehe singgeri: bat
ferembi: (**-ke**) **1**. to become old, to become worn out; **2**. to become deaf, to be deafened; **3**. to become giddy, to become dizzy
ferembumbi: (causative of **ferembi**)
ferenembi: to become worn out, to become decayed
ferešebumbi: (causative of **ferešembi**)
ferešembi: to take a sample
feretu: adjutant, assistant
ferge: **1**. the back claw of a fowl; **2**. the seam joining the two halves of a pair of trousers; **3**. ⟶ **ferhe**
fergecun: ⟶ **ferguwecun**
fergetun: a thumb ring used on the right hand in archery
fergimbi: to become numb, to sting
    fergime nimembi: to suffer from a sting
ferguwebumbi: (causative of **ferguwembi**)

ferguwecuke: strange, wonderful, astonishing, marvelous

    ferguwecuke fukjingga hergen: (奇字篆) a style of calligraphy

    ferguwecuke gungge poo: (神功礮) the name of a large cannon that weighed a thousand catties

    ferguwecuke horonggo bakcin akū poo: (神威無敵礮) the name of a large cannon that weighed three thousand catties

    ferguwecuke horonggo enduri: the name of a deity

    ferguwecuke horonggo kiru: the name of a banner used by the Imperial Escort and embroidered with dragons or serpents on a dark background

    ferguwecuke horonggo poo: (神威礮) the name of a large brass cannon weighing four hundred catties

    ferguwecuke karan: the Beijing observatory

    ferguweceke mangga: refined, exquisite

    ferguwecuke sabingga sence i fukjingga hergen: (芝英篆) a style of calligraphy

ferguwecun: **1**. auspicious sign, miracle; **2**. god, spirit

ferguwembi: to be astonished, to wonder at, to admire, to extol

ferguwen: **1**. efficacy, auspiciousness; **2**. efficacious, auspicious; **3**. an intelligent person; **4**. spirit, soul

    ferguwen acabun: efficacy, efficaciousness

ferguwendumbi: to wonder at (said of a group); also **ferguwenumbi**

ferguwenumbi: to wonder at (said of a group); also **ferguwendumbi**

ferhe: **1**. the thumb, the big toe; **2**. ⟶ **ferge**

    ferhe cecike: sparrow

    ferhe gidambi: in dividing up objects, to take the best for oneself

    ferhe sirge: the thickest string on a stringed instrument

ferhelembi: to grasp (a bowstring) with the thumb

feri: horse, donkey, or mule hide with the hair removed

ferimbi: to strive

ferkingge: experienced, knowledgeable, learned

ferten: wing of the nose (*ala nasis*)

fesen: ⟶ **fesin**

feser seme: **1**. broken into small pieces; **2**. frightened, stunned, astonished

    feser seme agambi: to drizzle, to rain lightly

    feser seme hūwajaha: broke into small pieces, shattered

    feser seme meijehe: broke into small fragments (said of porcelain)

feshebumbi: (causative of **feshembi**)

fesheku: ⟶ **fesheleku**

feshelebumbi: (causative or passive of **feshelembi**)

fesheleku: shuttlecock

feshelembi: **1**. to kick; **2**. to open up (border regions)

    fesheleme tabumbi: to string a bow by placing one's foot on one end

feshembi: to suffer

feshen: a tiered bamboo or wooden rack used for steaming various foods

    feshen efen: steamed bread, *mántou* 饅頭

feshešembi: to kick repeatedly

feshušembi: ⟶ **feshešembi**

fesin: handle, stock, grip, pole for a flag or banner

    fesin i toldohon: hilt of a sword

fesingge: having a handle

fesku: ⟶ **fesheleku**

fešen: ⟶ **fesin**

feššembi: ⟶ **feshešembi**

fetebumbi: (causative of **fetembi**)

fetecun: **1**. shortcoming, weak point, sore spot; **2**. criticism, criticism of someone's shortcomings

feteku: an ear-pick

fetembi: **1**. to dig, to dig out, to dig up; **2**. to criticize; **3**. to analyze, to scrutinize

    feteme alambi: to expose someone's shortcomings

    feteme gisurembi: **1**. to explain; **2**. to speak of someone's shortcomings

    feteme kimcimbi: to get to the bottom of something

    feteme niyamniyambi: to shoot under the target (at mounted archery)

    feteme toombi: to slander, to smear

feten: **1**. digging, excavation; **2**. fate; **3**. element (metal, wood, fire, water, or earth); cf. **sunja feten**

    feten acambi: to hit it off well, to be agreeable to one another

fetenumbi: to criticize each other's weak points

fetereku: overly critical, prone to criticism, harsh, mean, exacting, demanding, caustic

feterembi: **1**. to dig, to dig out; **2**. to criticize (faults), to reveal a person's faults; **3**. to investigate, to go into

    fetereme baimbi: to make a thorough investigation

    fetereme tucibumbi: to expose, to unmask

feteren: investigation

feteri: **1**. the wings of the nose; **2**. opening, small hole

    feteri feterilembi: to flare the nostrils while laughing

feterilambi: ⟶ **feteri feterilembi**

fethe: the dorsal fins of a fish

fetheku: oar

fethckulcmbi: to row

fethešembi: to paddle in water, to tread water

fethi: ⟶ **huwethi**

feye: **1**. nest, lair; **2**. wound; **3**. the eye of a needle

    feye baha: was wounded

    feye de edun dosimbi: a draft penetrates the wound

    feye fiyartun: scars of wounds

    feye tucike: an injury resulted

    feye tuwara hehe: woman coroner

    feye yebe oho: the wound has healed

    feye yeru: lair, hideout

feyelembi: **1**. to build a nest, to nest; **2**. to get wounded

feyengge: wounded, pertaining to a wound

feyesi: coroner

    feyesi tuwara niyalma: coroner

fi: writing instrument, writing brush, pen

    fi i dube: the tip of a writing brush

    fi i homhon: a cover for a writing brush

    fi i kitala: the shaft of a writing brush

    fi i nenggeleku: a stand for writing brushes

    fi i obokū: a washing basin for writing brushes

    fi i sihan: a vessel for holding writing brushes

    fi i ulgakū: a vessel for wetting writing brushes

    fi nikebumbi: to use a writing instrument, to put pen to paper

    fi šurgebuhengge fukjingga hergen: (戰筆書) a style of calligraphy

fib seme: wavering, unsteady

ficakū: **1**. a six-holed flute blown from one end; **2**. a whistle

    ficakū orho: a short reed that grows in mountainous areas

ficakūngge: pertaining to the flute

ficambi: **1**. to pipe, to blow (a flute), to whistle; **2**. to decoy game with a horn or flute

fican: blowing, piping, whistling

ficari: an eight-holed bamboo flute

fidembi: **1**. to dispatch (troops), to transfer (troops); **2**. to intrigue

    fideme icihiyambi: to dispatch (troops)

    fideme kadalara amban: (提督) Provincial Commander-in-Chief, *BH* 750

fidenembi: to go to transfer

fifambi: (**-ka**) **1**. to scatter, to stray, to disperse; **2**. to ricochet, to rebound (said of arrows)

    fifaka fosoko: in all directions, helter skelter

    fifaka fosoko urse: people who have fled and scattered

    fifame samsimbi: to be separated in flight, to be defeated and disperse

    fifame ukambi: to flee and scatter, to collapse in disarray

fifan: a plucked four-stringed instrument with frets, a lute

fifangga: pertaining to the lute

    fifangga niyehe: a kind of duck

fifari: a two-stringed instrument similar to a **fifan**

fiha yoo: **1**. syphilis, venereal sore; **2**. a blister

fihali: foolish, idiotic

fihalikan: rather foolish

fihanambi: to develop a blister or sore

fihašambi: to be at a loss for words

fihata: glans penis

fihe: the upper part of the foreleg of a quadruped, the flesh on the foreleg

fihebumbi: (causative of **fihembi**)

fihembi: (**-ke**) to be filled up, to be crowded, to be crammed in, to be stuffed full, to crowd into a narrow space

    fiheme jalukiyambi: to stuff full, to fill up

    fiheme labdu: abundantly full

    fiheme simbi: to stuff full

    fiheme tebumbi: to fill up, to cram full

    fihetele jalumbumbi: to fill to the brim

fihen biya: the second month of winter

fihenembi: to go to fill, to go to crowd in

fihenjimbi: to come to fill, to come to crowd in
fihete: foolish, silly
fihetembi: to weep, to sob
fijirembi: to scrape along the ground (arrows and birds)
fijirhi: a name for the wildcat; cf. **ujirhi**
fijiri: hemp seeds, sesame seeds
    fijiri nimenggi: sesame oil
fik fik seme: ⟶ **fik seme**
fik seme: in profusion, thickly, heavily, closely, densely
    fik seme banjimbi: to grow thickly
    fik seme jalukabi: filled completely, packed in tightly
fika: *Canarium album*: Chinese olive
    fika dengjan: a lantern shaped like a Chinese olive
    fika jahūdai: a boat pointed at both ends
    fika jinggeri: a nail pointed at both ends
    fika nimeku: a swelling of the abdomen due to constipation
    fika šoro: a bamboo basket narrow at both ends
    fika tungken: a drum narrow at both ends and bulging in the middle
fikaci: an olive-shaped, exotic fruit with a seven-layered skin
fikanambi: to have a bulging belly
fikatala: extremely far (a road)
fiksembi: to be in profusion; cf. **fik seme**
fiktan fiktu: discordant, cracked
fikte: foolish, dim
fiktu: **1**. crack, fissure; **2**. dissension, discord, grudge; **3**. pretext
    fiktu arambi: to use a pretext
    fiktu baimbi: to seek a pretext, to seek dissension
    fiktu deribumbi: to incite dissension, to stir up trouble
fila: a plate
filaingge: pertaining to plates
filan: a wood used in the manufacture of bows
filebumbi: (causative of **filembi**)
fileku: a pan for burning charcoal, a brazier, a stove
    fileku i tubi: a grate cover for a brazier
filembi: **1**. to warm oneself by a fire; **2**. to roast
filfin: barren, vacant, empty
    filfin ba: desolate place
    filfin beye: naked

fili: **1**. solid, filled; **2**. resolute, persevering
    fili feise: a kind of very hard brick
    fili feisei kūwaran: a factory for making a very hard variety of brick
    fili fiktu akū: without a solid reason
    fili na: solid earth
filikan: rather solid
filingga moo: red sandalwood; cf. **cakūran**, **dan mu**
filitahūn: ⟶ **filtahūn**
filtahūn: empty (place), unoccupied, vacant, bare
    filtahūn susu: abandoned, desolate
fimebumbi: (causative of **fimembi**)
fimembi: **1**. to test, to try; **2**. to sew the hem of a garment, to fold over and sew; **3**. to approach, to get near; **4**. to provoke
    fimeme etumbi: to try on (clothing)
    fimerakū: cannot happen
fimenembi: to go near, to approach
fina: ring at the end of the crupper
fing seme: firmly, resolutely, faithfully
fingge: tranquil, peaceful, serene, resolute
fingkabumbi: to have tenesmus, to feel an urgent need to defecate with straining but be unable to do so
fintabumbi: (causative of **fintambi**)
fintacuka: painful
fintaha: bag, satchel
fintambi: to have a pricking pain, to ache, to be painful
fintembi: to flee from fright, to run off in all directions
    fintehe gisun: rumor
    finteme genehe: fled, scurried
fio: ⟶ **fiyoo**
fio seme: directly, plainly
fioha: pullet, young tender chicken
fiokon: nonsense
    fiokon i fio: unheeded advice
fiokorombi: ⟶ **fiyokorombi**
fior seme: slurping, eating noisily
fiose: ⟶ **fiyoose**
fiota: fart
fiotambi: to fart; cf. **fiyotombi**
fir fir seme: ⟶ **fir fiyar seme**
fir fiyar seme: elegantly, gracefully
fir seme: quietly, calmly, imposingly, fluently
    fir seme arambi: to write fluently
firfin fiyarfin: with tears flowing, with copious tears

firgembi: (**-ke**) to leak out, to be revealed

firgembumbi: **1**. (causative of **firgembi**); **2**. to reveal (a secret), to let leak out (a secret)

firubumbi: (causative of **firumbi**)

firumbi: (**-ha**) **1**. to curse; **2**. to implore, to pray; **3**. to blaspheme

fisa: the back

    fisa wašakū: back scratcher

    fisai amargi: behind someone's back

    fisai nikeku: a back rest, a back support

    fisai šurden: a twirl of the sword over one's back when performing a sword dance

fiseke: ⟶ **fisembi** (subheading)

fiseku: the upturned eaves at the corners of Chinese buildings

    fiseku boro: an ancient-style summer hat with a wide brim

fisekulembi: to shield with the hand or an object

    fisekuleme tuwambi: to look while shielding the eyes with the hand

fisembi: (**-ke**) **1**. to project, to jut out; **2**. to fork, to branch; **3**. to spurt, to spew, to splash; **4**. to be oblique, to be slanting

    fiseke eyen: branch of a river

    fiseke fasilan: a slanting branch

    fiseme agambi: to rain in torrents

fisembumbi: **1**. (causative of **fisembi**); **2**. to relate, to narrate; **3**. to leave a wide margin when sewing

    fisembuhe jugūn: a suspended roadway built in mountainous areas

fiseme: ⟶ **fisembi** (subheading)

fisen: relation, offspring, progeny; cf. **durugan fisen**

fisengge: projecting, jutting out

    fisengge sihin: the upward projecting eaves of a Chinese building; cf. **fiseku**

fisha: the nut of the tree *Torreya nucifera*, torreya nut; cf. **fei dz**

fishaci: an exotic fruit resembling the **fisha**

fisihe: *Panicum miliaceum*: glutinous millet, broomcorn millet

fisihibumbi: (causative of **fisihimbi**)

fisihimbi: **1**. to sprinkle with the hands; **2**. to shake, to toss (one's sleeves)

fisihiyembi: ⟶ **fisihimbi**

fisikan: somewhat thick, somewhat dense, of rather good quality (meat)

fisiku: slow, negligent, sluggish

fisin: **1**. thick, dense; **2**. good quality (meat), lean

    fisin boso: finely woven linen

    fisin cece: finely woven silk crêpe

    fisin halfiyan sese giltasikū: silk with thick gold thread woven into it

    fisin hoošan: a coarse paper produced in Beijing

    fisin muheliyen sese giltasikū: silk with thick round gold threads woven into it

    fisin yali: lean meat

fisitun: a ritual vessel for offering millet

fisur seme: sluggishly, slowly

fita: fast, tight, taut

    fita mampimbi: to tie a hard knot

fithebumbi: **1**. (causative of **fithembi**); **2**. to set off (firecrackers)

fithejembi: to explode (said of firecrackers), to crackle

fitheku: a bow for fluffing cotton

    fitheku beri: crossbow

fithembi: **1**. to pluck, to play a stringed instrument; **2**. to rebound, to bounce back; **3**. to fluff (cotton); **4**. to flip (a **gacuha**); **5**. to tap on

    fitheme acanambi: to correspond exactly

fithen: a spark that flies out from a fire, crackling (of a fire)

fithengge yaha: charcoal that bursts while being burned

fituhan: a round stringed instrument resembling a Chinese zither

fiya: birch, tree of the genus *Betula*

    fiya moo: birch tree

fiyab seme: shying (said of livestock)

fiyabkū: thrush, a bird of the genus *Turdus*

fiyacumbi: to cry out in pain, to groan, to moan

fiyada: **1**. jawbone; **2**. term of abuse used toward persons of no ability

fiyafikū: ⟶ **fiyabkū**

fiyagambi: to harden, to dry up, to form a crust, to heal (said of a sore)

fiyagan: ⟶ **fiyahan**

fiyaganjabumbi: (causative of **fiyaganjambi**)

fiyaganjambi: **1**. to exchange, to change back and forth, to interchange; **2**. to make some accommodation in order to solve a problem

fiyahan: **1**. callus, hard skin; **2**. the sole of the foot; **3**. the bottom part of a hoof; **4**. agate, jade, tortoise shell, and other such precious objects

fiyahanambi: to harden, to form a callus

fiyaju: fawn, young deer

fiyajumbi: **1**. to be anxious about something beforehand; **2**. to be turbulent (said of clouds before a storm breaks)

fiyak fik seme: suddenly, with sudden movements, without deliberation

fiyak seme: suddenly, with a start

fiyaka: ⟶ **hejen fiyaka**

fiyakiyambi: to expose to the sun, to heat next to a fire

> **fiyakiyame halhūn**: hot from being exposed to the sun

fiyakiyan: heat of the sun, midday heat

> **fiyakiyan i dalikū**: a shelter from the sun

fiyaksa: *Taxus cuspidata*: Manchurian yew

fiyakūbumbi: (causative of **fiyakūmbi**)

fiyakūmbi: **1**. to heat, to dry by a fire, to dry in the sun; **2**. to bake

fiyakūnambi: to go to heat, to go to dry in the sun

fiyakūngga tubi: a bamboo implement used for drying things by a fire

fiyalanggi: a person who speaks in a straightforward manner, straightforward

fiyalar seme: **1**. in a straightforward manner; **2**. loosely, wildly (said of speech)

fiyalhū: evasive, fond of shirking work

fiyan: **1**. color, complexion; **2**. appearance; **3**. light (of a lamp); **4**. rouge, makeup; **5**. colored, bright

> **fiyan arambi**: to act in an affected way, to put on an act; cf. **fiyanarambi**

> **fiyan ilha**: colored flowers used to decorate bowls of vegetables or fruit

> **fiyan nemebumbi**: to have a nice appearance

> **fiyan tuwabumbi**: to show off one's military prowess before a battle

> **fiyan tuwara jebele**: a quiver used during a demonstration of prowess before a battle

fiyana: a frame used for carrying things on one's back, a pack frame

fiyanarakū: an iron

fiyanarambi: **1**. to pretend, to feign; **2**. to iron, to press; **3**. to act in an artificial, put-on manner

fiyancihiyan: abstemious, not fond of eating

fiyancihiyašambi: to have difficulties, to be in a difficult situation

fiyangga: **1**. colored, polychrome, motley, multicolored; **2**. decorated, fresh, good looking

> **fiyangga faidan**: cortege of the Imperial concubines of the sixth and seventh rank

> **fiyangga lakiyan**: decorative hangings made of colored cloth or paper

> **fiyangga ordo**: a pavilion-shaped object made of colored silk that was placed on a high table and used at the presentation of Imperial awards and rescripts

> **fiyangga tuhebuku**: colored hangings at the top of drapes or curtains, valances

> **fiyangga ulhūma**: a brightly colored pheasant

fiyanggū: youngest, least, smallest

> **fiyanggū simhun**: the little finger

> **fiyanggū sirge**: the thinnest string on a stringed instrument

fiyanggūšambi: to behave like a spoiled child

fiyangtahūn: large and strong, able-bodied

fiyangtahūri: large and robust

fiyangtanambi: to become large and strong

fiyanji: **1**. support, assurance, guarantee; **2**. rear guard, the rear (in a military sense)

> **fiyanji cooha**: the rear guard, reserves

> **fiyanji dalikū**: screen, shield

> **fiyanji ertun**: support and trust

fiyanjilabumbi: (causative of **fiyanjilambi**)

fiyanjilambi: to protect, to shield, to serve as the rear guard

fiyantoro ilha: a pink flower resembling the peach blossom

fiyar fir seme: right away, quickly

fiyar seme: right away, immediately

fiyaratala: in great quantity, very much, very many

fiyaringgiyabumbi: (causative of **fiyaringgiyambi**)

fiyaringgiyambi: to dry in the sun, to bleach in the sun

fiyartun: scar, blemish, spot

> **fiyartun giyalu**: crack in a bone or horn

fiyartunambi: to form a scar

fiyaru: maggot, larva

fiyarunambi: to get maggots

fiyarunahangge: maggoty (a term of abuse)

fiyarunarangge: ⟶ **fiyarunahangge**

fiyarunaru: ⟶ **fiyarunahangge**

fiyasambi: (**-ka**) to become dry (said of a bow), to dry out (firewood)

fiyasha: the wall at the two ends of a house
    fiyasha cecike: sparrow
fiyatar seme: foolishly, absurdly
fiyatarakū: a bush resembling the bird-cherry whose wood is used to make wild animal calls
fiye: *Pueraria thunbergiana*: kudzu vine, wild hemp
fiyegu moo: a tree that has been scratched by tigers to the point of bleeding sap
fiyehu mama: the goddess of mountain roads
fiyelebuku: a saddle used for practicing equestrian tricks
fiyeleku: **1**. a steep slope, a cliff; **2**. brazier, a small stove; cf. **fileku**
    fiyeleku hada: a steep cliff
fiyelembi: **1**. to do equestrian tricks; **2**. to fly in circles, to hover (said of falcons); **3**. to warm oneself by the fire
fiyelen: **1**. chapter, section of a book; **2**. *Amarantus mangostanus*: amaranth; **3**. yellow-beaked young birds; **4**. ringworm
fiyelenggu: capercaillie; cf. **horki**
fiyelesu: *Phytolacca acinosa*: Asian pokeweed
fiyelfe: a level area between high mountains or on the shore of a river
fiyen: **1**. powder; **2**. the feathers on an arrow shaft
    fiyen akū: without direction, unstable
    fiyen fiyan: complexion, makeup
    fiyen i ijukū: powder puff
    fiyen ijumbi: to apply powder
fiyene: frame for carrying a saddle
fiyenggu: a thick spot on a bear's belly
fiyengseri: an exotic yellow fruit with a white, powdery interior
fiyentehe: **1**. petal, clove (of garlic), a section, a slice, a strand; **2**. one row of feathers on an arrow; **3**. one part of a cloven hoof
    fiyentehe gisun: rumor
fiyentehejebumbi: (causative of **fiyentehejembi**)
fiyentehejembi: to crack, to fissure
fiyentehengge: having petals, cloves, sections, etc.
fiyenten: section of an official organization
    fiyenten i aisilakū: (寺副) the name of an official of the Court of Judicature and Revision
    fiyenten i icihiyakū: (寺丞) the name of an official of the Court of Judicature and Revision

fiyeolehe: a kind of sea fish with large scales
fiyerembi: ⟶ **fiyentehejembi**
fiyeren: fissure, fault (in the earth)
fiyerenembi: to form a crack or fissure
fiyereren: ⟶ **fiyeren**
fiyo: fart; cf. **fiyoo**, **fiota**
fiyoha: ⟶ **fioha**
fiyohombi: to toss the **gacuha**, using the thumb as a catapult
fiyokocombi: **1**. to rear (said of a horse), to kick (said of horses and mules); **2**. to snarl
fiyokojombi: ⟶ **fiyokocombi**
fiyokon: ⟶ **below**
    fiyokon i fiyoo: not giving a damn, indifferent
fiyokorombi: to talk foolishly, to act foolishly, to talk nonsense
    fiyokoroho gisun: absurd statement, nonsense
fiyolor seme: speaking thoughtlessly, untruthfully
fiyoo: **1**. dustpan; **2**. winnowing fan; **3**. a dance mask made from willow branches and painted with animal figures; **4**. ⟶ **fiyo**
fiyookorombi: ⟶ **fiyokorombi**
fiyoose: a gourd dipper, a ladle
fiyootambi: ⟶ **fiyotombi**
fiyootombi: ⟶ **fiyotombi**
fiyor seme: ⟶ **fior seme**
fiyorhon: *Dryocopus martius*: woodpecker
fiyorhūn: ⟶ **fiyorhon**
fiyotoho: ⟶ **fiyotombi** (subheading)
fiyotokū: black beetle
fiyotombi: **1**. to fart; **2**. to brag
    fiyotoho gisun: **1**. rubbish, nonsense, bullshit; **2**. bragging, boasting
fo: handle with an attached net for ladling chipped ice
fo sang hūwa ilha: hibiscus; cf. **fusuri ilha**
fo ulebumbi: to feed a child pre-chewed food
fodo: **1**. a willow branch used at shamanistic ceremonies; **2**. a pole hung with a quantity of various colored paper money and placed beside a grave
    fodo inggari: willow catkins
    fodo wecembi: to offer sacrifice in the presence of an erected willow branch
fodoba: a kind of small bird with plumage colored like willow leaves
fodoho: willow

fodoho abdaha i fukjingga hergen: (柳葉篆) a style of calligraphy

fodoho inggari: the fuzz or down from a willow tree

fodombi: (-ko) to pant, to gasp for breath

fodor fosok seme: raging, violently angry

fodor seme: seething, furious

fodorombi: (-ko) **1**. to pout, to purse the lips; **2**. to grow in the wrong direction (said of hair); **3**. to pant, to gasp; cf. **fudurambi**

fofilambi: to tie, to bind up

fohodombi: to get angry

foholokon: rather short

foholon: short

foholon ba: shortcoming

foholon jalgan: a short life

foifobumbi: (causative of **foifombi**)

foifokū: sharpener, strop for sharpening knives

foifombi: to sharpen

foihori: **1**. careless, superficial; **2**. accidental, by chance

foihori gisun: unfounded remarks

foihori gisurembi: to joke around

foihorilambi: **1**. to underestimate another's ability; **2**. to do carelessly, to neglect, to treat indifferently

foihorilame: carelessly, indifferently

foji: a skin covering for boots and shoes (worn in cold weather)

fokjihiyadambi: to act in a coarse or boorish manner

fokjihiyan: boorish, coarse

fokto: jacket made of grass linen

folgo: ⟶ **folho**

folho: a small iron hammer

folkolombi: to leave a space, to make an interval, to pause

folkolome: here and there, interspersed, at intervals

folobumbi: (causative of **folombi**)

foloho: **1**. ⟶ **folho**

foloho: **2**. ⟶ **folombi**

folombi: to carve, to engrave, to print

foloho acangga fukjingga hergen: (刻符書) a style of calligraphy

foloho hitha: engraved metal decoration on a horse's bridle

foloro faksi: engraver, carver, printer

folon: a carved inscription, something engraved or printed

folonggo: resembling something carved

fombi: (-ha) to chap

fome fiyahanambi: to form calluses from being chapped

fomci: ⟶ **fomoci**

fomilambi: to tuck in the clothing

fomoci: stockings, socks

fomon: a name for the wren; cf. **darha cecike**

fomorombi: to get tangled up

fompi: chapped

fon: time, season

fonde: when … (used after a participle)

fondo: through, thorough, completely

fondo gehun: transparent, translucent

fondo sabumbi: to see through something

fondo tokombi: to stab right through

fondo tucike: went through and came out the other side

fondojombi: to be broken or torn through, to be penetrated

fondolobumbi: (causative of **fondolombi**)

fondolombi: to penetrate, to go through

fondombi: ⟶ **fondolombi**

fongko: a small brass drum

fongsombi: (-ko) to become black from smoke

fongson: soot, dirt

fongsonggi: **1**. soot, dirt; **2**. a fish which resembles the red-sided culter and is found in the Sunggari River

fongsorombi: ⟶ **fongsombi**

foniyo: female roe deer

fonji: ⟶ **ere fonji**

fonjibumbi: (causative of **fonjimbi**)

fonjimbi: to ask

fonjin: question, questioning

fonjinambi: to go to ask, to enquire

fonjindumbi: to ask (said of a group); also **fonjinumbi**

fonjinggimbi: to send to ask

fonjinjimbi: to come to ask

fonjinumbi: to ask (said of a group); also **fonjindumbi**

fonjisi: **1**. questioner, interrogator; **2**. (理問) Law Secretary, *BH* 826

fontoho: **1**. small hole in an object; **2**. a kind of bottomless vessel

fontombi: ⟶ **fondolombi**

for: **1**. (onomatopoetic) the sound of slurping; **2**. the sound of spinning thread

for for: ⟶ **for**

for seme: the sound of crowing

forfoi: orangutan; cf. **furfu**

forgon: **1**. a season, the course of the year; **2**. fate, fortune

    forgon i ton: destiny, fate

    forgon i yargiyan ton: the official calendar

    forgon ufarambi: to miss an opportunity

    forgon wasimbi: to have bad luck

forgori ilha: *Rosa indica*: Chinese rose

forgošambi: ⟶ **forgošombi**

forgošobumbi: (causative of **forgošombi**)

forgošombi: **1**. to revolve, to rotate; **2**. to orbit, to circle around; **3**. to reverse, to transpose; **4**. to turn upside down, to invert; **5**. to transfer; **6**. to be reborn

    forgošome baitalambi: to transfer, to dispatch, to dispose

    forgošome banjimbi: to be reborn

    forgošome fiyelembi: to turn in the saddle while trick riding

    forgošome gūnimbi: to think back, to reconsider, to examine one's conscience

    forgošome niyamniyambi: suddenly to reverse direction while shooting from horseback

    forgošome yabumbi: to circulate

forhošombi: ⟶ **forgošombi**

foribumbi: (causative or passive of **forimbi**)

forikū: a wooden clapper

forimbi: to strike, to knock

foringga hūsun: a man who goes about at night striking the hours on a gong or clapper, night watchman

foringgiyambi: to test an arrow shaft by turning it between the fingers

forišambi: to strike hard

foritu: a stick with small bells attached to it (used by Buddhist monks)

forjin: a small knot or excrescence on a tree

    forjin moo: a tree that grows on riverbanks and has very hard wood

forko: spinning wheel

    forko i sabka sele: pivot on a spinning wheel

forobumbi: **1**. (causative of **forombi**); **2**. to pray, to chant incantations

forobun: **1**. rotation, chanting of incantations; **2**. vow

    forobun forobumbi: to make a vow

forohon cecike: a name for the hoopoe; cf. **indahūn cecike**

forombi: **1**. to spin; **2**. to turn, to turn around, to face, to turn toward

    foroho ici: the direction one is facing

foromimbi: ⟶ **foringgiyambi**

foron: **1**. swirl, curl, whirl; **2**. crown of the head, top, summit; **3**. rotation (of an arrow between the fingers)

    foron sain: the rotation of the arrow shaft is right, i.e., it is straight

foronjimbi: to turn in this direction, to turn this way

foronombi: to turn (in that direction)

forontu: curly, having curly hair

    forontu kara: a black horse with curly hair on the belly

    forontu morin: a horse with curly hair on the breast

fortohon: having a turned-up nose (said of animals)

foskiyambi: ⟶ **fosokiyambi**

fosoba: reflection, ray

fosobumbi: (causative or passive of **fosombi**, in either meaning)

fosok: (onomatopoetic) the sound of a wild beast leaping from cover

fosokiyambi: to get upset due to impatience, to fret, to become irritable

fosolhon: heat of the sun

fosombi (1): (**-ko**) to shine, to light up, to illuminate

fosombi (2): (**-ho**) to splash, to splatter

fosomikū tohon: a button for securing the hem while one is riding

fosomimbi: to tuck in the hem

foson: sunlight, sun's rays, the glow of a fire

fosonggi: ⟶ **fongsonggi**

fosonjimbi: to come shining, to shine in here

fosonombi: to go shining, to shine in there

fosopi: illuminated

fosor seme: many, in great quantity (said of wild animals)

fosorombi: (**-ko**) to shrink

fosor seme: seething (used to describe anger), foaming

    fosor seme obonggi dekdehe: produced white foam

fošor seme: foaming at the mouth (from anger)

fotor seme: **1**. bubbling (said of water), foaming, seething; **2**. furiously

    fotor seme fuyembi: to boil furiously

foyo: **1**. *ula* (*wūlā* 烏拉) sedge, carex grass: a soft grass-like plant used as padding in shoes and boots (*Carex meyeriana*); **2**. felt made from horsehair

    foyo faidambi: to divine by means of Eight Trigrams

    foyo orho: *ula* (*wūlā* 烏拉) grass, carex grass

foyodobumbi: (causative of **foyodombi**)

foyodombi: to divine

    foyodoro niyalma: diviner, fortune teller

foyodon: divination

foyonombi: to become matted (said of hair)

foyori: an exotic plum-like fruit

foyoro: plum

    foyoro moo: plum tree

    foyoro orho: ⟶ **foyo orho**

fu: **1**. an outside wall; **2**. prefecture; **3**. residence, mansion; **4**. charm, amulet; **5**. one dose (of medicine)

    fu bithe: a written charm

    fu cirgembi: to build a wall

    fu hecen: walls (around a town)

    fu i aisilara hafan: (治中) Sub-Prefect of the Metropolitan Prefecture, *BH* 793

    fu i aliha hafan: (府尹) Prefect of the Metropolitan Prefecture, *BH* 793

    fu i ilhi hafan: (府丞) Vice-Governor of Beijing, *BH* 793

    fu i saraci: (知府) Prefect, *BH* 848

fu fa seme: panting, feverish

fu gūwara: *Asio otus*: eared owl

fu nimaha: *Ctenopharyngodon idella*: white amur, grass carp

fu žin: lady, mistress

fu žung ilha: hibiscus; cf. **fusuri ilha**

fubihūn cecike: the Korean hoopoe

fubise: an exotic fruit from Tonkin

fubumbi: (causative of **fumbi**)

fucebumbi: (causative of **fucembi**)

fucembi: to get angry, to get mad

fucendumbi: to get angry (said of a group); also **fucenumbi**

fuceng: ⟶ **fu i ilhi hafan**

fucenumbi: to get angry (said of a group); also **fucendumbi**

fucihi: Buddha

    fucihi doro: the way of Buddha, Buddhism

    fucihi dzuši: Buddhist patriarch

    fucihi erhuweku: niche for a Buddha image

    fucihi huwejeku: the brightly ornamented background of a Buddha image

    fucihi i nomun: Buddhist sutra

    fucihi iktan: scriptures and valuables kept inside a Buddha image

    fucihi jombi: to pray to Buddha, to recite Buddha's name

    fucihi jondombi: to chant sutras, to invoke the Buddha

    fucihi miyoo: Buddhist temple

    fucihi nirugan: Buddhist image

    fucihi tacihiyan: Buddhist teaching, Buddhism

    fucihi ūren: Buddhist image

fucihingge: pertaining to Buddha, Buddhist

    fucihingge mahala: a liturgical hat surmounted with the images of the five Dhyāni-Buddhas (worn by monks during services)

fucihiyabumbi: (causative of **fucihiyambi**)

fucihiyalabumbi: (causative of **fucihiyalambi**)

fucihiyalambi: **1**. to burn hair off animal hide, to singe off; **2**. to straighten an arrow shaft using heat

fucihiyambi: to cough

fucihiyašambi: to heat in a flame

fucu faca: whispering

    fucu faca gisurembi: to whisper

fudambi: to vomit

fudangga: with the hair going the wrong way, bristly, unkempt

fudarambi: (-ka) **1**. to go backward, to be reversed, to be upside down; **2**. to go against, to oppose, to rebel; **3**. to go in the wrong direction (said of hair)

    fudaraka hūlha: rebel

    fudaraka niyalma: rebel, transgressor

    fudarame: conversely, on the contrary

    fudarame dosinambi: to rise (said of the tide or flood waters)

    fudarame etumbi: to wear inside out

    fudarame eyembi: to flow backward

    fudarame gisurembi: to refute, to rebut, to confute

fudarame yabumbi: to go in the wrong direction, to go backward

fudaran: opposition, rebellion

fudasi: recalcitrant, rebellious, obstinate

fudasi gūwara: a kind of owl

fudasi halai: recalcitrant and perverse

fudasihūlambi: to go mad, to lose one's mind

fudasihūn: **1**. upside down, inside out, reversed, inverted; **2**. rebellious, disloyal

fudasihūn lakiyambi: to hang upside down

fudasihūn nimeku: madness, insanity

fudebumbi: (causative of **fudembi**)

fudehun: ⟶ **fundehun**

fudejembi: to develop a flaw, to crack, to rip, to burst open, to split open

fudelebumbi: (causative of **fudelembi**)

fudelembi: to rip out a seam, to tear apart, to take apart

fudembi: **1**. to see off, to accompany; **2**. to accompany a trousseau; **3**. to give a gift on departure

fudehe jaka: dowry, trousseau

fudeme jurambumbi: to see off

fudenembi: to go to see off

fudenjimbi: to come to see off

fudešebumbi: (causative of **fudešembi**)

fudešembi: to dance in order to drive away evil spirits (to cure an illness) — specifically to dance in honor of the tiger god (**manggiyan**)

fudešere saman: a shaman who dances in honor of the tiger god

fudz: master (respectful term for teachers and elders)

fufa: (onomatopoetic) the sound of panting

fufen: **1**. one thousandth; **2**. a tenth of an inch

fufubumbi: (causative of **fufumbi**)

fufudambi: to cut

fufumbi: (-ha) to saw

fufun: a saw

fufungge: pertaining to a saw, saw-like

fufutambi: to be frustrated while doing a job, to engage in haggling, to bicker, to wrangle over trifles

fugu: ⟶ **fuhu**

fuhali: **1**. unexpectedly, surprisingly; **2**. completely, totally; **3**. seemingly, as if …

fuhašabumbi: (causative of **fuhašambi**)

fuhašambi: **1**. to do carefully, to do over and over; **2**. to examine; **3**. to exchange, to replace (old goods with new), to rotate

fuhašame gūninjambi: to reflect on carefully or intently, to turn over in the mind

fuhašame kimcembi: to study, to devote oneself to the study of

fuhašame sibkimbi: to do a careful study of

fuhen: **1**. the mold on the surface of fermenting substances; **2**. fuse made of grass or straw (used as kindling)

fuhešebumbi: (causative of **fuhešembi**)

fuhešeku orho: tumbleweed

fuhešembi: **1**. to roll, to roll over, to somersault, to tumble; **2**. to toss and turn (while sleeping); cf. **kurbušeme fuhešembi**

fuhešeme injembi: to double up with laughter

fuhešere moo: battle log (a weapon used in early times)

fuhešere wehe: a large stone rolled down from a height (used in warfare)

fuhiyembi: to get angry, to get mad

fuhu: wart

fuhu banjimbi: to develop a wart

fuhun: the appearance of anger or rage, enraged, angry

fuhun fuhun i: angrily, in a rage

fuhungge: having warts, covered with warts

fuifubumbi: (causative of **fuifumbi**)

fuifukū: kettle, pot for boiling liquids

fuifumbi: (-ha) **1**. to boil (transitive verb), to brew (tea); **2**. to boil down (as salt); **3**. to stew, to cook soft

fujin: wife of a feudal lord, wife of a **beile**, lady

fujisa: (plural of **fujin**)

fujiyang: (副將) Colonel, Regimental Commander, *BH* 752

fujulambi: ⟶ **fujurulambi**

fujun: gracious, refined

fujurakū: indecorous, unrefined, improper, inelegant

fujurakū hehe: prostitute

fujurakūngge: improper, dishonorable, indecorous, vulgar

fujuri: **1**. foundation, basis, origin; **2**. hereditary

fujuri amban: a hereditary dignitary

fujuri boo: a family in which men frequently followed official careers, a gentry family

fujuri niru: hereditary banner chief

fujurulabumbi: (causative of **fujurulambi**)

fujurulambi: **1**. to probe deeply, to get to the bottom of something, to make inquiries, to investigate; **2**. to visit, to call on

    fujurulame baicambi: to investigate

    fujurulame baimbi: to seek, to enquire

    fujurulame dacilambi: to seek news

    fujurulame fonjimbi: to make inquiries, to get to the bottom of something

    fujurulame sambi: to find out, to get to know

fujurun: prose poem, a *fù* (賦)

fujurungga: refined, elegant, graceful, sedate

    fujurungga šungkeri: elegant, refined, graceful

    fujurungga yangsangga: alluring, elegant and noble, graceful, charming

fuka: **1**. bubble, blister, pustule; **2**. circle, a circle in the Manchu writing system; **3**. enceinte in front of a city gate, bastion on a city wall; **4**. wild-animal cage

fukanambi: **1**. to bubble, to form bubbles; **2**. to form a blister

fukcihiyadambi: ⟶ **fukjihiyadambi**

fukcihiyan: ⟶ **fukjihiyan**

fukcin: ⟶ **fukjin**

fukdejembi: to reopen (a wound)

fukderembi: (-ke) **1**. to have a relapse (said of illness), to reopen (said of a wound), to flare up again (said of an illness); **2**. to bring up some matter again, to rake over past grievances

fukiyambi: to feel like throwing up; cf. **fuyakiyambi**

fukiyoo: floating bridge

fukjihiyadambi: to hurry, to be distraught, to be rushed

fukjihiyan: **1**. distraught, in a flurry, flustered; **2**. common, ordinary, despicable

fukjilambi: ⟶ **fukjišambi**

fukjin: beginning, origin, foundation

    fukjin doro: foundation, base, enterprise, undertaking

    fukjin doro be neimbi: to erect a foundation

    fukjin ilibumbi: to lay a foundation

    fukjin jise: first draft

fukjingga: original, ancient, primitive

    fukjingga hergen: (篆書) a style of calligraphy: seal characters

fukjingga hergen i kuren: (篆字館) an office in Beijing charged with developing a pseudo 'seal script' for Manchu

    fukjingga mahatun: a style of hat worn in ancient times

fukjišambi: to be restrained, to hold back, to feel constrained, to feel cramped

fuksuhu: large excrescence on a tree

    fuksuhu fiyoose: ladle made from a large tree excrescence

fuktala: *Pteridum aquilinum*: bracken fern

    fuktala sogi: edible bracken (used as a vegetable)

fulaburu: dark blue or black with a slightly reddish tinge, blue flecked with red or pink, plum-colored

    fulaburu gasha: *Cyanoptila cyanomelana*: Chinese blue and white flycatcher

fulacan: a bag for storing flint

fulahūkan: light pink, silver pink

fulahūn: **1**. pink, reddish; **2**. the fourth of the heaven's stems (丁); **3**. naked, bare, impoverished, barren, destitute

    fulahūn ba: barren ground, barren place

    fulahūn kokima: indigent, in dire need

    fulahūn susu: **1**. desolate, forsaken; **2**. ruins

    fulahūn yadambi: to be impoverished

fulahūri: deep red, fire red, crimson

    fulahūri kamtun: a deep red head scarf used during the Han dynasty

fulakcan: pouch for carrying a flint

fulan: a light-colored horse with dark mane and tail

fulana: *Prunus humilis*: bush cherry, Siberian crabapple

    fulana ilha: crabapple blossom

fularambi: (-ka) to become red, to redden, to blush

fulargan: a rust-colored swallow

fulari: of a red shade

    fulari cecike: ⟶ **fulgiyan sišargan**

    fulari ilha: an exotic red flower that blooms in autumn

fularikan: reddish, pink

fularilambi: to flash red, to lighten

fularjambi: to have a red appearance

fularšambi: ⟶ **fularjambi**

fulata: red-eyed, having red circles around the eyes

    fulata nisiha: a kind of small, red-eyed fish

fulca: an exotic sweet purple fruit (about the size of a man's finger)

fulcengge ilha: *Dianthus chinensis*: rainbow pink

fulcin: cheekbone, cheek

fulcu: an exotic fruit resembling the bird-cherry

fulcuhūn šulhe: *Pyrus betulaefolia*: birch-leafed pear

fulcun: a large exotic red fruit shaped like a man's finger

fuldun: grove, thicket, clump

> **fuldun fuldun i**: in clumps, in thickets

fuldurembi: (**-ke**) to break open (said of a wound), to split open

fulefun: for his sake (used in prayers)

fulehe: **1**. root; **2**. origin, source

> **fulehe be geterebumbi**: to root out, to eliminate totally

> **fulehe da šumin akdun**: deep rooted, engrained

> **fulehe obumbi**: to treat as the foundation, to view as the most important factor

> **fulehe suwaliyame**: together with the roots, including the roots

fulehengge: **1**. pertaining to or having roots; **2**. talented

fulehu: alms given to monks

fulehun: favor, kindness, good deed, alms

> **fulehun akū**: lacking kindness, devoid of good deeds

> **fulehun baimbi**: to beg for alms

> **fulehun i hafan**: (廕生) Honorary Licentiate, *BH* 958

> **fulehun i silgasi**: (恩貢) Senior Licentiate by Imperial Favor, *BH* 629A

> **fulehun i tacimsi**: (廕監) an Honorary Licentiate conferred upon certain joyous occasions, *BH* 959

> **fulehun isibumbi**: to bestow favor, to grant favors

fulehungge: gracious, kind

fulehusi: almsgiver, benefactor

fulenggi: ashes

> **fulenggi boco**: ash-colored

> **fulenggi niyanciha**: tender grass shoots

fulenggingge namu kuwecihe: a gray dove with black neck and red feet

fulfintu cecike: *Bombycilla japonica*: Japanese waxwing

fulgambi: ⟶ **fulhambi**

fulgidei: *Chrysolophus pictus*: golden pheasant

fulgike: *Calliope calliope*: rubythroat

fulgiyaci: short-haired summer deer pelts

fulgiyakan: light red, reddish

fulgiyan: **1**. red; **2**. the third of the heaven's stems (丙)

> **fulgiyan afaha**: voucher given for the use of a public horse, receipt for tax or toll

> **fulgiyan alan**: red birch bark that still has not dried out

> **fulgiyan caise**: a thin fried cake made from flour and honey

> **fulgiyan cibirgan**: a kind of red swallow

> **fulgiyan enggetu keru**: a kind of crow with red feet and beak

> **fulgiyan fulan**: a dark brown horse with dark mane and tail

> **fulgiyan gahangga kiru**: (赤烏旗) a banner of the Imperial Escort depicting a red crow

> **fulgiyan gasha**: a name for the wild goose; cf. **bigan i niongniyaha**

> **fulgiyan gashangga kiru**: (朱雀旗) a banner of the Imperial Escort depicting a small red bird

> **fulgiyan hafuka**: broke out with the measles

> **fulgiyan haksangga efen**: a kind of crunchy red cake

> **fulgiyan iletungge gu**: a round jade object with a hole in the center used for sacrifices at the altar of the sun

> **fulgiyan jamuri ilha**: a variety of red rose

> **fulgiyan jiyoo bing**: a kind of hard brown cake

> **fulgiyan jugūn**: equator

> **fulgiyan jugūn i hetu undu i durungga tetun**: an astronomical instrument used for observing the position of heavenly bodies in relation to the equator

> **fulgiyan jui**: baby, newborn infant

> **fulgiyan lefungge kiru**: (赤熊旗) a banner of the Imperial Escort depicting a red bear

> **fulgiyan mursa**: carrot, beet

> **fulgiyan nunggasun**: red felt

> **fulgiyan pilembi**: to endorse in red (said of the Emperor)

> **fulgiyan selbete**: the name of a wild grass

> **fulgiyan sisa**: small red beans, azuki beans

fulgiyan sišargan: *Carpodacus roseus*: Pallas's rose finch

fulgiyan suihetu coko: red-crested pheasant

fulgiyan suru: bay (color of a horse)

fulgiyan šungkeri ilha: *Bletilla chinensis*: red Chinese orchid

fulgiyan tosi: the red crest of a crane

fulgiyan tosingga fiyorhon: redcrested woodpecker

fulgiyan ujirhi: red wildcat

fulgiyan umiyesun: 'red sash' — the descendants of the six **Ningguta beile**

fulgiyan urangga moo: a tree of the *Clerodendrum* family

fulgiyan yarha: red leopard

fulgiyan yasa: trachoma

fulgiyangga: pertaining to red, red-haired

fulgiyari coko: rooster with very red feathers

fulgiyebumbi: (causative or passive of **fulgiyembi**)

fulgiyeku: **1**. blow gun, blowpipe; **2**. whistle, pipe; **3**. piper

fulgiyembi: to blow (with the mouth)

fulha: poplar, aspen

fulhambi: **1**. to produce pus, to flow (said of pus); **2**. to give vent to (one's anger or resentment); cf. **ki fulhambi**

fulheri: a round red exotic fruit

fulhumbi: to put out shoots, to sprout

fulhun: ⟶ **fulhuren**

fulhuntu: ⟶ **fulhutu**

fulhurembi: (**-ke**) to sprout, to germinate, to grow, to develop

fulhurembumbi: (causative of **fulhurembi**)

fulhuren: **1**. sprout; **2**. beginning, inception

fulhutu: a kind of ritual cap worn during the Zhou dynasty

fulhū: bag, sack

fulhūca: small sack

fulhūma: a kind of southern pheasant

fulhūsun: satchel, carrying bag

fulhūtu hūwašan: a mendicant monk

fuli: jerky, dried meat or fish

fulibumbi: to take form, to take shape

fulibume salgabumbi: to be endowed by nature

fuliburakū: does not take shape (used to describe a person grasping for words as he sobs or pants), hesitant in speech

fulimbumbi: ⟶ **fulibumbi**

fulin: **1**. form, shape; **2**. luck, lucky fate

fulingga: lucky, having good fortune

fuliyambi: **1**. to forgive, to pardon; **2**. to mend an arrow shaft

fulkūran moo: a kind of hawthorn

fulmai ilha: an exotic flower, the plant of which resembles wheat

fulmin: ⟶ **fulmiyen**

fulmiyebumbi: (causative of **fulmiyembi**)

fulmiyembi: to bind, to tie up, to tie together, to bundle together

fulmiyen: bundle, package

fulmun boihon: a bluish clay used for making molds when casting bronze

fulnaci ilha: *Pyrus halliana*, the red blossom of the Japanese cherry

fulniyeri ilha: a fragrant red exotic flower

fulsuri ilha: an exotic creeping plant with red blossoms

fulu: **1**. surplus, excess, left over, extra, additional; **2**. excelling, surpassing, better, superior; **3**. a sack-like protector for a wounded finger

fulu ba: advantage, strong point

fulu eberi: good and bad, superior and inferior

fulu elgiyen: abundant, plenteous

fulu gisun: excessive talk, gossip

fulu jeku: early grain

fulu len: a great deal larger

fulu nonggimbi: to increase

fulukan: somewhat excessive, somewhat better, a bit more

fulun: salary, emolument

fulun be kimcire tinggin: (稽俸廳) Salary Office of the Eight Banners

fulun caliyan i kunggeri: (俸糧科) Salary Section of the Board of War and the Court of Banqueting

fulun caliyan icihiyara ba: (俸餉處) Salary Office of the Board of Finance

fulun faitambi: to cut off one's salary as a punishment

fulun jembi: to receive official salary

fulungga: grand, majestic

fulungge: excessive, extra, left over

fuma: Imperial son-in-law; cf. **efu**

fumbi (1): (**-ha/-he**) to wipe, to wipe off

fumbi (2): (**-ngke, -mpi**) to become numb

fumerebumbi: (causative of **fumerembi**)

fumerembi: **1**. to mix up, to confuse, to stir together; **2**. to fight in a confused manner

fumereme afambi: to fight a fierce battle

fumereme banjimbi: to scrape by, to muddle along

fumereme kūthūmbi: to stir, to mix

fumerenumbi: to be mixed together

fun: **1**. one hundredth (of a Chinese foot); **2**. powder; **3**. fragrant odor

fun beye: an identical person or thing

fun fiyan: rouge, makeup

fun i fi: chalk (for writing)

funcebumbi: (causative of **funcembi**): to use sparingly

funcembi: to be left over, to be in excess

funceme: over, in excess

funcen: excess, left over

funcen daban: excessive, beyond limit

funcetele: to the point of excess

funde: **1**. (postposition) in place of, instead of, for; **2**. (adverb) substituting, in someone else's place

funde bošokū: Lieutenant, *BH* 727

funde orolohakū: without substitute

funde weilembi: to substitute for someone at work

fundehun: **1**. desolate, forsaken, deserted; **2**. pallid, ashen, pale

fundehun simacuka: desolate, forlorn, bleak

fundehun simeli: bleak, dreary

fundesi: animals and birds that have been released to avoid slaughter

funembi: to become numb

funfulambi: **1**. to order, to forbid; **2**. to get ready beforehand, to prepare

fung moo: **1**. maple; **2**. *Liquidambar acalycina*: sweetgum

fung šui: geomancy

fung tiyan goloi bolgobure fiyenten: (奉天清吏司) branch of the Board of Punishments in Mukden

funggaha: feather, down

funggala: tail feather, plume, feather in an official's hat

funggin: **1**. an old boar; **2**. the thick skin of a pig; **3**. the flesh of an old boar cooked with the skin — eaten in the twelfth month

funghūwang: phoenix

fungkeri hiyan: *Lysimachia foenum*: yellow loosestrife

fungkeri ilha: a kind of Chinese orchid found in marshes, marsh orchid

fungku: towel, cloth for wiping, kerchief

fungkū: log, block of wood

funglu: salary

fungnebumbi: to be enfeoffed

fungnehen: a document conferring enfeoffment, patent of nobility

fungnehen be kimcire bolgobure fiyenten: (驗封清吏司) Department of Grants, *BH* 338

fungnehen ejehe i kunggeri: (誥勅科) a section of the Board of War in charge of edicts, grants, and rescripts

fungnehen ejehe icihiyara ba: (誥勅房) a section of the Grand Secretariat in charge of edicts, grants, and rescripts

fungnehen icihiyara kungge yamun: (中書科) Imperial Patent Office, *BH* 137A

fungnembi: to enfeoff

fungsan: **1**. rank (the taste of mutton or beef); **2**. impoverished; **3**. the oil gland at the base of a bird's tail

fungsan yadahūn: destitute, impoverished

fungse: **1**. flour, meal; **2**. basin, pan

fungse orho: *Erigeron acer*: fleabane

fungšun: smelling of urine, smelly, malodorous

fungto: ⟶ **fungtoo**

fungtoo: envelope

funima: a poisonous sand fly; cf. **funjima**

funiyagan: tolerance, forbearance, magnanimity

funiyagan isheliyen: narrow-minded

funiyagan onco: broad-minded

funiyagangga: tolerant, forbearing, magnanimous

funiyaha: a parasitic worm that lives in the hair on the backs of horses and cattle

funiyahan: ⟶ **funiyagan**

funiyangga: ⟶ **funiyagangga**

funiyehe: hair, fur, nap

funiyehe dasitu: bangs worn by young boys in ancient times

funiyehe den cekemu: a kind of velvet with a thick surface

funiyehe i šošon: a lock of artificial hair worn by women over their natural hair

funiyehe sen: pore

funiyehe sindambi: to let down one's hair

funiyehe sulabumbi: to let one's hair grow long
funiyehelembi: to pull hair (while fighting)
funiyehengge: hairy, hirsute
funiyesen: ⟶ **funiyesun**
funiyesun: a kind of coarse woolen, felt
funjima: sand fly, gnat, midge
funtambi: (-**ka**) to become moldy
funtan: white mold on liquids, mold
funtanambi: to form mold
funtu: deer horn in velvet (used in medicine)
funtuhu: ⟶ **funtuhun**
funtuhulebumbi: 1. (causative or passive of
　　funtuhulembi); 2. to leave a gap, to make a
　　hole in something
funtuhulembi: 1. to make a gap, to leave a space, to
　　leave empty; 2. to be absent from one's post
funtuhun: 1. empty, barren, bleak, desolate; 2. gap,
　　opening, breach; 3. harelip; 4. quiet, still; 5.
　　pale, pallid
funtumbi: (-**ha**) 1. to brave (the rain, a storm, etc.);
　　2. to cross a river (said of livestock); 3. to
　　penetrate, to slip (into an enemy army); 4.
　　⟶ **funturambi**
funturabumbi: (causative of **funturambi**)
funturambi: to root, to dig with the snout
funturembi: ⟶ **funtumbi**
funturšambi: to root persistently
fur seme: 1. flowing slowly (said of perspiration); 2.
　　wafting, flowing gently; 3. having a smooth
　　appearance; 4. having a comfortable feeling
fur seme saikan: fresh and pretty
fur seme tucike: flowed lightly (sweat)
furanaha: dust, fine dirt, ashes
furangsi: France
furcan: a small, red-billed crane
furdan: 1. scar, wound; 2. pass, gateway; 3. eye of a
　　needle; 4. a twisted root
furdan dogon i kunggeri: (關津科) office in
　　the Board of War concerned with passes
　　and fords
furdan duka: gate at a pass
furdan i cifun: tariff, customs duty
furdan i temgetu bithei kunggeri: (關引科) a
　　section of the Board of War concerned with
　　issuing permits for passes
furdan kamni: narrow pass
furdehe: pelt, fur, fur jacket
furdehe kurume: a fur jacket

furdehe soforo: a saddle cushion made of fur
furelambi: to wipe
furfu: ape, orangutan
furfun farfan: in streams (tears)
furgi: 1. a bundle of willow branches or reeds used
　　to repair dams or dikes; 2. a stick with a tuft
　　of grass attached to the end (used in
　　shamanistic rites); 3. collar for draft
　　animals, yoke; 4. ⟶ **furgin**
furgi coko: a name for the turkey
furgi tai: dike terrace
furgibumbi: 1. (causative or passive of **furgimbi**);
　　2. to be silted up with sand
furgimbi: (-**he**/-**ha**) 1. to silt up, to pile up (said of
　　blowing sand or earth); 2. to surge (said of
　　the tide); 3. to foment: to bathe with a warm
　　medicated liquid
furgin: 1. tide; 2. hot (in taste), acrid, pungent
furgisi: a man who lays out **furgi** when the river
　　level is low
furgisu: ginger
furhūn cecike: a name for the hoopoe; cf. **indahūn**
　　cecike
furimbi: (-**ha**) 1. to dive, to swim under water, to
　　plunge; 2. to wallow
furitan: a name for the pelican; cf. **kūtan**
furitu niyehe: diving duck
furna: a bondman of the second generation
fursun: 1. shoots, sprouts (especially of a grain); 2.
　　sawdust
fursun sain: growth is good (said of domestic
　　animals)
fursun tebumbi: to set out seedlings
fursungga niyehe: a name for the wild duck
furu: 1. excrescence in wood; 2. canker, ulcer,
　　canker sore in the mouth; 3. tangled
　　branches; 4. cruel, violent
furu hatan: irascible
furu murikū: stubborn, unbending
furubumbi: (causative of **furumbi**)
furudambi: to act in a cruel or violent way
furukū: a grater
furumbi: (-**he**) to slice, to grate, to cut into fine
　　pieces
furun: meat scraped from a bone
furunambi: to develop a canker sore in the mouth
furungga hangse: finely cut noodles
furunumbi: to slice together

furusun tashari: a name for the eagle

fusa: Bodhisattva

fuse: unintentionally

> **fuse injehe**: laughed unintentionally

fusejembi: **1**. to burst (said of bubbles and boils), to explode; **2**. to break through, to develop holes; **3**. to break up (said of ice)

fuselembi: to break open, to make a hole in

fuseli: *Mylopharyngodon piceus*: the black carp whose gall is used as a medicine

fusembi: (**-ke, -ndere**) to propagate, to reproduce, to breed

fusembumbi: (causative of **fusembi**)

fusen: propagation

fusengge fulana ilha: a kind of wild red cherry blossom

fuserebumbi: (causative of **fuserembi**)

fuserembi: to trim, to edge, to put on a fur trimming

> **fuserehe mahala**: a hat with a fur-trimmed brim

fuserembumbi: ⟶ **fuserebumbi**

fuseri: *Zanthoxylum piperitum*: Szechuan pepper

> **fuseri moo**: Chinese prickly ash, Szechuan pepper

fushambi: to lose everything, to be wiped out

fushebumbi: (causative of **fushembi**)

fusheku: a fan

> **fusheku i heru**: the frame of a fan
>
> **fusheku i talgari**: a fan's covering
>
> **fusheku i temun**: the handle of a fan
>
> **fusheku i tuhebuku**: an ornament attached to the handle of a fan

fushembi: to fan

> **fushehe bongko**: cotton still in the boll, raw cotton

fushu: **1**. the top of the cooking stove; **2**. excrescence on a tree

> **fushu gurjen**: hearth cricket
>
> **fushu nahan**: a *kàng* (oven-bed) near the stove

fushubumbi: **1**. (causative of **fushumbi**); **2**. to set off (firecrackers)

fushumbi: **1**. to explode, to blow up, to blast, to go off (said of firecrackers), to crack (from overheating); **2**. to burst open (said of flower buds)

> **fushume sindambi**: to open fire, to shoot

fusi: **1**. base, ignoble, low-class, mean; **2**. contemptible person, wretch

> **fusi bahafi banjihangge**: a term of abuse

fusi bahambi: to give birth to a monstrosity as a result of ridiculing a person or thing

fusi baharahū: afraid of giving birth to a monstrosity

fusibumbi: (causative or passive of **fusimbi**)

fusihen: an erasable lacquer board used for writing

fusihūlabumbi: (causative or passive of **fusihūlambi**)

fusihūlambi: to look down upon, to despise

fusihūn: **1**. down, downward; **2**. westward; **3**. humble, low, cheap; **4**. junior, subordinate

> **fusihūn beye**: deferential form of first person pronoun
>
> **fusihūn nimeku**: venereal disease

fusihūšabumbi: (causative or passive of **fusihušambi**)

fusihūšambi: to look down upon, to despise

fusllaru: **1**. misbegotten, cretin, wretch (a term of abuse); **2**. slut, bitch

fusimbi: (**-ha**) **1**. to shave, to shave off, to cut one's hair; **2**. to trim the feathers on an arrow shaft

fusku: ⟶ **fushu**

fusu fasa: flustered, in a great rush, busy

fusubumbi: (causative of **fusumbi**)

fusuku: sprinkling can

fusumbi: (**-he**) to sprinkle (water), to spew, to spurt, to squirt, to jet; cf. **fosombi**

> **fusure tampin**: a sprinkling can

fusur seme: **1**. flaky and soft; **2**. steadily (said of a horse's gait); **3**. crackling, sputtering

> **fusur sere boihon**: loose earth

fusuri gunggulu: a parrot's crest

fusuri ilha: *Hibiscus mutabilis*: the cotton rose

fusuri niyehe: ⟶ **alhari niyehe**

fusurjembi: **1**. to crack, to become worn; **2**. to be eroded by alkali, to crack due to alkalinity

fušahū: a name for the scops owl; cf. **hūšahū**

fušarcan: a red-headed crane

fušargan: a name for the rose finch; cf. **fulgiyan sišargan**

futa: **1**. rope, cord, string; **2**. one *shéng* (繩; 180 Chinese feet)

> **futa fekucembi**: to jump rope
>
> **futa mishan**: a line for measuring the depth of water
>
> **futa tabumbi**: to tie a rope around someone
>
> **futa tatame wambi**: to kill by strangulation (a form of capital punishment)

futai kūwaran: rope factory

futahi: a first-generation bondman

futalabumbi: (causative of **futalambi**)

futalambi: to measure in *shéng* (繩); cf. **futa (2)**

    futalaha usin: extended land

fuwen: **1**. minute; **2**. one tenth of a Chinese inch; **3**. candareen

fuyakiyambi: to become nauseous, to become sickened

fuyambi: to feel like vomiting, to feel nauseated

fuyan: *Curcuma*, turmeric

fuyari niyehe: a kind of duck whose flesh has a nauseating smell — the same as **aka niyehe**

fuyebumbi: (causative of **fuyembi**)

    fuyebure tampin: a pot for boiling water

fuyembi: **1**. to come to a boil, to boil (intransitive verb); **2**. to skin (an animal)

    fuyere muke: boiling water

fuyendumbi: to skin together; also **fuyenumbi**

fuyenumbi: to skin together; also **fuyendumbi**

G ？

For words beginning with **g'**, see the section beginning on page 157.

gaba: three iron backpieces affixed to the *épaulière* on a suit of armor

gabsihiyalabumbi: (causative of **gabsihiyalambi**)

gabsihiyalambi: **1**. to be swift; **2**. to march with light baggage, to make a forced march; **3**. to form the vanguard

gabsihiyan: **1**. quick, clever, alert; **2**. light, mobile, convenient; **3**. vanguard

gabsihiyan etuku: martial attire

gabsihiyan hūsungge: valiant, intrepid

gabsihiyan i hiya: (前鋒侍衛) Imperial Guardsman of the Vanguard Division, *BH* 735

gabsihiyan i janggin: (前鋒參領) Colonel of the Vanguard Division, *BH* 735

gabsihiyan i juwan i da: (前鋒校) Sergeant of the Vanguard Division, *BH* 735

gabsihiyari: ⟶ **dersen gabsihiyari**

gabsiyan: ⟶ **gabsihiyan**

gabšambi: ⟶ **gabtašambi**

gabtabumbi: **1**. (causative of **gabtambi**); **2**. to shine (forth)

gabtakū orho: *Bidens bipinnata*: bramble bush

gabtama: nettles, brier, a kind of thorny plant

gabtambi: **1**. to shoot an arrow; **2**. to engage in unmounted archery; **3**. to shine, to radiate

gabtara niyamniyara: dismounted and mounted archery

gabtara ordo: archery pavilion

gabtara tungken: a small ball of felt used as a target

gabtan: **1**. archery; **2**. the distance an arrow can be shot

gabtanambi: to go to shoot

gabtandumbi: to shoot together; also **gabtanumbi**

gabtanjimbi: to come to shoot, to shoot in this direction

gabtanumbi: to shoot together; also **gabtandumbi**

gabtara: ⟶ **gabtambi** (subheading)

gabtašambi: to shoot a great number of arrows, to shoot repeatedly

gabula: glutton, gluttonous

gabula niyalma: glutton, gluttonous person

gabula sangga: the depression at the back of the neck

gacilabumbi: **1**. (causative or passive of **gacilambi**); **2**. to be in an awkward position, to find oneself in difficulties, to be in a predicament; **3**. to press, to squeeze

gacilambi: to put in an awkward position, to press, to deprive

gacilan: an awkward or embarrassing matter, predicament

gacuha: a toy or die made from the anklebone of a sheep or other animal

gacuha giranggi: the anklebone

gadahūn: grown tall or long, bulging (said of the eyes)

gadana: sole, only

gadana beye: all alone, on one's own

gadar seme: incessantly (said of talking)

gadarambi: (**-ka**) to become long, to grow stiff

gafa: having gnarled or twisted hands

gaga: ⟶ **gaha**

gaha: crow, raven, rook, jackdaw (general name of birds of the genus *Corvus*)

gaha cecike: *Dicrurus macrocercus*: black drongo

gaha garire beri: a kind of ancient bow

gaha hengke: *Trichosanthes cucumeroides*: snake gourd, a kind of gourd used as medicine against dysentery

gaha oton: *Momordica charantia*: bitter melon

gaha poo: puffball (a kind of mushroom)

gaha yasa: *Euryale ferox*: prickly water lily
gahacin: a name for the cormorant; cf. **suwan**
gahangga: pertaining to the crow
gahari: shirt, blouse
>**gahari uksin**: a shirt of armor, hauberk
gahū: **1**. curved toward the front, extended forward; **2**. with the mouth open, unable to speak
>**gahū fiha**: with the mouth agape
gahūmbi: to jut forward, to curve toward the front
gahūngga: jutting forward, curved toward the front
gahūri: projecting forward
gahūrilambi: to lean forward, to jut forward
gahūšambi: **1**. to stand with the mouth agape; **2**. to be so hungry that one is reduced to begging; **3**. to be unable to swallow; **4**. to remain speechless, to be unable to get the words out
>**gahūšame baimbi**: to beg with the mouth agape, to beg pitifully
gahūšatambi: (intensive form of **gahūšambi**)
gai: **1**. hey!; **2**. impediment, obstacle
>**gai mayabumbi**: to ward off some disaster through prayer
gaibumbi: **1**. (causative or passive of **gaimbi**); **2**. to be defeated, to be killed in battle
gaibušabumbi: (causative of **gaibušambi**)
gaibušambi: **1**. to be defeated due to lack of strength (at wrestling); **2**. to fear cold, to be unable to stand the cold
gaiha: ⟶ **gaimbi** (subheading)
gaihahū konggoro: a swift, dun-colored horse
gaihamsitu: wonderful, marvelous
>**gaihamsitu konggoro**: a wonderful dun-colored horse
gaihari: suddenly, sudden, all at once
gaiharilambi: **1**. to be sudden, to act suddenly, to realize something suddenly; **2**. to be stunned, to be amazed
>**gaiharilame**: suddenly
gaihasu: quick to obey
gaijambi: **1**. to take, to accept, to receive (goods); **2**. to pass (an examination); **3**. to confess; **4**. to marry (a man)
>**gaijara bithe**: receipt for receiving government goods
gaikabumbi: (causative of **gaikambi**)
gaikambi: **1**. to broadcast, to spread abroad, to praise; **2**. to be surprised, to marvel
>**gaikara gisun**: hearsay, rumor

gailambi: (**-ka**) to be possessed, to be hexed
gaimbi: (imperative: **gaisu**) **1**. to take, to take away, to take off; **2**. to marry (a woman)
>**gaiha gebui bithe**: a list of successful candidates in the examination for Metropolitan Graduate
gaindumbi: to take together, to contend; also **gainumbi**
gainumbi: to take together, to contend; also **gaindumbi**
gairalame: taking steadily
gaireleme: ⟶ **gairalame**
gaisilabumbi: **1**. (causative or passive of **gaisilambi**); **2**. to be entangled in, to be involved in, to be implicated
gaisilambi: to entangle, to catch up
gaisilan: entanglement, involvement
gaisilandumbi: to entangle one another; also **gaisilanumbi**
gaisilanumbi: to entangle one another; also **gaisilandumbi**
gaisin: ⟶ **gaisilan**
gaisu: (imperative of **gaimbi**)
gaitai: **1**. suddenly; **2**. accidently, by chance
>**gaitai andande**: suddenly
>**gaitai … gaitai …** : now … then …
>**gaitai gaitai**: all of a sudden
gajaraci: ⟶ **gajarci**
gajarci: a guide
gajarcilambi: to lead the way, to serve as a guide
gaji: ⟶ **gaju**
gajibumbi: (causative of **gajimbi**)
gajimbi: (imperative: **gaju**) to bring, to bring along
gajinjimbi: ⟶ **gajimbi**
gajiraci: ⟶ **gajarci**
gajirtai: guide
gaju: (imperative of **gajimbi**)
gajungga orho: aconite, wolfsbane, plants of the genus *Aconitum*
gakahūn: with gaping mouth, gaping (said of a crack), unable to speak, speechless, agape
gakarabumbi: (causative of **gakarambi**)
gakarambi: **1**. to crack open, to form a fissure; **2**. to become distant from one another (friends and relatives)
gakarashūn: separated, estranged
gakda: **1**. single, sole; **2**. crippled in one leg; **3**. blind in one eye

gakda bethe: lame in one leg, one-legged

gakda beye: alone, on one's own

gakda ton: odd number

gakda yasa: one-eyed, blind in one eye

gakdahūn: tall and lean

gakdahūri: a tall and skinny man

gakdun: debt, liability

gaksi: partner, companion, associate, fellow, member (of the same group)

gaksi dosimbi: to join a group

gaksi jafambi: to work as a group, to work in company, to form a group

gala: 1. hand, arm; 2. one of the sides of the encirclement in a battue; 3. arm's length, a measure equaling two Chinese feet and five inches; 4. (翼) one of the two 'wings' or divisions of the Eight Banners

gala aššambi: to take action, to set to work

gala baibumbi: to take time and energy

gala bethe aššame jabdurakū: to be caught unprepared

gala bethe hiyahalame fiyelembi: at trick riding, to ride with one's arms and legs crossed

gala bukdambi: to bend the forearm

gala dacun: quick-handed, dexterous

gala dambi: to take action, to make a move

gala endubumbi: to lose one's grip

gala fakcambi: to part company with

gala futa: a lasso for catching falcons

gala gidašambi: to wave the hand

gala isimbi: to set the hand to, to take action

gala joolambi: 1. to place one's hands in one's sleeves; 2. to join one's hands as a gesture of respect or greeting; 3. to have one's hands tied

gala monjimbi: to rub the hands from exasperation or regret

gala sidahiyambi: to turn one's sleeves back and uncover one's arms

gala unumbi: to put one's hands behind one's back

gala weile: handiwork, sewing and embroidery

galai amban: (前鋒統領) Commandant of the Vanguard Division, *BH* 735

galai amban i siden yamun: (前鋒統領衙門) Office of the Commandant of the Vanguard Division

galai bithe: manuscript

galai da: (翼長) Brigadier, *BH* 571, 737

galai falanggū: palm of the hand

galai falanggū be jorire adali: like pointing at the palm of the hand — very easy

galai falanggū i hergen: the lines on the palm of the hand

galai fileku: a small stove for warming the hands

galai huru: the back of the hand

galai ici: conveniently, easily

galai joolambi: to join the hands and bid farewell

galai mayan: arm, lower arm, wrist

galai oyo: glove

galai sujakū: an armrest

galai temgetu: signature

galai teyeku: a railing, a hand support

galai weile: ⟶ **gala weile**

galadambi: 1. to take action; cf. **gala dambi**; 2. to set the hand to, to begin work

galaktun: a protective sleeve made of mail

galambi: (-ka) to clear up (said of the weather), for the sun to come out

galamu: reel used in weaving

galangga tampin: a teapot with handles

galbi: good at hearing, possessing keen hearing

galbingga: a person with good hearing

galga: clear (said of weather)

galga gilga: clear and windless

galgan: ⟶ **galga**

galgibumbi: to be obstructed

galgirakū: no match for (at wrestling)

galgiyarakū: ⟶ **galgirakū**

gali: precocious, smart for one's age

galin cecike: a name for the oriole; cf. **gūlin cecike**

galirakū: below par, not up to standard, not comparable, inferior

galju: 1. slippery (said of ice); 2. quick and accurate (said of an archer)

galman: mosquito

galman hereku: *Sitta europaea*: Amur nuthatch

gamabumbi: (causative of **gamambi**)

gamambi: 1. to take (to another place); 2. to manage, to look after, to deal with, to execute (an order), to regulate, to dispatch; 3. to punish, to discipline

gaman: managing, method of dealing with something

gamji: greedy, covetous, avaricious, stingy

gamjidambi: to be covetous, to act in a greedy way

gamjilambi: ⟶ **gamjidambi**

ganabumbi: (causative of **ganambi**)

ganada: an arrow with a head resembling a duck's bill

ganambi: **1**. to fetch, to go to get; **2**. to gather

gancuha beye: all on one's own, alone, unaccompanied, carrying nothing with one

gancurgan: ⟶ **ganjuhan**

gang gang: (onomatopoetic) the sound of a flock of wild geese calling

gang ging: (onomatopoetic) crying loudly (said of a bird)

gang seme: (onomatopoetic) like wild geese crying

gangga: ⟶ **ganggan**

ganggada: a tall person

ganggadabumbi: (causative of **ganggadambi**)

ganggadambi: to be tall

ganggahūn: tall and skinny; cf. **gakdahūn**

ganggan: hard, tough, strong, staunch

    ganggan sijirhūn: staunch and upright

    ganggan tob: staunch and upright

ganggari: **1**. hard; **2**. the cry of the wild goose

    ganggari niongniyaha: a name for the goose

    ganggari tuhembi: to fall down hard, to fall on one's back

ganggata: tall in stature; cf. **ganggada**

ganggi: ten quadrillion

ganio: strange, odd, weird, extraordinary, inauspicious

    ganio aldungga: strange, peculiar

    ganio gisun: child's verse (usually containing some portent)

    ganio kukduri: weird, whimsical

ganiongga: odd, strange, unusual, queer, weird, uncanny

    ganiongga gasha: a kind of owl, the same as **yabulan**

    ganiongga gisun: a magic oath

    ganiongga hūšahū: ⟶ **hūšahū**

    ganiongga ibagan: monster, bogey

    ganiongga jaka: monster, uncanny thing

ganji: completely, all

ganjimbi: ⟶ **gajimbi**

ganjuhalambi: to fix on a saddle

ganjuhan: thongs for carrying gear attached to a saddle , saddle rigging

ganjurga: ⟶ **ganjuhan**

gaowa umiyaha: a kind of worm found in the stomachs of fish

gar: (onomatopoetic) a sound made when one is under pressure, the sound of shouting

    gar hūlambi: to cry out loudly

gar gar: (onomatopoetic) **1**. sound made by a small baby; **2**. sound made by cawing crows

gar gir: (onomatopoetic) the sound made by a flock of crows, the sound made by a group of people arguing

gar miyar: (onomatopoetic) the sound of many people shouting

gar seme: loudly

    gar seme jabumbi: to answer loud and clear

    gar seme surembi: to scream loudly

garbahūn: sparse, thin (said of branches in a tree)

gardambi: to hasten, to walk fast, to rush

gardari: an ax with a short handle

gardašambi: to walk vigorously, to walk swiftly, to walk in a race

gargalabumbi: (causative of **gargalambi**)

gargalambi: to be single, to be odd (said of a number)

gargan: **1**. branch, limb (of a tree or of the body); **2**. the earth's branches (地支); **3**. single, odd; **4**. branch of a river; **5**. leaf of a door; **6**. comrade, friend; **7**. brigade (of troops)

    gargan bira: river or stream branch

    gargan buhe: cartilage

    gargan eyen: tributary, affluent

    gargan inenggi: odd numbered days of a month

garganambi: **1**. to branch (said of a river); **2**. to put forth branches

gargangga: **1**. branching, having branches; **2**. fragmented, incoherent, missing the point

gargata: single, alone, odd

    gargata hergen: a single letter (of the alphabet)

gargimbi: to chirp

gargitai: at the risk of one's life

gargiyakan: rather sparse

gargiyan: sparse, skimpy (said of branches on a tree); cf. **garbahūn**

garhan: ⟶ **gargan**

garhangga: branched, having branches; cf. **gargangga**

garhata: ⟶ gargata

garhatalambi: ⟶ gargalambi

gari mari: asunder, in two, in twain, split

   gari mari seme: scattered

garici: a name for the cormorant

garilambi: to split asunder

garimbi: 1. to caw; 2. to copulate (said of dogs)

   garime gashūmbi: to swear, to vow

garimimbi: ⟶ garilambi

garin: 1. guard of a sword, pommel; 2. extra,
   supernumerary

   garin kutule: an extra or superfluous house
      slave

   garin morin: an extra horse (led by rope behind
      a rider)

garingga: lewd, bawdy, lustful, whore

   garingga hehe: lewd woman, whore

   garingga mama: mistress of a brothel

garja: ⟶ garjihūn

garjabumbi: 1. (causative of garjambi); 2. to split,
   to crush

garjambi: to split (intransitive verb), to break
   (intransitive verb)

garjashūn: 1. broken, split; 2. debilitated (said of a
   horse)

garjihūn: a large fierce dog

garlabumbi: (causative of garlambi)

garlambi: to break, to ruin, to destroy, to take apart,
   to dismember

garlan: ruin, destruction

garma: a four-pointed arrow used for shooting small
   game

garmibumbi: (causative of garmimbi)

garmimbi: to cut into small pieces, to tear into
   pieces, to break up

   garmime wambi: to execute by dismembering
      the body

garsa: 1. precocious, smart, intelligent, dexterous;
   cf. gali; 2. agile, dexterous, swift

   garsa gali: precocious, clever

   garsa jahūdai: a swift ocean-going vessel

garsakan: rather precocious, rather intelligent,
   rather dexterous

garša: a monk's habit

gartašambi: ⟶ gardašambi

garu: swan

garu turu: with combined effort

garudai: phoenix (male)

garudangga: like the phoenix

   garudangga ilha: an exotic, white,
      autumn-blooming flower with a short stem

   garudangga sejen: the carriage used by the
      Empress and Empress Dowager

   garudangga yengguhe: a brightly colored type
      of parrot

garukiyari: a kind of small green parrot

garun: long leggings used for mountain climbing

garunggū: the kalavinka: a mythical bird
   resembling a phoenix whose appearance is
   an omen of peace

   garunggū garudai fulgiyan hošonggo šun
     dalikū: a square red fan with kalavinka
     birds depicted on it

   garunggū garudangga fukjingga hergen: (鸞
     鳳書) a style of calligraphy

gasabumbi: (causative or passive of gasambi)

gasacun: resentment, discontent, complaint

gasambi: 1. to complain, to hold a grudge; 2. to
   grieve, to lament

gasan: 1. grief, woe, baneful influence; 2. carrion,
   the meat remaining after a bird of prey or
   predatory animal has killed and eaten

   gasan dulebumbi: to offer a young pig as a
      sacrifice outside the west wall of the house
      at dusk in order to drive off evil influences

gasandumbi: to hold a grudge against one another,
   to complain to one another; also gasanumbi

gasanumbi: to hold a grudge against one another, to
   complain to one another; also gasandumbi

gasha: (large) bird

   gashai songkonggo fukjingga hergen: (鳥蹟
     書) a style of calligraphy

gashan: calamity, disaster

gashangga: pertaining to large birds

   gashangga fukjingga hergen: (鳥書篆) a style
     of calligraphy

gashatu: a military standard with birds depicted on
   it

gashū: ⟶ gashūn

gashūbumbi: (causative of gashūmbi)

gashūmbi: to swear, to take an oath

   gashūha gisun: oath, pledge

   gashūme falimbi: to take a pledge, to take an
     oath

   gashūre bithe: written oath

gashūn: an oath, a pledge

gashūn i da: leader of an alliance

gashūngga: pursuant to an oath, sworn

gashūngga ahūn deo: sworn brothers

gashūre: ⟶ **gashūmbi** (subheading)

gashūtai: resolutely, even to the point of death, pledging one's life

gasihiyabumbi: **1**. (causative or passive of **gasihiyambi**); **2**. to suffer damage, to be ruined, to meet with disaster, to be ravaged; **3**. to perish, to drop dead, to perish on the road; **4**. to cause trouble for someone

gasihiyambi: **1**. to ruin, to waste; **2**. to harm, to damage, to destroy, to ravage; **3**. to humiliate; **4**. to harm someone for one's own profit; **5**. to annoy, to harass

gasihiyame efulembi: to damage

gasihiyame facuhūrambi: to disturb, to annoy, to harass

gasihiyame jobobumbi: to invade and harass

gasihiyandumbi: to ravage together; also **gasihiyanumbi**

gasihiyanumbi: to ravage together; also **gasihiyandumbi**

gašan: village, country (as opposed to the city)

gašan falan: the people of a village, community

gašan harangga: the inhabitants of a village

gašan i aha: village slave (a term of abuse)

gašan i caliyasi: village tax collector

gašan i da: village chief

gašan i saisa: the notables of a village

gašan tokso: villages and hamlets

gathūwa: a jacket made of weasel or sable fur

ge: **1**. brother-in-law: husband's elder brother; **2**. elder brother

ge ga seme: quarreling, wrangling

gebge gabga: tottering, wavering (said of a small child walking)

gebkeljembi: to glisten, to shine, to have an oily appearance, to have a satiny appearance

gebsehun: very skinny, emaciated

gebserembi: (**-ke**) to become very skinny

gebu: **1**. name, repute, fame; **2**. place in a competition; **3**. faction, sect

gebu afaha: list of names, roster

gebu akū simhun: the ring finger, the fourth finger

gebū algimbi: to become famous

gebu algin: fame, renown

gebu alibumbi: to sign up (for an examination), to register, to enter (a competition)

gebu arambi: to name, to sign one's name

gebu baha: became famous

gebu bithe: name card

gebu bumbi: to name, to bestow an honorary name on

gebu gaimbi: to gain fame, to obtain repute

gebu hala: name and surname

gebu hala i dangse: labor service roster

gebu isinaha: his name is established

gebu jergi: name and rank

gebu jergi be tucibume araha bithe: personal manifest

gebu kooli: general laws

gebu sindambi: to sign one's name

gebu tacihiyan: Confucian ethics

gebu teisu: social status

gebu tucike: became famous, famous

gebui afaha: calling card

gebukū: nameless

gebukū šumhun: the ring finger

gebulembi: to name, to call by name

gebungge: **1**. named, bearing the name … ; **2**. well-known, famous

gebungge tacihiyan: **1**. a well-known teaching; **2**. Confucian ethics

gecembi: to freeze, to frost

gecen: frost

gecen de hanggabumbi: to be obstructed by ice

gecen gecembi: there is a frost

geceri ilha: the name of an exotic flower that purportedly blooms in the depths of winter

gecetu niongniyaha: a name for the wild goose

gecuheri: brocade, satin with dragons or flowers depicted on it

gecuheri sijigiyan: a gown made of brocade

gecuhun: frost, frozen

gecuhun erin: a period cold enough to freeze water

gedacu: raw silk

gedehun: staring, gaping, unable to sleep

gedehun i šambi: to stare

gedubumbi: (causative of **gedumbi**)

gedumbi: to gnaw

gedurebumbi: (causative of **gedurembi**)

gedurembi: to graze, to munch on grass

gefehe: butterfly

gefehe ilha: pansy

geferi ilha: an exotic pink flower shaped like a butterfly

gege: **1**. elder sister, young lady (respectful term of address to young ladies); **2**. Princess

gegese: (plural of **gege**)

gehenakū: contemptible, obnoxious, ignoble

gehešembi: to nod (the head), to nod off

gehu gehulembi: to extend the neck (said of a bird while running)

gehuken: rather bright, somewhat bright

gehulembi: to nod (said of birds)

gehumbi: to bend the body forward, to bow

gehun: **1**. bright, shining, clear; **2**. wide open (said of the eyes); **3**. in vain

    gehun eldengge: glittering, translucent

    gehun gahūn: shining brightly (said of the sun)

    gehun gereke: (the sky) became very bright

    gehun gerembi: to break (said of dawn), to become light (said of the sky)

    gehun holtombi: to deceive openly, to lie blatantly

    gehun subuhūn: sober, clear-headed

    gehun šehun: brilliantly white, dazzling white

    gehun šun: daytime, bright sun

gehungge yoso: the Xuantong (宣統) reign period, 1909–11

gei seme: **1**. very thin (said of silk); **2**. light (said of mist or fog)

    gei sere talman: a light fog

geigehun: frail, delicate, feeble

geigen: **1**. a **gacuha** lying on edge; **2**. ⟶ **geihen**

geigerembi: (**-ke**) to be weakly

geihen: the shaft of the penis

geje gaja: petty, small

gejenggi: overly talkative, garrulous, irksome

geji: snare, trap (for birds)

    geji sindambi: to set a trap for birds

gejihešebumbi: (causative or passive of **gejihešembi**)

gejihešembi: to tickle under the arm

gejing gejing seme: ⟶ **gejing seme**

gejing seme: chattering, persistent, obnoxious, muttering, babbling

gejir seme: tiny, miniscule

gejun: halberd, spear

    gejun gijun i fiyenten: (戈戟司) Spear Section, *BH* 122

gejungge deji: a small amount of money taken from the winner at gambling games

gejurebumbi: (causative of **gejurembi**)

gejureku: **1**. harsh, cruel, overly demanding; **2**. embezzler, blackmailer

gejurembi: **1**. to extort, to blackmail, to exploit by usury, to embezzle; **2**. to mistreat, to act cruelly

gekde gakda: uneven, rough; ⟶ **kekde kakda**

gekdehun: skinny, skin and bones

geku: uvula

gekuhe: turtledove

gelambi: to come to, to wake up

gelebumbi: (causative or passive of **gelembi**)

gelecuke: frightful, frightening, fearful, terrible

gelecun: fright, fear

geleku: something frightful or terrifying

gelembi: to fear

gelendumbi: to fear together, to fear one another; also **gelenumbi**

gelenumbi: to fear together, to fear one another; also **gelendumbi**

gelerjebumbi: (causative of **gelerjembi**)

gelerjembi: to brim (with tears)

geleršembi: ⟶ **gelerjembi**

gelesu: timid, shrinking, careful

gelešembi: ⟶ **gelerjembi**

gelfiyeken: rather light (said of color)

gelfiyen: light, faint (said of color)

    gelfiyen fahala: rose-colored

    gelfiyen fulahūn: pink, light red

    gelfiyen sohon: pale yellow

    gelfiyen suwayan cecike: a name for the hawfinch; cf. **turi cecike**

    gelfiyen šanyan cecike: a name for the bullfinch; cf. **ūn cecike**

    gelfiyen yacin cecike: ⟶ **yacin ūn cecike**

gelgun: ⟶ **gelhun**

gelhun: timid, fainthearted

    gelhun akū: dare to … , fearlessly, boldly

    gelhun akū gisurembi: dares to speak, speaks without fear

geli: also, still, again

gelmerjembi: to shine, to glitter

gembi: **1**. to give a girl in marriage; **2**. to be married (said of a woman or girl)

gemu: **1**. all, in every case; **2**. even (adverb)

gemulembi: to make the capital

gemulehe ba: the place of Imperial residence, Imperial capital

gemun: the Imperial capital, the capital

gemun hecen: **1**. the capital city, Beijing; **2**. Urga (now Ulan Bator)

gemun hecen i dooli: (京畿道) Metropolitan Circuit, *BH* 213

gemun hecen i hafan i kunggeri: (京官科) Office of Metropolitan Officials in charge of hereditary appointments and enfeoffments

gemun i hafasai simnen: the examination given every three years for the officials of the capital

gemungge: pertaining to the capital

gemungge hecen: the capital city; cf. **gemun**

gemungge jecen: an area 500 *lǐ* around the capital

gen: the slightly protruding bone at the base of the back of the neck, the first thoracic vertebra

gen giranggi: bone at the base of the neck

gen gan akū: perplexed, muddled, mixed up

gene: ⟶ **genembi** (subheading)

gencehelebumbi: (causative or passive of **gencehelembi**)

gencehelembi: **1**. to strike with the back of a sword or like object; **2**. to land on the back (said of the **gacuha**)

gencehen: **1**. the back of an object (like a sword or mirror); **2**. heel of a shoe; **3**. the base of a wall; **4**. the edge of a field

gencehen mukšangga fukjingga hergen: (夊篆) a style of calligraphy

gencehengge: having a back or under side

gencehengge hengke: *Averrhoa carambola*: carambola

gencehešembi: to strike repeatedly with the back of a sword or like object

gencihelembi: ⟶ **gencehelembi**

genebumbi: (causative of **genembi**)

genembi: to go, to leave

gene oso: get going!

gene oso akū: Haven't you gone yet?

genereleme: stopping then going on

gengge gangga: all alone, on one's own, wandering about alone, vagrant

genggecembi: to wander from place to place, to lead the life of a vagabond

genggedembi: **1**. to walk unsteadily, to stagger; **2**. to be all alone

genggedeme banjimbi: to lead a vagabond's life

genggedeme ergen tambi: to be more dead than alive, to be half dead

genggedeme genggedeme: **1**. walking unsteadily, staggering; **2**. solitary and helpless

genggehun: bent forward, stooped

genggele coko: a name for the hoki pheasant; cf. **gunggala coko**

genggen: soft

genggen banin: a gentle, yielding personality

genggerembi: (**-ke**) to become weak and stooped

genggeri: wavering, staggering

genggeri ganggari: staggering, reeling

genggin: ⟶ **genggiyen**

genggitungga: illustrious, manifest

genggiyeken: rather clear

genggiyelebumbi: (causative of **genggiyelembi**)

genggiyelembi: to make clear, to make bright, to elucidate, to be clear about

genggiyen: **1**. bright, clear; **2**. enlightened; **3**. azurite blue

genggiyen abka: clear sky, blue sky, heaven

genggiyen abka gehun šun: in broad daylight

genggiyen biya: bright moon

genggiyen cai: green tea

genggiyen cai i boo: (清茶房) room in the palace used for the preparation of green tea

genggiyen cukūlu: night blind

genggiyen duwanse: bright blue satin

genggiyen ejen: an enlightened ruler

genggiyen i bulekušembi: to observe clearly, to judge wisely

genggiyen misun: soy sauce

genggiyen tugi: a light cloud

genggiyenakū: base, lowly, petty, unreasonable

genggiyengge: bright, illuminated, clear

genggiyesaka: rather bright, rather clear

genggiyesu: a fourth-generation house slave

genggumbi: to stand with the head inclined slightly forward, to incline forward (said of a wagon overladen in the front)

geo: **1**. a mare; **2**. female (horse, donkey, mule, etc.)

geo eihen: female donkey, jenny

geo morin: mare

geodebumbi: to seduce, to lure, to lead astray, to deceive

geodehen gasha: a poetic name for the pheasant

geoden: deceit, seduction, fraud,

> **geoden tuhebumbi**: to lead astray, to be deceived

geoge: a presumptuous or pretentious person, impudent, insolent

geogedembi: **1**. to be presumptuous, to be haughty, to be insolent; **2**. to flaunt, to show off

geohe: ⟶ **geoge**

geohedembi: ⟶ **geogedembi**

geolembi: to sneak up on (game), to hunt from concealment

geošen: *Esox reicherti*: pike

geošeri: beaver

ger: (onomatopoetic) the sound made by snarling dogs, the sound of many people talking together

ger gar: (onomatopoetic) the sound of shouting and quarreling

ger seme: incessantly (said of speaking)

> **ger seme wajirakū**: to talk incessantly, to prattle on and on

gerben garban: crawling spider-like, scraggly, walking in an irregular manner

gerci: accuser, one who brings suit, plaintiff

gercilebumbi: (causative or passive of **gercilembi**)

gercilembi: to report an offense, to inform against, to expose, to accuse, to inculpate, to denounce

> **gercileme tucibumbi**: to expose, to bring out into the open, to denounce

gereken: rather many, quite a few

gerembi: (**-ke, -ndere**) to become bright, to dawn

> **gerendere ging**: the last watch (just before dawn)

gerembumbi: **1**. (causative of **gerembi**); **2**. to await the dawn

geren: **1**. a crowd, a troupe, everyone; **2**. numerous, many, the various … ; **3**. of common origin, common, general; **4**. issue of a concubine; **5**. army

> **geren ci encu**: different from the common run, unusual

> **geren ci lakcambi**: to be preeminent

> **geren de tuwabumbi**: to expose publicly, to parade before the public

geren eme: father's concubine

geren fila: a percussion instrument consisting of ten small brass gongs

geren giltusi: (庶吉士) Bachelor, graduate of the lowest degree, *BH* 20

geren giltusi be tacibure kuren: (教習庶常館) Department of Study of the National Academy, *BH* 201

geren goloi baita be icihiyara bolgobure fiyenten: (職方清吏司) Department of Discipline, *BH* 415A

geren gubci: everyone, everybody

geren i tacin: custom, habit

geren irgen: commoners, ordinary people

geren jui: son of a concubine

geren kanggiri: a percussion instrument consisting of sixteen small metal gongs on a frame

geren leolen: public opinion

gerenembi: to become light, to dawn

gerenggele: before dawn

geretele: until dawn

gergembi: to dawn

gergen: **1**. yellowish tree cricket (*Oecanthus rufescens*); **2**. ⟶ **gerhen**

gergen gargan seme: continuously arguing and wrangling, chattering

gergen sembi: to prattle

gergiyen: ⟶ **gerhen**

gerguwengge coko: a name for the hoki pheasant; cf. **gūnggala coko**

gerhen: **1**. twilight; **2**. grain with small ears

> **gerhen mukiyeme**: at twilight

gerhin: ⟶ **gerhen**

geri: **1**. time, number of times; **2**. epidemic, pestilence, plague; **3**. dim, indistinct, unclear

> **geri fari**: **1**. indistinct, dim, unstable; **2**. worried, flustered, troubled, unsettled

> **geri farilambi**: to be worried

> **geri gari**: indistinct, unclear, dim, glimmering

> **geri garilame**: faintly, indistinctly

> **geri geri**: flashing, twinkling

> **geri gerilame**: dazzling, shining

> **geri goiha**: died in an epidemic (livestock)

> **geri nimeku**: epidemic, pestilence, plague

> **geri seme**: indistinctly

geri sukdun: pestilential vapors, unhealthy weather

gerilambi: **1**. to flash; **2**. to catch a glimpse of

gerilame gerišeme: glimmering

gerilaralambi: to flash, to flicker

gerinjembi: to move back and forth (said of the eyeballs)

gerisiku: ⟶ **gerišeku**

gerišeku: oscillating, wavering, irresolute

gerišembi: to waver, to oscillate, to twinkle

gerkušembi: to wink at, to make eyes at

gersi fersi: dawn, daybreak

gertele: ⟶ **geretele**

gerudei: the female phoenix

gerudengge: pertaining to the female phoenix

gese: **1**. (postposition) like, same; **2**. same, identical, equal

gese dendembi: to divide equally

gese sasa: matched evenly, similar, (lowering oneself) to the same level

gese tušan: same post, same official position

gesejembi: to unravel, to break from wear (said of a rope)

gesengge: the same

geser niyehe: a name for the little grebe; cf. **cunggur niyehe**

gesumbi: to come to, to regain consciousness, to wake up

gešan: **1**. lattice, lattice work; **2**. room divider, partition

gete: (plural of **ge**)

getebumbi: **1**. (causative of **getembi**); **2**. to wake up (transitive verb), to rouse from sleep

getehun: ⟶ **getuhun**

getehuri cecike: a name for the sparrow

getembi: to awaken, to become awake

geterakū: to make no progress in one's studies

geterembi: (-ke, -ndere) to be swept clean, to be washed clean, to be eliminated, to be rooted out

geterembumbi: **1**. (causative of **geterembi**); **2**. to sweep clean, to wash clean; **3**. to eliminate, to root out; **4**. to drive out (evil spirits)

geterilabumbi: (causative of **geterilambi**)

geterilambi: to beam with joy (the eyes)

getuhun: awake

getukelebumbi: (causative of **getukelembi**)

getukelembi: to make clear, to elucidate, to explain; cf. **genggiyelembi**

getuken: **1**. clear, lucid, understandable; **2**. completely recovered (from an illness)

getuken dacun: astute, shrewd

getuken šetuken: clear, lucid

getuken yargiyan: authentic, well-established

geye: *gāthā*: a Buddhist verse

geye gaya: stingy, petty

geyebumbi: (causative of **geyembi**)

geyembi: to carve, to engrave

geyeme gayame: uneven, serrated

geyen: carving, serration

gi bithe: ⟶ **geye**

gi buhū: *Muntiacus muntjac*: muntjac, barking deer

gi dzui furgi: rock-point dike

gi guwan ilha: cockscomb, celosia (a kind of flower)

gib seme: deafened (temporarily by a loud noise)

gibagan: crust, crust formed on the sides of a pot in which rice is cooked

gibaganambi: to form a crust, to become encrusted

gibalabumbi: (causative of **gibalambi**)

gibalambi: to paste on, to mount (pictures or calligraphy), to paste on wallpaper

giban: old cloth pasted together (used for making shoes)

gibanambi: to become encrusted

gicuhe: ⟶ **gicuke**

gicuke: shameful, disgraceful

gicuke manggi: shamefaced, embarrassed

gida: spear, lance

gida arga: spearmanship

gida mukšan: a long pointed wooden lance

gidabumbi: (causative or passive of **gidambi**)

gidabun: suppression, defeat

gidacan: **1**. ornament, decoration (on saddles, helmets, armor, bow-cases, belts, and rosaries); **2**. the two middle feathers in a falcon's tail

gidacun: ⟶ **gidacan**

gidaha: ⟶ **gidambi** (subheading)

gidakū: **1**. a press for metal; **2**. a decorative headband worn by Manchu women; **3**. a paper weight

gidalabumbi: (causative or passive of **gidalambi**)

gidalambi: to wield a spear, to pierce with a spear

gidambi: **1**. to press, to crush, to roll flat; **2**. to stamp (a seal); **3**. to force, to press (to do something); **4**. to quell, to crush, to defeat; **5**. to raid, to plunder; **6**. to suppress, to hold back (laughter); **7**. to close, to shut, to turn off; **8**. to hide, to deceive, to put on; **9**. to preserve (with salt, brine, honey, etc.), to pickle; **10**. to brood, to hatch; **11**. to build (granaries)

gidaha sogi: salted vegetables

gidaha weilengge niyalma: a criminal in custody

gidaha yali: salted meat, preserved meat

gidame arambi: to write in the semi-cursive script

gidame dabala: excessive, undue

gidame daldambi: to cover up, to conceal

gidame holtombi: to deceive, to conceal something

gidame omibumbi: to press someone to drink

gidame somimbi: to hide, to conceal, to secrete

gidara hergen: the semi-cursive script

gidarakū: without concealment, out in the open, frankly

gidanambi: to go to raid, to go to force

gidaname afambi: to attack

gidanjimbi: to come to raid, to come to force

gidara: ⟶ **gidambi** (subheading)

gidarakū: ⟶ **gidambi** (subheading)

gidashūn: somewhat bent forward, bent over

gidašabumbi: (causative or passive of **gidašambi**)

gidašambi: **1**. to beckon to come, to wave to; **2**. to take unfair advantage of, to wrong, to oppress, to deceive

gidašame fusihūlambi: to humiliate, to treat highhandedly

gidašame jobobumbi: to maltreat, to tyrannize

gidašara hūsun: pressure

gidu usiha: one of the stars of Ursa Minor

gidz: a clapper

gihi: deerhide, buckskin

gihi jibca: a jacket made of deer hide

gihintu lorin: a mule born from a mare

gihū šakdambi: to be stored away for too long (said of edibles)

gihūšambi: to beg

gihūšame baimbi: to beg persistently

gijan: fragments of meat left over after slicing

gijiri: rice straw used for weaving mats; cf. **jijiri**

gijun: a long three-pointed spear

gijungga gida: halberd

gikibumbi: (causative of **gikimbi**)

gikihangge: a term of abuse used toward an incompetent and greedy person

gikimbi: (**-ha**) to fill up, to fill in (a ditch)

gilacambi: to be feverish and agitated

gilahūn inenggi: cloudy day, overcast day

gilajan: **1**. bare, desiccated; **2**. an old desiccated tree without bark

gilajan hoto: a bald-headed man

gilajin: **1**. sharp and clear (said of a voice); **2**. ⟶ **gilajan**

gilbar keire: a horse with a reddish body and black tail and mane

gilembi: to advance in pairs to offer wine to a deceased person

gilerjembi: to be shameless, to know no shame

gileršembi: ⟶ **gilerjembi**

gilgabumbi: (causative of **gilgambi**)

gilgambi: to burn down to ashes, to come to the very end

gilha inenggi: a clear windless day

gilhambi: ⟶ **gilgambi**

gili: the base of an animal's horn; cf. **jili**

giljabumbi: (causative or passive of **giljambi**)

giljacuka: forgivable, pardonable, excusable

giljambi: to pardon, to forgive, to excuse

giljame gamambi: ⟶ **giljambi**

giljame gamarao: please excuse me!

giljame gūnimbi: to show sympathy to

giljame gūnireo: please forgive (me)

giljan: pardon, forgiveness

giljangga: compassionate, merciful, clement, forgiving

gilmahūn: shining, glistening

gilmari ilha: sunflower

gilmarjambi: to shine, to glow, to flash, to be brilliant

gilta gilta: shining, glowing

gilta gilti: glittering, gleaming

giltahūn: glittering, shining, clean

giltari: shining, glittering

giltari amihūn: flowers of sulphur, sublimed sulphur

giltari giltari: twinkling, glimmering

giltari nioweri: shiny, colorful, bright, resplendent

giltari sišargan: a name for the rose finch; cf. **fulgiyan sišargan**

giltarilambi: to shine, to glitter

giltarjambi: ⟶ **giltaršambi**

giltaršambi: to shine brightly, to gleam, to flash

giltasikū: silk brocade

giltukan: **1**. attractive, nice-looking, handsome; **2**. refined, elegant

giltungga: refined, talented

giltusi: (庶吉士) Bachelor (of the National Academy), *BH* 201

giluk: a good horse that can traverse a great distance in one day

gilun morin: ⟶ **giluk**

gimda: (甬) a constellation, the 1st of the lunar mansions, made up of the stars α and ζ in Scorpio

  gimda okdonggo kiru: (甬宿旗) a banner of the Imperial Escort depicting the constellation **gimda**

gimšu: the male quail

gin: **1**. scale, steelyard; **2**. catty

  gin i ilha: the scale of a steelyard

  gin i ton: number of catties

gin alha: colorful flower-patterned satin

gin ciyan gi: a variety of pheasant — probably the North China ring-necked pheasant; cf. **jihana coko**

gina: **1**. a trap for sable and squirrels, a deadfall; **2**. sheepskin decorated with gold leaf

  gina ilha: Chinese balsam, touch-me-not

gincihi: shiny due to continued long use

gincihinembi: to become shiny through wear

gincihiyan: **1**. fair, beautiful; **2**. bright, shining

  gincihiyan leke: a thin smooth cake made of honey, flour, and sesame oil

  gingcihiyan saikan: gorgeous, beautiful, resplendent

  gincihiyan šobin: flat baked wheat cakes with a smooth, shiny surface

  gincihiyan tuwabungga hoošan: a kind of slick paper used for public announcements

gincihiyari taiha: a kind of dog with long smooth hair

ginciri moo: *Cunninghamia sinensis*: China fir

gincitu moo: *Caryota ochlandra*: fishtail palm, a tall palm found in the Tonkin region

gindacan: tail feather

gindana: prison, jail

  gindana be kadalara hafan: (提牢) Inspector of Prisons, *BH* 457

  gindana be kadalara tinggin: (提牢廳) Prison Office, *BH* 457

ginderhen: a name for the crested lark; cf. **wenderhen**

ging: **1**. watch (of the night); **2**. scripture, sutra; **3**. capital (city)

  ging bithe: Buddhist scripture

  ging forimbi: to strike the watch (with a wooden clapper)

  ging forire niyalma: a night watchman

  ging forisi: watchman who strikes the night watch

  ging hecen: capital city; cf. **gemun hecen**

  ging hūlambi: to recite the scriptures

ginggacun: sadness, depression; cf. **gingkacun**

ginggambi: ⟶ **gingkambi**

gingge: clean, pure, honest, incorruptible

ginggembi: ⟶ **gingnembi**

ginggen: a catty — 0.5 kilograms

ginggin: **1**. a piece of wood attached to a dog's neck to keep him from biting; **2**. ⟶ **ginggen**

gingguhe: a name for the parrot

gingguji: respectful, chaste

  gingguji hehe: the wife of an enfeoffed official of the fourth rank

ginggulebumbi: (causative or passive of **ginggulembi**)

ginggulembi: **1**. to respect, to honor, to act respectfully; **2**. to write the standard form of the script

  gingguleme arambi: to write the standard form (*kǎishū* 楷書) of the script

  ginggulere hergen: (*kǎishū* 楷書): the standard form of the script

ginggulen: respect, attentiveness

ginggun: **1**. respect, honor, caution; **2**. respectful

  ginggun akū: without respect or honor, improper

  ginggun hoošan: a kind of thick paper made in Beijing

  ginggun ijishūn: respectful

  ginggun kundu: respect and honor

  ginggun nomhon: respectful and docile

  ginggun olhoba: prudent, cautious

  ginggun unenggi: respectful and sincere

gingkabumbi: **1**. (causative or passive of
  gingkambi); **2**. to be stifled, to suffocate, to
  be unable to breathe

gingkacuka: sad, depressing, depressed

gingkacun: sadness, depression

gingkambi: to feel stifled, to hold something inside,
  to bottle up one's feelings, to remain silent

gingli: (經歷) registrar, proctor

  gingli jergi hafan: official advisor

gingnebumbi: (causative of **gingnembi**)

gingnehen: picul (120 catties)

gingnembi: **1**. to weigh on a steelyard; **2**. to offer a
  cup with both hands at a sacrifice or
  shamanistic rite

gingsimbi: (-ha) **1**. to mumble; **2**. to growl while
  sleeping (said of a dog); **3**. to recite in a
  singsong fashion

ginji: golden pheasant; cf. **junggiri coko**

ginjule burga: *Salix alba*: white willow

gintala: *Oenanthe stolonifera*: Chinese tubular
  celery

gintehe: ⟶ **ayan gintehe**, **indahūn gintehe**

gintoho: a unit of weight equivalent to twenty-four
  Chinese ounces

gintu: a wooden frame for holding straw in place (in
  a yurt)

gio: **1**. roe deer (*Capreolus capreolus*); **2**. uncle:
  mother's brother

  gio holhon: *Atractylis ovata*

  gio ura: *Agaricus quercus*: a kind of mushroom

giocan: military exercise yard, parade ground

giodohon: quick, alert, lively, sprightly

giogin: the palm of the hand

  giogin arambi: to place the palms of the hands
  together (for prayer)

giogiohon: ⟶ **giyogiyan**

  giogiohon bethe: bound foot

giogiyan: well formed, fine, delicate

  giogiyan efen: small stuffed dumplings (usually
  boiled)

giogiyangga kiyoo: an open Imperial sedan chair
  carried by sixteen people

giohambi: to beg (for alms)

giohombi: ⟶ **giohambi**

giohošombi: to beg persistently

giohoto: beggar

gioi dz: tangerine

gioi ilha: chrysanthemum; cf. **bojiri ilha**

gioi ši: **1**. a recluse, a retired scholar; **2**. lay Buddhist

gioi žin: (舉人) Provincial Graduate, *BH* 629B

gioingge jahūdai: a warship with a flat keel

gioise: tangerine; cf. **jofohori**

giolu: skull

giose: **1**. pongee (silk); **2**. ⟶ **giyose**

gioošeri: ⟶ **geošeri**

giowan: **1**. copper; **2**. section of an old-style Chinese
  book (*juàn*)

  giowan gasha: cuckoo

giowandz: examination paper

giowanse: **1**. coarsely woven raw silk (used for
  painting); **2**. a scroll

giran: corpse, dead body

  giran be tuwambi: to examine a corpse

  giran benembi: to take part in a funeral
  procession, to attend a funeral

  giran icihiyara mcnggun: burial expenses

  giran jafambi: to cremate a corpse

  giran jafara ba: crematorium

  giran sindara ba: graveyard, burial place

  giran tucibumbi: to escort a body to the
  cemetery

  giran tuwara niyalma: coroner

giranggi: **1**. bone; **2**. blood relative

  giranggi acan: bone joint

  giranggi jalan: joint

  giranggi pai: domino

  giranggi sasukū: ⟶ **giranggi pai**

  giranggi yali: relatives, relations

giranggilambi: to be wounded to the bone

giratu: big-boned (said of livestock)

giratungga: big-boned, stocky

girdan: **1**. cloth or strips of pelts cut with scissors;
  2. evenly cut slices of meat; **3**. pennant; **4**.
  border trim on a banner; **5**. streamer on a
  shaman's hat

  girdan kiltan i fiyenten: (旛幢司) Flags and
  Signals Section, *BH* 120

girdangga: outfitted with strips of pelt or cloth

girdu cecike: ⟶ **derdu cecike**

girha: (箕) a constellation, the 7th of the lunar
  mansions, made up of four stars (θ, η, γ, δ)
  in Sagittarius

  girha tokdonggo kiru: (箕宿旗) a banner
  depicting the constellation **girha**

giri cecike: a name for the myna

giribumbi: (causative of **girimbi**)

girikū: a small knife for trimming skin, paper, or cloth

girilambi: to cut into long strips

girimbi: (**-ha**) to trim with a knife or scissors, to cut evenly, to cut a strip

girin: **1**. strip; **2**. section, area, region

    girin efulembi: to break river ice in autumn to catch fish

    girin i boo: house facing the street, house overlooking a street

girinjambi: to exert oneself

girkūmbi: to act intently, to act with a single purpose, to concentrate

giru: **1**. appearance, aspect, form; **2**. a wooden bow before it is laminated with horn

    giru sacimbi: to cut out the wooden shaft of a bow

    giru sain: good looking

girubumbi: **1**. (causative or passive of **girumbi**); **2**. to shame, to bring shame to, to be disgraced

girucuke: shameful, disgraceful

girucun: shame, disgrace, disgraced

girudai: the phoenix of the south

girumbi: (**-ha**) to be ashamed, to feel ashamed, to be embarrassed, to be shy

girungga: handsome, having a nice appearance

girutu: having a sense of shame, a person who has a sense of shame

    girutu akū: shameless

gisabumbi: **1**. (causative of **gisambi**); **2**. to wipe out, to annihilate

    gisabume wambi: to annihilate

gisambi: (**-ka**) to be wiped out, to perish utterly

gisan: **1**. perishing, annihilation; **2**. hair that falls out

    gisan halambi: to have the hair fall out and be replaced by new

gise: prostitute, whore

    gise hehe: whore, prostitute

    gise hehe i falan: house of prostitution, brothel

gishe: vine of a cucurbitaceous plant; cf. **jushe**

gisiha: hazelnut tree; cf. **jisiha**

gista: **1**. end of a tendon; **2**. devious, cunning

gisucembi: ⟶ **gisurecembi**

gisuhe: ⟶ **gishe**

gisun: **1**. speech, word, language; **2**. drumstick

    gisun aifumbi: to break one's word

    gisun akdun: true to one's word

gisun anaburakū: obstinate, unyielding in speech

gisun banjinarakū: not to have the words (to express one's anger or indignation)

gisun be gaijara temgetun: (納言旌) one of the pennants of the Imperial Escort

gisun be gaimbi: to obey

gisun bederebumbi: to take back a reply, to announce the completion of a mission

gisun bumbi: to give one's word, to assent

gisun dahambi: to obey, to keep one's word, to redeem a promise

gisun fuliburakū: cannot get the words out, remains speechless

gisun fulu: talkative, gossipy

gisun fulu niyalma: busybody, a gossip

gisun gaimbi: to obey

gisun goicuka: what was said is to the point

gisun hese: speech

gisun i fesin: an object of talk (criticism or gossip), a pretext for gossip, a subject for ridicule

gisun lakcan: phrase

gisun mudan: **1**. language, speech; **2**. tone (of one's speech), manner of speaking

gisun ulambi: to pass on a message

gisun yabun: words and deeds

gisurebumbi: (causative of **gisurembi**)

gisurecembi: to talk together, to discuss

gisurembi: to speak, to talk

    gisurehei ayambumbi: to persuade, to move with words

    gisurere hafan: (給事中) Junior Metropolitan Censor, *BH* 210

gisurembumbi: ⟶ **gisurebumbi**

gisuren: talk, discussion

gisurendumbi: to talk to one another; also **gisurenumbi**

gisurenembi: to go to talk

gisurenjimbi: to come to talk

gisurenumbi: to talk to one another; also **gisurendumbi**

gita loodan: very small

gitala: ⟶ **gintala**

gitarilambi: ⟶ **giltarilambi**

gituhan: a zither-like instrument with twelve strings

gitukū: name of the bamboo partridge in southwest China

giya: ⟶ **giyai**

giya siyan leke: a steamed cake with a sugar and jujube filling

giya ša etuku: a monk's habit

giya še dzun: Kāśyapa Buddha; cf. **g'asib**

giyab: (onomatopoetic) the sound made by the Pekingese dog

giyabalabumbi: (causative of **giyabalambi**)

giyabalambi: **1**. to press, to hold between two objects; **2**. to punish by applying a press to the feet

giyaban: **1**. a foot-press used for punishing criminals, pressing sticks; **2**. board, plank

   giyaban gidambi: to apply the pressing sticks

   giyaban gūlha: boots made from the thigh skin of horses, mules, or donkeys

giyabsahūn: emaciated, thin and weak

giyabsarambi: (**-ka**) to be emaciated, to become skinny

giyabumbi: (causative of **giyambi**)

giyaduraka: chaotic, in every direction

giyaha: fallen leaves, dried leaves

   giyaha sihambi: leaves fall

giyahalcambi: to move agilely (said of horses)

giyahanjambi: to be criss-crossed, to interlock; cf. **hiyahanjambi**

giyahūha cecike: a name for the wren; cf. **jirha cecike**

giyahūn: accipitrine birds: hawks, falcons, etc.

   giyahūn baksi: falconer

   giyahūn cecike: shrike; cf. **mergen cecike**

   giyahūn i ošoho: a hawk's claws

   giyahūn maktambi: to launch a falcon

   giyahūn ujire ba: a place where falcons are kept

   giyahūn yasa: a moss-like plant (*Lycopodium clavata*), club moss

giyai: street

   giyai girin: the street front, facing the street

giyai yuwan: (解元) number one in the provincial examination

giyajalambi: to serve as an attendant

giyajan: **1**. attendant of a **beile**, **beise**, or Prince; **2**. large shears

giyaji: fragile, attractive but not sturdy

giyajilambi: ⟶ **giyajalambi**

giyakda: a small curved knife

giyakdalambi: to cut with a small curved knife

giyakta: fallen leaves; cf. **giyaha**

giyaktu cecike: brown bush warbler; cf. **enggetu cecike**

giyalabumbi: (causative of **giyalambi**)

giyalabun: interval, space, pause

giyalaganjambi: ⟶ **giyalganjambi**

giyalahabumbi: ⟶ **giyalgabumbi**

giyalakū: **1**. separation, compartment, section; **2**. divider, separator, partition; **3**. interval, space

giyalamaha: headband, diadem

giyalambi: to make a space or pause between, to separate, to be separated (by an interval), to be intermittent, to be in between

giyalamtun: in the Zhou dynasty, the name of a small table on which flesh was offered

giyalan: **1**. space between, interval, interstice; **2**. measure word for rooms and houses; **3**. room or cabin on a boat

   giyalan lakcan akū: without interruption

giyalanambi: to form a divider, to form an interval

giyalgabumbi: (causative of **giyalgambi**)

giyalgambi: to neglect to give something its due, to omit, to delete

   giyalgame marimbi: to return with empty hands

giyalganjambi: to do by turns

giyalhūha: dry wood split up for burning

giyalin gaha: jackdaw

giyaltu: *Trichiurus lepturus*: largehead hairtail, a kind of sea fish

giyalu: crack, fissure, defect

   giyalu baimbi: to look for defects

   giyalu giyapi: defect

giyalunambi: to crack, to develop a defect

giyambi: to pare, to whittle, to split

   giyara moo: split firewood

giyamulabumbi: (causative of **giyamulambi**)

giyamulambi: to go by the relay-post system

giyamun: **1**. relay station, relay post, military post station; **2**. post horse, relay horse

   giyamun be kadalara hafan: (驛站官) official in charge of a post station

   giyamun be kadalara yamun: (驛站監督衙門) Office of an Inspector of Military Post Stations, *BH* 754

   giyamun dedun: post-house, relay station

giyamun i caliyan bodoro kunggeri: (驛傳科) Military Posts Section, *BH* 425

giyamun i falgangga: (館所) a Board of War office in charge of matters relating to post stations

giyamun i haha: manservant at a post station

giyamun i hūsun: post-station worker

giyamun i morin: post horse

giyamun tebumbi: to establish a string of relay posts

giyamusi: (驛丞) Inspector of a Post Station, *BH* 754

giyan: **1**. reason, right, principle, order; **2**. reasonable, right, in order, proper; **3**. measure word for rooms and buildings; cf. **giyalan**

giyan be jorikū: (中允) an official in the Supervisorate of Imperial Instruction just under the **erdemu be neileku**

giyan be murimbi: to be unfair

giyan de acanambi: to be reasonable

giyan de acanarakū: unreasonable

giyan fiyan: reasonable, orderly

giyan fiyan i: methodically, systematically, in an orderly way, reasonably

giyan giyan i: in proper order, in an orderly and reasonable manner, in detail

giyan i: on principle, by right

giyan šeng: (監生) collegian of the Imperial Academy of Learning

giyanakū: **1**. (usually used preceding **udu**) How much (or how many) could there be?; **2**. few, a certain number of

giyanakū šolo bio: could there still be time?

giyanakū udu: how much could there be?

giyanceo: raw silk

giyancihiyan hoošan: a kind of thin shiny paper

giyandu: (監督) inspector

giyang: **1**. river, especially the Yangtze; **2**. ginger; **3**. (onomatopoetic) the sound of a dog barking

giyangdu: **1**. *Virga sinensis*: cowpeas; **2**. a pastry made of cowpeas

giyangga: reasonable, moral

giyanggiyan: reasonable

giyangguhe: a name for the myna

giyangka beri: a gripless bow made from the horns of the water buffalo

giyangkū: a shirker

giyangkūšambi: always to be shirking one's duty or work

giyangnabumbi: (causative of **giyangnambi**)

giyangnakū: **1**. one who insists that he is always right, an arguer, one who talks back; **2**. reluctant to admit mistakes

giyangnakūšambi: always to be insisting on one's own views, to talk back

giyangnambi: to explain, to comment on

giyangnan: Jiangnan 江南, the area south of the Yangtze River

giyangnan goloi bolgobure fiyenten: (江南清吏司) a section of the Board of Finance concerned with Jiangnan

giyangnan goloi falga: (江南甲) Office of the Board of Civil Appointments concerned with Jiangnan

giyangnandumbi: to explain (said of a group); also **giyangnanumbi**

giyangnanumbi: to explain (said of a group); also **giyangnandumbi**

giyangsimbi: to yelp (said of dogs that are tied up and want to escape)

giyansi: spy, enemy agent

giyantu: a whip-like weapon with a four-cornered iron tip

giyapi: peeled, having a raised crust

giyapi šobin: a kind of baked cake with a raised crust

giyapinambi: to rise in layers, to be layered

giyar gir: (onomatopoetic) the sound made by monkeys and birds

giyar giyar: (onomatopoetic) the same as **giyar gir**

giyargiyan seme: scolding constantly

giyaribumbi: (causative of **giyarimbi**)

giyarici: patrolman, policeman

giyarimbi: **1**. to patrol, to make a tour of inspection; **2**. to go away from home to fast; **3**. to split

giyarime dasara amban: (巡撫) Governor, *BH* 821

giyarime kederembi: to make a tour of inspection

giyarime kederere hafan: (巡視官) guard officer

giyarire jahūdai: patrol boat

giyarimsi: **1**. (巡檢) Sub-District Magistrate, *BH* 857; **2**. patrolman, policeman

giyarinambi: to go to patrol, to go to inspect

giyarinjimbi: to come to patrol, to come to inspect

giyase: **1**. stand, frame; **2**. border; cf. **jase**

giyaselambi: to prop up, to erect

giyatarabumbi: (causative or passive of **giyatarambi**)

giyatarambi: **1**. to embezzle (bit by bit), to extort; **2**. to chip away at, to erode

   giyatarame singgebumbi: to embezzle, to misappropriate

giyebumbi: (causative of **giyembi**)

giyei tiyei: announcement

giyei ucuri: kalpa; cf. **g'alab**

giyembi: to carve, to incise

giyen: indigo

   giyen gasha: *Cyanoptila cyanomelana*: Chinese blue and white flycatcher

   giyen lamun: indigo blue

giyengge: ⟩ **cunggur niychc**

giyengge cecike: ⟶ **jirha cecike**

giyo: ⟶ **gio**

giyob seme: (onomatopoetic) the sound of an arrow flying close by

giyogiyan: ⟶ **giogiyan**

giyoholombi: to rage, to rave

giyohombi: ⟶ **giohombi**

giyok seme: with a bang, with a crash

giyolo: the crown of the head

   giyolo i šurden: the swirling of a sword above the head while dancing

giyomo: (角) the third note in the classical pentatonic scale

giyong seme: (onomatopoetic) the sound made by the wings of a phoenix in flight

giyoo: flood dragon

   giyoo muduri: ⟶ **giyoo**

giyoocan: a practice field for archery

giyoose: ⟶ **giyose**

giyoosi: teacher, instructor

giyor seme: (onomatopoetic) the sound made by the belly growling when one is hungry, borborygmus

giyorobumbi: to be beaten into unconsciousness

giyorombi: (-ko) to lapse into unconsciousness (from a beating)

giyos seme: with a bang

giyose: a kind of meat pastry, a meat-filled dumpling

   giyose efen: ⟶ **giyose**

giyowan: ⟶ **giowan**

giyūn: a measure of weight equivalent to thirty catties

go: a golden neck ornament worn by married women at court ceremonies

gobi: desert, wasteland

gobimbi: to hew, to chop

gobolobumbi: (causative of **gobolombi**)

gobolombi: **1**. to leave out deliberately, intentionally to divide unfairly, to distribute unfairly; **2**. to alight on a tree (said of pheasants)

goci moo: *Sophora japonica*: the Chinese scholar tree

goci tata: restless, unsettled

gocibumbi: (causative of **gocimbi**)

gocihiyašambi: ⟶ **gūwacihiyašambi**

gocika: pertaining to the Imperial bodyguard

   gocika amban: (御前大臣) Adjutant General, *BH* 101

   gocika bayara: (親軍) Imperial Bodyguard, *BH* 98, 100

   gocika bayarai juwan i da: (親軍校) Lieutenant of the Imperial Bodyguard, *BH* 100

   gocika hiya: (御前侍衛) Guard of the Antechamber, *BH* 99

gocikangga: pertaining to the Imperial Bodyguard

   gocikangga mukšan: a mace carried by the Imperial Bodyguard

gocikū: **1**. an apron or shirt of armor; **2**. leggings

gocima: drawer

   gocima dere: a table with drawers, a chest of drawers

gocimbi: (-ka) **1**. to draw, to pull; **2**. to play a stringed instrument; **3**. to withdraw (troops); **4**. to extract, to press out (oil); **5**. to fall, to recede (said of water), to draw back; **6**. to become skinny (said of a horse); **7**. to appear, to come out (said of a rainbow); **8**. to sew with long stitches; **9**. to suck in, to smoke (tobacco)

   gocime bederembi: to retire, to resign from a post

gocimbumbi: **1**. (causative of **gocimbi**); **2**. to suffer cramps; **3**. to freeze solid

   gocimbure nimeku: cramps

gocime: ⟶ **gocimbi** (subheading)

gocingga buren: a long horn made from wood, a woodwind instrument

gocingga mudan: the entering tone of Chinese

gocishūdambi: to be modest, to act modestly

gocishūn: modest, humble

gocišambi: to shrink back, to draw back

godohon: erect, tall and straight

   godohon ilibumbi: to set up straight

godombi: to leap high out of the water (said of fish)

godomimbi: to mumble to oneself

godondumbi: to leap high out of the water (said of many fish); also **godonumbi**

godonumbi: to leap high out of the water (said of many fish); also **godondumbi**

godor seme: mumbling, chattering

godori: leaping up suddenly, all at once

godorilambi: to leap up, to spring up

gofoho: a snare for catching small birds in trees

gofoholombi: to be intertwined, to be entangled

gofoloko: a wooden lantern holder placed on a rafter

goho: 1. elegant, dainty, adorned; 2. fop, dandy; 3. fond of showing off

   goho goiman: frivolous, flighty

gohodombi: 1. to adorn oneself, to make up; 2. to show off, to put on an act, to be ostentatious

goholobumbi: (causative of **goholombi**)

goholombi: to hook, to put on a hook

gohon: a hook

   gohon i jiha sele: three iron rings on the leather strap of a quiver

gohonggo: having a hook, provided with hooks, hook-shaped

   gohonggo sujahan: a hook for holding a window or a plaque

   gohonggo wase: a hook-shaped tile at the corners of a roof

gohorombi: (-ko) to bend (intransitive verb), to form the shape of a hook, to curl (intransitive verb)

gohošombi: 1. to hook in; 2. to take amiss, to get entangled in an argument

gohoto: a wooden cylinder used for rolling or pounding grain

gohū: ⟶ **goho**

goibumbi: (causative or passive of **goimbi**)

goicuka: 1. hindering, in the way; 2. to the point, appropriate, apt, suitable; 3. attention drawing, out of the ordinary

   goicuka akū: unhindered, without obstacle

   goicuka ba: hindrance, obstacle

goidabumbi: (causative of **goidambi**)

goidambi: 1. to last for a long time, to endure; 2. to be late, to delay, to take a long time

   goidahakū: before long, in a short while

   goidame elgiyen calu: a granary located in Shandong

goidašambi: to pound

goihorombi: (-ko) to be dispirited, to be dejected, to be in low spirits, to be lacking in courage

goihošambi: ⟶ **giohošombi**

goiman: charming, enticing, elegant, romantic

goimangga: possessing enticements or charm, alluring

goimarambi: to adorn oneself, to make oneself attractive, to entice with one's charms, to play the coquette

goimbi: (-ha) 1. to take a hit, to be struck (e.g., by an arrow or bullet); 2. to be affected by, to suffer from

goisu: (imperative of **goimbi**)

goito: a calk placed on the bottom of snowshoes to prevent slipping

goitobumbi: to do in vain

goji: a person with a crooked finger

gojime: (a word used to connect two clauses with a somewhat contrary meaning: **baturu gojime bodohon akū** 'brave but without strategy'; **gojime** can generally be translated 'but' or 'however'; in other contexts 'only, although, even if' may be more appropriate)

gojingga: ⟶ **gojinggi**

gojinggi: fast-talking

gojong seme: fast and unclear (said of speech)

gojonggi: fast-talking, a fast talker

gojor seme: chattering, talking endlessly

gokci: the handle of a plow

gokji: a molting bird

gokjibumbi: (causative of **gokjimbi**)

gokjimbi: to knot up, to plait, to plait with silk thread, to wrap and sew colored thread around a pouch or belt

goko: (onomatopoetic) the sound of chickens cackling

goksi: ceremonial court dress lacking flared shoulder pieces

golafungga moo: yew tree

golambi: to shoot off an arrow with a flourish of the hand

golbon: a clothes rack

golcehen coko: a long-tailed chicken

golderen: a long table used for transacting official business

golin: copper, bronze (Sibe)

golmikan: rather long

golmin: long

>**golmin asari de tugi fisin i mudan**: music played in the Hanlin Academy during banquets

>**golmin foholon**: length

>**golmin fungku**: a long towel or wiping cloth

>**golmin hecen**: the Great Wall

>**golmin jan**: a kind of long whistling arrow

>**golmin temgetu**: a small, long, official seal used by petty provincial officials

>**golmin uncehengge šanyan baibula**: the paradise flycatcher; cf. **baibula**

golmishūn: rather long, longish

golo: **1**. river bed; **2**. province, district; **3**. saddlebow

>**goloi amban**: (外省大臣) provincial officials of high rank

>**goloi beise**: feudal Prince

>**goloi hafan**: (外省官員) provincial official

>**goloi hecen**: provincial capital

golobumbi: (causative of **golombi**)

golocun: fright, fear

golohon: fright

>**golohon gaimbi**: to douse a frightened child with water

golohonjombi: **1**. to be exceedingly frightened; **2**. to wake up trembling from fright (said of children)

goloi: ⟶ **golo** (subheading)

golombi: **1**. to be startled, to be scared; **2**. to be sprained, to be twisted

golon tuwa: a fire that starts on a cloudy night and causes birds to land, a fire kindled on a dark night

golondumbi: to be startled (said of a group); also **golonumbi**

golongge: ⟶ **golonggo**

golonggo: pertaining to a province or district

golonjombi: to fear continually

golonombi: to freeze along the banks of a river

golonumbi: to be startled (said of a group); also **golondumbi**

golorombi: to go to another province

golotome simnembi: to take the examination for the degree of provincial graduate

golton: the charred remains of a tree after it has been burned

gombi: (**-ha**) to go back on one's word, to break a promise, to renege

gon gan: (onomatopoetic) the cry of a goose or swan

gondoba: ⟶ **hondoba**

gonggibumbi: (causative of **gonggimbi**)

gonggimbi: to send (someone) to get

gonggohon: listless, restless, bored, a listless person

gonggohori: listless, bored, idle

>**gonggohori ilimbi**: to stand about idly, to loiter

gonggon: standing upright (said of the **gacuha**)

gonggori: with a start

>**gonggori ilimbi**: to stand up suddenly with a start

gonjambi: **1**. to take a turn for the worse; **2**. to regret what one has promised

gorbi moo: sandalwood tree

gorgi: clasp on the girth (saddle belly-strap) of a horse

gorgin: flame; cf. **gūrgin**

gorgin moo: *Phellodendron amurense*: Amur cork tree; see also **gūrgin moo**

goro: **1**. far, distant; **2**. a tree of the *Sophora* family

>**goro aigan gabtara kacilan**: an arrow used for long range target shooting

>**goro mafa**: maternal grandfather

>**goro mama**: maternal grandmother

>**goro omolo**: daughter's child

>**goro yasai buleku**: telescope

goroki: distant, distant place

>**goroki be bilure bolgobure fiyenten**: (柔遠清吏司) Department for Receiving Princes of Outer Mongolia, *BH* 495

gorokin: a southern barbarian

gorokingge: a person from a distant place, a distant place

>**gorokingge be tohorombure bolgobure fiyenten**: (徠遠清吏司) Department of Eastern Turkestan, *BH* 495

gorokon: rather far

goromilambi: ⟶ **goromimbi**

goromimbi: to do from afar, to go a long distance

goromime bodombi: to plan from afar, to take a long-range view

goromime gūnimbi: to think of from afar, to take one's time in deliberation, to plan far ahead

goromime yabumbi: to go a long distance

gosibumbi: (causative or passive of **gosimbi**)

gosicuka: **1**. pitiful; **2**. lovable

gosicuka kenehunjecuke: pitiful and suspicious

gosicungga: merciful, compassionate

gosihabi: ⟶ **gosimbi** (subheading)

gosiholombi: **1**. to be bitter; **2**. to act in a miserable or distressed manner, to be miserable or distressed

gosihon: **1**. bitter; **2**. miserable, suffering

gosihon duha: the small intestine of a sheep

gosihon suingga: misery, suffering

gosihori: a large bitter exotic fruit

gosihūn: ⟶ **gosihon**

gosimbi: **1**. to pity, to have mercy; **2**. to love, to cherish; **3**. to be painful (said of a skin abrasion); **4**. to appear sporadically (said of pocks)

gosihabi: few pocks have appeared

gosin: pity, mercy, love

gosindumbi: to love one another

gosingga: loving, compassionate, cherished, beloved

gosingga gucu: a cherished friend

gositambi: to like, to love

goslambi: to release the hand upward after shooting an arrow

gotor seme: fast and unclear (said of speech); cf. **gojong seme**

gu: **1**. father's sister; **2**. jade, jadeite, nephrite

gu dengjan ilha: a fragrant red exotic flower that blooms at night

gu dzung: a kind of thin woolen

gu fileku ilha: an exotic white flower that resembles a hand warmer

gu fiyahan: gems and tortoise shell, jewels and precious stones

gu honggo ilha: a white, bell-shaped, exotic flower

gu i ciktengge fukjingga hergen: (玉筋篆) a style of calligraphy

gu i cincilan: a jade tube used in antiquity for observing the heavens

gu i deyen tugi jeksengge mudan: music played while wine was offered during great banquets in the palace

gu i yamun de yebken urse be isabure mudan: music played while food was served during a banquet at the Hanlin Academy

gu lujen: the name of one of the Imperial chariots

gu niyanjan: the name of one of the Imperial coaches

gu orho: *Hyoscyamus agrestia*: a kind of henbane found in Vietnam and Guangdong

gu sifikū ilha: *Hosta glauca*: short-cluster plantain lily

gu suje i hithen: a ritual vessel for holding jade and silk at sacrifices

gu wehe: unrefined jade, raw jade

gubci: universal, all, entire

gubci abkai muheliyen durungga tetun: a global map of the heavens at the Beijing observatory

gubci elgiyengge: the Xianfeng (咸豐) reign period, 1851–61

gubcingge: universal, whole

gubirnator: governor (Russian)

gubsu: bud (of a flower), measure word for flowers

gubulembi: to grow entangled, to be intertwined, to become overgrown, to grow in thick clumps

guceng: jewels worn at the girdle

gucihi: term of address used between the two wives of one man, rival (female)

gucihiyereku: **1**. jealous; **2**. rival, a person who is jealous of another

gucihiyerembi: to be jealous, to be a rival

gucihiyerendumbi: to be jealous of one another; also **gucihiyerenumbi**

gucihiyerenumbi: to be jealous of one another; also **gucihiyerendumbi**

gucu: friend, comrade, companion

gucu arambi: to treat as a friend, to become friends

gucu arame: together, in a group

gucu duwali: a group of friends, a clique

gucu falimbi: to make friends

gucu gargan: friends and acquaintances, friends

gucu giyajan: (王府隨侍) attendant in the palace of a Prince

guculembi: to make friends, to be friends with

gucung seme: ⟶ **gojong seme**

gucuse: (plural of **gucu**)

gudešembi: to strike repeatedly with the fist

gudz: **1**. the frame of a fan; **2**. Buddhist nun

gufan: a precious stone from the state of Lu

gufu: husband of father's sister

gufute: (plural of **gufu**)

gugio: black jade

gugioi: a jade girdle ornament

gugu gugu: **1**. sound used to call chickens; **2**. the sound made by the turtledove

gugui: ⟶ **gugioi**

gugun gasha: a bird of Fujian having a gray head, green wings, blue tail, and red and black feet — possibly a cuckoo

gugur seme: stooped, bent over

gugurecembi: to bow together

gugurembi: (**-ke**) to stoop, to be bent over with old age, to shrink up with cold

guguršembi: to bow before superiors

gug'an: red jasper

guhe: saltpeter

guheren ilha: an exotic flower with large leaves, a purple stalk, and sack-like blossoms

guhūtun: the name of a sacrificial jade of the Xia dynasty

guh'ang: ⟶ **guceng**

gui: turtle, tortoise

gui hūwa: osmanthus (a small fragrant white flower); cf. **šungga ilha**

gui pi: cinnamon

guifei: an Imperial Concubine of the second rank

guifun: a ring (for the finger)

guigu: vigorous, healthy (said of an old person)

guikeri: *Hovenia dulcis*: Japanese raisin tree

guilebumbi: (causative of **guilembi**)

guilehe: apricot

  guilehe boco: apricot-colored

guilembi: to invite, to make an appointment, to arrange a meeting, to summon

guilendumbi: to invite one another

guilenembi: to go to invite

guilenjimbi: to come to invite

guileri: *Malus prunifolia*: plumleaf crabapple, Chinese apple

guini: (鬼) a constellation, the 23rd of the lunar mansions, made up of four stars ($\theta, \eta, \gamma, \delta$) in Cancer

guini tokdonggo kiru: (鬼宿旗) a banner depicting the constellation **guini**

guioi: a high quality nephrite

guise: cabinet, chest, counter

gujehe: the name of the cuckoo in Jiangdong

gujiri ilha: the passion flower

gujung seme: assiduously, concentratedly, diligently

gukdu gakda: with ups and downs, uneven, unlevel

gukduhun: high, elevated

  gukduhun ba: rise, a high place

gukdun jofohori: *Citrus reticulata*: Mandarin orange

gukdurembi: to rise up, to tower

guki moo: an exotic tree resembling the weeping willow

gukio: a kind of precious stone

guklong: hyacinth (a gem)

gukjurembi: (**-ke**) to become crooked

guksen: a short burst of rain, a blast of wind, a measure word for clouds

  guksen guksen: in bursts, in spells, one by one (clouds)

  guksen guksen agambi: to rain in bursts or spells

guksu: ⟶ **guksen**

gukubumbi: **1**. (causative of **gukumbi**); **2**. to annihilate, to wipe out

gukubun: annihilation, extinction

gukumbi: to be annihilated, to be wiped out, to perish, to be extinguished

gukung: a jade-like stone

gukunggele: at the point of annihilation

gulan: a pearl-like stone

gulbu: mayfly, ephemerid

gulejembi: to come loose (said of a knot)

gulhuken: rather complete

gulhun: complete, intact, entire, whole

  gulhun dubengge suihe: a tassel untrimmed at the end

  gulhun emu inenggi: all day

  gulhun funglu jetere hafan: full-salaried official

  gulhun sindambi: to inter, to bury

  gulhun suwanda: a head of garlic

  gulhun šoge: whole ingots

  gulhun teksin: neat, orderly

guli jušen halangga niyalma: ⟶ **jušen**

gulin cecike: a name for the oriole; cf. **gūlin cecike**

guliyatun: the name of an ancient ritual vessel

gulu: **1**. simple, pure, unadulterated, unrefined, in a natural state; **2**. innocent; **3**. white, plain in color

gulu fulgiyan: one of the eight banners: the pure red banner

gulu fulgiyan suje kiru: a pure red banner used by the escort of an Imperial Concubine of the first rank

gulu haksan bocoi suje sara: a pure gold-colored silk parasol used by the escort of an Imperial Concubine of the third rank

gulu haksan bocoi suje šun dalikū: a pure gold-colored silk fan-parasol used by the escort of an Imperial Concubine of the first rank

gulu hošonggo šušu bocoi sara: a pure purple square umbrella

gulu jiramin: pure and honest

gulu lamun: one of the eight banners: the pure blue banner

gulu nomhon: simple, plain, honest and forthright

gulu suje: plain silk

gulu suwayan: one of the eight banners: the pure yellow banner

gulu šanyan: one of the eight banners: the pure white banner

guluken: rather plain, rather unadorned

gulung seme: chattering, idly (said of talking)

gulungge: **1**. simple, plain, homely; **2**. honest and sincere

gulur seme: stuttering

gulurjembi: to stutter

gumen: a kind of red gem

gun etuku: the official dress of the Zhou king

gunda ilha: an exotic flower said to bloom in the moonlight

gung: **1**. duke; **2**. palace; **3**. merit; **4**. a mine; **5**. effect

gung de wesimbi: to return to the palace

gung diyan: palace; cf. **gurung**

gung ilgambi: to judge merit

gung ni gege i efu: the son-in-law of a duke

gung ni jui gege: the daughter of a duke

gung šeng: a scholar recommended by the local government on the basis of accomplishment and virtue

gungceo: silk prepared by the Imperial factory

gungcu: ⟶ **gungceo**

gungcun: ⟶ **gungceo**

gungdz: young master, son of a noble or wealthy family

gungge: **1**. merit, accomplishment; **2**. meritorious

gungge amban: a meritorious official

gungge amban i ulabun icihiyara kuren: (功臣館) an office charged with compiling the biographies of meritorious officials

gungge be saišara goroki be bilure temgetun: a banner of the Imperial Escort on which **gungge be saišara goroki be bilure** was written

gungge faššan: feat, exploit

gungge gebu: accomplishment and fame

gungge ilgambi: to judge merit

gungge mutebumbi: to succeed

gunggu: having a protruding occiput, protruding (said of the back of the head)

gungguceme genggeceme: irresolute, shrinking from decision or responsibility, apprehensive

gungguhun cecike: one of the names of the hoopoe; cf. **indahūn cecike**

gunggule: ⟶ **gunggulu**

gunggulembi: to shoot upward (an arrow)

gunggulu: crest on a bird's head

gunggulun coko: a crested chicken

gunggulungge: crested

gunggulungge niongniyaha: a crested goose

gunggulungge saman cecike: a crested lark

gunggulungge še: a crested eagle

gunggumbi: **1**. to feel apprehension; **2**. to be overwhelmed (with sadness); **3**. to cower, to shrink away

gunggume tembi: to sit cowering

gunggun ganggan: indecisive, shrinking from decision or responsibility, apprehensive

gunghun: (宮) one of the musical notes of the pentatonic scale

gungju: Princess

gungkeri ilha: magnolia

gungmin: honest, sincere, fair

gungnebumbi: (causative of **gungnembi**)

gungnecuke: respectful

gungnecuke gingguji: respectful

gungnecun: respect

gungnembi: to show respect to, to salute

gungnenembi: to go to show respect

gungsen gungsen: hanging down, drooping

gungši: (供事) clerk; cf. **baita de afaha hafan**

gunirembi: (-ke) **1**. to become slack, to loosen, to become lax; **2**. after drawing a bow taut, to let the string slacken; **3**. to diminish somewhat (said of anger); **4**. to shut by itself (said of a door or gate), to slam shut

guniyerembi: ⟶ **gunirembi**

gupai: mah-jongg piece, domino

gur gar seme: sound made by wild geese

gur seme: **1**. snarling, growling; **2**. grumbling; **3**. used to describe someone who talks too much

gurehe: **1**. the broad tendons on a cow's throat; **2**. lazy but crafty, given to shirking work

gurehedembi: always to be shirking one's duty

gurehelebumbi: (causative of **gurehelembi**)

gurehelembi: to wrap with sinew (from a cow's neck)

> **gurehelehe beri**: a bow that has been wrapped with tendons from a cow's neck

gurelji: click beetle

gurembi: ⟶ **gurumbi**

gurgu: wild animal, beast, game

> **gurgu darimbi**: the animals pass very close (at a battue)

gurgungge: decorated with animal figures

gurgušembi: to hunt wild animals

gurgutu: animal heads carved on the four corners of a building

gurhu: ⟶ **gurgu**

guribumbi: **1**. (causative of **gurimbi**); **2**. to move (transitive verb), to transfer

> **guribume fungnembi**: to transfer a title of enfeoffment to one's father or grandfather

> **guribure bithe**: a document circulated among all the subdivisions of a governmental organ

gurimbi: to move, to transfer (intransitive verb)

> **gurime tembi**: to move to a new residence

gurinembi: to go to move, to move to another place

gurinjembi: **1**. to move around, to wander around; **2**. to accommodate oneself to, to give in to

gurinjimbi: to come to move, to move here

guriwa ilha: an exotic flower whose leaves and stalk resemble bamboo

gurjen: a cricket

gurjen butambi: to hunt crickets

gurjendumbi: to chirp

gurlun gūwara: eared owl; cf. **fu gūwara**

gurubumbi: (causative of **gurumbi**)

gurumbi: (1) (-he) to dig up, to dig out, to collect (vegetables, herbs)

gurumbi: (2) (-ke) to redden, to become inflamed, to swell

gurun: **1**. country, tribe, people; **2**. ruling house, dynasty; **3**. country-side

> **gurun be dalire gung**: (鎮國公) Prince of the Blood of the fifth degree, *BH* 20

> **gurun be dalire janggin**: (鎮國將軍) Noble of the Imperial lineage of the ninth rank, *BH* 24

> **gurun be tuwakiyara janggin**: (泰國將軍) Noble of the Imperial lineage of the eleventh rank, *BH* 26

> **gurun boo**: the Court

> **gurun de aisilara gung**: (輔國) Prince of the Blood of the sixth degree, *BH* 21

> **gurun de aisilara janggin**: (輔國將軍) Noble of the Imperial lineage of the tenth rank, *BH* 25

> **gurun gūwa**: an outsider

> **gurun i bodogon**: statecraft, national strategy

> **gurun i doro yoso**: national system

> **gurun i efu**: (固倫額駙) husband of a **gurun i gungju**

> **gurun i ejen**: monarch, ruler, king, Emperor

> **gurun i gungju**: (固倫公主) Princess born to an Empress, *BH* 14

> **gurun i jase**: national boundary

> **gurun i juse be hūwašabure yamun**: (國子監) Imperial Academy of Learning, *BH* 412

> **gurun i suduri**: national history, dynastic history

> **gurun i suduri be asarara yamun**: (皇史宬) the storage place for the national historical archives

> **gurun i suduri kuren**: (國史館) State Historiographer's Office, *BH* 205

> **gurun i tacikū**: (太學) the literary designation of the Imperial Academy of Learning, *BH* 412

> **gurun i yoso**: national prestige

gurunembi: to go to dig out, to go to gather

gurung: **1**. palace; **2**. constellation, one of twelve celestial mansions

   gurung de wesimbi: to return to the palace

   gurung deyen: palace

gurunumbi: to dig out (said of a group)

gurutun: a sacrificial vessel of Emperor Shun

guse: **1**. a Buddhist nun; **2**. ⟶ **gudz**

   guse miyoo: Buddhist nunnery

gushembi: **1**. to develop (into something), to succeed; **2**. to be of use, to be of value

   gusherakū: worthless, unreliable, immature, good-for-nothing

   gusherakū baita: malevolent action

gushumbi: ⟶ **gushembi**

gusio: a kind of precious stone

gusucembi: ⟶ **gusucumbi**

gusucuke: out of humor, annoyed, dull, annoying, depressing

gusucumbi: to be out of humor, to feel bored, to be annoyed

gusucun: annoyance, dejection, sadness, depression

gusui: a precious stone worn at the girdle; cf. **guceng**

gute: (plural of **gu**)

guti: a kind of precious stone

guwa: the eight trigrams used for divination

   guwa maktambi: to cast the trigrams

   guwa tuwambi: to consult the trigrams

guwa miyan: fine dried noodles

guwafu: **1**. crutch; **2**. oars; **3**. punting pole

   guwafu moo: a short pole, used as a weapon, with a piece of wood attached at right angles to one end

guwaidz: crutch, walking stick

guwaige: ⟶ **guwafu**

guwalase: a wild sour-tasting plant similar to shepherd's purse

guwalasun: a short sleeveless jacket worn by women

guwali: dwellings located on both sides of the city gates outside of a city, suburb, outskirts of a town

guwan: **1**. Daoist monastery; **2**. fence; **3**. a string of 1000 coins; **4**. mountain pass

guwan dz: pot, jar

guwan in pusa: the bodhisattva Avalokiteśvara

guwandz: a short nine-holed bamboo flute

guwang mucen: a kind of iron cooking pot made in Guangdong

guwangga ilha: *Jasminum grandiflorum*: poet's jessamine

guwanggun: undependable person, villain, rascal

guwanggusa: (plural of **guwanggun**)

guwanggušambi: to behave like a rascal, to act villainously

guwanglambi: to stroll, to walk about

guwangse: **1**. leg-irons, manacles; **2**. a crossbar of a fence with holes provided for the vertical poles

   guwangse sangse etubumbi: to put on leg-irons and handcuffs

   guwangse tabumbi: to put in stocks and shackles

guwangselambi: to put in fetters or shackles, to put in manacles

guwangsi: banquet attendant

   guwangsi tebumbi: to station a banquet attendant

guwangša: fine silk from Canton

guwanni: lazy, indolent, prone to shun work

guwanse: a cap

guwase: long thin cakes

guwatalambi: to divide into equal portions

guwebuhen: amnesty, pardon

guwebumbi: to remit, to pardon, to grant amnesty, to spare

   guwebure hese: a writ of amnesty

guwecehe: pale

guwecihe: pigeon, dove; cf. **kuwecihe**

guweciheri: bluish gray, dove-gray

guwei dz šeo: executioner; cf. **erumci**

guwejihe: stomach

   guwejihe da: the opening of the stomach, appetite

guweke: **1**. careful, attentive; **2**. beware of …

guwele gala: on the lookout, furtive, stealthy

guwele mele: stealthy, furtively, like a thief

guwelecembi: to act furtively, to peek, to spy on

guweleku: concubine

guwelembi: to act stealthily, to spy

guwelke: **1**. careful, attentive to detail; **2**. (interjection) pay heed to

guwembi (1): **1**. to be spared, to be pardoned; **2**. to avoid, to escape

guwembi (2): (**-ngke, -ndere**) to chirp, to tweet, to quack, to clang, to make a noise (like a drum), to sound

    guwendere še i kiru: (鳴鳶旗) a banner of the Imperial Escort with a kite depicted on it

guwembumbi: (causative of **guwembi [2]**)

guwenci: chirping, tweeting, quacking, cackling

guwendehen: a name for the myna

guwendembi: **1**. to chirp, to tweet, to quack, to cackle; **2**. to make a continual clanging or drumming sound

guwenden cecike: a kind of small red bird with yellow feet

guwendengge itu: a name for the partridge; cf. **itu**

guwendere: ⟶ **guwembi (2)** (subheading)

guwenderhen: *Alauda arvensis*: the lesser skylark

guwešembi: **1**. to lead astray; **2**. to bruise

guye: **1**. the heel of the foot; **2**. a piece of iron at the end of a sword's handle

    guye sele: an ornamental iron corner piece on bow cases and quivers

guyoo: green jasper

gūbadambi: to jump about wildly, to raise a ruckus, to rage, to be fit to be tied

    gūbadame koikoljombi: to stir up trouble, to fan the flames of disorder

gūbadašambi: to jump back and forth, to jump up and down

gūbcibumbi: (causative of **gūbcimbi**)

gūbcimbi: **1**. to tie a saddle pad on the back of a horse; **2**. to place a cover over something

gūbimbi: to tie down a load on a wagon with rope

gūbiri: *Sagittaria sagittifolia*: old-world arrowhead

gūca: female goat, nanny

gūcihiyalambi: ⟶ **gūwacihiyalambi**

gūcihiyašambi: ⟶ **gūwacihiyašambi**

gūcila: a partially burned log

gūdu gada: prattling, chattering, chatting

gūdumbi: to spawn

gūi gūi: **1**. (onomatopoetic) a sound made by hunters chasing game; **2**. a sound used to call the saker falcon

gūje: a sound used to call a falcon

gūju: ⟶ **gūsu**

gūla: original, originally,

    gūla beye: oneself, one's own person

gūlabumbi: (causative of **gūlambi**)

gūlakū: precipice, steep cliff, deep canyon

gūlambi: **1**. to back up, to come back into the pipe (said of smoke); **2**. to roll down, to precipitate

    gūlame tuhenjihe: rolled down from a high place

    gūlame wasimbi: to come rolling down from a height

gūldarakūlambi: to develop a stiff neck (said of livestock that cannot lower its head to eat or drink)

gūldargan: *Hirundo rustica*: eastern house swallow

gūldarhan: ⟶ **gūldargan**

gūldun: arch, tunnel

    gūldun boo: bridal chamber

    gūldun jugūn: tunnel

gūldurakū yoo: a sunken boil from which great quantities of blood and pus flow forth

gūldurambi: **1**. to penetrate, to sneak through a hole, to make a hole to gain entry; **2**. to make a tunnel or passageway; **3**. to act obsequiously, to curry favor; **4**. to sink inward (said of a boil)

    gūldurame: secretly, privately

    gūldurame eyembi: to flow underground, to flow through a tunnel

    gūldurame fetembi: to excavate

gūlduri: a passage for water at the foot of a dike, a drain, a discharge duct, a culvert

gūldusi: spy, agent

gūlga: ⟶ **gūlha**

gūlganambi: to grow upward (a defect in an animal's hoof)

gūlgi: *in the following expressions*:

    gūlgi foyo: *ula* (*wūlā* 烏拉) sedge; cf. **foyo orho**

    gūlgi orho: *ula* (*wūlā* 烏拉) sedge; cf. **foyo orho**

gūlgirakū: unrelenting, refusing to forget, cannot forget, to have in one's mind constantly

gūlha: boot

    gūlha foyo: *ula* (*wūlā* 烏拉) grass; cf. **foyo orho**

    gūlha šusen: a leather strap attached across the heel of a boot

gūlhi wehe cinuhūn: the best quality cinnabar

gūli gali: (onomatopoetic) the call of the oriole

    gūli gali sembi: to cry like an oriole

gūlibumbi: (causative of **gūlimbi**)

gūlidambi: to call (said of the oriole)

gūlimbi: (-ka) to be on good terms, to be in agreement, to share similar views, to find one another congenial, to hit it off

gūlika gucu: intimate friend, bosom buddy

gūlime acabumbi: to get together to plan mischief

gūlime ildumbi: to make friends, to hit it off

gūlin cecike: *Oriolus chinensis*: oriole

gūlindumbi: to be on mutually good terms

gūljambi: 1. to refloat a grounded boat downstream by pulling from behind with a tow rope; 2. to become intimate with, to become close

gūljargan: ⟶ guljarhan

gūljarhan: the grip of a whip or other similar article that has been wrapped with cord or thongs

gūlmahūn: 1. rabbit, hare; 2. the fourth of the earth's branches (卯)

gūlmahūn biya: the second month

gūlmahūn erin: the period from five AM to seven AM

gūlmahun i asu: a net for catching rabbits

gūlmahūngga aniya: the year of the rabbit

gūlturakūlambi: ⟶ gūldarakūlambi

gūlu gala: (onomatopoetic) the sound of whispering or mumbling

gūman: frequenter of brothels, whoremonger

gūmbi: 1. to growl; 2. to cut out (meat from a bone)

gūn halambi: to molt, to shed the skin (said of snakes)

gūna: three-year-old cow

gūnan: ⟶ gūna

gūng gang: (onomatopoetic) the sound made by a wild goose

gūnggala coko: *Crossoptilon mantchuricum*: the hoki pheasant

gūnggari niongniyaha: a kind of wild goose found in Qinghai

gūngkali: a recessed area at the foot of a riverbank

gūngkambi: to be hot and humid, to be sultry

gūngkan: Adam's apple, larynx

gūngkanambi: to have a protruding Adam's apple

gūnibumbi: (causative or passive of **gūnimbi**)

gūnicun: 1. longing, yearning, nostalgia; 2. a kind of verse expressing yearning

gūnigan: thought, opinion, feeling

gūnigangga: thoughtful, knowledgeable

gūnihakū: unexpectedly

gūnijan: thought, reflection, meditation

gūnimbi: to think, to reflect, to consider, to intend

gūnin: 1. intention, thought, opinion, feeling, sense; 2. mind, spirit; 3. token (of one's feelings or intention)

gūnin acabumbi: to set forth one's views

gūnin acambi: to have similar views

gūnin acinggiyabumbi: to be moved, to be aroused emotionally

gūnin akū: unintentional

gūnin akūmbumbi: to do one's very best, to exhaust all effort

gūnin arbun: temperament, disposition, mood, intention

gūnin aššambi: to be moved emotionally, to have one's passions aroused, to become excited

gūnin bahambi: to be pleased, to get an idea

gūnin baibumbi: to have one's plans upset, to be upset, to worry, to be vexed

gūnin baimbi: to ask for an opinion

gūnin be tebumbi: to harbor an intention

gūnin be tucibumbi: to express one's intentions

gūnin be ujimbi: to cultivate one's thoughts or intentions (especially toward one's parents)

gūnin cihai: as one wishes, willfully

gūnin cinggiya: indecisive, vacillating

gūnin dahambi: to be convinced

gūnin de acambi: to correspond to one's views

gūnin de icišambi: to follow one's purpose

gūnin de tebumbi: to be concerned about, to keep in mind, to pay attention to, to be careful

gūnin de teburakū: unconcerned, unperturbed about something

gūnin dekderšembi: to have vain hopes, to be carried away with one's thoughts

gūnin den: proud, haughty

gūnin eberembi: to be dispirited

gūnin efujembi: to be deeply hurt, to be very sad

gūnin elehun: content, satisfied

gūnin erki: willful, bull-headed

gūnin falabumbi: to have confused thoughts, to be confused

gūnin fayambi: to go to a lot of trouble

gūnin forgošombi: to reconsider, to have second thoughts, to change one's mind

gūnin fulu: suspicious

gūnin geren: suspicious

gūnin girkūmbi: to concentrate one's attention, to be absorbed

gūnin hafirabumbi: to be in an embarrassing situation, to be ill at ease

gūnin hiri oho: became disappointed

gūnin hūlimbumbi: to be obsessed, to be perplexed

gūnin hūsun: mental powers

gūnin i cihai: as one likes, in accordance with one's wishes

gūnin i ici: in accordance with someone's wishes

gūnin i saligan: arbitrary action

gūnin icakū: not satisfied

gūnin isibumbi: to announce one's intentions

gūnin isika: one's intention is realized, satisfied

gūnin isinaha ba: hope, wish, intention

gūnin isinambi: to hope for

gūnin jafambi: to have a firm intention

gūnin jafatambi: to restrain oneself, to control one's thoughts

gūnin mujilen: mood, state of mind, mentality

gūnin musembi: to suffer a setback, to have one's plans frustrated

gūnin niorombi: to be profoundly affected by something

gūnin saha gucu: a bosom friend

gūnin sandumbi: to be on intimate terms, to like one another

gūnin sindambi: the mind is at ease, to be calm, not to worry

gūnin subumbi: to put one's mind to rest

gūnin suilambi: to take a lot of trouble

gūnin sukdun: disposition, temperament, train of thought

gūnin sulabumbi: to relax, not to worry

gūnin tarhūn: overbearing, domineering

gūnin tatašambi: to be anxious, to be very worried, to cherish a deep feeling

gūnin tebumbi: to keep in mind, to harbor an intention

gūnin tuksitembi: to be tense

gūnin unenggi: sincere

gūnin usambi: to be disappointed, to be disheartened

gūnin wacihiyambi: to exhaust all effort

gūnin waliyabumbi: to be confused, to be bewildered

gūnin werešembi: to pay attention, to be careful

gūnin yenden: interest, enthusiasm

gūnin yojohošambi: to itch to show off one's skill

gūninambi: to have a thought come to mind, to recall

gūningga: full of ideas, reflective

gūninjacuka: worthy of consideration, worthy of reflection

gūninjambi: to consider, to think over carefully, to reflect upon

gūr gar: (onomatopoetic) the sound made by a flock of flying birds

gūr gūr seme: (onomatopoetic) sound of flying birds

gūrakūšambi: to peer, to leer, to look around furtively

gūran: 1. cord for tying a bundle; 2. a male roe deer, roebuck; cf. gio

gūrbambi: to shun, to shy: to start in fright

gūrbi: cattail, reed

    gūrbi orho: reeds, cattails

gūrgi: a clasp

    gūrgi foyo: a kind of swamp-growing reed that is somewhat taller than *ula* (*wūlā* 烏拉) grass; it is used as padding in boots

gūrgilabumbi: (causative or passive of gurgilambi)

gūrgilambi: 1. to inflame, to burn; 2. to clasp, to buckle

gūrgimbi: ⟶ gūrgilambi

gūrgin: flame

    gūrgin dalikū: the lid of a stove or heater

    gūrgin moo: *Phellodendron amurense*: Amur cork tree; see also gorgin moo

    gūrgin muduri dardan: satin with a pattern of flames and dragons

gūsa: banner

    gūsa be kadalara amban: (都統) Lieutenant-General (of a banner), *BH* 719

    gūsa i ejen: (都統) Lieutenant-General (of a banner), *BH* 719

    gūsai baitai kunggeri: (都統科) Office of Banner Affairs in the Board of War

    gūsai beise: (固山貝子) Prince of the Blood of the fourth degree, *BH* 19

gūsai da: (協領) Colonel of a Regiment of the Provincial Manchu Garrisons, *BH* 746

gūsai efu: (縣統儀賓) husband of a Princess of the eighth rank

gūsai ejen: lieutenant general of a banner

gūsai fujin: the wife of a **beise**

gūsai gege: the daughter of a **beise**

gūsai yamun: (都統衛門) headquarters of a banner

gūsangga: pertaining to a banner, belonging to a certain banner

gūsici: thirtieth

gūsihiya: border, boundary

    gūsihiya acambi: to have a common border

gūsin: thirty

gūsinggeri: thirty times

gūsita: thirty each

gūsu: thick, heavy rope

    gūsu futa: hawser, heavy rope

gūsulambi: to tie up with heavy rope

gūtubumbi: **1**. to spoil, to besmirch, to sully; **2**. to shame, to defile, to dishonor

gūtucun: shame, disgrace, defilement

gūwa: other, another

    gūwa niyalma: someone else

    gūwai beye: third party, disinterested party

gūwabsi: to another place, elsewhere

gūwacihiya: with a start, with a wince

    gūwacihiya gūwacihiya aššambi: to wake up with a start

    gūwacihiya tata: with a start

gūwacihiyalabumbi: **1**. (causative of **gūwacihiyalambi**); **2**. to startle

gūwacihiyalacuka: startling, amazing

gūwacihiyalambi: to be startled, to be alarmed

gūwacihiyašambi: to feel jittery, to feel unsettled, to have the flesh creep

gūwahiyan: **1**. a hole for cooking used by soldiers in the field; **2**. a tripod used for supporting a cooking pot over a hole; **3**. a constellation in Lyra

    gūwahiyan arame ilihabi: have set up camp

gūwai: ⟶ **gūwa** (subheading)

gūwaidabumbi: (causative of **gūwaidambi**)

gūwaidambi: to lean on, to lean to one side

gūwaidame dedumbi: to lie on one's side

gūwaidame ergembi: to rest lying on one's side

gūwaidanambi: to walk swaying from side to side, to stagger

gūwaimarambi: ⟶ **goimarambi**

gūwaimbi: ⟶ **goimbi**

gūwainambi: to come to a certain price

gūwaingge: someone else's

gūwaisuntumbi: to pretend not to notice, to slight someone

gūwaliyabumbi: (causative of **gūwaliyambi**)

gūwaliyambi: (**-ka, -ndara**) **1**. to change (intransitive verb); **2**. to spoil (said of food); **3**. to fade (said of colors); **4**. to become faint

gūwaliyambumbi: (causative of **gūwaliyambi**)

gūwaliyandarakū: unchangeable, constant

gūwaliyašakū: **1**. changeable, fickle; **2**. someone who frequently changes his or her mind

gūwaliyašambi: **1**. to change frequently; **2**. to get worse (said of an illness); **3**. to have frequent internal disorders

gūwambi: to bark

gūwambumbi: (causative of **gūwambi**)

gūwancihiyan: unappetizing

gūwang gūwang: (onomatopoetic) the sound of barking

gūwanumbi: to bark (said of a group of dogs)

gūwar gūwar: (onomatopoetic) the cry of dogs, ducks, frogs, or doves

gūwar sembi: to quack, to croak

gūwarimbi: to croak (said of frogs)

gūwasihiya: *Egretta alba*: eastern egret

gūwašabumbi: to be blamed or rejected (by spirits and demons)

gūwašambi: (**-ka**) to spoil (said of sour things)

gūwaššabumbi: (causative of **gūwaššambi**)

gūwaššambi: **1**. to cut meat into strips; **2**. to throb, to twitch (said of the eyelids)

gūwaššan: thin strips of meat

gūyambi: **1**. to brush against trees during the mating season (said of deer), to be in rut; **2**. to roar (said of dragons)

gūyandumbi: to mate, to jump about (said of mating deer)

G'

For words beginning with **g**, see the section beginning on page 129.

g'abala: skull, cranium

g'abišara: a name for the pheasant

g'aci: one tenth to the seventeenth power

g'alab: **1**. Kalpa, world period; **2**. disaster, ruin

g'amuliyang: chameleon

g'an: steel

    g'an i siren: steel wire

g'an lan: Chinese olive

g'andz: sugar cane

g'ang: ⟶ **g'an**

g'angg'a: the Ganges

g'anje: sugar cane

g'angse: a carrying-pole carried by two men

g'anjur nomun: the Ganjur

g'anse: tangerine, mandarin orange

g'aodz: salve, ointment

g'aoming: document for posthumous enfeoffment of officials above the fifth rank

g'aosy: proclamation, announcement

    g'aosy bithe: proclamation, announcement

g'aoši bithe. ⟶ **g'aosy bithe**

g'aoyoo: salve, ointment

g'arsi: monk's habit; cf. **garša**

g'asib: Kāśyapa Buddha

g'o: one tenth of a *shēng* 升

g'odarg'a: chicken (word of Sanskrit origin)

g'ogin: widower

g'ona ilha: an exotic light red flower

H ᠠ

Although the Manchu alphabet contains a letter **h'**, this dictionary contains no words beginning with it and no separate section for it.

ha: **1**. a small net for catching pheasants; **2**. (onomatopoetic) a sound made by breathing on frozen objects; **3**. (onomatopoetic) a sound made when eating something hot or salty; **4**. (onomatopoetic) the cry of a bird of prey when it sees a man

ha hak gosihon: pungent, hot (said of food)

habcihiyadambi: to treat affectionately or warmly, to show sympathy to

habcihiyan: affable, friendly, sympathetic, affectionate, harmonious

habgiyambi: to yawn

habšabumbi: (causative or passive of **habšambi**)

    habšabuha niyalma: the accused, the defendant

habšambi: **1**. to accuse, to bring to court; **2**. to report to, to be responsible to

    habšaha niyalma: accuser, plaintiff

    habšame alambi: to report to a superior

    habšame duilere weile: legal case, lawsuit

    habšara baita: grievance

    habšara bithe: letter of accusation, indictment

habšan: accusation, complaint, lawsuit, legal case

    habšan bithe: legal case, legal document

    habšan i sefu: legal counsel, lawyer

habšanambi: to go to accuse, to go to report, to go to court

habšandumbi: to accuse together, to accuse one another; also **habšanumbi**

habšanjimbi: to come to accuse, to come to report

habšanumbi: to accuse together, to accuse one another; also **habšandumbi**

habta: **1**. the wing of a saddle; **2**. wing

    habta habtalambi: **1**. to soar, to glide (said of large birds); **2**. to tuck back the wings

    habta habtašambi: to soar, to glide (said of large birds)

habtaha: a wide girdle used to protect a man's midsection in battle

habtalambi: **1**. to squint, to wink, to blink; **2**. ⟶ **habta habtalambi**

habtambi: ⟶ **habtalambi**

habtašambi: **1**. to wink or blink repeatedly; **2**. to soar, to glide

haca: handful, skein

hacihiyabumbi: (causative of **hacihiyambi**)

hacihiyambi: **1**. to urge, to press, to force; **2**. to rush, to hurry; **3**. to entreat to eat or drink

hacihiyan: compulsion, urging, pressing

hacihiyanambi: to go to urge, to go to force

hacihiyandumbi: to press or urge together; also **hacihiyanumbi**

hacihiyanjimbi: to come to urge, to come to force

hacihiyanumbi: to press or urge together; also **hacihiyandumbi**

hacika: ⟶ **hacuka**

hacilambi: **1**. to separate according to type, to classify; **2**. to itemize, to recount point by point

    hacilaha dardan: silk with many kinds of flowers woven in it

    hacilame: point by point, item by item, every kind

    hacilame wesimbure kunggeri: (建言科) office concerned with preparing itemized reports for the Emperor

hacin: **1**. kind, sort, class, item; **2**. article, paragraph; **3**. condition, intention; **4**. the fifteenth day of the first month (the lantern festival), festival, holiday

    hacin aname: in every respect

    hacin arambi: to celebrate a holiday

hacin geren: full of deceit, full of tricks, holding unorthodox or unconventional views

hacin hacin i: all kinds of, various kinds of

hacin i ucuri: the lantern festival, the days around the lantern festival

hacin i yamji: the evening of the lantern festival

hacin inenggi: **1**. holiday; **2**. the fifteenth day of the first lunar month, the lantern festival; **3**. the name of various auspicious days during the year

hacin meyen: item, kind, clause

hacin meyen i dangse: land record books

hacin tome: each kind, every item, item by item, altogether

hacingga: all kinds of, every sort of

hacinggai: in every way

hacuhan: **1**. a small cooking pot; **2**. ⟶ **huwešere hacuhan**

hacuhiyan: a large three-legged vessel of ancient times, a tripod

hacuka: **1**. dirty, lewd, defiled, unseemly, base, vulgar; **2**. stingy, miserly

hacukadambi: to commit dirty acts, to commit lewd acts

hacukadara nirugan: lewd pictures, pornography

hacumbi: (-ka) **1**. to become dirty, to become defiled; **2**. ⟶ **hacukadambi**

hada: **1**. a crag, a small cliff, rocky summit; **2**. peak

hada cibin: *Ptyonoprogne rupestris*: rock-martin

hada wehe: gravel, broken stones, scree

hadabumbi: (causative of **hadambi**)

hadafun: ⟶ **hadufun**

hadagan: ⟶ **hadahan**

hadaha: ⟶ **hadahan**

hadaha usiha: the North Star

hadahai: ⟶ **hadambi** (subheading)

hadahan: a nail or peg of iron, bamboo, or wood

hadahan nisiha: a small fish shaped like a tent peg

hadai: tenon, plug, wedge

hadala: horse's bridle

hadala etubumbi: to put a bridle on a horse

hadala multulembi: to remove a horse's bridle

hadala šaban: cleats — four iron teeth placed on a round frame and attached to the soles of shoes to prevent slipping on a slippery or steep surface

hadala yoo: a sore on a horse's mouth caused by a bridle

hadama burga: a kind of willow that grows alone — it has white bark and its wood is good for making arrows

hadambi: **1**. to nail, to tack; **2**. to sting (said of insects); **3**. to sole (shoes or boots); **4**. to fix the eyes on

hadahai: fixedly (said of looking)

hadahai ejembi: to keep firmly in mind

hadahai feksimbi: to run with an arrow stuck in the body

hadanambi: to fix the eyes on, to stare

hadara: *Salmo thymallus*: grayling, a small fish that lives in clear cold water

hadubumbi: (causative of **hadumbi**)

hadufun: scythe, sickle

haduhūn: salty; cf. **hatuhūn**

hadumbi: to cut with a sickle, to reap

hadunjimbi: to go to cut with a sickle, to go to reap

hadunumbi: to reap together

hafa šoro: a basket made of brambles (used for carrying vegetables and similar things)

hafan: official, officer

hafan bahambi: to obtain an official position

hafan efujembi: to be dismissed from office

hafan efulembi: to dismiss from office

hafan hali: an official

hafan hergen: official rank

hafan i bithe: a license obtained by merchants from an official source

hafan i boo: (吏房) Office of Personnel of the Court of Colonial Affairs

hafan i jurgan: (吏部) Board of Civil Appointments, *BH* 333

hafan i jurgan i kungge yamun: (吏科) section of personnel of the Censorate

hafan i tangkan: an official grade or rank

hafan i temgetu i kunggeri: (憑科) an office of the Board of Civil Appointments charged with issuing orders to local officials who were appointed monthly and with checking on the terms of those previously appointed

hafan i yamun: official office, government office

hafan jergi: official rank

hafan sindambi: to appoint an official

hafan sindara bolgobure fiyenten: (錄勳清吏司) Department of Inner Mongols, later **jasak dangsei bolgobure fiyenten**

hafan sirambi: to inherit an official position

hafan tembi: to occupy an official post, to serve as an official

hafan wesimbi: to be promoted to a higher official rank

hafasa: (plural of **hafan**)

hafasi: scholar, minor official

hafasi daifasa: scholar-officials

hafasi šufatu: a head wrapping worn by **hafasi**

hafin: clamp, vise, clip

hafin moo: the two pieces of wood that hold a ship's mast in place

hafirabumbi: **1**. (causative or passive of **hafirambi**); **2**. to be embarrassed, to find oneself in difficult circumstances

haifirabume afambi: to mount a pincer attack

hafiraha: ⟶ **hafirambi** (subheading)

hafirahūn: **1**. narrow, cramped; **2**. pressing, critical; **3**. in dire straits, hard up, in a predicament

hafirahūn mejige: bad news

hafirakū: **1**. pincers, pliers; **2**. crab's claws

hafirakū sibiya: metal fasteners that secure an axle to a cart

hafirakū simhun: a sixth finger

hafirambi: **1**. to pinch, to press or hold between two objects; **2**. to hold under the arm; **3**. to press a seam together; **4**. to put pressure on, to compel; **5**. to put in a difficult situation; **6**. to threaten

hafiraha afaha: a memorandum pressed between the leaves of a document

hafiran: seam on a boot

hafirhūn: ⟶ **hafirahūn**

hafiršambi: to use economically

hafiršambumbi: (causative of **hafiršambi**)

hafiršanumbi: to use economically (said of a group)

hafišambi: to pat affectionately, to flatter

hafišangga: obsequious, flattering

hafitambi: **1**. to press or hold on both sides of an object, to pinch; **2**. to inlay

hafitame afambi: to attack from two sides, to mount a pincer attack

hafitame geyembi: to engrave on two sides

hafitara fulhun: one of the six minor scale pipes

hafu: **1**. penetrating, going through; **2**. thorough, comprehensive; **3**. enlightened, possessing understanding; **4**. (as a postposition) through

hafu bulekušembi: to have a thorough understanding, to see clearly

hafu giyai: thoroughfare

hafu hafu: penetrating, thorough, throughout, total, comprehensive

hafu hiyoošungga: thoroughly filial

hafu sambi: to know clearly

hafu ulhimbi: to understand clearly

hafukiyambi: to inform in detail, to give a thorough rundown on

hafulambi: **1**. to penetrate, to go through, to pierce; **2**. to do thoroughly; **3**. to forbid someone to do something

hafumbi: (**-ka, -re/-ndara**) **1**. to penetrate, to go through, to soak through; **2**. to understand thoroughly, to comprehend; **3**. to communicate, to have relations with, to have free passage

hafundarakū: impenetrable

hafumbubumbi: (causative of **hafumbumbi**)

hafumbukū: interpreter, translator

hafumbukū hafan: an official translator

hafumbukū kamcihabi: accompanied by a translator

hafumbumbi: **1**. (causative of **hafumbi**); **2**. to convey a message, to inform, to let know, to announce; **3**. to dredge, to clear out an obstruction; **4**. to understand

hafumbume: thoroughly, completely

hafumbume acinggiyambi: to move, to affect

hafumbume efulembi: to destroy completely

hafumbume ulhibumbi: to proclaim, to make public

hafumbume weilembi: to dredge

hafun: **1**. transparent, permeable; **2**. smooth, successful; **3**. the eleventh hexagram of the *Yijing*

hafun cece: smooth transparent silk gauze

hafunambi: to connect with another place, to form a free passage to another place

hafundarakū: ⟶ **hafumbi** (subheading)

hafungga: **1**. penetrating, going through, connecting, passable; **2**. pertaining to free passage

    hafungga boo: a central room that connects with both front and back rooms in a house

    hafungga mahatun: a hat with openings on both sides

    hafungga omolo: a descendant of the sixth generation

    hafungga talu: a thoroughfare, passage

hafunjibumbi: (causative of **hafunjimbi**)

hafunjimbi: to come through (in this direction), to come straight through

haga: fish bone

hagabukū: a four-inch wooden hook with an iron tip used to catch black carp

hagambi: **1**. to get something caught in the throat; **2**. to form a hard abscess in the breast

haha: male, man

    haha i deji: a superior man, champion

    haha jui: boy, son

    hahai erdemu: martial skill, manly arts

hahabukū: ⟶ **hagabukū**

hahama ancun: **1**. a precious stone hanging on a bag of fragrance; **2**. an earring with a single gem; **3**. an earring with a single pearl

hahangge: male, masculine

haharambi: to act like a man, to act in a manly way

hahardambi: to become a man, to grow to manhood

hahasi: (plural of **haha**)

hahi: urgent, hurried

    hahi cahi: hurried, agitated, urgent, critical

    hahi edun: a strong wind, a storm

    hahi gisun: harsh words

    hahi hatan: irritable, irascible

    hahi jobolon: grave danger, adversity

    hahi mejige: urgent message, urgent news

    hahi nimeku: acute illness

    hahi oshon: cruel, ruthless, brutal

    hahi oyonggo: critical, urgent, crucial

hahiba: quick, nimble

hahikan: rather urgent

hahilambi: to act quickly or urgently, to hurry

hahūbumbi: (causative of **hahūmbi**)

hahūmbi: to show delayed growth (said of feathers)

hahūrabumbi: **1**. (causative of **hahūrambi**); **2**. to get stuck in the throat

hahūrakū: choker used for restraining a dog

hahūrambi: **1**. to grab by the throat, to choke; **2**. to occupy a militarily strategic point

hahūršambi: **1**. to hold by the throat continually, to throttle; **2**. to accuse obstinately

haicing: the peregrine falcon; cf. **šongkon**

haidan: a large hook on which frogs and small fish were used as bait

    haidan sisimbi: to fish with a **haidan**

haidarabumbi: (causative of **haidarambi**)

haidarambi: to lean, to lean to one side, to droop, to hang the head

haidaršambi: to lean to one side while walking

haidu: lopsided, leaning to one side

haifirambi: ⟶ **hafirambi**

haifiršambi: ⟶ **hafiršambi**

haifitambi: ⟶ **hafitambi**

haigari: ⟶ **haihari**

haigū: ⟶ **haihū**

haiha: **1**. mountain slope; **2**. spool for yarn or thread

haihabumbi: (causative of **haihambi**)

haihambi: to incline

haihan: **1**. welt of a shoe or boot; **2**. bone, feathers, hemp stalks, hair fed to falcons to clean out their stomachs

haiharambi: to lean to one side, to topple, to incline

haiharame: along the slope of a hill

haihari: ⟶ **heiheri haihari**

haiharilambi: to reel from side to side

haiharšambi: to stagger, to reel, to sway, to slant

haihashūn: inclined, leaning, awry

haihū: **1**. soft; **2**. staggering, weaving from side to side

haihūljambi: to sway, to rock, to shake, to flutter, to waver

    haihūljame oksombi: to walk in a graceful manner (said of women)

haihūn: a name for the otter; cf. **hailun**

haihūna: *Melanocorypha mongolica*: Mongolian lark

haihūngga: soft, supple

    haihūngga sufa: a new-style handkerchief

haihūwa: bream

haihūwan: weak, delicate, yielding

haijan: a mode of Manchu singing during which the singer imitates the movements of a snake

haijung seme: reeling under a heavy load

hailambi: to scorn an offering, to reject a shamanistic libation

hailami: ⟶ **hailambi**

hailan: **1**. elm tree, tree of the genus *Ulmus*; **2**. vexation, scorn

    hailan gaibumbi: to be vexed, to be distressed

    hailan gaimbi: 1, to make things difficult for someone, to make someone feel awkward, to vex, to distress; **2**. to be vexed, to feel distressed

    hailan sence: a kind of yellow fungus that grows on elms

hailashūn: **1**. precipitous, steep; **2**. awry, crooked

hailun: *Lutra lutra*: otter

    hailun cecike: *Halcyon smyrnensis*: turquoise kingfisher

hainuk: first-generation hybrid of a bull and a female yak

hairabumbi: (causative of **hairambi**)

hairacuka: **1**. pitiable, pitiful; **2**. Too bad!, What a shame!; **3**. lovable, likeable

hairacun: pity, regret

hairaka: ⟶ **hairakan**

hairakan: **1**. regrettable; **2**. what a shame!

hairambi: (**-ka, -ndara**) **1**. to regret, to begrudge, to be unwilling to part with; **2**. to love tenderly

    hairame narašambi: to be reluctant to part with, to linger over

hairan: regret, begrudging, compassion, tenderness

    hairan jaka: an object that one is loath to part with

    hairan niyalma: a person that one is very fond of

hairandambi: to begrudge, to stint on

haisanda: wild garlic

haita: a large wild pig

haitang: crabapple, tree of the genus *Malus*; cf. **yonggari**

hajan: wooden palisade surrounding a fortress

haji: **1**. dear, beloved; **2**. affection; **3**. fond of, addicted to: **nure de haji** 'fond of liquor'; **4**. scarce, lean (year), famine

    haji aniya: a year of famine, a lean year

    haji gucu: a dear friend

    haji hairan: tender love

    haji halhūn: ardent, amorous

    haji sain: on intimate terms

    haji yuyun: famine

hajilambi: **1**. to love, to be fond of, to fall in love; **2**. to become intimate with, to make love; **3**. to fish with a net stretched across a stream

    hajilame acabumbi: to be intimate, to make love to

hajilan: love, intimacy

hajin: affection

hajingga: intimate, close, affectionate

    hajingga baibula: one of the names of the paradise flycatcher; cf. **baibula**

hajun: **1**. weapon, tool; **2**. a sickle-like knife used in tiger traps

hak: (onomatopoetic) the sound of clearing one's throat

hakcin: **1**. quick-tempered, rash, brusque; **2**. high and steep, precipitous

hakda: old grass left over from the previous year, a spot of grass remaining in an area that has been burned over

haksabumbi: **1**. (causative or passive of **haksambi**); **2**. to scorch, to become scorched

haksambi: (**-ka**) **1**. to become scorched, to get dark from contact with sunlight or fire; **2**. to turn red in the rising or setting sun (clouds); **3**. to have a burning sensation in the stomach

    haksaha tugi: reddish clouds, clouds at dawn or dusk

    haksame olhombi: to become dried out in the sun

haksan: **1**. steep, precipitous, dangerous, treacherous; **2**. swift (said of a current); **3**. cruel, brutal; **4**. golden, reddish brown

    haksan bocoi junggidei kiyoo: a yellow sedan chair carried by eight men and used by concubines of the second rank

    haksan bocoi suje de aisin dambuha garudangga kiru: a banner used by the escort of concubines of the second class, with a phoenix embroidered upon a yellow background

    haksan enggeleku: cliff, precipice

    haksan hakcin: precipitous, high, steep

    haksan oyonggo: strategic and inaccessible

    haksan sehehuri: perilous, precipitous

    haksan umiyesun: a yellow sash worn by members of the Imperial clan

haksan weilen: work fraught with danger, dangerous work

haksangga: scorched, brown from cooking

haksangga efen: a kind of baked wheat cake

hakšabumbi: (causative or passive of **hakšambi**)

hakšambi: **1**. to fry in fat; **2**. to render fat or oil; **3**. to become scorched

hakšan: scorching, scorched

hala: **1**. clan, family, family name; **2**. kind, style, sort

hala hacin: all sorts of

hala halai: every sort of, miscellaneous

hala umiyaha: a small red insect found in wells

halabumbi: (causative or passive of **halambi**)

halahai: nettle

halai fudasi: **1**. rebellious, disloyal, perverse; **2**. in confusion

halambi: **1**. to exchange, to change (clothing), to take the place of; **2**. to correct, to emend, to change; **3**. to burn, to scald

halame aliyambi: to regret, to repent

halame arambi: to rewrite, to revise

halame etumbi: to change clothes

halame jurume: changing back and forth

halame jurume etumbi: to change clothes a number of times

halan: **1**. menstruation; **2**. exchanging

halan ilimbi: menstruation ceases

halanambi: to go to exchange, to go closer to

halandumbi: to exchange with one another; also **halanumbi**

halangga: belonging to the same clan or family

halanjambi: to exchange in turn, to take turns

halanjame dedumbi: to gang-rape

halanjame latumbi: to take turns sexually assaulting someone, to gang-rape

halanjimbi: to come to exchange

halanumbi: to exchange with one another; also **halandumbi**

halar: (onomatopoetic) the sound made by jade pendants hitting together, tinkling

halar hilir: (onomatopoetic) the sound of bells on a girdle, the sound made by a shaman's sword

halašakū: **1**. a pampered child; **2**. coquette, flirt, flirtatious woman; **3**. joker, funny person

halašambi: **1**. to act spoiled, to act up, to pout; **2**. to wiggle and squirm about, to act unsettled before the onset of a fever or smallpox

halba: **1**. the shoulder blade, a scapula; **2**. toy made from a pig's scapula with a red cord and coins attached

halbaha: **1**. a small knob on a helmet, the decoration on the top of a banner pole, a finial; **2**. the wide part of an arrowhead; **3**. a spoon

halbaha moo: a three-holed, two-foot long wooden plank used in ceremonies in the shamanistic shrine

halbahan: spoon-bill pelican

halbišambi: to curry favor, to fawn

halbubumbi: (causative of **halbumbi**)

halbulha: one who gives shelter to bandits and thieves

halbumbi: **1**. to give entrance to, to take into one's home, to give shelter to; **2**. to cover, to conceal

halda: sturgeon's spleen (used as a medicine for boils)

halda yoo: a boil between the shoulder blades

haldaba: flatterer, an obsequious person, a sycophant

haldabašambi: to be obsequious

haldarambi: to slip and fall

halfiri: a flat hollow fruit about the size of a tangerine

halfiyakan: somewhat flat

halfiyan: flat, thin

halfiyan nimaha: flatfish, flounder

halfiyan turi: *Dolichos lablab*: flat bean

halfiyangga: flat-shaped

halfiyangga jahūdai: a kind of flatboat used on the Yangtze River

halfiyangga tungken: a flat drum used in religious services

halgan: ⟶ **halhan**

halgibumbi: **1**. (causative or passive of **halgimbi**); **2**. to be tongue-tied

halgimbi: (-ka) to wrap around, to wind, to entwine

halhan: plowshare

halhimbi: ⟶ **halgimbi**

halhūkan: rather hot

halhūn: hot

halhūn bederembi: one of the divisions of the solar year — falling on the 23rd or 24th of August

halhūn calimbi: to suffer from heat prostration

halhūn goimbi: to have heat stroke, to be affected adversely by hot weather

halhūn jailambi: to escape the heat of summer

halhūn mucen: pot with charcoal in a center chimney, used for chafing meat, hotpot, chafing pot

halhūn šahūrun bulukan necin: hot, cold, warm, even (used to describe the nature of medicines)

halhūn šeri: hot spring, spa

halhūri: pepper

hali: **1**. marshland, swamp, untilled land, virgin land; **2**. official; cf. **hafan hali**

hali bigan: wilderness, wilds

hali ulhū: marsh grass

halman: soap, soap for the face

halmari: **1**. a sword used by shamans; **2**. ⟶ **ibagan halmari**

halmun: a bushing: an iron ring placed in the hub of a wheel into which an axle is inserted

haltan yoo: ⟶ **halda yoo**

halu: fine flour or meal

halu hacin: ⟶ **hala hacin**

halukan: warm

halukan edun: a warm wind

halukan nesuken: pleasantly warm

halukū: thick cotton trousers

halungga gūlha: fur-lined boots

hamgiya: **1**. skullcap (*Scutellaria baicalensis*); **2**. plants resembling sagebrush or mugwort

hamgiya suiha: dry brush, overgrowth

hamgiyari: one of the names for the wild pig

hamibumbi: (causative of **hamimbi**)

hamimbi: (-ka) **1**. to approach, to be close to, almost to reach, to be within reach; **2**. to suffice; **3**. to bear, to tolerate

hamika: almost, within reach

hamime: about to, on the point of

hamirakū: **1**. unbearable; **2**. insufficient; **3**. unattainable; **4**. unsuccessful

haminambi: **1**. to go near to, to approach; **2**. almost to reach, to be close to, to be near attaining something

haminjimbi: to come near to, to approach

hamišambi: to go right up to, to approach closely, to come close to, almost to reach

hamtabumbi: (causative of **hamtambi**)

hamtakū: a child who defecates where he ought not

hamtambi: to defecate

hamtanambi: to go to defecate

hamtu: felt hat

hamu: excrement, feces

hamu dundambi: 'feeds with feces' — an expletive

hamu sere yoo: hemorrhoids

hamutambi: ⟶ **hamtambi**

han: Emperor, Khan

han i araha: commissioned by the Emperor

han i hese: Imperial edict

han i pilehe: endorsed by the Emperor

han i uksun i ejehe: the genealogy of the Imperial clan

han i uksun i ejehe kuren: (玉牒館) Bureau for the Compilation of the Genealogical Record of the Imperial Clan

han tembi: to ascend the throne, to become Emperor

han usiha: the second star of the Great Dipper

han dung: reservoir, tank

hana: a section of the lattice wall of a yurt

hanci: near

hanci fimembi: to approach, to come near to, to come close

hanci latumbi: to come near, to approach

hanci šurdeme: in the vicinity of

hancikan: rather near

hanciki: near, near place, nearby, vicinity

hanciki niyalma: relative, person from the same town

hancikingge: that which is near, one who is nearby

hancingga: near, proximate

hancuha mucen: a three-legged cooking pot, tripod

handa: a pock mark, a scar

handu: **1**. the rice plant; **2**. leaven for making soy sauce

handu bele: late maturing rice

handu boihon: mud in a rice paddy

handu cise: a rice paddy, flooded rice field

handu cyse: wet field (for rice); cf. **handu cise**

handu iri: ⟶ **handu cise**

handu orho: rice stalks, rice straw

handu tarire kūwaran: (稻田廠) Imperial Agricultural Office, *BH* 90A

handu umiyaha: the rice worm

handucun: a song of the rice harvest

handumbi: to plant in a paddy field

handutun: a round vessel for holding offerings at sacrifices

hanggabumbi: **1**. to block, to obstruct, to impede; **2**. to be obstructed, to be congested; **3**. to grow slowly (due to drought)

hanggai: packsaddle

>**hanggai enggemu**: ⟶ **hanggai**

>**hanggai niru**: an unpolished, rusty arrowhead

hanggambi: to moisten by sprinkling

hanggi: ⟶ **hangki**

hanggir hinggir: (onomatopoetic) the tinkle of bracelets and anklets

hanggir seme: tinkling, jingling

hanggisun: a fringed sash worn by women, a scarf, a kerchief

hangki: *Melia japonica*: China-berry tree

hangnabumbi: (causative of **hangnambi**)

hangnambi: to solder, to weld, to repair metal pots

>**hangnara faksi**: a repairer of pots

>**hangnara okto**: solder

hangnan: solder

hangnasi: borax

hangse: noodles

hangsi: **1**. a kind of very thin silk; **2**. the spring festival falling on the 5th or 6th of April

>**hangsi inenggi**: the Spring Festival

hangšara: ⟶ **kangsiri**

hani majige: ⟶ **hani tani**

hani tani: tiny, little; cf. **heni tani**

hanja: incorrupt, honest, clean, pure

>**hanja bolgo**: incorrupt and clean

>**hanja genggiyen**: upright and incorruptible

>**hanja gingge**: honest and clean

>**hanja girutu**: incorrupt and possessing a sense of shame

hanjadambi: to act honestly, to act incorruptly

hanjambi: to be covetous, to be greedy

hanjan: ⟶ **hanja**

hao: one ten-thousandth of a Chinese foot

har seme: pungent, having a sharp odor

hara: **1**. a short autumn coat of sable or lynx; **2**. *Setaria viridis*: a common weed, foxtail; **3**. black (said of horses)

>**hara orho**: foxtail, bristlegrass

harambi: to watch, to observe

haran: reason, cause

haranambi: to produce foxtails, to produce weeds

harangga: **1**. subordinate, subject to, belonging to, vassal to; **2**. (the one) in question, the said … , the appropriate … ; **3**. one of the divisions of the Green Banner

>**harangga aiman be aliha bolgobure fiyenten**: (典屬清吏司) Department of the Outer Mongols, *BH* 495

>**harangga ba**: a dependent or subordinate area

>**harangga hafan**: subordinate (official)

haratu: subordinate, underling, subject

hardakū: carp

hardame: ⟶ **herdeme hardame**

harga: ⟶ **harha**

hargasi: ⟶ **harkasi**

hargašabumbi: (causative of **hargašambi**)

hargašambi: **1**. to look up, to look up to, to look into the distance from a high place; **2**. to go to court, to have an audience at court; **3**. to admire

>**hargašame buyembi**: to admire, to esteem

>**hargašame dorolombi**: to make obeisance, to pay respects (to a sovereign)

>**hargašame goidaha**: "I have longed to meet you."

>**hargašame tuwambi**: to look up, to look into the distance

>**hargašara dorolonggo kunggeri**: (朝儀科) a bureau charged with checking the credentials of those granted Imperial audiences

hargašan: the court

>**hargašan de hengkilenjire bolgobure fiyenten**: (王會清吏司) Department for Receiving Princes of Inner Mongolia, *BH* 495

>**hargašan i boo**: palace

>**hargašan yamun**: the Imperial Court

hargašanambi: to go to court

hargašandumbi: to look up together; also **hargašanumbi**

hargašanjimbi: to come to court

>**hargašanjire acanjire kunggeri**: (朝參科) a bureau of the Imperial Patent Office concerned with Imperial audiences

hargašanumbi: to look up together; also **hargašandumbi**

hargi: **1**. a place where water flows very swiftly, rapids; **2**. mustard

hargi sogi: mustard (the plant), mustard greens

hargi šurdeku: whirlpool, eddy

harha: the leather between the sole and the leg of a boot

harhū: mire, mud, silt, sludge

harhū boihon: the mud at the bottom of a body of water, slime, mire

harhū umiyaha: *Cicindela chinensis*: tiger beetle, a small worm with black and yellow spots that is used to cure the bite of a mad dog

harhūdambi: to stir up the mud on the bottom of a river or lake in order to stifle fish

hari: **1**. crooked, bent, curved, awry, inclining; **2**. cross-eyed; **3**. a net bag for holding deer's innards

haribumbi: **1**. (causative or passive of **harimbi**); **2**. for the face and ears to become frozen, to be frozen (said of crops), to suffer cold damage

harikū: an iron (for pressing clothing), a cauterizing iron

harima efen: a kind of baked cake

harimbi: **1**. to cook on a griddle, to grill; **2**. to iron (clothing); **3**. to cauterize sores on cattle; **4**. to be partial, to cover up someone's failings, to have a prejudice in favor of someone

hariha efen: flat bread baked on a griddle

hariha gese nimembi: to hurt like hell

harime dasambi: to cauterize a wound on livestock

harime gosimbi: to be partial toward, to show a preference for

haringga: ⟶ **garingga**

harkasi: various febrile diseases: influenza, typhoid fever, etc.; fever accompanied by headache and muscle pain

harkasi nimeku: a febrile disease like influenza

harsa: *Martes flavigula*: yellow-throated marten

haršakū: partial, someone who shows partiality

haršambi: **1**. to protect, to defend; **2**. to cover up for; **3**. to be partial to

haršame daldambi: to shield, to protect, to cover up

haršame dalimbi: to shelter, to protect

haršame gosimbi: to be partial

haršame tuwambi: to show partiality, to treat with partiality

haršandumbi: to cover up for one another, to protect one another; also **haršanumbi**

haršanumbi: to cover up for one another, to protect one another; also **haršandumbi**

hartungga: **1**. subordinates, subjects; **2**. (標) Chinese banner troops in the provinces

harun: ⟶ **haran**

hasa: hurriedly, quickly

hasa gene: go quickly!

hasaha: scissors, shears

hasaha umiyaha: centipede

hasahalambi: to cut with scissors or shears

hasahangga fukjingga hergen: (剪刀篆) a style of calligraphy

hasak seme: (onomatopoetic) the sound of rustling paper

hasala: a fast-running cow

hasalabumbi: (causative of **hasalambi**)

hasalakū: shears, scissors, shears for cutting metal

hasalambi: to cut with scissors, to shear

hasan: mange, itch, scabies

hasanambi: to get the mange or scabies

hasha: ⟶ **hasaha**

hashalabumbi: (causative of **hashalambi**)

hashalambi: to erect a fence or palisade, to mark off

hashan: a fence of wood or kaoliang stalks, a palisade

hashan jafambi: to erect a fence or palisade

hashan umiyaha: millipede

hashū: **1**. left; **2**. erroneous, improper, depraved

hashū ergi fiyenten: (左司) First Department (of a government organ)

hashū tonggo tabumbi: to fasten thread on the left side

hashūtai: **1**. heterodox, depraved; **2**. left-handed, a left-handed person; cf. **hasutai**

hashūtai doro: heterodoxy, black magic

hasi: **1**. persimmon; **2**. eggplant

hasi boco: the color of eggplant

hasi funta: the white powder-like material found on persimmons

hasi šatan: large dried persimmons

hasiba: protective, prone to defending

hasihan: ⟶ **hašahan**

hasihimbi: **1**. to go hurriedly, to scurry; **2**. to hope to attain something by good fortune

hasikū: ⟶ **hašakū**

hasima: *Rana amurensis*: Manchurian wood frog

hasingga: pertaining to the persimmon, persimmon-shaped

   hasingga tampin: a persimmon-shaped container

hasiri: the color of eggplant, eggplant purple

hasrun sirga: a white horse with red spots around the nose and eyes

hastai: ⟶ **hashūtai**

hasu orho: a kind of climbing plant whose melon-like fruit can be salted and eaten

hasukiyalambi: ⟶ **hašukiyambi**

hasuralabumbi: (causative of **hasuralambi**)

hasuralambi: ⟶ **hasurgalambi**

hasuran: the bark of the Chinese wild peach (*Prunus davidiana*)

   hasuran moo: the tree from which **hasuran** is taken

hasurgalambi: to cover (arrows) with the bark of the wild peach tree

hasutai: **1**. left-handed, with the left hand, left-handed person; **2**. heterodox, depraved

   hasutai banin: odd temperament, stubbornness

   hasutai doro: ⟶ **hashūtai doro**

haša: a small storage house

   haša boo: ⟶ **haša**

hašabumbi: (causative of **hašambi**)

hašahan: **1**. a cloth covering (for vehicles); **2**. a grain container made of mats sewn together; **3**. the felt covering for a section of a Mongolian yurt; **4**. a device for catching fish; **5**. tablecloth, table covering

hašakū: a scrubbing brush (made from gaoliang stalks or the stalks of other grains)

   hašakū dengjan: lanterns placed on the four corners of the yellow tent in temples and at altars on days of sacrifice

hašambi: **1**. to scrub; **2**. to surround, to encompass; **3**. to cover, to shelter from, to bank with earth

hašan: drapery, curtain, hangings

hašatambi: to protect carefully

hašukiyambi: to hasten, to hurry

hata: a thin belt or strip of cloth

hatabumbi: (causative or passive of **hatambi**)

hataburu: hateful — an expletive

hatacuka: hateful, detestable, loathsome

hatakan: rather strong, somewhat hard

hatambi: **1**. to loath, to find repugnant, to hate; **2**. to immerse red-hot metals into water to harden them, to temper; **3**. to fire (ceramics or pottery)

   hatame deijimbi: to temper (metals), to fire (pottery, brick, etc.)

hatan: **1**. violent, fierce, hot-tempered; **2**. strong (said of liquor); **3**. fiery, blazing, scorching; **4**. hard (said of metal)

   hatan furu: cruel, savage, fierce

   hatan nure: strong liquor

hatarambi: to fall ill suddenly, to have a sudden pain, to have a fit of temper

hatuhūn: salty, brackish

   hatuhūn muke: brackish water

   hatuhūn sogi: salted vegetables

   hatuhūn usiha: a kind of sour fruit from the South

hayabumbi: (causative or passive of **hayambi**)

hayadambi: to act lewdly

hayaha: ⟶ **hayambi** (subheading)

hayahan: border, trim (on clothing)

   hayahan dahū: a court garment trimmed with sable, lynx, or black fox

   hayahan i ergume: a fur-trimmed court dress

   hayahan i ulhun: a sable-trimmed shoulder piece

   hayahan undurakū: trimmed "dragon satin"

hayakta: a wild pig with upturned tusks

hayaljambi: to wind, to twist, to slither

hayambi: **1**. to coil, to wind, to wreathe, to spiral; **2**. to hem, to edge, to trim (a garment), to add a border

   hayaha hiyan: coiled incense

   hayaha meihe usiha: (騰蛇) the name of a Chinese constellation that has the appearance of a coiled snake

   hayaha undurakū: bordered "dragon satin"

   hayame banjimbi: to grow in a coiled fashion

   hayame dedumbi: to lie coiled up (like a snake)

hayan: licentious, loose, dissolute, lewd, lascivious

   hayan hehe: wanton woman, woman with loose morals

   hayan koiman: indecent, overly familiar

   hayan mujilen: lust, sexual desire

hayandambi: ⟶ **hayadambi**

hayandumbi: to wreathe around

hayarilambi: ⟶ **hayaljambi**

hayarlambi: ⟶ **hayaljambi**

he: stretcher, litter

he dz: garment made of coarse cloth

he fa seme: (onomatopoetic) gasping, panting

he gi: the hoki pheasant; cf. **gūnggala coko**

hebdebumbi: (causative of **hebdembi**)

hebdembi: to discuss, to talk over, to consult

hebdenembi: to go to talk over

hebdenjimbi: to come to talk over

hebdenumbi: to discuss together

hebdešembi: to talk over carefully or thoroughly

hebe: **1**. consultation, deliberation, planning; **2**. plan, plot, intrigue

  hebe acambi: to hold a consultation, to come together to deliberate

  hebe arambi: to plot, to deliberate

  hebei: with forethought, deliberately

  hebei amban: (參贊大臣) Councillor, *BH* 867, 880

  hebei antaha: assistant to a high official

  hebei ba: (議政處) an office in charge of receiving and handling memorials concerning affairs of state

  hebei hafan: strategist, officer in charge of planning

  hebei latumbi: to have an adulterous affair

  hebei saisa: advisor, adjutant

  hebei ubašambi: to plot a revolt

  hebei urse: advisors

  hebei wambi: to kill treacherously, to murder

hebedembi: ⟶ **hebdembi**

  hebedere saisa: strategist

hebei: ⟶ **hebe** (subheading)

hebengge: **1**. of one mind, in agreement, open to discussion; **2**. obedient to the pull of the reins

heberembi: to investigate, to inquire into

hebešebumbi: (causative of **hebešembi**)

hebešembi: to discuss, to talk over, to consult about, to plot

  hebešeme toktobumbi: to come to agreement, to settle through consultation

hebešendumbi: to discuss with one another

hebešenjimbi: to come to discuss

hebte ihan: a cow with white hair on both sides of the belly

hebtehe: a wide waistband (worn by women)

hebtešembi: **1**. to struggle for breath, to gasp; **2**. to greet someone with bows and raised hands; **3**. to curry favor, to ingratiate oneself

hebu: the end of a thread, a snag, the broken end of a thread

hebunembi: to form thread ends or snags

hecebumbi: (causative of **hecembi**)

hecembi: **1**. to scoop out completely; **2**. to use up, to do something thoroughly

  heceme gamame: completely, thoroughly

  heceme herembi: to scoop up completely, to catch up everything in a net

  heceme kimcimbi: to make a thorough investigation

hecen: city, city wall

  hecen i fu: city wall

  hecen i keremu: parapet, rampart

  hecen sahambi: to build a city wall

  hecen ulan: moat

heceri ilha: an exotic yellow flower that blooms in spring

hede: **1**. what remains after a boil or sore heals, scar; **2**. something left behind (offspring, property), progeny, offspring; **3**. stubble (of wheat or grass); **4**. sediment, dregs; **5**. charred portion of a candle wick

  hede bi: has offspring

  hede da: descendant

  hede lakcambi: to have no offspring

hedei: a bunghole, a mortise

hederebumbi: (causative or passive of **hederembi**)

hedereku: a rake

  hedereku orho: ivy

hederembi: to rake, to rake in, to scratch (said of thorns)

hederenumbi: to rake together

hedu: an itch, scabies

  hedu fiyelen: scabies and ringworm

hefa seme: ⟶ **he fa seme**

hefeli: belly, womb

  hefeli aššambi: to have diarrhea

  hefeli de toktonombi: to be reborn in the womb

  hefeli dorgi jui: fetus

  hefeli hūwaitakū: a maternity girdle

  hefeli nimembi: to have a belly ache, to suffer gastric distress

  hefeli wakjahūn: the belly hangs down in a paunch

hefeliye: ⟶ **hefeli**

hefeliyebumbi: (causative of **hefeliyembi**)

hefeliyembi: **1**. to carry at the bosom, to hold in one's arms; **2**. to cherish

hefeliyen: **1**. bosom; **2**. ⟶ **hefeli**

hefeliyenembi: to have diarrhea

    hefeliyenere nimeku: dysentery

hehe: woman, female, wife

    hehe dethe: the smaller feathers on a bird's wing

    hehe doose: a Daoist nun

    hehe feyesi: female undertaker, female coroner

    hehe gaimbi: to take a wife, to marry

    hehe han: Empress, female khan

    hehe hūwašan: Buddhist nun

    hehe jui: girl, female child

    hehe keli: husband's brother's wife

    hehe nakcu: aunt: wife of mother's brother

    hehe tohon: loop for a button

    hehei lang: young girl

hehengge: female, pertaining to women, feminine

heherdembi: to become a woman, to become nubile

hehereku: womanish, showing female pettiness

heherembi: to act in a feminine way

    hehereme arbušambi: to act in a feminine way (said of men)

heheri: **1**. palate; **2**. indentation, groove, crevasse

    heheri faitame: cutting across a crevasse

    heheri madaha: "the palate has swollen" (a sign of sickness in cattle)

hehesi: (plural of **hehe**)

hei hai: (onomatopoetic) the sound of crying

heihedembi: to stagger, to reel (said of a drunk person)

heiherembi: to stumble along

heiheri haihari: staggering, reeling, with graceful and sinuous movements

heiheri haiharilambi: to reel, to stagger

heiherilembi: to sway, to stagger

heihule: a small round fish with a small mouth, possibly a kind of dace

heihuwe: fish cut into small pieces and then fried in its own fat

hejembi: **1**. to mend by stitching threads in a criss-cross pattern; **2**. to have difficulty in breathing, to gasp; **3**. to make a betrothal, to be betrothed, to get engaged

    hejere jaka: betrothal gift

hejen fiyaka: a dogsled

hejihe: **1**. a steep area of a mountainside; **2**. the horizontal wooden bar on a pounder or pestle (for rice)

hejiheleme: along the steep part of a mountainside

hejimbi: ⟶ **hejembi**

hekcehun: falling (said of the flood waters in autumn)

hekcembi: to ebb, to go out (said of the tide)

hekderehun: ⟶ **hekderhen**

hekderembi: to go across a steep area on a mountainside

hekderhen: a steep slope

hekderhun: steep

hekterembi: (**-ke**) to lose consciousness

hele: **1**. mute, dumb; **2**. ⟶ **helen**

    hele hempe: stuttering

    hele hempe akū: speechless, without talent for speaking

heledembi: to stutter

helen: **1**. a spy, an informer, an enemy captive who gives information; **2**. ⟶ **hele**

    helen akū: **1**. having difficulty speaking; **2**. speechless, inarticulate; cf. **hele hempe akū**

    helen burubumbi: to lose one's ability to speak (due to illness)

    helen hempe: stuttering; cf. **hele hempe**

    helen hempe akū: ⟶ **hele hempe akū**

    helen jafambi: to catch an enemy in order to extract information from him

heleri halari: careless, neglectful, sluggish

helfišembi: to lean to one side, to waver; cf. **kelfišembi**

heliyen: **1**. stone pestle, device for hulling rice, foot-operated pestle; **2**. praying mantis

    heliyen sebsehe: praying mantis

helme: ⟶ **helmen**

helmehen: spider

    helmehen i asu: spider web

helmeku: spider; cf. **helmehen**

helmembi: to spin a web

helmen: **1**. shadow, shade; **2**. reflection

    helmen uran: shadows and echoes, reaction

helmenembi: to cast shadows

helmešembi: to reflect light, to cast a shadow

helnebumbi: (causative of **helnembi**)

helnembi: to invite, to go to invite

    helneme solimbi: to invite

helnere šusihe: a silver identification plaque carried by dignitaries while on an inspection

hemhimbi: to grope one's way along

hemilembi: to gather up (the hem of a garment)

hempe: stuttering, stutterer

hen: **1**. a small portable chair made of wood or bamboo; **2**. a small amount

hen tan i: **1**. needy, in need; **2**. with difficulty, barely

hencebumbi: (causative or passive of **hencembi**)

hencehen: a small hoe-shaped implement (for scraping the sides of cooking pots), trowel, small spade

henceku: mortar for pounding grain

hencembi: to pound in a mortar, to smash, to crush

henden: ⟶ **hente**

hendubumbi: (causative of **hendumbi**)

hendumbi: to say, to speak

heng o enduri: the moon goddess Heng E

hengge: ⟶ **hengke**

henggenembi: to have an unkempt appearance, to be uncombed and dirty

henggilembi: ⟶ **hengkilembi**

hengke: melon, cucurbitaceous plants

hengkeri: a kind of small melon

hengkeri fulana ilha: *Pirus spectabilis*: Chinese crabapple

hengki: (shortened imperative of **hengkilembi**)

hengkilebumbi: **1**. (causative of **hengkilembi**); **2**. to have shares apportioned equally according to the number of people

hengkileku: **1**. a clamp for holding together broken objects; **2**. trigger on a musket; **3**. one who kowtows

hengkileku umiyaha: snapping beetle, click beetle

hengkilembi: to kowtow, to prostrate oneself

hengkilendumbi: to kowtow together; also **hengkilenumbi**

hengkilenembi: to go to kowtow, to go to court

hengkilenjimbi: to come to kowtow, to come to court

hengkilenumbi: to kowtow together; also **hengkilendumbi**

hengkin: a kowtow, a prostration

hengkin i tuwabun: list of the names of officials granted audiences at court

hengkin i tuwabun i kunggeri: (啟疏科) an office of the Court of Banqueting concerned with the above-mentioned list

hengkišembi: to kowtow repeatedly

heni: **1**. a little, a bit; **2**. a pinch (the amount one can pick up with four fingers); **3**. at all (with negative expressions), not the least bit

heni akū: not in the slightest

heni heni: a small amount, a little

heni sereme bahakū: did not foresee at all

heni tani: a bit, a little, only

henjembi: ⟶ **hencembi**

henjimbi: to come to invite, to invite to come here

hente: **1**. full-grown wild pig; **2**. pitchfork

hente niru: a forked arrow

hentelembi: to use a pitchfork

heo: (侯) marquis

heo seme: **1**. calm, at ease, unhurried; **2**. sufficient, enough to get by on; **3**. pretty good, not bad, fairly well

heo seme banjimbi: to get by fairly well

heo seme isika: sufficient

heoledembi: to be careless, to be negligent, to be idle, to be disrespectful toward

heoleken: rather negligent

heolen: **1**. neglect, negligence, laziness, carelessness; **2**. negligent, careless

heolen banuhūn: negligent, lazy, indolent

heolen sula: lax and negligent

heošembi: to be hesitant, to be undecided

heperebumbi: (causative of **heperembi**)

heperembi: **(1)** **(-ke)** **1**. to dodder from old age; **2**. to drink to excess, to act silly when drunk

hepereme sakdambi: to become a doddering old man

hepereme soktombi: to get soused, to become very drunk

heperembi: **(2)** to rake in greedily, to grab up greedily

her har: (onomatopoetic) ahem! (sound of clearing one's throat)

her har seme: paying attention, heeding

her har serakū: does not speak to anyone, does not pay attention to anyone, haughty, snobbish

hercibumbi: (causative of **hercimbi**)

hercimbi: to wind thread onto a spool

hercun: aforethought, attention

hercun akū: unconsciously, not paying attention, inattentively, unintentionally

hercun akū de: without realizing it

herdembi: **1**. to wander about begging, to be in dire straits; **2**. to pick up from the ground, to pick up from horseback

herdeme hardame: roaming about begging

herebumbi: (causative of **herembi**)

hereku: a ladle for lifting things from water

hereku maša: a perforated spoon for lifting things from water

herembi: **1**. to ladle out, to fish for, to drag for, to take out of water with a net, to scoop up; **2**. to produce (paper)

heren: corral, stable

heresu: (*Salicornia herbecea*: glasswort, a grass growing along the edges of salt marshes, eaten by camels)

hergebumbi: (causative of **hergembi**)

hergembi: **1**. to strain, to skim fat from the surface of a liquid; **2**. to produce paper

hergen: **1**. writing, written characters, letter; **2**. design, lines on the palm; **3**. receipt; **4**. rank, title

hergen aname: word by word, graph by graph

hergen arambi: to write

hergen dasakū: (正字) a clerk in the Supervisorate of Imperial Instruction

hergen efujembi: to be dismissed from one's rank

hergen foloro falga: (刻字處) engraving office in the Imperial Library

hergen hengkilebumbi: to pay close attention to wording, to be fussy about the use of words

hergen i kemun: lined paper, paper with cells for characters

hergen i uju: a unit of the Manchu syllabary

hergen niyalma: person with a title

hergen sirambi: to inherit a title

hergen takambi: to be literate

hergen tušan: official title

hergenembi: to form designs or characters

hergenehe cece: silken gauze with characters woven in

hergenehe suje: silk with characters woven in

hergengge: having an official title

hergesi: (儒士) a clerk of the Board of Rites

hergibumbi: (causative of **hergimbi**)

hergice: thread wound onto a spool from a hank, a reel

hergimbi: **1**. to wind (thread); **2**. to wander, to be a vagabond; **3**. to circle (said of predatory birds)

hergime hejeme: winding and criss-crossing

hergin: **1**. the border or margin of a net; **2**. rule, regulation, order, discipline; **3**. outline; **4**. ⟶ **sunja hergin**, **hešen hergin**

hergin be teksilere hashū ergi fiyenten: (肅紀左司) the name of a section of the Board of Punishments in Mukden

hergin fafun: discipline

hergin šošohon: outline, general, account

herginembi: ⟶ **hergenembi**

hergitu: reel (said of thread), skein

herin: a high spot in the bed of a body of shallow water

heristos: Christ

hersembi: to be attentive

herserakū: inattentive, paying no attention to others

hersu: ⟶ **kersu**

heršembi: ⟶ **hersembi**

heru: **1**. spokes of a wheel; **2**. frame of a fan

hese: **1**. Imperial order, edict; **2**. divine decree, fate; **3**. ⟶ **gisun hese**

hese wasimbi: to give a command, to issue an edict

hese wasimbumbi: to issue an edict

hesei: by Imperial order, by decree

hesei bithe: Imperial edict

hesei buhengge: ordained by decree, bestowed by decree

hesei kiru temgetu: a banner sent by the Emperor to dignitaries in the border regions

hesebumbi: to ordain, to determine

hesebuhe ton: fate

hesebun: fate, determination

hesebun be aliha usiha: the stars ι, κ, λ, μ, ν, and ξ in Ursa Major

hesebun forgon: fate, predestination

hesei: ⟶ **hese** (subheading)

hesihešembi: to saunter along, to look about as one walks along, to grope along

hesihetembi: to stumble along

hesitembi: ⟶ **hesihetembi**

hešelembi: to pull in a fish net
hešemilambi: ⟶ **hešemimbi**
hešemimbi: to close a bag with a drawstring
hešen: **1**. cord or rope along the edge of a net, head
    rope on a fishing net; **2**. guiding principle,
    fundamental principle, rule of conduct; **3**.
    boundary, border, shore, margin
    hešen be feshelembi: to expand the border
    hešen hergin: **1**. guiding principles; **2**. social
        order and law
    hešen i camhari: boundary marker, boundary
        stone
    hešen i wehe: boundary stone
    hešen ilibumbi: to set up a boundary marker
    hešen ulhun: basic principles, leading
        principle, outline
hešenembi: to wear tattered or dirty clothes
hešerembi: to place around the edge of something
hešu hašu: **1**. sporadic, scattered, piecemeal; **2**.
    trifling, trivial, petty
    hešu hašu baita: trifling matter, trivia
    hešu hašu niyalma: petty, small-minded person
hešurebumbi: (causative of **hešurembi**)
hešureku: rake
hešurembi: **1**. to rake in, to rake up; **2**. to do
    completely, to do thoroughly
hetebumbi: (causative of **hetembi**)
hetehen: a nail or hook used for hanging objects
hetembi: **1**. to roll up, to turn back (the sleeves of a
    garment), to lift up (the hem of a garment);
    2. to fold, to fold up; **3**. to perform a half
    kowtow in the Manchu fashion (said of
    women); **4**. to recede (said of fog); **5**. to
    bring to a conclusion
    heteme gisabumbi: to intercept and wipe out
    heteme goholombi: to grab one leg and pull up
        on it (at wrestling)
    heteme heturembi: to intercept, to obstruct
    heteme ilha: a cup-shaped piece of iron atop a
        helmet
    heteme šufatu: a kind of rolled turban
    heteme tasihimbi: to grab after the sole of the
        foot and push (at wrestling)
heterembi: ⟶ **hederembi**
hethe: **1**. property, possessions, wealth; **2**.
    occupation, undertaking; **3**. stalk, stubble; **4**.
    bridle without a metal buckle; **5**. line on the
    crupper; **6**. pressed cuff on a court garment

hethe garjambi: to go bankrupt
hethebumbi: (causative of **hethembi**)
hethembi: **1**. to pluck out (grass); **2**. to scald, to
    place in boiling water for an instant (a
    method of cooking)
hetu: **1**. horizontal; **2**. stocky, broad (said of a
    person's build); **3**. located at the side,
    peripheral; **4**. woof (in cloth); **5**.
    inauspicious, unexpected
    hetu baita: gossip, scandal
    hetu boo: wings on both sides of the main
        house, side rooms
    hetu dalangga: dam on a river
    hetu edun: a sudden wind
    hetu ficakū: a horizontal flute
    hetu hitha: ornament on the girth (saddle
        belly-strap) of a horse
    hetu lasha: transversing, crossing
    hetu niyalma: a third party, a third person, an
        outsider, someone else
    hetu šambi: to look askance at
    hetu tacikū: unorthodox teaching
    hetu tembi: to sit at the side of
    hetu tuwambi: ⟶ **hetu šambi**
    hetu ulin: windfall, ill-gotten wealth
    hetu undu: **1**. horizontal and vertical, warp and
        woof; **2**. in disorder, hither and yon
    hetu undu sarkū: does not know anything,
        does not know up from down
    hetu weile: ⟶ **hetu baita**
    hetu yabumbi: to run amok, to run wild
    hetu yasa: an icy look
    hetu yasai tuwambi: to look askance at
hetuken: rather stocky
hetuliyan: rather horizontal
hetumbi: (**-he/-ke**) to transverse, to pass across, to
    cross, to spend (a period of time)
hetumbumbi: **1**. (causative of **hetumbi**); **2**. manage
    to get by; **3**. to raise through the winter
heturebumbi: (causative of **heturembi**)
heturembi: **1**. to cut off, to block, intercept, to
    interrupt; **2**. to intercept and rob, to ambush
    hetureme gisurembi: to interrupt what
        someone is saying
heturen: a horizontal beam or rafter
heturhen: *Falco subbuteo*: hobby
heturi: **1**. peripheral, unimportant; **2**. ordinary,
    everyday; **3**. sudden

heturi ba de tembi: to live in seclusion

heturi bade: in private life, in one's unofficial life

heturi baita: private matter, peripheral matter

heturi dasargan: a popular remedy, an unauthorized prescription

heturi etuku: ordinary clothing, everyday clothes worn by an official

heturi faidan: an ordinary escort

heturi faidan i kiyoo: a sedan chair with gold-colored curtains, carried by eight men

heturi fasilan: side issues, unexpected complications

heturi gisun: digression (from a main topic)

heturi jobolon: unexpected calamity, sudden misfortune

heturi sarin: private banquet

heye: discharge from the eyes

heyen: ⟶ **heye**

heyenembi: to discharge matter from the eyes; cf. **abka heyenehebi**

hi cy: a name for the mandarin duck; cf. **ijifun niyehe**

hib seme: striking solidly (said of an arrow shot at an animal), striking a hard blow

hibcan: **1.** scarce, needy, meager; **2.** frugal, sparing

hibcan eden: scarcity, lack

hibcan gulungge: frugal and unassuming

hibcan hafirahūn: in dire straits, indigent

hibcan malhūn: frugal

hibcarabumbi: (causative of **hibcarambi**)

hibcarambi: to be frugal, to act frugally, to live in a frugal fashion

hibcarandumbi: to be frugal together; also **hibcaranumbi**

hibcaranumbi: to be frugal together; also **hibcarandumbi**

hibcilakū: frugal person, miser

hibsa: ⟶ **hiyabsa**

hibsu: honey

hibsu ejen: honeybee

hibsu ejen i hitha: beehive

hibsu i da: queen bee

hibsu šugi: candied fruit, fruit preserved in honey

hibsungge: pertaining to honey

hibsungge usiha: a chestnut-like fruit

hibta: **1.** a protective shoulder pad of felt for carrying things; **2.** a kind of shawl or cape worn by women

hican: frugal, abstemious, simple in one's way of life, uncorrupted

hican getuken: pure, incorrupt

hican kemungge: thrifty, frugal

hicu: fault, defect, slip-up, mistake

hicu kicembi: to find fault with

hicumbi: **1.** to look for faults in someone, to find fault; **2.** to cause difficulties, to criticize

hicume tuhebumbi: to cause harm to someone

hida: **1.** curtain made of bamboo or reeds; **2.** bamboo grating used for steaming food, grid, grate

hidakū: a curtain in front of a door or window to protect from rain

hidambi: to wind yarn onto a wooden spindle

hife: *Echinochloa crusgalli*: barnyard grass, tares, darnel

hife bele: grain from barnyard grass

hife hara: a kind of barnyard grass with spreading ears

hihajambi: ⟶ **hiyahanjambi**

hihalambi: **1.** to consider rare, to consider precious; **2.** to value, to esteem, to consider worthwhile, to deign

hihan: rare, precious

hihan akū: ⟶ **hihanakū**

hihanakū: not precious, worthless, not worthy

hihūn budun: listless, lacking enthusiasm, depressed, uninterested, desultory, disappointed, gloomy, somber

hija: stove, furnace, smelter, hearth for melting metals

hija dabumbi: to light a stove

hija i niyalma: smelter

hija i nuhaliyan: a heated oven-bed

hija i tukda: grate on stove

hija tuwambi: to watch a furnace in order to regulate the heat

hijada: a person in charge of smelting stoves

hijuhūn: blind

hilteri: armor scales worn visibly on the outside of a mail skirt

hilterilembi: to attach **hilteri** to a mail skirt

himci: in two, asunder

himci genehe: broke in two

hin giranggi: the tibia, shinbone; cf. **sudu**

hina: one ten-thousandth of a Chinese foot

hinceo: silk woven from twisted thread, worsted silk

hinci: ⟶ **himci**

hincu: ⟶ **hinceo**

hing je: mendicant (Buddhist) monk

hing seme: **1**. honest, sincere, earnest; **2**. concerned, solicitous; **3**. serious (said of an illness)

   hing seme nimembi: to have a serious illness

hing tsai: ⟶ **hinggari**

hinggan: mountain range, forested mountains

hinggari: *Nymphoides peltatum*: floating heart

hingge: school of fish, swarm of fish

hinggeri: (虛) a constellation, the 11th of the lunar mansions, made up of two stars, β in Aquarius and α in Equuleus

   hinggeri tokdonggo kiru: (虛宿旗) a banner depicting the constellation **hinggeri**

hingke: land not suitable for agriculture

   hingke usin: poor land, land unsuitable for cultivation, unproductive field

hingneci: **1**. mallow; **2**. *Brasenia schreberi*: watershield (an edible water plant)

   hingneci šu ilha: water lily

hingsengge: sincere, honest

hio seme: sighing deeply

hiohūn: ⟶ **hihūn**

hiong seme: (onomatopoetic) the sound of wings flapping

hionghioi gasha: *Lanius sphenocercus*: the Chinese great shrike

hionghūwang: realgar

hir hir seme: sad, morose, worried

hir seme: sad, bereaved

hiracambi: to keep looking askance, to spy on intently, to stare at

   hiracame guwelecembi: to covet, to cast greedy eyes on

hiralambi: to spy, to look furtively

hirambi: to look askance at, to spy on, to peek

hirandumbi: to spy on one another

hirga: ⟶ **hirha**

hirgambi: ⟶ **hirhambi**

hirgen: the dried bed of a creek or river

hirha: flint

hirhabumbi: (causative of **hirhambi**)

hirhambi: to cut off, to shear off

hirhelembi: to flow along

hirho: corsac; cf. **kirsa**

hirhūbumbi: (causative or passive of **hirhūmbi**)

hirhūmbi: **1**. to scrape; **2**. to irritate, to provoke; **3**. to scrape against a wall or tree to stop itching (said of animals)

hiri: **1**. firmly, fast (asleep); **2**. disappointed

   hiri akdambi: to trust firmly

   hiri amgambi: to sleep soundly

   hiri oho: became disappointed

   hiri onggoho: completely forgot

   hiri ubiyambi: to despise, to dislike intensely

hirinjambi: to be distressed

hirsa: corsac; cf. **kirsa**

hisalabumbi: (causative of **hisalambi**)

hisalambi: to pour a libation of liquor in honor of the dead

hisdakū: cymbals

hise: actor, actress

hishabumbi: (causative of **hishambi**)

hishakū: a brush

hishambi: **1**. to brush, to brush against, to scrape; **2**. to strike (a flint); **3**. to sharpen, to whet

   hishame: (used as a postposition) right next to, very close to

hishan: dirty spot, dirt adhering to something, stain

hishanambi: to form a dirty spot, to become dirty

hishūn: **1**. shy, modest, restrained; **2**. too ashamed to show one's face

hisy: a very steep and dangerous spot on a mountainside

hitaha: ⟶ **hitha**

hitahūn: **1**. fingernail, toenail; **2**. pick for a stringed instrument

hitahūšambi: to press firmly with a fingernail

hitarhūn: wrinkled

hitaršambi: to wrinkle

hiterebumbi: (causative of **hiterembi**)

hiterembi: (**-ke**) to knit the brow, to frown

hiterenembi: to bunch up in wrinkles (said of clouds that are piled one atop another like fish scales)

hiterešembi: to frown continually

hitha: **1**. ornament on a horse's bridle or crupper; **2**. a scale of armor; **3**. beehive, honeycomb; **4**. ⟶ **šu ilhai hitha**

hithalambi: to make a beehive

   hithalame giyalambi: to make cells in a beehive

hithari: an exotic red fruit whose skin resembles armor scales

hithembi: **1**. to sprinkle water; **2**. to sprinkle water using chopsticks (at shamanistic rites)

hithen: chest, trunk

hithūn: ⟶ **hitahūn**

hiya: **1**. guard, page, chamberlain (more specifically an Imperial guard who wore peacock feathers; cf. *BH* 99); **2**. dry; **3**. reel, spool

hiya aniya: drought year

hiya gashan: drought

hiya gurun i sirdan: a kind of ancient arrow

hiya kadalara dorgi amban: (領侍衛內大臣) Chamberlain of the Imperial Bodyguard, *BH* 98

hiya kadalara dorgi amban i ba: (領侍衛內大臣處) Office of the Chamberlain of the Imperial Bodyguard

hiya silmen: female sparrow hawk (*Accipiter virgatus*)

hiyai idui janggin: (侍衛班領) Commander of a Relief of the Bodyguard, *BH* 99

hiyai juwan i da: (侍衛什長) Sergeant of the Imperial Bodyguard, *BH* 99

hiyab seme: quickly, swiftly

hiyaban: coarse hempen cloth, grass cloth, cloth made from ramie

hiyabsa: **1**. a press; **2**. two boards bound by cords used as a cover for books or documents; **3**. two boards placed on the necks of draft animals or boards placed on the backs of such animals to secure the saddle blanket; **4**. splint for a broken limb

hiyabsa enggemu: pack saddle, small wooden saddle (for horses pulling a load)

hiyabsa jahūdai: a kind of large seagoing vessel

hiyabsalabumbi: (causative of **hiyabsalambi**)

hiyabsalambi: **1**. to splint a broken limb; **2**. to tie a horizontal board on an ox's horns

hiyabsambi: to lick (as a mother cow its young)

hiyabulakū: a lantern rack

hiyabun: a hemp stalk to which chaff or sesame stalks are attached and ignited — a kind of lantern used by the Manchus

hiyadabumbi: (causative of **hiyadambi**)

hiyadambi: **1**. to plait, to weave (a net or basket); **2**. to darn, to mend

hiyadan: **1**. a rack of shelves, a cabinet for books; **2**. compartments in a closet or chest

hiyadangga kunggeri: (架閣科) a section of the Office of Discipline in the Board of War

hiyaganjambi: to be in disorder, to be confused; cf. **hiyahanjambi**

hiyaganjame tuheke: fell in heaps (said of the corpses of bandits that have been executed)

hiyahabumbi: **1**. (causative of **hiyahambi**); **2**. to mess up, to create confusion; **3**. to knit

hiyahalabumbi: (causative or passive of **hiyahalambi**)

hiyahalambi: **1**. to cross one another, to cross back and forth, to criss-cross; **2**. to involve, to implicate

hiyahalame tabumbi: to string a bow by bending it with the knees

hiyahali cecike: *Loxia curvirostra*: crossbill

hiyahaljambi: ⟶ **hiyahalambi**

hiyahambi: to cross, to criss-cross

hiyahan: **1**. an abatis — a means of military defense consisting of pointed stakes jutting outward from a central shaft; **2**. crosspiece on a crupper; **3**. an object shaped like a cross

hiyahan i enggemu: a saddle with a support on it for holding a child

hiyahan mulan: **1**. chair with a back; **2**. folding chair

hiyahan mulan i iletu kiyoo: an open litter with a folding chair

hiyahan siltangga jahūdai: a ship with crossing masts

hiyahan tehe: cross (a means of crucifixion)

hiyahanjambi: to be piled up, to lie in a confused heap, to criss-cross, to intersect, to be interlaced

hiyahanjame tembi: to live intermingled in one place (said of different ethnic groups)

hiyahanjame tuheke: ⟶ **hiyaganjame tuheke**

hiyahū: wheezing, a rattling sound in the throat, asthma

hiyahū nimeku: asthma

hiyai: ⟶ **hiya** (subheading)

hiyak seme: furious, in a rage

hiyalambi: **1**. to carry a child on one's back; **2**. to wear a hairnet

hiyalar seme: the sound of metal or porcelain falling

hiyalhūwa: hemp stalks

hiyalhūwari: a match (made from hemp stalks)

hiyalu: a carrying bag made of netting, a hairnet

hiyaluri ilha: an exotic small white flower that resembles a net made from silk thread

hiyamtun: the name of a small sacrificial vessel of the Xia dynasty

hiyan: **1**. incense, perfume; **2**. *xiàn* 縣, county, district

    hiyan ceng: (縣丞) Assistant District Magistrate

    hiyan dabukū: incense burner

    hiyan dabukū i sindakū: a table on which an incense burner is placed

    hiyan dere: a table used for burning incense

    hiyan fila: a dish on which incense is burned

    hiyan i caliyasi: (縣總) District Tax Clerk

    hiyan i ejesi: (典史) Jail Warden, *BH* 857

    hiyan i fangšakū: a bag in which incense is placed

    hiyan i hoseri: a box for incense

    hiyan i jumanggi: a small bag for holding incense

    hiyan i saraci: (知縣) District Magistrate, *BH* 856

    hiyan i sihan: a cylindrical container used for burning incense

    hiyan i siramsi: (縣丞) Assistant District Magistrate, *BH* 857

    hiyan i tacibukū hafan: (教諭) District Director of Schools, *BH* 857

    hiyan sisikū: a flat wooden or clay vessel for incense

hiyanci: a hunting rifle with a long thin barrel

hiyancilambi: to form a herd (said of deer in summer)

hiyancuhū nimaha: salted fish

hiyang be: eunuch

hiyang bing: cake of incense

hiyang ca: jasmine tea

hiyang cun moo: *Cedrela sinensis*: Chinese toon tree

hiyang hing seme: **1**. energetically, vigorously; **2**. strictly

hiyang seme: vociferously, energetically

hiyangci: chess

hiyangci sindambi: to play chess

hiyangci undehen: chessboard

hiyangcilambi: ⟶ **hiyangci sindambi**

hiyanglu: an incense burner; cf. **hiyan dabukū**

hiyangtaršambi: to act overbearingly, to be arrogant

hiyangtu: somewhat squint-eyed

hiyanjuhū nimaha: ⟶ **hiyancuhū nimaha**

hiyari: squint-eyed

hiyaribumbi: to wither up because of drought

hiyaršambi: to get up and leave, to evade

hiyasa: (plural of **hiya**)

    hiyasai budai boo: (侍衛飯局) kitchen of the Imperial Bodyguard

hiyase: **1**. box; **2**. a box of offerings attached to the top of a pole (used by shamans); **3**. a Chinese peck, a container holding one peck

hiyaseku: a person who watches over weights in a market place

hiyatahan: a bejeweled goblet of the Xia dynasty

hiyatan: railing

hiyatari: railing on a street, palisade, paling, grill

hiyatu: fringe of warp threads left on cloth after it is removed from the loom, thrum

hiyebele: *Milvus lineatus*: black-eared kite

hiyedz: ⟶ **hiyese**

hiyekden moo: ⟶ **fiyatarakū**

hiyena: hyena

hiyenakū: **1**. unstable, unsettled, uneasy, restless; **2**. frivolous

hiyese: scorpion

hiyo šeng: student

hiyob seme: (onomatopoetic) the sound of a bone-headed arrow striking

hiyohoton: having a protruding hip

hiyok seme: (onomatopoetic) the sound of sighing

hiyong seme: (onomatopoetic) the sound of an arrow flying through the air

hiyoošulabumbi: (causative of **hiyoošulambi**)

hiyoošulambi: to be filial, to act filially

hiyoošun: filial, filial piety

    hiyoošun akū: unfilial

    hiyoošun i doro: filial piety

hiyoošundumbi: ⟶ **hiyoošuntumbi**

hiyoošungga: filial, a filial person

hiyoošuntumbi: to show one's filial piety through offerings to one's deceased parents and grandparents

hiyoošuri gaha: a name for the crow

hiyor hiyar: (onomatopoetic) the sound of a horse neighing

    hiyor hiyar seme: **1**. neighing; **2**. strongly, obstinately

hiyor hiyor sembi: to be robust

hiyor seme: (onomatopoetic) the sound of the feathers on a flying arrow

hiyoši: scholar

hiyotohon: curved up at both ends, arched

    hiyotohon deretu: a table with curved ends

hiyotonggo son: curved eaves on a house

hiyotonggo ulhūma: a poetic name for the pheasant

hiyotorobumbi: (causative of **hiyotorombi**)

hiyotorombi: (-ko) to curve up at the ends, to turn up at the ends

hiyotoršombi: to walk erratically due to a lack of strength, to stagger under a heavy load

ho gi: a turkey

ho ha: (onomatopoetic) the sound of sighing; cf. **hiyok seme**

ho ha seme: (onomatopoetic) the sound made when suffering from extreme cold

ho hoi: the sound made by hunters to scare animals out of hiding

ho hūwa ilha: lotus

ho juweng gurun: the United States of America

ho lan: Holland, Dutch

    ho lan gurun: Holland, the Netherlands

    ho lan gurun i loho: a kind of Dutch sword

hob seme: **1**. shoving, pushing; **2**. (onomatopoetic) the sound of an arrow striking

hobai: printed calico or chintz

hobo: coffin

    hobo musen: bier, inner and outer coffin

hobolon: *Sambucus javanica*: elder tree

hoboo: ⟶ **hobo**

hoborho: the outer coffin (in ancient times)

hocikon: beautiful, attractive, pretty

    hocikon gege: a beauty, a beautiful girl or woman

hocikosaka: **1**. attractive; **2**. in good health, in good condition

hodan gasha: the name of a bird that resembles a chicken and cries both day and night (possibly the hoki pheasant)

hode: perhaps, maybe, possibly

hodori: the fry of the Siberian salmon

hodz: a gold medallion worn around the neck by women as part of their court attire

hofin: a small porcelain vase

hofiyan: nimble, quick, dexterous, prompt

hofun: bubbles or foam on the surface of muddy water

hogi: turkey

hohan: ⟶ **hoohan**

hoho: **1**. pod, peapod, cluster of grapes; **2**. earlobe

    hoho efen: boiled meat pastries shaped like peapods; cf. **giyose**

hohoco ilha: a flower that resembles the flower of the bamboo and produces seeds in a pod

hohocu: an exotic cherry-like fruit that grows on a vine

hohodokū: a speaking tube, a device for magnifying one's voice

hohodombi: to cup the hands and call through them to someone far away

hohon: **1**. a barrel for holding liquor; **2**. a hollow tree in which a bear spends the winter

hohonggo moo: *Sophora japonica*: pagoda tree, Chinese yellow-berry

    hohonggo mooi use: the seed of the yellow-berry tree used for making yellow dye

hohonombi: **1**. to form pods, to hang down in pod-like fashion; **2**. to form icicles

hohori: the soft cartilage jutting from the side of an aural cavity

    hohori jan: a whistling arrow made from a cow's horn

hoi: ⟶ **hūi**

hoidz: ⟶ **hoise**

hoifalabumbi: (causative of **hoifalambi**)

hoifalambi: to dye black with a concoction of the leaves and stems of the Amur maple; ⟶ **wence moo**

hoifan: a dye made from the leaves and stems of the Amur maple; ⟶ **wence**

hoihalambi: to go on the winter hunt

hoihan: the area of a battue

    hoihan abalambi: to hunt in a battue formation, to form an encirclement when hunting

    hoihan sindambi: to form a battue formation

hoiho: a tailless chick

hoilabumbi: (causative of **hoilambi**)

hoilacambi: to look to both sides, to glance to both sides, to glance furtively to both sides

hoilalambi: to glance backward

hoilambi: (**-ka**) to be dirty, to be soiled, to be worn out (said of clothing)

hoilambumbi: (causative of **hoilambi**)

hoilantu: a kind of monkey indigenous to western China

hoilashūn: **1**. faded, worn out; **2**. broken down, dilapidated; **3**. low, humble, wretched

    hoilashūn manashūn: soiled and tattered

hoilembi: to apply lime or mortar

hoise: Moslem, Uyghur

    hoise i tacihiyan: Islam

    hoise niru: chief of a Moslem banner

    hoise tacikū: a Moslem school

hoji: coriander

hojigon: ⟶ **hojihon**

hojihon: son-in-law

hojihosi: (plural of **hojihon**)

hojiko: a name for the chicken; cf. **coko**

hojiri ilha: a white or violet aster

hojo: **1**. beautiful, attractive, pretty; **2**. gratifying, satisfying

    hojo faha: pupil of the eye

hojon ilha: *Papaver Rhoeas*: corn poppy

hoju: ⟶ **hojo**

hokci: a wild edible plant with thin stems and pointed leaves

hoki: **1**. group, party, band, gang, faction, clique; **2**. partner, accomplice; **3**. clerk in a store

    hoki acambi: to form a faction or clique

    hoki duwali: members of a clique or faction

    hoki isambi: to form an association

    hoki jafambi: to form a clique

hokilambi: to form a group of friends, to form a clique, to work as partners, to form a partnership

hokobumbi: (causative of **hokombi**)

    hokoburakū: without cease

hokombi: **1**. to part, to take leave from; **2**. to abandon, to reject; **3**. to divorce; **4**. to resign from

hokotoi: divorced (said of a woman)

    hokotoi genembi: to return home (said of a divorced woman), to go and not return

hoksombi: to be depressed, to be melancholy

hoksoncombi: to be depressed often

hokton: **1**. cork; **2**. float (on a fishing line or net)

    hokton moo: *Phellodendron amurense*: Amur cork tree

hoktošombi: to hunt on high ground during a flood

holbobumbi: **1**. (causative or passive of **holbombi**); **2**. to be connected, to be related, to get joined

    holbobuha baita: related matter, relevant matter

    holbobume ušabumbi: to be involved, to be implicated

holbohon: **1**. one person of a pair; **2**. connection, link

holbokū: fastener, clamp

holbombi: **1**. to connect, to join; **2**. to pair, to mate, to get married; **3**. to implicate

    holbome acabumbi: to get married

    holbome toodambi: to repay twofold

    holboro bithe: marriage document

holbon: **1**. pairing, a pair; **2**. mate; **3**. marriage; **4**. agreement

    holbon be hejembi: to arrange a marriage

    holbon i baita: marriage

    holbon i hithan: joint, hinge

holbonggo: connected, paired

    holbonggo fukjingga hergen: (填篆) a style of calligraphy

    holbonggo hoošan: paper produced from two or four layers of bamboo

holboro: ⟶ **holbombi** (subheading)

holboto ilha: bindweed, morning glory

holdon: **1**. signal fire, beacon; **2**. falling star, meteor; **3**. Siberian pine (*Pinus sibirica*)

    holdon i karan: ⟶ **holdon tai**

    holdon moo: Siberian pine

    holdon tai: beacon tower

    holdon tuheke: a star fell

    holdon tuwa: beacon fire

holhoci: *Atractylis ovata*

holhon: the lower part of the leg, shank

    holhon giranggi: the bone of the lower part of the leg, the shin, tibia

    holhon gocimbumbi: to pull a muscle in the calf

holimpa: a grain resembling maize

holin: the inside of the cheek

holkon: moment, instant

    holkonde: suddenly, in an instant

holo: **1**. valley; **2**. ravine, furrow, a tile drain, ditch; **3**. false, spurious, not genuine; **4**. aurochs

    holo cai: low quality tea

    holo cilburi: martingale

    holo gebu: alias, false name

    holo gisun: lie, falsehood, gossip

    holo jibca: a jacket of artificial fur

    holo kūdarhan: a cloth crupper

    holo ulhisungge: hypocritical, unctuous

holokon: rather false, somewhat spurious

    holokon uluken: rather false and spurious

holon gaha: jackdaw (general name for birds of the genus *Corvus*)

    holon weijun: stork; cf. **weijun**

holor: (onomatopoetic) sound of a bell

    holor halar: (onomatopoetic) the sound of many bells

holtobumbi: (causative or passive of **holtombi**)

holtombi: to deceive, to lie, to act deceitfully

    holtoho gisun: falsehood, lie

    holtome boolambi: to make a false report

    holtome gisurembi: to lie, to tell a falsehood

holton: ⟶ **holdon**

holtonumbi: to deceive one another, to lie to one another

holtošombi: to deceive often

holtu cecike: the name of a small bird

homholombi: to stick in a scabbard, to sheathe

homhon: scabbard, top for a writing brush, sheath

homida cecike: a name for the goat-sucker; cf. **indahūn cecike**

homin: hoe

homitu gūwasihiya: a name for the egret; cf. **gūwasihiya**

homso: a shuttle

    homso maktambi: to pass a shuttle back and forth

homsori bele: rice that has turned red from long storage

hon: very, most, too

honci: sheepskin

honcihin: ⟶ **hūncihin**

honcun: ⟶ **huncun**

hondoba: **1**. a kind of foxtail-like grass that can be eaten by horses; **2**. sheath for a whip

honggoco: small white-bellied fish that have been frozen in the ice of a stream

honggocon: willow herb, plants in the genus *Epibolium*

honggolon niyehe: ⟶ **honggon niyehe**

honggon: small bell

    honggon cecike: a small bird with a bell-like voice

    honggon niyehe: a kind of wild duck

honggono cecike: ⟶ **honggon cecike**

honggonombi: **1**. to form bubbles, to form small bells; **2**. to crumble, to come apart, to shatter

    honggonome gecehe: has frozen into small pieces

honggori: a bell-shaped fruit from Sichuan used as a medicine

    honggori ilha: the flower of the bead tree

hongko: **1**. end; **2**. mountain spur; **3**. a place where level land ends; **4**. head of a pestle; **5**. the forward part of a boat, bow; **6**. small footbridge over a mountain stream

    hongko cecike: a small, yellow-breasted black bird whose cry resembles that of the swallow

hongkolo galman: a large yellow mosquito-like insect

hongkū: ⟶ **hongko**

honika: the young of fish, fry

honiki: a small bear with short front legs

honin: **1**. sheep; **2**. the eighth of the earth's branches (未)

    honin biya: the sixth month

    honin erin: period of the day from 1 PM to 3 PM

    honin i deberen: lamb

honingga: pertaining to sheep

    honingga aniya: the year of the sheep

hono: still, yet

honokta: **1**. a small white sea fish lacking scales; **2**. ⟶ **honggoco**

hontahan: ⟶ **hūntahan**

hontoho: **1**. half; **2**. a bannerman with half salary; **3**. section of an organization

    hontoho inenggi: for a long time

    hontoho moo: an identification plaque in two pieces that can be fitted together for verification

hontoholobumbi: (causative or passive of **hontoholombi**)

hontoholombi: to divide into halves, to halve

hontohon: ⟶ **hontoho**
hontohoto: half each, a half for each person
hoo: one ten-thousandth of a Chinese foot
hoo hio seme: **1**. bravely, decisively, powerfully, intrepidly; **2**. unrestrained, bold, uninhibited, forthright, magnanimous, free and easy
hoo hoo seme: **1**. brave, valiant; **2**. torrentially
hoo seme: surging, flooding, torrential, mightily
    hoo seme dambi: to blow violently (said of the wind)
    hoo seme jolhombi: to surge mightily
    hoo seme yabumbi: to go in an elated manner
hoocang etuku: coat made of feathers
hoohan: a kind of heron
hooho: ⟶ **hoo hoo seme**
hoošan: **1**. paper; **2**. ⟶ **hūwašan**
    hoošan afaha: a sheet of paper
    hoošan dahabumbi: to burn paper on which charms have been written (done by a shaman for a sick person)
    hoošan herembi: to produce paper
    hoošan hergembi: ⟶ **hoošan herembi**
    hoošan i pai: paper playing cards
    hoošan i tuku: the surface of a paper fan
    hoošan jiha: paper money
    hoošan sasukū: ⟶ **hoošan i pai**, playing card
hoošang: ⟶ **hūwašan**
hoošari moo: *Broussonetia papyrifera*: paper mulberry
hopai: a tally used by official post riders for drawing provisions
hopen: fire basin, small charcoal stove
hor seme: neighing, whinnying, snoring
horgikū: **1**. pivot, fulcrum, hinge; **2**. socket, socket of the hip joint; **3**. a pole with a wheel on top, to which swings are attached
horgimbi: **1**. to sway, to rock; **2**. to rotate, to spin
horgin: the rounded end of the thigh bone
horho: **1**. upright cabinet, wardrobe; **2**. pen, cage; **3**. outer coffin; cf. **horhū**
horhodombi: to take shelter, to seek refuge
horhotu: a large wooden cage for catching tigers and leopards
horhū: outer coffin; cf. **horho**
horibumbi: (causative or passive of **horimbi**)
horigan: pen, corral, cage

horilakū asu: a long net cast from two boats into still water
horimbi: to enclose, to put in a pen, to imprison
horin: **1**. cage; **2**. ⟶ **horho**
horki: *Tettao parvirostris*: the Siberian capercaillie
horo: eel; cf. **hūwara**
horoki: having a senile aspect, old-looking
horolambi: ⟶ **horolombi**
horolombi: **1**. to show severity, to intimidate, to frighten; **2**. to use poison
    horolome bucebumbi: to kill by poisoning
horon: **1**. majesty, authority, awe, power; **2**. poison, venom
    horon aisilaha daifan: (武翼大夫) an honorary military title of the third rank second class
    horon akdun aisilaha hafan: (武信佐郎) an honorary military title of the sixth rank second class
    horon akdun hafan: (武信郎) an honorary military title of the sixth rank first class
    horon algin: reputation, prestige
    horon arambi: to display one's might
    horon be algimbuha amban: (建威大夫) an honorary military title of the first rank first class
    horon be badarambuha amban: (振威大夫) an honorary military title of the first rank second class
    horon be iletulehe daifan: (昭威大夫) an honorary military title of the fourth rank first class
    horon be selgiyehe amban: (武顯大夫) an honorary military title of the second rank first class
    horon be selgiyere temgetun: an insignia of the Imperial Escort
    horon be tucibuhe daifan: (宣武大夫) an honorary military title of the fourth rank second class
    horon bodohonggo hafan: (武略郎) an honorary military title of the fifth rank second class
    horon dube: the tongue of a snake
    horon encehen: power, influence
    horon erdemungge hafan: (武德郎) an honorary military title of the fifth rank first class

horon fafuringga aisilaha hafan: (奮武佐郎) an honorary military title of the seventh rank second class

horon fafuringga hafan: (奮武郎) an honorary military title of the seventh rank first class

horon giranggi: small curved bones from the breast of a tiger (used as medicine)

horon goimbi: to be poisoned

horon gungge amban: (武功大夫) an honorary military title of the second rank second class

horon hūsun bisire sula hafan: powerful gentry

horon i okto: poison

horon sindambi: to put one's power on display

horon toose: authority, power

horon tuwabumbi: to put on a show of force, to display one's prowess

horon tuwancihiyangga aisilaha hafan: (修武佐郎) an honorary military title of the eighth rank second class

horon tuwancihiyangga hafan: (修武郎) an honorary military title of the eighth rank first class

horonggo: **1**. powerful, terrible, awe-inspiring, possessing great authority, majestic, regal; **2**. poisonous, venomous

horonggo cecike: a mythical bird that was supposed to drive off evil influences — its carved image was often attached to the end of a pole

horonggo cecikengge mukšan: a pole with an image of the **horonggo cecike** attached to the end

horonggo gurgu: a fabulous beast with a long tail and two horns

horonggo gurgungge kiru: (辟邪旗) a banner of the Imperial Escort with the image of the **horonggo gurgu** embroidered on it

horonggo jaka: poison, poisonous substance, toxin

horonggo yangsangga deyen i bithe weilere ba: (武英殿修書處) Printing Office and Bookbindery at the Throne Hall, *BH* 94

horontu mahatun: a hat used in ancient times by the bodyguard of a ruler

hosan ilha: an exotic flower resembling the osmanthus and blooming monthly throughout the year

hose: box

hoseri: ⟶ **hose**

hoseri dengjan: a fireworks box

hoshori: curly (hair)

hoshori indahūn: a curly-haired dog

hoshorilabumbi: (causative of **hoshorilambi**)

hoshorilambi: to curl, to crinkle

hoshorinambi: to become curly

hoso hasa: (onomatopoetic) the sound of paper being shaken

hosori: **1**. dandruff, flakes of skin; **2**. soot; **3**. earwax; **4**. crust, filings, iron shavings, iron filings

hosorinambi: to be disheveled, to be unkempt

hošang. Buddhist monk, cf. **hūwašan**

hošo: **1**. corner, angle; **2**. area, region; **3**. direction; **4**. edge; **5**. square

hošo baimbi: to present **hoho efen**, liquor, cattle, etc. before a wedding

hošo muheliyen: square and round

hošo sahambi: ⟶ **hošo baimbi**

hošo taktu: a four-cornered observation tower of the examination hall

hošoi cin wang: (親王) Prince of the Blood of the first degree, *BH* 15

hošoi duka: a side door, a corner door

hošoi efu: (郡主儀賓) the son-in-law of a **hošoi cin wang**

hošoi ejen: tetrarch

hošoi fujin: (親王福晉) the wife of a **hošoi cin wang**

hošoi gege: (郡主) the daughter of a **hošoi cin wang**

hošoi gungju: (和碩公主) the Daughter of the Emperor by an Imperial Concubine, *BH* 14

hošoi gungju i hošoi efu: (和碩額駙) the husband of a **hošoi gungju**

hošon: **1**. quarter, precinct; **2**. square

hošonggo: square, four-sided

hošonggo sijirhūn: upright, righteous

hošošombi: ⟶ **hoššombi**

hošotolobumbi: (causative of **hošotolombi**)

hošotolombi: **1**. to let a corner protrude; **2**. to make into a square

hošotonggo: having corners, angular

hošotonggo šufatu: a square-shaped turban
hoššobumbi: (causative or passive of **hoššombi**)
hoššombi: **1**. to deceive, to entice, to mislead; **2**. to coax a child to take medicine for sleep
   hoššome ergelembi: to entice (under threat of force)
   hoššome gamambi: to abduct, to kidnap
hoto: **1**. gourd; **2**. cranium, bald head, skull; **3**. a piece of iron over the shoulder piece of a suit of armor; **4**. (as an adjective) bald
   hoto cekemu: flowery Japanese satin
   hoto guwejihe: the third stomach of a ruminant
   hoto hengke: gourd, squash
   hoto yoo: favus, scald-head — a disease in which parts of the scalp become bald
hotoci: coconut
   hotoci mahatun: an ancient-style hat made from a coconut
hotoho: ⟶ **hotohon**
hotohon: turned up, bulging (said of the lips)
hotombi: to sulk, to pout
hoton: walled city, city wall
   hoton fekumbi: to assault a city
   hoton i da: (城守尉) Military Commandant of a Minor Manchu Garrison in the Provinces, *BH* 746
   hoton i enduri: guardian deity of a city
   hoton mandal: a small shelter in which Buddhist monks recite scriptures
hotong: Moslem, Turk, Moslem inhabitant of Turkestan
hotorombi: (**-ko**) to curve up at one end
hu: ⟶ **hū**
hubtu: a long padded gown made of cotton
hude: the stern of a ship, a rudder
   hude jafambi: to guide the rudder, to steer
hufumbi: ⟶ **hūfumbi**
huhu: leaven for making liquor
   huhu i suwaliyan: a mixture of millet and oat bran
huhucu: *Adenophera* (bellflower) — a medicinal drug
huhun: **1**. breast; **2**. (human) milk
   huhun ci aljabumbi: to wean from the breast
   huhun i eme: wet-nurse
   huhun i eniye: wet-nurse
   huhun i tumiha: teat, nipple
   huhun jembi: to suck the breast

   huhun sidakabi: milk has filled the breasts
   huhun simimbi: to suck the breast
   huhun sindambi: to lactate (said of a new mother)
   huhun ulebumbi: to nurse, to feed a baby breast milk
huhuri: unweaned, suckling
   huhuri gebu: a baby name
   huhuri jui: a child still not weaned
huidz: ⟶ **hoise**
hujengge gasha: a name for the owl; cf. **yabulan**
huju: **1**. trough; **2**. a hollowed-out piece of wood held together with rings and used for transporting silver
hujubumbi: (causative of **hujumbi**)
hujuku: bellows
hujumbi: **1**. to operate a bellows; **2**. to prostrate oneself, to bow deeply, to cower, to crouch, to bend down
hujurebumbi: (causative of **hujurembi**)
hujureku: a small mortar or mill for grinding sesame seeds, soy beans, etc.
   hujureku cifun: milling tax
hujurembi: to grind, to mill
hujuri: a wind tube used for making fires in the open
hujurukū: ⟶ **hujuku**
huksa: ⟶ **hukšen**
huksidembi: to rain violently
huksumbi: ⟶ **hukšumbi**
hukšebumbi: (causative of **hukšembi**)
hukšembi: **1**. to carry on the head, to wear on the head; **2**. to pile earth around the roots of a young plant; **3**. to appreciate, to thank, to be thankful to; **4**. to swell; cf. **hukšumbi**
   hukšeme šufatu: a head covering consisting of a flat board with cloth hanging on both sides
hukšembumbi: to put a hood on a falcon
hukšen: a falcon raised for more than a year at home, a falcon kept in the house
   hukšen garudai: an old phoenix
hukšenumbi: **1**. to carry on the head (said of a group); **2**. to pile earth around the roots of a young plant (said of a group)
hukšeri bele: rice that has turned brown from long storage
hukšumbi: (**-ke**) **1**. to swell; **2**. ⟶ **hukšembi**
huktambi: ⟶ **hūktambi**

huktu: a long padded gown made of cotton; cf.
    hubtu
hukturi: ⟶ **kukduri**
hukun: dirt, refuse, manure, fertilizer
    hukun boihon: refuse, muck
    hukun buktan: a pile of refuse, garbage dump,
        dunghill
hule: a measure of volume equaling ten lesser
    pecks, a bushel
hulun murakū: a whistle used for luring deer
hulur seme: squeaking
humsuhun: craw of a bird, crop, gizzard
humsun: **1**. craw of a bird, crop; **2**. eyelid
    humsun i teile: 'with only the eyelid' — with
        little effort
    humsun kamnimbi: to close the eyes (before
        sleep)
humše. *Strix aluconi*. Manchurian wood owl
humtu: hunchbacked
humudu: *Otis tarda*: bustard
huncu: sleigh, sled
hundu: ⟶ **humtu**
hunggiyanglambi: to play cards
hungken: ⟶ **emu hungken jiha**
hungkerebumbi: (causative of **hungkerembi**)
hungkerembi: **1**. to pour out into a hole or
    receptacle; **2**. to cast (metal), to pour into a
    mold; **3**. to water (plants); **4**. to make
    candles
    hungkereme: in profusion, copiously
    hungkereme agambi: to rain cats and dogs
    hungkereme buyembi: to yearn for, to admire
        greatly, to desire ardently
    hungkereme feksimbi: to run at breakneck
        speed
    hungkereme gisurembi: to have a good talk, to
        have a long chat, to have an earnest talk
        with, to have a heart-to-heart talk
    hungkereme sindambi: to give free rein to a
        horse
hungkimbi: to mash, to crush, to pulverize
hunio: water bucket, pail, tub
hurcembi: to find fault with, to criticize
huren: **1**. the ridge of the nose; **2**. a hole on a stove
    near the cooking pot where a light
    (**hiyabun**) is placed; **3**. a badger trap
    huren wase: arched tile used on the roofs of
        temples and palaces

hurenembi: to arch, to form a vault
hurgen: team and plow (used as a measure of a
    person's wealth)
hurhu: ⟶ **hurku**
hurhui cecike: a name for the goat-sucker; cf.
    indahūn cecike
hurku: sulphur
hurkun gūwara: a name for the eared owl; cf. **fu**
    gūwara
hurse: an earthen cooking pot
huru: **1**. turtle or tortoise shell; **2**. the back of a bird;
    3. the back of the hand; **4**. a rise, a high
    place; cf. **kuru**
hurugan: tortoise shell
hurunembi: ⟶ **hurenembi**
hurungge: having a shell (like a turtle)
huterembi: (**-ke**) to wrinkle; cf. **hiterembi**
huthe: scab
huthenembi: to form a scab
huthubumbi: (causative or passive of **huthumbi**)
huthumbi: to tie up, to bind
hutu: **1**. ghost, devil, disembodied spirit; **2**. an ugly
    man
    hutu bušuku: ghosts and goblins
    hutu enduri: ghosts and deities
    hutu geleku: an exotic fruit that can be made
        into rosaries
    hutu ibagan: ghosts and monsters
hutucembi: to curve up at the ends
hutungge: **1**. devilish, demonic; **2**. hateful, deceitful
huturcembi: ⟶ **kuturcembi**
hutuse: (plural of **hutu**)
huwaca: hole through which an oven-bed is lit
huwejebumbi: (causative of **huwejembi**)
huwejehen: a screen
huwejehengge tojin: a peacock with its tail feathers
    spread
huwejembi: **1**. to screen off, to cover; **2**. to set up a
    screen
huwejen: **1**. screen; cf. **huwejehen**; **2**. a board for
    covering the top of an oven-bed; **3**. a weir
    for catching fish in fast water
    huwejen cambi: to set up a screen
    huwejen ilibumbi: to erect a screen
huwejengge duka: gate separating the inner and
    outer courts of a house
huweki: fertile, fruitful, luxuriant
huwekiyebubumbi: (causative of **huwekiyebumbi**)

huwekiyebumbi: **1**. (causative of **huwekiyembi**); **2**. to admonish, to guide, to incite zeal, to encourage

huwekiyebun: encouragement, advice, admonition

huwekiyembi: to be enthusiastic, to do zealously, to expend great effort, to rouse oneself, to be happy

huwekiyen: enthusiasm, happy mood, zeal, excitement

huwekiyen yendembi: to show interest, to have a good feeling, to be in a good mood

huwekiyendumbi: to be enthusiastic together; also **huwekiyenumbi**

huwekiyenumbi: to be enthusiastic together; also **huwekiyendumbi**

huwelen: ⟶ **heolen**

huwengge: luxuriant, abundant

huwengkiyembi: to peck out of a shell (said of chicks)

huwenji: a wooden cup or bowl with a handle

huwerke: a window-shutter made from wood or matting

huwesi: knife

huwesiku: ⟶ **huwešeku**

huwesilembi: to stab or pierce with a knife

huwesišembi: to stab repeatedly with a knife

huwešebumbi: (causative of **huwešembi**)

huwešeku: iron (for pressing clothing)

huwešembi: to iron, to press (clothing), to brand, to sear

huwešere hacuhan: a flatiron

huwešen: Buddhist nun

huweten: *Buteo hemilasius*: upland buzzard

huwethi: seal (a sea mammal)

huye: a pit (dug close by a riverbank) from which a hunter shoots birds of prey that come to take the bait he has put out

huye tembi: to sit in a pit in order to catch quail

hū: **1**. a paste made of boiled rice or other grain, paste; **2**. the back of the neck; **3**. one millionth of a Chinese foot; **4**. a unit of measure equaling five small pecks

hū i da: the base of the back of the neck, the first thoracic vertebra; cf. **gen**

hū tukiyere hūsun: granary worker charged with weighing rice

hūba: amber

hūbalabumbi: (causative of **hūbalambi**)

hūbalambi: to paste, to mount, to paste paper over a window

hūbalara faksi: a person who mounts paintings and calligraphy

hūban: **1**. a tablet carried in the hand during audiences in ancient times; **2**. a jade implement pointed at one end and square at the other (used during important ceremonies in ancient times)

hūbarak: clergy, clerical

hūberi: a fur neckpiece worn by women in winter

hūbilabumbi: **1**. (causative or passive of **hūbilambi**); **2**. to be caught in a trap, to be deceived

hūbilambi: to trap, to trick, to snare

hūbin: trap, snare

hūbin de dosika: fell into a trap

hūbišabumbi: (causative of **hūbišambi**)

hūbišambi: to set a trap or snare, to deceive

hūbumbi: (causative of **hūmbi**)

hūcin: a well

hūcin fekumbi: to jump down a well (a form of suicide)

hūcin šodombi: to clean out a well

hūcingga: pertaining to a well

hūda: **1**. business; **2**. price, value; **3**. goods

hūda arambi: **1**. to convert to cash, to sell off; **2**. to fix a price, to evaluate, to appraise

hūda boo: store, inn

hūda bumbi: to fix a price

hūda ja: cheap, inexpensive

hūda maiman: business

hūda mangga: expensive

hūda nonggimbi: to raise the price

hūda toktobumbi: to set a price

hūda toktosi: dealer, broker, middleman

hūda wasika: the price has fallen

hūda wesike: the price has risen

hūdai ba: market, market place

hūdai bai hūda: market price

hūdai cifun: tax on trade

hūdai jaka: merchandise

hūdai jaka ejere afaha: (ship's) manifest

hūdai niyalma: merchant

hūdašabumbi: (causative of **hūdašambi**)

hūdašambi: to engage in business, to trade

hūdašara niyalma: businessman, merchant, tradesman

hūdukala: Fast!, Hurry!

hūdukan: rather fast

hūdulabumbi: (causative of **hūdulambi**)

hūdulambi: to hurry, to hasten, to quicken, to accelerate

hūdun: fast, quick

    hūdun fuifukū: a vessel for heating up tea or liquor

    hūdun hafuka: a boil having red lines in it

    hūdun yoo: boil, carbuncle

hūdungga: speedy, swift

hūfan: company, partnership, troupe

hūfubumbi: (causative of **hūfumbi**)

hūfumbi: to run aground

hūfun: gruel used to feed domestic animals

    hūfun ulebumbi: to prepare gruel for feeding to livestock

hūha: **1**. a rope made of silken floss; **2**. a knot of silken floss at the end of a whip

hūhūba: a long gown without slits at the side

hūhūcan: ⟶ **hūhucu**

hūhucu: *Adenophora*: a medicinal herb

hūhūli: a name for the scops owl; cf. **hūšahū**

hūi: **1**. red felt edging on the lower part of a saddle blanket; **2**. an exclamation: 'Now, then … '; **3**. meeting, assembly, association; **4**. as one pleases

hūi hai seme: dizzy, unsteady

hūi hiyang: fennel

hūi hūwa ilha: a kind of fragrant orchid

hūi kui: (會魁) a title bestowed on those who placed between sixth and thirteenth on the Imperial examination, *BH* 629C

hūi seme: **1**. dizzy; **2**. surging; cf. **hūwai seme**

hūi šoro: a matted basket used for pressing oil

hūi tai: frivolous, dawdling

hūi yuwan: (會元) those who placed second to fifth in the Imperial examination, *BH* 629C

hūifan: ⟶ **hoifan**

hūise: Moslem; cf. **hoise**

hūjaci: policeman, constable

    hūjaci be kadalara ba: (管轄番投處) Office of the Controller of the Police Bureau, *BH* 81

    hūjaci be kadalara fiyenten: (番子司) Police Division of the Office of the Banner General of Mukden

hūjibumbi: (causative of **hūjimbi**)

hūjimbi: **1**. to rouse a recumbent tiger by shouting; **2**. to make a noise (said of trees in a windstorm)

    hūjime dambi: to sough (said of the wind), to blow so as to set the leaves of trees in motion

hūjiri: alkaline, alkali, soda, bittern

    hūjiri ba: an alkaline place

hūju: a Central Asiatic pearl

hūk seme: suddenly (become tired)

hūk hūk seme: fitfully

hūkcumbi: to surprise, to catch unaware, to appear suddenly

hūkjun: a name for the stork; cf. **weijun**

hūktambi: **1**. to be hot and moist, to be steaming; **2**. to ferment; **3**. to stew slowly (intransitive verb)

    hūktame halhūn: steaming hot, sultry

hūktambumbi: **1**. (causative of **hūktambi**); **2**. to stew, to braise, to steam (rice)

hūlabumbi: (causative of **hūlambi**)

hūlambi: **1**. to shout, to call; **2**. to read aloud; **3**. to crow

    hūlara hafan: (贊禮郎) Herald, Ceremonial Usher, *BH* 79, 382B, 391

hūlan: chimney, smoke hole

hūlanabumbi: (causative of **hūlanambi**)

hūlanambi: to go to call, to go to read

hūlandumbi: to call together, to read together; also **hūlanumbi**

hūlanumbi: to call together, to read together; also **hūlandumbi**

hūlangga coko: a name for the chicken; cf. **coko**

hūlangga gasha: ⟶ **hūlangga coko**

hūlanjimbi: to come to call, to come to read

hūlara: ⟶ **hūlambi** (subheading)

hūlašabumbi: (causative of **hūlašambi**)

hūlašambi: to exchange, to barter, to trade, to exchange places with

hūlašandumbi: to exchange with one another

hūldurambi: ⟶ **gūldurambi**

hūlga: ⟶ **hūlha**

hūlgi: ⟶ **hūlhi**

hūlgican niyehe: a name for the wild duck known as **yargican niyehe**

hūlha: **1**. bandit, robber, thief; **2**. rebel; **3**. secret, on the sly

    hūlha baita: a case involving robbery

hūlha be jafara tinggin: (捕盜廳) Bureau of Police Affairs, *BH* 795A-D

hūlha da: bandit chieftain

hūlha holo: robbers and thieves, bandits

hūlhai feniyen: a gang of thieves

hūlhai feye: den of bandits

hūlhai hoki: a bunch of bandits, a gang of thieves

hūlhabumbi: (causative or passive of **hūlhambi**)

hūlhambi: **1**. to rob, to steal; **2**. to act secretly, to act furtively, to act on the sly

hūlhame arambi: to do secretly

hūlhame tuwambi: to take a peek

hūlhame ukambi: to slip away, to escape secretly

hūlhanambi: to go to steal

hūlhandumbi: to steal (said of a group); also **hūlhanumbi**

hūlhanjimbi: to come to steal

hūlhanumbi: to steal (said of a group); also **hūlhandumbi**

hūlhatu: swindler, thief, brigand, inveterate thief

hūlhi: muddled, confused, bewildered, mixed up

hūlhi eberhun: muddled, stupid

hūlhi eberi: muddleheaded, nutty

hūlhi lampa: **1**. primeval chaos; **2**. confused, bewildered, only half conscious

hūlhi modo: foolish, stupid

hūlhidambi: to act in a confused manner, to be in a daze

hūlhikan: somewhat confused

hūlhitu: a muddleheaded person, a blockhead, a dunce

hūlibun: deception, delusion, perplexity

hūlimbumbi: **1**. to be led astray, to be deluded, to be deceived; **2**. to lead astray, to delude

hūlimbume yarumbi: to seduce, to lead astray

hūluri malari: careless, lax, hasty, sloppy

hūman: talent, capability, skill, ability, technique

hūmarabumbi: (causative of **hūmarambi**)

hūmarambi: (-ka) **1**. to have a dirty face, to be soiled; **2**. to soil, to make dirty

hūmbi: to plait, to braid

hūmbur seme: profusely (said of sweating)

hūnambi: to form a paste, to form a mess, to become all tangled up

hūncihin: relative, of the same clan or family

hūng hiyong: (onomatopoetic) **1**. the sound of the tide; **2**. the sound of running horses

hūng i poo: a European cannon

hūng moo gurun: Holland, Europe

hūng seme: (onomatopoetic) the sound of a fire

hūngko: the front part of a ship, the bow; cf. **hongko**

hūngniyoolambi: to rain while the sun is shining

hūngsi: **1**. pebble; **2**. Chinese little grebe (*Poliocephalus rufficollis*)

hūngsibumbi: (causative of **hūngsimbi**)

hūngsimbi: **1**. to fling, to hurl, to hurl to the ground, to throw away, to discard; **2**. to talk nonsense, to talk wildly

hūngsitambi: to fling continually

hūngsitu gasha: ⟶ **kuringge gasha**

hūnoolambi: to cause an uproar

hūnta: hemp, cannabis, ramie

hūntahan: cup, mug, glass

hūntahan bederebumbi: to return a toast at a banquet

hūntahan i tokton: rack for cups used at offerings

hūntahan jafambi: to offer a glass of liquor

hūntahan taili i cargilakū: cup and plate rocket — a kind of fireworks

hūr har seme: shying (said of horses)

hūr hūr seme: flaming, blazing

hūr seme: flaming, blazing

hūr seme jilidambi: to fly into a rage

hūr sehe: became a bit tipsy

hūrfu: orangutan

hūrga: ⟶ **hūrhan**

hūrga sogi: watercress

hūrgadambi: ⟶ **hūrhadambi**

hūrgan: ⟶ **hūrhan**

hūrgibumbi: (causative or passive of **hūrgimbi**)

hūrgikū: whirlpool, vortex, eddy

hūrgimbi: to spin, to turn around; cf. **horgimbi**

hūrgime dambi: to blow in whirls

hūrgime yabumbi: to go for a stroll

hūrgire edun: whirlwind

hūrha: ⟶ **hūrhan**

hūrhadabumbi: (causative of **hūrhadambi**)

hūrhadambi: to catch fish in a large net

hūrhan: a large fishing net

hūrhan i weihe: protruding teeth

hūri: pine nut

hūri bahiya: pinecone

hūri faha: pine nut

hūri faha i šobin: cake baked with pine nuts

hūrka: a horsehair snare used to catch small birds

hūru: a mouth harp made of cow's horn and bamboo

hūrudambi: to play the mouth harp

hūse: beard

hūsetai: bearded

hūsha monggon: windpipe

hūshūri coko: a chicken with curly feathers

hūsiba orho: ivy

hūsibumbi: **1.** (causative or passive of **hūsimbi**); **2.** to be beset by (illness); **3.** to be wrapped up, to be entangled in

hūsibuha nimeku: chronic illness

hūsiha moo: wild walnut

hūsihan: (woman's) skirt

hūsikū: wrapping; cf. **monggon hūsikū**

hūsimbi: to wrap, to wrap up, to envelop

hūsime: entirely, completely, whole

hūsime šufatu: a linen hat worn in ancient times

hūsingga sijigiyan: a broad-sleeved habit worn by Buddhist and Daoist monks

hūsiri moo: *Quercus dentata*: Mongolian oak

hūsitun: a leg-binding, especially the type worn by men

hūsubure hafan: ⟶ **hūsun bure hafan**

hūsun: **1.** strength, power, might; **2.** laborer, worker

hūsun acambi: to exert oneself to the utmost, to do one's very best

hūsun aisilambi: to give aid to

hūsun bumbi: to expend effort, to be diligent

hūsun bure hafan: a diligent official

hūsun de haminambi: to have the strength to accomplish something

hūsun etuhun: powerful, healthy

hūsun faksi i kunggeri: (夫匠科) Section Concerned with Laborers and Artisans, in the Board of Works

hūsun hamirakū: not within one's power

hūsun i durimbi: to carry away by force

hūsun i ebsihe: with all one's might

hūsun i hojihon: a son-in-law who lives in his wife's parents's house

hūsun isibumbi: to devote oneself to

hūsun tucimbi: to perform labor, to render service, to exert oneself

hūsun turimbi: to hire laborers

hūsun uncambi: to sell one's labor, to do hard labor

hūsun yabumbi: to work, to do physical labor

hūsungge: powerful, mighty

hūsungge boo: a powerful rich family

hūsuri: earwax; cf. **hosori**

hūsutulebumbi: (causative of **hūsutulembi**)

hūsutulembi: to do with power, to use strength, to strain

hūša: *Pueraria Thunbergiana*: kudzu-vine, a plant used for making a kind of coarse linen fabric

hūša siren: a vine with three-pronged leaves that grows on pine and cypress trees

hūšahū: *Otus scops*: scops owl

hūšaju: *Colocasia esculenta*: taro

hūthūmbi: ⟶ **kūthūmbi**

hūthūri: ⟩ **kūthūri**

hūtung: alley, lane

hūturi: good luck, good fortune, blessing

hūturi baimbi: to pray for good fortune

hūturi fengšen: good fortune

hūturi fengšen aisimbi: to bestow good fortune and prosperity

hūturi fengšen jalafun: good fortune, prosperity (many sons), and long life

hūturi imiyambi: good fortune arrives in abundance

hūturi isibumbi: to bring good fortune

hūturi isimbi: good fortune arrives

hūturi nure: wine offered by the Emperor at state sacrifices

hūturingga: possessing good fortune, fortunate

hūwa: **1.** courtyard, yard, garden; **2.** in two, asunder, apart

hūwa jafambi: to construct a courtyard

hūwa hūwa seme: in two, asunder

hūwacarambi: to snore

hūwacihiyan enggemu: a saddle with a horn-shaped saddle horn

hūwafihiya: **1.** a wooden tool shaped like a halved bamboo used for smoothing arrow shafts; **2.** a pastry of flour, honey, and sesame shaped like the tool described above

hūwafihiyabumbi: (causative of **hūwafihiyambi**)

hūwafihiyambi: to shave smooth an arrow shaft

hūwai mukengge kiru: (准旗) a blue banner of the Imperial Escort depicting waves on a green background

hūwai seme: **1**. surging, in great quantity (said of water), billowing; **2**. boundless, limitless

hūwai tolon: a bonfire lit to announce to the people some important event

hūwaidanambi: to dry up, to wither

hūwaise: *Sophora japonica*: pagoda tree, the Chinese yellow-berry; cf. **hohonggo moo**

hūwaitabumbi: (causative of **hūwaitambi**)

hūwaitakū: something that is tied on; cf. **tobgiya hūwaitakū**, **hefeli hūwaitakū**

hūwaitambi: to tie, to tie up, to bind

hūwajalambi: to sign a contract or agreement

hūwajambi: to break (intransitive verb), to tear, to crack

hūwajan: painter, artist

hūwajiyoo moo: *Zanthoxylum piperitum*: Sichuan pepper tree

hūwakiyabumbi: (causative of **hūwakiyambi**)

hūwakiyambi: **1**. to peel, to peel off; **2**. to take away, to revoke, to abrogate

hūwakšahalabumbi: (causative of **hūwakšahalambi**)

hūwakšahalambi: to erect a wooden railing or fence

hūwakšahan: stave in a wooden railing or fence

hūwakšan: a small stave used in card playing to show whose turn it is

hūwaksiha: ⟶ **hūwakšahan**

hūwala ihan: an isabella (buff-colored) cow

hūwalabumbi: (causative of **hūwalambi**)

hūwalama usiha: wild walnut

hūwalambi: **1**. to break up, to cut up, to split, to break open; **2**. to rip up; **3**. to cut (one's hair); **4**. to gouge out; **5**. to play the finger game

hūwalar: (onomatopoetic) the sound of wading in water, the sound of splashing

hūwalar hilir: (onomatopoetic) the sound of fish nets in water

hūwalar seme: (onomatopoetic) the sound of flowing water, the sound of splashing

hūwaliyambi: (-ka) to harmonize, to unite, to reconcile, to conciliate, to get along well together, to live in harmony

hūwaliyambumbi: (causative of **hūwaliyambi**)

hūwaliyan: harmony, good terms, friendly relations

hūwaliyandumbi: to harmonize with one another

hūwaliyapi: in full concord

hūwaliyasun: **1**. harmony, concord, peace; **2**. friendliness; **3**. harmonious, gentle

hūwaliyasun edun: a gentle wind

hūwaliyasun i doro: peace treaty

hūwaliyasun necin: peaceful, gentle, moderate

hūwaliyasun sain: cordial, friendly

hūwaliyasun sukdun: cordiality, politeness

hūwaliyasun tob: the Yongzheng (雍正) reign period, 1723–35

hūwaliyasun tugi kumun be halanjame deribure mudan: a piece of music played during the offering of wine at the end of the plowing ceremony

hūwamiyambi: to peel, to shell

hūwang be: *Phellodendron amurense*: a kind of oak whose bark is used in Chinese medicine, Amur cork tree

hūwang doo: the ecliptic

hūwang guifei: (皇貴妃) Imperial Concubine of the First Rank, *BH* 6

hūwang li: ⟶ **hūwangli**

hūwang taidz: (皇太子) the Heir Apparent, *BH* 12

hūwang taidz i fei: (皇太子妃) Concubine of the Heir Apparent

hūwangdan: yellow lead ore

hūwangdana: *Emberiza aureola*: yellow-breasted bunting

hūwangdi: Emperor

hūwangga: on good terms with, in concord

hūwanggar hūwalar: roaring and splashing

hūwanggar seme: surging and roaring

hūwanggar seme agambi: to rain copiously

hūwanggiyambi: to prevent, to stand in the way

hūwanggiyara aibi: what difference does it make?

hūwanggiyarakū: there is no harm, it does not stand in the way, it makes no difference, there is nothing wrong

hūwanggiyan: a quiver worn on one's back

hūwangheo: Empress

hūwangli: calendar, almanac

hūwangse: orpiment

hūwanta: bare, uncultivated, bald (said of a mountain), lacking vegetation

hūwanta alin: bare mountain, bald mountain

hūwanta sebsehe: a yellow locust-like insect with small wings

hūwantahūn: barren, bald (said of mountains)

hūwantahūn tala: barren steppe, wasteland

hūwantanambi: to become barren

hūwar: (onomatopoetic) the sound of a thing being dragged on the ground

hūwar hir: **1**. (onomatopoetic) the sound of clothing rubbing together; **2**. profuse (said of tears)

hūwar hir seme: ⟶ **hūwar hir**

hūwar seme: ⟶ **hūwar hir**

hūwara: **1**. a file; **2**. eel; cf. **horo**

hūwarabumbi: (causative of **hūwarambi**)

hūwaradambi: to file, to plane

hūwarakan: window shutter made of willow twigs

hūwarambi: to file

hūwasa hisa: (onomatopoetic) the sound of stepping on dry leaves

hūwasar: **1**. (onomatopoetic) the sound made by desiccated plants in the wind; **2**. coarse, rough

hūwasar seme: coarse, rough

hūwašabukū: a kind of local school in ancient times

hūwašabumbi: **1**. (causative or passive of **hūwašambi**); **2**. to raise, to bring up, to nourish, to bring to maturity or fruition, to accomplish, to foster

hūwašabure cooha: a young man brought up at state expense who was destined for military service and therefore exempt from the corvée

hūwašada: (僧官) abbot, Buddhist superior

hūwašambi: to grow up, to mature, to develop

hūwašan: a Buddhist monk

hūwašan be kadalara fiyenten: (僧錄司) section on monastic affairs

hūwašan doose i kunggeri: (僧道科) Office of Buddhist and Daoist affairs in the Board of Rites

hūwašasa: (plural of **hūwašan**)

hūwayalambi: to sign (a contract)

hūwayambi: to sign a contract or agreement

hūya: **1**. a sea snail; **2**. cup made from a sea snail's shell; **3**. a half-grown roe deer

hūya efen: a wheat cake made in the form of a sea snail

huyambi: to cry (said of eagles, falcons, etc.)

hūyan: rheumatism in the shoulder

hūyan dekdembi: to have muscle pain in the upper back (especially after influenza)

hūyanambi: to form a crust of dirt on the face

hūyasun: foot fetters (for hawks and falcons)

hūyukū šoro: a basket that is lowered into a soy vat to press out the clear soy sauce

hūyušembi: to exchange (temporarily), to transfer, to remit

hūyušeme bojilambi: to remit (money)

I ㅈ ㄱ ㅓ

i: **1**. he, she; cf. **ini**, **inde**, **inci**; **2**. (the genitive particle); **3**. (the instrumental particle); **4**. an interjection used to get the attention of subordinates

i ci: an interjection of regret

i i: **1**. (onomatopoetic) the sound of sobbing; **2**. an interjection of derision

i seme: sneering, scornful, derisory

ibadan: *Ulmus laciniata*: mountain elm, the wood of which was used for making spears

ibagan: **1**. monster, apparition, phantom; **2**. a madman

    ibagan dailaha: went stark raving mad

    ibagan gailaka: ⟶ **ibagan dailaha**

    ibagan hiyabun: the seed-bearing portion of a reed (used as kindling or as filler for a mattress)

    ibagan halmari: the pod of the honey locust tree, used as soap

ibagasa: (plural of **ibagan**)

ibagašambi: to act strangely while possessed by a spirit or phantom, to act like one possessed

ibahan: ⟶ **ibagan**

ibahašambi: ⟶ **ibagašambi**

ibakabumbi: (causative of **ibakambi**)

ibakambi: to shorten; ⟶ **ibkambi**

ibakci: a thorny bush resembling the bird-cherry that bears an inedible fruit

ibašen muke: water from melting snow

ibebumbi: **1**. (causative of **ibembi**); **2**. to offer, to present

    ibebume wesimbure kunggeri: (進呈科) an office in charge of petitions and memorials, in the Grand Secretariat

ibedembi: to advance gradually

ibeden: gradual advance

ibehen: the end of a bow

ibelembi: to advance slowly

ibembi: **1**. to advance, to go forward; **2**. to give more feed to; **3**. to stoke a fire, to advance a wick for better light

ibenembi: to go forward, to advance

ibenjimbi: to come forward

ibenumbi: to advance together

iberi: the back part of a helmet, a neck-guard

ibešembi: to advance gradually

ibete: rotten tree, rotten wood

ibge: ⟶ **ibehen**

ibiri: ⟶ **iberi**

ibiyaburu: loathsome creature!

ibiyacuka: loathsome, disgusting

ibiyacun: **1**. loathing, disgust; **2**. disgusting person

ibiyada: ⟶ **ibiyacuka**; cf. **ubiyada**

ibiyaha: well-developed ears of grain

    ibiyaha jafambi: to select good ears of grain to lay aside for use as seed

ibiyahalambi: to select choice ears of grain for seed

ibiyambi: to loathe, to detest; cf. **ubiyambi**

ibiyon: detestable, hateful

ibkabumbi: (causative of **ibkambi**)

ibkambi: to shorten, to diminish, to reduce, to abbreviate

ibkašambi: to advance step by step

ibte: an outgrowth on a tree that has begun to rot; cf. **ibete**

ibtenembi: to rot, to decay (said of trees)

    ibtenehe moo: a rotted tree

    ibtenehe oforo: a nose that has turned red due to drinking, brandy nose

iburšambi: to crawl, to creep

    iburašame aššambi: to wriggle, to squirm

    iburašame yuburšambi: to wriggle (said of insects)

ica: *Heemisalanx prognathus*: a kind of long white ocean fish with no fins — called the 'noodle fish' in Chinese

icabumbi: ⟶ **acabumbi**

icakū: **1**. unpleasant, unfitting, uncomfortable; **2**. anxious, uneasy

icakūliyan: rather unpleasant

icakūšambi: **1**. to be unpleasant, to lose favor with; **2**. to affront, to offend

icambi: **1**. to neigh; **2**. ⟶ **acambi**; **3**. ⟶ **isambi**

icangga: **1**. tasty, delicious; **2**. interesting, delightful, pleasing; **3**. convenient, comfortable

icangga buda: choice foods, delicacies

icangga gisun: gentle words, tactful expressions

icangga šungkeri: graceful, refined

ice: **1**. new, fresh; **2**. the first ten days of the month; **3**. beginning, at the beginning, the first day of a lunar month; **4**. recently

ice aniya: the New Year

ice biya: new moon

ice boo: bridal chamber

ice cai: bud tea

ice calu: a granary near Mukden

ice donjin: news

ice hafan: inexperienced official

ice hojihon: bridegroom

ice ilhangga suje: new-style flowered silk

ice inenggi: the first day of a lunar month

ice jecen: Xinjiang

ice nimaha: fresh fish

ice niyalma: bride

ice tušan: new incumbent

ice urun: bride

icebumbi: **1**. (causative or passive of **icembi**); **2**. to be stained, to be contaminated, to be infected

icebun: contamination, smearing, stain

iceburakū: uncontaminated

iceken: rather new, rather fresh

icekesaka: quite new or fresh

iceku: pigment, coloring, dyestuff

iceku orho: madder (from which red dye is made)

iceleme: at the beginning of the month

icembi: **1**. to dye; **2**. to bleach; **3**. to contaminate; **4**. to stain

icere faksi: dyer

icemlebumbi: (causative of **icemlembi**)

icemlembi: **1**. to make new, to renew; **2**. to do anew, to do over

icemleme arambi: to redo

icere: ⟶ **icembi** (subheading)

icereme: during the first ten days of the month; cf. **ice**

ici: **1**. right (as opposed to left); **2**. direction, dimension; **3**. (postposition) in accordance with, along with, after, according to, facing, on the side of, toward

ici acabumbi: to cater to, to be obsequious, to pander, to flatter

ici acabume gisurembi: to speak in a flattering way

ici acabume weilembi: to act in conformity, to act in an obsequious way

ici acarakū: not suitable, inappropriate

ici akū: ⟶ **icakū**

ici baharakū: not following a definite course of action, not setting a goal

ici ergi: the right-hand side

ici ergi fiyenten: (右司) second department of a governmental organ

ici fambumbi: to lose one's sense of direction

ici kani akū: at variance, disagreeing

icihi: spot, blemish, flaw

icihi akū: spotless, without blemish

icihi dasihi: spot, blemish

icihiyabukū: manager, person in charge

icihiyabumbi: (causative of **icihiyambi**)

icihiyambi: **1**. to arrange, to manage, to take care of; **2**. to put in order, to tidy up; **3**. to get oneself ready, to groom; **4**. to prepare a corpse for burial

icihiyame dasambi: to handle, to manage

icihiyame forgošombi: to plan and manage, to operate

icihiyame gamambi: to manage, to cope with

icihiyame sindambi: to inter, to bury

icihiyara etuku: shroud, clothing for the dead

icihiyara hafan: (郎中) Departmental Director, *BH* 290

icihiyandumbi: to manage together; also **icihiyanumbi**

icihiyanjambi: to put in order carefully, to order reasonably

icihiyanumbi: to manage together; also **icihiyandumbi**

icihiyara: ⟶ **icihiyambi** (subheading)

icihiyasi: (吏目) Departmental Police-master and Jail Warden, *BH* 851A

icikūšambi: ⟶ **icakūšambi**

icingga: **1**. having direction, purposeful; **2**. experienced, competent, skilled, expert at

    icingga akū: inexperienced, incompetent, unskilled

icišambi: **1**. to exploit a situation, to take advantage of an opportunity; **2**. to go in the direction of; **3**. to curry favor

icitai: right-handed (especially at archery)

icu: a fur coat or jacket without an outer covering

icuhiyan: ⟶ **acuhiyan**

idaliya: Italy

idambi: ⟶ **idumbi**

idarambi: to gasp for breath, to feel pain while breathing

idaršambi: to have a pain in the chest or belly

    idaršame nimembi: to have dull pain

idu: a turn at duty, shift

    idu alibumbi: to pass one's duty on to the next shift

    idu alimbi: to be on duty, to go on duty

    idu arambi: to take one's turn

    idu dosimbi: to go on duty, to take up one's turn

    idu fekumbi: to skip one's turn

    idu gaimbi: ⟶ **idu arambi**

    idu halabumbi: to change shifts

    idu halanjambi: to do alternately by turns, to do in rotation

    idu i boo: a guardroom

    idu ilibumbi: to pass on one's turn to another

    idu jafambi: to take turns

idukan: rather coarse

idumbi: to glue feathers onto an arrow shaft

idun: coarse, rough, uneven

idurabumbi: (causative of **idurambi**)

idurambi: to do duty in turn, to serve in turn

    idurame kederembi: to patrol at fixed intervals

idurembi: ⟶ **idurambi**

ifibumbi: (causative of **ifimbi**)

ifimbi: (-ha) to sew

    ifire faksi: tailor, seamstress

ifin: **1**. sewing, needlework; **2**. seam

    ifin akū: seamless

ifire: ⟶ **ifimbi** (subheading)

igan: ⟶ **ihan**

igehe: the stem of a fruit or melon

igen: the two ends of a bow

    igen šukumbi: to attach the ends of a bow

igengge: pertaining to the origin

igeri usiha: the herd boy — the star Altair

ihaci: cowhide

ihan: **1**. bovine, cow, ox, bull; **2**. the second of the earth's branches (丑)

    ihan biya: the twelfth month

    ihan bula: the honey locust tree

    ihan buren: a signal horn made of brass

    ihan erin: period of the day from 1 AM to 3 AM

    ihan honin i adun i baita be kadalame icihiyara uheri da: (牛羊館總監) Superintendent of Livestock in the Board of Rites

    ihan morin i cifun be kadalara yamun: (牛馬稅務監督衙門) Office in Charge of Taxes on Horses and Cows in the Mukden Board of Revenue

    ihan mušu: a kind of small yellow quail

    ihan nimaha: cowfish — a kind of scaleless fish about a yard long that bears some resemblance to a cow

    ihan sejen: ox cart

    ihan tuwa: bonfire

    ihan uncehen: a scaleless fish somewhat larger than a perch with a round tail and sharp stickers on its back

    ihan yaksargan: *Phragomaticola aedon*: reed warbler

ihangga: pertaining to the cow

    ihangga aniya: the year of the cow

ihasa: (plural of **ihan**)

ihasi: rhinoceros

ihasingga kiru: a banner embroidered with the image of a rhinoceros

ihida: the bits of meat left over after an animal has been butchered

ii: ⟶ **i i**

ija: gadfly

    ija cecike: *Parus parus*: great titmouse

    ija niyehe: *Podiceps ruficollis*: little grebe

ijari ilha: *Magnolia fuscata*: banana shrub

ijarlambi: to smile

ijaršambi: **1**. to smile cheerfully; **2**. to polish

ijasha mahala: a hat topped with a chrysanthemum-shaped ornament (used by high officials)

ijibumbi: (causative of **ijimbi**)

ijifun: comb

ijifun niru: an arrow with a shaft shaped like the back of a comb

ijifun niyehe: *Aix galericulata*: mandarin duck

ijilabumbi: (causative of **ijilambi**)

ijilambi: to become accustomed to one another (livestock)

ijimbi: (**-ha**) **1**. to comb; **2**. to put vertical threads on a loom; **3**. to put in proper order, to regulate

ijime wekjimbi: to straighten out something tangled, to put in order

ijire wekjin: basic principle

ijin: **1**. warp; **2**. taut, tight; **3**. tautness, tightness, tension

ijin wekjin: **1**. warp and woof; **2**. order and rule

ijire: ⟶ **ijimbi** (subheading)

ijishūn: **1**. obedient, submissive, docile, filial; **2**. favorable, smooth, without a hitch

ijishūn dasan: the Shunzhi (順治) reign title, 1644–61

ijishūn hehe: posthumous title given to the main wife of an official of the fifth rank

iju: stunted, undersized

ijubumbi: (causative of **ijumbi**)

ijukū: a tool for spreading ointment or powder; cf. **fiyan ujukū**

ijumbi: (**-ha**) to smear, to spread

ijume darime gisurembi: to speak sarcastically, to intimate something bad about a person

ijurabumbi: (causative or passive of **ijurambi**)

ijurambi: **1**. to rub, to scrape; **2**. to satirize, to mock, to jeer

ijuršambi: **1**. to rub vigorously; **2**. to make sarcastic remarks

ikdaki: the white hair on the sides of a roe's tail

ikengge: **1**. original; **2**. chief, great, large

ikiri: **1**. pair, twins; **2**. in pairs, in succession, one after another; **3**. along the way, on the road

ikiri afaha: a book in which records of official money transactions were kept (it was divided into two parts, one of which was given to the payee as a receipt and the other was kept by the government)

ikiri coko: a name for the chicken; ⟶ **coko**

ikiri jungken: a set of sixteen bronze bells hung in pairs, each producing a different tone

ikiri kingken: a set of sixteen L-shaped stones hung in pairs, each producing a different tone

ikiri mulu: a ridgepole that extended through two different buildings

ikiri tecembi: to sit together in a row

ikiri usiha: Altair (name of a star)

ikirilame: forming a pair, along the border

iktabumbi: (causative of **iktambi**)

iktambi: (**-ka**) to accumulate, to pile up, to collect, to gather

iktambumbi: (causative of **iktambi**)

iktan: **1**. accumulation, piling up; **2**. in Buddhist writings, **skandha**

iktangga: implicit, hidden

ikūbumbi: (causative of **ikūmbi**)

ikūmbi: to shrink, to contract

ikūn: contraction, shrinking

ikūrsun: marrow of the spine

ikūršambi: to crawl (like a snake or worm), to creep along

ikūrulambi: to get up, to stand up (said of horses)

ilacambi: ⟶ **ilambi**

ilaci: third

ilaci de oci: in the third place

ilaci jalan i omolo: great-great-grandchild

ilaci jergi hiya: attendant of the third class

iladala: unstable, inconstant

iladambi: **1**. to jump forward with the legs crossed (a kind of game); **2**. to be unstable, to be inconstant, to act irresolutely

iladame faitambi: in cutting out clothes, to cut down the dimensions so that one part is smaller

ilafibumbi: (causative of **ilafimbi**)

ilafimbi: to turn back, to curl back

ilagi: vapor from dew

ilaha: the green bark of the willow

ilambi: (**-ka**) to bloom

ilan: three

ilan acangga hergen: three Chinese characters used to represent the sound of a Manchu word

ilan bethengge hūntahan: a three-legged gold or jade wine vessel used for sacrificial purposes

ilan biya: the third month

ilan dedume fudembi: to accompany to the third stage of a journey

ilan dorolon i bithei kuren: (三禮館) Office in Charge of Editing the Classics of Ritual

ilan erdemu: the three powers: heaven, earth, and man

ilan fafun i yamun: (三法司) Three High Courts of Judicature, *BH* 215

ilan fu: the hottest time of the summer occurring right after the summer solstice

ilan gūsai menggun afabure toksoi da sabe kadalara ba: (管理三旗銀兩莊頭處) Office for Collecting Rents on Imperial lands, *BH* 78A

ilan hafu bithei kuren: (三通館) Office in Charge of Compiling the Santong

ilan hešen: the three moral relationships: Prince-subject, father-son, husband-wife

ilan irungge mahatun: an ancient-style hat with three high ridges on top

ilan jaifan: three bones that join together in the croup of a horse

ilan mulfiyen i suje: silk having three-tier round pattern

ilan namun i dangse boo: (三庫檔房) Business Office of the Three Palace Storehouses (for silver, textiles, and pigments)

ilan niyakūn: the ceremony of kneeling thrice

ilan siden i calu: the three granaries of the Imperial household

ilan šanyan: the three hottest ten-day periods of summer

ilan tacihiyan: the three teachings: Confucianism, Buddhism, Daoism

ilan tuhebuku i mahatu: an ancient-style hat topped with three jeweled pendants

ilan unggala miyoocan: a three-barreled musket

ilanggeri: three times

ilanofi: three persons

ilari boso: a kind of very wide white cloth

ilarsu: three-tiered, three-leveled, three-storied

ilase: three years old

ilata: three each

ilbabumbi: (causative of **ilbambi**)

ilbakū: trowel for applying plaster

ilbambi: to plaster (a wall)

ilbara faksi: stonemason, plasterer

ilban: **1**. plaster; **2**. the plastered surface of an oven-bed

ilbara: ⟶ **ilbambi** (subheading)

ilbarilambi: to smile

ilbašambi: to laugh while putting tongue-pressure against the lips

ilbeke: fond of eating fatty foods

ilcambi: ⟶ **incambi**

ildambi: to be quick-witted, to be agile, to be bright

ildamu: **1**. elegant, refined; **2**. quick-witted, bright

ildamungga: elegant, graceful, tasteful, charming, appealing

ildedei: a name for the turkey

ildefun: the back of the head, the juncture of the neck and the cranium

ildehe: bast, the bark of the linden tree

ildubi: a name for the **yabulan** (a kind of owl)

ildubumbi: (causative of **ildumbi**)

ildufun giranggi: ⟶ **ildefun**

ildumbi: (**-ka**) to be well acquainted with, to be friends with

ildun: **1**. convenient, comfortable; **2**. convenience, opportunity

ildun de: conveniently, in passing, incidentally, taking advantage of something

ildun duka: side door

ildungga: convenient, handy

ildungga afaha: a summary of official documents

ildungga duka: side door, side gate

ildušambi: to take advantage of an opportunity

ile: a kind of hunting net

ilebumbi: (causative of **ilembi**)

ilekesaka: rather clear

ilembi: **1**. to lick; **2**. to strip the outer skin from hemp stalks

ilenggu: **1**. tongue; **2**. the trigger of a trap; **3**. a wooden stick hanging from the nose ring of a domestic beast; **4**. the clapper of a bell

ilenggu dasakū: tongue scraper

ilenggu dube: the tip of the tongue

ilenggu halgimbi: to be tongue tied

ilenggu foholon: in the wrong, not on solid ground

ilerebumbi: (causative or passive of **ilerembi**)

ilerembi: to tether with a long rope, as for grazing

iletu: **1**. well known, clear, out in the open, manifest, obvious, public; **2**. not shy, open to others; **3**. publicly, openly

    iletu cooha: troops in the open

    iletu getuken: clear, obvious

    iletu hūlha: bandit who operates in the open

    iletu kiyoo: an open sedan chair

    iletu targacun: warning, object lesson

    iletu temgetu: clear proof, clear sign

    iletu yabumbi: to act openly

iletuken: rather clear, rather open

iletulebumbi: (causative of **iletulembi**)

iletulehe: ⟶ **iletulembi** (subheading)

iletulehen: a horizontal tablet over a door or gate

iletulembi: **1**. to reveal, to expose, to make public; **2**. to appear, to become well known; **3**. to do in a clear manner

    iletulehe mukun: prominent family, distinguished clan

    iletuleme wesimbure bithe: a memorial presented to the throne on festive occasions

iletun: **1**. elucidation, clearing up; **2**. chart, table; **3**. ⟶ **iletu**

iletungge: bright, clear, obvious

    iletungge gu: a jade ornament, symbolic of a male child and used in ceremonies in ancient times

iletusaka: clearly, obviously, openly

ilga: ⟶ **ilha**

    ilga sabsimbi: to tattoo

ilgabumbi: (causative or passive of **ilgambi**)

ilgabun: **1**. discernment, judgment; **2**. difference

ilgacun: difference, differentiation

    ilgacun akū: without difference

ilgambi: **1**. to distinguish, to differentiate; **2**. to select; **3**. to evaluate, to assess

    ilgame faksalambi: to differentiate

    ilgame sonjombi: to select, to choose

    ilgame takambi: to identify, to recognize

ilganambi: ⟶ **ilhanambi**

ilgandumbi: to distinguish (said of a group)

ilgangga: ⟶ **ilhangga**

ilgari: paper strips attached to a willow branch (used as an offering to spirits)

    ilgari tucibumbi: to hang out willow branches with paper streamers on them (used by shamans for driving off evil spirits)

ilgašambi: **1**. to visit friends or relatives; **2**. to go for a walk, to go sightseeing

ilgašanambi: to go to visit

ilgin: skin from which the hair has been removed, rawhide

    ilgin i šošonggo mahala: an ancient-style of rawhide hat used during wartime

ilgiri niyehe: a small diving duck with oily flesh, the same as **aka niyehe**

ilha: **1**. flower, blossom; **2**. patterned, colored, polychrome; **3**. gradations on a scale; **4**. pox, measles

    ilha akū sirgeri: plain white silk yarn

    ilha akū turtun: plain thin pongee

    ilha boso: colored cloth

    ilha bulha: brightly colored

    ilha cecikengge loho: a sword decorated with colored bird patterns

    ilha i felhen: flower stand

    ilha i fengse: a vessel with a miniature landscape in it

    ilha fiyen: pollen

    ilha i simen: nectar

    ilha i šugi: myrrh

    ilha muke: wild strawberry; cf. **ilhamuke**

    ilha noho dardan: satin with large patterns on it

    ilha šeolembi: to embroider

    ilhai dobokū: flower vase

    ilhai hungkereku: a watering can for flowers

    ilhai niyaman: calyx

    ilhai suku: a clump of flowers

    ilhai sulku: flower stand

    ilhai tebuku: a sack used for carrying flowers

    ilhai tubi: a protective cover placed over flowers

    ilhai ukdun: a warm pit used for forcing plants

    ilhai yafan: flower garden

ilhakū moo: fig tree

ilhakū tubihe: fig

ilhamuke: wild strawberry

ilhanambi: **1**. to bloom; **2**. to grow dim (said of the eyes), to have blurred vision

ilhangga: colored, patterned, flowery

    ilhangga cuse moo: golden bamboo

    ilhangga dengjan: festive lantern (displayed on the lantern festival)

    ilhangga fungkū: a brightly colored carved or embroidered stool

    ilhangga moo: rosewood

ilhangga sirgeri: thin silk cloth having a brightly colored pattern

ilhangga šobin: cakes with colored patterns stamped on them

ilhangga toose: lace

ilhangga turtun: brightly patterned thin silk

ilhangga wehei niowarikū: malachite green

ilhangga yabihan: coffered ceiling

ilhari: ⟶ **ilgari**

ilhi: **1**. next, subsequent; **2**. vice-, sub-, assistant; **3**. dysentery

ilhi anambi: to ascend to the next rank

ilhi aname: in order, one after the other

ilhi bayarai jalan i janggin: (副護軍參領) Lieutenant-Colonel, *BH* 734

ilhi bodome: according to rank, in order

ilhi hafan: (少卿) subdirector, vice-president

ilhi hafumbure hafan: (通政副使) Deputy Commissioner of the Transmission Office, *BH* 928

ilhi hefeliyenembi: to have dysentery

ilhi ilhi: in order, in succession

ilhi jalan i janggin: (副參領) Lieutenant-Colonel, *BH* 658

ilhi jorisi: (副指揮) Assistant Police Magistrate, *BH* 796A

ilhi kadalara da: (副管) Assistant Director of the Imperial Clan School; cf. *BH* 717

ilhi ome: in a rank, in single file, one after another

ilhi tacibukū hafan: (訓導) Subdirector of Schools, *BH* 857

ilhi tacibure hafan: (司業) Assistant Director of the National Academy of Learning

ilhi takūrakū: (副使) Assistant Overseer, Assistant Inspector; cf. **takūrakū**

ilhi tušan: deputy position

ilhi tušan i hafan: Assistant Magistrate

ilhi uju i jergi: grade one-B

ilhici: deputy; cf. **dabsan juwere ilhici**

ilhin: ⟶ **ilgin**

ilhinembi: to have dysentery

ilho: ⟶ **ilhū**

ilho moo: the tree *Idesia pylocarpa*: wonder tree

ilhuru: the name of a small colorful bird

ilhuru dudu: a multicolored dove

ilhuru giyahūn cecike: a kind of shrike

ilhū: **1**. upright, vertical; **2**. appropriate, suitable

ilhūngga: lying straight (said of hair on an animal)

ilibumbi: **1**. (causative of **ilimbi**); **2**. to erect, to set up; **3**. to stop, to end, to bring to an end; **4**. to add to one's possessions

ilibuci ojorakū: without being able to stop

ilibunjimbi: to come to establish

ilicambi: to stand together

ilifimbi: to curl (said of metals)

ilihai: immediately, on the spot

ilihai andande: immediately

ilihai waha: killed him on the spot

ilihangga: strong, durable (said of silk products)

ilihen: (艮) the third of the eight trigrams of the *Yijing* (symbolizing mountains)

ilimbahabumbi: (causative of **ilimbahambi**)

ilimbahambi: (**ilimbaha**) **1**. to become accustomed, to get used to; **2**. to be at peace with, to be calm

ilimbi: (-ha) **1**. to stand, to get up; **2**. to stop, to cease; **3**. to raise (troops); cf. **cooha ilimbi**; **4**. to serve as; cf. **ejen ilimbi**

ilire tere be ejere yamun: (起居注衙門) Office for Compiling the Records of the Emperor's Daily Activities

ilimeliyan: in a standing position

ilin: standing, standing position

ilin akū: no place to stop or stand

ilinambi: to go to stand on, to settle down, to stop (on)

ilingga hengketu: a wooden emblem carved in the shape of a melon

ilingga hiyan: incense in the form of long sticks

ilinjambi: **1**. to come to a stop, to stand around, to loiter; **2**. to cease, to stop; **3**. to be just able to stand (said of a child)

ilinjimbi: to come to stand (on)

ilire: ⟶ **ilimbi** (subheading)

ilkidun: a name for the partridge; cf. **jukidun**

ilmaha: uvula

ilmahū: a wooden device used for tightening the threads on a loom

ilmen: lead or stone weights placed on the bottom of nets

ilmerembi: (-ke) to break loose, to escape from its reins (a horse)

ilmoho usiha: (伐星) one of the stars in the constellation of Orion

ilmun han: the ruler of the underworld

ilten: a high shoulder piece or collar on court garments

imahū: *Naemorhedus goral*: goral

imalan: the tree *Maclura cochinchinensis*: a member of the mulberry family

imari: *mǔ* 畝: a Chinese measure of land area, about one sixth of an acre

imata: **1**. completely, all, totally, thoroughly; **2**. only, exclusively

imbe: (accusative form of **i**)

imci: ⟶ **imcin**

imcin: a kind of drum used by shamans

imcišambi: to beat an **imcin**

imengge moo: *Triadica sebifera*: Chinese tallow tree

imenggi: vegetable oil

    imenggi dabukū: oil lamp

imenggilembi: to oil, to rub with oil, to lubricate

imete: a small nail (used on armor)

imeten ilha: *Syringa vulgaris*: lilac

imhe: (翼) a constellation, the 27th of the lunar mansions, made up of twenty-two stars distributed between Crater and Hydra

    imhe tokdonggo kiru: (翼宿旗) a banner depicting the constellation **imhe**

imisun: ⟶ **imiyesun**

imiyaha: insect, bug; cf. **umiyaha**

imiyahanambi: to get worms; cf. **umiyahanambi**

imiyambi: to assemble, to gather

    imiyara sabintungga kiru: (遊麟旗) a banner with the image of a unicorn on it

imiyan: assembly, gathering

imiyantu: a sacrificial hat of the Xia dynasty

imiyara: ⟶ **imiyambi** (subheading)

imiyelembi: to gird oneself; cf. **umiyelembi**

imiyesun: belt, girdle; cf. **umiyesun**

imseke: the young of the otter

in: the female or negative principle — Chinese yin

    in i simen: vaginal discharge, menstrual discharge

    in yang: the male (positive) and female (negative) principles

in du gurun: India

ina: the son of one's sister — nephew

    ina jui: nephew on the mother's side

    ina sargan jui: niece on the mother's side

    ina urun: wife of one's sister's son

incambi: to neigh

inci: (ablative of **i**): from him, from her, than him, than her

indahūlambi: to fall simultaneously (in wrestling)

indahūn: **1**. dog; **2**. the eleventh of the earth's branches (戌)

    indahūn biya: the ninth month

    indahūn cecike: *Upupa epops*: the hoopoe, a kind of bird

    indahūn erin: the period from 7 PM to 9 PM

    indahūn fekun: dog gallop — a kind of gallop that resembles a dog running

    indahūn gintehe: a kind of tree with colored bark and red and white flowers and that grows near rivers

    indahūn holdon: *Pinus sibirica*: Siberian pine, masson pine

    indahūn i derhuwe: a dog-fly

    indahūn manggisu: a name for the badger; cf. **dorgon**

    indahūn mucu: wild grape

    indahūn nacin: a kind of falcon

    indahūn sindambi: to set dogs (on game)

    indahūn soro: wild jujube

    indahūn soro debse: cake made of sour jujubes

    indahūn ujire ba: kennel

indahūngga: pertaining to dogs

    indahūngga aniya: the year of the dog

indan: an arrow lacking an arrowhead

inde: (dative or locative of **i**): to him or her

indebumbi: (causative of **indembi**)

indehen: malaria

indembi: to rest (on a journey), to spend the night, to halt, to spend time

    indeme: separated by a night

inden: a two day stay, stopover (on a journey)

inderi: a mare or cow that gives birth to young after a year's gap

ine mene: at will, willingly, as one pleases, may just as well (do something)

ineku: **1**. same, this (day, month, year); **2**. likewise, in like manner, in the same way, still, as before

    ineku aniya: this year

    ineku biya: this month

    ineku inenggi: today

    ineku jihe fucihi: Tathāgata (epithet of Buddha used by Buddha when speaking of himself)

ineku omolo: a descendant of the sixth generation

ineku sile: broth, water in which meat has been cooked

inemene: ⟶ **ine mene**

inenggi: **1**. day, daytime; **2**. date, point in time; **3**. a kind of sea fish resembling the bream

inenggi abkai tampin: the upper part of a water clock

inenggi anambi: to postpone, to defer

inenggi aname: day by day, per diem

inenggi bilambi: to set a time limit, to fix a deadline

inenggi dobori akū: both day and night, ceaselessly

inenggi dulime: during the daytime, in the middle of the day

inenggi dulin: midday, noon

inenggi dulin amala: afternoon

inenggi dulin onggolo: forenoon, morning

inenggi erin: time

inenggi goidabumbi: to extend the amount of time

inenggi goidambi: for a considerable amount of time to pass

inenggi halambi: to change a deadline

inenggi hetumbi: to make a living

inenggi hetumbumbi: to live, to get by

inenggi sidaraka: the days have become longer

inenggi šun de: in the daytime

inenggi šuntuhele: the whole day

inenggi tome: every day

inenggi tulimbi: to exceed a deadline

inenggi wame banjimbi: to while away the time

inenggidari: every day

inenggishūn: around noon, close to midday

ing: **1**. camp, military encampment; **2**. battalion

ing hadambi: to pitch camp, to camp

ing ilimbi: to set up camp

ing jafambi: to establish camp

ing cing: sapphire

ing gasha: oriole, eagle

ing hūng: ruby

ing lo: tassel

ing ši wehe: limestone from Yingde county in Guangdong (used for building rockeries)

ingga moo: a kind of camphor tree

inggaha: **1**. down, fluff; **2**. the fuzz of a cattail or willow tree, catkin

inggaha cece: a kind of very light fabric made of down

inggaha cekemu: velvet

inggaha suje: a kind of tightly woven thick woolen that resembles satin

inggaha šufanaha suri: a kind of silk crêpe

inggali: wagtail, a bird of the genus *Motacilla*

inggari: the down or fuzz from the blossom of the willow tree

inggari orho: duckweed

inggarilambi: to produce fuzz (said of plants)

inggiri: England

inggiri gurun: England

ingguhe: ⟶ **yengguhe**

ingtori: cherry

ingturi: ⟶ **ingtori**

ingyang seme: (onomatopoetic) buzzing (said of flies)

ini: (genitive of **i**): his, her

ini beye: he himself, she herself, personally

ini cihai: at will, at random, as one pleases, willfully

ini cisui: on one's own initiative, by itself, of its own accord

iningge: his, hers

iniyaha: looper, measuring worm

injaha: the young of the gazelle; cf. **jeren**

injahan: ⟶ **injaha**

injebumbi: (causative of **injembi**)

injecembi: to laugh together

injecuke: funny, humorous, amusing

injeku: **1**. joke; **2**. funny, amusing

injeku arambi: to joke

injeku gisun: funny story, joke, jest

injekungge: comical, gay, jovial

injekušembi: to ridicule, to laugh at

injembi: to laugh

injemeliyan: smiling

injendumbi: to laugh (said of a group); also **injenumbi**

injenumbi: to laugh (said of a group); also **injendumbi**

injesi: joker, clown

injiri: veil on a woman's hat used to protect her face from the sun

intu cecike: the name of a small brown bird that chatters incessantly

inu: **1**. also, too; **2**. even (adverb); **3**. so, yes; **4**. correct

io: oil, paint, lacquer

io g'ang cing: a kind of brown cloth

iodan: an oilcloth raincoat

iogi: (遊擊) Major; cf. **dasihire hafan**

ioi: **1**. a musical instrument shaped like a lying tiger — the serrated ridge down the back is stroked with a wooden stick at the conclusion of a musical selection; **2**. one of the five tones; cf. **yumk'a**

ioimtun: a ritual vessel used by King Shun

iojan: a painter

iolebumbi: (causative of **iolembi**)

iolembi: to oil, to paint, to lacquer

    iolehe hoošan: oil paper

    iolere faksi: a lacquer worker, a painter

iose: pomelo

iowan: ⟶ **yuwan**

iowanboo: ⟶ **yuwamboo**

iowei: ⟶ **yuwei**

ira: a small variety of glutinous millet that matures early (smaller than **fisihe**)

    ira buda: cooked millet

    irai nure: liquor made from glutinous millet

irahi: **1**. ripple; **2**. a shaft of light coming through a crack in a door or window

iren: **1**. ripples and foam caused by swimming fish; **2**. wild reindeer, caribou (*Rangifer tarandus*)

irenembi: to cause ripples (said of fish)

ireshūn: sunken, sloping down toward the front (said of animals)

irga: ⟶ **irha**

irgašambi: to flirt with the eyes, to wink at

irge honin: a castrated ram, a wether

irgebumbi: to compose verse, to recite or chant poetry

irgebun: poem, verse

    irgebun mudan: rhyme

    irgebun yoro: ballad, folk poetry

irgece moo: the name of a black and deep-red colored tree that grows in Tibet

irgece niyehe: a name for the mandarin duck; cf. **ijifun niyehe**

irgen: people, the common people

irgen i banin: situation of the people

irgen i gūnin: popular will

irgen i kunggeri: (民科) Section of Civil Affairs (of various governmental organs)

irgen sere temgetu: pass used at local examinations by nonofficial participants

irgese: (plural of **irgen**)

irha: remnants of cloth

iri: **1**. plot, bed (in a vegetable or flower garden); **2**. fifty *mǔ* 畝; cf. **imari**

irkimbi: to provoke a person to anger

irkinjimbi: to come to provoke

irmu: a name for the quail; cf. **mušu**

irubumbi: (causative or passive of **irumbi**)

irudai: the phoenix of the north

irukū: lead sinker on a net

irumbi: (-ha) to sink, to drown

    irume bucembi: to die from drowning

irun: **1**. tiles laid facing downward; **2**. rows of grain in a field; **3**. raised path between fields; **4**. the inside part of an oven-bed, channels in an oven-bed for the passage of smoke

irungge mahatun: an ancient-style hat that indicates rank by the number of ridges on top

irushūn: **1**. sunken, submerged, secret, hidden; **2**. high at the back and lower in front

irusu hiyan: incense made from agarwood (*Aquilaria agallocha*)

isabumbi: **1**. (causative of **isambi**); **2**. to gather, to assemble, to collect together

isabun: gathering, assembly, collection

isakū: convener of a meeting

isambi: **1**. to come together, to gather, to assemble; **2**. to plait

isamjambi: to accumulate, to collect

isan: gathering, assembly, meeting, association

    isan neimbi: to hold a meeting

isanambi: to go to assemble

isandumbi: to gather together; also **isanumbi**

isangga mekten: a game of chance in which a number of people make bets on a monthly drawing of tallies

isanjimbi: to come to assemble

isanjingga boo: the antechamber of the throne room where those who awaited audiences assembled

isanumbi: to gather together; also **isandumbi**

isarlambi: to be assembled

ise: chair

    ise i sektefun: a chair cushion

isebumbi: **1**. (causative of **isembi**); **2**. to punish, to reprimand; **3**. to intimidate

isebun: **1**. punishment, reprimand; **2**. intimidation

isecun: fear, fright

iseku: one who is afraid, coward, afraid

    iseku akū: unafraid

iselebumbi: (causative of **iselembi**)

iseleku: scorpion

    iseleku ilha: an exotic flower that grows in the mountains of Guizhou

    iseleku umiyaha: scorpion

iselembi: to oppose steadfastly, to defy, to resist

isembi: to fear, to lack courage, to be timid

isha: **1**. Siberian jay (*Garrulus glandarius*); **2**. greedy and covetous person

isheliyeken: rather narrow

isheliyen: narrow

ishu: reel or skein of thread

ishulembi: to face one another, to meet face to face

ishun: **1**. (postposition) toward, facing, opposite; **2**. next; **3**. forward; **4**. cf. **ishunde**

    ishun aniya: next year

    ishun biya: next month

    ishun cashūn: **1**. opposite, incoherent, contradictory; **2**. facing and back to back, in two directions at once, with a wringing motion

    ishun duka: facing gate, a gate on the opposite side

    ishun edun: head wind

    ishun jabumbi: **1**. to contradict, to take an unyielding position in an argument; **2**. to talk back to

    ishun muduri: facing dragons (on satin)

    ishun sefere: the two hands joined exactly together, thumb to thumb, forefinger to forefinger

ishunde: mutually, to one another, in succession, one after another

    ishunde bahambi: to get along well with one another

isi: *Larix sibirica*: larch

isibubumbi: (causative of **isibumbi**)

isibumbi: **1**. (causative of **isimbi (1, 2)**); **2**. to send, to take to, to deliver, to pass to (someone);

3. to bestow; **4**. to cause, to bring about; **5**. to repay, to return a favor; **6**. to begin the training of falcons and hunting dogs

    isiburakū: (with **de**) cannot or will not go so far as, unlikely

isihai: ⟶ **isimbi (1)** (subheading)

isihibumbi: (causative of **isihimbi**)

isihidabumbi: (causative or passive of **isihidambi**)

isihidambi: **1**. to grab hold of and shake; **2**. to give a stern look, to reprove

isihimbi: (**-ha**) to shake, to wave, to shake out, to shake off

isika: ⟶ **isimbi (1)** (subheading)

isimbi (l): (**-ka, -pi**) l. to reach, to arrive; **2**. to approach, to come up to; **3**. to be enough, to be sufficient: **baitalara de isimbi** 'to be sufficient for use'; **4**. (with **de**) to be as good as; **5**. to be about to (with the imperfect participle: **jetere isika** 'about to eat')

    isihai: (postposition) including, together with

    isika: (with imperfect participle) almost, about to, soon to

    isika joo: that is quite enough!

    isime: approximately

    isimeliyan: approximately (with numbers)

    isirakū: (with **de**) not as good an alternative as … , it is better to … , not as good as …

    isirei: imminent, approaching, impending

isimbi (2): (**-ha**) to pull up (grass), to pluck

isimbumbi: (causative of **isimbi (1)**)

isime: ⟶ **isimbi (1)** (subheading)

isimeliyan: ⟶ **isimbi (1)** (subheading)

isinambi: **1**. to reach, to arrive (at that place); **2**. to go so far as to …

    isinahala ba: everywhere

isingga: sufficient, adequate

    isinggai: sufficiently

isinjimbi: (imperative: **isinju**) to arrive (at this place), to reach (here)

    isinjiha be ejembi: to record incoming documents

isinjio: ⟶ **isinju**

isinju: (imperative of **isinjimbi**)

isirakū: ⟶ **isimbi (1)** (subheading)

isirei: ⟶ **isimbi (1)** (subheading)

isitai: ⟶ **icitai**

isitala: up to, until

isohon: bezoar: concretions found in the bellies of ruminant animals and used as medicine

isu: plain black satin

isuhe: ⟶ **ishu**

isuhūn: weak, delicate, sickly (said of children)

isuka: golden eagle

isungge šufatu: a military head covering of ancient times made from black satin

isus: Jesus

itele: one hundred-trillionth (of a Chinese foot)

iten: a two-year-old cow

itu: *Perdix dauurica*: Chinese partridge

itulhen: *Falco cherrug*: saker, Shanhan falcon

iturhen: ⟶ **itulhen**

ituri: a nestling cuckoo; cf. **dumin cecike**

J ᠵ

ja: 1. cheap, inexpensive; 2. easy; 3. ordinary,
    unimportant
    ja akū: 1. wonderful, marvelous; 2. not easy; 3.
        not cheap
    ja be bodombi: to do the easy way, to save
        trouble or work
    ja de baharakū: not easy to obtain
    ja ja de: easily
    ja tuwambi: to look down on
ja fu bithe: ⟶ jafu bithe
ja ja: 1. a sound used to scare off children or
    animals; 2. (onomatopoetic) the sound
    made by a bird when it is caught
ja ji: (onomatopoetic) the sound of many people
    screaming
jabarhan: an iron hoop
jabcacun: reproach, blame, regret, complaint
jabcambi: 1. to regret; 2. to blame, to reproach; 3.
    to complain; 4. to swarm (said of insects)
jabcan: regret, blame, complaint
jabcandumbi: to regret (said of a group), to blame
    (said of a group); also jabcanumbi
jabcanumbi: to regret (said of a group), to blame
    (said of a group); also jabcandumbi
jabdubumbi: (causative of jabdumbi)
jabdugan: 1. interval, pause; 2. free time, leisure,
    spare time
    jabdugan akū: lacking sufficient time (to do
        something)
jabduhai: ⟶ jabdumbi (subheading)
jabduhakū: ⟶ jabdumbi (subheading)
jabduhangga: at leisure, relaxed, natural, leisurely
jabdumbi: 1. to be at leisure, to have the time to; 2.
    to complete (successfully), to hit the mark,
    to make a successful attempt; 3. to strike a
    blow
    jabduhai teile: as time permits, as opportunity
        allows

jabduhakū: did not have time to, did not
    succeed in
jabdurakū: 1. does not have time to; 2. taken
    unawares, taken by surprise
jabdungga: leisurely
jabdurakū: ⟶ jabdumbi (subheading)
jabhū: (張) a constellation, the 27th of the lunar
    mansions, made up of six stars in Hydra
    jabhū tokdonggo kiru: (張宿旗) a banner on
        which the constellation jabhū was depicted
jabjan: python, large snake
jabkū: a small bag of arrows carried at one's side
jabsun: a hundred billion
jabšabumbi: (causative of jabšambi)
jabšaki: (undue) advantage, (unearned) gain, cheap
    bargain
    jabšaki be baimbi: to seek an (unfair)
        advantage
    jabšaki be yabumbi: to live hoping for
        advantage, to live depending or hoping for
        good fortune
jabšambi: 1. to succeed, to gain, to win; 2. to gain
    an advantage, to benefit from; 3. to be a
    matter of good fortune
    jabšara ufarara: gain and loss, success and
        failure
jabšan: 1. good luck, good fortune, advantage; 2.
    cheap, inexpensive
    jabšan baimbi: to seek good luck, to look for
        an advantage, to depend on good fortune
    jabšande: fortunately, by good luck
jabtundumbi: to regret mutually, to regret (said of
    a group)
jabubumbi: 1. (causative of jabumbi); 2. to confess
jabumbi: to answer, to respond
jabun: 1. answer; 2. deposition (at law), testimony
    jabun gaimbi: to take a deposition
    jabun i bithe: written confession, statement
        made under interrogation, a deposition

jaci: **1**. too, very; **2**. frequently, apt to, susceptible to
   jaci elehun: too aloof (to one's relations)
   jaci fahūn amba: too bold (used to scold people)
   jaci ohode: all the time, often, no matter what
jacin: second, other
jacingge: second born
jadagalambi: ⟶ **jadahalambi**
jadagan: **1**. disability, paralysis; **2**. disabled, paralyzed
jadaha: ⟶ **jadagan**
jadahalambi: to be disabled, to be crippled
jadahan: ⟶ **jadagan**
jafabumbi: (causative of **jafambi**)
jafaha: ⟶ **jafambi** (subheading)
jafakū: handle, grip, grip on a bow
   jafakū hadambi: to nail a grip on (a bow)
   jafakū urhubuhe beri: a bow with a beveled grip
jafakūngga: having a handle
   jafakūngga dengjan: a lantern with a handle
   jafakūngga tungken: a large drum with a handle
jafambi: **1**. to take in the hand, to grasp, to seize, to hold, to grip, to take hold of one's opponent (at wrestling); **2**. to offer; **3**. to pick (fruit); **4**. to collect (taxes); **5**. to drive (a chariot or wagon); **6**. to freeze; **7**. to cremate; **8**. to erect, to build; cf. **jase jafambi**, **ing jafambi**; **9**. to arrest, to take into custody
   jafaha gūnin: aspiration, ambition
   jafara bithe: arrest warrant
jafan: **1**. bridal gift, dowry; **2**. gifts presented to a senior or teacher when visiting for the first time; **3**. driving of chariots or wagons
jafanabumbi: (causative of **jafanambi**)
jafanambi: to go to seize, to offer
jafangga: pertaining to holding, easy to handle, easy to grasp
jafanjimbi: to come to seize, to come to offer
jafanumbi: to grasp one another, to wrestle; cf. **jafunumbi**
jafara: ⟶ **jafambi** (subheading)
jafašakū: ⟶ **bithei jafašakū**
jafašambi: to hold continually, to keep groping for, to hold fast
jafata: a hawk that leaves the nest of its own free will

jafatambi: to restrain, to constrain, to control, to keep in rein
jafu: **1**. felt, wool blanket; **2**. directive, decree
   jafu bithe: directive, decree
   jafu fomoci: wool socks, socks made of felt
   jafu sektefun: a felt cushion or pad
jafukūngga: economical, thrifty, good at managing a household
jafunambi: to become like felt, to form felt
jafunubumbi: (causative of **jafunumbi**)
jafunumbi: to grasp one another, to wrestle
jafuta: ⟶ **jafata**
jaguri tungken: a foot-long drum used by the Imperial Escort
jaha: a dugout with a sharp front end and straight stern, a light boat
jahala: a horse with red or brown stripes around its neck
jahaltu sirga: a horse with silver stripes on its neck
jahara: **1**. ⟶ **jahari**; **2**. multicolored
jahari: pebbles and stones found along a river bed
   jahari dalangga: a dam of pebbles and river stones
   jahari wehe: pebble, rock
jahūdai: boat, ship; cf. **cuwan**
   jahūdai fekumbi: to board a ship (in battle)
   jahūdai giyalan: cabin on a boat
   jahūdai i falgari da: (船署長) chief of the river constabulary
   jahūdai i hongko: prow of a boat
   jahūdai ilire ba: wharf, dock
jai: **1**. next, following, second; **2**. still, again, more; **3**. later; **4**. and
   jai coro: two days from tomorrow, three days from now
   jai inenggi: the following day
   jai jalan i omolo: great-grandchild
   jai jergi: second class
   jai jergi dosikasi: second-class metropolitan graduate
   jai jidere aniya: the year after next
   jai yaya akū: there is no one else
   jaide: in the second place, secondarily
jaici: second
jaida: kitchen knife, cleaver
jaidakū: **1**. bronze cymbals; **2**. small knife
jaidalambi: to cut with a cleaver
jaidambi: to exorcise, to drive out (demons)

jaidari: a kind of small cymbal

jaifan: confluence of the sources (small streams) of a river

jaifiyan: ⟶ **jaifan**

jailabumbi: **1**. (causative of **jailambi**); **2**. to move aside, to ward off, to parry; **3**. to depose (the Emperor); **4**. to set aside

    jailabume balhambi: to try to get rid of smallpox by offering a pig and sacrificial cakes

jailambi: to avoid, to get out of the way of, to shun, to hide

jailanambi: to go to hide

jailandumbi: to hide together, to avoid together; also **jailanumbi**

jailanumbi: to hide together, to avoid together; also **jailandumbi**

jailatambi: to shun continually, to act furtively, to conceal oneself

jaira: *Euarctos thibetanus*: female black bear

jaisang: (Mongolian) clan chieftain

jajabumbi: (causative of **jajambi**)

jajambi: to carry on one's back

jajanambi: **1**. to go carrying on one's back; **2**. to swarm, to exist in great numbers

jaji: an interjection of praise used toward small children

jajigi: *Erythroculter erythroculter*: red-sided culter, a valued food fish

jajihi: ⟶ **jajigi**

jajilabumbi: (causative of **jajilambi**)

jajilambi: to stack sorghum stalks, grass, or wood into a large pile

jajimbi: ⟶ **jajilambi**

jajin: a big pile or heap of stalks, grass, or wood

    jajin yali: meat from the face of a pig

jajuri: thicket, dense grove

jajurinambi: to form a thicket

jak jik: (onomatopoetic) the sound of birds screaming in flight

jak moo: *Haloxylon ammodendron*: saxaul — a low bush that can be used as fuel even when green

jaka: **1**. thing, object; **2**. material, stuff; **3**. side, edge, border; **4**. crack, fissure; **5**. interval, fault; **6**. area in front of something, place near something; cf. **jakade**; **7**. (particle used after the imperfect converb) just, as soon as, about to; cf. **saka**

jaka baimbi: to look for faults

jaka fiyeren: flaw, fissure, loophole

jaka jahūdai: cargo ship

jaka jaman: things, goods, possessions

jaka šolo: free time, free interval

jakade: (see separate entry below)

jakai cese: inventory list

jakaci: from oneself

jakade: **1**. (after the imperfect participle) because of, when; **2**. (postposition) in the vicinity of, to the presence of, close to

jakaderi: through a crack

jakalabumbi: to make a space between two things

jakambi: to fit joints together in the framework of a house

jakan: **1**. just, just now, not long (in duration), recently; **2**. ⟶ **jaka**

jakanabumbi: **1**. (causative of **jakanambi**); **2**. to sow discord, to drive a wedge between, to instigate

jakanambi: to crack, to split, to form a fissure, to divide (intransitive verb)

jakangga: having a crack, cracked

jakanjambi: to investigate carefully, to study assiduously, to research

    jakanjame: assiduously, thoroughly, to the utmost, sparing no effort

    jakanjame fonjimbi: to interrogate, to question carefully

    jakanjame gisurembi: to sow discord, to drive a wedge between

jakarabumbi: (causative of **jakarambi**)

jakarakū: the crack between the high end wall of a house and the roof

jakarambi: (-ka) **1**. to open slightly, to crack, to form a fissure; **2**. to break up with (friends or relatives); **3**. to get a little better (said of an illness); **4**. for mountains to become visible just before dawn

jakarame: (postposition) along, along the side of

jakdan: pine, trees of the genus *Pinus*

    jakdan i šugi: resin, pine sap

jakdu: one one-hundred-billionth

jakjahūn: cracked, split open, breached, having a fissure

jakjarambi: (-ka) to form a crack

jaksambi: (**-ka, -pi**) to turn bright red, to turn red (said of clouds)

jaksan: rose-colored clouds (at dawn or dusk)

jaksangga: dusk-colored, rose-colored

> **jaksangga moo**: *Lagerstroemia indica*: crape-myrtle

> **jaksangga gurung**: (紫宮) the name of a constellation

> **jaksangga ilha**: crape-myrtle flower

> **jaksangga ten**: (紫极) the name of a constellation, also called **dergi bikita**

jaksari moo: a tree with red branches and purple blossoms that reportedly grows in the South Sea islands

jaksun: *Abies firma*: fir, momi fir

jaktahan ilha: an exotic purple cup-shaped flower

jakūci: eighth

jakūn: eight

> **jakūn biya**: the eighth month

> **jakūn edungge kiru**: the eight-wind banners

> **jakūn fafun**: the eight proscriptions

> **jakūn faidan**: eight rows (of dancers)

> **jakūn gūsa**: the eight banners of the Manchus

> **jakūn gūsai kunggeri**: (八旗科) Office in Charge of the Eight Banners' Affairs in the Board of Civil Appointments in Mukden

> **jakūn gūsai ne beidere baita icihiyara ba**: (八旗現審所) Summary Court for Banner Affairs

> **jakūn gūsai turun**: (八旗大纛) the great standard of the eight banners — a banner in the colors of the eight banners

> **jakūn gūsai uheri ejetun bithei kuren**: (八旗通志館) office in charge of compiling the **jakūn gūsai uheri ejetun bithe** (called the *Bāqí tōngzhì* 八旗通志 in Chinese)

> **jakūn hergen**: the eight cyclical signs of one's birth

> **jakūn hergen tuwambi**: to examine the eight cyclical characters of one's birth (a form of fortune telling)

> **jakūn jijuhan**: the Eight Trigrams

> **jakūn kuluk**: the eight valiant steeds

> **jakūn meyen**: the eight sections of an 'eight-legged' classical essay

> **jakūn mudan**: the tones of the eight materials: metal, stone, silk, bamboo, gourd, earth, rawhide, and wool

jakūn niyalma tukiyere haksan bocoi kiyoo: a golden sedan chair carried by eight porters and used by Imperial concubines

jakūn ubu de dosika gung: a duke who possessed the eight privileges

jakūn ubu de dosimbuhakū gurun be dalire gung: (不入八分鎮國公) Prince of the Blood of the Seventh Degree, *BH* 22

jakūn ubu de dosimbuhakū gurun de aisilara gung: (不入八分輔國公) Prince of the Blood of the Eighth Degree, *BH* 23

jakūn ubui narhūngga fukjingga hergen: (八分書) a style of calligraphy

jakūnggeri: eight times

jakūnju: eighty

jakūnjuci: eightieth

jakūnjute: eighty each

jakūri suje: silk woven from eight different types of thread

jakūru: a measure equaling eight Chinese feet, a fathom (the length of the outstretched arms)

jakūse: eight years old

jakūta: eight each

jala: **1**. a marriage go-between, matchmaker; **2**. measure word for fences or walls

> **jala niyalma**: matchmaker

> **jala yabumbi**: to act as a go-between

jalabumbi: **1**. (causative of **jalambi**); **2**. to point out (a mistake)

jalafun: long life

> **jalafun arambi**: to celebrate a birthday (said of an older person)

> **jalafun hergengge šun dalikū**: an escort's parasol with the word **jalafun** written on it

jalafungga: possessing long life, long-lived

> **jalafungga ilha**: the flower *Tupistra chinensis*, China ruffles

> **jalafungga kiltan**: a pennant of the Imperial Escort bearing the word **jalafungga**

> **jalafungga toro**: flat peach, a variety of sweet, white-fleshed peach resembling a doughnut

jalafuri ilha: an exotic white flower from an evergreen plant

jalahi: cousin or nephew of the same surname

> **jalahi ahūn deo**: male cousins on the paternal side

> **jalahi jui**: nephew (son of one's brother)

jalahi sargan jui: niece (daughter of one's brother)

jalahi urun: the wife of a nephew

jalaktalambi: to leave a space, to pause (in music)

jalaktalara mudan: rhythm

jalaktambi: 1. ⟶ **jalaktalambi**; 2. to become uneven (said of a bird's plumage)

jalaktan: 1. pause, space; 2. meter, beat (in music), rhythm

jalakū: a bird lure

jalambi: (-ka, -ra/-ndara, -pi) 1. to pause, to leave a space, to be disconnected; 2. to let up (said of a pain or illness); 3. for a short time to pass

jalandarakū: without pause, uninterrupted

jalapi: after a pause, after a while

jalarakū: ⟶ **jalandarakū**

jalan: 1. joint, a section (of bamboo, grass, etc.); 2. generation, age; 3. world; 4. subdivision of a banner, ranks; 5. measure word for walls and fences

jalan aname: one generation after another

jalan baita: affairs of the world

jalan ci aljahabi: has passed away, has departed this world

jalan fon: the universe, the cosmos

jalan gurun: the world

jalan halame: generation after generation

jalan halame bošoro niru: hereditary banner chief

jalan i arbun: ways of the world

jalan i janggin: (參領) Colonel, *BH* 658, 659

jalan i wa: the mundane world

jalan jalan i: in turn, in succession, section by section, generation after generation, joint by joint

jalan jalan wasimbi: each generation is worse than the preceding one

jalan jecen: the world

jalan si: a **jalan**, subdivision of a banner, ranks

jalan sirambi: to continue for generations, to be hereditary

jalan sirara hafan: (世襲官) hereditary official

jalan waliyambi: to pass away, to die

jalangga: 1. measured, temperate, economical; 2. chaste; 3. pertaining to a generation

jalangga hehe: chaste woman — usually refers to a widow who has remained unmarried

jalapi: ⟶ **jalambi** (subheading)

jalarakū: ⟶ **jalambi** (subheading)

jalari: one quintillionth (of a Chinese foot)

jalasu: 1. an emblem or token carried by emissaries; 2. an Imperial document conferring enfeoffment

jalasu ilha: the flower *Stachyuras praecox*, spiketail

jalbarilambi: ⟶ **jalbarimbi**

jalbarimbi: to pray, to supplicate

jaldambi: to deceive, to cheat

jaldašambi: to deceive thoroughly

jalgambi: to put back together (broken things), to rejoin, to attach

jalgan: 1. length of life, span; 2. fate, destiny, lot

jalgan i dubembi: to die of old age

jalgan se: lifespan

jalgan ton: years of life, predestined age

jalgangga: pertaining to long life

jalgangga moo: tree of heaven

jalgari monio: ⟶ **jalhari monio**

jalgari moo: 1. a bamboo-like tree growing eight or nine feet tall; 2. tamarisk

jalgasu moo: *Cedrela sinensis*: Chinese toon tree

jalgiyabumbi: (causative of **jalgiyambi**)

jalgiyambi: 1. to fill out by taking from an abundance and adding to a scarcity, to add, to make even, to share one's abundance; 2. to compromise, to bend the rules for someone

jalgiyanjabumbi: (causative of **jalgiyanjambi**)

jalgiyanjambi: 1. to make even, to balance out; 2. to come to an understanding, to compromise, to break a precedent in order to accommodate someone

jalhambi: ⟶ **jalgambi**

jalhari monio: a kind of monkey with an extremely long lifespan

jali: 1. a red inedible fruit resembling the hawthorn; 2. wicked, traitorous; 3. plot, intrigue

jali arga: wickedness, deceit

jali deribumbi: to cook up a plot

jalidambi: to plot against, to intrigue against

jalimi: ⟶ **jalmin**

jalin: 1. reason, motive, occasion; 2. (postposition) because of, on account of: **mini jalin** 'on my account'; **3**. in order to, for the purpose of; **4**. concerning, *in re …*

jalinde: (postposition) for the sake of, in order to

jalingga: traitorous, wicked, crafty

   jalingga anggalinggū: treacherous, crafty

   jalingga butemji: malicious

   jalingga kiyangkiyan: wicked and violent

   jalingga koimali: wicked and deceitful

   jalingga oshon: crafty and cruel, malevolent

   jalingga šuban: a wicked official, a subordinate

jaliyūn: the question form of **jalin**: is it for this reason?

jalmin: *Polygonum hydropiper*: knotweed

jalu: **1**. full, fullness; **2**. self-satisfied, full of oneself

   jalu eldembure dengjan: a hanging lantern in which a number of candles burn

   jalu gurun: the entire nation

jalukan: somewhat full

jalukiyabumbi: (causative of **jalukiyambi**)

jalukiyambi: to be full, to become full, to be sufficient

   jalukiyame: fully, sufficiently

jalumbi: (-ka, -ndara, -pi) **1**. to be full, to be fulfilled; **2**. to fulfill

jalumbumbi: (causative of **jalumbi**)

jalun: fullness

jalungga: full, filled

jaman: quarrel, row

jamarambi: **1**. to quarrel, to have a row; **2**. to shout, to make a commotion

   jamarame daišambi: to make a racket

jamaran: quarrel, wrangle

jamarandumbi: to wrangle with one another; also **jamaranumbi**

jamaranumbi: to wrangle with one another; also **jamarandumbi**

jamaršambi: to be quarreling continually

jambi: to exorcise an illness by burning charms and reciting incantations

jamdan hiyan moo: sandalwood tree

jampan: curtain, mosquito-net

jampangga cece: fine gauze used for curtains

jampin: **1**. ⟶ **jampan**; **2**. ⟶ **jempin**

jamu: **1**. pink, peach-colored; **2**. Daurian rose (*Rosa davurica*), the fruit of the Daurian rose

   jamu ilha: **1**. rose; **2**. an odorless, exotic red rose

jamuhari ilha: an exotic light purple flower resembling a rose

jamuri: **1**. one hundred-quadrillionth (of a Chinese foot); **2**. hedgerose

   jamuri ilha: hedgerose

   jamuri orho: *Lithospermum officinale*: gromwell

jan: a perforated whistling arrow with a bone head

janambi: to exorcise an illness by burning paper charms and by reciting incantations

jancuhūkan: rather sweet

jancuhūn: sweet, pleasant, agreeable

   jancuhūn hengke: *Cucumis melo*: sweet melon

   jancuhūn jofohori: tangerine

   jancuhūn muke: nectar

   jancuhūn mursa: carrot

   jancuhūn silenggi: sweet dew

   jancuhūn uslha: chestnut

   jancuhūn yoo: a small boil or pustule on the skin, impetigo

jancuhūnje: sugar cane

jancuhūri orho: licorice

jang: **1**. ten Chinese feet; cf. **juda**; **2**. a pole used for beating criminals

jang bithe: account books

jang jing: (onomatopoetic) **1**. the sound made by birds looking for one another, chirping; **2**. sobbing; **3**. the sound of musical instruments

jang loo: elder

   jang loo hūwašan: Buddhist abbot

jangca: a cape worn by lamas

jangci: a felt cape worn during snow or rain

jangcin: ⟶ **jangci**

jangdz: the son of a Prince of the second class

jangga moo: *Cinnamomum camphora*: camphor tree

jangga niru: a whistling arrow with a bone head

janggalcambi: to amble (said of horses)

janggalibumbi: (causative of **janggalimbi**)

janggalimbi: to be in dire straits, to be hard pressed

janggin: (章京) **1**. Secretary in various government organs; **2**. Adjutant (of a banner), *BH* 724, 874

   janggin deli: a large stone used to bar a gate

   janggin hadahan: linchpin on a cart

   janggin šufatu: a kind of turban worn by military officers in ancient times

janggisa: (plural of **janggin**)

jangguci: **1**. river deer (*Hydropotes inermis*); **2**. in ancient times a derogatory name for the Miao

janggūwan: pickled or preserved vegetables, melons, etc.

jangju: chess

jangju cekemu: a kind of velvet produced in Changzhou 常州

jangkiri coko: a name for the peewit; cf. **niyo coko**

jangkū: a long-handled sword

janglabumbi: (causative of **janglambi**)

janglambi: to beat with a pole (as a punishment)

jangnambi: to take hold of

jangturi: a village head

janjuri: *Myrica rubra*: red bayberry

janumbi: to be spiteful, to harbor enmity

jar: (onomatopoetic) **1**. the sound made by men working hard; **2**. the sound made by crickets or grasshoppers; **3**. the sound made by a bone-headed arrow

jar jar: (onomatopoetic) the sound made by crickets

jar jir: (onomatopoetic) the sound made by birds early in the morning

jargima: locust, grasshopper

jargisu: ginger produced in Fujian

jargiyalakū asu: a kind of large fish net

jargū: ⟶ **jarhū**

jargūci: judge

jarhū: *Cuon alpinus*: red wolf, dhole

jarhūn: ⟶ **jarhū**

jari: a shaman's helper

jarimbi: to chant prayers (said of a shaman)

jarin: musk

jarin cai: fragrant tea

jarin moo: musk tree (grows in the valleys in the region south of the Yangtze River)

jarji cecike: a name for the oriole; cf. **gūlin cecike**

jarkin coko: a name for the peewit; cf. **niyo coko**

jasak: chief of a Mongol banner

jasak i dangsei bolgobure fiyenten: (旗籍清吏司) Department of the Inner Mongols, *BH* 495

jasambi: ⟶ **jasimbi**

jase: **1**. border, boundary, frontier; **2**. border region; **3**. water gate; **4**. palisade, barricade; **5**. cf. **giyase**

jase jafambi: to erect a barricade or palisade

jase jecen: frontier, border region

jasei amargi ba: area north of the Great Wall

jasei amargi fiyelenggu: *Bonasa bonasia*: the Mongolian hazel grouse

jasei dukai janggin: (關口守尉) banner-chief of a frontier gate

jasei hafan: frontier official

jaselambi: to establish a frontier, to secure a border

jasibumbi: (causative of **jasimbi**)

jasigan: **1**. letter, mail; **2**. things posted to a distant place

jasihan: ⟶ **jasigan**

jasihiya: a name for the eastern egret; cf. **gūwasihiya**

jasimbi: to post, to mail, to send (a letter)

jasinambi: to go to mail

jasindumbi: to write to one another, to correspond

jašu: the name of the quail in early autumn; cf. **muša**

jata: mediocre (person), untalented, good-for-nothing

jaya: a birchbark canoe (with a turned-up front)

jayabumbi: (causative of **jayambi**)

jayambi: **1**. to cut the jaw off a slaughtered animal; **2**. to stutter

jayan: the jaw joint

jayan i hūsun: with clenched teeth, obstinate

je: **1**. affirmative interjection: yes; **2**. foxtail millet (*Setaria italica*); **3**. grain in general

je bele: foxtail millet

je falan: threshing floor

je je wajiha: That's all!, Forget it!

je sembi: to agree

je ja: (onomatopoetic) the sound made by men working

je ja seme: screaming, shouting loudly

jebele: **1**. quiver; **2**. right wing, right side

jebele dashūwan i fiyenten: (弓矢司) Bow and Arrow Section, *BH* 119

jebele dube: the third **jalan** of a banner

jebele gala: the right wing, i.e., the four right banners: Plain Blue, Plain Red, Bordered Red, and Bordered Blue

jebele meiren: the second **jalan** of a banner

jebeletu: designation of the third adjutant of a camp or battalion

jebkelebumbi: (causative of **jebkelembi**)

jebkelembi: **1**. to guard against, to take precautions against, to be careful about; **2**. to prevent

jebkešembi: to be very cautious

jebsehe: an insect that eats the joints on the stalks of grain

jebumbi: (causative of **jembi**)

jecen: border, frontier

jecen acambi: to border on

jecen akū: borderless, limitless

jecen dalin: shore, shoreline

jecen i dolo: within one's territory, inside the country

jecuheri: ⟶ **jecuhuri**

jecuhunjembi: to hesitate, to be hesitant, to waver

jecuhuri: **1**. hesitant, in doubt, undecided, vacillating, wavering; **2**. askew, crooked

jedebule: a meaningless word occurring at the beginning of verses of Manchu songs

jedz: a folded memorial sent to the Emperor; cf. **bukdari**

jefalan: ⟶ **je falan**

jefeliyen: field rations; cf. **jufeliyen**

jefohon: an exotic fruit resembling the pomelo

jefu: (imperative of **jembi**)

jeja: ⟶ **je ja**

jeje: father

jekde moo: a tree resembling the pear tree (its dark reddish bark is used for decorative purposes; possibly a kind of myrtle)

jekdun: chaste, pure, chastity, purity

jekdun be tuwakiyambi: to guard one's purity

jekdun moo: *Ligustrum lucidum*: Manchurian privet

jekdun sargan jui: a chaste maiden, a virgin

jekdungge: chaste, pure; cf. **jekdun**

jeke: (perfect participle of **jembi**)

jekenembi: to go to eat

jekenjimbi: to come to eat

jekse: **1**. a burned-over place on the steppe; **2**. a place not touched by rain; **3**. an empty place among red clouds at sunset or at dawn

jeksibumbi: (causative of **jeksimbi**)

jeksimbi: **1**. to dislike; **2**. to be timid, to be anxious, to be frightened; **3**. to be hesitant, to falter

jeksitembi: to be frightened often, to be anxious constantly

jekšembi: ⟶ **jeksimbi**

jekšun: sharp-tongued, caustic

jeku: grain, provisions, food

jeku aga: one of the twenty-four divisions of the solar year — falling on April twentieth or twenty-first

jeku be baicara tinggin: (盤糧廳) grain control office along the waterways used for grain transport

jeku be faringgiyambi: to cut grain and lay it out to dry

jeku be kadalara tinggin: (糧廳) Grain Administration Bureau

jeku bele: grain, rice and other grains

jeku giyamun: grain distribution point

jeku hara: ⟶ **hara**, definition (**2**)

jeku i dooli: (糧道台) grain intendant

jeku i fiyenten: (糧储司) Office of Grain Matters of the Board of Revenue in Mukden

jeku juwere hafan be ilgara kunggeri: (督糧科) Office of Grain Administration in the Board of War

jeku kunesun: grain ration

jeku teksilehe: the grain has become even (i.e., is near maturity)

jekui baita be tefi icihiyara yamun: (坐糧廳衙門) Office of the Supervisor of Government Granaries in the capital

jekui cuwan: boat for transporting grain

jekui kunggeri: (糧科) Grain Section in the Board of Revenue in Shaanxi

jekuju: the god of millet, the shrine to the god of millet

jekunembi: to swell and form pus

jelambi: to stop (said of rain), to clear up

jelbe: young of the salmon trout; cf. **jelu**

jele: ⟶ **jelen**

jele mele: clever, smart

jeleme cecike: a gray sparrow with blackish spots

jelen: doubt, vacillation

jelgin: ⟶ **jelgiyen**

jelgiyen: a chin strap of a hat

jelken: *Mustela sibirica*: Siberian weasel

jelmin: rape (a vegetable), rape-seed oil (used as a hair dressing by women)

jelmin imenggi: rape-seed oil, canola oil (used in ancient times as a hair dressing by women)

jelu: *Hucho taimen*: salmon trout

jembi: (**1**) (imperative: **jefu**; **-ke, -tere**) to eat

jeke beri: a bow on which the horn facing does not reach to the notches for the bowstring

jeke yadaha: contesting the original owner's right to something

jeke yadaha genehe: left without paying attention to others

jeke yadaha i burulaha: fled without regard to others

jembi: (**2**) (**-ngke, -ndere, -mpi**) to bear, to put up with, to tolerate

jemdelembi: to cheat, to practice fraud, to be corrupt

jemden: **1**. mishap, disorder; **2**. corruption, malpractice, cheating, mismanagement

jemden banjinambi: to go wrong

jemden be geterembumbi: to abolish what is harmful

jemden yabumbi: to cheat

jeme: wet nurse

jemengge: food, foodstuffs

jemetu lorin: mule born from a jenny (female ass)

jemgetu: sign of misfeasance, fraud, falsification

jemin: a dose

jempi: **1**. patient, long-suffering; **2**. perfect converb of **jembi** (**2**)

jempilembi: to fry cakes

jempin: fried cakes of buckwheat or wheat filled with meat or vegetables

jempin inenggi: the second day of the second month when pan-fried cakes are eaten

jen žin: a Daoist immortal

jenderakū: cannot bear, unbearable; cf. **jembi** (**2**)

jendere: (imperfect participle of **jembi** [**2**])

jendu: secretly, on the sly, quietly

jendu alhūdambi: to imitate on the sly

jendu gisurembi: to talk softly, to speak in a low voice

jenduken: secretly on the sly, quietly

jendukesaka: secretly, in secret

jendumbi: **1**. to secrete, to keep secret; **2**. to eat one another

jendun: secrecy, secret

jengdun: chaste, chastity, purity

jengdz: (正字) title of one of the heir apparent's tutors

jengge: **1**. food, provisions; **2**. pure, incorruptible

jengge niyalma: (a Daoist term) a person who has attained enlightenment or immortality

jengke: perfect participle of **jembi** (**2**)

jenglung: steamer, vessel for steaming food; cf. **teliyeku**

jenumbi: **1**. to eat together; **2**. ⟶ **jendumbi**

jeo: department (a political subdivision)

jeo i beidesi: (州判) Second Class Assistant Department Magistrate, *BH* 851A

jeo i dooseda: (道正) Superior of the Daoist Priesthood in a Department, *BH* 573B

jeo i erin sonjosi: (典術) Departmental Inspector of Petty Professions, *BH* 851A

jeo i hūwašada: (僧正) Superior of the Buddhist Priesthood in a Department, *BH* 573A

jeo i saraci: (知州) Department Magistrate, *BH* 855

jeo i tacibukū hafan: (學正) Departmental Director of Schools, *BH* 851A

jeo i uheci: (州同) First Class Assistant Department Magistrate, *BH* 851A

jeo pan: (州判) Second Class Assistant Department Magistrate, *BH* 851A

jeofi: a hut with a round birchbark roof

jeofingge boo: a hermit's hut, sometimes refers to a Buddhist convent

jerde: sorrel horse

jerempe: ⟶ **jerpe**

jeren: *Procapra gutturosa*: Mongolian gazelle, zeren

jergi: **1**. rank, step, grade; **2**. order, sequence; **3**. layer, level; **4**. time; **5**. and so forth, et cetera; **6**. ordinary, rank and file

jergi akū: strange, unusual, extraordinary

jergi ci dabambi: to go beyond one's station

jergi ci encu: unusual, uncommon

jergi hergen: rank

jergi ilhi: sequence, succession

jergi jergi: in layers, rank upon rank

jergi niyalma: an ordinary person, the average person

jergi nonggimbi: to promote, to upgrade

jergi tangkan: official rank

jergi tangkan i alin: a small bronze monument on which the ranks of officials were inscribed, located in the courtyard before the main throne room in Beijing

jergi tušan: official rank

jergi waka: out of the ordinary, unusual

jergicelembi: to rank, to put in order

jergilebumbi: 1. (causative of **jergilembi**); 2. to rank, to put in order

jergilembi: 1. to be in order, to be arranged according to rank; 2. to be equal to

jergilen: ranking, ordering

jergingge: 1. of the same rank, of the same sort, of the same layer, consisting of layers; 2. ordinary, routine

    jergingge dalangga: a dam built in layers resembling fish scales

    jerginnge hoseri: boxes containing food arranged layer-like on a rack

jergišembi: ⟶ **jerkišembi**

jerguwelebumbi: (causative of **jerguwelembi**)

jerguwelembi: to make a railing or fence

jerguwen: 1. railing, fence; 2. the horizontal posts of a railing; 3. the horizontal stones of a stone railing; 4. horizontal stones or steps to the palace

    jerguwen i bongko: a railing post knob

    jerguwen i dengjan: red lantern hung on the post knobs of a railing at the New Year

jerin: 1. edge, border; 2. anvil

jeringge wase: tile with decorative borders

jerkin: dazzling light

    jerkin ilha: *Cornus kousa*: kousa

jerkingge ilhangga loho: a sword made of highly polished steel

jerkišembi: to blind (said of light), to dazzle, to be dazzled

jerpe: a growth on the lip

jerun: a measure equaling eight Chinese feet

jeseri: arrow with a bone head (used for hunting birds)

jeten: (軫) a constellation, the 28th of the lunar mansions, made up of four stars (γ, ε, δ, β) in Corvus

    jeten tokdonggo kiru: (軫宿旗) a banner depicting the constellation **jeten**

jetere: (imperfect participle of **jembi**)

    jetere fiyancihiyan niyalma: a person who eats little

    jetere jaka: foodstuffs, victuals, food

jeyen: blade, sharp edge, sword

    jeyen i dube: point (of a knife's blade)

jeyengge: having a blade, sword, knife

ji gida: halberd

ji ilha: safflower

jibca: a short fur jacket or coat

jibcalambi: to wear a fur jacket or coat

jibcan: ⟶ **jibca**

jibci: pincushion, needle-cushion

jibegun: having narrow eyes

jibehun: 1. cover, quilt; 2. ⟶ **jibegun**

jibembi: to cover with a quilt

jiberembi: (-ke) to squint, to narrow the eyes

jibge: 1. stingy; 2. slow, negligent, sluggish

jibgehun: close, dense, impenetrable

jibgešembi: 1. to move slowly, to act sluggishly; 2. to pace up and down, to wander about; 3. to be stingy, to begrudge, to be unwilling to part with

    jibgešeme narašambi: to be reluctant to leave

    jibgešeme tutambi: to tarry, to stop on a journey

jibin: fine-meshed

    jibin asu: a fine-meshed net

jibsibumbi: (causative or passive of **jibsimbi**); 2. to overlap, to superimpose; 3. to be piled up, to be overlapping

jibsigan: ⟶ **sektefun i jibsigan**

jibsimbi: 1. to place in layers, to layer, to add on an extra garment, to add an extra layer, to double up; 2. to pile up, to stack up; 3. to mount a painting

    jibsime edelembi: to pile up (said of debts)

    jibsime fusembi: to increase manyfold

    jibsime isabumbi: to accumulate, to amass

    jibsime muhaliyambi: to pile up, to accumulate

jibsinumbi: to be folded over one another

jibsirge: gold and silver filigree

jibumbi: (causative of **jimbi**)

jidere: (imperfect participle of **jimbi**: coming, future, next)

    jidere aniya: next year, the coming year

    jidere biya: next month, the coming month

    jidere omolo: great-great-great grandchild

jiduji: after all, finally, in fact, really, surely, in the end

jidun: the back side of a mountain

jidurambi: to be jealous

jifebumbi: (causative of **jifembi**)

jifembi: to fill in cracks in the hull of a boat or in a tub, to calk

    jifere faksi: a calker

jifu nunggele: *Catalpa ovata*: Chinese catalpa
jifubumbi: to get stuck in wood (said of saws and awls)
jifun: soft and yielding, lacking crispness, hard to cut because of a soft, yielding consistency
jifunumbi: to be elastic, to lack crispness, to be extendable
   jifunure sukdun: mirage
jiganambi: ⟶ **jihanambi**
jigeyen: **1**. hard of hearing (because of old age); **2**. slow, slow moving, sluggish
jigiyen: ⟶ **jigeyen**
jiha: **1**. money, copper coin; **2**. tenth of a tael
   jiha butambi: to earn money
   jiha efimbi: to gamble
   jiha efire falan: gambling hall
   jiha efire jaka: gambling paraphernalia
   jiha fafun i yamun: (錢法堂) Coinage Office, *BH* 460A
   jiha fesheleku: shuttlecock made from a copper coin and feathers
   jiha fesku: ⟶ **jiha fesheleku**
   jiha fila: a small plate
   jiha hungkerere kūwaran i takūrakū i yamun: (作廠大使衙門) Operations Office of the Mint
   jiha i fafun: law dealing with currency matters
   jiha i kemneku: a board with a depression in it into which a certain number of coins will fit (used for counting large numbers of coins)
   jiha ilha: yellowhead, a flower of the genus *Inula*, the buds of which resemble coins
   jiha mektembi: to gamble
   jiha šufambi: to pool money for some purpose
   jiha tekdebumbi: to burn sacrificial paper money
   jiha toodambi: to return borrowed money
   jiha ulin: wealth, money
   jihai temgetu: bank note, paper money
jihana bojiri ilha: *Inula britannica*: the same as **jiha ilha**
jihana coko: Mongolian ring-necked pheasant
jihana yarha: a spotted leopard
jihanambi: to bloom (said of grains)
jihari yanggali: the name of a small bird whose neck feathers resemble a string of cash
jiji jaja: (onomatopoetic) twittering
jijirgan: a poetic name for the house swallow

jijiri: a mat woven from fine straw (used in summer)
   jijiri orho: a kind of grass (*Anthistiria ciliata*) used for weaving mats and shoes
jijubumbi: (causative of **jijumbi**)
jijugan: ⟶ **jijuhan**
jijuhan: diagram, trigram, or hexagram of the *Yijing*
   jijuhan be tuwambi: to consult the *Yijing*
   jijuhan i kūbulin: changes of the *Yijing* diagrams
jijumbi: (**-ha**) to draw lines, to draw, to write, to cast lots
jijun: **1**. stroke, line; **2**. whole or broken lines making up the eight trigrams of the *Yijing*
jijungge: pertaining to divination
   jijungge nomun: the *Yijing*
jikū: destination, outcome
jilabumbi: (causative of **jilambi**)
jilaburu: pitiful person
jilacuka: pitiful
jilacungga: compassionate, merciful
jilahabi: ⟶ **jilambi** (subheading)
jilakan: pitiable, pitiful, poor
jilambi: (**-ka/-ha**) **1**. to pity, to have compassion for, to love; **2**. to form pockmarks
   jilahabi: 'has been merciful toward' — i.e., has formed only a few pockmarks
jilan: **1**. compassion, pity, love; **2**. a place where a fast current prevents water freezing
   jilan mukengge kiru: (濟旗) a banner of the Imperial Escort with a design of flowing water depicted on a green background
jilangga: compassionate, benevolent, philanthropic
jilari gaha: ⟶ **holon gaha**
jilbi: ⟶ **jilbin**
jilbimbi: to sew a gold border onto clothing
jilbin: a thin gold border
jilehun: unabashed, audacious, shameless
jilekun: ⟶ **jilehun**
jilerjembi: ⟶ **jileršembi**
jileršembi: **1**. to ignore (someone) deliberately, to feign ignorance; **2**. to be shameless; **3**. to brim with tears
jilga: ⟶ **jilha**
jilgambi: to make a sound, to sing (said of birds)
jilgan: sound, noise, voice
   jilgan i bulekušere toosengge fusa: Bodhisattva Avalokiteśvara
   jilgan mudan: (regional) accent

jilgan sibumbi: to lose one's voice

jilgandumbi: to shout together

jilgangga gasha: the name of a bird that sings at night (its voice can be heard, but its form is never seen)

jilgibumbi: (causative of **jilgimbi**)

jilgimbi: to remove the hair from a hide

jilha: stamen and pistil of a flower

jilhambi: to burn to ashes; cf. **gilgambi**

jilhangga ilha: the name of an exotic flower (it has a stem and leaves resembling the camellia, has large buds, and is very fragrant)

jili: **1**. anger, temper; **2**. the base of the horn on deer, roe, etc.

jili banjicuka: annoying, vexing

jili banjimbi: to get angry

jili dambi: to become angry, to vent one's anger; cf. **jilidambi**

jili dosombi: to hold back one's anger

jili guribumbi: to vent one's anger on an innocent person

jili hatan: quick to anger, fiery, volatile, irascible

jili mangga: blunt, gruff, quick to anger

jili nukibumbi: to be piqued, to act out of spite, to get fed up, to become angry

jilidambi: to get angry, to become mad

jilidame facihiyašambi: to become angry and agitated

jilihangga: **1**. ardent, intense; **2**. upright, chaste

jilihangga hehe: a widow who does not remarry

jilihangga sargan jui: a betrothed girl who commits suicide upon hearing of the death of her fiancé

jilinambi: **1**. for a hole to form in river ice; **2**. ⟶ **jili banjimbi**

jilkilambi: to wind onto a skein

jilkin: skein, hank, tuft, lock, strand

jilun: pitiable, poor; cf. **jilakan**

jima: sesame

jima malanggū: white sesame

jima nimenggi: sesame oil

jima šobin: a baked wheat cake filled with red bean paste and sprinkled with sesame seeds

jimalambi: to attach a spearhead to the shaft

jimbi: (imperative: **jio, -he, -dere**) to come, see also **jidere**

jin: ⟶ **jing**

jin ši: ⟶ **dosikasi**

jing: **1**. just, just at the time when, on the point of; **2**. often, frequently, all the time, keep on … ; **3**. a watch of the night; cf. **ging**

jing geneki serede: just on the point of going, just about to go

jing seme: all the time, keep on …

jing jiyang: (onomatopoetic) the sound of flutes and stone bells, the sound of weeping

jing yang: (onomatopoetic) the sound of birds singing harmoniously

jinggeri: **1**. a small nail with a large head; **2**. a nail on armor

jinggeri fangkambi: to drive in an armor nail

jinggiya: a sty on the eye

jingjan: small and colorless

jingjanambi: to be very small or short

jingjara: **1**. yellow-browed bunting (*Emberiza chrysophrys*); **2**. the common sparrow

jingji: **1**. heavy, steady, firm; **2**. grave, ceremonious

jingjing jangjang: (onomatopoetic) **1**. the sound of various types of flutes and pipes; **2**. the sound of a flock of birds singing in the springtime

jingkini: **1**. honest, upright, orderly, regular; **2**. chief, main, principal; **3**. authentic, legitimate, genuine, true

jingkini beye: one's own person, in person

jingkini cifun: chief tax, main tax, regular tax

jingkini doron jafaha hafan: chief magistrate

jingkini hafan: (子爵) viscount

jingkini ilhi: chief and subordinate

jingkini kadalara da: (宗學總管) Director of the School for Imperial Clansmen; cf. *BH* 717

jingkini uju jergi: rank l-A, chief rank of the first order

jingkini wesimbure bithe: the original copy of a memorial (i.e., the one read by the Emperor; the second copy went to the archives)

jingnembi: to advance by pairs to offer a libation of wine at a funeral

jingse: knob on an official cap indicating rank

jingse i aligan: the support on an official cap for a knob

jingse kiyamnambi: to attach a knob to an official hat

jingse umiyesun bisirengge: 'possessing knob and sash' — an official

jingsitun: (井) a constellation, the 22nd of the lunar mansions, made up of eight stars in Gemini

jingsitun tokdonggo kiru: (井宿旗) a banner with the constellation **jingsitun** depicted on it

jinjaha: testicles

jinjiba: white-eye, bird of the genus *Zosterops*

jinjiha: ⟶ **jinjaha**

jinjima: a kind of small bean very hard to cook soft

jinjiri janjiri: (onomatopoetic) noise of a group of children

jio: (imperative of **jimbi**)

jir jar seme: (onomatopoetic) twittering (said of birds)

jir jir seme: (onomatopoetic) **1**. the sound of bubbling water; **2**. the crying of crickets, birds, or mice

jira: close together, dense, thickly spaced

jirahūn: obstinate, stubborn

jiramikan: rather thick

jiramilabumbi: (causative of **jiramilambi**)

jiramilambi: **1**. to make thick, to thicken; **2**. to treat generously, to treat courteously

jiramilanjimbi: to come to treat generously

jiramin: **1**. thick; **2**. generous, kind

jiren: ⟶ **jerin**

jirgabumbi: **1**. (causative of **jirgambi**); **2**. to put someone at ease

jirgacun: comfort, ease

jirgambi: **1**. to be at ease, to enjoy leisure, to be comfortable, to lead an easy life, to lead a life of pleasure; **2**. not to be employed in an official capacity; **3**. to die (said of the Emperor)

jirgame banjimbi: to live comfortably

jirgame tembi: to live in leisure

jirgeku: a sprayer used to put out fires

jirgembi: to twitter, to chirp

jirgembumbi: to disclose, to leak

jirgio: a kind of waterfowl

jirha cecike: *Troglodytes troglodytes*: North China wren

jiri: ten trillion

jirin: ⟶ **jeren**

jirumtu suru: a fine white horse

jirun: ten million

jisa: storehouse at a lamaist temple

jise: a draft of writing, a rough draft

jise icihiyara boo: (稿房) office for preparing drafts in the Court of Colonial Affairs

jise toktobumbi: to put a draft into final form

jiselembi: to make a rough draft, to draft

jisiha: hazelnut tree

jisubumbi: (causative of **jisumbi**)

jisumbi: to cut leather and similar material in a straight line

jiya: (an emphatic sentence particle; cf. **jiye**)

jiyan hoošan: a slip of paper

jiyang wang asu: a large fish net used from a boat in still water; cf. **horilakū asu**

jiyang žung: velvet

jiyanggiyūn: **1**. general; **2**. (將軍) Manchu General-in-Chief, *BH* 744

jiyansi: spy, enemy agent; cf. **giyansi**

jiye: (an emphatic sentence particle; cf. **jiya**)

jiyei: **1**. older sister, miss; **2**. a tasseled tally used by Princesses as an emblem

jo: a Chinese pint

jo banjimbi: to belch, to regurgitate acidic substances

jobai: ⟶ **joobai**

jobobumbi: (causative of **jobombi**)

jobocuka: causing concern, disquieting, worrisome, distressing

jobocun: worry, affliction, grief, sorrow

joboho: ⟶ **jobombi** (subheading)

jobolon: harm, trouble, disaster, calamity, sorrow, mourning, funeral

jobolon baita: funeral

jobolon gashan: disaster

jobolontu: inauspicious

jobombi: **1**. to suffer, to be in need; **2**. to worry, to be distressed

joboho arambi: to compensate for trouble caused to someone

joboro suilara: worry and pain, suffering

jobon: distress

joborakū ilha: an exotic flower that is said to bloom when it is caressed by a woman

joboro: ⟶ **jobombi** (subheading)

joboshūn: **1**. concerned, worried; **2**. worry, concern

jobošombi: to suffer deeply, to be very distressed, to worry much

jocibumbi: **1**. (causative of **jocimbi**); **2**. to annihilate, to finish off, to murder; **3**. to reduce to dire straits

jocimbi: **1**. to be in need, to be at the end of one's means; **2**. to lose one's life, to perish, to be murdered

jocin: ⟶ **jojin**

jodoba: *Plantago major*: common plantain, a kind of herb

jodobumbi: (causative of **jodombi**)

jodohūn cecike: a name for the hoopoe; cf. **indahūn cecike**

jodombi: **1**. to weave; **2**. to come and go unexpectedly, always to be coming and going

jodoro arara yamun: (織造府) Office of the Superintendent of the Imperial Manufactories

jodoro faksi: weaver

jodoro icere kūwaran: (織染局) Imperial Weaving and Dyeing Office, *BH* 96

jodoro sargan jui: the Weaving Girl — the name of a star; cf. **jordorgan usiha**

jodoro weilere kunggeri: (織造科) section on weaving and manufacturing in the Board of Works

jodon: grass linen, grass cloth, kudzu-hemp cloth

jodon i wase: footwear made of grass linen

jodongga cece: gauze of coarse linen

jodorgan usiha: 'the weaving girl' — the star Vega in the constellation Lyra

jodorho: *Rhizoma alismatis*: oriental water plantain

jodoro: ⟶ **jodombi** (subheading)

jofoho: **1**. point, edge; **2**. corner, angle; **3**. harpoon for spearing fish

jofoho acabumbi: to match the points

jofohoci: *Citrus decumana*: shaddock

jofoholobumbi: ⟶ **jofoho acabumbi**

jofohon: pomelo

jofohonggo: pointed, projecting

jofohori: citrus fruit, orange, tangerine

jofohori šatan: orange cake

jofohoto: *Citrus acida*, a kind of lime fruit

johibumbi: (causative of **johimbi**)

johimbi: to heal (said of a boil or sore)

joholimbi: (-**ka**) to be pudgy, to be flabby, to gain weight

johombi: to belch, to burp

jojin: horse's bit

jojin be sudamimbi: to slacken the reins

jojin i songgiha: crossbar on a bit

jojingga: pertaining to a bit

jok seme: abruptly, suddenly (said of stopping)

jokjabumbi: (causative or passive of **jokjambi**)

jokjambi: **1**. to beat severely, to thrash; **2**. to gulp down

joksi: a wooden dipper without a handle

joksikū: a small adze with a curved blade

joksilambi: to stuff oneself, to be a glutton

joksinambi: to be overweight, to eat to excess

jokson: **1**. first stage, beginning, inception; **2**. at first; **3**. skinny (said of horses)

joktonda: *Lilium japonicum*: Japanese lily

jokū: fodder knife

jolabumbi: ⟶ **joolabumbi**

jolacambi: to bow, to stoop, to be obsequious

jolambi: ⟶ **joolambi**

jolbonombi: to become dull

joldombi: to buy back things one has given or sold to someone else, to redeem one's former goods

jolfo: oyster

jolgocombi: **1**. to gush forth in abundance; **2**. to press forward in a rage, to stampede, to rush off in a fury

jolhocombi: ⟶ **jolgocombi**

jolhombi: to gush up, to well up, to boil over

joli: a ladle with many small holes in it used for straining; cf. **jooli**

jolibumbi: (causative of **jolimbi**)

joligan: **1**. ransom money, ransom; **2**. hostage

jolikū: ⟶ **joolikū**

jolimbi: **1**. to redeem, to ransom; **2**. to row

jolinambi: to go to redeem

jolinjimbi: to come to redeem

jolo: **1**. doe, female deer; **2**. hateful, hideous; **3**. monster; **4**. ⟶ **giyolo**

jolo buhū: doe, female deer

joman: edge, seam, end

joman acabumbi: to join (folded) edges (in sewing)

jombi: (**1**) (-**ha**) to cut with a fodder knife

jombi: (**2**) (-**ngko, -ndoro, -mpi**) **1**. to bring to mind, to recall, to mention, to bring up; **2**. to move in the womb

jombumbi: **1**. to mention, to point out, to bring up; **2**. to advise, to exhort; **3**. to mollify, to mediate

    jombume ulhibumbi: to remind

jon: memory, recall

jondobumbi: (causative of **jondombi**)

jondombi: **1**. to recall to mind, to mention, to bring up, to concentrate on; **2**. to recite the scriptures

jong jong seme: grumbling, complaining

    jong jong seme gasambi: to grumble from discontent

jongdon: bright satin with gold threads woven through it

jongginambi: to knit the brow from anxiety

joni: the name of the magpie in the Ganjur

jonombi: ⟶ **jondombi**

joo: **1**. an Imperial order; **2**. interjection: Enough!, Stop!, It will not do!

    joo bai: interjection: Enough!, Stop!

    joo bithe: Imperial edict

    joo ele oho kai: That's enough!, Sufficient!

joo siowan hafan: (招宣) Commander of the Military Police

joobai: ⟶ **joo bai**

joocin: ⟶ **jojin**

joocina: let it be!

jookū: ⟶ **jokū**

joolabumbi: to turn over one's duty to another at relief time

joolacambi: ⟶ **jolacambi**

joolambi: **1**. to join the two hands, to join the hands behind one's back, to join the hands in greeting; **2**. to have the hands bound; **3**. to explain, to hand over (an official position)

    joolame jafambi: to hold both of a person's hands

jooli: a bamboo ladle for lifting things from water; cf. **hereku**

joolibumbi: (causative or passive of **joolimbi**)

jooligan: ransom, redemption payment; cf. **joligan**

joolikū: oar

joolimbi: **1**. to ransom, to redeem; **2**. to row

joolinambi: to go to redeem

joolingga: pertaining to ransom, ransom money

joolinjimbi: to come to redeem

jooman: **1**. the base of a fingernail; **2**. ⟶ **joman**

joombi: **1**. ⟶ **jombi (1)**; **2**. to cease, to desist; cf. **joo**, **joocina**

jor: (onomatopoetic) the sound of many humans, dogs, chickens, or animals screaming

jor jar: (onomatopoetic) the sound of people or birds screaming

joran: fast amble

    joran morin: ambling horse

jordabumbi: (causative of **jordambi**)

jordambi: to amble (said of horses and mules)

jorgimbi: to chirp, to twitter, to hum

jorgindumbi: to chirp, to hum (said of a group of birds or insects)

jorgirhen: *Alauda arvensis*: lesser skylark

jorgon biya: the twelfth month

jorgon inenggi: the eighth day of the twelfth month

jorho: a pointed arrowhead with holes on each side

    jorho cecike: a name for the wren; cf. **jirha cecike**

    jorho fodoho: *Salix gracilistyla*: rosegold pussy willow, a kind of willow from which arrow shafts were made

    jorho singgeri: mole

jorhon: ⟶ **jorgon**

joribumbi: (causative of **jorimbi**)

joriha: ⟶ **jorimbi** (subheading)

jorihū: one of the stars in the Great Dipper

jorikū: pointer, index finger

jorilambi: ⟶ **jorišambi**

jorimbi: **1**. to point, to indicate, to point out; **2**. to instruct, to give instructions, to command; **3**. to aim (at a target); **4**. to use a pretext

    joriha jurgan: directive, instructions

    jorime toktobumbi: to appoint, to designate, to assign

    jorime wakalabumbi: to censure, to reprimand

    jorime wakašambi: to reprove, to reprimand

    jorire simhun: the index finger

jorin: **1**. aim, goal; **2**. intent, meaning, elucidation

    jorin i gisun: words of elucidation or direction (on a document)

    jorin sain: good shot, steady aim

joringga: theme (on an examination)

    joringga hoošan: examination paper

    joringga i acabun: the second part of a formal essay (immediately following the **joringga i faksabun**)

joringga i faksabun: the first two sentences of a formal essay

joringga i tucibun: the section following the introduction (**deribume fiyentehe**) in a formal essay

joringga i yarun: the part of an official essay following the opening expositon (**deribume giyangnan**)

jorire: ⟶ **jorimbi** (subheading)

jorisi: magistrate

jorišambi: to point out continually, to indicate continually, to give guidance

joro: a kind of arrow with a horn head

joro singgeri: vole

joron: *Lophatherum gracile*: wild beans, a straight plant with large leaves and flowers resembling the blossoms of the bean plant (used as feed for horses)

jortai: **1**. deliberately, willfully; **2**. pretending

jortanggi: ⟶ **jortai**

jotombi: always to be coming and going

ju: **1**. imperative of **jimbi**; **2**. a musical instrument shaped like a square peck measure — it was used as a signal for other musical instruments to begin

ju sy muke i sekiyen golmin i mudan: a musical piece used by the Board of Rites when it entertained the hereditary duke who was a descendant of Confucius

juben: story, tale

juben alambi: to tell a story

jubengge: tale-carrier

jubesi: storyteller

jubešebumbi: (causative or passive of **jubešembi**)

jubešembi: to slander someone behind his back

jubki: an islet in a river, a sand bar

jubu: (主簿) clerk, recorder, registrar; cf. **dangse jafašakū**

jubungga: **1**. pertaining to a clerk; **2**. pretext for gossip

jubungge: ⟶ **jubengge**

juburambi: ⟶ **jiberembi**

juburšembi: to catch diphtheria, to get an inflammation of the throat, to have acute tonsillitis

jubušembi: to ponder, to judge

juce: **1**. pond, pool (with clear, deep water); **2**. a guard post, checkpoint, police precinct

juce tembi: to stand watch, to stand guard duty

jucelebumbi: (causative of **jucelembi**)

jucelembi: to stand guard, to stand a watch

jucen: ⟶ **juce**

jucerhen: a leather line attached to a saddle at the place where the pommel and the frame of the saddle join

juciba: firefly

jucuba: ⟶ **juciba**

juculembi: to sing Chinese opera, to act

juculesi: actor, opera performer

jucuma: a face mask worn for protection against small insects

jucun: play, opera, theatrical performance

jucun i hūfan: a theatrical troupe

jucungge: pertaining to the stage, theatrical

jucungge karan: stage in a theater

juda: ten Chinese feet, about 3.3 meters

judun: mountain ridge

judura: a domestic pig colored like a wild pig

judura ihan: a cow with a white stripe down its spine

judurakū: striped silk

judurame: along a mountain ridge

juduran: **1**. stripe, line; **2**. the grooves on a file; **3**. fold, crease

jufeliyebumbi: (causative of **jufeliyembi**)

jufeliyembi: to prepare dried provisions for a long journey

jufeliyen: dried provisions used on a long journey, field provisions

jugembi: to offer night sacrifice to the Big Dipper

jugūn: **1**. road, way, street; **2**. the name for a province during Song and Yuan times

jugūn andala: on the way, halfway along

jugūn arambi: to give way to, to yield

jugūn bahabumbi: to create an opportunity, to make a way for

jugūn be heterembi: to block the way

jugūn be jafame: on the way

jugūn cinggiya: the way is (unexpectedly) short

jugūn de tosombi: to cut off a road, to ambush on the way

jugūn dedun: post station

jugūn durimbi: to make a quick getaway

jugūn faitambi: to block someone's way, to cut off a road

jugūn fambumbi: to lose one's way, to get lost

jugūn giyai be kadalara tinggin: (街道廳) Roadway Office, *BH* 796A

jugūn giyai be kadalara tinggin i hafan: (街道廳官) head of the Roadway Office

jugūn i andala: on the way, along the way

jugūn i niyalma: traveler, wayfarer

jugūn i on: the distance traveled, journey

jugūn i yarun: pass, travel permit, a road pass carried by officials

jugūn jukimbi: to repair a road

jugūn malhūn: the way is unexpectedly long

jugūn neimbi: to open a way (by force)

jugūn on: distance traveled, the way to somewhere

jugūn yabumbi: to travel

jugūn yabure andala: halfway along (on a trip)

juhe: ice

juhe akiyahabi: 'the ice has dried' — i.e., has frozen solid

juhe dukdurekebi: the ice has swollen up, the ice has formed a raised spot

juhe fusejehe: the ice has become brittle

juhe gecebumbi: to make ice, to make water freeze

juhe hujurembi: the ice grinds together (in the spring when it starts to melt)

juhe jafaha: the ice has frozen solid

juhe orome gecehebi: 'the ice has formed a thin crust' — a thin crust of ice has formed on the surface of water

juhe sicakabi: the ice has cracked

juhe sulhumbi: the ice is thawing

juhe šatan: sugar-candy

juhe tuheke: the ice has fallen (into the water at the thaw)

juhen singgeri: mammoth frozen in the ice in Siberia

juhenembi: to form ice

juhimbi: to heal, to grow back together (said of an abscess); cf. **johimbi**

juhiyan: **1**. a precious head ornament made of pearls and other jewels; **2**. a group of workers searching for pearls, fish, honey, ginseng, etc.

juhiyan i da: (朱顯達) chief of workers who searched for fish, pearls, honey, ginseng, etc.

jui: **1**. child; **2**. son

jui be durimbi: to place child in a cradle

jui jalan: the generation of one's children (including nephews and nieces)

jui jongko: the child has moved in the womb

jui sumbi: to have a miscarriage

jui taksiha: has become pregnant

juingge: pertaining to children or sons

jujin: a name for the peacock; cf. **kundujin**; **tojin**

juju jaja: (onomatopoetic) mumbling, muttering, chattering

jujumbi: (-ha) to mark out a line with a needle (in sewing)

jujurambi: to act in a petty way, to be small about things

jujuri majari: handling a matter in a tedious way

jukden: *Alnus mandshurica*: alder

juke: a kind of cake made of crumbled **toholiyo** cakes

juke efen: ⟶ **juke**

juken: **1**. just right, just enough; **2**. ordinary, common; **3**. inferior, of poor quality

juken isika: just sufficient

juken sain: just right

juki: not drawn taut (said of a bow)

jukibumbi: (causative of **jukimbi**)

jukidun: *Perdix dauurica*: Daurian partridge

jukimbi: (-ha) **1**. to fill, to fill up, to fill in; **2**. to supplement, to bring up to full strength

jukimbumbi: ⟶ **jukibumbi**

jukja: ⟶ **jokja**

jukjambi: to treat unfairly; cf. **jokjambi**

jukjuhu niyehe: a black-footed wild duck that is very good at diving

jukte: **1**. a long strip of something; **2**. long, thick piece

juktehen: temple, shrine

juktehen i sarasi: (知觀) assistant to the priest in charge of a Daoist temple

juktelebumbi: (causative of **juktelembi**)

juktelembi: to cut into small slices or pieces

juktembi: to offer sacrifice to, to worship

jukten: **1**. offerings to one's ancestors, offerings, sacrifice, worship; **2**. ancestral temple

jukten be aliha hafan: (主祠) master of ceremonies (at a sacrifice)

jukten be sirambi: to continue the family line

jukten i boo: shrine where offerings were made to one's ancestors or famous men

jukten i usin: land belonging to a temple

juktesi: sacrificial attendant

juktu: stout, developed, strong

jukturi: a two-year-old bear

julan: a place in a river where the fast current prevents freezing in winter

julebumbi: to cause to chant or tell stories

julefun: for his sake, in his stead (used in prayers for **terei jalin**)

julehen: ⟶ **emu julehen**

julen: story, tale

> **julen alambi**: to tell a story

> **julen bithe**: book of stories, novel

julergi: **1**. front, in front of, before; **2**. south

> **julergi bithei boo**: (南書房) the name of a study used by the Emperor

> **julergi colhon i kiru**: a banner depicting the southern holy mountain

> **julergi fisembuhe boo**: a veranda in front of a house

> **julergi hecen**: the southern part of a city

> **julergi ice calu**: a storehouse in Beijing belonging to the Board of Finance

> **julergi juwere jekui kunggeri**: (南漕科) Office of Grain Transport in Yunnan

> **julergi kūwaran i calu**: (南館倉) a storehouse in Mukden

> **julergi nahan**: a *kàng* (oven-bed) on the south wall

julergingge: **1**. pertaining to the front; **2**. southern

juleri: front, in front

> **juleri gaimbi**: to take the lead, to try to be first

> **juleri karun**: advanced outpost

> **juleri yabumbi**: to lead the way

> **juleri yarhūdan**: (洗馬) an official in the Supervisorate of Imperial Instruction

julesi: forward, toward the front, southward

> **julesi bumbi**: to offer an animal in sacrifice; cf. **metembi**

> **julesi jorikū**: compass

julesiken: a little bit forward

juletun: ancient vessels and objects, antiques

julge: antiquity, ancient times

> **julgeci ebsi**: from antiquity until now

> **julgei fonde**: in ancient times, in the distant past

> **julgei tetun**: antique, curio

> **julgei ulasi**: monument of antiquity

julgen: good fortune, lucky chance

julgen sain: 'luck was good' (said of a safe return from a journey or a hunt)

julgume: short boots worn by women

julgū: ⟶ **julhū**

julhun: ⟶ **julkun**

julhū: reins

julhūmbi: to polish an arrow shaft with wood filings, hair, or lint

julibumbi: to become swollen (said of the face)

julimbi: (**-ka**) to swell

julishūn: having blurry vision

juliyambi: **1**. to spit out something one cannot chew; **2**. to bulge (said of the eyes)

julkiyembi: ⟶ **jukimbi**

julkun: **1**. the depression at the base of the neck or throat; **2**. the depression on the chest of animals

julungga: docile, obedient

jumalambi: to attach a spearhead to a shaft

juman: a level area above the opening of a stove

jumangga ilha: the name of an exotic blue flower

jumanggi: a small bag

jumanggilambi: to put into a small bag

jumara: *Citellus dauricus*: suslik, a kind of squirrel

jumargan: another name for the suslik, a kind of squirrel; cf. **jumara**

jumbali: right in, straight into, straight away

jumbi: (**-ngke, -mpi**) to clench one's teeth

jun: **1**. stove, kitchen range, hearth; **2**. tissue, pulp of a tree; **3**. vein; **4**. ⟶ **juwen**; **5**. brick; ⟶ **jun wehe**

> **jun ejen**: the kitchen god, the god of the hearth

> **jun gajimbi**: ⟶ **juwen gajimbi**

> **jun i bilha**: smoke outlet of a stove

> **jun i ejen**: the kitchen god

> **jun i nuhaliyan**: a depressed area near the opening of a stove

> **jun i šenggin**: an area jutting from the front of a stove (used for adding fuel)

> **jun i wecen**: sacrifice to the kitchen god

> **jun tonggo**: strong three-strand thread

> **jun wehe**: brick

junafi: ⟶ **juwe nofi**

junara: a name for the partridge; cf. **jukidun**

jung: bell — the same as **jungken**

> **jung forimbi**: to ring a bell

jung yuwan: the Yellow River Plain

junggala: the inside of a stove — the firebox

jungge: veined

> **jungge suje**: veined silk

> **jungge suri**: veined satin

junggebumbi: (causative of **junggembi**)

junggembi: to transfer a person's possessions secretly to another place

junggeri: ⟶ **junggiri coko**

junggidei kiyoo: a sedan chair carried by sixteen men and used by the Imperial concubines

junggila gasha: a name for the turkey; cf. **ildedei**

junggin: brocade

> **junggin abuha ilha**: *Malva sylvestris*: common mallow

jungginambi: 'to become like brocade' — to get furrows on the forehead, to worry

junggingge hoošan: 'brocade paper' — a strong paper with a pattern on it

junggiri coko: *Chrysolophus pictus*: the golden pheasant

junggisun: ⟶ **garunggū**

> **junggisun coko**: a kind of phoenix resembling the pheasant

> **junggisun ilha**: *Diervilla albiflora*: bush honeysuckle

junggitu: an ancient name for the pheasant

jungguhe: a spotted myna

jungken: bell

> **jungken mucihiyangga fukjingga hergen**: (鐘鼎篆) a style of calligraphy

jungkengge: **1**. a measure of volume equaling six bushels and four pecks; **2**. pertaining to a bell

jungšu: (中書) Secretary of the Grand Secretariat, *BH* 137

jungšun: water or wine poured in a sacrificial pig's ear

junihin: **1**. an ancient land measure — a plot of land; **2**. a kind of ancient land tax

> **junihin usin**: a plot of land on which a tax was levied

juningge: a measure of volume equaling eighteen pecks; cf. **hiyase**

juniru: a measure of length equaling sixteen Chinese feet

junofi: ⟶ **juwe nofi**

junta: an animal path

jurambi: (**-ka, -ndara**) to set out, to begin a journey

jurambumbi: **1**. (causative of **jurambi**); **2**. to send on one's way; **3**. to dispatch a memorial

juran: point of departure, place from which a journey begins

juranumbi: to set out together

jurcebumbi: (causative of **jurcembi**)

jurcehen: disobedient, obstinate, disobedience

jurcembi: **1**. to disobey, to go against, to go against one's word, to turn one's back on, to oppose (in battle); **2**. to differ from, not to conform to, not to be uniform; **3**. to miss (a deadline); **4**. to violate, to contradict

jurcen: disobedience

jurcendumbi: to oppose one another, to contend, to fight with one another; also **jurcenumbi**

jurcenjembi: **1**. to differ from one another, to be inconsistent with one another, to diverge; **2**. to do by turns, to alternate, to criss-cross

> **jurcenjeme alibumbi**: to take turns in toasting guests

> **jurcenjeme halabumbi**: to rotate, to take turns

> **jurcenjeme tašarambi**: to diverge and err

jurcenumbi: to oppose one another, to contend, to fight with one another; also **jurcendumbi**

jurcit: Jurchen: the rulers of the Jin dynasty and ancestors of the Manchus

jurgalambi: **1**. to make lines, stripes, or creases; **2**. to form lines or stripes; **3**. to mark lines on cloth (said of tailors)

jurgan: **1**. line, column; **2**. righteousness, moral courage, devotedness, loyalty; **3**. ministry, board (an organ of government); **4**. meaning, significance, gist

> **jurgan akū**: **1**. disloyal; **2**. unjust, unrighteous

> **jurgan be fekumbi**: to fail in one's duty

> **jurgan be yabubumbi**: to perform one's duty

> **jurgan gocimbi**: to draw a line

> **jurgan i ama**: foster father

> **jurgan jorimbi**: to command (an army)

> **jurgan jurgan**: line by line, row by row, column by column

> **jurgan moo**: piece of wood used for drawing lines, straight edge

> **jurgan singgeri**: a kind of short-tailed rodent (when a number of them move, they align themselves by carrying in their mouths the tail of the one ahead)

> **jurgan tacikū**: free school

jurgan tondo: the trajectory is straight (said of an arrow)

jurgangga: **1**. honorable, loyal, upright, morally courageous, righteous; **2**. for the public benefit

jurgangga calu: a public granary

jurgangga eyun: adoptive older sister

jurgangga gasha: a name for the wild goose

jurgangga haha: a widower who remains unmarried

jurgangga hehe: a widow who remains unmarried; cf. **jalangga hehe**, **jilihangga hehe**

jurgangga inenggi: the day on which the sixty-day cycle begins anew

jurgangga saisa: an honorable man, a devoted and generous person

jurgangga taciku: a tree school

jurgangga yabun: a proper act, an act of loyalty

jurgatu gasha: a name for the ptarmigan

jurgimbi: **1**. to split wood by using a wedge; **2**. ⟶ **jorgimbi**

jurguntu cecike: a bird with black beak and tail and striped wings, resembling the magpie

jurha usiha: the constellations Cancer and Leo

jurhu: colored coarse linen cloth

jurhu fungku: a towel made of colored coarse linen cloth

jurhu suri: a cloth made partly of silk and partly of colored coarse grass linen

jurhun: **1**. a Chinese inch; cf. **tsun**; **2**. clothesline, rope for drying clothes

jurjun: a game resembling backgammon; cf. **šuwanglu**

jurjun cecike: a name for the goatsucker; cf. **simari cecike**

jursan gio: a two-year-old roedeer

jursi: Borneo camphor

jursu: **1**. two-layered, double, complex, complicated; **2**. pregnant; **3**. padded (said of clothing)

jursu etuku: padded clothing, clothing made in two layers

jursu fomoci: padded socks

jursu hida: a double curtain

jursu mulu moo: a piece of wood nailed over the foot of a ship's support

jursu ombi: to become pregnant

jursu oyo: a felt cover for the smoke hole of a yurt

jursu sijigiyan: a padded gown

jursulebumbi: (causative of **jursulembi**)

jursulembi: to double, to add a layer to, to fold over, to be doubled

juru: **1**. pair, couple, peer; **2**. even (number)

juru acabumbi: to become man and wife

juru akū: without peer, incomparable

juru biya: even-numbered months

juru gargan: doubled and single, even and odd

juru gisun: a matched couplet

juru gisun i dengjan: a matched couplet hung on the 'myriad year lantern' in the palace during the first month of the year

juru holbon: joining in pairs

juru holbon ombi: to enter into marriage

juru kotoli jahudai: a 'double-sailed ship' — the name of a large warship

juru muduringga suwayan šun dalikū: an escort's parasol with a pair of dragons embroidered on it

juru niyaman: parents

juru sirha: the stars α and β of Ursa Minor

juru songgiha fitheku beri: a crossbow with a double mechanism

juru usiha: the stars α and β of Ursa Minor

jurucilen: a text of paired couplets of four or six words

juruken: in pairs, paired

juruken i maksimbi: to dance in pairs

jurulebumbi: (causative of **jurulembi**)

jurulembi: to make a pair, to pair, to join in pairs

jurumbi: (**-ha**) to vomit

jurume ilimbi: to stand with head hanging down (said of horses)

jurun: a rat- or mousehole, the hole of any small animal

jurungge: doubled, paired

jurungge gasha: a name for the mandarin duck; cf. **ijifun niyehe**

juse: (plural of **jui**)

juse bayan: children are many, having many children

juse dasu: children

juse deote: sons and younger brothers, youngsters

juse jira: children are closely spaced

juse omosi: sons and grandsons — descendants

jusei halbulha: a lair where kidnapped children are kept (usually for prostitution)

jusei oron: womb, uterus

juseki: childish, juvenile

jusetu moo: *Ixora chinensis*

jushe: the vine of cucurbitaceous plants, tendril

jusibumbi: (causative of **jusimbi**)

jusihun: ⟶ **jušuhun**

jusikū: ⟶ **jusukū**

jusimbi: ⟶ **angga be jusimbi**: to jabber, to engage in idle talk

jusin: ⟶ **jušen**

jusku: ⟶ **jusukū**

justalabumbi: (causative of **justalambi**)

justalambi: to form strips

    justalaha sirdan juhe: icicle

    justalame carcinambi: to form icicles

justan: a strip, a stripe, any elongated object

    justan i fempi: a strip used for sealing houses or vessels

justangga soro: striped jujube

jusubumbi: (causative of **jusumbi**)

jusukū: a block of lead used for drawing lines on paper

jusumbi: (**-ha**) **1**. to draw a line on paper; **2**. to cut into strips

juša: cinnabar

jušembi: (**-ke**) to sour, to have a sour stomach

jušembumbi: (causative of **jušembi**)

jušempe: *Physalis alkekengi*: alkekengi, Chinese lantern plant

jušen: **1**. serf of the Manchus; **2**. an earlier ethnonym referring to the Manchus

    jušen boo: serf's quarters

    jušen halangga niyalma: a serf of the Manchus

jušuci: lemon

jušuhe: a small wild pear the skin of which is used as a medicine

jušuhuken: rather sour

jušuhun: sour

    jušuhun jofohori: an orange

    jušuhun muyari: *Nephelium lappaceum*: rambutan

jušuhuri: an exotic sour fruit

jušuk: a sour fruit about the size of an egg that grows in South China

jušun: **1**. vinegar; **2**. a metaphor for jealousy

jušun muke: 'vinegar water' — a drink made of cucumbers, vegetables, and cabbage

jušuri: fruit of the *Prunus mume*

jušuru: a Chinese foot, a ruler

jušutu: *Prunus tomentosa*: Nanking cherry

jušutun: an exotic fruit grown in Sichuan

juteo: scroll

jutuhan: a five-stringed musical instrument played with a bamboo pick

jutungga jodon: a piece of coarse grass linen sufficient for the production of two articles of clothing

juturi cecike: one of the names of the hawfinch; cf. **yacin ūn cecike**

juwabumbi: (causative of **juwambi**)

juwajiri orho: *Pinellia tuberifera*: green dragon, the name of an herb

juwali: a small green frog

juwambi: (**-ngka, -mpi**) to open the mouth

juwan: **1**. ten; **2**. biography, account

    juwan biya: the tenth month, ten months

    juwan booi da: chief of ten households in a village

    juwan cikten: the ten celestial stems (天干)

    juwan hergen: cross

    juwan i da: (護軍校) Lieutenant, *BH* 734

    juwan jakūn simnere boo: (十八方) the eighteen examination rooms in the national examination hall

    juwan juwe gargan: the twelve earthly branches (地支)

    juwan juwe tuhebuku i mahatu: an ancient-style hat with twelve pendants

    juwan juwe uju bithe: the twelve divisions of the Manchu syllabary

    juwan tumen: one hundred thousand

juwanci: tenth

juwanda: chief of ten, decurion

juwangduwan: colored satin with gold threads woven in

juwangga: preserved cucumbers

juwanggeri: ten times

juwanta: ten each

juwaran: ⟶ **joran**

juwarantambi: ⟶ **jordambi**

juwari: summer

    juwari be bodoro hafan: (夏官正): Astronomer for the Summer, *BH* 229

juwari dosika: one of the twenty-four solar divisions of the year (falling on May sixth or seventh)

juwari gūldargan: a name for the western house swallow; cf. **gūldargan**

juwari ten: the summer solstice

juwarikten: the summer sacrifice to the ancestors

juwaringga junggidei: the mountain pheasant with its summer plumage

juwase: ten years old

juwata: ten each

juwe: two

juwe biya: the second month, two months

juwe dube šolonggo: pointed at both ends

juwe irungge mahatun: an ancient-style hat with two ridges on top

juwe jeyengge suhe: a double-edged ax

juwe mujilen: disloyalty, duplicity

juwe muru: the two regulators: yin and yang

juwe nofi: two persons, two people

juwe sidende: between two

juwe ujan: both ends

juwe ujan šolonggo: ⟶ **juwe dube šolonggo**

juwe urhu: two finger-widths, one inch; cf. **jurhun**

juwebumbi: (causative of **juwembi**)

juweci: second

juwedebumbi: (causative of **juwedembi**)

juwedembi: **1**. to be conflicting, to contain contradiction; **2**. to be of two minds, to have divided loyalty, to be disloyal, to be unfaithful

juwedeme iladame: in an undecided manner, in a vacillating manner

juwederakū: loyal, consistent, uncontradictory

juwedere mujilen: unfaithfulness, duplicity

juwembi: to transport, to ship, to transfer, to move

juwere bira: canal

juwere birai angga: canal junction

juwere data: (旗甲) chiefs of bannermen charged with transporting grain

juwere hafan: transport official

juwere hahasi: (旗丁) bannermen charged with transporting grain

juwere hūsun: porter, transportation worker

juwere jeku: tribute grain

juwere jekui baita be tefi icihiyara hafan: (坐糧廳官) Supervisor of the Government Granaries at the Capital, *BH* 565

juwere jekui baita be uheri kadalara amban: (漕運總督) Director-General of Grain Transport, *BH* 834

juwere jekui calu: a granary located in Henan

juwere niyalma: grain porter

juwere turigen: porter's wages

juwen: debt, loan, borrowing

juwen bumbi: to lend, to give on loan

juwen gaimbi: to borrow

juwen sindambi: ⟶ **juwen bumbi**

juwen usen: loans and debts

juwenggeri: twice

juwenofi: ⟶ **juwe nofi**

juwenusi: porter, stevedore, one who loads grain at a water lock

juwere: ⟶ **juwembi** (subheading)

juwerge: a two-stringed musical instrument

juwete: two each

juyedun: a name for the partridge; cf. **jukidun**

juyehen yali: tenderloins

juyembi: (-ke) to become difficult to open (said of the jaws)

juyen: a short padded cotton jacket

jy cuwang nimeku: hemorrhoids

jy gi: a long-tailed pheasant: cf. **nikan ulhūma**

jy jeo: (知州) Department Magistrate, *BH* 855

jyfu: (知府) Prefect, *BH* 848

jyhiyan: (知縣) District Magistrate, *BH* 856

jyjeo: ⟶ **jy jeo**

jyjoo bithe: license, authorization, pass

jyši: (知事) **1**. Archivist, *BH* 830A; **2**. Deputy Police Superintendent

jytu: the fourth note in the classical pentatonic scale

K ʔ

For words beginning with **k'**, see the section beginning on page 245.

ka ka seme: (onomatopoetic) laughing, giggling

kab kib seme: snapping at each other (said of dogs fighting or biting)

kab seme: snapping, biting (said of a pack of dogs)

kaba: in pairs, paired

    kaba bojiri ilha: a double chrysanthemum

    kaba jui: twin

    kaba šu ilha: two lotus flowers growing on one stem

kabahūn: flat (said of the nose)

kabalambi: to form a pair

kabangga: paired, twin

    kabangga jui: twin; cf. **kaba jui**

kabarabumbi: ⟶ **kaparabumbi**

kabari: 1. a Pekingese dog; 2. a growth on the noses of horses and donkeys

    kabari indahūn: Pekingese dog

    kabari tuwambi: to make bubbles (said of fish in the water)

kabcihūn: flat, level

kabkalambi: to bite, to snap (said of dogs)

kabkašambi: to answer impudently, to talk back to

kabsidambi: ⟶ **kabsitambi**

kabsitambi: to speak foolishly, to answer disrespectfully, to talk back to

kabšambi: ⟶ **kabsitambi**

kabumbi: (causative or passive of **kambi**)

kacang seme: hard (said of foods), sound made when hitting something hard

    kacang seme mangga: stiff and hard

kacar kicir: (onomatopoetic) 1. sound of walking on gravel; 2. sound of biting something hard or gritty

kacar seme: not cooked soft, undercooked, hard and stiff, coarse and hard

kaciki: a ragged coat of deer or roe hide

kacilan: an arrow used for target practice

kadalabumbi: (causative or passive of **kadalambi**)

kadalaci: (主管) administrator, person in charge

kadalakū: manager, director

kadalambi: to administer, to manage, to control, to be in charge of, to rule, to lead (troops)

    kadalame bošoro ba: (督催所) Office of Encitement, *BH* 493

    kadalame simnere hafan: (監臨官) Supervisor (of an examination), *BH* 652F

    kadalara niyalma: responsible person, person in charge

kadalan: 1. administration, control; 2. (關防印) a rectangular-shaped seal used by high provincial officials, *BH* 984

kadalangga: 1. (總兵) Brigade General, *BH* 751; 2. garrison

kadalara: ⟶ **kadalambi** (subheading)

kadalasi: ⟶ **dabsun juwere kadalasi**

kadalatu: (管勾) clerk of a Confucian temple

kadarakū: daring, brave

kadurambi: to contest, to dispute with

kaduršambi: always to be disputing

kafur kifur: 1. agile, quick; 2. (onomatopoetic) the sound made when stepping on snow or ice

kafur seme: 1. (onomatopoetic) the sound of walking on ice or snow (crunching); 2. decisive, straightforward, without further ado; 3. generously, without stint, without fuss

    kafur seme mokcoho: broke with a snap

    kafur seme yabumbi: to act in a straightforward manner

kaha: ⟶ **kambi** (subheading)

kai: (sentence particle showing emphasis)

kaica: a basket made of birch bark

kaicabumbi: (causative of **kaicambi**)

kaicambi: to shout, to yell

kaicame injembi: to laugh loudly, to guffaw

kaican: **1**. shouting, yelling; **2**. the shouting of hunters on a battue after roe

kaicandumbi: to shout together; also **kaicanumbi**

kaicanumbi: to shout together; also **kaicandumbi**

kaicari: ⟶ **kaiciri**

kaici: border, boundary between two patrol areas

kaici acambi: to patrol the area between two guard posts

kaiciri: a box that hangs from the belt for holding toothpicks and ear cleaners

kaideo: ⟶ **kaidu**

kaidu: lone (said of a horse), single (said of a horse)

kaidu morin i yabumbi: for a single rider to ride along on a lone horse

kaikada: askance

kaikamari: ⟶ **kaikari**

kaikarambi: to be slanted or crooked, to look askance at

kaikarafi tuwambi: to look askance at

kaikari: giant shellfish from which mother-of-pearl is produced, pinna

kaikata: ⟶ **kaikada**

kailan: a kind of large soft-shell river turtle

kailari orho: *Leonurus sibiricus*: honeyweed — a medicinal herb

kailun: a brown horse with black mane and tail

kailun niongniyaha: a brown wild goose

kaipi: a covered basket made of willow branches used to hold sewing materials; cf. **kapi**

kaitu: ⟶ **kaidu**

kajabumbi: (causative of **kajambi**)

kajambi: to gnaw, to crunch with one's teeth, to break with one's teeth

kajilan: ⟶ **kacilan**

kaka: feces of children

kaka faka: (onomatopoetic) the sound of many people laughing

kaka kiki: (onomatopoetic) the sound of happy laughter

kaka seme: (onomatopoetic) laughing, tittering

kakabumbi: (causative of **kakambi**)

kakambi: to defecate (said of children)

kakari fakari: (onomatopoetic) the sound of many people laughing

kaki: **1**. violent, quick-tempered; **2**. strong (said of liquor); **3**. small, narrow (said of clothing), cramped

kakiri: **1**. hot pepper, capsicum; **2**. *Zanthoxylum piperitum*: an aromatic tree, Sichuan pepper

kakitu: a tight-fitting sleeveless jacket

kaksaha: a name for the magpie; cf. **saksaha**

kaksimbi: **1**. to cough up (blood or phlegm); **2**. to loosen something tangled

kakū: water gate, lock, sluice, floodgate

kakū i angga: sluiceway

kakū undehen: the horizontal boards that cut off the flow of water in a water gate

kakūng kikūng: (onomatopoetic) the sound made by a heavily loaded cart or by a heavy load

kakūng seme: gritting one's teeth, with hate, with effort

kakūr: (onomatopoetic) the sound of gritting one's teeth

kakūr kikūr: (onomatopoetic) the sound made by ropes and pegs when securing a load on a wagon

kakūr sere asuki: sound of gritting one's teeth

kalang: (onomatopoetic) the sound of metal or stone objects banging together

kalang kiling: (onomatopoetic) the same as **kalang**

kalang seme: ⟶ **kalang**

kalar kalar: (onomatopoetic) the sound of metal objects hitting one another

kalar kilir: (onomatopoetic) the sound of keys or small bells jingling

kalar seme: kindly, courteously, harmoniously

kalbi: ⟶ **kalbin**

kalbikū: an arrow with a small head and a slender shaft used for shooting at distant targets

kalbimbi: to shoot a **kalbikū**

kalbin: the lower part of the belly

kalbin tucike: 'the belly has protruded' — to have a paunch

kalbiyambi: ⟶ **kalbimbi**

kalca: ⟶ **kalja**

kalcuhūn: having a broad forehead

kalcun: spirit, energy

kalcun sain: in good spirits, energetic, full of vitality

kalcunggi: **1**. high-spirited, energetic, robust, full of vitality, vivacious, lively; **2**. a high-spirited or energetic person

kalfimbi: ⟶ **kalbimbi**

kalfin: **1**. the distance the **kalbikū** is shot; **2**.
    ⟶ **kalbin**

kalfini: sea flounder, flatfish
    kalfini mudan ilha: bleeding-heart (flowering
        plant: *Dicentra spectabilis*)

kalfiyambi: ⟶ **kalbimbi**

kalfiyan: ⟶ **halfiyan**

kalibumbi: (causative of **kalimbi**)

kalimbi: to soar, to glide (said of hawks, eagles,
    etc.)

kalimu: whale

kalinambi: to fly far off, to soar away

kalja: **1**. white stripe or a bare strip on the head of
    an animal; **2**. white spot on a horse's nose;
    3. bald head
    kalja seberi morin: a horse with white feet and
        a white spot on the forehead
    kalja sele: the horizontal piece of iron (on a
        bridle that goes over the nostrils)
    kalja yali: fresh bacon, streaky pork

kaljakū weijun: a name for the stork; cf. **weijun**

kaljangga ijifun niyehe: a mandarin duck with
    white stripes

kalju: ski pole (the end of the pole is shaped like a
    spoon)

kalka: shield
    kalka gida: shields and spears — metaphor for
        war

kalkangga: pertaining to a shield
    kalkangga cooha: troops carrying shields
    kalkangga loho: a sword carried along with a
        shield

kaltara: **1**. a brown horse with white around the
    mouth and eyes; **2**. slick, shining (said of
    bird's feathers)
    kaltara niyehe: mallard; cf. **borjin niyehe**

kaltarabumbi: **1**. (causative or passive of
    kaltarambi); **2**. to suffer a fall (by slipping)

kaltarambi: to slip (and fall)
    kaltarame tuhembi: to slip and fall

kaltarashūn: slippery

kaltaršambi: to be slippery
    kaltaršara ba: a slippery spot

kaltashūn: awkward, recalcitrant, uncooperative

kaltu multu: just, almost, almost but not quite
    within reach

kalu mulu: careless, sloppy, overly hasty

kalumimbi: to pierce the skin but not the flesh (said
    of an arrow)

kambi: **1**. to surround, to lay siege; **2**. to obstruct, to
    ward off, to stop, to impede; **3**. to go on an
    errand; cf. **alban kambi**
    kaha be subumbi: to lift a siege
    kame abalambi: to go on the winter hunt
    kame afambi: to surround and attack, to
        ambush
    kame dalimbi: to defend, to resist
    kame gisurembi: to hinder someone from
        speaking, to interrupt someone
    kame heturembi: to intercept

kambuljambi: to be soft and damp (the earth), to be
    swampy

kamcibumbi: (causative of **kamcimbi**): to be
    annexed

kamcigan: Chinese people and criminals who were
    enrolled in the Eight Banners after
    submitting to the Manchus

kamcikū mulan: folding chair or stool

kamcimbi: to place close together, to be together, to
    be in the same place, to serve concurrently,
    to act at the same time
    kamcifi icihiyambi: to manage concurrently, to
        serve concurrently
    kamcifi tuwašatambi: to give consideration to
        two or more things, to take two or more
        things into account
    kamcime tebumbi: to pack together

kamcin: **1**. concurrent, consolidated, in one place;
    2. annexation
    kamcin i gurun: vassal state, dependency

kame: ⟶ **kambi** (subheading)

kamkū: a brown silk from which hats were made

kamni: a narrow pass, a strategic pass
    kamni angga: a narrow pass

kamnibumbi: (causative or passive of **kamnimbi**)

kamnimbi: **1**. to sew together, to bring together, to
    put back together, to close (the eyelids or
    lips); **2**. to grow together, to heal (said of a
    wound)
    kamnime tabumbi: to button up

kamtu: felt hat, felt liner in a helmet

kamtun: a coarse silken cloth used in ancient times
    for tying the hair

kanagan: pretext, pretense, excuse
    kanagan arambi: to make excuses

kanagan baimbi: to seek a pretext

kanagan jorimbi: to make an excuse

kanahan: ⟶ **kanagan**

kancambi: ⟶ **kanjambi**

kanda: the soft skin under the neck of a cow, dewlap

kandagan: ⟶ **kandahan**

kandahan: *Alces alces*: Manchurian moose

kandahan tohoma: saddle skirt: a piece of moose hide hanging from the sides of a saddle to protect the rider's legs from dirt and mud

kandarhan: a decoration attached to the bridle that hangs down from the horse's jaw

kang seme: aloud, out loud

kanggarambi: **1**. to slip slightly, to skid; **2**. to pierce the skin with an arrow; **3**. to miss (an opportunity), to let go by

kanggarsambi: to keep on slipping

kanggasikū: show-off, braggart, conceited person

kanggasitambi: to act in an insolent way, to parade one's skill, to be conceited

kanggašambi: to act in an insolent way, to swagger

kanggili: slim, shapely, possessing a fine delicate build, lanky

kanggiljambi: (-ka) to become slim and shapely

kanggir: (onomatopoetic) the sound of metal or porcelain falling

kanggir kinggir: (onomatopoetic) the sound of bells

kanggir seme: (onomatopoetic) the sound of metal or porcelain falling

kanggiri: **1**. metal strips (hung under the eaves) that tinkle in the wind; **2**. a bronze decoration attached to a box below a lock

kanggiri ilha: an exotic flower that grows in clusters and flutters even when there is no wind

kanggū niyehe: *Mergellus albellus*: smew, a kind of duck

kanggūr kinggūr: (onomatopoetic) the sound of a large structure collapsing

kanggūr seme: **1**. (onomatopoetic) the sound of a wall falling; **2**. foolhardy, reckless, impudent

kangkambi: to be thirsty

kangkašambi: to be very thirsty

kangkašara nimeku: diabetes

kangnambi: **1**. to leap onto a bareback horse, to leap on and straddle

kangsambi: to shave hair off a pelt

kangsanggi: arrogant, reckless, conceited, overbearing

kangsiri: ridge of the nose, the top of the nose ridge just below the eyes

kangsiri foribumbi: to meet with a rebuff, to run up against a brick wall

kangsiri forimbi: to rebuff, to refuse, to deal a blow to

kangtarambi: **1**. to rise up in the front (said especially of a cart that is loaded too heavily at the rear); **2**. to tie the reins of a horse to the pommel of a saddle so as to keep the horse from wandering; **3**. to hold the head high

kangtaršambi: to walk with the head high, to act in a proud manner, to act boldly

kangtaršame arbušambi: to put on airs, to go about with one's head in the air

kani: **1**. faction, clique; **2**. like-minded; **3**. ⟶ **ai kani**

kani acarakū: not compatible, unable to get along with people

kani akū: not amiable, uncongenial, unable to get along with people

kanin: **1**. kelp, edible seaweed; **2**. ⟶ **kani**

kanin akū: ⟶ **kani akū**

kaningga: **1**. having a relationship, related, of the same sort; **2**. amiable, able to get along with others

kanirakū: ⟶ **kani akū**

kanjambi: to play with the **gacuha**

kanjidu: a name for the eastern great bustard; cf. **humudu**

kanjiha ihan: a cow with a white nose

kanjiha niongniyaha: a small wild goose with a red beak and a red fleshy crest on the head

kanjimbi: to come to surround, to come to lay siege

kanumbi: to surround together, to besiege together

kapahūn: flat, compressed, pressed down, small in stature

kapahūn deduhebi: is lying flat

kaparabumbi: (causative or passive of **kaparambi**)

kaparambi: (-ka) to be pressed flat, to be pressed together, to be flat

kapi: a sewing basket with a cover; cf. **kaipi**

kapihūn: ⟶ **kapahūn**

kar seme: defensive, defending one's own possessions

kara: **1**. black (generally of animals or plants); **2**. layperson (as opposed to a monastic)

kara cai: strong black tea (drunk with added milk)

kara cecike: a name for the myna

kara fulan: an iron-gray horse

kara hūna: a tree whose fiber is used to fasten arrowheads to the shaft

kara indahūn: a black dog

kara keire: a dark brown horse

kara kiongguhe: a black myna

kara lama: a lama who has returned to secular life

kara muke: the Amur River

kara saksaha: a black magpie

kara yarha: a black panther

kara fara: hot-tempered

karaba: supportive, protective, solicitous

karabumbi: (causative of **karambi**)

karahi weijun: a white stork with black feathers on the breast

karaki: a crow

karalja: a name for the coot; cf. **karan kalja**

karaltu: a name for the sparrow hawk; cf. **silmen**

karambi: to look down from a height, to gaze into the distance

karara dengjan: a lantern that shines very far at night, a signal lantern

karan: **1**. lookout tower, watchtower, platform; **2**. stage (in a theater); **3**. ⟶ **kara**

karan kalja: *Fulica atra*: coot

karanambi: to go to look from a height

karandumbi: to look together from a height; also **karanumbi**

karandun: ⟶ **karanidun**

karangga taktu: watchtower, sentry tower

karanidun: *Faleo columbarius*: merlin

karanjimbi: to come to look from a height

karanumbi: to look together from a height; also **karandumbi**

karasu: a name for the cormorant; cf. **suwan**

karcabumbi: (causative or passive of **karcambi**)

karcambi: to run into, to collide with, to bump into

karcame guwembi: to make a noise by rubbing the wings together (locusts, crickets, etc.)

karcandumbi: to bump into one another, to collide, to clash; also **karcanumbi**

karcanumbi: to bump into one another, to collide, to clash; also **karcandumbi**

karcin: a kind of spotted or speckled hawk resembling the black-eared kite

kargama: croup of a horse or mule

kargama hūwalame niyamniyambi: to turn around and shoot over the croup of a horse (in archery)

kargibumbi: (causative of **kargimbi**)

kargimbi: **1**. to cut evenly; **2**. to pluck, to pull up (grass); **3**. to shave a criminal's head (a form of punishment in ancient times)

karhama: ⟶ **kargama**

karimbi: ⟶ **kalimbi**

karjambi: ⟶ **garjambi**

karka cecike: *Capella gallinago*: common snipe

karkakū: 'scraper' — a musical instrument shaped like a tiger and having a corrugated back over which a bar can be run to produce a grating sound; cf. **ioi**

karkala: ⟶ **karkalan**

karkalan: **1**. Siberian pea tree (*Caragana arborescens*); **2**. Chinese wild peach (the inner bark of which is used for attaching arrowheads to the shaft); cf. **hasuran**

karkambi: **1**. to scrape with a wooden or bamboo stick; **2**. to keep time by scraping a chopstick on a dustpan

karkan cecike: ⟶ **karka cecike**

karkimbi: ⟶ **kargimbi**

karmabumbi: (causative of **karmambi**)

karmacun: protection

karmakū: protector

karmambi: **1**. to protect, to take care of, to safeguard; **2**. to be concerned about

karmame aitubumbi: to rescue

karmame dalimbi: to ensure, to safeguard

karman: ⟶ **karmacun**

karmandumbi: to protect together, to protect one another; also **karmanumbi**

karmangga: (衛) First Class Transport Station (on the Grand Canal), *BH* 834

karmani: a written charm; cf. **tarni**

karmanumbi: to protect together, to protect one another; also **karmandumbi**

karmarambi: ⟶ **karmambi**

karmasi: protector, patron

karmatambi: to protect continually

karmatangga: protective

karmatu mahatun: a hat worn in ancient times by the officers of the Imperial bodyguard

karu: **1.** retribution, recompense, reward, revenge; **2.** gratitude; **3.** (adverb) in return, in retribution

   karu alambi: to report back

   karu bithe: return letter, reply to a letter

   karu bumbi: **1.** to repay, to recompense; **2.** to give a reply

   karu de karu: having a reciprocal relationship, exchanging favors

   karu gaimbi: to exact revenge

   karu jasigan: reply to a letter

   karu temgetu: receipt for a document issued by the authorities

karulabumbi: (causative of **karulambi**)

karulambi: **1.** to repay, to recompense; **2.** to requite, to get revenge; **3.** to reply

karulan: **1.** recompense; **2.** karma

karun: outpost sentry, border guard

   karun cooha: troops on sentry duty

   karun i ba: an outpost, sentry post

   karun i cuwan: patrol boat

   karun i niyalma: sentry, border guard

   karun sabumbi: to see the first signs of smallpox

   karun sindambi: to position a sentry, to send an officer to an outpost to manage affairs

karušambi: to do in return, to reciprocate, to persist in repaying

   karušame acabumbi: to engage in social activities, to do as a courtesy

   karušame arbušambi: to socialize

   karušame tantambi: to strike back

   karušame toombi: to talk back, to retort

kas kis: swift, agile

kas seme: **1.** (onomatopoetic) sound of a grazing arrow; **2.** the sound of a knife or scissors cutting; **3.** swift

kasari: ⟶ **kabari**

kaskan: what arrogance! (an oath)

kaskanambi: to become arrogant or conceited, to treat with disrespect

kata fata: in a rush, in a flurry, concerned, anxious

kata kiti: (onomatopoetic) **1.** the sound of shoes treading on a hard surface; **2.** squeaking, scraping

katabumbi: **1.** (causative of **katambi**); **2.** to dry in the open air

kataha: ⟶ **katambi** (subheading)

kataha fadu: the name of a bird whose call sounds like **kataha fadu**

katak: (onomatopoetic) the sound of a lock clicking shut

   katak kitik: (onomatopoetic) the sound of an object falling from a high place

katambi: to dry out, to become dry

   kataha yali: dried meat

katang seme: **1.** very hard, solid; **2.** loud and clear, sonorous

katangga soro: jujubes dried in the sun

katar tatar: **1.** affable, warm; **2.** with all one's might, to the best of one's ability

katar seme: dried out, dried up

katarabumbi: (causative of **katarambi**)

katarambi: to trot

kati: brocade embroidered in silk

   kati jongdon: grass linen with brocade embroidery on it

katun: **1.** sturdy, robust, healthy and strong, hale and hearty, energetic; **2.** effort, exertion; **3.** queen

katungga: robust, healthy, energetic

katunjambi: to endure, to stick it out, to force oneself, to exert effort, to persevere in, to manage with effort

   katunjame hacihiyambi: to exert oneself, to make a great effort

katur kitur: (onomatopoetic) the sound of eating hard brittle things (like ice)

katur seme: (onomatopoetic) making a brittle, crunching sound

katuri: crab, crayfish

ke: **1.** interjection of surprise; **2.** a quarter of an hour; cf. **kemu**

keb kab seme: affectionate, warm, affable, sincere

keb seme: **1.** warm, affable; **2.** exhausted; **3.** falling, dropping

   keb seme gisurembi: to have an earnest talk

   keb seme šadambi: to become very tired

kebisu: ⟶ **keibisu**

kebse: a little too much

kebse ekiyehe: diminished too much, diminished considerably

kebsembi: ⟶ **keb seme**

kebsimbi: **1**. to slap the legs against leather saddle skirts; **2**. to click or snap loudly

kebsisu: ⟶ **keibisu**

kebsu: ⟶ **keibisu**

kecembi: ⟶ **hecembi**

kecer seme: in large quantity (said of very small objects)

kecer seme adambi: to fit many small pieces together

keci maci: stingy

kecu: fierce, cruel, savage, hard-hearted

kecu gūnin: malice, hard-heartedness

kecu horon: vicious, venomous

kecu mudan: abusive language, harsh voice

kecudembi: to be fierce, to act fiercely, to show cruelty

kederebumbi: (causative of **kederembi**)

kederelembi: ⟶ **kederembi**

kederembi: to patrol, to go on patrol, to make the rounds

kedereme baicambi: to make a tour of inspection

kedereme baicara hafan: (巡邏官) an official who patrols the examination hall, proctor

kedereme seremšembi: to patrol

kederešembi: ⟶ **kederšembi**

kederšembi: to hurt with harsh words, to attack verbally, to ridicule

kefucen: brittle, fragile; cf. **kufuyen**

keibiri ilha: an exotic flower — when growing very close together they resemble a brightly colored carpet

keibisu: carpet, rug

keifu: the name of an arrow used for shooting tigers, bears, and buck deer

keifulembi: to pierce, to go through (arrows)

keike: **1**. severe, exacting; **2**. unkind, harsh, mean, caustic; **3**. partial, unfair

keike fetereku: harsh, caustic

keike nekeliyen: mean, unkind

keike oshon: severe, vicious, venomous, black-hearted

keikedembi: to act in an unfair or prejudiced manner, to act harshly toward someone

keikeljembi: to lean to one side, to act partially

keikembi: ⟶ **keikedembi**

keikuhen: a kestrel

keilen: *Alligator sinensis*: Yangtze alligator

keire: a dark brown horse with a black tail and mane

keišembi: **1**. to implore, to beg; **2**. to heal, to dry up (said of a sore on a horse)

kejeme: ⟶ **kejine**

kejime: ⟶ **kejine**

kejine: **1**. a long while, a long time; **2**. a lot, many

kejine ba gaiha: traveled a long distance

kejine daha: (snow, rain) fell in abundance

kejine inenggi oho: many days passed

kejine labdu: a great many, a lot

kejine ofi: after a long while

kejini: ⟶ **kejine**

kek sembi: to be pleased, to be gratified, to be refreshed

kekde kakda: not level, bumpy (said of a place where one is walking)

keke: elder sister of husband or wife — sister-in-law

keke kaka: (onomatopoetic) stuttering, stammering, the sound of giggling

kekerembi: **1**. to belch; cf. **jo banjimbi**, **johombi**; **2**. to put on airs

kekeri tatambi: to act conceited

keki kaka: (onomatopoetic) laughing, cackling

keksebuku: a good-luck scepter, a scepter made in a fantastic shape

keksebumbi: **1**. (causative of **keksembi**); **2**. to satisfy, to please, to gratify

keksembi: to be pleased, to be gratified; cf. **kek sembi**

keksen: gratification, satisfaction

keksengge: satisfying, gratifying, satisfactory

keksengge gohon: a hook shaped like a good-luck scepter and used for hanging curtains

kekte kakta: uneven, rough (surface), bumpy

kektehun: **1**. stooped, humpbacked; **2**. skin and bones

keku: the uvula; cf. **ilmaha**

keku umiyaha: a kind of multicolored caterpillar that appears in large groups on trees

kekuhe: *Cuculus canorus*: Asiatic cuckoo

kekutu: a variety of cuckoo

keleng kalang: slack, loose, lax

keleng kalang umesi sula: limp, tired out (said of horses and cows)

keler kalar: **1**. undone, unraveled (said of seams); **2**. careless, negligent, absentminded; **3**. lax, loose; **4**. tired, exhausted (said of horses)

keler kalar seme: loose, lax

keler kalar seme aššambi: to be loose (undone) and move

keleri: slack, loose

keleri kalari: loose, lax, slack

kelfimbi: (-ke) **1**. to lean, to tilt; **2**. to be past the zenith (said of the sun), to incline (said of the sun)

kelfišembi: **1**. to lean to one side (said of a ship in a storm), to list; **2**. to waver, to be irresolute, to be in doubt

kelfišeme feksimbi: to run (said of wild animals)

kelfiyedembi: ⟶ **kelfišembi**

kelfiyelembi: ⟶ **kelfišembi**

kelfiyembi: ⟶ **kelfimbi**

kelfiyešembi: ⟶ **kelfišembi**

keli: men who have married sisters — brothers-in-law

kelmembi: ⟶ **kemnembi**

keltehe: golden carp; cf. **onggošon**

kelterhen: a kind of swallow (has a short beak, black body, speckled breast, and a loud cry)

kemin: marrow, medulla, porous matter in the bones

kemki kamki: shameless, forward, obtrusive

kemkimbi: to chase and bite (said of dogs, geese, etc.)

kemnebumbi: (causative of **kemnembi**)

kemneku: a measuring device

kemnembi: **1**. to measure, to weigh; **2**. to moderate, to use with measure, to use temperately, to be frugal

kemneme baitalambi: to use frugally, to use economically

kemneme bodoro bolgobure fiyenten: (虞衡清吏司) Department of Weights and Measures, *BH* 460A

kemneme malhūšambi: to act frugally

kemnere olhošoro namun: (節慎庫) the name of a silver depository of the Board of Works

kemnen: measure, measuring

kemnen akū: without measure, intemperate

kemšu: a name for the Chinese button quail; cf. **niyo mušu**

kemu: a quarter of an hour; cf. **ke**

kemu i tampin: a water clock, clepsydra

kemu tampin tuwara hafan: (挈壺正) Keeper of Clepsydra, *BH* 231

kemuhen: norm, standard, scale, model

kemun: **1**. measure, dimension, model, ruler, rule, regulation; **2**. a marker beyond which one is not allowed to step when competing in archery; **3**. a point beyond which one is not allowed to go

kemun akū: without measure, without rule, immoderate, unlimited

kemun ci dabanambi: to go beyond a limit

kemun durun: dimension, scale, model, standard, system

kemun gaimbi: to take measurements

kemun i jiha: a model coin — a model from which other copper coins were cast

kemun i suje: silk used for offerings

kemun ici: norm, yardstick

kemun kooli: measure, rule, regulation

kemun miyalin: measure, dimension

kemun ton: **1**. reckoning, measuring; **2**. quota

kemun yangse: manners, deportment

kemungge: **1**. having measure, frugal; **2**. limited, measured, simple

kemuni: **1**. often; **2**. still, yet

kemuni jafašambi: to practice constantly (what one has learned)

kemuni unde: not yet, still not

kemuri coko: a name for the chicken; cf. **ikiri coko**

kendele nisiha: a small fish resembling the chum salmon

kenderhen: the long hair under the neck of a camel

kenderhen niongniyaha: a name for the wild goose; cf. **jurgangga gasha**

kenderhen niyehe: *Sythya fuligula*: the tufted duck

kenehunjebumbi: (causative or passive of **kenehunjembi**)

kenehunjecuke: doubtful, suspicious

kenehunjembi: to doubt, to suspect, to be in doubt, to vacillate

kenehunjere ba akū: there is no doubt, doubtless

kenehunjen: doubt, suspicion

keng: (onomatopoetic) the sound of coughing

keng kang: (onomatopoetic) the sound of many people coughing or clearing their throats

keng keng: (onomatopoetic) the sound of kowtowing

keng seme: ⟶ **kek sembi**

kengcembi: to break, to collapse (said of soft things)

kenggehun: **1**. emaciated; **2**. empty, vacant

　kenggehun kanggahūn: empty, vacant

kenggeri: **1**. the breast of a slaughtered animal; **2**. the clavicle (of a fowl)

kenggin: a kind of large sea mammal, perhaps a kind of whale

kengkembi: **1**. to dry out, to be dried up; **2**. to be famished, to be very hungry and thirsty

kengkešembi: to crave, to desire greatly

kengse: **1**. resolute, determined; **2**. in two, asunder

　kengse bijambi: to break in two

　kengse lasha: decisive, resolute

　kengse lashalambi: to be decisive

kengsejembi: to become worn (said of ropes and fine objects)

kengselebumbi: (causative of **kengselembi**)

kengselembi: **1**. to break in two, to break asunder; **2**. to decide, to determine

kengsimbi: **1**. to cough, to hack, to clear the throat; **2**. to call (said of the cuckoo)

kengšembi: ⟶ **kengsimbi**

kengtehun: **1**. stooped, hunched; **2**. towering above the herd

　kengtehun amba: larger than the rest of the herd

kenje: small in stature, stunted

kenšembi: ⟶ **kengkešembi**

keo keo seme: fervent

ker: (onomatopoetic) the sound of a belch

kercibumbi: (causative of **kercimbi**)

kercimbi: to cut up or dissect a slaughtered animal, to butcher

　kercihe yali: chunks of meat from a butchered animal

keremu: rampart, battlement, citadel

　keremu de aktalame: straddling a rampart

kerkenembi: to become severely pockmarked

kerkeri: a pockmarked person; cf. **mase**

kerkimbi: **1**. to bark incessantly, to yap; **2**. to scrape a winnowing fan with a bamboo stick during the 'snake song'

kerkin karkan: uneven, rough, bumpy

kerme: a sea fish resembling the **tubehe**

kermeyen nimaha: a sea fish similar to the **heihule**

kersen: the skin and flesh between the breast and front legs on sheep and wild animals

kersu: the flesh from the breast of a sheep

keru: a young crow — the same as **holon gaha**

kerulembi: to impose a reparation or compensation as a punishment, to impose a fine

kerun: compensation, fine, reparation

　kerun gaimbi: to demand compensation

kes: as if cut off with a knife, sharp, sheer

　kes seme: sharp, sheer, cut off

　kes seme lakcaha: severed smoothly, broke sharply

　kes sere ba: a precipitous place that looks like it has been cut off with a knife, a sheer drop

　kes sere hada: sheer cliff

kese masa: **1**. in dire need; **2**. crude, unkempt, careless

kesembureo: idler, sluggard, scoundrel — a term of derision

kesemburu: ⟶ **kesembureo**

keser seme: (onomatopoetic) the sound of chewing hard things

kesi: kind act (from above), favor, grace, kindness, graciousness

　kesi akū: unfortunately

　kesi be selgiyere fulehun be isibure temgetun: the name of an insignia of the Imperial Escort

　kesi be tuwakiyara gurun be dalire gung: (奉恩鎮國公) Prince of the Blood of the fifth degree, *BH* 20

　kesi be tuwakiyara gurun de aisilara gung: (奉恩輔國公) Prince of the Blood of the sixth degree, *BH* 21

　kesi be tuwakiyara janggin: (奉恩將軍) Noble of the Imperial lineage by Imperial Favor, *BH* 27A

　kesi bele i calu: a granary of the Board of Finance in Beijing

　kesi de hengkilembi: to kowtow as an act of thanksgiving for the Emperor's favor

　kesi fulehun: favor, grace

kesi isibumbi: to bestow favor

kesi menggun i namun: a treasury located in every banner for rewarding the troops

kesi selgiyembi: to bestow favor

kesi simehe: his grace has permeated (everywhere)

kesi šangnahan i kunggeri: (賞賜科) Office of Rewards and Bestowals in the Board of Rites

kesi yali: meat used as offerings

kesike: cat

kesike fatha: a wild herb whose leaves resemble cat's paws

kesingge: blessed with good fortune, blessed, favored

kesingge hafan: (恩騎尉) a hereditary rank of the ninth grade, *BH* 944

kesiri masiri: **1**. coarse, unkempt; **2**. careless, worthless; **3**. barely, with difficulty

kesiri masiri baita: dirty actions, coarse behavior

kesiri masiri gisun: coarse speech, bad language

kesitu: blessed, favored

kete kata: **1**. (onomatopoetic) the sound of horse's hooves striking stone; **2**. snacks (dried fruit and biscuits) eaten by children

ketek katak: (onomatopoetic) the sound of cartwheels on a rough surface

keteri: labia (part of the female genitalia), *labia minora*

ki: **1**. breath, vapor; **2**. anger; **3**. banner

ki be tucibumbi: to vent one's anger

ki fulhambi: to vent one's anger or resentment

ki kū: (onomatopoetic) the sound of sniggering or giggling

ki pai hafan: (旗牌) police commissioner

ki yang jodon: a kind of coarse grass linen produced in Qiyang 祁陽 in Hunan

kib seme: (onomatopoetic) **1**. the sound of hitting something with the fist; **2**. the sound of tripping and falling

kican: one hundred sheets of paper

kicebe: diligent, assiduous, industrious, hardworking

kicebe malhūn: industrious and frugal

kicebumbi: (causative of **kicembi**)

kicembi: **1**. to strive, to exert oneself, to be diligent, to apply oneself, to concentrate on, to be intent on, to study; **2**. to make plans, to strive to obtain; **3**. to seek, to pursue (a goal)

kiceme baicambi: to investigate diligently

kiceme faššambi: to work diligently, to put forth effort

kicen: **1**. diligence, exertion, striving; **2**. task, undertaking, lesson; **3**. vīrya, one of the six pāramitā

kicen faššan: industriousness, hard work

kicendumbi: to strive together; also **kicenumbi**

kicenumbi: to strive together; also **kicendumbi**

kidubumbi: (causative or passive of **kidumbi**)

kidulambi: ⟶ **kiyangdulambi**

kidumbi: (-ha) to think about, to long for, to miss someone

kidun: longing

kidun cecike: *Suthora webbiana*: the Hebei crow-tit

kifur: (onomatopoetic) the sound of crunching or teeth gnashing

kifur seme: crunching, grinding (said of sounds)

kijimi: **1**. trepang, sea slug; **2**. an oath used toward children

kik kik seme: anxious, troubled, confused

kiki kaka: (onomatopoetic) the sound of many people laughing

kikūr: (onomatopoetic) the sound made by cartwheels, the sound of teeth gnashing

kikūr seme: **1**. ⟶ **kikūr**; **2**. heavy, thick (said of cloth)

kila: *Rosa acicularis*: wild rose

kila ilha: **1**. ⟶ **kila**; **2**. lily

kilahūn: seagull, gull, birds of the genus *Larus*

kilakci: a very small cooking pot

kilang kalangga: (onomatopoetic) the sound of ringing or tingling

kilhana: *Bidens bipinnata*: bramble-bush

kilin: a unicorn, *qílín* 麒麟

kilingga: pertaining to a unicorn

kiltan: banner, pennant

kiltangga: bearing a banner or pennant

kiltari: signal flag

kiluk: a black-spotted horse

kima: *Sida ziliaefolia*: Sichuan hemp

kima suse: mortar mixed with hemp fibers

kimcibumbi: (causative of **kimcimbi**)

kimcikū: **1**. checker, examiner; **2**. thorough, exact, careful

kimcimbi: (**-ha**) to examine, to check, to investigate, to look into carefully, to do carefully

  kimcime acabumbi: to proofread

  kimcime baicakū: (檢討) Corrector, *BH* 200C

  kimcime baicambi: to investigate carefully

  kimcime baicara ba: (稽查房) an office of the Grand Secretariat

  kimcime baicara boo: (查核房) Inspection Office of the Printing Office and Bookbindery

  kimcime bodombi: to calculate carefully, to assess

  kimcime ekiyembumbi: to trim (expenditures), to reduce (spending)

  kimcime gūnimbi: to think over carefully

  kimcime toktobumbi: to check and ratify, to appraise

  kimcime yargiyalambi: to verify carefully

kimcin: examination, investigation, checking

kimcindumbi: to examine together; also **kimcinumbi**

kimcinumbi: to examine together; also **kimcindumbi**

kimcisi: (照磨) Commissary of the Seal or Correspondence Secretary, *BH* 826

kimu: ⟶ **kimun**

kimulebumbi: (causative of **kimulembi**)

kimulembi: to harbor enmity, to harbor a grudge, to get revenge

kimun: enmity, grudge, a feud, revenge

  kimun baita: a matter of enmity, feud, a matter for revenge

  kimun bata: enemy, bitter foe

  kimun be fulhambi: to vent one's enmity, to get revenge

  kimun be karulambi: to get revenge

  kimun falimbi: to become enemies, to start a feud, to incur hatred

  kimun gaimbi: to get revenge

  kimun jafambi: to harbor a grudge

kimundumbi: (**-he**) to get revenge on one another, to have a grudge against one another

kimungge: **1**. inimical, hostile; **2**. harboring a grudge, vengeful; **3**. a personal enemy

  kimungge niyalma: enemy, foe

kimuntumbi: ⟶ **kimundumbi**

  kimuntuhe niyalma: enemy, foe

kin: the seven-stringed lute; cf. **kituhan**

  kin še: lute and harp

kina ilha: *Impatiens balsamina*: garden balsam

kinamu ilha: *Lawsonia inermis*: henna

king: **1**. (onomatopoetic) the sound of a heavy object falling; **2**. musical stone; **3**. land measure equal to one hundred *mǔ* 畝, about 6.7 hectares

kinggir seme: clinking, clattering

kinggiri: a name for the hill myna

kinggiri seme: (onomatopoetic) the sound of breaking into many small pieces, the sound of something collapsing

kingguhe: a name for the myna

kingken: musical stone

kingkiri seme: (onomatopoetic) crashing loudly

kintala: ⟶ **kitala**

kinumbi: to loathe, to despise, to harbor a grudge

kiongguhe: *Acridotheres cristatellus*: myna of South China

kionggun: firm, unshakable

kiongguri ilha: hydrangea

kior seme: (onomatopoetic) the sound of a bird taking off suddenly

kiraga: attentive, observant

kirfu: *Acipenser schrenkii*: Amur sturgeon

kirho: lettuce

kiriba: **1**. a patient person; **2**. patient, long-suffering; **3**. cruel

kiribumbi: (causative of **kirimbi**)

kirica: female demon (a Buddhist term)

kiricun: patience, forbearance

kirijy: demons

kirikū: one who endures, sufferer

kirimbi: (**-ha**) **1**. to endure, to tolerate, to suffer; **2**. to lie still (said of animals who sense a nearby danger)

kirinjambi: to worry, to be upset

kirsa: *Vulpes corsac*: corsac, fox of the steppes

  kirsa cabi: the white breast and belly pelt of the corsac

kiru: **1**. flag, banner; **2**. a small banner worn on a soldier's back

kiruda: red signal flag

kirulambi: ⟶ **karulambi**

kirumbi: to seek out a mare (said of a stallion)

kirusi: battle banner

kisari: a sterile mare

kišan: fresh, new, neat, bright

kišimiši: small green seedless grape

kitala: **1**. the stock of a writing brush; **2**. quill

kitari: a kind of wild pig with white hair on its neck and legs

kitir seme: fast (galloping)

kituhan: the seven-stringed lute

    kituhan fithembi: to pluck a lute

    kituhan i kuyerhen: knots on the cords of a lute

    kituhan i murikū: the pegs of a lute

    kituhan i sujakū: the base of a lute

kituhangga: pertaining to the seven-stringed lute

kiya: honeycomb, cell

kiyab kib seme: sprightly, nimbly, smartly

kiyab seme: **1**. quickly; **2**. snug fitting, just right; **3**. concentrated; **4**. tight

    kiyab seme gene: go quickly

    kiyab seme jio: come quickly

kiyadambi: to inlay (pearls or jewels)

kiyafur kifur: (onomatopoetic) **1**. the sound of chewing hard objects; **2**. the sound of something smashing

kiyak: (onomatopoetic) the sound of dried wood breaking

    kiyak kik: (onomatopoetic) the sound of a large tree splitting

    kiyak seme: ⟶ **kiyak**

kiyakiyabumbi: (causative of **kiyakiyambi**)

kiyakiyambi: **1**. to sigh; **2**. to click the tongue in admiration, to praise, to admire

    kiyakiyame ferguwembi: to click the tongue in amazement, to sigh in admiration

    kiyakiyame saišambi: to admire and praise

kiyakū: *Pseudobagrus fulvidraco*: a species of catfish, Korean bullhead

kiyakūha: a hawk of mixed breed — considered useless for falconry

kiyakūng: (onomatopoetic) the sound made by a heavily loaded wagon, with a rumbling sound

    kiyakūng kikūng: ⟶ **kiyakūng**

    kiyakūng seme: with a clang, the sound of metal hitting something hard

    kiyakūng seme guwembi: to make a rumbling sound (said of a heavy wagon)

kiyalabumbi: (causative of **kiyalambi**)

kiyalambi: to bind (books)

    kiyalara dobtoloro falga: (做書作) bookbindery in the Printing Office and Bookbindery; cf. *BH* 94

kiyalang: (onomatopoetic) **1**. the sound of a single bell; **2**. the sound of metal colliding with another object

    kiyalang sembi: to ring, to clang

kiyalmabumbi: (causative of **kiyalmambi**)

kiyalmagan: an inlaid ornament

kiyalmambi: to inlay pearls, jewels, or coral in gold or silver

kiyambi: to inlay (jewels or pearls in gold or silver)

kiyamnambi: to inlay — the same as **kiyalmambi**

kiyamnan mahatun: an ancient-style hat adorned with golden cicadas and sable tails

kiyan: **1**. a paper measure equaling twenty-five sheets, a quire; **2**. anything folded or bound together

kiyangdu: **1**. agile, adroit, quick; **2**. prone to using force, overbearing, forceful; **3**. eager to excel

kiyangdukan: **1**. rather agile; **2**. rather prone to using force

kiyangdulabumbi: (causative or passive of **kiyangdulambi**)

kiyangdulambi: to use force, to take by force, to throw one's weight around

kiyangkiyan: having exceptional ability, intrepid, robust, powerful

    kiyangkiyan haha: a bold and unconstrained man, a gallant man

    kiyangkiyan mangga: bold, intrepid, powerful

kiyangkiyašabumbi: (causative or passive of **kiyangkiyašambi**)

kiyangkiyašambi: to offer powerful resistance, to show strength, to flaunt one's might

kiyangkiyatu mahatun: a style of hat worn in ancient times by heroes

kiyangsimbi: to squeal loudly (said of pigs); cf. **giyangsimbi**

kiyar: (onomatopoetic) the sound made by a wild hawk

    kiyar kir: (onomatopoetic) the cry of alarm made by birds of prey and martens

    kiyar seme: shrieking fiercely (to keep someone from advancing)

kiyaribumbi: (causative of **kiyarimbi**)

kiyarimbi: **1**. to chop firewood; **2**. to decimate, to slaughter; **3**. to cackle (after laying an egg)

kiyarime waha: totally decimated

kiyarkiya seme: annoying someone by talking too much, wearisome

kiyas: (onomatopoetic) the sound of something brittle breaking

kiyata: *Oncorhynchus keta*: keta, chum (a kind of Pacific salmon)

kiyatar seme: rumbling, roaring

kiyatar seme injembi: to laugh uproariously

kiyatubumbi: (causative of **kiyatumbi**)

kiyatumbi: to be famished, to suffer hunger

kiyatur kitur: (onomatopoetic) the sound of clods being crushed under wagon wheels

kiyei nan hiyang: a kind of incense

kiyob seme: (onomatopoetic) the sound of arrows striking a target

kiyokan: a small pointed knife used by an arrow maker

kiyokiyon: the name of an edible wild plant with hollow stems

kiyokiyon giranggi: the end of the tail bone

kiyokiyūn: ⟶ **kiyokiyon**

kiyolorjombi: to put on airs, to behave in an affected manner

kiyoo: **1**. sedan chair, litter; **2**. bridge

kiyoo cambi: to throw a bridge (across a stream)

kiyoo doombi: to cross a bridge

kiyoo niongniyaha: a small black-headed wild goose

kiyoo sejen: sedan chair

kiyoo tukiyembi: to carry a sedan chair

kiyooka: wood chips used as kindling; cf. **šašun**

kiyookan: ⟶ **kiyooka**

kiyor seme: (onomatopoetic) **1**. cackling; **2**. rumbling like thunder

ko: **1**. ditch, sewer; **2**. (onomatopoetic) sound of gagging

ko ka: (onomatopoetic) sound made when something gets caught in the throat, the sound of gagging

ko sangga: sewer, ditch

ko moo: a species of oak

kob seme: **1**. right on the mark, right on target; **2**. wholly, totally; **3**. without more ado, forthwith

kob seme gamaha: took it away forthwith

kob seme genehe: went without any ado

kob seme tehe: sat down without any ado

kobcihiyadambi: to put on airs, to strut about, to act in an affected or frivolous manner

kobcihiyan: fond of dressing up, fond of adornment, pretentious, affected

kobcimbi: to become detached, to fall off, to peel off

kobdolombi: to keep in a **kobdon**

kobdon: a container for arrows or tools

kobi: **1**. concave place, depression; **2**. the depressions on both sides of the nose

kobkolombi: to remove (paper that has been stuck to some surface), to tear off something pasted to some object

kobsohon: **1**. long-nosed; **2**. something floating on the surface of water

kobsohon sabumbi: to see something floating on water

kobsoljombi: to brag about small things, to be a petty braggart

kobsoljome arbušambi: to behave like a petty braggart

kobto: respectful, awed

kobtolombi: to treat respectfully

kobton: respect, reverence

kobtonggo: respectful, deferential

koco: **1**. angle or corner in a house; **2**. an out of the way place

koco mudan: winding, sinuous, twisting, curved

koco wai: angular, curved, crooked

kodo: the third stomach of sheep and cows that is eaten filled with blood

kofon suje: a kind of porous silk material

kofor seme: rotten or soft on the inside (said of food)

kofori: **1**. fluffy, porous, puffy, spongy; **2**. a kind of fruit resembling the pomelo

kofori efen: a kind of very porous pastry

kofori ilha: a very fragrant exotic white flower that blooms toward the end of spring

koforinambi: to become hollow, to become porous

kohodombi: to cry (said of pheasants in autumn)

kohong kohong: (onomatopoetic) the sound of repeated coughing

koika: **1**. scalp; **2**. short plants growing thickly together that resemble human hair; **3**. bricks made of clay and plant roots; **4**. sod, sward

koika fu: a wall built of sod

koika hoton: a mud wall

koikalambi: to scratch the scalp, to hurt the scalp

koikašabumbi: (causative of **koikašambi**)

koikašambi: **1**. to mix together; **2**. to scuffle

koikohon: floating high on the surface

koikoljombi: to behave in a reckless or peculiar fashion, to stir up trouble

koikon: short fine feathers that appear on the tails of fowl — their appearance on a hen indicates the hen is no longer willing to sit on eggs

    koikon dekdehebi: 'tail feathers have appeared' (said of a person who has become fed up or obstinate, or has lascivious thoughts)

koimali: cunning, tricky, shifty, deceitful

koimalidambi: to act cunningly, to act in a tricky manner, to act deceitfully

koiman: tricky, cunning, deceitful

koimangga: cunning, tricky

koimasitambi: to act always in a tricky manner

koitolombi: to employ tricks, to act deceitfully

koiton: **1**. deceitful, tricky; **2**. enticing, coquettish

    koiton mama: mistress of a brothel

koitonggo: cunning, tricky

kojohombi: to prevent, to obstruct

koki: tadpole

kokima: poverty-stricken, indigent

kokingga fukjingga hergen: (蝌蚪書) a style of calligraphy

kokirabumbi: (causative or passive of **kokirambi**)

kokirakū: **1**. one who harms other people; **2**. harmful, cruel

kokirambi: **1**. to harm, to damage, to injure, to wound; **2**. to be harmed, to suffer a loss

kokiran: damage, harm, injury

kokirandumbi: to harm one another

kokirangga inenggi: a day on which the earth's branch overcomes the heaven's stem

koko: (onomatopoetic) the sound made by chickens

kokoli: **1**. a garment without lapels that is pulled on over the head; **2**. baby's clothing; **3**. the name of a small bird that resembles the woodcock

kokolibumbi: (causative of **kokolimbi**)

kokolimbi: to remove, to take off, to strip off (clothing)

koksimbi: **1**. to cackle; **2**. to cry (said of pheasants in springtime)

koksin ulhūma: 'cackling pheasant' — the cackling by a pheasant when it senses an oncoming storm

kolabumbi: (causative of **kolambi**)

kolambi: to skin, to remove the tile from a roof, to remove thatch

    kolame arambi: to record item by item, to record carefully

koloi: channel, furrow

kolongso: bad body odor, the odor of the armpits

    kolongso wa: body odor

kolor seme: too large, loose fitting (shoes, boots, etc.)

komo: a felt blanket placed under a camel's saddle

komolobumbi: (causative of **komolombi**)

komolombi: to put on a felt saddle blanket, to put a felt pad on a camel

    komoloho enggemu: a saddle with felt padding for skinny or saddle-sore horses

komon: ⟶ **komo**

komso: few, little, a little bit

    komso dulin: minority

    komso i tomilambi: to appoint an insufficient number of people for some task

komsokon: rather little, rather few

komsolabumbi: (causative of **komsolambi**)

komsolambi: to become little or few, to decrease, to reduce

komsolombi: ⟶ **komsolambi**

komsongge: what is few, that which is little

konggir: (onomatopoetic) the sound of a small bell

    konggir kanggir: (onomatopoetic) the sound of many small bells

    konggir seme: (onomatopoetic) ringing, tinkling

konggohon: **1**. sunken (eyes); **2**. emaciated

    konggohon i tuwambi: to look at with infatuation

konggolo: the crop of a bird

konggor: (onomatopoetic) the sound of pouring water

    konggor seme: flowing swiftly

konggoro: grayish yellow (said of horses)

konggur: (onomatopoetic) the sound of thunder

kongsimbi: to speak nonsense in a loud voice

konjisun: ⟶ **konjosu**

konjosu: the end of the large intestine

konsun: hemorrhoidal swelling

koojiha: globefish eaten after the winter solstice; cf. **kosha**

koolambi: ⟶ **kolambi**

kooli: **1**. rule, norm, statute, codex, decree, law; **2**. custom, habit; **3**. document; **4**. method

kooli akū: **1**. without regulation, without a rule; **2**. unreasonable

kooli be fetembi: to cite a precedent

kooli durun: rule, regulation

kooli durun i bolgobure fiyenten: (儀制清吏司) Department of Ceremonies, *BH* 376A

kooli hacin: regulations and precedents

kooli hacin i bithei kuren: (則例館) division of regulations and precedents (one in every Board and important organ of government)

kooli icihiyara ba: (辦例處) Office of Regulations of the Imperial Household

kooli kemun: norm, standard, criterion

kooli obumbi: to make into a rule, to make the norm

kooli songkoi: in accordance with the rules

kooli yarun: quotation

kooli yoso: rules and regulations

koolingga: prescribed, ordered, ordained, in accordance with propriety

koosa: ⟶ **kūwasa**

kor: (onomatopoetic) the sound of sniffling or snoring

kor kor seme: gobbling, gorging

korambi: ⟶ **kūrambi**

kordon: a person good on skis or snowshoes

kordonggo: alert, quick, quick-witted

koribumbi: **1**. (causative or passive of **korimbi**); **2**. to be washed away (by a river current), to be undermined by a swift current

korikū: gouge, chisel, small curved knife

korimbi: to erode, to hollow out, to dig out, to cut out

korkong korkong: (onomatopoetic) the sound of repeated coughing

koro: sorrow, regret, damage, injury, offense, wound, punishment

koro akū: harmless, innocuous

koro arambi: **1**. to harm, to hurt, to injure; **2**. to be harmed

koro baha: **1**. was wounded, was injured; **2**. sustained loss

koro bahambi: to suffer loss, to be at a disadvantage, to be hurt

koro de dailambi: to fight a vendetta

koro gosihon: sorrow and suffering

koro isibumbi: to bring harm to, to harm, to poison

korombi: to resent, to harbor a grudge

korsobumbi: (causative or passive of **korsombi**)

korsocombi: to regret continually

korsocuka: regrettable, annoying

korsocun: regret, annoyance, resentment

korsocun be fulhambi: to vent one's resentment or annoyance

korsombi: **1**. to regret, to miss; **2**. to be annoyed at, to hate, to be angry at, to resent

korsome gasambi: to regret, to resent

korsome gūnimbi: to be sorrowful

korsondumbi: to be mutually annoyed, to regret mutually; also **korsonumbi**

korsonumbi: to be mutually annoyed, to regret mutually; also **korsondumbi**

kos seme: suddenly (got away or became skinny)

kos seme ukcaha: suddenly got away

kos seme wasika: suddenly became skinny

kosha: globefish, swellfish, fish of the genus *Fugu*

kosihimbi: **1**. to strive for, to aspire to; **2**. to go quickly, to scurry (to gain an advantage)

koskon kaskan: assiduous, busy, urgent

kotoli: sail (of a ship)

kotoli kiru: flag on a ship's mast

kotong: hard and dry

kotong katang seme: hard and dry

kotor: (onomatopoetic) the sound of pheasants flying

kotor katar: (onomatopoetic) **1**. the sound of hard things rattling together or falling; **2**. the sound of a flock of pheasants flying

kotor seme: **1**. in one gulp; **2**. (onomatopoetic) the sound of pheasants taking off

koyorholombi: to kill and skin the horse of a deceased man — after the offering at the grave the horse's skin and saddle are burned together with paper money

ku: **1**. soot (from cooking); **2**. storehouse, warehouse

ku gidambi: to build granaries

ku i menggun: silver money minted by the government, money in the treasury, deferred pay given to bannermen

ku ijumbi: to smear (the face) with soot

ku namun: storehouse

kub seme: out of energy, exhausted, (fell) in a heap

kubcen: ⟶ **kubcin**

kubcin: **1**. hem of a skirt; **2**. border at the top of boots or socks

kuberhen: welt caused by a whip or cane

kuberhenembi: to raise a welt, to cause a swelling (said of insects)

kubsuhun: **1**. brawny, burly, muscular; **2**. large, awkward

kubsuhuri: **1**. ⟶ **kubsuhun**; **2**. massive, unwieldy

kubsurembi: (**-ke**) to swell

kubuhe: ⟶ **kubumbi** (subheading)

kubuhen: border, edging, hem

kubumbi: to edge, to add a border to, to hem, to face a garment

kubuhe fulgiyan: bordered red (said of a banner)

kubuhe lamun: bordered blue (said of a banner)

kubuhe suwayan: bordered yellow (said of a banner)

kubuhe šanyan: bordered white (said of a banner)

kubun: **1**. cotton; **2**. willow catkins

kubun fithembi: to tease cotton with a bow

kubun fomoci: cotton stockings

kubun i etuku: cotton clothing, padded clothing made of cotton

kubun sektembi: to spread out cotton to make a quilt or a padded garment

kubunembi: to become mushy (said of melons)

kubungge hoošan: a kind of soft thin paper

kubungge moo: a tree that grows in Sichuan with fruit resembling cotton and which can be woven into cloth

kuburgen: scar, cicatrice

kuburhen: grape vine

kuciker fulan: a horse with dark mane and tail

kucung seme: diligent, assiduous

kude: a plaited basket for feeding cows

kude šoro: feeding basket woven from brambles

kudebumbi: (causative of **kudembi**)

kudembi: to tie up (a boat)

kudešembi: to beat the back with both hands (a kind of massage)

kufan: two partitioned rooms at both sides of the main house

kufang: ⟶ **kufan**

kufumbi: to run aground on a sandbar

kufur seme: the sound of eating something crisp

kufuyen: crisp, brittle, the pleasant sound of someone chewing brittle things

kufuyen šulhe: a kind of juicy pear

kuhen: **1**. one of the main channels of vital energy (**sukdun**), attached to the spine and connected to the internal organs; **2**. sprout on a tree; **3**. groove on a sword or knife, groove on an arrowhead

kuhengge: Swollen up lout! (oath used toward a lazy person)

kui hūwa: mallow; cf. **hingneci**

kuilebumbi: (causative of **kuilembi**)

kuileku: a form used for maintaining the shape of quivers, shoes, boots, and hats, a last

kuilembi: to place on a form (**kuileku**)

kuini: spoon

kuinihe: (奎) a constellation, the 15th of the lunar mansions, made up of sixteen stars divided between Andromeda and Pisces

kuinihe tokdonggo kiru: (奎宿旗) a banner depicting the constellation **kuinihe**

kukduri: **1**. braggart, boaster; **2**. boastful

kuke noor: the province of Qinghai

kukele alha: a red and white spotted horse

kuken: a horizontal piece of wood at the base of a window, window sill

kukji: a response used in group singing

kukjuhūn: ⟶ **kumcuhun**

kukjurembi: (**-ke**) to be bent over, to be stooped

kuku: **1**. blue-gray, gray; **2**. a kind of incense

kuku fulan: a blue-gray horse

kuku ihan: a gray cow

kuku ulhūma: a blue-gray pheasant

kuku kaka: (onomatopoetic) the sound of many people laughing

kuku seme injembi: to laugh unintentionally, to titter, to giggle

kukule: ⟶ **kukulu**

kukulembi: to foment (bathe medicinally) a serious wound in the open breast of an animal kukulu: forelock of a horse

kukurembi: to call a mate, to call the female (said of birds)

kukuri: a flat vessel for tea and milk

kuk'an: a board along the edge of an oven-bed

kulge: (in Buddhism) vehicle: **amba kulge** 'Mahayana — the Great Vehicle'

kulkuri suru: a white horse good in mountain terrain

kulu: healthy, vigorous, strong

kuluk jerde: sorrel

kulun: one of the eight trigrams of the *Yijing* (representing heaven)

kuluri malari: gradually

kulutu fulan: a gray steed

kumbi: (-**ke**/-**he**) to swell, to bloat

kumcuhun: bent forward, stooped, crooked, humpbacked

    kumcuhun i yabumbi: to walk hunched over

    kumcuhun wase: tiles used on the roof ridge

kumcun muke tashari: a name for the eagle; cf. **ing gasha tashari**

kumcurembi: to have stooped posture

kumdu: empty, hollow

    kumdu gūnin: modesty, open-mindedness

    kumdu mujilen: humility, humble

    kumdu untuhun: the void, emptiness

kumdulebumbi: (causative of **kumdulembi**)

kumdulembi: to be empty or hollow

kumdun moo: a tree six or seven (Chinese) feet tall that grows in mountain valleys, with light reddish bark

kumgetu: a red staff with one hundred vermilion lacquered bamboo rods and velvet tassels hanging from it (used to direct music)

kumuci: **1.** master of music in antiquity; **2.** official of the Board of State Music

    kumuci da: (署使長) Bursar of the Board of State Music

kumuda: (司樂) Master of Music, Director of Music; cf. *BH 391*

kumun: music

    kumun be aliha amban: (大士) an official in antiquity charged with musical matters

    kumun be aliha hafan: (太師) an official in antiquity who was in charge of musical matters

kumun be kadalara hafan: (典樂) an official in charge of music

kumun de baitalara jaka: musical instrument

kumun i ahūra: musical instrument

kumun i faidasi: (奉鑾) director of music

kumun i jurgan: (樂部) the Board of State Music, *BH 387*

kumun i karmangga: (旗手衛) Standard-bearers Section, *BH 122*

kumun i mudan: tonal rules for *cí* (**uculen**) poetry

kumun i niyalma: musician

kumun i tetun: musical instrument

kumungge: noisy, festive, exciting, lively, animated

    kumungge ba: an exciting place

    kumungge simengge: noisy and exciting, full of bustle and excitement, lively

    kumungge wenjehun: exciting, festive, bustling

kumusi: **1.** dancer (in the palace); **2.** musician

    kumusi i da: the chief dancer (of the palace)

    kumusi mahatun: a hat worn in ancient times by dancers

kundu: respect, honor, respectful

    kundu akū: impolite

kundujin: a name for the peacock; cf. **tojin**

kundulebumbi: (causative or passive of **kundulembi**)

kundulecuke: worthy of respect, respectable

kundulembi: to respect, to treat with respect, to honor, to entertain an honored guest

    kundulere kobtoloro: honor and respect

kundulen: respect, honor

kundulendumbi: to show mutual respect; also **kundulenumbi**

kundulenumbi: to show mutual respect; also **kundulendumbi**

kundulere: ⟶ **kundulembi** (subheading)

kundun: respectful

kunesun: provisions (for a journey)

    kunesun honin: a sheep to be used as food on a trip

    kunesun i menggun: money for provisions

    kunesun ufa: grain provision

kung: (onomatopoetic) the sound of a large object falling to the ground

kung cang: (onomatopoetic) the sound of drums and cymbals

kung cang seme banjimbi: to live on a a grand scale

kungge yamun: a section (of an organization)

kungger seme: incessantly

kunggeri: bureau

kunggeri seme: ⟶ **kungger seme**

kungguhen: ⟶ **kungguhun**

kungguhun: having sunken eyes

kunggur: (onomatopoetic) **1**. the sound made by empty wagons; **2**. the sound of heavy thunder; **3**. in great number

kunggur kanggar: (onomatopoetic) the sound of thunder

kunggur seme: **1**. in large numbers, in a throng; **2**. the sound made by wagons; **3**. the sound of heavy thunder

kunggur seme yamulambi: to go to the *yámen* in droves

kungguri seme: ⟶ **kunggur seme**

kungšuken: a little burned or scorched

kungšumbi: to burn, to scorch, to boil (milk)

kungšun: burned, scorched, scalded

kungšun wa: the odor of something scorched or scalded

kunusun: ⟶ **kunesun**

kur: (onomatopoetic) the sound of growling

kurbu: a flat ridge on an arrowhead

kurbulambi: to turn around

kurbumbi: to roll about, to roll on the ground, to tumble about

kurbušembi: **1**. to turn around and around, to turn over, to toss and turn, to roll about; **2**. to be upset, to be anxious

kurbušeme fuhešembi: to toss and turn restlessly, to be unable to sleep

kurbušeme forgošombi: to toss and turn

kurbušetembi: to turn over repeatedly, to be very anxious

kurbutembi: ⟶ **kurbušembi**

kurce: the name of a white sea fish

kurcilembi: to harden an arrow shaft by wrapping it in wood shavings and firing it

kurcilehe sirdan: an arrow hardened by fire

kurcin: a scaleless short white river fish with dark spots

kurdun: **1**. a Buddhist cycle, **samsara**; **2**. wheel; cf. **mukei kurdun**

kure: a river fish similar to the grass carp but with poor quality flesh

kurehu: *Dryocopus martius*: the great black woodpecker

kurelembi: to form cavalry into squadrons

kuren: **1**. squadron, detachment; **2**. establishment, office, depository; **3**. chestnut-colored, dark brown

kurene: weasel

kuri: **1**. spotted, striped, dappled; **2**. a dog striped like a tiger

kuri alan: spotted birch bark

kuri damin: a striped eagle

kuri hiyahali cecike: a striped crossbill

kuri ihan: a spotted cow

kuri kara: spotted black and yellow

kuri weifutu: a black-spotted dog

kuringge: spotted, striped

kuringge gasha: a black-headed bird with a spotted body

kuringge hoohan: a black-striped crane

kurku: **1**. a children's toy cast from lead in a hollowed-out bone (used like dice); **2**. head, chief, ringleader, instigator

kurne: ⟶ **kurene**

kuru: height, elevation, rise; cf. **huru**

kuruken: a somewhat elevated place

kurume: a coat or garment worn over one's other garments

kurune: ⟶ **kurene**

kus seme injembi: unable to keep from laughing

kuskun seme: steadily, without rest, assiduously

kuskurembi: to ruffle the feathers and beat the dirt with the wings (said of birds)

kušulebumbi: (causative or passive of **kušulembi**)

kušulembi: to dislike, to find annoying, to be tired of, to be disgusted

kušun: **1**. disgusted, sick of, unwell, uncomfortable; **2**. ill-fitting (clothes)

kušungge suri: silk crêpe

kuteci: a horse herder, stableboy, groom

kutitu lorin: a mule born from a jenny, a hinny

kutule: **1**. serf, banner slave, footman, attendant; **2**. horse herder, groom

kutulebumbi: (causative of **kutulembi**)

kutulembi: **1**. to lead (animals); **2**. to hold hands

kutung: (onomatopoetic) the sound of a large object falling to the ground

kutur fatar: **1**. affectionate, friendly, affable; **2**. with all one's might, to the best of one's ability

kutur seme: (onomatopoetic) **1**. the sound of incessant drumbeating; **2**. the sound of horses galloping; **3**. the sound of horses shaking themselves off

kuturcembi: to behave deferentially toward, to act solicitously

kuturšembi: ⟶ **kuturcembi**

kuwai šeo: bailiff

kuwalar: ⟶ **kūwalar, hūwalar**

kuwang cang seme: ⟶ **kūwang cang seme**

kuwanggar seme: ⟶ **hūwanggar seme**

kuwangse: basket

kuwecehe: ⟶ **kuwecihe**

kuwecicehe: ⟶ **kuweciheri**

kuwecihe: pigeon, dove

    kuwecihe boco: dove-gray, light gray

kuweciheri: dove-gray, light bluish gray

kuwedan: ⟶ **huweten**

kuwelembi: to remove the skin and the layer of fat attached to it (from bears and pigs)

kuweten: ⟶ **huweten**

kuyerhen: knot on a bowstring

kū ca: (onomatopoetic) the sound of fighting

kūbulibumbi: (causative of **kūbulimbi**)

kūbulimbi: **1**. (**-ka**) to change, to become altered (in appearance); **2**. to revolt

kūbulin: **1**. change, alteration; **2**. revolt

    kūbulin de acabumbi: to act according to a changing situation

    kūbulin ilenggu cecike: a name for the myna

kūca: a male goat

kūdargalambi: to grasp the crupper

    kūdargalame dorime fiyelembi: to trick ride at a gallop holding the crupper

kūdargan: crupper (on a horse)

    kūdargan dabame cashūn fiyelembi: to ride backward passing over the crupper (equestrian acrobatics)

    kūdargan tatame cashūn fiyelembi: to ride backward pulling on the crupper (equestrian acrobatics)

    kūdargan tataralame kurbume fiyelembi: to turn about while pulling on the crupper (equestrian acrobatics)

kūdarhan: ⟶ **kūdargan**

kūlan: **1**. a yellow horse with black tail and mane; **2**. wild ass

kūlhūri mumuri: toothless

kūlibumbi: (causative of **kūlimbi**)

kūlimbi: (**-ka**) to be scared stiff, to be stunned (from fear), to lie silently because of fear (animals), to cower

kūlin calin: frivolous, not serious, inconstant, furtive

kūlincambi: to be stupefied, to be dumbstruck, to stare blankly

    kūlincame tuwambi: to look with hostility

kūlisidambi: ⟶ **kūlisitambi**

kūlisitambi: **1**. to be petrified by fear, to be extremely frightened; **2**. to be frivolous, to be irresponsible, to act furtively

kūme: ⟶ **kūwarame**

kūngga: deep valley, canyon

kūr kar: (onomatopoetic) **1**. the sound made when something is caught in the throat; **2**. the sound made by the intestines

kūrambi: to engage in sexual intercourse, to have sex

kūrca: black (from smoke)

kūrcalambi: to blacken (with smoke)

kūrcan: *Grus grus*: eastern common crane

kūrcanambi: to become black with soot

kūrdakū: stirring stick; cf. **misun i kūrdakū**

kūrdambi: to stir up, to mix up

kūru: a kind of sour cake made from cow or mare's milk and liquor, a kind of Mongolian cheese

kūtambi: to mix

kūtan: *Pelecanus philippensis*: pelican

    kūtan morin: a white horse with red breast

kūthūbumbi: (causative or passive of **kūthūmbi**)

kūthūmbi: to mix, to mix up, to stir, to stir up, to mingle, to confuse

    kūthūme afambi: to fight a fierce battle

kūthūri: a decorative cloud form used on the tops of boots, yurts, and other objects

    kūthūri šufatu: a turban decorated with cloud designs and worn in ancient times

kūtka: the young of the Tibetan black bear; cf. **mojihiyan**

kūtu fata: hurrying, rushed

kūtu kata: (onomatopoetic) the sound of walking feet

kūtuktu: a living Buddha, a reincarnate lama

kūwa: light-yellow (said of a horse)

> **kūwa damin**: a light-yellow eagle

kūwaca: **1**. an inkstone made of horn (carried on trips); **2**. an ink vessel used by carpenters to draw straight lines; **3**. an object babies can suck on, a pacifier

> **kūwaca i beri**: a vessel made of horn used for holding gunpowder, powder horn

> **kūwaca yoro**: a large bone arrowhead used for mounted archery

kūwacambi: to cry (said of deer)

kūwacarabumbi: (causative of **kūwacarambi**)

kūwacarambi: **1**. to hollow out, to clean out the inside of some object with a small knife, to scrape; **2**. ⟶ **hūwacarambi**: to snore

kūwaha: the name of a small, thin-beaked bird that cries at night

kūwahalambi: to open the mouth wide

> **kūwahalafi injembi**: to laugh out loud, to rock with laughter

kūwai fai seme: frivolous and talkative, shallow, empty-headed

> **kūwai fai seme hūwaliyasun**: affable, friendly in a frivolous sort of way

> **kūwai fai seme weihuken**: thoroughly frivolous

kūwaici: **1**. a fastener on the crupper; **2**. with the toes pointing outward

kūwaicidambi: to walk with the toes pointing outward

kūwak cak: (onomatopoetic) the sound of fighting with poles or sticks

> **kūwak cak seme**: **1**. careless, coarse, carelessly boasting; **2**. (onomatopoetic) the sound of fighting with sticks

> **kūwak cak seme arbušambi**: to act in a careless, boastful manner

kūwala: pale yellow

> **kūwala ihan**: a light-yellow cow

kūwalabumbi: (causative of **kūwalambi**)

kūwalaci: a board over which hides are stretched for removing the hair

kūwalambi: to skin, to peel; cf. **kolambi**

kūwalar seme: straightforward, friendly

> **kūwalar seme gisurembi**: to speak in a straightforward manner

kūwang: (onomatopoetic) **1**. the sound of an explosion; **2**. the sound of knocking on wood

kūwang cang: (onomatopoetic) the sound of drums and cymbals

kūwang seme: (onomatopoetic) the sound of many people talking, noisily

kūwangkar seme: ⟶ **hūwanggar seme**

kūwangtahūn: **1**. an area without trees or plants; **2**. barren, waste

kūwar: (onomatopoetic) the sound of a seam ripping

kūwara megu: a wild mushroom of a faint greenish color

kūwara sence: ⟶ **kūwara megu**

kūwarabumbi: (causative or passive of **kūwarambi**)

kūwaracanambi: to look askance at

kūwarambi: to surround, to encircle, to circle (an erroneous word), to include

kūwaran: **1**. enclosure, encirclement, corral; **2**. camp (military), barracks; **3**. workshop, plant, factory; **4**. market place; **5**. yard of a monastery or temple

> **kūwaran faidan usiha**: (勾陳星) the name of a constellation

> **kūwaran i boo**: barracks

> **kūwaran i calu**: the granary of the troops of the green banner and of the garrison troops

> **kūwaran i da**: a commander elected by the officers of a camp

> **kūwaran i kunggeri**: (營科) the Barracks Office of the Board of War

> **kūwaran jafambi**: to set up a military camp

> **kūwaran meyen**: military ranks, the military

kūwaranambi: to encircle, to circle

kūwas: (onomatopoetic) **1**. the sound of chopping wood; **2**. the sound of a falcon striking an object with its wings; **3**. the sound of a breaking rope

> **kūwas kis**: (onomatopoetic) **1**. the sound made by someone dragging his feet; **2**. the sound of a sickle mowing; **3**. the sound of sacks of grain being dragged on a floor; **4**. the sound of a breaking stick

> **kūwas seme**: the sound of something breaking or splitting

kūwasa: braggart, boastful

> **kūwasa gisurembi**: to brag, to boast

kūwasadambi: to brag, to boast wildly

kūwata kiti: (onomatopoetic) the sound of a hard object striking something

kūwatar seme: spooked (said of an excitable horse)

kūwatiki: a year-old bear

kūwatiri: a small animal resembling the bear, with scant shiny hair

K'

For words beginning with **k**, see the section beginning on page 224.

k'ambi: (Tibetan) abbot

k'amduri: (亢) a constellation, the 2nd of the lunar mansions, made up of four stars (κ, ι, ϕ, λ) in Virgo

    k'amduri tokdonggo kiru: (亢宿旗) a banner depicting the constellation **k'amduri**

k'arsi: ⟶ **garša**

k'o: section (of an organization) — same as **kunggeri**

k'olke: Nepal

k'ose: a figured textile woven from gold and silk threads on a gauze background

L ᠯ

la li akū: lacking energy, out of sorts

la li sembi: capable, adept

la li seme: **1**. quick-witted, sharp; **2**. neatly, efficiently

    la li seme akū: slow, slow-witted, desultory, lethargic

la tai: a candleholder

la žeo: cured meat

la žu yali: smoked meat; cf. **la žeo**

lab seme: with the mouth packed full

laba: a horn; cf. **buleri**

labarhūn: face upward, on one's back, lying supine

labari: **1**. a large wooden cup for liquor; **2**. canopy over an image of the Buddha

labdahūn: hanging down, drooping

    labdahūn suduli i fukjingga hergen: (倒薤篆) a style of calligraphy

labdarambi: to hang down

labdu: **1**. many, much; **2**. wide, extensive (said of learning)

    labdu erecuke: quite hopeful

labdukan: rather a lot, rather many

labdulambi: to increase, to make more

labdungge: much, many

labi: **1**. diaper; **2**. protective curtain for defense against arrows on warships and battle wagons

labsa: **1**. greatly, substantially; **2**. difficult to obtain, rare; **3**. disappointed

    labsa bahara jaka: a rare item, something difficult to obtain

    labsa ekiyehe: considerably diminished

    labsa oho: become disappointed

labsambi: to fall in large flakes (said of snow), to rain in large drops

labsan: snowflake, raindrop

labsari ilha: the name of a snow-white flower

labsimbi: **1**. to become soiled all over, to become covered with sores; **2**. to speak foolishly; **3**. to gulp down, to devour

    labsime jembi: to gulp down food

labsitambi: to speak uninterrupted nonsense

labta labta: in tatters, in rags

lacadambi: to apply a lacquer seal

    lacadaha bithe: letter sealed with lacquer

ladu: a round quiver made of pigskin

ladurambi: to scuffle, to pull at one another when quarreling, to drag back and forth

lafihiyan: stupid, clumsy, awkward

lafu sogi: *Brassica sinensis*: Chinese cabbage

lagu: **1**. a kind of small frog, smaller than the **hasima** (used as bait on bird traps); **2**. a kind of beetle

    lagu yoo: a large sore on the hand

laha: **1**. straw mixed with mortar (used for making walls); **2**. catfish

lahari: a kind of small oak

lahin: complicated, troublesome

    lahin tabumbi: to involve in a troublesome matter

    lahin taha: got involved in a troublesome matter, became burdened with

lahū: **1**. not adept, unskilled (especially at hunting and dealing with livestock); **2**. scoundrel, hoodlum

lahūta: a kind of small, rather incompetent hawk

lahūtan ilga: ⟶ **hosan ilha**

lai coko: bustard

laidabumbi: (causative or passive of **laidambi**)

laidakū: **1**. lapwing, peewit; **2**. mischievous, ill-behaved, self-willed (children); **3**. shameless

    laidakū jui: scoundrel, rascal

laidambi: **1**. to welsh, to refuse to recognize one's debts or promises, to disavow; **2**. to blame someone else for one's own errors; **3**. to be mischievous, to be self-willed

laifa: a kind of small wild bean suitable for horse's fodder, vetch

laifan: ⟶ **laifa**

laifarambi: (-ka) to collapse (from exhaustion), to wither and fall (said of flowers)

laihū: **1**. a person who repudiates his debts or promises, a person who blames others for his own mistakes, shameless, unreliable; **2**. a self-willed child, a mischievous child

    laihū jui: profligate, undependable rascal

laihūdambi: to refuse to recognize one's debts or deeds, to be obstinate

laihūn: an undependable person, a good-for-nothing, a rogue

laihūšambi: **1**. to behave like a good-for-nothing, to act like a rogue; **2**. to be self-willed and obstinate (said of children)

laihūwa: ⟶ **laihū**

laju: clumsy, awkward, heavy, cumbersome, unwieldy

    laju ujen: clumsy, awkward

lajukan: rather clumsy, rather cumbersome

lak: convenient, appropriate

    lak akū: inconvenient, inappropriate, not right, ill at ease, unhappy

    lak lik seme: clever, adroit, capable

    lak oho: appropriate, just right

    lak se: Quickly!, Hurry up.

    lak seme: just right, right on the nose, it happened that …

    lak seme akū: inappropriate, not proper

lakacan nisiha: eelpout, burbot

lakca nimaha: the name of a large-bellied sea fish with a head resembling the catfish (has an unusually large liver)

lakcabumbi: (causative of **lakcambi**)

lakcambi: **1**. to break off (intransitive verb), to snap; **2**. to come to an end; **3**. to be outstanding; **4**. to be remote

    lakcafi colgorokū: preeminent, excelling

    lakcafi encu: totally different, vastly different

    lakcaha: superb, excellent

    lakcaha jecen: remote region, distant area

    lakcame: (adv.) extremely, most

    lakcarakū: ceaselessly, without end

lakcan: interruption, breaking off, pause

    lakcan akū: uninterrupted

    lakcan i sirabun: one of the six yang tones

lakcashūn: broken off, interrupted

lakda: simple, foolish; cf. **lokdo lakda**

    lakda likdi: drooping, hanging down

lakdahūn: drooping, hanging down

    lakdahūn tuheke: fell into a drooping position

lakdahūri: fully drooping, hanging all the way down

lakdari: just then, all of a sudden (caught or grasped)

    lakdari nambuha: grabbed all of a sudden

    lakdari taha: suddenly caught in a trap or net

lakdarilambi: to happen all of a sudden, to occur just at the right time

lakdaršambi: to hang down, to droop

lakiyabumbi: **1**. (causative or passive of **lakiyambi**); **2**. to be in need, to be hard-pressed, to be in difficult straits

lakiyaha: ⟶ **lakiyambi** (subheading)

lakiyakū: rod for hanging things

    lakiyakū hacuhan: a hanging pot

lakiyambi: to hang, to let hang, to hang up, to suspend

    lakiyaha ulmengge fukjingga hergen: (懸針篆) a style of calligraphy

lakiyan: **1**. a string of cash; **2**. hanging, suspension

lakiyangga: hanging, suspended

    lakiyangga hangse: noodles that are hung out to dry

    lakiyangga huwejehen: a screen that is hung on the wall

lakiyanjimbi: to come to hang

lakiyari monio: spider monkey

laku: thick padded cotton trousers

lakū: ⟶ **lahū**

lala: **1**. end, last, final, last throw with the **gacuha**; **2**. cooked glutinous millet or rice

    lala buda: steamed glutinous millet or rice

    lala dube: final, last

    lala dube isinjimbi: to arrive last

    lala juhe efen: four-cornered dumplings made of glutinous rice wrapped in rush or bamboo leaves and boiled

lalaha: soft, weak

lalahūn: soft, lithe, supple (said of cloth)

lalakai: mushy, pulpy

lalanji: **1**. very soft, mushy, pulpy, tender; **2.** exhausted, spent; **3.** repeatedly; **4.** very

lalanji henduhe: said repeatedly

lalanji heperembi: to get very drunk

lalanji oho: **1**. became overcooked; **2.** became exhausted; **3.** become very drunk

lalanji soktombi: to become dead drunk

lalanju: ⟶ **lalanji**

lali: spry, lively, brisk, quick, nimble, dexterous, agile

lali akū: lacking agility, slow, desultory

lali seme: quickly, agilely

lalibumbi: (causative of **lalimbi**)

lalimbi: **1**. to be soft, tender, pulpy; **2.** to be weakened from hunger

lalin: open, direct, straightforward

lalin dacun: sensitive, keen, acute

laluri dudu: the name of a green turtle dove with heavy plumage, same as **ilhuru dudu**

lama: **1**. lama, monk; **2.** Catholic or Russian Orthodox priest

lama niyehe: in older Manchu used for **anngir niyehe** and later used for **ijifun niyehe**

lama tacihiyan: lamaism

lamasai tehe juktehen: lamaist temple

lampa: chaos, disorder, chaotic, disordered

lampa i fon: primeval chaos

lampalambi: to be mixed up, to be chaotic

lampangga: desolate, primitive

lamu: indigo

lamu orho: indigo plant

lamudai: ⟶ **garunggū**

lamukan: light blue, bluish

lamuke: *Cyanosylvia svecica*: Eastern red-spotted bluethroat

lamun: blue

lamun bojiri ilha: *Callistephus chinensis*: China aster

lamun cecike ilha: an exotic blue flower that resembles a small bird

lamun funggala: (藍羽侍衛) Junior Bodyguard (wearing the Blue Feather), *BH* 99

lamun funggala be boro de hadambi: to attach a blue feather to a summer hat

lamun garudai: a blue phoenix

lamun gūsai falga: (藍旗甲) Office for the Blue Banners in the Board of War

lamun gūwasihiya: *Ardea cinerea*: Eastern gray heron

lamun hoohan: ⟶ **lamun gūwasihiya**

lamun lahūta: a black kite, a black vulture

lamun muheliyengge gu: a flat piece of blue jade with a hole in the center (used in sacrifices to heaven)

lamun narhūngga holbonggo hoošan: a kind of blue paper used for mounting things

lamun samsu: a kind of fine blue linen

lamun ulgiyan cecike: *Halcyon pileata*: black-capped kingfisher

lamurcan: a bird that resembles the crane (over three Chinese feet tall and is raised in gardens)

lamurhan: a name for the heron

lan: **1**. indigo; cf. **lamu**; **2.** Chinese orchid; ⟶ **lan ilha**

lan diyan hūwa ilga: indigo flower

lan gaimbi: to attest, to base oneself on good evidence

lan ilha: *Cymbidium goeringii*: Chinese spring orchid

lan orho: indigo plant; cf. **lamu orho**

lang giyūn: young man, young gentleman

lang lang seme: (eating) with the mouth stuffed full

langca: garnet

langgabumbi: **1**. (causative or passive of **langgambi**); **2.** to be down and out

langgabume oitobumbi: to be down on one's luck

langgambi: to be detained, to be held up, to be impeded, to be stranded away from home, to be delayed

langgašambi: to be indecisive

langgū: pumpkin

langju: one ten-millionth (of a Chinese foot)

langka: the flower of reeds or rushes, florescence of reeds

langlai: dung beetle

langse: dirty, unclean

langse gisun: filthy language, obscenity

langse moo: the horizontal wooden supports at both ends of a wagon or sedan chair

langsedambi: to act or speak in a dirty manner, to be dirty

langsedame toombi: to revile using obscenities

langtanambi: to have a large head, to be thick or heavy at one extremity

langtangga: ⟶ **langtungga**

langtu: a large double-headed hammer for use on iron

langtulambi: to hit with a double-headed hammer

langtungga: large-headed

langtušambi: to beat with a two-headed hammer

lar lir seme: **1**. profuse, abundant; **2**. sticky

lar seme: **1**. talkative, long-winded; **2**. sticky, viscous, gluey

lar seme dalhūn: viscous and sticky

larbahūn: weary, worn out, weak and limp

largikan: rather profuse

largin: **1**. profuse, abundant, complicated; **2**. annoying

largin facuhūn: confused, jumbled

largin geren: various, of every sort

largin labdu: various, multifarious

largin lampa: complex, intricate

largin mangga: troublesome, convoluted, entangled

largin subsi: confused, chaotic, complicated but trivial, convoluted

largišambi: to act in a diffuse, complicated way

largišame gisurembi: to speak in a confused, complicated manner

larhūn: *Ipomoea batata*: sweet potato

larin: a name for the donkey

larsen: soggy, doughy, pulpy, cooked too soft

larsenda: *Dioscorea japonica*: Chinese yam

larturi: *Menispermum dauricum*: moonseed

lasan: a consolation toss in playing with **gacuha**

lasari: hanging so as to form a canopy (said of leaves and branches)

lasari moo: a tree with thick drooping branches

lasari šufatu: an ancient-style hat with tassels hanging in back

lasarinambi: to hang down (said of branches)

lasha: **1**. asunder, into sections, in two, into pieces; **2**. decidedly, definitely

lasha genehe: broke in two

lasha lasha: in sections, asunder, in two

lasha obumbi: to break off, to make a break with

lasha sarkū: do not know at all

lashajambi: to break off, to break in two (intransitive verb)

lashalabumbi: **1**. (causative of **lashalambi**); **2**. to cut off, to terminate

lashalambi: **1**. to break off, to break in two (transitive verb); **2**. to terminate; **3**. to make a decision, to act decisively

lashalame icihiyambi: to manage decisively

lashalan: cutting off, decision

lashangga jahūdai: a boat used in rapids or shallows

lashatai: decisively, decidedly, definitely

lasihibumbi: (causative or passive of **lasihimbi**)

lasihidabumbi: (causative or passive of **lasihidambi**)

lasihidambi: **1**. to shake hard, to shake off; **2**. to toss to and fro, to rock, to sway, to wobble

lasihikū: **1**. thongs with balls at the end that are attached to a drum and that strike the drum when shaken; **2**. a weapon consisting of a pole with a shorter pole attached to its end by a chain, a flail

lasihikū tungken: a hand drum with attached thongs that have balls at the ends

lasihimbi: **1**. to shake, to toss around, to brandish; **2**. to write the cursive script; **3**. to parry, to fend off

lasihime arambi: to write the cursive script

lasihire hergen: grass script — the most cursive of the Chinese scripts

lasihire jangkū: a sword with a very long handle (more like a spear with a long curved blade)

lasiri: ⟶ **lasari**

lata: **1**. slow; **2**. dull, not clever

lata jata: untalented, not up to par

lata moyo: slow, dull-witted

lata moyo erdemu akū: dull-witted and untalented

latai: a candlestand

latakan: rather slow, rather dull

latihi: torn piece of a mat

latubuha: ⟶ **latubumbi** (subheading)

latubukū: a sticky pole used for catching birds

latubumbi: **1**. (causative or passive of **latumbi**); **2**. to be seduced or raped

latubuha afaha: a page pasted to the back of a document

latukū sogi: a wild plant with yellow flowers and prickly leaves that can be cooked and eaten — similar to **hūrga sogi**

latumbi: **1**. to adhere, to stick to; **2**. to be attached; **3**. to have an illicit affair with, to commit adultery; **4**. to become dirty, to become stained, to become greasy; **5**. to be contagious, to be infectious; **6**. to be near, to come near; **7**. to incite, to provoke

latunambi: **1**. to go near, to approach; **2**. to go to commit an illicit sexual act; **3**. to go to incite, to go to provoke

latungga: **1**. sticky, adhesive; **2**. fond of interfering, fond of causing dissension, fond of butting into other people's business

latunjimbi: **1**. to come near, to approach; **2**. to come to commit an illicit sexual act; **3**. to come to provoke

layabumbi: (causative of **layambi**)

layambi: (**-ka**) to wilt, to wither

le la seme: (going) all together, coming and going all together

leb seme: unexpectedly, spontaneously

lebdehun: **1**. lacking energy, sluggish; **2**. slow-witted, thick-headed, lacking talent

lebderembi: (**-ke**) **1**. to be sluggish, to be out of energy; **2**. to go limp, to droop (said of birds' wings)

lebenggi: swampy, marshy, damp, muddy

    lebenggi ba: marsh, swamp

    lebenggi lifakū: muddy, miry, swampy

    lebenggi usin: muddy field, field in a swampy area

lebkidembi: ⟶ **lekidembi**

ledehun: ⟶ **letehun**

leder seme: slow (said of a flying object)

    leder seme deyembi: to fly slowly

ledurembi: to beat up on someone (said of a group)

lefu: bear

    lefu i fiyahan: bear's paw (a culinary delicacy)

    lefu šan: *Senecio integrifolius*: a kind of groundsel

lehebumbi: (causative of **lehembi**)

lehele: **1**. whore, procuress; **2**. illegitimate, born of a whore, bastard

    lehele jui: bastard, child of a whore

    lehele mama: mistress of a brothel

lehembi: **1**. to remain unsatisfied after obtaining something; **2**. to continue to complain after some matter is concluded; **3**. to go back on one's word

lehendumbi: to complain together; also **lehenumbi**

lehenumbi: to complain together; also **lehendumbi**

lejirhi: a name for the wildcat; cf. **ujirhi**

lekcehun: ⟶ **lekdehun**

lekde lakda: **1**. hanging in shreds or rags; **2**. hanging like fruit on a plant; **3**. following closely behind

lekdedembi: ⟶ **lekderembi**

lekdehun: hanging down and screening something

    lekdehun dalibumbi: to hang down and screen something

lekderembi: (**-ke**) to have an unkempt or dirty appearance, to hang in disarray, to be disheveled

lekderi: disheveled, shaggy

    lekderi niongniyaha: a name for the wild goose; cf. jurgangga gasha, **kenderhen niongniyaha**

    lekderi niyehe: a name for the wild duck

leke: **1**. a whetstone, a grinding stone; **2**. a kind of honey pastry made in the form of a whetstone

lekebumbi: (causative of **lekembi**)

lekedembi: ⟶ **lekidembi**

lekembi: to sharpen, to grind on a whetstone

lekerhi: **1**. *Latax lutris*: sea otter; **2**. otter skin

lekerhin: a seal (animal)

lekeri: **1**. a spiral shell used as a horn; **2**. ⟶ **lekerhin**

leketembi: ⟶ **lekidembi**

lekidembi: to wave one's hands over the head while dancing, to wave one's hands and feet while wrestling

leksei: all together, in unison

leli: **1**. extensive, vast, wide; **2**. protective armor for the chest

    leli amba: vast

lemban: ⟶ **lempen**

lempen: **1**. a tent of rush mats used as a sunshade, awning; **2**. a protective shelter of rush mats for cattle, cow shed

lempi: prematurely gray, having white hairs among the black

lempinembi: to turn prematurely gray, to get white hairs among the black

len: immense, strong and big

    len coko: a name for the chicken; cf. **kemuri coko**

lenggeri: a kind of large rat

lenggetu: the name of a ceremonial hat of the Xia dynasty

lengken: rather big and strong

lenglen langlan seme: sloppy, careless, slovenly

lengseki: awkward, clumsy, lacking in agility, coarse

lengsenggi: ⟶ **lengseki**

lengtenembi: to be crude or awkward

leo: basket

leodz: basket

leolebumbi: (causative of **leolembi**)

lcolcccmbi: to discuss together

leolembi: to discuss, to talk over

leolen: discussion, disputation, principle, theory

leolendumbi: to discuss together, to talk over; also **leolenumbi**

leolenumbi: to discuss together, to talk over; also **leolendumbi**

leombi: (**-ha**) to perform feats of military prowess on horseback in front of enemy troops in order to frighten them

leose: multistoried building, tower, building

ler biyar seme: walking slowly

ler lar seme: **1**. fluttering; **2**. luxuriant; **3**. leisurely, slowly

ler ler seme: **1**. walking slowly, sauntering; **2**. serious, upright; **3**. friendly, amiable

ler seme: **1**. imposing, impressive; **2**. luxuriant, profuse (said of vegetation); **3**. agilely, gracefully, gently, lightly, flittingly; **4**. relieved

    ler seme agambi: to rain a fine rain

    ler seme banjihabi: grows profusely

    ler seme dambi: to blow gently (said of the wind)

lergin: ⟶ **lergiyen**

lergiyen: broad-minded, magnanimous

leserembi: (**-ke**) to ripple, to form ripples

lesumbi: **1**. to go at a fast trot; **2**. to skim the earth (said of birds)

    lesume šodome: galloping without stopping

lete lata: **1**. heavy (said of a load); **2**. lagging behind and trying to catch up

letehun: large or wide at the top

letuhun: ⟶ **letehun**

leyecun: ballad

leyembi: to sing without accompaniment

li: one thousandth (of a Chinese foot), one thousandth of a tael; cf. **eli**

li jy: litchi; cf. **mase muyari**

lib seme: right through, piercing (said of a spear thrown at an animal)

libki: **1**. a worn-out horse, a horse that has been beaten with a whip; **2**. scorching hot, sweltering (weather)

libkimbi: (**-ha**) to be worn-out (said of horses)

libu: one billionth (of a Chinese foot)

licise: the name of an exotic fruit that resembles a crossbow projectile

lidu: *Phaseolus mungo*: mung bean

    lidu fungse: mung bean flour

lifa: deep (into), penetrating

    lifa daha: penetrated deeply (said of an arrow)

    lifa dosika: penetrated deeply

    lifa gidalaha: pierced deeply

lifabumbi: (causative or passive of **lifambi**)

lifadambi: to sink slightly (into mud or mire)

lifagan: ⟶ **lifahan**

lifahan: mud, muck, mire, slime, muddy, miry

    lifahan cifahan: mud and slime

lifahanambi: to become muddy

lifakū: swamp, morass, swampy, muddy

lifambi: **1**. to become muddy, to be muddy; **2**. to sink into mud, to get bogged down

    lifame irumbi: to sink into mud

lifan: **1**. a stone or wooden vessel used to catch oil and wine from a press; **2**. one of the eight trigrams of the *Yijing* (representing heaven)

lilci: down, downward

    lilci tuheke: fell downward

limu: (吏目); ⟶ **icihiyasi**

ling: finger games

    ling deribumbi: play finger games (while drinking)

    ling yabumbi: ⟶ **ling deribumbi**

ling pai: tally with a charm written on it (used by Daoist priests)

ling seme: heavy, burdensome

lingdan: a miraculous medicine, an elixir

lingge: a shining deed, a glorious deed

lingjy: *Fomes japonicus*: a kind of auspicious fungus

lingse: **1**. a kind of thin satin-like material, damask; **2**. collar

lingsika: a name for the tiger

lio hūwang: sulphur; cf. **hurku**

lio kio gurun i kuren: (琉球館) an establishment for taking care of Ryukyuan emissaries

lio sing usiha: meteor

lioho: a white-striped sea fish

liohūwang: ⟶ **lio hūwang**

lir liyar seme: smooth and sticky (like a good paste)

lirha: (柳) a constellation, the 24th of the lunar mansions, made up of eight stars in Hydra

    lirha tokdonggo kiru: a banner depicting the constellation **lirha**

liyan dz: lotus seed

liyanse: curtain

liyar seme: thin and sticky (said of phlegm, glue, or paste), slimy

liyase: a hanging, a curtain or drape

liyeliyebumbi: (causative of **liyeliyembi**)

liyeliyefi: ⟶ **liyeliyembi** (subheading)

liyeliyehun: dizzy, faint, delirious

liyeliyembi: to become dizzy, to become faint, to be dazed and confused, to become delirious

    liyeliyefi tuhembi: to faint

liyeliyen ilha: a purple flower whose odor causes faintness

liyeliyendumbi: to become faint together; also **liyeliyenumbi**

liyeliyenumbi: to become faint together; also **liyeliyendumbi**

liyeliyešembi: to be (constantly) faint, to be very dizzy, to become confused

liyoliyo: an interjection of derision used toward untalented, worthless people

liyoo: fodder, forage

    liyoo orho: fodder

liyor seme: **1**. exhausted, without strength; **2**. soft, yielding

lo: **1**. cymbal, gong; **2**. silk gauze, crêpe

    lo suje: a very thin, light silk gauze for autumn clothing

lo ca: *rakša*, a demon in Hindu mythology

lo han: an arhat

lo la seme: unexpectedly, all of a sudden

lob seme: suddenly dark

lobi: gluttonous, ravenous

    lobi hutu: the ghost of an evil person who can never satisfy his hunger or thirst, Sanskrit preta

lobin: ⟶ **lobi**

loca: ⟶ **lo ca**

lodan: the anklebone of a cow or sheep (used in a dice-like game); cf. **gacuha**

lodur seme: ⟶ **ludur seme**

loho: sword

    loho usiha: ⟶ **lohū usiha**

lohobumbi: to be in dire straits, to be down and out

lohū usiha: the unlucky star Rahu — υ in the constellation Pegasus

lok seme: suddenly, unexpectedly

lokdi: dense, thick

lokdo lakda: clumsy, awkward

lokdohon: sitting alone, alone and quiet

lokdori: unexpectedly, in an unforeseen manner

lokseme: ⟶ **lok seme**

loksimbi: to speak foolishly or crazily

loksin: foolishness, nonsense

loksinambi: to become pudgy, to become obese

loksobumbi: to be despondent, to be depressed or dejected

lokson: vexation, annoyance (at being teased)

loktohon: ⟶ **lokdohon**

loktorombi: (-ko) to sit alone

loli fodoho: *Salix babylonica*: weeping willow

loli fulana ilha: *Pyrus spectabilis*: a crabapple with hanging branches

lolo: the anklebone of a pig (used as a die)

lolo seme: boasting idly, chattering foolishly

lomi: rice kept in storage for a number of years — the same as **hukšeri bele**

lomikte: a pale yellow gem resembling the cat's-eye

long long seme: ⟶ **long seme**

long seme: talking foolishly, speaking nonsense

longko: a cooking pot made of bronze or copper

longkon: a gong or cymbal

longsikū: **1**. a person who chatters on and on; **2**. indiscrete in speech, talking nonsense

longsimbi: to chatter on and on, to talk foolishness

longto: halter, headstall

longtolobumbi: (causative of **longtolombi**)

longtolombi: to wear a halter or headstall

longtu: ⟶ **longto**

loo: **1**. prison; **2**. gong; cf. **lo**
    loo be tuwakiyara niyalma: jailer; cf. **loo dz**
    loo de horimbi: to jail, to imprison
    loo dz: jailer
loo loo: maternal grandmother
loo niyang: old lady, lady of the household
loo siyan šeng: old man, old gentleman
loodan: **1**. old female role in Chinese opera; **2**.
    ⟶ **lodan**
loombi: to bark or growl fiercely
loomi: ⟶ **lomi**
    loomi bele: rice that has been stored for a long
      time
looye: **1**. master of the household; **2**. master, lord
looyese: (plural of **looye**)
lor seme: speaking incessantly, talkative
lorbodo: three-year-old deer
lorin: mule
losa: ⟶ **lorin**
lose: ⟶ **lorin**
loshan: a basket woven from willow branches and
    used for carrying preserved vegetables; cf.
    šangšaha
loso: slushy, muddy (refers especially to the spring
    when the fields are still too muddy to plow)
lostu jahūdai: a small, wide river boat with low
    sides
lu la seme: unexpectedly
lu lu seme: ⟶ **lulu seme**
lu nimaha: a kind of perch; ⟶ **sahamha**
lu šui muke: brine in which bean curd is prepared
ludahūn: (數) a constellation, the 16th of the lunar
    mansions, made up of three stars (β, γ, α)
    in Aries
    ludahūn tokdonggo kiru: a banner depicting
      the constellation **ludahūn**
ludun: a reed basket for grain
ludur seme: thick and sticky (said of liquids)
    ludur seme halhūn: sticky hot
ludz: oven, stove
lugiya hengke: *Momordica charantia*: bitter melon
luhu: a headless arrow with a dull point resembling
    a pestle (used for shooting sitting birds and
    for target practice)
    luhu cecike: one of the names of the snipe; cf.
      karka cecike
luhulebumbi: (causative of **luhulembi**)
luhulembi: to shoot a headless arrow (**luhu**)

lujen: an Imperial coach
luju: one hundred-millionth
lujuri: pelt of a black fox
    lujuri dobi: black fox
luk seme: strongly, intensely, thickly, in
    considerable quantity, densely
    luk seme dushun: intensely dark
    luk seme farhūn: pitch dark, dark as night
    luk seme halhūn: hot and windless
    luk seme talmaka: a thick fog has descended
    luk sere talman: dense fog
luka: the young of the lynx; cf. **silun**
lukderembi: ⟶ **lukdurembi**
lukdu: dense
    lukdu lakda: wobbling, flopping about, flabby,
      pudgy
    lukdu lukdu: lush, dense (said of plants)
lukduhun: ruffled, disheveled (said of the feathers
    on sick birds)
lukdurembi: (**-ke**) to become ruffled or disheveled
    (said of the feathers on birds)
luksimbi: to throb (said of a festered wound or
    sore), to be unable to sit still
luku: **1**. thick, dense (said of hair and plants); **2**.
    caterpillar
    luku fisin: (of vegetation) lush, dense, luxuriant
    luku umiyaha: caterpillar
lukuken: rather thick, rather dense
lulu: ordinary, common, average (said of ability)
    lulu lala: muddled, illogical
    lulu seme: ordinary, average
    lulu seme wajimbi: to die in obscurity
lumbabumbi: (causative or passive of **lumbambi**)
lumbambi: to smear with glue or paste
lumbanambi: to become covered with dirt or mud
lumbimbi: (**-ha**); ⟶ **lumbambi**
lumbu: suddenly flowing slowly (said of a place in a
    stream)
    lumbu muke: slow-flowing water
    lumbu oho: suddenly became slow-flowing
lumbur: flowing slowly
lumburjambi: **1**. to be soft, not firm (said of wet
    earth); **2**. to flow slowly
lung seme: ⟶ **luk seme**
lunggu: a male sable; cf. **seke**
lur seme: thick, viscous, concentrated
lurgiken: rather rough (said of the voice)
lurgin: rough, coarse (said of the voice), gruff

lurgišembi: to change (said of an adolescent's voice), to be rough (said of the voice)

lurgiyen: ⟶ **lurgin**

luse: stove

lushun: tired, weary

lusu šobin: a pastry with walnut filling

lusumbi: (**-ke**) to become tired, to become weary

luši: (錄事) Secretary in a Board, of the eighth or ninth rank

luwan: the male of a colorful phoenix-like bird that was considered a symbol of concord between Prince and minister as well as between husband and wife

luwanggon: small bells on the bits of horses that drew the Imperial coach

M ᠮ

ma: here! (said when handing something to another person)

mabu: a cloth for wiping off objects

mabulabumbi: (causative of **mabulambi**)

mabulakū: mop, swab (a rag attached to a pole used for wiping the floor)

mabulambi: to wipe, to wipe off, to mop

maca: a bitter-tasting wild plant resembling garlic

    maca duha: large intestine of horses, donkeys, and mules

maci: an iron ring on the crupper of beasts of burden

macibumbi: (causative of **macimbi**)

maciha: ⟶ **macika**

macihi: the observation of the Buddhist commandments

    macihi jafambi: to meditate and observe the Buddhist commandments

macika: border or edge of a mat or net

    macika arambi: to weave the rope border of a hunting or fishing net

macimbi: **1**. when patching a garment, to gather the edges of the patch on the inside while smoothing out the outside surface; **2**. to lay squares of grass to form a lawn

macumbi: to become thin, skinny

madabumbi: **1**. (causative of **madambi**); **2**. to cause to rise (said of dough); **3**. to grow (said of interest)

madaga: ⟶ **madagan**

madagan: interest (on money)

madage: an affectionate expression used while patting an old person or child on the back

madambi: **1**. to expand, to swell, to grow (said of interest); **2**. to stand on end (said of hair)

madangga: fluffy, puffy

madari: a large beast

    madari uju: an animal head made of bronze with a ring in its mouth (attached to a door to facilitate opening and closing)

madasu: leaven, fermenting agent

madiyoo: mah-jongg tiles; cf. **sasuri**

mafa: (paternal) grandfather, ancestor, old man

mafangge: having a grandfather or ancestor

mafari: (plural of **mafa**)

    mafari miyoo: ancestral temple

    mafari soorin: ancestral tablets

mafuta: **1**. a buck deer, stag; **2**. rope made of hemp

    mafuta buhū: a buck deer

mager: a wild plant with edible roots — the white variety is known as **šanggiyan selbete**, the red variety as **monggo sedo**

magi: ⟶ **maki**

mahala: **1**. hat, cap — especially the round fur winter hat of Manchu officials; **2**. target

    mahala delbin: brim of a hat

    mahala elbeku: a cover for a hat (used when raining)

    mahala gaha: a crow with a large body and a white head

    mahala goiha: hit the target

    mahala ihan: a cow with head and body of different colors — usually black and white

    mahala maktame tuwambi: to look upward

    mahala tukiyeku: a hat rack

mahalalambi: to wear a hat

    mahalalaha asita: a young man entering adulthood

mahatu: **1**. hat worn in ancient times by high officials and nobles; **2**. hat worn by the Emperor, crown

mahatun: a hat of ancient times

mahila: stalk, stem

mahū: **1**. a (devil) mask; **2**. a leather hood covering the head, neck, and shoulders

mahūlabumbi: (causative or passive of **mahūlambi**)

mahūlambi: **1**. to wipe out, to strike out (errors when writing), to erase; **2**. to humiliate, to disgrace; **3**. to wear a hood

mahūntu: another name for the large black monkey called **elintu**

maidari: Maitreya, the coming Buddha

maifaraha: a motherless child

maigu: deaf; cf. **dutu**

maikan: tent

mailaci: *Iris ensata*: water iris

mailambi: to get infected

mailan: *Iris pallasii*: Chinese small iris

    mailan i use: the seeds of *Iris pallasii*

mailaru: 'Won't you get infected please!' (an oath)

mailasun: arbor vitae, cypress

maimadambi: to walk weaving from side to side, to stagger

maiman: business, trade; cf. **hūda**

    maiman arambi: to engage in business, to do business

    maiman tinggin: trading outpost

maimašambi: to do business

maise: wheat

    maise efen: steamed bun made from wheat flour

    maise ufa: wheat flour

    maise urembi: 'wheat ripens,' the ninth solar term — June fifth, sixth, or seventh

    maisei wekji suse: wheat husk, chaff from wheat

maisha: ⟶ **maishan**

maishan: **1**. a decorative clasp on the crupper of beasts of burden; **2**. wolfberry (*Fructus lyeii*); **3**. bitter willow; cf. **maishan moo**

    maishan halu: a meal made from the fruit of the wolfberry

    maishan halu i sacima: a pastry made from sesame and the fruit of the wolfberry

    maishan moo: *Salix sinopurpurea*: bitter willow

maisiri: a club held in one hand (a kind of weapon)

maitu: a pole heavier at one end than the other (a weapon), mace

maitulambi: to hit with a pole or club

maitun da: a pea-like plant with an edible root that secretes a white juice

maitušabumbi: (causative or passive of **maitušambi**)

maitušambi: to beat with a pole

majan: a long arrow with a long narrow head used for fighting

majige: **1**. a little, a little bit; **2**. somewhat, about

    majige andande: short while

    majige endebuku: somewhat of an error, a trifling error

    majige ome: in a short while

maka: an introductory particle of doubt or questioning: I wonder … , could it really be that…?

makambi: to become muddled, to become confused in one's thinking

makarambi: to become feeble due to old age

    makarame sakdaka: became old and decrepit

maki: tassel on a banner, yak-tail pendant on a banner

makitu: a yak-tail banner

makjahūn: short, dwarf-like

makjan: short, midget, dwarf

    makjan niyalma: dwarf, midget

makjanambi: to be short, to be a midget

maksibumbi: (causative of **maksimbi**)

maksikū: dancer

    maksikū moo: a horizontal stick on a banner pole from which the banner hangs

maksimbi: **1**. to dance; **2**. to wave, to brandish (a weapon)

    maksire garudangga kiru: a banner on which a dancing phoenix is embroidered

maksin: a dance, dancing

maksinambi: to go to dance

maksinjimbi: to come to dance

maksisi: dancer

    maksisi mahatun: a hat worn by dancers in ancient times

maktabumbi: **1**. (causative or passive of **maktambi**); **2**. to get lost, to lose one's way, to be abandoned; **3**. to be prostrate with illness; **4**. to be blown ashore, to be tossed ashore

maktacuka: praiseworthy

maktacun: praise

maktambi: **1**. to throw, to toss; **2**. to throw a rider (said of a horse); **3**. to let loose, to release (a hawk); **4**. to praise, to extol; **5**. to act haughtily

maktandumbi: to throw together, to praise together; also **maktanumbi**

maktanjimbi: **1**. to come to throw; **2**. to come to praise

maktanumbi: to throw together, to praise together; also **maktandumbi**

maktašambi: to throw around, to toss about, to fling

mala: a wooden mallet

malahi: **1**. a striped yellow wild cat; **2**. sometimes used to mean 'rabbit'

malanggū: sesame

malanggū abdaha efen: thin sesame cakes used by the Manchus at offerings in the sixth month

malanggū cai: tea with sesame added

malanggū haksangga efen: baked wheat cakes garnished with sesame seeds

malanggū ira fisihe maise turi: the five grains: sesame, small grain glutinous millet, broomcorn millet, wheat, and beans

malanggū misun: sesame paste

malanggū nimenggi: sesame oil

malanggū šobin: baked wheat cakes covered with sesame seeds

malari: crowded, cluttered, disorderly; cf. **hūluri malari**

malašambi: to beat to death fish caught under ice

malfun cece: transparent cloth that has holes resembling sesame seeds

malhūkan: rather a lot, quite a few

malhūn: **1**. economical, frugal; **2**. seemingly near but really far, long and dull (road); **3**. thick at one end

malhūn yokcingga: modest and (still) good looking

malhūngga: **1**. frugal; **2**. sufficient for use; **3**. long and boring (said of a road)

malhūšabumbi: (causative of **malhūšambi**)

malhūšambi: to use frugally, to be sparing with, to save

malhūšame banjimbi: to live frugally

malhūšandumbi: to use together frugally; also **malhūšanumbi**

malhūšanumbi: to use together frugally; also **malhūšandumbi**

maljiha: an anklebone die (**gacuha**) polished on both sides

malta: name of a large sea mammal, possibly the white whale or dolphin

malta beri: a bow covered with water buffalo horn

maltakū: a tool for scraping dirt or mud

malu: a bottle (for liquor)

maluka: ⟶ **malukan**

malukan: abundant, in large quantities

mama: **1**. (paternal) grandmother, female ancestor, old lady; **2**. pocks, smallpox

mama eršembi: for pocks to appear, to get smallpox

mama ilha: pock

mama tucimbi: ⟶ **mama eršembi**

mama yadahūn: the pocks are few

maman: support for a rafter; cf. **bangtu**

mamarambi: ⟶ **namarambi**

mamari: (plural of **mama**)

mamfin: ⟶ **mampin**

mamgiyabumbi: (causative of **mamgiyambi**)

mamgiyakū: extravagant, lavish, wasteful, luxurious

mamgiyambi: to be extravagant, to squander, to dissipate

mamgiyame fayambi: to squander, to waste

mamgiyan: lavish, extravagant

mamgiyandumbi: to squander together, to spend lavishly together; also **mamgiyanumbi**

mamgiyanumbi: to squander together, to spend lavishly together; also **mamgiyandumbi**

mampi: ⟶ **mampin**

mampibumbi: (causative of **mampimbi**)

mampilambi: to tie a knot

mampimbi: to tie a knot, to knot

mampin: knot

mampingga ilha: the name of a pale yellow flower, *Edgeworthia chrysantha*, paper bush

mamugiya: *Malus prunifolia*: pear-leafed crabapple

mamuhan: used for ventilation, ventilating

mamuhan fa: a skylight

mamuhan sangga: ventilation hole in the wall of a house

mamuhan sihan: bamboo air pipe inserted for ventilation into grain in storage

mamuhan tura: a short pillar between the upper and lower beams of the ceiling

mamuke: a name for the rabbit

mamun akū: listless, dejected, depressed, without any enthusiasm left

mamyari: an exotic fruit from Tonkin and South China (from a tree that resembles the litchi)

man i niyalma: a southern aborigine

manabumbi: (causative or passive of **manambi**)

managa: diapers

managan: ⟶ **managa**

manaha: ⟶ **manambi** (subheading)

manambi: **1**. to be worn-out, to be tattered, to be old (not new); **2**. to be dispersed (troops); **3**. to come to an end, to wane, to diminish

    manaha biya: last month

    manaha sabu: worn-out shoe

    manaha šaniyaha: torn and tattered

manao: agate

manashūn: **1**. worn-out, old, tattered; **2**. waning, end, the month's end

manda: slow, late

mandakan: rather slow, a little slow

mandal: (a Buddhist term) the mandala

    mandal bolgomimbi: to purify the cult objects with incense and recite a portion of scripture (on the day of a religious service)

    mandal ilha: *Datura alba*: thorn apple flower

    mandal moo: *Datura stramonium*: thorn apple

mandalambi: to be slow, to be late

mandara: (a Buddhist term) the tree of paradise

mandarawa ilha: *Ficus carica*: fig bloom

mandubumbi: (causative of **mandumbi**)

mandumbi: to mature, to grow up

mang orho: *Miscanthus sinensis*: Chinese silver grass

    mang orho usenembi: one of the divisions of the solar year falling on June 7th or 8th

mangga: **1**. hard (not soft), difficult; **2**. expensive; **3**. expert at, strong in, capable; **4**. expertly made, well-crafted; **5**. strong, fierce, a strong man

    mangga aburi: vicious, brutal

    mangga arambi: to show off one's strength, to intimidate

    mangga beri: crossbow

    mangga beri cambi: to set oneself against, to oppose

    mangga bithe: a written amulet used by Daoists to expel evil

    mangga buda: pastry

    mangga cece: hard silk gauze

    mangga ceceri: a kind of hard, strong silk

    mangga doose: a skilled Daoist

    mangga fili: hard and fast

    mangga moo: oak, tree of the genus *Quercus*

    mangga moo i usiha: acorn

    mangga niyalma: a man of iron, a person of great integrity

    mangga niyecen: leather patch attached to the inner side of a boot's heel

    mangga tangga: tough, too hard to chew

    mangga tuwabungga hoošan: a kind of hard, thick poster paper

    mangga urse: capable people

manggaburu: causing difficulty to someone

    manggaburu ba: things that have caused difficulty to another person

manggai: merely, simply, no more than

    manggai oci: if worse comes to worst, if it is with difficulty, in extreme cases

manggakan: rather hard, difficult capable, etc.

manggalambi: to be difficult, to be serious (said of an illness), to worsen, to act in a hard or vigorous manner

    manggalaha nimeku: intractable illness

    manggalame: severely, with force

    manggalame maktabumbi: to become very serious (said of an illness)

    manggalame saimbi: to bite down hard

    manggalame tantambi: to beat severely

manggantu: good horse, steed

manggasa: (plural of **mangga**): strong men

manggašabumbi: (causative of **manggašambi**)

manggašacuka: difficult, embarrassing

manggašambi: **1**. to have difficulties, to be in an awkward position, to be in an embarrassing position; **2**. to be shy, to be hesitant

    manggašara ba: difficult matter, embarrassing circumstances

manggi: **1**. after (after the perfect participle or imperative); **2**. simply, no more than; cf. **manggai**; **3**.

    manggi ... geli ... both ... and ...

manggici: if worse comes to worst

manggir: (Mongolian) wild onion

manggisu: badger; cf. **dorgon**

manggiyan: **1**. nasal discharge from glanders in horses and livestock; **2**. a spirit that descends into a shaman who has invoked the tiger god, causing the shaman to dance

manggiyan weceku wasika: the spirit who causes the shaman to dance has descended

manggiyanambi: to produce nasal discharge (said of livestock with glanders)

manggo: ⟶ **manggao**

mangkan: sand dune

mangkan gūwara: another name for the **elben gūwara**

mangkara: a horse or dog with white hair on the head, eyes, and muzzle

mangkara gaha: **1**. white-headed crow; **2**. ⟶ **mahala gaha**

mani: prayer beads, rosary

mani tolombi: to pray using prayer beads

mani tolome genembi: to walk slowly

manja: tea used in ceremonial offerings in lamaist temples

manjiha: came late, came slowly

manju: Manchu

manju bithe: Manchu writing, Manchu text

manju dangse boo: (滿檔房) Record and Registry Office (also in charge of preparing Manchu documents), *BH* 379

manju gūsa: Manchu banner, general of a Manchu banner

manju hergen: Manchu script, Manchu letter (of the alphabet)

manju monggo bithe ubaliyambure boo: (滿州蒙古翻譯房) the Manchu and Mongolian translation Office of the Court of Colonial Affairs

manju wesimbure bithei ba: (滿本堂) Manchu Copying Office, *BH* 138

manjurabumbi: (causative of **manjurambi**)

manjurambi: **1**. to speak or write Manchu; **2**. to act like a Manchu, to behave in the Manchu manner

manjusa: (plural of **manju**)

manjusai mukūn hala be uheri ejehe bithe weilere kuren: (滿州民族通譜館) office concerned with Manchu genealogies

manjusiri: Mañjuśrī — the name of a bodhisattva

manoo: agate

mansui: brightly colored satin with golden cloud and dragon designs

mansui undurakū: ⟶ **mansui**

mantu: steamed bread, **mantou**

mantumbi: ⟶ **mandumbi**

maobin hoošan: a kind of paper made from bamboo pulp

maokala: a kind of hawk

marabumbi: (causative of **marambi**)

marakū: **1**. one who declines or rejects; **2**. an obstinate person

marambi: to decline, to reject, to turn down, to refuse

marandumbi: to refuse or to decline together; also **maranumbi**

maranumbi: to refuse or to decline together; also **marandumbi**

maratambi: to decline weakly, to refuse moderately

margan: the young of the roe deer

marhan: ⟶ **margan**

mari: time, occasion (same as **geri** and **mudan**)

mari nakū: in an instant

maribumbi: (causative of **marimbi**)

marimbi: **1**. to return, to go back, to turn around, to about-face; **2**. to fall off (said of pocks)

marimbu wehe: agate

marin: turning around, return, return trip

marma nisiha: a small red-spotted sea fish

maru: a school of fish; cf. **hingge**

marulambi: to form a school, to school (said of fish)

marutu cecike: *Lonchura punctulata*: spice finch

masakū: a swing hung from a rafter inside a building

masambi: to swing in a **masakū**

masan: the sediment of sesame seeds left after the oil has been extracted

masan dehe: a fishhook with a bait of sesame sediment

mase: **1**. pockmarks; **2**. a pockmarked person; cf. **kerkeri**

mase muyari: litchi

mase usiha: walnut

mase usiha i faha: the edible part of the walnut

maselakū: a snare for catching birds

masikan: weighty, robust

masilabumbi: (causative of **masilambi**)

masilambi: to exist in abundance, to strain one's powers, to do forcefully

masilame: in abundance, plentifully, forcefully, tightly (said of tying)

masilame hūwaitambi: to tie tightly

masilame jafambi: to hold on to tightly

masiri: an exotic fruit that tastes like walnut

maša: dipper, ladle

mašalakū: a piece of wood above a window with holes (in which the pivots of the casement turn)

mašan: support, handle, idea

   mašan bahambi: to obtain support, to get something to hold on to, to get an idea

   mašan baharakū: lacking something to hold onto

mašangga niyalma: a person who understands how to manage affairs well

matabumbi: (causative of **matambi**)

matalambi: to stamp the earth with the hind hoof, to kick with hind feet

matambi: to heat in order to bend (bone, horn, wood, bamboo, etc.)

matan: a kind of sweet food made from barley, malt candy

matangga: caved in (cheeks), sunken and pursed (lips)

   matangga wase: a ridge tile

matarakū: a round straw pad that is placed on the head for carrying things

matašambi: to dig up, to dig out, to dig with the claws

mateo: wharf, landing site

matun: a watch station on a city wall

maya: a dipper with a spout

mayabumbi: **1**. (causative of **mayambi**); **2**. to exorcise, to break a spell, to dispel, to eliminate

mayalambi: to carry on the forearm

mayambi: (-ka/-ha) to diminish, to subside, to go down (said of swelling), to calm down, to be freed from a spell

mayambumbi: ⟶ **mayabumbi**

mayan: **1**. lower arm (including wrist and elbow); **2**. cubit (a measure); **3**. blood from a wounded animal; **4**. good luck, good fortune

   mayan baha: 'obtained a kill', won at dice, was lucky, won at gambling

   mayan ehe: having an unsuccessful or unfavorable outcome

   mayan gaiha: encountered good luck, was lucky

   mayan sain: **1**. many animals were killed on the battue; **2**. smoothly, without a hitch, favorable, having a good outcome

   mayan tatabumbi: to hold back using the elbow

me: pulse, vein; cf. **sudala**

   me jafambi: to take the pulse

   me tuwambi: to check the pulse

mede: news, information, intelligence

   mede isibumbi: to deliver a message

medebumbi: to give news, to bring news

   medebure dengjan: a red lantern that was hoisted as a signal at certain intervals while the Emperor was traveling

medeci: messenger

medege: news, information

   medege gasha: seagull

   medege niyehe: ⟶ **medege gasha**

medegeri cecike: **1**. one name for the seagull; **2**. a bird that announces the arrival of guests by crying and flying

medehe: ⟶ **medege**

medergu ilha: *Rhododendron sinicum*

mederi: sea

   mederi angga: mouth of a river

   mederi dalan: seawall, breakwater

   mederi dalin: seashore, seaside

   mederi debembi: for a tidal wave to form

   mederi dorgon: sea otter; cf. **lekerhi**

   mederi eihen: seal; cf. **lekerhin**

   mederi gubci taifin necingge mudan: a piece of music played at great banquets while tea was brought in

   mederi hūlha: pirate

   mederi jaka: sea product, seafood

   mederi jakarame: along the seacoast

   mederi jakarame golo: maritime province

   mederi jugūn: sea route, seaway

   mederi juwere calu: a Beijing granary of the Board of Finance

   mederi katuri: sea crab (of the North China Sea)

   mederi kilahūn: seagull; cf. **medege gasha**

   mederi kiongguhe: the sea myna of Fujian

   mederi melkešembi: the sea produces a mirage

   mederi morin: **1**. beluga, white whale; **2**. seahorse

   mederi onggolo: seaport, bay

   mederi sampa: sea shrimp, prawn

   mederi ulhūma: a black sea bird resembling the pheasant

medesi: messenger

megu: mushroom; cf. **sence**

mehe: a spayed sow

> **mehe ulgiyan**: sow, female swine

mehejen: sow

mehele: ⟶ **mehejen**

> **mehele jui**: piglet, shote

mehen: a sow that has not yet farrowed

meheren: a sow that has given birth

mehete: having a short upper lip

mehubumbi: (causative of **mehumbi**)

mehumbi: to bow, to make a bow to, to bow down

mehun: ⟶ **mehen**

mei gui: rose (the flower)

mei ilha: *Prunus mume*: Chinese plum blossom

mei meni: individually; cf. **meni meni**

mei muke: the name of a sweet beverage

mei yaha: (fossil) coal

meifehe: slope of a hill

meifen: neck

> **meifen be gidaralame tasihimbi**: to press on the neck and kick the leg from the side (in wrestling)
>
> **meifen buktakabi**: got a crick in the neck
>
> **meifen dabali niyamniyambi**: to shoot at under the neck of a horse
>
> **meifen i šurden**: neck-ring used during sword play
>
> **meifen ikūhabi**: took fright

meihe: **1**. snake; **2**. the sixth of the earth's branches (巳)

> **meihe biya**: the fourth month
>
> **meihe bulunambi**: the snake is hibernating
>
> **meihe cecike**: the name of a small bird that has a long neck and a sharp tongue
>
> **meihe erin**: the period from 9 AM to 11 AM
>
> **meihe geleku**: castor-bean plant
>
> **meihe geleku i use**: castor bean
>
> **meihe giranggi**: Snake bones! (an oath)
>
> **meihe gūn halambi**: the snake changes its skin
>
> **meihe šari**: *Cichorium intybus*: endive, chicory
>
> **meihe yoo**: a red eruption on the skin

meiheguweleku: ⟶ **meihe geleku**

meihen singgeri: mongoose

meihengge: pertaining to the snake

> **meihengge aniya**: the year of the serpent

meiherebumbi: (causative of **meiherembi**)

meiherembi: to carry on the shoulder, to lift to the shoulder

> **meiherefi maktambi**: to lift to the shoulder and throw down (in wrestling)

meihetu: *Apterigia immaculata*: mud eel

> **meihetu hengke**: *Luffa cylindrica*: fiber melon, luffa

meijebumbi: **1**. (causative of **meijembi**); **2**. to shatter, to pulverize, to crush

meijembi: **1**. to shatter, to fragment, to break (intransitive verb); **2**. to become powder

meilebumbi: (causative of **meilembi**)

meilembi: to carve up, to dissect (a carcass), to cut off, to cut out (transitive verb)

meimeni: every one, severally, individually, respectively; ⟶ **meni meni**

meiren: **1**. shoulder, upper arm; **2**. on a battue, the two banners marching on both sides of the center; **3**. side-, vice-, sub-; **4**. the sides of a bow grip; **5**. the large beads on both ends of a Buddhist rosary

> **meiren adame**: shoulder to shoulder, side by side
>
> **meiren giranggi**: shoulder bone
>
> **meiren hiyahanjambi**: to cross one's arms
>
> **meiren i janggin**: (副都統) Lieutenant-General, *BH* 658

meirengge: having shoulders

meiretu: the shoulder piece of a suit of armor

meise: the fruit of *Prunus mume* (Japanese apricot)

meisile: pale yellow amber

meitebumbi: (causative of **meitembi**)

meitembi: to cut off, to cut in two, to excise, to sever, to reduce

mejige: news, information

> **mejige alambi**: to report news
>
> **mejige ba**: information point, place where news can be obtained
>
> **mejige gaimbi**: to collect information, to gather news

mejigelebumbi: (causative of **mejigelembi**)

mejigelembi: to make inquiries, to seek information, to look for news

mejigešembi: to make repeated inquiries

mejin cecike: a long-tailed bird with a black neck and back whose cry announces good luck

mekcerembi: to bend forward, to incline the shoulders forward

mekcerefi ilihabi: stands bent forward

mekceršembi: to bend very far forward

meke: the side of a **gacuha** without a hole

meke ceke tuwambi: to see who is better, to compete

mekele: in vain, vainly, emptily, merely

mekeni: mouth harp

mekenimbi: to play the mouth harp

mekeniyen: ⟶ **mekeni**

mekerebumbi: (causative of **mekerembi**)

mekerembi: to be decrepit, to be disabled, to be beaten to a pulp

mektebumbi: (causative of **mektembi**)

mektembi: to bet, to wager, to contest, to contend, to compete

mekten: **1**. bet, wager; **2**. competition, contest

mekterembi: ⟶ **mektembi**

melbiku: oar

   melbiku jahūdai: a short, light rowboat

melbimbi: to row

melbin moo: a tree used for making oars

mele: on the lookout

melebumbi: **1**. (causative of **melembi**); **2**. to overlook, to neglect, to omit, to forget

melembi: **1**. to water (livestock); **2**. to sneak away, to hide

melendumbi: to water together; also **melenumbi**

melenembi: to go to water

melenjimbi: to come to water

melenumbi: to water together; also **melendumbi**

melerhi: a name for the manul, cat of the steppes; cf. **ujirhi**

melerjembi: to sneak off, to shrink away

meleršembi: **1**. ⟶ **memeršembi**; **2**. ⟶ **melerjembi**

melešetembi: to shrink back, to fear stepping forward

meli: jasmine

meljebumbi: (causative of **meljembi**)

meljembi: to compete, to compete in, to engage in a contest, to gamble, to race, to bet

melken: vapor rising from the earth, mirage

melkešembi: to rise (said of vapor from the earth), to form a mirage

   melkešere dengjan: magic lantern: darkened room or box in which an image is projected through refraction (an entertainment before the era of the photograph)

melketu: an imaginary creature capable of causing a mirage

melmen: blood clot

melmenembi: to clot, to coagulate

membe: (accusative form of **be**): us

meme: wet nurse; ⟶ **meme eniye**

   meme ama: husband of a wet nurse

   meme eigen: husband of a wet nurse

   meme eniye: wet nurse

memema: husband of a wet nurse

memeniye: wet nurse (of a noble family)

memereku: stubborn, firm, obstinate, pigheaded

memerembi: **1**. to be stubborn, to remain fixed in one's opinions; **2**. to be greedy for, to covet

memeren: stubbornness, obstinacy

memerjembi: to shrink back because of fear

memeršembi: to be indecisive, to act in a sluggish manner, to have a dull look (said of the eyes)

men šen enduri: the gate god

menci: (ablative of **be**): from us, than us

mende: (dative of **be**): to us, for us

menderembi: (**-ke**) to get one's speech confused (said of old people)

mendz: doorkeeper

mene: **1**. indeed, actually, truly, honestly; **2**. ⟶ **menen**; **3**. ⟶ **ine mene**

menehun: stupid, not intelligent

meneken: **1**. rather paralyzed, a bit paralyzed; **2**. stunned, stupefied

menekesaka: **1**. glassy eyed, as if paralyzed; **2**. dejected, miserable

menen: **1**. paralyzed, invalid, disabled; **2**. stupid, silly

   menen nimeku: paralysis

menerembi: (**-ke**) **1**. to be stupid, to be silly, to be in a daze; **2**. to be numb, to be asleep (said of parts of the body); **3**. to be paralyzed

mengde: a window that does not open, a blind window

mengdelembi: to nail tight, to nail shut

mengge: tough, hard (said of foods), hard to chew

menggin: ⟶ **menggun**

menggun: silver, money

   menggun guilehe: ginkgo, the fruit of the ginkgo

   menggun i namun: (銀庫) silver depository, treasury, Bullion Vaults, *BH* 71, 497

menggun inggali: the name of a small white bird

menggun jalungga namun: the name of a silver depository in Datong, northern Shanxi

menggun nisiha: silverfish — a tasty white fish that is taken from frozen water in the winter

menggun urebumbi: to mine silver ore

menglen: vain, futile

mengse: a curtain, drapery

mengseku: curtain made of cloth or felt hung before a door

mengseku i lakiyakū: rod for hanging a door curtain

mengseku i namun: depository of door curtains belonging to the Board of Works

meni: (genitive of **be**): our

meni meni: each, every, severally, individually, one by one, separately, respectively; cf. **meimeni**

meningge: ours

menji: turnip

mentehe: missing a tooth, toothless

mentehejembi: to have missing teeth, to be gap-toothed

mentu: steamed bread (usually round in shape); cf. **mantu**

mentuhudembi: to behave stupidly, to act in a silly fashion

mentuhuken: rather stupid, rather silly

mentuhun: stupid, silly

mentuhurebumbi: (causative or passive of **mentuhurembi**)

mentuhurembi: to speak stupidly, to behave stupidly, to act in a silly fashion

mentun: ⟶ **mentu**

mere: buckwheat

mere jempin: fried cakes made of buckwheat

mere nimanggi: snow that has frozen into small beads the size of a grain of buckwheat

mere ufa: buckwheat flour

meren ilha: an exotic white flower that resembles crushed rice

mergedembi: to be an excellent hunter or fisherman, to excel, to be outstanding

mergembi: ⟶ **merhembi**

mergen: **1**. a very good hunter or fisherman, an intelligent or wise man; **2**. outstanding, wise, worthy, skilled, adept

mergen arga: brilliant scheme

mergen cecike: another name for the shrike; cf. **giyahūn**

mergen gala: a skilled person

mergen hehe: title of honor of the third rank conferred upon the wife of a meritorious official

mergen šuwe: sagacious, sagacious person

mergengge mahatun: a hat worn by worthies and scholars in ancient times

mergese: (plural of **mergen**)

merhe: a double-edged fine-toothed comb

merhebumbi: (causative of **merhembi**)

merhembi: to comb with a **merhe**

merke: ⟶ **merhe**

merkimbi: to recollect, to recall, to bring to mind, to ponder

merkihe seme baharakū: be unable to recollect

merkime baimbi: to ponder, to mull over

merkime gūnimbi: to be deep in thought, to be pensive

merkime kidumbi: to think about constantly, to long for

merkin: recall, memory, consciousness

merkingge: alert, conscious

merpingge niyehe: a name for the common duck

mersen: freckle, spot on the face

mersenembi: to get freckles

mersengge: spotted, freckled

mersengge asha: a quail with small spots on its wings

mersengge cuse moo: spotted bamboo

mersengge dudu: a small spotted purple dove

merseri: betel nut; cf. **binse**

mersetu coko: a name for the turkey; cf. **suihetu coko**

mešebumbi: (causative or passive of **mešembi**)

mešembi: **1**. to shove in; **2**. to copulate, to make sexual connection with (a female)

meteku: a pole for offerings

metembi: **1**. to pay a vow to a god; **2**. to offer animals in sacrifice to heaven

metu: a name for the partridge; cf. **jukidun**

meye: brother-in-law: younger sister's husband (in the older language it also meant wife's younger brother)

meyelebumbi: (causative or passive of **meyelembi**)

meyelembi: **1**. to cut into sections; **2**. to form a group or squad

meyen: **1**. section, segment, division, piece, chapter; **2**. group, squadron, team, rank (of troops), row; **3**. measure word for a poem, stanza

    meyen banjibumbi: to form into ranks, to organize into a team

    meyen i afaha: a list on which was written the number of the group that was to have an audience with the Emperor

    meyen i amban: (領隊大臣) Commandant of the Forces, *BH* 865

    meyen meyen i: section by section, piece by piece, etc.

meyengge cargilakū: firecrackers that explode in rapid succession

meyete: (plural of **meye**)

mi mi sere mudan: decadent tune

mi orho: ⟶ **mijiri orho**

mibsehe: rice worm, grain eating insect

mibsehenembi: to develop rice worms

miburi: one sextillionth

miceo: cloth made from silk remnants

miciha arambi: to make rope for fishing and hunting nets

micihiyan: **1**. shallow; **2**. narrow-minded

    micihiyan be fetembi: to dredge the shallows of a river

    micihiyan de hūfumbi: to run aground

    micihiyan fetere cuwan: boat used in dredging, dredger

micika: ⟶ **micihiyan**

micubumbi: **1**. (causative of **micumbi**); **2**. to beat someone so that he cannot get up

micudambi: to crawl around (said of children)

micumbi: (**-he**) to crawl

micuršembi: to crawl continuously

mida: ⟶ **midada**

midada: the name of a plant whose sweet-tasting roots resemble the roots of the sow thistle; cf. **šari sogi**

midaha: leech

midaljambi: **1**. to move back and forth, to move in a zigzag way, to slither (like a snake); **2**. to

shake the body so as to make the bells on the belt ring (said of shamans)

migan: ⟶ **mihan**

mihacan: the young of the wild pig

mihadambi: to throw a tantrum, to make a scene, to jump up and down

    mihadame aidahašambi: to run amok, to rampage

    mihadame subadambi: to throw a fit, to stomp and shout loudly

mihan: a young pig

mijirebumbi: **1**. (causative of **mijirembi**); **2**. to beat someone until he cannot move

mijirembi: to crawl forward, to crawl on the knees

mijiri orho: *Ligusticum*: Sichuan lovage

mijurabumbi: **1**. (causative of **mijurambi**); **2**. to beat someone until he cannot move

mijurambi: to move back and forth while sitting, to drag the feet while walking

    mijurame dodobumbi: to beat into submission

mikcan: **1**. one name for the musk deer; cf. **miyahū**; **2**. musk; cf. **jarin**

mila: **1**. open, wide open; **2**. Be off!, Be gone!; **3**. pale yellow amber

    mila neimbi: to open wide

milacambi: ⟶ **milarambi**

milahūn: wide open, gaping

    milahūn moro: bowl with a thick rim and wide opening

milambi: to go away, to be off

milan: water in which rice has been rinsed

milarabumbi: (causative of **milarambi**)

milarambi: (**-ka**) **1**. to open wide; **2**. to shun, to dodge, to stay far away from

milarcambi: ⟶ **milarambi**

milata: wide open, agape

miltahūn: bare, vacant

mimbe: (accusative of **bi**): me

mimi: a kind of large fly, flesh fly

mimimbi: (**-ha**) to close (the mouth)

mimiralambi: to close the mouth

mimsoro: a jujube-like exotic fruit

minci: (ablative of **bi**): from me, than me

minde: (dative of **bi**): to me, for me

mindz: a brush

    mindz buleku: goggles

mingga: ⟶ **minggan**

minggaci: thousandth

minggada: chiliarch, chief of one thousand

minggaha: the name of an exotic fruit that grows on a vine, has up to two hundred seeds in a pod, and tastes like a chestnut

minggalambi: to number in the thousands

minggan: one thousand

minggan tumen: ten million

mingganggeri: one thousand times

minggari: one thousand square *lĭ*

minggata: one thousand each

minggatu: (千總) Chiliarch, Lieutenant, *BH* 752E, 796, etc.

mingmiyaha: **1**. corn earworm; **2**. a small green bug found on the mulberry tree

mini: (genitive of **bi**): my, of me

mini beye: myself

miningge: mine

miodori miodori: walking with difficulty (because of a sore back)

miomiohon: ⟶ **miyoomiyoohūn**

miori: ⟶ **miyori**

miosihodombi: **1**. to act or speak in a false and heretical way; **2**. to distort, to misrepresent, to twist

miosihon: evil, false, heretical, heterodox

miosihon ibagan: evil spirit, demon

miosihon sukdun: evil influence

miosihon tacin: heretical teaching, heretical doctrine, sorcery

miosihūn: ⟶ **miosihon**

miosiri: smiling

miosiri miosirilambi: to smile, to have a smile on the face

miosirilambi: to smile

miošorombi: (**-ko**) to become crooked or bent, to become askew

misan: tub, vat; cf. **misen**

mise: slack, loose (said of a bow with a loose string)

misen: a large jar with a wide mouth

misha: ⟶ **mishan**

mishabumbi: (causative of **mishambi**)

mishabure dalangga: a dam through which the current is regulated

mishalabumbi: **1**. (causative of **mishalambi**); **2**. to get caught in a trap or net

mishalabume bethe tambi: to get a foot caught in a trap

mishalakū: vessel for holding the inked string used by carpenters for marking straight lines

mishalakū hūrka: snare for catching wild animals

mishalambi: **1**. to mark a straight line with an inked string; **2**. to restrain, to detain in a trap

mishambi: to shun, to avoid, to dodge

mishan: **1**. an inked string used by a carpenter for marking straight lines; **2**. criterion, standard

misihiyadambi: to walk in an affected way, to swing the hips from side to side

misjan: mason

misu hūsiha: magnolia vine (*Schizandra chinensis*)

misuijan: ⟶ **misjan**

misun: a thick sauce, jam, fermented bean paste

misun boco: the color of fermented bean paste — brown

misun i kūrdakū: a wooden stirring stick for bean paste

misuru: brown, reddish brown

mišun: one hundred trillion

mita: an iron ornament on the end of a crupper

mita jafu: a sack for catching the feces of draught animals, a bag hanging under an animal's tail to catch dung

mita uše: a leather thong used to attach the **mita jafu**

mitabumbi: (causative of **mitambi**)

mitaljambi: ⟶ **midaljambi**

mitambi: **1**. to spring back (said of a bow when the string is removed); **2**. to oppose

mitan: **1**. sweet rice porridge; **2**. ⟶ **mita**

mitandumbi: **1**. to spring back together; **2**. to oppose together

miyaha: ⟶ **mihan**

miyahū: *Moschus moschiferus*: musk deer

miyahū fungsan: musk

miyahūtu: the muntjac of South China

miyalibumbi: (causative of **miyalimbi**)

miyalida: the man who measures grain in a granary

miyalikū: **1**. measurer, measure; **2**. powder measure (for guns)

miyalimbi: to measure

miyalin: a measure

miyamibumbi: (causative of **miyamimbi**)

miyamiga: ⟶ **miyamigan**

miyamigan: **1**. ornament, jewelry; **2**. makeup; **3**. decoration, adornment; **4**. cover-up, whitewash

    miyamigan gisun: words used to cover up something

miyamihan: ⟶ **miyamigan**

miyamikū: a person fond of making up or dressing up

miyamimbi: **1**. to adorn, to decorate; **2**. to make up, to dress up; **3**. to cover up, to whitewash, to conceal

    miyamime gisurembi: to conceal the truth when speaking

    miyamime holtombi: to cover up, to hide the truth

miyamin: decoration, ornamentation

miyamišakū: fond of making up, one fond of making up

miyamišambi: to adorn oneself, to decorate, to dress up

miyamiyahan: ⟶ **miyamigan**

miyan ceo: a fine cotton fabric; cf. **miceo**

miyan diyan gurun: Burma

miyan gin: gluten

miyandz: Burma, Burmese

    miyandz hūlha: Burmese bandit

miyang: (onomatopoetic) the sound of a child crying

    miyang ming: (onomatopoetic) **1**. the sound of many children crying; **2**. the sound made by the young of deer, roe, and sheep

miyanggin: wheat gluten

miyants hūlha: Burmese bandits

miyar mir: (onomatopoetic) the sound of children crying

miyar miyar: (onomatopoetic) **1**. the sound made by a baby crying; **2**. the sound made by young deer, roe, and sheep

miyar seme: **1**. bleating; **2**. nagging

miyarga: ⟶ **miyarha**

miyarha: clitoris

miyaridambi: to sway, to shake, to fly unsteadily (said of arrows); cf. **miyasidambi**

miyarimbi: to bleat, to baa

miyasi miyasi: ⟶ **miyasihi miyasihi**

miyasidambi: to walk unsteadily, to fly unsteadily (said of an arrow)

miyasihi miyasihi: unsteady, staggering

miyasihidambi: to walk unsteadily

miyasihitambi: ⟶ **miyasihidambi**

miyasirilambi: to pucker the mouth as if ready to cry

miyasitambi: ⟶ **miyasidambi**

miyegu: crust (formed on rice or gruel when it turns cold)

    miyegu efen: a food made from steamed glutinous millet flour

    miyegu wecembi: to offer **miyegu** pastry

miyehu: ⟶ **turi miyehu**: bean curd, tofu

miyehudembi: to jump about, to hop around (said of wild animals)

miyehunembi: **1**. to form a crust; **2**. to have trouble moving around, to become decrepit

miyehusu: bean-curd skin

miyekudembi: ⟶ **miyehudembi**

miyoo: temple, shrine

miyoocalabumbi: (causative of **miyoocalambi**)

miyoocalambi: to fire a musket, to fire a gun

miyoocalandumbi: to fire muskets together; also **miyoocalanumbi**

miyoocalanumbi: to fire muskets together; also **miyoocalandumbi**

miyoocan: musket, flintlock, firearm, gun

    miyoocan goimbi: to be hit by a shot from a gun, to be shot

    miyoocan i cooha: musketeers, musket troops, riflemen

    miyoocan sindambi: to fire a gun, to fire a musket

miyoociyang: ⟶ **miyoocan**

miyoodz: the Miao minority of South China

miyoomiyoohūn: bent outward, protruding (lips)

miyori: a second (of time)

miyosirilambi: ⟶ **miosirilambi**

miyošori: ⟶ **miosiri**

    miyošori miyošorilambi: to smile

miyošorobumbi: (causative of **miyošorombi**)

miyošorombi: **1**. to bend, to be deflected; cf. **miošorombi**; **2**. to pout

mo: **1**. one ten-trillionth; **2**. Chinese acre, *mǔ* 畝 (one sixth of an acre)

mo li ilha: jasmine

mo seme: right in the face, right to one's face

    mo seme basumbi: to make fun of someone to his face

mobin hoošan: a kind of writing paper made from bamboo

mobsehe: ⟶ **mibsehe**

mociko: askance, crooked, askew; cf. **waiku**

mocin: a fine smooth cotton, usually dark brown or black

　mocin samsu: a fine smooth brown or black cotton cloth

mocinji: ⟶ **mojihiyan**

moco: incompetent, unskillful, stupid, blunt, tactless

　moco simhun: the index finger

mocodombi: to act in an incompetent, stupid, or tactless manner

mocokon: rather incompetent, rather stupid

modan ilha: *Paeonia suffruticosa*: woody peony

modo: slow-witted, dull, lacking agility, clumsy, careless

　modo gasha: a name for the cuckoo; cf. **kekuhe**

modokon: rather dull, rather clumsy

mohobumbi: **1**. (causative or passive of **mohombi**); **2**. to do in a thorough or complete way; **3**. to suffer serious harm

　mohobume fonjimbi: to question thoroughly

moholo: a hornless castrated bovine

mohombi: **1**. to be exhausted, to be depleted, to run out; **2**. to be in dire need, to be destitute, to be impoverished; to become dull

mohon: exhaustion, depletion, end, finish, need

　mohon akū: endless, boundless, without limit, eternal, inexhaustible

　mohon wajin: end, termination

mohori sohori: **1**. careless, sloppy, shabby; **2**. scattered about, in disorder

mohoto: hairless (a horse's tail); cf. **mokto**

mojihiyan: *Euractos thibetanus*: Tibetan black bear

mokcombi: to break off, to break in two

moko: (昂) a constellation, the 18th of the lunar mansions, made up of seven stars in Taurus

　moko tokdonggo kiru: a banner depicting the constellation **moko**

mokso: asunder, in two, in the center

　mokso genehe: went asunder, broke in two

　mokso mokso: in pieces, broken in two

moksolobumbi: (causative or passive of **moksolombi**)

moksolombi: to break in two (transitive verb), to cleave, to chop off

mokto: **1**. docked off, bobbed; **2**. bare, bald (said of an animal's tail); **3**. irascible, surly

　mokto šošonggo mahala: an ancient-style hat similar to the **mahatu** but without a fringe

molho: the large intestine of the wild pig

molhūri: a hornless bovine; cf. **moholo**

moli ilha: jasmine; cf. **meli**

molo: maple tree, trees of the genus *Acer*

molodombi: to glue back together

molojin: the name of the peacock in Buddhist scriptures

molori moo: *Photinia serrulata*: Chinese photinia

momohon: silent, speechless (from embarrassment)

momohori: sitting together silently, sitting still (said of a group), sitting erect

momokon: silent because of shyness, retiring

momorombi: to sit silently (said of a group), to sit erect, to stay in one's seat

momoršombi: to be tense (when shooting from horseback)

moncon: chrysanthemum-shaped knob on a cap

monggo: Mongolia, Mongolian

　monggo aisin hergengge loho: a sword with a Mongolian inscription in gold letters

　monggo bithei ba: (蒙古堂) Mongolian Copying Office, *BH* 138

　monggo boo: Mongolian yurt, felt tent

　monggo buda: a broth made of meat and rice

　monggo buren: a long horn used by Mongolian lamas

　monggo cibin: Mongolian swallow

　monggo cooha: Mongolian troops

　monggo dashūwan dube: the second **jalan** of the Mongols

　monggo gūsa: **1**. Mongolian banner; **2**. Lieutenant-General of a Mongolian banner

　monggo hergen: the Mongolian written language, Mongolian writing or letters

　monggo jebele dube: the first **jalan** of the Mongols

　monggo jurgan: another name for the **Tulergi golo be dasara jurgan**: Court of Colonial Affairs, *BH* 491

　monggo sedo: the name of a wild plant with edible stalks — the same as **fulgiyan selbete**

　monggo tala: the Mongolian plateau, Mongolia

monggo yoro: an arrow with a square birch-wood head with holes in it (used for shooting rabbits on rocky terrain)

monggoi buren: a horn used by lamas

monggocon: a bottle with a narrow mouth and long neck

monggocun: ⟶ **monggocon**

monggoi: ⟶ **monggo** (subheading)

monggolibumbi: (causative of **monggolimbi**)

monggolikū: **1**. something worn around the neck; **2**. ornamental neckband worn by women; **3**. dog collar

monggolimbi: to wear on the neck

monggon: neck, throat

monggon faitambi: to cut the throat

monggon hūsikū: **1**. a protective piece of armor for the neck; **2**. a collar around the neck

monggon soyombi: to draw in the neck

monggorobumbi: (causative of **monggorombi**)

monggorokū: a bordered collar fixed to a jacket

monggorokū hūsikū: neckpiece, neck scarf

monggorokū sijigiyan: a gown with collar and cuffs trimmed in brocade

monggorokū ulhi wahan: collar and cuffs trimmed in brocade

monggorombi: **1**. to act in a Mongolian manner; **2**. to speak Mongolian, to use Mongolian, to write Mongolian; **3**. to kick the shuttlecock

monggorome: in the Mongolian manner, in the Mongolian language

monggorome gisurembi: to speak Mongolian

monggorome tembi: to sit in the Mongolian manner — i.e., with one foot under the buttocks

monggorome ubaliyambumbi: to be translated into Mongolian

monggoso: (plural of **monggo**)

monggošun: *Carassius carassius*: crucian carp

monggū: ⟶ **monggo**

mongniohon: **1**. gasping for breath; **2**. compressing the lips when angry

monio: monkey, ape; cf. **bonio**; **2**. a term of endearment used toward children and one's intimates

moniocilambi: to behave like a monkey, to monkey around

monjibumbi: (causative of **monjimbi**)

monjimbi: to rub, to knead, to massage

monjirambi: **1**. to rub with the hand, to knead; **2**. to wring the hands (in frustration, etc.), to be in an agitated state

monjiršambi: **1**. to rub vigorously, to knead vigorously; **2**. to sit rocking back and forth in anger; **3**. at wrestling, to keep pressing an opponent down

monjišambi: to massage

moo: **1**. tree; **2**. wood; **3**. stick, pole; **4**. a bamboo stick used for beating; **5**. ⟶ **moo ihan**

moo bujan: forest, woods

moo faksi: carpenter, woodworker

moo garma: an arrow with a four-sided wooden head with a barb sticking out from each side (used for shooting pheasants and rabbits)

moo hasi: *Diospyros kaki*: persimmon

moo hengke: *Pseudocydonia sinensis*: Chinese quince

moo i ada: wooden raft

moo i beri: a wooden bow used for preparing cotton

moo i calu i kunggeri: (木倉科) Office of Wood Storehouses in the Board of Works

moo i cikten: beam of wood

moo i fuktala: mistletoe

moo i hasi: persimmon; cf. **moo hasi**

moo i hoton: a wooden wall

moo i jun: lumber, wood (as opposed to the other parts of a tree)

moo i kemneku: ⟶ **moo i kemun**

moo i kemun: set square, used for measuring wood

moo i noran: a pile of wood

moo i urge: wooden figurine

moo i ūren: wooden puppet

moo ihan: yak

moo lujen: the name of a six-horse Imperial coach with a roof consisting of four pieces of wood

moo morin: **1**. stilts; **2**. a wooden horse used by children at play

moo sacimbi: to chop wood, to cut firewood

moo sacire niyalma: a woodcutter

moo sika i keibisu: a carpet made of palm fiber

moo šu ilha: *Magnolia liliflora*: lily magnolia

moo usiha: the planet Jupiter

moo yaha: charcoal

mooi calu: wood warehouse of the Board of Works

mooi faksi: carpenter

mooi hasi boco: persimmon-colored

mooi kemneku: set square used for measuring lumber

mooi šolon: wooden image

mooi tuhen: wooden rack, wooden frame

moodasi: a person in charge of planting and caring for trees, a forester

mooi: ⟶ **moo** (subheading)

moositun: a kind of ancient sacrificial vessel (豆)

mooyen ilha: *Hibiscus syriacus*: Rose of Sharon

morho: *Medicago hispida*: alfalfa, toothed bur clover

morici: a person who watches horses at official establishments

morilabumbi: (causative of **morilambi**)

morilambi: to mount a horse, to ride a horse, to go by horse

morilaha wehe: stones placed near a gate to help people mount horses

morilara wehe: stones placed on both sides of the main gate of a house

morin: **1**. horse; **2**. the seventh of the earth's branches (午)

morin bargiyambi: to rein in a horse, to round up horses

morin biya: the fifth month

morin cooha: cavalry

morin deleri etehe ucun: a piece of music played during the greeting of a general

morin erin: the period from 11 AM until 1 PM, midday

morin gajimbi: to lead one's horse to a target (in mounted archery)

morin hūwaitambi: 'to tie up the horse' — euphemism for going to the toilet

morin i baita: horse affairs, horse-related matters

morin i baitai kunggeri: (馬政科) Office of Horse Affairs in the Board of War

morin i jalin wecembi: to make an offering to the horse god

morin i toron: branding iron for horses

morin jalmin: polygonum, knotweed

morin jurcembi: to join battle on horseback

morin mangga: skillful at riding

morin sejen belhere bolgobure fiyenten: (車駕清吏司) Remount Department, *BH* 415A

morin silmen: a female kite

morin sindambi: to give the horse its head

morin torho: *Asarum sieboldi*: wild ginger

morin turgen: ⟶ **morin torho**

morin weihe: a sore in children's mouths

moringga: **1**. pertaining to the horse, mounted; **2**. horseman, rider

moringga aniya: the year of the horse

moringga cooha: cavalry, mounted troops

moringga faidan: the mounted Imperial Escort

moringga hūjaci: mounted police

moringga hūlha: mounted bandit

moringga uksin: armor for a horse

morisa: (plural of **morin**)

moro: **1**. bowl; **2**. a dry quart

moro hiyase: a dry quart

moroi dobton: covering for a bowl

morohon: big and round (said of eyes)

morohon neimbi: to open wide (the eyes)

morohon tuwambi: to look at with wide open eyes

morombi: to open wide (the eyes)

moselabumbi: (causative or passive of **moselambi**)

moselakū: a large millstone

moselakū i lifan wehe: stone trough for a stone roller

moselakū wehe: millstone

moselambi: **1**. to mill, to grind; **2**. to sit with the feet tucked under the body

moselame: with the feet tucked under the body

moselame tembi: to sit with the feet tucked under the body

mosike: the name of a small monkey-like animal from Tonkin that is very adept at catching rats

mošuse: an exotic purple fruit resembling the walnut

moton hoošan: a kind of strong paper made from hemp

motoro: *Cydonia japonica*: a kind of sour, astringent quince

motoro gaha: a kind of crow that nests in forests

moyaci ilha: an exotic red flower of South China that blooms in spring and autumn — it resembles hibiscus

moyo: **1**. dull; **2**. chicken-pox

moyoro: an exotic fruit resembling the quince but somewhat larger

mu: a *mǔ* (畝) about one sixth of an acre; cf. **imari**

muce: ⟶ **mucen**

mucejun: a name for the stork; cf. **weijun**

mucen: cooking pot, caldron

mucengge: **1**. pertaining to a cooking pot; **2**. a measure equaling 6 pecks and 4 quarts

mucesi: a cook

>**mucesi i kunggeri**: (廚役科) an office in charge of preparing sacrificial animals

muciha: **1**. bamboo splints or rushes for making baskets and mats; **2**. the center part of a grass or rush mat

>**muciha futa**: a bamboo rope used for hauling boats

>**muciha i hoseri**: a container woven from thin bamboo splints or reeds

>**muciha mahatun**: an ancient-style hat made from bamboo splints

mucihiyan: a tripod vessel

mucitu mahatun: an ancient-style hat made of bamboo splints and decorated with lacquer on the outside

mucitun: a sacrificial vessel of antiquity woven from bamboo

mucu: **1**. Amur grape (*Vitis amurensis*); **2**. the imported wine grape

>**mucu bocoi haksangga efen**: crisp grape-colored cake

>**mucu bocoi jiyoo bing**: ⟶ **mucu bocoi haksangga efen**

>**mucu halu i sacima**: cake made of flour, sesame oil, sesame seeds, sugar, and grapes

>**mucu nure**: grape wine

>**mucu yafan**: vineyard

mucunggai gasha: one of the names of the spotted kingfisher; cf. **cunggai**

mudaci ilha: *Papaver rhoeas*: corn poppy

mudacilambi: to make a continuous sound

mudakiyambi: to walk on a sinuous path, to turn (corners)

mudali: ⟶ **mudari**

mudalimbi: **1**. to turn (a corner); **2**. to go the long way around, to make a detour; **3**. to be sinuous, winding

>**mudalime**: via a detour, in a roundabout way

mudalin: a round piece of cloth that can be used for patches

mudaliyan: circuitous and long, winding, tortuous

mudambi: to return

mudan: **1**. curve, bend, curved, bent; **2**. detour, roundabout way; **3**. sound, tone, melody, rhyme; **4**. expression, tone of voice, implication; **5**. out of the way, remote; **6**. time, as in one time, two times, etc.; **7**. peony; **8**. ⟶ **mudan efen**; **9**. curved piece of wood on a catapult

>**mudan arambi**: to knead to and fro (dough)

>**mudan baha**: started to sweat — after the crisis in an illness

>**mudan dari**: every time

>**mudan de acabumbi**: (諧聲) to form characters according to the phonetic principle

>**mudan efen**: a deep-fried twisted pastry made of millet, rice, and buckwheat flour

>**mudan gaime yabumbi**: to go by a roundabout way

>**mudan hūwaliyambumbi**: to harmonize, to blend sounds in a pleasing way

>**mudan hūwaliyambure falgari**: (和聲署) Music Office, *BH* 388

>**mudan i acabumbi**: to match in sound — i.e., to form new characters by compounding a phonetic and semantic element

>**mudan i ba**: a remote place

>**mudan mudan**: every time

>**mudan mudan de**: at various times, periodically

>**mudan nurhūme**: repeatedly, time and again

>**mudan tebumbi**: to set a trap for someone

>**mudan wai**: a remote place in the mountains, a precipitous and inaccessible place

>**mudan waka**: absurd

>**mudan yoho**: a remote area

mudandari: ⟶ **mudan dari**

mudangga: **1**. curved, bent; **2**. having sound or tone

>**mudangga dalan**: a dike that follows the curves of a river

>**mudangga fesin i haksan bocoi suje sara**: a yellow silk umbrella with a crooked handle used as an insignia by the Imperial concubines

>**mudangga jugūn**: a crooked road

mudangga nahan: a crooked oven-bed

mudari: there and right back

mudumbi: to file, to file smooth

mudun: **1**. a file for working wood, horn, or bone; **2**. spur off the foot of a mountain

>**mudun futa**: a snare for catching lynx

muduri: **1**. dragon; **2**. the fifth of the earth's branches (辰)

>**muduri biya**: the third month

>**muduri duka**: the name of the ceremonial arch behind the second door of the Examination Hall

>**muduri dukai dalangga**: a dam with a sluice

>**muduri erin**: the period from 7 AM to 9 AM

>**muduri garudai suwayan suje šun dalikū**: a large fan made of yellow satin embroidered with phoenixes and dragons

>**muduri garudai tumin lamun suje kiru**: a dark blue satin banner embroidered with phoenixes and dragons

>**muduri jahūdai**: dragon boat (used for racing)

>**muduri morin**: a fine horse

>**muduri muyame tasha murame**: roaring like a dragon and growling like a tiger

>**muduri ošohonggo fukjingga hergen**: (龍爪篆) a style of calligraphy

>**muduri soorin de wesimbi**: to ascend the Dragon Throne

>**muduri ujungge girdan**: the dragon-headed pennant — the name of an insignia of the escort

mudurikū: tile figures of dragons on both ends of the roof-ridge of a palace

muduringga: pertaining to the dragon

>**muduringga aniya**: the year of the dragon

>**muduringga doyonggo**: gold brocade with walking dragons woven in

>**muduringga fukjingga hergen**: (龍書) a style of calligraphy

>**muduringga giyancihiyan hoošan**: letter paper with a dragon design

>**muduringga hiyan moo**: *Dryobalanops camphora*: Borneo camphor

mufi ilha: *Magnolia kobus*: lily magnolia

mufuyen: **1**. blunt, rounded, having rounded edges and corners; **2**. dull-witted

>**mufuyen modo**: **1**. blunt and dull; **2**. dull and slow-witted

mugūn: ⟶ **mukūn**

muhaliyabumbi: (causative of **muhaliyambi**)

muhaliyambi: to pile up, to stack up

>**muhaliyaha orho**: haystack, pile of grass

>**muhaliyame sindambi**: to place in a pile

muhaliyan: **1**. ball, sphere, bead, round projectile, pellet; **2**. bullet, shell; **3**. pile, stack

muhan: a male tiger or panther

>**muhan sebsehe**: walking stick (a kind of insect)

>**muhan tasha**: a male tiger

>**muhan yarha**: a male panther

muhandumbi: ⟶ **muhantumbi**

muhantumbi: to copulate, to breed (said of cows, tigers, and cats)

muhari: an exotic fruit about the size of a crossbow projectile with a taste like that of chestnut

muharšambi: **1**. to have pain in the eye from rubbing; **2**. to suffer angina

muhašan: bull

muheliyeken: rather round

muheliyen: round

>**muheliyen fa**: window shaped like the moon

>**muheliyen jan**: a round whistling arrow — an arrow with three holes in the head that was used for shooting deer and roe

>**muheliyen moo**: a wooden ball on the end of a stick

>**muheliyen muhun**: the round earthen altar at the Temple of Heaven

muheliyengge: round, spherical

>**muheliyengge gu**: round flat piece of jade with a hole in the center (used in ceremonies in ancient China)

muheren: **1**. wheel; **2**. ring, earring; **3**. a metal ring used as a paperweight; **4**. the end of an axle

muheri ilha: *Kerria japonica*: Japanese yellow rose

muhešembi: to carry mud in the beak (said of swallows)

muhi: **1**. a sable (or other animal's) tail attached to the front of a fur jacket below the lapel; **2**. a curved board on the back of a wagon to which the ropes that hold the load are fastened; **3**. wooden ring to which the ropes of a swing are attached

muhiyan ilha: *Rosa banksiae*: banksia

muhu: a high ridge or mound

muhun: a mound on which funerary offerings to the nobility were made in ancient times

muhuru: female sockeye salmon; cf. **cime**

muhūlu: a yellow dragon-like creature without horns

muhūri: rounded off, leveled off

mujakū: **1**. extremely, truly; **2**. many

mujan: carpenter

mujangga: truly, indeed, actually, true, real, correct

mujanggai: half way, almost

>**mujanggai soktombi**: to become half drunk

mujanggao: is it true that … ?, can it be that … ?

mujanggo: ⟶ **mujanggao**

muji: *Hordeum vulgare*: barley

mujilen: mind, intention, heart (in a figurative sense)

>**mujilen akūmbumbi**: to exhaust all efforts, to do one's best

>**mujilen ališambi**: to be perturbed, to be upset

>**mujilen bahabukū**: (啟心郎) an official title used at the beginning of the Manchu dynasty (ranking just below **ashan i amban**)

>**mujilen bahambi**: to understand, to realize

>**mujilen baibumbi**: to be upset, to have one's plans upset

>**mujilen be cashūlambi**: to betray one's lover, to be an ungrateful lover

>**mujilen be tucibumbi**: to have an intimate conversation

>**mujilen de acambi**: to be satisfied, to be content

>**mujilen de dekdembi**: to develop suspicions

>**mujilen de elembi**: to find pleasing

>**mujilen de tebumbi**: to be concerned about, to keep in mind

>**mujilen deribumbi**: to be aroused, to be swayed

>**mujilen efujembi**: to be distressed, to grieve

>**mujilen farfabumbi**: to be confused in one's mind

>**mujilen fayabumbi**: to go to a lot of trouble

>**mujilen fereke**: fainted, lost consciousness

>**mujilen ferimbi**: to exert all effort, to strive

>**mujilen geren**: suspicious

>**mujilen girkūmbi**: to concentrate one's efforts

>**mujilen gūnin**: thoughts, intention

>**mujilen gūwaliyambi**: to have a change of heart or intentions

>**mujilen halambi**: to cease to be faithful, to break faith, to change one's loyalty

>**mujilen hungkerehe**: repented, was remorseful

>**mujilen hūdun**: quick-tempered

>**mujilen icakū**: ill-pleasing, unsatisfactory

>**mujilen isheliyen**: narrow-minded, petty

>**mujilen jancuhūn**: willing, content, pleased

>**mujilen jempi**: having the heart to do something

>**mujilen jobombi**: to be troubled

>**mujilen juwenderakū**: steadfast, loyal

>**mujilen niyaman**: feeling, sincerity

>**mujilen niyaman i gese niyalma**: a trusted friend

>**mujilen sesulambi**: to be startled

>**mujilen sidarambi**: to be calm or tranquil in grief or difficulty

>**mujilen sindambi**: to relax, to feel at ease, to calm down

>**mujilen sithūmbi**: to concentrate one's efforts

>**mujilen suilambi**: to be troubled, to be upset

>**mujilen sula**: relieved

>**mujilen teng seme jafambi**: to make a strong resolution, to have a strong intention

>**mujilen tookabumbi**: to while away the time, to divert oneself

>**mujilen tuksitembi**: to be anxious

>**mujilen usambi**: to grieve, to be sad

>**mujilen usatala oho**: fell into grief or despair

mujilengge: **1**. having purpose or aim; **2**. spirited, stout-hearted

mujimbi: (-ha) to moan (during an illness), to cry, to roar

>**mujime soksimbi**: to sob, to cry inconsolably

mujin: ambition, aim, will, aspiration

>**mujin be ujimbi**: to nurture an ambition, to follow the goal that one's parents have set

>**mujin be wesihulere tanggin**: name of the third hall of the east gallery of the Imperial Academy of Learning

>**mujin de acabumbi**: to attain one's ambitions

mujingga: strong-willed, ambitious, spirited

mujuhu: carp; cf. **hardakū**

mujuku: ⟶ **mujuhu**

muk mak seme: obstinate, stubborn, awkward

mukcuhun: having a deformed hip that protrudes forward

mukdan moo: *Codium mucronatum*: China cypress

mukdehen: root or branch of a desiccated tree, a desiccated tree

mukdehun: altar

mukdehuri: an exotic sweet fruit that grows in Fujian (somewhat larger than a jujube)

mukdembi: (-ke/-he) **1**. to rise, to go upward; **2**. to flourish; **3**. to soar upward, to increase

mukdembumbi: (causative of **mukdembi**)

mukden: **1**. rising, ascent, flourishing, prosperous; **2**. Mukden

mukden i boigon i jurgan: (盛京戶部) the Board of Finance in Mukden

mukden i ilan munggan i kadalan jafaha hafan i yamun: (盛京三陵掌關防衙門) the Office of the Official in Charge of the Three Mausoleums of Mukden

mukdendembi: to rise

muke: **1**. water; **2**. river, stream

muke bahanambi: to know how to swim

muke bahanara niyalma: a good swimmer

muke be necin obure tampin: the third vessel of a water clock

muke de sindambi: to bury in a body of water, to bury at sea

muke dendere tampin: a vessel located behind the **muke be necin obure tampin** on a water clock

muke gaha: a name for the cormorant; cf. **suwan**

muke gahacin: another name for the cormorant

muke gocimbi: **1**. to recede (said of a flood); **2**. to suck up water

muke gocire beri: bow with a hollow stock through which water can be sucked

muke hasi: *Solanum nigrum*: sunberry

muke hūšahū: a kind of gull that resembles the owl

muke ibadan: a tree whose bark resembles that of the elm

muke ihan: a water buffalo

muke maktambi: to sprinkle water

muke noho ba i usin: field covered with water, field with standing water

muke tasha: the name of a predatory fish, the same as the **edeng**

muke tashari: the Siberian white crane

muke tebuku: a container for water used for making ink

muke tuwa: extreme misery

muke usiha: the planet Mercury

mukei aisi: water conservancy

mukei aisi be yendebure tinggin: (水利廳) office of an official in charge of water conservancy, irrigation, etc.

mukei cifun: water taxes

mukei dababukū: a long tin pipe used for siphoning water

mukei dalin: bank of a stream

mukei eyebuku: a water pipe, a drain pipe

mukei feise: unfired, sun-dried brick

mukei foron: whirlpool, eddy

mukei gasha: waterfowl

mukei gashan: flood

mukei hujureku: a small water-run mill

mukei hūsun: boatman

mukei ihan: water buffalo

mukei ihan i uihe beri: a bow made from the horn of a water buffalo

mukei isihikū: a pole with wet hemp attached to the end (used for extinguishing fires)

mukei jugūn: water route

mukei kurdun: waterwheel

mukei moselakū: a large water mill

mukei mudan: river cove, bend in a river

mukei nimeku: dropsy, edema

mukei niowangga moo: *Xylosma japonicum*: bush holly, a tree that grows near water

mukei nure: clear wine, wine clear as water

mukei on: water route, journey by boat, voyage

mukei singgeri: water mouse

mukei šurdeku: a water wheel

mukei talgan: the surface of water

mukei tebun: a container for water

mukei wasihūn: downstream

mukei weilen be icihiyara bolgobure fiyenten: (都水清吏司) an office concerned with water conservancy in the Board of Works

mukei wesihun: upstream

mukelembi: to water, to irrigate

mukelu ilha: hyacinth

mukenembi: to turn to water, to melt

mukeri: watery, weak (said of tea)

mukiyebumbi: **1**. (causative of **mukiyembi**); **2**. to extinguish, to put out; **3**. to wipe out, to annihilate

mukiyembi: to go out (fire), to be extinguished, to expire, to perish, to cool off

mukiyen: extinction, annihilation

mukjambi: to be stubborn

mukjuri makjari: idle (talk), paltry, petty, inconsequential

mukjuri mukjuri: running slowly (said of short people)

mukjuršembi: to bow deeply

mukšalabumbi: (causative or passive of **mukšalambi**)

mukšalambi: to beat with a stick

mukšan: stick, club, cudgel

mukšan fu: roach (kind of fish: *Rutilus rutilus*)

mukšatu nimaha: minnow, tench

muktehen: temple, monastery

muktembi: ⟶ **mektembi**

muktuhun: sand grouse; cf. **nuturu**

muktun: mole, animals of the family *Talpidae*

mukūmbi: to hold a liquid in the mouth

mukūn: **1**. clan, extended family, kindred; **2**. fleet; **3**. herd, flock

mukūn falga: clan

mukūn i ahūn deo: all the boys of one generation in a clan, brothers and cousins of the same surname

mukūn i urse: members of a clan

mulan: **1**. a stool; **2**. an ironing board

mulderhen: lesser skylark; cf. **guwenderhen**

mulfiyen: **1**. something round, disk; **2**. bull's-eye; **3**. circles woven into a textile

mulhūri: a cow without horns

mulinambi: to swallow, to gulp down

muliyan: **1**. the curve of the jawbone under the ear; **2**. the curve at the base of the wings of birds

mulmen: a kind of fish hawk, possibly the same as **suksuhu**

multujembi: to come loose, to come off, to get free, to leave

multulembi: to take off, to remove, to loosen (a knot), to disconnect, to slip off, to slacken

multumbi: ⟶ **multulembi**

mulu: **1**. ridgepole, beam; **2**. support pole of a tent or yurt; **3**. mountain ridge; **4**. the back line on a pelt

mulu i fere moo: supporting beam in a ship's cabin

mulu i hetu moo: a horizontal beam in the ship's cabin

mulu tukiyembi: to place a beam in position, to hoist a beam

mulunombi: (**-ho, -ro**) to form a ridge, to form a mound

mulurame: along a mountain ridge

muluse: an exotic fruit that grows inside the bark of a tree — it is a four- or five-inch long sweet, yellow fruit

mumanambi: (**-ka**) to wallow in mud (said of deer)

mumin: very deep, profound, unfathomable

mumin wehe: lapis lazuli

mumuhu: **1**. ball, football (often made from a pig's bladder); **2**. a term of abuse

mumuhun: ⟶ **mumuhu**

mumurembi: **1**. to buck, to kick (said of horses and other livestock); **2**. to go around in circles

mumurhūn: vague, indistinct, blurred

mumuri: **1**. toothless, missing a tooth; **2**. worn smooth

munahūn: morose, surly, out of humor, annoyed, displeased, sorrowful

munari: a round exotic fruit that tastes bitter when first eaten, but then turns sweet in the mouth

mung mang: (onomatopoetic) sound made by cattle or deer

mung mang seme: lowing, bellowing, roaring

mung mung seme: ⟶ **mung mang seme**

mungga: ⟶ **munggan**

munggan: **1**. low hill, mound, tumulus; **2**. tomb, mausoleum

mungge niongniyaha: a name for the wild goose

munggirembi: to play boisterously, to romp

mungkeri ilha: *Magnolia splendens*: laurel magnolia

mungku: a fish frozen in the ice

munjimbi: (**-ha**) to cry out in pain; cf. **mujimbi**

mur mar seme: obstinate, stubborn

muradambi: to roar in rage

murakū: a whistle for calling deer

murambi: **1**. to roar, to low, to bellow, to neigh; **2**. to call deer with a whistle

murame dosimbi: to hunt deer at the time of the mating season

muran: a battue held at the time of the deer-breeding season

muran i aba: a battue for deer during the mating season

muratambi: to roar continually, to howl

murca: a wooden crossbar for holding fast the ropes that keep down a load

murcakū: **1**. spiral, whorl, helix; **2**. snail-shaped ornament on a hat

murcakū fara i iletu kiyoo: an open sedan chair with a spiral shaft

murcan: a small gray crane, the same as **ajige kūrcan**

murfa: highland barley (grown in Tibet and Qinghai)

murhu: unclear, vague, blurred

murhu farhūn: now clear and then unclear, first blurred then distinct, indistinct (in the mind), dazed

murhūn: ⟶ **murhu**

muribumbi: **1**. (causative or passive of **murimbi**); **2**. to sprain, to wrench; **3**. to wrong someone

murigan: ⟶ **murihan**

murigan weceku: a deity to whom sacrifice was offered at the north wall of a house

murihan: a curved place on a road or path

murihan boo: a house with a curved front

murikū: **1**. obstinate, stubborn, headstrong, perverse; **2**. peg (of stringed instruments)

murikū moo: a board for tying down the ropes that hold the load on a wagon

murimbi: (**-ha**) **1**. to twist, to wring, to wring out, to pinch; **2**. to be stubborn, to be obstinate; **3**. to go around; **4**. to force, to compel; **5**. to roll up (as a quilt)

murime: with legs tucked under the body; cf. **moselame**

murime fudarambi: to be defiant

murime wambi: to kill by strangling

murin tarin: difficult to manage, recalcitrant, stubborn, unreasonable

murinjambi: to be stubborn, to act recalcitrantly

murishūn: **1**. wronged, unjustly judged, treated unjustly; **2**. stubborn

muritai: obstinate, stubborn, stubbornly, insistently

murkibumbi: (causative of **murkimbi**)

murkimbi: to trim off the corners, to round out, to round off

mursa: **1**. radish, daikon (large white Chinese radish); **2**. an engraved round ornament

murtai: obstinate, recalcitrant; cf. **muritai**

murtambi: to cry out, to scream

murtashūn: **1**. absurd, preposterous; **2**. eccentric; **3**. recalcitrant, uncooperative

murtashūn leolen: fallacy, false or absurd theory, absurd notion

muru: **1**. form, shape, appearance, lay (of the land), style, manner; **2**. nearly, almost; cf. **amba muru**

muru akū: **1**. out of shape; **2**. unreasonable, absurd

muru be tuwame: from the look of things

muru tucike: has taken form

murung: a spotted wildcat

murungga: **1**. similar in appearance; **2**. exemplary, model

murušembi: **1**. to do in outline, to do only in a general way, to do in an approximate way; **2**. to take form, to obtain a shape

murušeci: in general, in outline

murušeme: in general, in outline, approximately

murušeme bodombi: to estimate

murušeme tucibumbi: to give a general account

muse: we (inclusive)

musebumbi: (causative of **musembi**)

museingge: ours; ⟶ **muse**

musembi: (**-ke**) **1**. to become bent or warped; **2**. to feel thwarted

musembumbi: **1**. (causative of **musembi**); **2**. to make crooked, to warp, to bend; **3**. to disappoint, to thwart

musen: **1**. bending, warping; **2**. grave, hole prepared as a grave; **3**. outer coffin

musengge: ⟶ **museingge**

musha: a short-haired tiger — one name for the tiger; cf. **tasha**

musi: parched flour (used to make a broth to which sugar is added)

musi cai: tea to which parched flour is added

musi wehe: soapstone

musiha moo: *Quercus serrata*: a kind of oak

musihi: a wooden dipper with a long handle

musiren: *Calamus rotang*: rattan

musumbi: ⟶ **musembi**

mušeku: ⟶ **musihi**

mušu: *Coturnix coturnix*: quail

mušu algan: a snare for quail

mušu congkibumbi: to set quail to fighting (a sport)

mušu gidara asu: a net, four feet square, used by one man for catching quail

mušuhu: excrescence on a tree, a gnarl

mušuhuri: just, just now, just right

mušurhu: **1**. the yellow fish that is supposed to turn into a quail in the ninth month; **2**. yellow croaker (*Johnius dussumeri*)

mušuri: a kind of linen produced in Korea

mutebukū: a kind of local school in ancient times

mutebumbi: **1**. (causative of **mutembi**); **2**. to achieve, to bring about; **3**. to fill (a post)

mutembi: **1**. to be able, can, to be possible; **2**. to be completed, to be achieved

mutehe be simnere bolgobure fiyenten: (孝功清吏司) office for examining merit in the Board of Civil Appointments

muterei teile: doing all one can, with all one's ability, to the extent of one's power, to the best of one's ability

muten: **1**. capability, potentiality; **2**. achievement, skill, art

muten akū: without skill or talent

muten arambi: to show off one's abilities or talents

mutengge: skilled, talented, capable

mutubumbi: **1**. (causative of **mutumbi**); **2**. to raise to maturity

mutulhen: a kind of fish hawk (possibly identical to **suksuhu**)

mutumbi: (-ha) **1**. to grow, to grow up, to mature; **2**. to rise (said of water)

mutun: **1**. growth, stature, size; **2**. share, portion

muwa: **1**. coarse, crude, rough, thick; **2**. heavy-set, brawny; **3**. careless; **4**. boorish

muwa albatu: coarse and rough, simple and crude

muwa boso: coarse cloth

muwa duha: the large intestine

muwa edun tuwambi: euphemism for 'to defecate'

muwa funiyesun: coarse woolen fabric

muwa honci: the skin of a large sheep

muwa suse: coarse, unrefined, crude

muwa suseri hoošan: a kind of paper made from bamboo

muwa uhungge hoošan: a kind of coarse yellow wrapping paper

muwa wehe: uncarved stone

muwakan: rather coarse, crude, rough

muwarungga fukjingga hergen: (大篆) a style of calligraphy — the great seal

muwašambi: **1**. to be coarse, crude, or rough; **2**. to do in a sketchy way

muwašame: roughly, in a sketchy fashion

muya: the broken stalks of grain, chaff, straw

muya suse: chaff and straw

muyahūn: complete, intact, unblemished

muyahūn akū: incomplete, not intact

muyahūn sain: in good condition, in excellent shape

muyambi: **1**. to roar; **2**. to be angry without speaking of it

muyari: *Nephelium longana*: 'dragon's eye', longan

mūnggu: bird's nest — the edible nest of a kind of swallow

N ᠨ

na: **1**. earth, land, field; **2**. background (of a design on a textile), base; **3**. local; **4**. (sentence particle for expressing surprise or weak interrogation)

na aššambi: for an earthquake to occur, to have an earthquake

na bešekebi: the earth has become saturated with rain

na de fekumbi: to throw oneself to the ground

na i aisi: geographical advantage

na i enduri dobon: the hall where sacrifices to the earth were offered

na i gindana: (Buddhist) hell

na i giyan: the lay of the land, configurations of the land, geography

na i hafan: local magistrate

na i loo: hell, the underworld

na i mangga ba: firm earth

na i oilo hetu i durungga tetun: the name of an astronomical instrument in the Beijing observatory

na i oilo hetu undu i durungga tetun: the name of an astronomical instrument in the Beijing observatory

na i sihiyakū: the earth's axis

na i tan: the altar to earth

na sulhumbi: the earth is spongy (at the spring thaw)

naca: brother-in-law: wife's elder brother

naceo: a kind of silk with designs woven in

nacihiyabumbi: (causative of **nacihiyambi**)

nacihiyambi: to comfort, to console, to soothe

nacihiyame fonjimbi: to express sympathy

nacihiyame sumbi: to mollify, to appease

nacin: *Falco peregrinus*: the peregrine falcon

nadaci: seventh

nadaju: ⟶ **nadanju**

nadan: **1**. seven; **2**. goods, possessions; **3**. paper money hung on a long pole and offered at the grave on the seventh and forty-ninth day after a person's death

nadan biya: the seventh month

nadan irungge mahatun: an ancient-style hat with seven ridges on top

nadan jaka: goods, merchandise

nadan sen: the seven orifices of the body

nadan tuhebuku i mahatu: an ancient-style cap with seven tassels

nadan usiha: the Big Dipper, Ursa Major

nadan waliyambi: to offer sacrifice every seven days after a person's death

nadanci: seventh

nadangga: pertaining to the number seven

nadangga hoošan: seven-layered paper

nadangga inenggi: the seventh day of the seventh month

nadanggeri: seven times

nadanju: seventy

nadanjuci: seventieth

nadanjuta: seventy each

nadanjute: ⟶ **nadanjuta**

nadase: seven years old: **nadan se**

nadata: seven each

nagalambi: ⟶ **nahalambi**

nagan: ⟶ **nahan**

nag'a ilha: the 'naga flower,' which has a white blossom surrounded by six leaves (Ceylon ironwood, *Mesua ferrea*)

nahalambi: to lie sick on the oven-bed, to be bed-ridden with illness

nahan: *kàng*, oven-bed of North China and Manchuria

nahan i baita: sexual intercourse

nahan i hosori: soot from an oven-bed

nahan i irun: chimney of an oven-bed

nai: a large sacrificial tripod used in ancient China

naihū: the Big Dipper, Ursa Major; cf. **nadan usiha**

naihū de sucunangga loho: a sword that glitters when it is drawn from the scabbard

naihūbumbi: (causative of **naihūmbi**)

naihūmbi: to tilt, to lean to one side, to stagger

naiji ilha: spikenard

naimisun: the hem of a fur jacket's lining; cf. **afin**

nainai: housewife, mistress of a household

nairahūn: gentle, kind, warm and generous

nairahūn arambi: to pretend to be gentle or kind

najihiyan: a name for the **mojihiyan**, the Tibetan black bear

nakabumbi: **1**. (causative of **nakambi**); **2**. to dismiss, to let go, to discharge; **3**. to stop, to impede; **4**. to retire from office

nakambi: **1**. to stop, to cease, to desist; **2**. to leave (a post); **3**. to leave a perch (chicken)

naka bai: Stop!, Cease!

nakcu: uncle: mother's brother

nakcuse: (plural of **nakcu**); cf. **nakcuta**

nakcuta: (plural of **nakcu**)

nakū: after (used after the imperative)

nama: ⟶ **naman**

nama gida: a small spear used by the vanguard

nama sirdan: a military arrow with a head shaped like a spearhead

namalabumbi: (causative of **namalambi**)

namalambi: to stick with a needle, to practice acupuncture

naman: a needle used for acupuncture

namarabumbi: (causative or passive of **nanalambi**)

namarambi: to fight for more, to demand more, to take up again (a quarrel), to raise (a price)

namašan: (used after the participles) at the point of, just when, right after, about to

nambumbi: **1**. to be caught, to be captured; **2**. to be discovered; **3**. to have something fall into one's hand

nambuha nambuhai: unintentionally, unexpectedly, randomly, by chance

namgin: a red persimmon-like fruit of Hainan

nami: a garment made of cured deerskin

namki: saddle blanket or pad

namkū: the name of a famous sword kept in the arsenal

namsi namsi: at random, haphazard

namšan: (used with the participles) at the point of, just when, when about to; cf. **namašan**

namšuri: an exotic fruit from a bush over three feet tall that blooms in winter

namu: **1**. ocean, sea; **2**. overseas, foreign; **3**. a large-leafed green vegetable eaten raw, lettuce, celtuce, stem lettuce (*Lactuca sativa*)

namu angga: port, harbor

namu coko: a peacock; ⟶ **tojin**

namu dengjan: a lamp made of a sheep's horn hung before a Buddha image

namu niyehe: a sea duck or foreign duck with a white body, spotted head and wings, and a red flesh growth on the bill

namu sika moo: a variety of South Sea palm

namu ulgiyan: dolphin

namu urangga moo: a kind of conifer in Annam

namuci: ⟶ **namusi**

namun: storehouse, granary

namun asaran: storage in a granary

namuri: name of a flax-like plant from which fabric can be woven

namusi: keeper of a warehouse or granary

nan: (男) baron

nandabumbi: (causative of **nandambi**)

nandambi: to ask for, to beg, to demand

nanggin: porch, veranda, gallery, corridor

nanggišambi: to show off one's charms, to ingratiate oneself with, to allure with one's charms

nanggitu coko: a name for the turkey; cf. **junggila gasha**

nanggū: a trap for badger and raccoon-dogs

nantuhūn: **1**. dirty, filthy; **2**. corrupt

nantuhūn gebu: infamy, notoriety

nantuhūn hafan: corrupt official

nantuhūrabumbi: (causative or passive of **nantuhūrambi**)

nantuhūrambi: to dirty, to make filthy, to soil, to foul

naracuka: regrettable, causing feelings of longing and attachment

naracun: longing, attachment

narahūnjambi: to long for continually

narambi: (**1**) to be reluctant to part with, to begrudge, to want to hang on to, to pine away, to cling to

narambi: (**2**) (**-ka**) to become emaciated, to look haggard

naranggi: finally, after all, really

narašambi: to feel ardently drawn to, to yearn for, to pine for

narašembi: ⟶ **narašambi**

narga: harrow, rake

nargabumbi: (causative of **nargambi**)

nargambi: to level with a harrow, to rake

narhūdambi: to be stingy, to be miserly

narhūn: **1**. fine, thin; **2**. detailed, minute; **3**. secret, confidential; **4**. sparing, economical, frugal; **5**. grazing the target (at archery)

    narhūn arga: secret plan, plot, ruse

    narhūn ba: (密本房) Office of Secret Communications in the Board of War

    narhūn baita: a secret matter

    narhūn boso: fine cloth

    narhūn duha: the small intestine

    narhūn edun: euphemism for urine

    narhūn edun tuwambi: euphemism for 'to urinate'

    narhūn ferguwecuke: exquisite

    narhūn funiyesun: a kind of fine woolen

    narhūn gala: soft, delicate hand (of a woman)

    narhūn honci: lambskin

    narhūn muciha futa: a thin bamboo tow rope

    narhūn nimeku: **1**. tuberculosis; **2**. hernia

    narhūn selei futa: fine wire

    narhūn wehe: a stone polished smoothly

narhūngga: fine, refined, detailed

    narhūngga fukjingga hergen: (小篆) a style of calligraphy — the small seal

narhūnjambi: ⟶ **narahūnjambi**

narhūšabumbi: (causative of **narhūšambi**)

narhūšambi: **1**. to be fine, to be minute; **2**. to be sparing, to be economical; **3**. to do carefully, to do minutely; **4**. to do secretly; **5**. to make (an arrow shaft) thin

    narhūšame alambi: **1**. to report in detail; **2**. to make a secret report

    narhūšame bodombi: to calculate carefully

    narhūšame fempilere ba: Bureau for Sealing (examination papers)

    narhūšame fempilere falgangga: (彌封所) the same as **narhūšame fempilere ba**

    narhūšame fempilere hafan: (彌封官) Sealer of Examinations, *BH* 652F

    narhūšame gisurembi: to speak of in detail

narhūšembi: ⟶ **narhūšambi**

nari: female brown bear; cf. **nasin**

nasa: ⟶ **nasan**

nasabumbi: (causative of **nasambi**)

nasacuka: regrettable, lamentable, mournful

    nasacuka ucun: dirge, mournful song

nasacun: regret, lament, grief, sorrow

nasambi: **1**. to mourn, to grieve, to feel sorrowful, to be disconsolate; **2**. to lament, to regret

    nasara bithe: obituary, memorial essay for a deceased person

nasan: salted cabbage, preserved vegetables

    nasan gidambi: to make salted cabbage

    nasan hengke: cucumber

    nasan sogi: pickled cabbage

nasandumbi: to lament together, to grieve together

nashūlabumbi: (causative of **nashūlambi**)

nashūlabun: opportunity

nashūlambi: to meet with an opportunity, to take advantage of an opportunity, to seize a chance

nashūn: **1**. opportunity, opportune moment, chance; **2**. circumstances, situation, occasion

    nashūn be acabumbi: to take advantage of an opportunity

    nashūn be amcambi: to take advantage of an opportunity

    nashūn be tuwame: taking advantage of an opportunity

    nashūn de acabumbi: to rise to the occasion, to act in accordance with circumstances

    nashūn giyan: principle of action, reason

    nashūn ufarambi: to miss an opportunity

nasin: *Ursus arctos*: large brown bear

nasucungga: regrettable, pitiable

naya: brother-in-law: younger brother of one's wife

ne: **1**. now, at present, current; **2**. sentence particle of mild interrogation

    ne aniya: the current year

    ne belen: ready, available

    ne bisire: still alive

    ne je: immediately, right now

    ne jen belhehe: already prepared

ne menggun: cash

ne tušan: current post

ne tušan i: currently in office

nece: sister-in-law: the wife of one's wife's elder brother

necibumbi: (causative or passive of **necimbi**)

necihiyebumbi: (causative of **necihiyembi**)

necihiyembi: **1**. to level, to smooth out; **2**. to console, to calm down; **3**. to subjugate, to subject, to pacify

necihiyen: peaceful, tranquil, serene

necihiyenembi: to go to pacify, to go to subdue

neciken: rather level

necimbi: **1**. to encroach, to violate, to transgress, to infringe, to trespass; **2**. to provoke, to tease; **3**. to attack, to raid; **4**. to harm, to hurt; **5**. to commit a crime

 necime nungnembi: to invade and harass (a border region)

necin: **1**. level, flat, even; **2**. peaceful, tranquil, calm

 necin cibsen: calm, tranquil

 necin ekisaka: calm, quiet

 necin elhe: peace, safety

 necin hūda: fair price, lower price

 necin miyalimbi: to weigh rice after smoothing off the top of a container with a piece of wood

 necin mujilen: even temper, gentle disposition

 necin na: level land, level ground, level place

 necin nesuken: gentle, mild (temperament)

 necin tondo: fair, equitable

necindumbi: to attack one another

necinembi: to go to encroach or provoke, to go to attack

necingge: level, flat

 necingge karan: watchtower, lookout tower

 necingge kemun: level: instrument for testing if something is level or not

 necingge mahatun: an ancient-style hat with a flat board on top

 necingge mudan: the level tone of Chinese

 necingge saifi: a flat spoon

necinjimbi: to come to encroach, to come to provoke, to come to attack

nege: (see below)

 nege negelembi: to learn how to stand (said of a small child), (metaphorically) to be barely able to do something

negelembi: to be unsteady, to wobble (said of things just placed in an erect position)

nehū: (this word and the next two have the peculiar spelling of soft **h** before **ū**): slave girl, maidservant

nehūji: slave girl, maidservant

 nehūji mama: an old slave woman

nehūse: (plural of **nehū**)

nei: sweat, perspiration

 nei funiyehe: body hair

 nei taran: perspiration

 nei tucimbi: to sweat

 nei yoo: heat rash

 nei yoo dekdembi: to get heat rash

neibumbi: **1**. (causative of **neimbi**); **2**. to come to one's senses

 neibume ulhimbi: to realize suddenly

neibushūn: open, frank, candid

neigecilebumbi: (causative of **neigecilembi**)

neigecilembi: to divide equally, to even out

neigelembi: to make even, to make uniform, to act uniformly, to behave equally

neigen: even, uniform, equal, average

 neigen akū: uneven, unequal

 neigen necin: equal, equivalent

neigenjebumbi: (causative of **neigenjembi**)

neigenjembi: to make even, to make uniform, to divide evenly, to share equally

 neigenjeme dendembi: to divide equally

neihen: ⟶ **neigen**

neiku sithan: small hinge on a box

neilebukū: tutor of the heir-apparent during the Three Kingdoms Period

neilebumbi: (causative of **neilembi**)

neilebun: introduction, exposition (a kind of essay)

neileku: ⟶ **erdemu be neileku**

neilembi: to disclose, to elucidate, to introduce to something new — especially knowledge, to enlighten, to reveal

neilen: introduction, disclosure, primer, letter (from a superior)

neileshūn: beginning, beginning of spring

neimbi: to open, to open up

 neime badarambumbi: to open up (a frontier region)

 neime suksalambi: to open up (wasteland)

nekcu: uncle: the wife of one's mother's brothers

nekcute: (plural of **nekcu**)

nekeliyeken: rather thin, rather flimsy

nekeliyelembi: to make thin, to make scanty, to make unimportant, to treat as unimportant

nekeliyelenembi: to go to make thin

nekeliyen: 1. thin, flimsy, fine; 2. unimportant, trifling; 3. scanty, meager; 4. unkind, mean (said of someone's attitude)

    nekeliyen ceceri: a variety of thin silk

    nekeliyen duyen: inconstant, fickle, heartless

    nekeliyen holbonggo hoošan: a variety of strong thin paper made from bamboo

    nekeliyen oshon: harsh, unkind

    nekeliyen šobin: a thin baked cake made of flour, sugar, walnuts, and lard

neku: a woman's female friend, sworn sister, female companion

nekulambi: ⟶ nekulembi

nekulembi: 1. to take advantage of (a friend's good offices, an opportunity, someone's misfortune); 2. to rejoice over another's misfortune or weakness; 3. to be only too glad to do something

nelhe: peaceful, healthy

nemebumbi: 1. (causative of nemembi); 2. to increase

nemegin: a measure equal to thirty catties

nemehen: 1. addition, increment; 2. something extra added when trading things of unequal value

nemeku omolo: a descendant of the fifth generation

nemembi: 1. to add, to increase; 2. to remove the husks from grain

    nememe: 1. moreover, on the contrary, especially; 2. still more

nemendumbi: 1. to add together; 2. to hull together

nemergen: ⟶ nemerhen

nemerhen: a raincoat made of reeds

nemeri: tender, young (said of fruits and vegetables)

nemerku: a raincoat, rain jacket

nemešembi: to add to repeatedly

nemeyeken: rather tender, rather graceful

nemeyen: tender, gentle, graceful, docile, easygoing

    nemeyen ceceri: a soft silk used for women's garments

    nemeyen hojo: gentle and charming, tender and beautiful

nemgiyan: ⟶ nemgiyen

nemgiyen: affectionate, gentle, tender

    nemgiyen nesuken: gentle, mild, tender

nemkibumbi: (causative of nemkimbi)

nemkimbi: 1. to sew the outer part of a fur garment to the lining, to fold over and sew the underarm seam of an unpadded garment; 2. to tack (sew with loose stitches)

nemkiyambi: ⟶ nemkimbi

nemselembi: to add more, to intensify, to make more serious (an illness), to aggravate (someone's anger)

nemsuri bele: a variety of rice that is cultivated in dry fields in the south

nemšeku: avaricious, insatiable, an insatiable person

nemšembi: to vie for first place, to put (profit) first, to be avaricious, to be dissatisfied and seek more, to try to be first

nemu: mineral deposit, ore, ore deposit, mine

nemuri: mine (for minerals)

nendebumbi: (causative of nendembi)

nendembi: to be in front, to put first, to come before, to be prior, to act first, to take the lead

    nendeme yabumbi: to go ahead, to be in the lead

    nendere be nemšembi: to try to do first, to strive to be best

nenden: first, beforehand, prior, premature

    nenden amaga: first and latter, successively

    nenden bojiri ilha: a variety of chrysanthemum that blooms in the seventh month

    nenden ilha: *Prunus mume*: Chinese plum flower

    nenden ilhai giyen: the name of a dark blue dye

    nenden usiha: *Elaeagnus pungens*: thorny olive

nenembi: to be first, to be ahead, to do something first, to act first; nendembi

    nenehe: former, prior, which went before

    nenehe adali: as before, as usual

    nenehe aniya: former year, previous year

    nenehe biya: previous month

    nenehe enduringge saisa: former holy sages, sages of antiquity

    nenehe inenggi: former day, previous day

    nenehe jalan: former age, previous age

    nenehe tušan: former post

    neneme: formerly, previously, beforehand, first, in advance

    neneme amala: one after another, successively, early or late, from first to last

nengge: slight corneal opacity, nebula, a film covering the eye

nenggelebumbi: to cushion, to support, to prop up

nenggeleku: ⟶ **fi i nenggeleku**

nenggelembi: **1**. to prop up, to cushion; **2**. to raise the heels, to stand on tiptoe

nenggerebumbi: **1**. to prop up; **2**. to delay, to avoid

nenggereshun: cushioned, supported

nenggeshun: ⟶ **nenggereshun**

neombi: **1**. to roam, to wander away from home; **2**. to float, to drift

neore tugi: a floating cloud, a lone moving cloud

nere: **1**. a three-legged prop for a cooking pot; **2**. a hole used for cooking purposes; **3**. stove, cooking range

nere fetembi: to dig a cooking hole

nere jun: a portable stove made of iron (used when traveling)

nerebumbi: **1**. (causative or passive of **nerembi**); **2**. to shoot a wounded animal again; **3**. to vilify further, to add insult to injury, to blame an innocent party

nereku: a sleeveless rain cape made of leather or oilskin

nereku nerembi: to put on a rain cape

nerembi: to throw (clothing) over the shoulders

nergen: ⟶ **nergin**

nergi: smart, clever, sharp

nergin: **1**. moment, short space of time, occasion, opportunity; **2**. temporary

nergin de: **1**. just at this time, at that moment, on some occasion; **2**. temporarily

nergin i: temporary

nergin i hūsun: a temporary worker

nerginde: by chance, it happened that …

nergingge: clever at grasping opportunities

nerkimbi: to open, to open out (a scroll, roll of cloth, etc.)

nerku: ⟶ **nereku**

neshun: flat

nesi: **1**. right now, just at this minute; **2**. a crack on an animal's hoof

nesidun: one of the names of the partridge; cf. **jukidun**

nesuken: gentle, tender, mild

nesuken hehe: posthumous title of wives of sixth-rank officials

nesuken nemeyen: gentle and easygoing

neye: the wife of one's wife's younger brother

ni: **1**. (genitive particle after words ending in **-ng**); **2**. (interrogative particle at the end of a clause); **3**. (a particle used at the caesura in archaic verse); **4**. (an exclamation of wonder)

ni gidambi: to record (someone's mistakes), to note (one's merits and errors)

nicangga tungken: a large drum on a stand

nicarambi: ⟶ **nijarambi**

nicuhe: pearl

nicuhe boobai: valuables, jewels

nicuhe šungkeri ilha: a kind of Chinese orchid with fragrant purple blossoms

nicuhei šurdehen: a sphere inlaid with pearls that in ancient times was used for observing the sun, moon, and stars

nicuheri moo: a variety of arbor vitae whose leaves resemble pearls

nicuhūn: ⟶ **nincuhūn**

niculambi: to wink, to blink

nicumbi: (**-ha/-he**) to close the eyes

nicun ilha: *Spiraea thunbergii*: baby's breath, spiraea

nicušambi: ⟶ **niculambi**

nidumbi: to groan, to moan

nihešulembi: ⟶ **niohušelembi**

nijarabumbi: (causative of **nijarambi**)

nijarakū: a vessel for grinding hard materials into powder, mortar

nijarambi: to grind fine (as in a mortar)

niji: path around a swamp or damp place

nijihe: small bits of grain produced during the husking and milling process

nikacilambi: to act like a Chinese person

nikacilarakū: non-Chinese, acting in a non-Chinese manner

nikai: (an emphatic sentence particle)

nikan: **1**. Chinese; **2**. southern Chinese, southern barbarians

nikan bithei kunggeri boo: (漢科房) Chinese Copying Office, *BH* 138

nikan dangse boo: (漢檔房) Translation Office (for Manchu and Chinese)

nikan gūldargan: a small type of swallow that is fond of chirping

nikan hengke: *Cucumis melo*: a variety of sweet-tasting melon somewhat larger than the 'sweet melon'

nikan hergen: Chinese character, Chinese writing, the Chinese written language

nikan ulhūma: *Syrmaticus reevesii*: the long-tailed pheasant, Reeve's pheasant

nikan uli: a kind of sour apple that is often preserved

nikan wesimbure bithei ba: (漢本堂) Office of Chinese Memorials of the Grand Secretariat

nikan yoo: a pustule or boil on the skin, venereal sore

nikarabumbi: (causative of **nikarambi**)

nikarambi: **1**. to speak Chinese, to act in a Chinese manner; **2**. to act like a barbarian

nikaramc ubaliyambumbi: to translate into Chinese

nikasa: (plural of **nikan**)

nikcabumbi: **1**. (causative or passive of **nikcambi**); **2**. to smash, to destroy

nikcambi: **1**. to shatter, to disintegrate, to be destroyed; **2**. to be at a disadvantage, to suffer loss

nikde: the part of an animal's back that supports a saddle (on horses, mules, and donkeys), withers

nikebuku: a prop, doorstop

nikebumbi: **1**. (causative of **nikembi**); **2**. to prop up, to support, to serve as a support; **3**. to undergo (a punishment); **4**. to entrust to, to hand over to; **5**. to confer (on), to bestow; **6**. to impose (a burden)

nikebun: painted representation of a deity or plaque with a deity's name written on it, ancestral tablet

nikedembi: **1**. to make do with, to make the best of, to accommodate oneself to; **2**. to assume, to take on; **3**. to come near, to approach

nikedeme: just enough, just a little

nikeku: a support, something to lean on

nikeku mulan: a chair

nikeku mulan i dasikū: covering or cushion on a chair

nikekungge sektefun: cushion or padding on the back of a chair

nikembi: **1**. to lean, to lean on; **2**. to rely on, to depend on; **3**. to approach, to draw near, to neighbor on; **4**. to remain in confinement for a month after childbirth; cf. **niyarhūlambi**

niken: support, reliance

nikendumbi: to support one another, to support together

nikenembi: **1**. to go to lean on; **2**. to draw near to

nikenjimbi: **1**. to come to lean, to come to rest on; **2**. to draw near to

nikešembi: to limp slightly

niketu: support, reliance

niketu akū: without means of support

niksimbi: (**-he**) to shiver with cold

niktan: a divine elixir, an elixir of cinnabar that is supposed to confer immortality

niktan okto: elixir, efficacious medicine

niktan siktan: ⟶ **niktan**

niktembi: to slap one's legs against the saddle skirt; cf. **kebsimbi**

nikton: at peace, peaceful

niktongga: peaceful, tranquil

niktongga gecuheri: a kind of silk produced in Nanjing and decorated with dragon figures

niktongga suri: a fine silken fabric from Nanjing

niktongga undurakū: a silken fabric from Nanjing with a design of prancing dragons

nilabumbi: (causative of **nilambi**)

nilakū: small roller for crushing or grinding objects, crusher, grinder

nilambi: to polish, to buff, to grind (a lens), to make smooth and shiny

nilara yonggan: fine sand used for polishing jade, glass, etc.

nilembi: ⟶ **nilambi**

nilgiyan: shiny, glistening, slick, smooth, oily, glossy, satiny

nilgiyan suje: a variety of shiny satin

nilgiyangga: lustrous, brilliant, shining

nilhi: dysentery; cf. **ilhi**

nilhi hefeliyenembi: to have dysentery

nilhūdambi: **1**. to slip, to skid, to slide; **2**. to be slippery

nilhūma: a name for the pheasant

nilhūn: slippery, slick

nilhūšambi: to be slick (said of ice)

niltajabumbi: (causative or passive of **niltajambi**)

niltajambi: to be damaged by rubbing, to be abraded

niltubumbi: to singe hair off of a skin

niltumbi: to shed hair or fur

niluga: ⟶ **nilukan**

nilukan: smooth, glossy, not rough

nimaci: goatskin

nimada: hornless dragon

nimadan: a kind of tree that grows in valley groves and produces a hard, fine-grained wood

nimaha: fish

    nimaha butambi: to fish

    nimaha butara jahūdai: fishing boat

    nimaha butara niyalma: a fisherman

    nimaha gabtara šaka: an arrow with a five-pronged forked head used for shooting fish

    nimaha usiha: a star in the Milky Way located north of the constellation **weisha**

    nimaha yasa: a corn on the foot

nimahašambi: to fish

nimala: ⟶ **nimalan**

nimlalan: *Morus alba*: mulberry tree

    nimalan moo: ⟶ **nimalan**

niman: goat

nimanggi: snow

    nimanggi iktambi: snow piles up, the snow is drifting

    nimanggi ilha: snowflake, snow crystal

    nimanggi kiyalmambi: (the wind) drives the snow in whirls

    nimanggi labsan: snowflake

    nimanggi wenembi: the snow is melting

nimarambi: to snow

nimargan: *Alcedo atthis*: little kingfisher

nimari: **1**. goatskin; **2**. snow-like

    nimari gūwasihiya: the eastern egret; cf. **gūwasihiya**

    nimari ilha: *Hibiscus rosa-sinensis*: rose-of-China

    nimari yanggali: a small bird with snow-white feathers — when it sings it is supposed to snow

nimasi: a name for the kingfisher; cf. **ulgiyan cecike**

nimašakū: a small two-man boat made from a tree trunk

nimašan: **1**. water from melting snow; **2**. the sea eagle (*Haliaeetus albicilla*)

nimašan muke: water from melting snow

nimebumbi: (causative of **nimembi**)

nimecuke: **1**. painful, excruciating; **2**. frightful, fierce, cruel; **3**. strong (said of liquor)

    nimecuke horonggo poo: the name of an iron cannon four feet eight and one-half inches long

nimeku: **1**. sickness, illness; **2**. pain; **3**. defect, weakness

    nimeku bahambi: to get an illness

    nimeku de darubumbi: to be prone to frequent illnesses

    nimeku de hūsibuhabi: is afflicted by a chronic illness

    nimeku turgen: the illness is acute

nimekulebumbi: (causative of **nimekulembi**)

nimekulembi: to become ill, to develop an illness

nimekungge: ill, sick, one who is ill

nimembi: to ache, to be painful, to suffer from pain, to be ill

    nimeme bucembi: to die of an illness

    nimeme dedumbi: to lie ill in bed

    nimeme maktabumbi: to fall ill, to be laid up with illness

nimenggi: oil, fat; cf. **imenggi**

    nimenggi noho: covered with oil, full of fat

    nimenggi yasa: the two depressions near a person's hipbone

nimenggilembi: to grease, to oil, to press oil, to produce oil

nimetembi: to be ill together, to suffer mutually

nimheliyen ilha: *Viburunum roseum*: snowball

nincuhūn: smelling of fish or raw meat, smelly, smelling of blood

nindaršambi: to pay compliments to, to flirt

ningceo: Nanjing silk

ningcu: ⟶ **ningceo**

ningdan: a growth on the neck, goiter

ningdangga: having a growth on the neck, having a goiter

ningge: the one which … , he who …

ninggišambi: ⟶ **nindaršambi**

ninggiya: **1**. water caltrop, horn chestnut (*Trapa natans*); **2**. anchor; **3**. a weapon used for stopping enemy horses, an iron weapon with sharp barbs

    ninggiya bula: *Tribulus terrestris*: puncture vine

ninggiya efen: small meat-filled dumplings boiled in soup

ninggiya moo: wooden anchor

ninggiya sele: **1.** an iron anchor; **2.** a horseshoe with teeth or cleats

ninggiyan: ⟶ **ninggiya**

ninggu: top, on top, upper surface

ningguci: sixth

ninggude: (postposition) on top of

ninggule: linden tree; cf. **nunggule**

ninggun: **1.** six; **2.** ⟶ **ninggu**

ninggun acan: **1.** the six directions: north, south, east, west, up, and down; **2.** the entire world

ninggun biya: the sixth month

ninggun fu: the internal organs: stomach, gall bladder, large intestine, small intestine, and three visceral cavities

ninggun irungge mahatun: an ancient-style hat with six ridges on top

ninggun muten: the six skills: rites, music, archery, chariot-driving, calligraphy, and arithmetic

ninggun yangsangga inenggi: the six auspicious days of the year

ninggunggeri: six times

ninggureme: on top, over, upward

ningguse: six years old

ninggute: six each

ningkabumbi: to be inflated, to become puffed up, to feel suffocated

ningniyen: ⟶ **ninggiya**

niniyarambi: to suffer a sharp pricking pain, to ache (said of a tooth)

niniyarilambi: to get a pain in the back, to wrench the back

niniyaršambi: to set one's teeth on edge (by eating sour or hard things)

ninju: sixty

ninju dulefun i durungga tetun: an astronomical instrument of the Beijing observatory used for observing the variation in degrees among the equator, ecliptic, sun, moon, and stars

ninjuci: sixtieth

ninjute: sixty each

ninkimbi: **1.** to search for a doe (said of buck deer); **2.** to search for fawns (said of a mother doe); cf. **nirkimbi**

ninkime baimbi: to search for fawns (said of a mother doe)

nintehe ilha: a fragrant white blossom of Hainan that resembles jasmine

nintuhū: having a crooked neck, a crooked-necked person

nintuhū hari: a crooked-necked man

ninuri: a name for the cat

nio: **1.** (an interrogative sentence particle); **2.** (an emphatic particle)

niobombi: to tease, to taunt with words

nioboro: deep green

niocuhe: ⟶ **nicuhe**

niohan: (牛) a constellation, the 9th of the lunar mansions, made up of six stars in Capricorn

niohan tokdonggo kiru: a banner depicting the constellation **niohon**

niohe: wolf

niohe sube: a wild plant whose leaves are used as padding for saddles

niohe ujungga: having the head of a wolf

niohe yoo: lupus, small red eruptions on the skin

nioheri: a kind of mythical wolf

niohobumbi: ⟶ **niyohobumbi**

niohokon: light green, greenish

niohombi: to engage in sexual intercourse, to have sex; cf. **niyohombi**

niohon: **1.** light green, greenish (also used for various shades of green and blue); **2.** the second of the heaven's stems (乙)

niohon abka: the vault of heaven, the blue sky

niohon elbengge fukjingga hergen: (碧落篆) a style of calligraphy

niohon jili banjimbi: to fly into a blue rage

niohon senggi: blood shed in a just cause

niohon talkiyangga loho: the name of a kind of sword

niohon temgetungge gu: a flat piece of jade with a hole in the center used at certain feudal investitures and at sacrifices

niohubumbi: (causative of **niohumbi**)

niohuken: somewhat pea green

niohumbi: **1.** to pound, to stamp; **2.** to construct a pounded earth wall

niohun: pea green

> **niohun teišun**: bronze

niohurembi: to act fiercely, to put on a fierce expression

niohušulebumbi: (causative of **niohušulembi**)

niohušulembi: to go naked, to be naked

niohušun: naked

niojan niyehe: *Podiceps ruficollis*: Chinese little grebe

niokan: a small arrow made from a willow branch and used by children for play

> **niokan bolgombi**: to throw small play arrows or chopsticks into a pot — a drinking forfeit game

niokji: moss on stones in water; cf. **niolmonggi**

niokso: a string-like form of algae found on the surface of water

niolhucembi: 1. to be rabid (said of a dog); 2. to plunge headlong, to rush forward

> **niolhucehe indahūn**: mad dog, rabid dog

niolhumbi: to run swiftly, to gallop, to give a horse its head, to let go at a fast pace

niolhumbumbi: (causative of **niolhumbi**)

niolhun: 1. the sixteenth day of the first month, the end of the New Year festivities; 2. slippery; cf. **nilhūn**

> **niolhun efen**: round boiled pastries filled with walnut and sesame that are eaten on the evening of the fifteenth day of the first month

> **niolhun ilha**: a red flower resembling the quince that blooms around the sixteenth of the first month

niolhušembi: to slip, to lose one's footing

niolhūdambi: to slip and fall, to lose one's footing, to slide

niolhūn: ⟶ **niolhun**

niolmon: 1. moss; 2. rainbow; cf. **nioron**; 3. entering battle without armor

> **niolmon beye**: a soldier without helmet and armor

niolmongge: 1. naked; 2. lacking fur or scales

niolmonggi: moss on rocks in water; cf. **niokji**

niolmuhan: ⟶ **ilmun han**

niolmukan: 1. ⟶ **nilukan**; 2. greasy

niolmun: ⟶ **nioron**

niolocuka: too greasy, too oily, disgusting

niolombi: to get stuck in the throat because of being too greasy, to gag on something because it is disgusting

niombi: (-ho) to be frozen to the bones

> **niome nimembi**: to have the bones ache with cold

> **niome šahūrun**: cold that penetrates to the bones

niomere: octopus

niomošon: *Brachymystax lenok*: Siberian salmon

niomšun: ⟶ **niomošon**

nionggajambi: to be scratched, to be injured (the surface of some object), to be damaged on the surface due to a hard blow, to be grazed

> **nionggajara adali**: as if pierced (on seeing something pitiful)

> **nionggajarahū**: oh that he may not be hurt!

nionggalabumbi: (causative or passive of **nionggalambi**)

nionggalambi: to damage slightly the surface of some object, to scratch, to abrade

niongnio: 1. the largest feather on a bird's wing; 2. outstanding, best, superior

> **niongnio dethe**: the largest and toughest feather on a bird's wing

> **niongnio tucike**: preeminent, outstanding, best

niongniyaha: goose

> **niongniyaha i be**: the name of a plant that is the same as **meihe šari**

nionio: 1. pupil of the eye; 2. an expression of affection used by adults to children

> **nionio faha**: the pupil of the eye

nionioru: a small basket tray

niori: ⟶ **niowari nioweri**

niorombi: (-ko, -pi) 1. to turn green or blue; 2. to develop a bruise on the skin; 3. to be moved profoundly; 4. to be infatuated with, to be charmed by, to be bewitched by; 5. to appear (said of a rainbow)

niorombumbi: 1. (causative of **niorombi**); 2. to make iron shine

nioron: rainbow

> **nioron burubuha**: the rainbow became covered with clouds

> **nioron gocika**: the rainbow appeared

> **nioron gocingga loho**: a sword that sparkles like a rainbow

> **nioron samsiha**: the rainbow has disappeared

nioronggo dabtangga loho: a sword forged like a rainbow

nioronggo kiltan: a pennant of the Imperial Escort that is colored like a rainbow

niorumbi: (**-ke**) ⟶ **niorombi**

niošuhulembi: to change color when angry

niošumbumbi: ⟶ **nišumbumbi**

niowancihiyan: smelling of new-mown hay or grass, having the fragrance of grass

niowangga ilha: *Lychnis fulgens*: brilliant campion

niowangga moo: *Ilex pedunculosa*: longstock holly

niowanggiyakan: apple-green, light green, greenish

niowanggiyan: **1**. green; **2**. the first of the heaven's stems (甲)

    niowanggiyan derhuwe: a green fly

    niowanggiyan fiyorhon: a green woodpecker

    niowanggiyan fulan: a blue-black horse

    niowanggiyan fulha: a green poplar

    niowanggiyan gu: green jade, jasper

    niowaggiyan gurjen: katydid, long-haired grasshopper

    niowanggiyan muduringga kiru: a banner of the Imperial Escort embroidered with a green dragon

    niowanggiyan tu i cooha: Chinese troops of the green banner

    niowanggiyan turi: green pea, green bean

    niowanggiyan turun: the green banner, i.e, the Chinese troops of the provinces

    niowanggiyan turun cooha: the Chinese troops of the green banner

    niowanggiyan uju: a green lacquered tablet on which a person granted an audience with the Emperor wrote his name and rank

    niowanggiyan yasai tuwambi: to look on greedily or covetously

    niowanggiyan yenggehe: a green parrot

    niowanggiyan yenggetu: a kind of macaw

niowaniori hiyaban: light green summer cloth

niowargi gasha: turquoise kingfisher

niowari: shiny green or blue

    niowari bojiri ilha: a blue chrysanthemum

    niowari cecike: siskin

    niowari niori: the same as **niowari nioweri**

    niowari nioweri: bright green, shiny green

niowarikū: jasper green

niowarimbu wehe: emerald

niowarišambi: to be green, to become green

niraha: ⟶ **nirga**

nirehe: (女) a constellation, the 10th of the lunar mansions, made up of four stars (ε, μ, *4*, *5*) in Aquarius

    nirehe tokdonggo kiru: a banner depicting the constellation **nirehe**

nirfa: Nirvana

nirga: short, sparse (said of hair)

nirgakan: rather short, rather sparse (said of hair)

nirhūwatu: a name for the bamboo partridge; cf. **cuse moo i itu**

nirkimbi: to look for a doe (said of a buck deer); cf. **ninkimbi**

niru: **1**. a large arrow for shooting game and people; **2**. a **niru**, a banner company of a hundred men; **3**. (佐領) the head of a banner, Captain, *BH* 726

    niru belhere ba. (備箭處) the place where arrows were made for the Emperor's use

    niru ejen: commander of a banner company

    niru faksi: an arrow maker, fletcher

    nirui falga: the meeting place of a banner company

    nirui janggin: (佐領) Captain, *BH* 726

nirubumbi: (causative of **nirumbi**)

nirugan: picture, chart, map, diagram, drawing, painting

    nirugan i temun: a round stick on which paintings are rolled

niruhan: ⟶ **nirugan**

nirumbi: (**-ha**) to draw, to paint

    nirure ceceri: silk used for painting

nirwan: Nirvana, paradise

    nirwan tuwabumbi: to die (said of monks)

niselembi: to fend off

nisiha: **1**. a small fish; **2**. the name of a card game

    nisiha efen: flat boiled cakes made from wheat flour and eaten with cream

    nisiha umiyaha: bookworm, insect that damages books

nisihai: along with, together with, along with so as to make a complete set

nisikte: a kind of grass growing in clumps in a forest (used for weaving nets)

nisubumbi: (causative of **nisumbi**)

nisukū: skates, shoes used for walking on ice

nisumbi: (**-ha**) to slide, to glide, to skid, to skate (on ice)

nisundumbi: to skate together on the ice, to slide together

nisuri: a device attached to the grip of a bow to allow it to release smoothly

niša: **1.** strong, heavy, solid, firm; **2.** sufficiently, in sufficient quantity, in ample quantity, fully

  niša aciha: a heavy load

  niša bumbi: to give in sufficient quantity

  niša dambi: to blaze brightly

  niša gaimbi: to take in ample quantity

  niša gidambi: to press firmly

  niša isebumbi: to punish severely

  niša tantambi: to administer a sound beating

  niša tebumbi: to pack in firmly

nišakan: rather strong, rather heavy

nišalabumbi: (causative of **nišalambi**)

nišalambi: **1.** to act forcefully, to do with force, to hit solidly; **2.** to pick off lice

  nišalame: with due care, seriously

  nišalame afabumbi: to entrust solemnly

  nišalame tantambi: to beat severely

nišan: an undyed spot on both ends of a piece of silk cloth, a mark, a sign

nišargan: skin eruption, boil, sore, carbuncle

niše: one millionth

nišui faksi: a mason

nišumbumbi: to stick into, to insert, to fit into

nitan: **1.** weak, diluted, insipid, dulled, bland; **2.** without worldly desires

  nitan aisin: gold that is not 100 percent pure

  nitan boco: light color

  nitan cai: weak tea

  nitan menggun: silver that is not 100 percent pure

  nitan nure: weak liquor

  nitan sogi: lightly salted vegetables

nitarabumbi: **1.** (causative of **nitarambi**); **2.** to dilute

nitarambi: (-ka) **1.** to become weak or diluted; **2.** to calm down, to be appeased; **3.** to become less severe

nitumbi: ⟶ **nidumbi**, to groan, to moan (in pain)

nituri cecike: a snipe with a white beak

niyabumbi: (causative of **niyambi**)

niyada: late in maturing, slow in growing

  niyada jeku: late grain

niyadaha: a late maturing pear from the south

niyagara: ⟶ **niyahara**

niyahan: puppy, whelp

niyahara: tender sprouts, tender leaves, tender buds

  niyahara i yarun: one of the six yang tones

  niyahara nimala: tender leaves of the mulberry tree

niyaharanambi: ⟶ **niyaharnambi**

niyahari ilha: 'child's flower' — a small flower that grows in thick clusters

niyahari nunggele moo: *Catalpa Bungei*: the catalpa tree

niyaharnambi: to put forth tender shoots or buds

niyahašabumbi: (causative of **niyahašambi**)

niyahašambi: **1.** to set a dog on game; **2.** to drive cattle; **3.** to limp (said of horses and cattle with damaged hooves)

niyajiba: *Capsella bursa-pastoris*: shepherd's purse

niyaki: pus, nasal and bodily discharge, nasal mucus

  niyaki sirimbi: to blow the nose, to wipe the nose

niyakinabumbi: (causative of **niyakinambi**)

niyakinambi: to form pus

niyakitu: a dirty-nosed child

niyakūn: genuflection, kneeling

niyakūrabumbi: (causative of **niyakūrambi**)

niyakūrambi: to kneel, to genuflect

niyalhūnjambi: to get dizzy from heat or hunger

niyalma: **1.** man, person; **2.** another person, someone else, others; **3.** philtrum: the line or groove running from the bottom of the nose to the upper lip

  niyalma anggala: population

  niyalma de holbombi: to get married

  niyalma henduhe balama: people say so, such is the popular opinion

  niyalma i urkin de yabumbi: to go along with other people's actions, to go along with the crowd

  niyalma irgen: the people

  niyalma nimaha: **1.** a creature that is half fish, half man; **2.** seal

  niyalma tatara boo: inn, hotel

  niyalma uncara hūdaci: a person who deals in slaves, especially girls and children

  niyalma usiha: the name of five stars in the Milky Way

  niyalmai baita: human affairs

  niyalmai duwali: mankind, humankind

  niyalmai jalan: the human world

niyalmai sabi: a hundred-year-old man, a very old man

niyalmaingge: belonging to someone else

niyamala: moss found on trees and stones

niyamalambi: to honor (one's parents), to serve (one's parents)

niyaman: **1**. heart; **2**. pistil of a flower; **3**. center, innermost part; **4**. relative, parent; **5**. trusted friend, intimate; **6**. wick of a candle

niyaman acambi: to find congenial, to be in agreement

niyaman arambi: to marry, to get married

niyaman be tatambi: to be on tenterhooks, to be in great suspense

niyaman be ujimbi: to take care of one's parents

niyaman daribumbi: to be related in some manner

niyaman de acanambi: to visit one's parents or elders

niyaman dubembi: to pass away (said of one's parents)

niyaman feliyembi: to discuss marriage

niyaman fintambi: to suffer chest pain

niyaman gabtakū: the beams that connect the ridge beam and the horizontal beams in a roof

niyaman hadahan: the iron pegs on a harness to which the reins are fastened

niyaman haksambi: to have a burning sensation in the stomach

niyaman holbombi: to contract a marriage

niyaman hūncihin: blood relative, relatives

niyaman i baita: affair of the heart, marriage, matchmaking

niyaman i juktehen: shrine to one's parents

niyaman iliha: the ears appeared (on grain)

niyaman jafambi: to marry

niyaman jaka: the center of the chest, the pit of the stomach

niyaman jaka nimembi: to have a pain in the chest, to have a pain in the heart, to have a pain in the pit of the stomach

niyaman tuksimbi: the heart beats

niyaman ufuhu: intimate friend

niyamanambi: **1**. to form a center, to form a heart; **2**. to be uncooked in the center, to be undercooked (said of rice)

niyamangga: related (by blood), having an innermost part

niyamani: a term of endearment used toward young children and elderly people

niyamarambi: to treat as an honored relative

niyamarcambi: to be jealous of others, to envy, to be inwardly contemptuous

niyamašambi: to live on an islet

niyamašan: **1**. islet in a river; **2**. center, middle part

niyambi: to rot, to decay, to go bad

niyaha hecen: a tottering wall, a wall about to fall

niyaha omo: polluted pool

niyaha yali: **1**. rotten meat; **2**. laggard, lazybones, lazy person, an annoying or importunate person

niyambulu: weakling

niyamciri: grass and leaves placed under hides by a tanner

niyamniyabumbi: (causative of **niyamniyambi**)

niyamniyambi: to shoot (arrows) from horseback, to practice mounted archery

niyamniyara mahala: a hat worn for mounted archery

niyamniyan: an arrow used in mounted archery

niyamniyan gabtan: ⟶ **niyamniyan**

niyamniyanambi: to go to practice mounted archery

niyamniyandumbi: to practice mounted archery together; also **niyamniyanumbi**

niyamniyanumbi: to practice mounted archery together; also **niyamniyandumbi**

niyan: Imperial carriage

niyancakū: a wooden stick for beating starched clothes while washing

niyancambi: **1**. to starch; **2**. ⟶ **šun niyancambi**

niyancan: **1**. starch; **2**. vitality, courage, vigor

niyancan akū: **1**. unstarched, limp; **2**. lacking courage

niyancan bijaha: **1**. to become limp (said of starched cloth); **2**. lost courage

niyancan bijambi: to grow limp, to lose courage

niyancan bilambi: to break someone's courage, to break someone's spirit

niyancan eberembi: to lose heart, to be disheartened

niyancangga: **1**. starched, strong, firm; **2**. long-lasting

niyancanggangge: one who is brave, strong, that which is strong, firm, hard

niyanci hiyan: a mountain plant with fragrant willow-like leaves that are burned like incense at sacrifices

niyanciha: green grass, green plants, verdant growth

niyanciri hamgiya: *Artemisia capillaris*, wormwood

niyandz: a small ball of some material that has been rolled between the fingers

niyang: girl

niyang niyang: (Daoist) goddess

niyangdz: lady, mistress (of a household)

niyanggu je bele: a kind of white millet

niyanggūbumbi: (causative of **niyanggūmbi**)

niyanggūmbi: **1**. to chew; **2**. to backbite, to criticize

niyangniya: clear (after clouds have dispersed)

niyangniya tucike: it has become clear (after clouds have parted or dispersed)

niyangniyahūn: grimacing (from pain or fatigue)

niyangniyang: goddess

niyangniyarambi: (-ka) to grimace (from pain or fatigue)

niyanhūn: puppy, whelp; cf. **niyahan**

niyaningjiji: *Polygonum filiforma*: jumpseed, a medicinal plant

niyaniombi: **1**. to chew; **2**. to backbite

niyaniyun: betel nut

niyanjan: an Imperial chariot

niyanjari ilha: an exotic bloom with purple petals, a white center, and an odor that inhibits sleep

niyanse: ⟶ **niyandz**

niyara: sweetened grain that has been allowed to ferment (in making liquor), fermented glutinous rice sweetened and served as a dessert

niyaran: ⟶ **niyara**

niyarangga tara: a mixture of sour milk, sugar, and **niyara**

niyarhoca: the young of the Manchurian moose; cf. **kandahan**

niyarhūkan: rather fresh

niyarhūlambi: to remain in confinement for a month after the birth of a child

niyarhūn: fresh

niyari: wet land, muddy area, marsh

niyasi yali: flesh that is between the teeth

niyasubumbi: (causative of **niyasumbi**)

niyasumbi: (-ka) to come to a head (said of a boil), to fester, to discharge pus

niyaša: ⟶ **niyasi**

niyecebumbi: (causative of **niyecembi**)

niyecebun: ⟶ **niyececun**

niyececun: **1**. filling out, supplementing, mending; **2**. benefit, advantage, aid

niyecembi: **1**. to mend; **2**. to fill in, to fill (a post); **3**. to supplement; **4**. to nourish (said of food or medicine)

niyeceme jukimbi: to compensate, to reimburse

niyeceme sindambi: to fill a vacancy

niyecen: a patch, a small piece of cloth

niyecetembi: to mend continually, fill in regularly

niyehe: the duck

niyehe tatara asu: a long net for catching wild ducks

niyehe tungge: the name of an edible wild plant that creeps along the earth, a kind of edible fern

niyehe umhan i toholiyo: a pastry made of duck's eggs, sugar, honey, rice, and flour and fried in lard

niyei pan: Nirvana

niyekdecuke: **1**. spoiled, rancid; **2**. hateful, loathsome, detestable

niyekdembi: (-ke) to spoil, to become rancid, to become sour

niyekeje: the male sockeye salmon

niyekse: light, thin (said of clothing)

niyeksembi: (-ke) to thaw on the surface (while still frozen underneath)

niyekserhen: a bird of Fujian that eats fish and shrimp (has a yellow head, black back, yellow-striped feathers, and long legs)

niyeksu: ⟶ **niyokso**

niyelebumbi: (causative of **niyelembi**)

niyelejembi: to be abraded (said of the skin), to be chaffed

niyeleku: **1**. a stone roller, upper millstone; **2**. a stick for washing

niyeleku i alikū wehe: the lower millstone

niyeleku wehe: a stone roller for separating grains from the ear, a millstone

niyelembi: **1**. to roll, to mill (grains); **2**. to roll fabrics with a stone roller; **3**. to read out loud

niyemcin: German (a word of Russian origin)

niyemperembi: to thaw on the surface (while still frozen underneath)

niyengceri ilha: *Lychnis fulgens*: brilliant campion

niyenggari cecike: a name for the myna

niyengguweri cecike: ⟶ **niyenggari cecike**

niyengniyeltu cecike: the name of a bird that has a white head and neck, black wings, and that sings incessantly during the spring

niyengniyeri: **1**. spring (season); **2**. sexual love

    niyengniyeri be bodoro hafan: (春官正) Astronomer for Spring, *BH* 229

    niyengniyeri boco: spring scenery

    niyengniyeri dosimbi: 'spring enters' — one of the twenty-four divisions of the solar year falling on the 4th or 5th of February

    niyengniyeri dulin: the vernal equinox

    niyengniyeri enduri: the name of a god to whom sacrifice is offered on 'spring enters'

    niyengniyeri fiyan de urgunjere mudan: a piece of music played while tea was brought in to the banquet after the spring plowing ceremony

    niyengniyeri mujilen: amorous feelings, sexual arousal

    niyengniyeri nirugan: erotic pictures

    niyengniyeri okto: aphrodisiac

    niyengniyeri šungga ilha: a fragrant white flower with six petals and a yellow center

niyengniyerikten: the spring offering to the ancestors

niyeniye: **1**. weak willed, lacking initiative; **2**. hibernation of snakes and insects

niyeniyedembi: ⟶ **niyeniyeršembi**

niyeniyehudembi: to be weak willed, to be lacking in initiative

niyeniyehun: weak willed, lacking initiative

niyeniyehunjembi: to be weak willed, to lack initiative, to be weak of character

niyeniyen: ⟶ **niyeniye**

niyeniyeršembi: **1**. to bite gently; **2**. to be too timid to take action, to be unable to take decisive action

niyere: **1**. weak, feeble, slight; **2**. light, flimsy (said of clothing); **3**. fragile (said of vessels)

niyerebumbi: (causative of **niyerembi**)

niyereken: rather weak, flimsy, light

niyerembi: **1**. to wear light clothing; **2**. to be lacking protective garb (armor, helmet, etc.); **3**. to swim (said of fish and animals)

    niyereme: lightly attired

    niyereme beye: without helmet and armor

niyerengge: one who wears light clothing

niyeri: ⟶ **niyengniyeri**

niyo: swamp, marsh, bog, slough

    niyo coko: *Vanellus vanellus*: peewit, lapwing

    niyo i ba: marsh, slough

    niyo i hoohan: a kind of bittern

    niyo i lefu: a marsh bear

    niyo ilha: *Nymphaea tetragona*: pygmy water lily

    niyo mušu: *Turnix tanki*: Chinese button quail

    niyo saksaha: marsh magpie

niyobumbi: (causative of **niyombi**)

niyociki: a small bird that resembles the bittern

niyohombi: to have sexual intercourse, to engage in sex; cf. **niohombi**

niyokdoko: ravine, gully, defile

niyokso: floss-like green algae

niyolmon: ⟶ **niolmon**

niyolocuka: ⟶ **niolocuka**

niyolodo: hateful, detestable (in speech), rascally, roguish

niyombi: to scrape meat from bones

niyomošun: drifting ice

niyoolocuka: oily, greasy, fatty; cf. **niolocuka**

niyorombi: ⟶ **niorombi**

no: a sentence particle marking a question

nofi: person (used after numbers higher than one)

noho: covered, filled, saturated: **muke noho ba** 'a place covered with water'

nokai: very

    nokai ja: very easy

nokcimbi: to get very angry

nomhokon: rather tame, rather docile

nomhon: docile, quiet, tame, guileless, unobtrusive, simple minded, honest

    nomhon morin i fiyenten: (馴馬司) Equestrian Section, *BH* 118

    nomhon sufan i falgangga: (馴象所) Elephant-training Section, *BH* 122

    nomhon sufan ujire boo: (馴象房) elephant-training house

nomin: **1**. lapis lazuli, lazurite; **2**. fat of fish and frogs, milt, soft roe

nomohon: ⟶ **nomhon**

nomulambi: to preach, to expound the scriptures

nomun: **1**. classic book, classic; **2**. sutra, scripture; **3**. law, holy teaching, religion; **4**. preaching

    nomun be kadalara yamun: (司經局) library in the palace where sutras were kept

    nomun bithe nadan afaha šu fiyelen: the seven purports of the classics

    nomun han: Dharma king, Dharmarāja

    nomun hūlambi: to recite sutras

    nomun jibehun: a funeral garment with *dhāraṇīs* embroidered on it

    nomun mandal: a Buddhist or Daoist scripture reading service in a temple or private home

    nomun tarni kuren: (經咒館) an office for the copying of *dhāraṇīs* in Manchu, Chinese, Mongolian, and Tibetan

non: younger sister

nonggibumbi: **1**. (causative or passive of **nonggimbi**); **2**. to advance, to increase

    nonggibure gucu: an intimate friend

nonggibun: increase

nonggimbi: **1**. to add, to add to; **2**. to increase (in rank)

    nonggime fungnembi: to raise to a higher rank as a sign of favor

nongginambi: to go to add, to go to increase

nonggindumbi: to add together, to increase together

nongginjimbi: to come to add, to come to increase

nono: *Allium hakeri*: water scallion

nonte: ⟶ **nota**

nontoho: shell, skin, rind; cf. **notho**

noor: (Mongolian) lake

norambi: to pile up wood or plants

noran: a pile of wood or plants

noro: (in some place-names) lake; ⟶ **noor**

norobumbi: (causative of **norombi**)

norombi: **1**. to remain still in one place, to remain at home, to remain in the nest, to lie without moving; **2**. to be reluctant to leave, to recall with nostalgia

    norome amhambi: to sleep soundly

noron: longing, attachment; cf. **naracun**

nosiki: an excellent hunter

nota: (plural of **non**)

notho: skin, rind, bark of a tree

nothori: a sweet-tasting exotic fruit

noyan: **1**. a title of Mongolian nobility; **2**. Prince lord

nu: **1**. a sentence particle expressing mild interrogation; **2**. crossbow

    nu beri: a crossbow

nuhakan: rather at ease

nuhaliyan: marshy, swampy, low-lying

    nuhaliyan ba: low-lying area prone to flooding, swamp, bog

    nuhaliyan hali: swamp, swampy

nuhan: at ease, easy-going; cf. **elhe nuhan**

nuhasi: a name for the rhinoceros

nuheci: hide of the wild boar

nuhen: a year-old wild pig

nuhere: **1**. a puppy seven or eight months old; **2**. sleepy head (said of children)

    nuhere dafaha: the female chum salmon; cf. **dafaha**

    nuhere mafa jihe: 'puppy grandfather came' (said to small children by old people who want to keep them awake to play)

nuheri: ⟶ **nuhere**

nuhu: a high place, an area higher than a surrounding depression

nujalambi: to beat with the fist

nujan: fist

    nujan aššarakū: the fist is not moving (at archery)

    nujan bargiyambi: to clench the fist

nujangga maitu: a red-lacquered pole with a golden fist on the end

nujašambi: to beat all over with the fists

nukabumbi: (causative or passive of **nukambi**)

nukacuka: **1**. sharp, pointed; **2**. to the point, apt

nukajambi: **1**. to be stuck painfully by thorns, to have a prickly pain, to suffer stinging pain; **2**. to have a sharp pain in the eye

nukambi: to be stuck, to be pricked, to have a stinging pain

nukcibumbi: **1**. (causative of **nukcimbi**); **2**. to provoke (someone who is already angry), to incite, to agitate

nukcimbi: (-ke) **1**. to become enraged, to act in ire; **2**. to advance, to rush to; **3**. to be routed (said of bandits), to make a desperate retreat; **4**. to act energetically; **5**. to be aroused, to be excited

nukcime yabumbi: to advance valiantly or fiercely

nukcishun: **1**. excited, aroused; **2**. fierce, vehement

nukibumbi: **1**. (causative or passive of **nukimbi**); **2**. to incite, to agitate, to stir up, to stimulate

nukimbi: to be stirred up, to be incited, to be agitated, to be stimulated

nukte: an area in which nomads lead their flocks and herds following water and grass; **2**. baggage carried on pack animals

nuktebumbi: (causative of **nuktembi**)

nuktembi: to lead a nomadic life, to wander with one's flocks or herds, to be nomadic

nukteme yabumbi: to nomadize, to wander

nuktere ba: nomadic area, grazing lands

nuktendumbi: to lead the nomadic life together; also **nuktenumbi**

nuktenembi: to go to lead a nomadic life

nuktenjimbi: to come to lead a nomadic life

nuktenumbi: to lead the nomadic life together; also **nuktendumbi**

nuktere: ⟶ **nuktembi** (subheading)

nunggalambi: to stew slowly

nunggalaha yali: stewed meat

nunggari: **1**. down, fine fur or hair; **2**. fuzz (on plants)

nunggari fathangga kuwecihe: *Syrrhaptes paradoxus*: sand grouse

nunggari funggaha: a name for the quail; cf. **mušu**

nunggari funiyesun: a kind of woolen

nunggari jafu: fuzzy felt

nunggasun: a material woven from down or fine wool

nunggasun suje: a satin-like material woven from down

nunggele: linden tree, trees of the *Tilia* genus

nunggembi: to swallow

nunggile: ⟶ **nunggele**

nunggimbi: ⟶ **nunggembi**

nungnebumbi: **1**. (causative or passive of **nungnembi**); **2**. (euphemistic) to be murdered

nungnecun: harm, injury

nungneku: troublemaker, teaser

nungnembi: **1**. to harm, to wrong, to injure; **2**. to encroach, to infringe; **3**. to provoke, to incite, to harass; **4**. (euphemism) to murder

nungnenjimbi: to come to provoke, to come to harm

nungneri monio: a name for the monkey

nunjibumbi: to be lulled to sleep (by storytelling, singing, etc.)

nuran: **1**. a liquor cask with holes; **2**. funnel

nure: undistilled liquor, (rice) wine

nure belhere falgari: (良醞署) the wine section of the Court of Banqueting

nure dagilambi: to serve liquor

nure de soktombi: to get drunk on wine

nure huhu: leaven for making wine

nure jušun i boo: (酒醋房) wine, vinegar, and soy sauce factory for the palace

nure subumbi: to sober up

nure targambi: to abstain from wine

nure tebumbi: to make undistilled spirits

nurei efin: drinker's wager game

nurei ekšun: sediment from undistilled spirits (sometimes used in cooking)

nurhūmbi: to be connected, to be in series

nurhūme: connected, in a row, in a series, continually, repeatedly

nurhūme afambi: to fight continually

nushumbi: to rush (toward), to charge, to storm, to assail

nuturu: *Syrrhaptes paradoxus*: sand grouse

O ᡩ ᡩ

o: **1**. an interjection of reply; **2**. armpit; cf. **oho**; **3**. the depression of a mortar; cf. **ogo**; **4**. (sentence particle of interrogation)

    o mayan: armpit; ⟶ **ogu**, **oho**

o a: (onomatopoetic) the sound made by small children trying to talk

o guwa: pumpkin

o nimaha: alligator, crocodile

o šo seme: coddling, fondling

    o šo seme gosimbi: to love tenderly

o umiyaha: moth

obdombi: (-ko) to become tasteless

    obdoko yali: meat of game that has been exhausted and has thereby become tasteless

obgiya: a hook on a long pole used to catch birds on water

obihiya yali: the meat from the shoulder blade of an animal

obo: (Mongolian) mound of stones, cairn used as a landmark, border marker

obobumbi: (causative of **obombi**)

oboko: ⟶ **obokū**

obokū: a basin used for washing, a basin for washing the face, a vessel for writing brushes

    obokū efen: cake made of egg yolks, flour, sugar, and wine — a filling made of jujubes was sometimes added

obombi: to wash

obonggi: bubble, foam, froth

    obonggi arki: a bubbling distilled liquor made by the Manchus

    obonggi dekdembi: to foam, to froth, to bubble

obongginambi: to form foam, to foam, to bubble

obonggo hiyan: dragon spittle incense

obonjimbi: to come to wash

obonombi: to go to wash

obubumbi: (causative of **obumbi**)

obumbi: **1**. (causative of **ombi**); **2**. to make, to make into, to cause to become, to consider as

oca: ⟶ **ooca**

ocan: **1**. seam; **2**. loop for a button

oci: (conditional of **ombi**) a particle used to set off the subject: 'as for'

ocibe: (concessive form of **ombi**) although

ocir: the head of a Buddhist rosary

ododon: a name for the crested lark; cf. **wenderhen**

odoli: an ornamental iron hook attached to the ring of a horse's bit

odontu kailun: a horse that has spots resembling stars

odz: Japan, Japanese

ofi: **1**. a snare for catching pheasants; **2**. (perfect converb of **ombi**) because

ofoho: a plowshare

ofordombi: ⟶ **oforodombi**

oforo: **1**. nose; **2**. outcropping on a mountain

    oforo acabumbi: to tell tales, to gossip about, to backbite, to incite by slander

    oforo dambagu: snuff

    oforo feteri feterilembi: to move the sides of the nose

    oforo i da: nose ridge

    oforo i dube: the end of the nose

    oforo i sangga: nostril

    oforo niyaki: nasal discharge, nasal mucus

    oforo sangga: ⟶ **oforo i sangga**

    oforo songgiha: tip of the nose

    oforo tura: the small ridge that separates the two nostrils

oforodombi: to incite by slander, to engage in malicious gossip

oforonggo: slanderer, gossip, nosy person

ogo: **1**. the depression of a mortar; **2**. the holes on an iron plate that is used for making the heads of nails; **3**. armpit

ogū: ⟶ **oho**

oha: **1**. agreed, consented; **2**. ⟶ **ooha**
ohakū: would not agree or permit, not permissible
oho: **1**. armpit; cf. **o, o mayan, ogū**
  oho da: the top of a sleeve
oho: **2**. ⟶ **ombi** (subheading)
ohode: ⟶ **ombi** (subheading)
ohodombi: to support by holding under the arms
oholiyo: a double handful, the cupped hands: ten
  oholiyo is the equivalent of one **moro**, ten
  sefere comprise one **oholiyo**
oholiyombi: to hold in both hands, to take in both
  hands
oholji: ⟶ **oholjon**
oholjombi: to make a loose knot
  oholjome hūwaitambi: to tie a loose knot
oholjon: **1**. a loose knot; **2**. a loose snare for
  catching pheasants
oholjun: ⟶ **oholjon**
ohoršombi: to feel nauseated, to be disgusted
ohotono: mole, an animal of the *Talpidae* family
oi: **1**. exclamation used to attract people's attention;
  2. sound used to call animals
oibobumbi: (causative of **oibombi**)
oibombi: (**-ko**) to become decrepit, to become old
  and unable to move steadily, to be confused,
  to be senile
oibumbi: ⟶ **oibombi**
oifo: frivolous, thoughtless, superficial
oihori: **1**. careless, superficial; **2**. fine, splendid; **3**.
  exceedingly, very
  oihori sain: exceedingly good, how splendid!
  oihorio: Isn't it wonderful?, Wouldn't it be
    nice?
oihorilabumbi: (causative or passive of
  oihorilambi)
oihorilambi: **1**. to take lightly, to slight, to insult, to
  neglect, to behave carelessly; **2**. to receive a
  light wound (said of hunted game)
  oihorilame fiohorilambi: to act in a rash or
    indiscrete way
  oihorilame tuwambi: to look down on, to slight
oilo: **1**. surface, outside; **2**. (adv.) openly, in the open
  oilo sain: nice on the outside
oilohodombi: to act frivolously, to be frivolous
oilohon: frivolous, superficial, not serious
  oilohon balama: very frivolous, flighty, unruly
  oilohon dabduri: flippant, impetuous
  oilohon hakcin: impetuous, flippant

oilohon nekeliyen: flirtatious, frivolous
oilokon: rather superficial, frivolous
oilon: surface
  oilon i bele: the top layer of grain in a granary
oilorgi: surface, outside
  oilorgi yangse: ostentatious, showy, ornate
oilori: **1**. on the surface, on the outside; **2**. cursory,
  superficial, frivolous, flighty; **3**. without
  cause or reason, accidentally
  oilori deleri: superficial, trivial, frivolous
  oilori nambuha: fell into someone's hands
    accidently
  oilori oilori: extremely frivolous, flighty
oitobumbi: to be in dire straits, to be hard pressed
  oitobume mohombi: to fall into dire poverty
ojin: a long sleeveless court garment worn by
  women
ojirakū: ⟶ **ojorakū**
ojojo: an interjection of derision
ojombi: to kiss
ojorakū: it will not do (to), one may not … ; cf.
  ombi
ojoro: (imperfect participle of **ombi**)
ojorongge: that which is, that which is permissible
ok: (onomatopoetic) **1**. the sound made when
  frightened; **2**. the sound of gagging and
  vomiting
okcilabumbi: (causative of **okoilambi**)
okcilambi: to cover, to put on a cover
okcin: **1**. a cover, covering; **2**. shell (of a crab)
okcingga moro: a covered bowl or cup
okdobumbi: (causative of **okdombi**)
okdojimbi: ⟶ **okdonjimbi**
okdombi: (**-ko**) **1**. to go to meet, to meet halfway, to
  greet, to welcome; **2**. to engage (an enemy)
  okdoro kumun: a piece of music played during
    the return of the Emperor from sacrifices
okdombumbi: ⟶ **okdobumbi**
okdomo: one of two leather straps on the left side of
  a saddle that are put through the clasps of
  the saddle girth (belly-strap)
okdonambi: ⟶ **okdonombi**
okdonjimbi: to come to meet
okdonombi: to go out to meet, to go to greet, to go
  to welcome
okdonumbi: to meet together, to welcome together
okdori ilha: *Jasminum nudiflorum*: forsythia, winter
  jasmine

okdoro: —→ okdombi (subheading)

oke: aunt: the wife of father's younger brother

okete: (plural of oke)

oki yoro: a large wooden arrowhead

okjiha: 1. reed, rush; 2. calamus, sweet-flag (*Acorus calamus*)

okjiha sektefun: a cushion made of rushes

okjiha uhuri: a container woven from rushes, rush bag

okjihada: the roots of the calamus

okjoslambi: 1. to speak or handle carelessly; 2. to act hastily or rashly, to act irreverently

okjoslame koro bahambi: to suffer loss due to a careless action

oksibumbi: 1. (causative or passive of oksimbi); 2. to come out of a scabbard, to fall out of a quiver

oksimbi: to spit out, to spit up, to vomit up

oksobumbi: (causative of oksombi)

oksombi: to step, to go step by step, to take a step

okson: step, pace

okson be ilinjambi: to halt, to go no farther

okson fuliburakū: unable to take a step

oksonjombi: to make small steps (said of children learning to walk)

oktalambi: to cut off the nose — an ancient punishment

okto: 1. drug, medicine; 2. gunpowder; 3. dye; 4. poison

okto acabumbi: to mix medicine

okto fangdz: drug prescription

okto fushubumbi: to set off gunpowder

okto gurumbi: to dig for herbs

okto i boo: apothecary

okto i dasarhan: —→ okto fangdz

okto i siren: fuse

okto latumbi: to apply medicine, to apply salve to a wound

okto muhaliyan: bullet

okto niru: a poisoned arrow

okto omimbi: to take medicine

okto orho: medicinal herb

okto sihan: an implement for measuring gunpowder

oktoi afaha: medicated plaster

oktoi horon: action of a poison

oktoi puseli: drugstore, apothecary

oktoi šugi: salve, ointment

oktoi wambi: to poison

oktolombi: 1. to treat with medicine; 2. to poison

oktolome wambi: to poison, to kill by poisoning

oktorohon: overly hungry, so hungry that one is incapable of eating

oktorohon banjiha: became overly hungry

oktoron: rabbit's tracks

oktosi: doctor, physician; cf. daifu

oktosi be kadalara yamun: (太醫院) the Imperial Medical Department, *BH* 233

oktosi be kadalara yamun i aliha hafan: (太醫院院使) Commissioner of the Imperial Medical Department, *BH* 235

oktosi be kadalara yamun i ilhi hafan: (太醫院院判) Vice-Commissioner of the Imperial Medical Department, *BH* 236

oktosilabumbi: (causative of oktosilambi)

oktosilambi: to treat (sickness), to cure

olbihiyan: —→ olfihiyan

olbo: 1. a short padded outer jacket; 2. (敖爾布) Manchurian Orbo, Private of the Second Class (in the Chinese banners), *BH* 731

olboro yali: meat from the cheeks of a bear

olfihiyan: impatient, negligent, frivolous

olgoba: —→ olhoba

olgocuka: —→ olhocuka

olgombi: —→ olhombi

olgon: —→ olhon

olgošombi: —→ olhošombi

olhoba: careful, attentive, cautious, circumspect

olhobumbi: (causative of olhombi)

olhocuka: frightful, scary, dangerous

olhocun: fear, terror, sense of danger

olhokon: rather dry, rather thirsty, rather afraid

olhombi: 1. to fear; 2. to dry, to dry up

olhon: 1. dry, dried up; 2. dry land

olhon be yabumbi: to travel by land

olhon buda: dry rice (as opposed to gruel or porridge made from rice)

olhon feye: a surface wound, contusion

olhon jugūn: land route

olhon monggon: the windpipe, trachea

olhon usin: dry field (as opposed to a flooded rice field)

olhošombi: 1. to be cautious, to be careful; 2. to respect, to revere

olhošon: cautious, careful, respectful

olhotun: in Chinese medicine, the three visceral cavities housing the internal organs

oliha: cowardly, shy, timid

    oliha budun: timid and weak, cowardly, timorous

    oliha niyalma: a coward

olihadambi: to be cowardly, to be shy, to be timid

olimbi: to avoid the road, to veer to the side, to wind, to go around

    olime mudalime: twisting and turning

    olime yabumbi: to go avoiding the road

olji: **1**. captive, prisoner of war; **2**. booty, loot, plunder

oljilabumbi: (causative or passive of **oljilambi**)

oljilambi: to capture (a prisoner during wartime)

olo: hemp, flax

    olo foyo: a plant that resembles shredded flax and is used as padding in boots

    olo futa: rope made from hemp

    olo sabu: hempen shoes

olobumbi: (causative of **olombi**)

olohoi: interjection of surprise

olombi: to wade, to cross a stream, to wade across, to ford

olon: girth (saddle belly-strap) of a horse

olongdo: long boots used for mountain climbing

olosi: a wader, i.e., one who fishes standing in shallow water wearing leather trousers

ološon: long leather trousers used for wading in shallow streams

ombi: (imperfect participle **-joro**, imperative: **oso**) **1**. to become, to change into; **2**. to be, to exist; **3**. to be proper, to be permissible

    oho siraha ahūn: elder brother of the same mother but with different fathers

    ohode: (perfect participle of **ombi** plus **de**) if

omcoko: harelip, having a harelip

omi sangga: a hole used by rats and squirrels for storing food

omibumbi: (causative of **omimbi**)

omicambi: to drink together

omicanambi: to go to drink together

omiha: ⟶ **omimbi** (subheading)

omiholambi: ⟶ **omiholombi**

omiholobumbi: (causative of **omiholombi**)

omiholombi: to suffer hunger, to starve

omihon: hunger, starvation, starving, hungry

omilabumbi: (causative of **omilambi**)

omilambi: to ford a stream (said of horses)

omimbi: **1**. to drink; **2**. to smoke (tobacco); **3**. to take (medicine)

    omiha hūsun de: under the influence of wine

omin: famine, year of famine

ominambi: to go to drink

omingga: drink, beverage

ominjimbi: to come to drink

omkiya: flying squirrel, an animal of the genus *Sciuropterus*

omo: lake, pond

    omo cise: pond, pool, tank

    omo dabsun: salt distilled from a lake

omoktu konggoro: a yellow horse

omolo: grandson

    omolo sargan jui: granddaughter

    omoloi omolo: great-grandson

omosi: (plural of **omolo**)

    omosi mama: Manchu goddess of good fortune and fecundity

omšoko: harelipped

omšon biya: the eleventh month

on: stage of a journey, distance

    on dosombi: to be able to travel a long distance (said of horses, camels, etc.)

    on gaimbi: to travel hard, to travel twice the usual rate

    on gaime yabumbi: to make a forced march

    on temšembi: to travel hard

onasu: giraffe

onco: **1**. broad, wide; **2**. generous

    onco leli: broad, vast

    onco umiyesun: the leather belt from which the quiver hangs

oncodobumbi: (causative of **oncodombi**)

oncodombi: to forgive, to grant amnesty, to act leniently

    oncodome gamambi: to forgive

    oncodome guwebumbi: to forgive, to pardon

oncohon: **1**. lying on one's back, facing upward; **2**. overbearing, arrogant

    oncohon dedumbi: to lie on one's back

    oncohon maktambi: to turn upward

    oncohon tuhembi: to fall onto one's back

    oncohon tuwambi: to look upward

    oncohon umušuhun: on the back and on the stomach

oncohošombi: **1**. to be arrogant, to be overbearing; **2**. to exult

oncokon: rather wide, broad

ondobumbi: (causative or passive of **ondombi**)

ondombi: **1**. to act foolishly, to fool around, to play (with something); **2**. to engage in sex, to have sex

   ondome arbušambi: to act indecently, to engage in sexual activity

ondonumbi: to engage in sexual intercourse together

ong seme: (onomatopoetic) the sound made by an arrowhead called **oki yoro**

onggobumbi: (causative or passive of **onggombi**)

onggocon: a short two-stringed musical instrument

onggola: root of the ear

onggolo: **1**. before, previous, ago; **2**. in front; **3**. a river port, river cove

onggolokon: a little before

onggombi: to forget

   onggoro cecike: jay

   onggoro ilha: the blossom of *Hemerocallis graminea*, the flower of forgetfulness, the daylily

   onggoro mangga: ⟶ **onggotai**

   onggoro orho: *Hemerocallis graminea*: daylily

onggon: the space between a saddle and an animal's back, bare back of a horse

onggoro: **1**. the hammer bone of the inner ear (worn by children as a charm against forgetfulness); **2**. forgetful; **3**. ⟶ **onggombi** (subheading)

onggosu: **1**. absentmindedness, forgetfulness; **2**. forgetful, absentminded

onggošon: *Carassius auratus*: golden carp

onggotai: forgetful, absentmindedly, forgetfully

ongkimbi: to flee (said of animals when they see or smell an approaching person)

ongko: pasture, pastureland

ongnika: *Gulo gulo*: wolverine

ongton: boorish, rustic, unsophisticated, rude

ongtori: boorish, ignorant

onon: the male zeren; cf. **jeren**

oo nimaha: the great sea turtle

ooca: *Gobia fluviatilis*: gudgeon

ooha: *Siniperca chuatsi*: mandarin fish, Chinese perch

oolambi: to step aside, to make way

oološombi: to move out of the way

oome: used for **ome** (imperfect converb of **ombi**)

oori: **1**. semen; **2**. essence, spirit, energy

   oori simen: vigor, spirit, energy

   oori sukdun: energy, essence, basic principle

   oori turibumbi: to ejaculate, to have a nocturnal emission

   oori ushe: semen

ooron: ⟶ **oron**

or: (onomatopoetic) **1**. sound made by tigers; **2**. sound of vomiting; **3**. ⟶ **or ir**

or ir: (onomatopoetic) sound of chanting sutras

or seme: (onomatopoetic) the sound of chanting

ora: a long sleeveless jacket made of satin with a dragon design

orcun: ⟶ **orhoco**

ordo: **1**. palace, palace in the form of a pavilion; **2**. pavilion

oren: ⟶ **ūren**

orgi: the sharp edges of an arrowhead

orgilambi: to graze (said of an arrow)

orgon: ⟶ **orhon**

orho: grass, hay, plant

   orho da: ginseng; cf. **orhoda**

   orho i kūwaran: a place in Mukden for the storage of hay

   orho jodon: coarse grass linen

   orho liyoo: fodder

   orho muke amcarakū: 'cannot reach grass and water' (said of ill horses and cattle)

   orho ordo: grass hut

   orho šoforokū: the name of two feathers on the right wing of a hawk (and other birds of prey)

orhoco: very small (said of a newborn baby)

orhoda: ginseng

   orhoda gurure temgetu bithe: a license issued for the gathering of ginseng

   orhoda icihiyara kūwaran: bureau in charge of matters relating to ginseng

orhon: white and black feathers on the tails of falcons

orhonggo: pertaining to grass, grassy

   orhonggo kiltari: signal flag with feathers attached to it

ori: **1**. a rosary of glass beads worn around the neck; **2**. ⟶ **oori**

orici: twentieth

orima: the name of a sea fish that resembles the burbot

orimbi: to walk in one's sleep

orin: twenty

orinci: twentieth

orinta: twenty each

orita: ⟶ **orinta**

orobuhangge: various foods made from curdled milk

orobumbi: (causative of **orombi**)

oroko: ⟶ **orombi** (subheading)

orokū: something curdled or coagulated, clabber

orolokū: substitute, one who fills in

orolombi: to fill in, to put a substitute in, to fill a vacancy, to fill in for, to substitute for

    orolome simnembi: to sit in for someone else at an examination

orombi: (-**ko**) to form a layer on the surface (said of gruel or other liquids), to rise to the surface (said of fat or cream in a liquid)

    oroko nimenggi: fat that has risen to the surface of a liquid, cream

    oroko niowarikū: verdigris

oromo: ⟶ **oromu**

oromu: cream

oron: **1**. position, place; **2**. vacant post, vacancy; **3**. constellation, one of the twelve celestial palaces; **4**. the earthly or physical soul; **5**. domestic reindeer; **6**. negative intensifier, (not) at all

    oron akū: **1**. altogether lacking, completely without; **2**. without a vacancy; **3**. without a trace

    oron akū gisun: baseless talk, nonsense, senseless gossip

    oron buhū: a tame reindeer

    oron de: at a post, in a position

    oron ejelesi: incumbent who puts his position up for sale

    oron gurgu: domestic reindeer

    oron i kunggeri: (缺科) office concerned with vacant posts — part of the Board of Civil Appointments

    oron i šusi: (天文生) the name of an official of the Imperial Board of Astronomy

    oron soorin: point of the compass, bearing

oronco i niyalma: a reindeer herder

oronde: ⟶ **oron de**

oronggo: *Procapra przewalski*: Przewalski's gazelle

oros: Russia, Russian, foreign

    oros bithei kuren: (俄羅斯文館) the name of an institution for the study of Russian

    oros kuren: (俄羅斯館) hostel in Beijing for Russian emissaries and merchants

    oros niru: a banner company composed of Russians and their descendants

    oros tacikū: (俄羅斯學) the Russian school in Beijing

orson nimembi: to have pains in the abdomen after childbirth

ose: Japanese; cf. **odz**

oshodombi: to be cruel, to be brutal, to mistreat, to act in a cruel or tyrannical way

oshon: **1**. cruel, brutal, tyrannical; **2**. ⟶ **osohon**

    oshon ehe: cruel, ruthless, vicious, evil-minded

    oshon erun: cruel torture, inhuman torture

oso: (imperative of **ombi**)

    oso nakū: not yet, still has not …

osohokon: rather small

osohon: small, little

    osohon beye: **1**. person of low position, humble person; **2**. small stature, short stature; **3**. (a deferential term used for oneself)

    osohon budai erin: the period just before the midday meal

osokon: ⟶ **osohon**

    osokon niyengniyeri: Indian summer

ošo: a three-fingered leather glove used for holding falcons

ošoho: claw, talon; cf. **wasiha**

ošoholombi: to catch in the claws

ošohonggo: having claws

ošonggo ilha: an exotic flower whose petals resemble falcon's claws

otala: ⟶ **odoli**

otgo: a drake's tail that flares frontward

otho: ⟶ **otgo**

otolo: until (terminal converb of **ombi**)

oton: wooden tub without handles or feet, trough, vat

otori: a small scale battue in springtime

otorilambi: to hunt (on a battue) in springtime

oyo: **1**. roof (of a house, tent, or sedan chair), top of a grave; **2**. crown of a hat; **3**. sandfly, gnat

    oyo funima: sandfly, gnat

oyo gaimbi: to perform a Manchu sacrifice that involves throwing pieces of meat onto the roof

oyo jafara alikū: a vessel used for making offerings to deities

oyo oyo: (onomatopoetic) sound used for calling small dogs

oyobumbi: (causative of **oyombi**)

oyoki: hasty, hurried

oyolombi: ⟶ **oyombi**

oyombi: (1) (-**ho**) to bend, to curve, to arch, to roll up, to coil up, to rock

oyome sahambi: **1**. to build an enceinte before a city gate; **2**. to build a bridge arch

oyombi: (2) (-**ko**) **1**. to go more than halfway (on a trip); **2**. to be more than half finished, to be almost done; **3**. to be quite exhausted; **4**. to be important or urgent

oyombumbi: to hurry, to hasten, to do more than half

oyomburakū: not urgent, unimportant

oyombure ba akū: there is nothing urgent

oyombure baita: important matter

oyombure baita waka: it is not an urgent matter

oyome: ⟶ **oyombi** (**1**) (subheading)

oyomeliyan: somewhat bent or curved

oyon: peak

oyonde isinaha: to have arrived at the peak (said of destitution)

oyonggo: important, urgent, essential

oyonggo baita: urgent or important matter

oyonggo jecen: an important border area

oyonggon: important matter, important point, crucial point

oyotonggo mahatun: a hat of Qin and Han times with an arched top

oyoyo: (an expression of derision)

P ᡦ

page: a small stone used in the **gacuha** game

pai: **1**. playing card, card; **2**. inscribed tablet

pai biyan: horizontal inscribed tablet

pai efimbi: to play dominoes, to play cards, to play mah-jongg

pai fang ilibumbi: to erect a **pailu**

pai pai lu: ⟶ **pailu**

pai siyoo: a musical instrument consisting of twelve joined pipes

pailu: *páilóu* 牌樓: temporary arch (or other structure over a street) bearing slogans or holiday greetings

pailuri: a small **pailu**

pak: (onomatopoetic) **1**. the sound of exploding firecrackers; **2**. the sound made by a hard object falling to the floor

pak pik: (onomatopoetic) the sound of many small firecrackers going off

pak seme: **1**. ⟶ **pak**; **2**. dry and hard, lacking oil (said of rice)

palta wehe: diamond

paltari: diamond, a small piece of diamond used for drilling in porcelain

pampahūn: swollen (said of the face)

pampu: a thick padded coat

pan: **1**. a metal disk hung in temples that is struck by the devout to attract the attention of the gods; **2**. clapper

pancalambi: to use as travel expenses, to give for travel expenses

pancalara jiha: travel expenses

pancan: money for a journey, travel expenses

pandz: measure word for a game of *go* or chess, chessboard

pang: a sail, the same as **kotoli**

pangduwan: Jiangsu silk

panghai: crab, the same as **katuri**

pangse jahūdai: a kind of war junk

pangtanambi: to get fat

panlo: riotously, uproariously

panse: chessboard, measure for games of chess

pao: ⟶ **poo**

parpahūn: short and pudgy

parpanambi: to become corpulent, to grow pudgy

parsu: one ten-trillionth

pase: a rake; cf. **hedereku**

pasha: Easter, Passover

pata piti: **1**. (onomatopoetic) the sound of fruit falling from a tree; **2**. reeling under a heavy load

patak: (onomatopoetic) the sound of a hard object falling to the ground

patar pitir: (onomatopoetic) the sound made by struggling fish and birds

pei: **1**. (onomatopoetic) the sound of spitting; **2**. interjection expressing rejection

pei pai: (onomatopoetic) the sound of repeated spitting

pekte pakta: perplexed, dismayed, dumfounded

pelehe: ⟶ **pelehen**

pelehen: a name for the crane

pelembi: to cover the ceiling with a mat awning

pelerjembi: to toss the head when the reins are pulled (said of horses)

pen: **1**. a thatched shed; cf. **elben i boo**; **2**. a sail; cf. **kotoli**, **peng**

peng: **1**. a large mythical bird, a roc; **2**. sail of a boat; cf. **kotoli**, **pen**

per par: (onomatopoetic) the sound of birds or flying insects beating their wings

per pir: (onomatopoetic) the sound of a grasshopper taking off

per seme: (onomatopoetic) the sound of wings beating

pes: (onomatopoetic) the sound of something soft being torn or broken

pes pas: (onomatopoetic) **1**. the sound of something soft ripping; **2**. the sound of galloping

pes pis: (onomatopoetic) the sound of a horse galloping

pes seme: (onomatopoetic) with a ripping sound (said of soft objects)

petur seme: sobbing

pi ba g'o: loquat

pi siyoo: a tanner

pi šuwang okto: arsenic

picar seme: ⟶ **picir pacar seme**

picik pacak: (onomatopoetic) the sound of walking in mud

picir pacar seme: in profusion (said of small objects)

picir seme: ⟶ **picir pacar seme**

pijan: **1**. a leather case, a leather box; **2**. a leatherworker

pila: ⟶ **pulu pila seme**

pilembi: to act on (a document), to criticize, to write critical comments or judgments on a document

  pilehe bithe: a document with instructions written on it

pilgican niyehe: a name for the little grebe; cf. **cunggur niyehe**, **niojan niyehe**

pilu fucihi: Vairochana Buddha

pilutu: a hat worn by lamas during services — it has pictures of the Vairochana Buddha around the edge

pimpinambi: to have a pudgy face

pin: an Imperial Concubine of the fourth rank

ping di jeo: smooth crêpe

ping g'o: apple; cf. **pinggu**

ping orho: duckweed

ping sembi: to be bloated, to be swollen

pingdz: ⟶ **pingse**

pinggari: *Marsilia quadrifolia*: ground clover

pinggiyen boso: a kind of smooth linen

pinggo: ⟶ **pinggu**

pinggu: apple

pingguri: ⟶ **pinggu**

pingse: **1**. scale, balance; **2**. vase, bottle

pingselebumbi: (causative of **pingselembi**)

pingselembi: to weigh on a balance

pio seme: floating, wafting, light (in weight)

pipa: loquat; ⟶ **pipuri**

pipag'o: ⟶ **pipa**

pipuri: *Eriobotrya japonica*: loquat

  pipuri ilha: the flower of the loquat tree

piyak: (onomatopoetic) the sound of slapping

piyan: chessboard

piyan piyan: lightly, gracefully

piyang seme: chirping (said of crickets)

piyas pis seme: **1**. tactless, unrefined, clumsy; **2**. spitting (to show contempt)

piyas seme: agile, nimble

piyat piyat: (onomatopoetic) the sound of shoes dragging on the floor

piyata gaimbi: to hit the wrist with two fingers (a game)

piyatang seme: ⟶ **piyatar seme**

piyatar seme: talking on and on, prattling

piyoo: credential, pass, ticket, certification

  piyoo bithe: ⟶ **piyoo**

piyoociyan: evaluative note attached to a memorial for the Emperor's attention

po gin mahala: a soft, limp hat

pocok: (onomatopoetic) the sound of things hitting water

pocong: ⟶ **pocok**

podao: dagger

podz: **1**. an old lady; **2**. firecracker

pojan: firecracker

pok: (onomatopoetic) **1**. the sound of hitting something; **2**. the sound of an arrow hitting something

pok seme: (onomatopoetic) the sound of striking something, the sound of things colliding

pokcohon: short and fat, uncomely (appearance)

pokita: a bone arrowhead without holes

poksohon: plump, fat (said of a child), plump person

poksohori: ⟶ **poksohon**

polori: a large basket tray

poluri: ⟶ **polori**

pongcun: paunchy, short and paunchy

pongtonombi: to get fat and clumsy

poo: cannon

  poo i cooha: artillery troops

  poo i karan: fort, battery

  poo i niyalma: gunner, artilleryman

  poo i okto: gunpowder

  poo i unggala: magazine or powder chamber

  poo sindambi: to fire a cannon

  poo šeo: gunner

poojan: ⟶ **pojan**

popornombi: ⟶ **porponombi**

porong seme: crude, coarse, boorish

porpa: liberal, generous

porpon parpan: with the nose and eyes both running (said of weeping)

porponombi: to become fat and clumsy

pos gurun: Persia

pos pos: (onomatopoetic) the sound of heavy breathing

pos seme: (onomatopoetic) **1**. the sound of (an arrow) piercing an object; **2**. blurting out

potor patar: (onomatopoetic) the sound of a group of birds flying

pu: **1**. (onomatopoetic) the sound of blowing with the mouth; **2**. courier station

    pu i cooha: a soldier entrusted with delivering a message

    pu i da: person in charge of a courier station

pudanai: malva nut: the fruit of *Scaphium scaphigerum*

puhū: shopkeeper

puk pak seme: rough, coarse

puk seme: (onomatopoetic) sound of someone falling

pul: (Uyghur) money

pulu: ⟶ **puru**

pulu pala: disorderly, careless, crude

pulu pila seme: ⟶ **pulu pala**

pun: **1**. sail of a ship (cf. **kotoli**); **2**. an awning, covering for a wagon

    pun bargiyambi: to take in a sail

    pun tatambi: to hoist a sail

pupai: a temple servant

pur seme: (onomatopoetic) the sound of birds taking flight

puru: a coarse Tibetan wool from which lamas' winter hats are made; cf. **cengme**

pus pos: (onomatopoetic) the sound of silk or leather tearing

pus seme: **1**. (onomatopoetic) the sound of piercing something; **2**. unintentionally (said of laughing)

    pus seme injembi: to burst out laughing

pusa: bodhisattva

puse: **1**. insignia of rank on the official and court clothing of officials and nobles; **2**. store, shop; cf. **puseli**

    puse kurume: a court garment with the insignia of rank on it

    puse noho cece: silken gauze with insignias of rank on it

    puse noho niktongga suri: Nanjing silk bearing insignia of rank

    puse noho suje: silk with a design of dragons in golden circles

puseli: store, shop

    puseli ejen: proprietor, store owner

    puseli sindambi: to open up a store

puti moo: *Ficus religiosa*: bo tree, bodhi tree

putu pata: **1**. (onomatopoetic) the sound of many small things falling in succession; **2**. hurried, pressed, in haste

putur: (onomatopoetic) the sound of a large bird taking off

putur patar: flapping, fluttering

putur seme: **1**. drop by drop, bit by bit, gradually, unevenly; **2**. slowly dripping (said of tears); **3**. (onomatopoetic) the sound of a bird landing

    putur seme songgombi: to sob, to whimper

R ✈

rakca: ⟶ **rakša**

rakša: **1**. a man-eating demon, ogre; **2**. Russian

ridi: magic, supernatural power

S ᠰ

For words beginning with **š**, see the section beginning on page 340.

sa: **1**. shaft or thill of a cart or sedan chair; **2**. feather grass from which the outside surface of summer hats are made; cf. **deresu**; **3**. (plural suffix, sometimes written separately)

sabarambi: **1**. to drip, to trickle; **2**. to scatter, to disperse

sabcirambi: to rear (said of horses)

sabdabumbi: (causative of **sabdambi**)

sabdambi: to leak, to drip, to trickle, to fall in drops

    sabdara silenggingge fukjingga hergen: (垂露篆) a style of calligraphy

sabdan: **1**. a drop; **2**. leaking

    sabdan i aligan: rain drain under the projection of a roof

    sabdan sabdan: drop by drop

sabdangga wase: roof tile that permits water to drip down

sabe: (the plural marker **sa** plus the accusative particle **be**)

sabi: **1**. omen, sign, portent; **2**. propitious

    sabi acabun: marital predestination, a meant-to-be marriage, a marriage made in heaven

    sabi ferguwecun: propitious omen

    sabi ferguwen: good omen, auspicious sign

sabibumbi: to give a sign

sabingga: propitious, pertaining to a good omen, auspicious

    sabingga cecike: a dark gray bird with a strong wide red beak — the male and female are always found together

    sabingga darudai: a name for the phoenix

    sabingga hoošan: good-luck paper money hung on doors and gates at the New Year

    sabingga moo: the name of a mythical tree in which the Chinese characters for 'universal peace' are supposed to appear

    sabingga orho: the fungus *Fomes japonicus* before it forms its cap

    sabingga sence: the fungus *Fomes japonicus*, a sign of good fortune

    sabingga sence i fukjingga hergen: (芝英篆) a style of calligraphy

    sabingga sence i šušungge saracan: a purple parasol of the Imperial Escort embroidered with a figure of the auspicious fungus *Fomes japonicus*

sabintu: a female unicorn

sabintungga fukjingga hergen: (麟書) a style of calligraphy

sabirambi: ⟶ **sabarambi**

sabirgan cecike: a small black bird with a white forehead

sabirgan orho: *Reineckia carnea*: a perennial plant with violet flowers that supposedly open when happy events occur

sabirgi: an insignia of rank worn on the official and ceremonial clothing of officials and nobles; cf. **puse**

    sabirgi kurume: ⟶ **puse kurume**

    sabirgi noho cece: ⟶ **puse noho cece**

    sabirgi noho niktongga suri: ⟶ **puse noho niktongga suri**

    sabirgi noho suje: ⟶ **puse noho suje**

sabiri ilha: *Daphne odora*: water daphne

sabitun: the (male) unicorn

sabka: chopstick

    sabka sele: **1**. linchpin; **2**. iron pin used on a loom

sabkalambi: to pick up with chopsticks, to eat with chopsticks

sabsibumbi: (causative of **sabsimbi**)

sabsikū: garment, religious habit

sabsimbi: **1**. to sew tightly (boots and saddle pads); **2**. to brand characters on the face and arms of criminals; **3**. to trim a horse's mane

sabta: **1**. a stick used for spreading glue; **2**. a small bone or piece of cartilage in the knee, elbow, or shoulder joint

sabtarambi: to mark with an ax, to incise slightly

sabtari wasika: the area above the hoof has swollen (causing the horse to be lame)

sabu: shoe

sabubumbi: **1**. (causative or passive of **sabumbi**); **2**. to appear, to look like

sabugan: experience, perception, knowledge of the world

    sabugan akū: inexperienced, easily impressed by trifling matters

    sabugan be sabuhakū: has not seen much of the world, has not experienced real life

sabuhū: ⟶ **ebuhu sabuhū**

sabula: pubic hair

sabumbi: to see, to perceive

    saburakū oho: disappeared

sabun: **1**. sight, vision; **2**. visage, appearance

sabunambi: to go to see

sabundumbi: to see together, to see one another; also **sabunumbi**

sabunjimbi: to come to see

sabunumbi: to see together, to see one another; also **sabundumbi**

saburakū: ⟶ **sabumbi** (subheading)

saca: helmet

    saca i temgetu: an insignia the color of the wearer's banner that was attached to the back of the helmet and on which the name and rank of the banner chief was written

sacalabumbi: (causative of **sacalambi**)

sacalambi: to wear a helmet

sacalandumbi: to wear helmets (said of a group); also **sacalanumbi**

sacalanumbi: to wear helmets (said of a group); also **sacalandumbi**

sacibumbi: (causative or passive of **sacimbi**)

sacikū: **1**. hoe, mattock; **2**. chisel

    sacikū sirdan: a flat-headed arrow

    sacikū umiyaha: a kind of beetle

sacima: a small pastry made of noodles, sugar, and sesame seeds and cooked in sesame oil

sacimbi: **1**. to chop, to hack, to chop off; **2**. to hoe; **3**. to chisel; **4**. to clip (a horse's hooves)

    sacime wambi: to behead

    sacime wara weile: an offense for which beheading was the punishment

sacimri loho: a large sword used during battle for chopping the legs of horses

sacinambi: to go to chop

sacindumbi: to chop together, to hoe together; also **sacinumbi**

sacinumbi: to chop together, to hoe together; also **sacindumbi**

sacirambi: to hack, to chop at, to chop into pieces

sacu: grains of buckwheat

    sacu fungse i ufa: strained buckwheat flour

    sacu ufa: buckwheat flour

sacurambi: **1**. to grind buckwheat; **2**. to fall in grain-like flakes (said of snow)

sada: pine needle, any needle-like leaf from a plant

sadasihiyambi: ⟶ **sidahiyambi**

sade: (the plural suffix plus the case particle **de**)

sadulambi: to form an in-law relationship, to betroth

sadun: related by marriage, a relative by marriage

    sadun hala: relative by marriage

    sadun jafambi: to form an in-law relationship, to betroth

sadusa: (plural of **sadun**)

safulu: swim bladder of a fish

sagambi: ⟶ **sahambi**

sagin: an exotic sour-sweet fruit about the size of the fruit of the lacquer tree

saha: **1**. hunting, a small-scale battue

saha: **2**. ⟶ **sambi** (1) (subheading)

sahabumbi: (causative of **sahambi**)

sahadabumbi: (causative of **sahadambi**)

sahadambi: **1**. to hold a small-scale battue; **2**. to hunt in autumn

sahahūkan: the color of (Chinese) ink, ink-black

sahahūn: **1**. blackish, rather black; **2**. the tenth of the heaven's stems (癸)

    sahahūn muke tashari: a kind of crane

sahahūri: jet black

sahalca: pelt of a black sable

sahaldai: a black gibbon

    sahaldai monio: ⟶ **sahaldai**

sahaliyakan: rather black, blackish

sahaliyan: **1**. black; **2**. the ninth of the heaven's stems (壬)

  sahaliyan bonio: a black monkey

  sahaliyan dobihi: a black fox pelt

  sahaliyan faha: black pupil, black eye

  sahaliyan fatha: a kind of quail with black feet

  sahaliyan giranggi coko: a kind of chicken with fuzzy white feathers and black bones and skin

  sahaliyan gu: a kind of black gem

  sahaliyan ihan: a black cow

  sahaliyan kekuhe: a black pigeon or dove

  sahaliyan malanggū: black sesame

  sahaliyan moo: ebony

  sahaliyan nilgiyan hoošan: paper made from bamboo fiber and coated with gold

  sahaliyan turi: small black beans

  sahaliyan tuyeku yonggan: a black sand used in casting bronze

  sahaliyan ujungga: 'the black-headed ones' — the common people

  sahaliyan ula: Amur river

  sahaliyan yarha: a black panther

sahalja: a black coot

sahaltu: having a black face

  sahaltu cecike: the name of a black-headed bird somewhat larger than a sparrow with a white neck, back, and dark yellow wings with white spots

sahambi: **1**. to pile up, to stack; **2**. to build a wall or other structure by laying bricks

  sahame weilembi: to build up, to erect

sahamha: *Labrax luyu*: sea perch

sahan: pile, stack, a stack of **gacuha** piled up by a winner

saharabumbi: (causative of **saharambi**)

saharambi: (-ka) to turn black, to blacken

sahari: into a heap

  sahari tuhembi: to be thrown (in wrestling)

sahiba: obsequious, fawning, groveling

saibigan: birthmark

saibihan: spoonbill pelican; cf. **halbahan**

saibumbi: (causative or passive of **saimbi**)

saiburu: canter (of a horse), slow amble

saicungga fengšen: the Jiaqing (嘉慶) reign period, 1796–1820

saifa weihe: the molars, the back teeth

saifatu: a four-year-old horse

saifi: a spoon; cf. **kuini**

saifilambi: to scoop out with a spoon

saiha: **1**. anklebone; **2**. ⟶ **alin i saiha**; **3**. brush, undergrowth; cf. **suiha**

  saiha giranggi: anklebone

  saiha i doko: the inside of the anklebone

  saiha i tuku: the outside of the anklebone

saihada: shinbone, tibia

saihūwa: a bramble plant with round leaves and a red blossom (used for weaving baskets and as an implement for beating criminals), brambles, possibly a kind of vitex

  saihūwa bula: brambles, thorny undergrowth

saihūwada: the light rod, a bamboo rod used for flogging; cf. **cy**

saihūwadalabumbi: (causative or passive of **saihūwadalambi**)

saihuwadalambi: to flog with a light bamboo rod

saika: ⟶ **saikan**

saikan: **1**. pretty, good-looking, beautiful; **2**. rather well, nicely, properly

  saikan arbungga ilha: *Rosa semperflorens*: blowing rose

  saikan arbungga ilha i suwayan suje sara: a silver parasol of the escort embroidered with yellow, red, and black blowing rose (*Rosae semperflorentes*)

  saikan ejembi: to keep well in mind

  saikan eldengge: bright-colored and beautiful, gorgeous

  saikan hojo: very beautiful, very attractive

saikū: snacks to go with liquor

saikūngge: pertaining to snacks

saimbe: ⟶ **sain be**

saimbi: to bite, to chew

saimengge: worth tasting, good to eat

sain: **1**. good, well; **2**. auspicious, favorable

  sain acabun: good omen

  sain be fonjimbi: to ask after someone's health

  sain be ibebure temgetun: a banner of the escort bearing the inscription **sain be ibebure**

  sain de aisilakū: (贊善) a court title just below that of **giyan be jorikū**

  sain dorolon: wedding

  sain holbon: a good marriage match

  sain i yabu: have a good trip!

  sain inenggi: an auspicious day, a clear day

sain irgen: common people

sain sabi: a good or auspicious omen

sainambi: to go to bite

saintu: good, excellent (used in posthumous names)

sainumbi: to bite one another

saisa: **1**. a man proficient in letters and good in his speech and conduct, scholar, gentleman; **2**. hero, stalwart

saisa be baire kunggeri: (求賢科) Office for the recruiting of candidates for official service

saisaha: ⟶ **saishan**

saise: small cake, cracker, biscuit

saisha cecike: a name for the sparrow

saishan: a basket (with a handle) that can be carried in the hand at one's side

saišabukū: flatterer

saišabumbi: (causative or passive of **saišambi**)

saišacuka: praiseworthy, worthy of commendation

saišakūšambi: to look for praise, to seek praise

saišambi: to praise, to commend

saišandumbi: to praise or commend together; also **saišanumbi**

saišangga: famous, renowned, praiseworthy

saišanumbi: to praise or commend together; also **saišandumbi**

saitu: minister, man of high rank, senior official

saiyūn: interrogative form of **sain**: **si saiyūn**? 'How are you?'

saja: a million

sajingga deo: younger (in respect to speaker) student of the same teacher

saka: **1**. fish or meat cut up fine, mixed with seasonings and eaten raw; **2**. clause particle used after the imperfect converb: just, as soon as — the same as **jaka**; **3**. an adjectival suffix: as if, like, somewhat, rather: **necikesaka** 'rather level'; **hocikon saka** 'rather nice'

sakalambi: ⟶ **šakalambi**

sakda: **1**. old (said of people); **2**. old man; **3**. sow, specifically a four-year-old wild sow

sakdabumbi: (causative of **sakdambi**)

sakdaki: having the aspect of old age (said of someone young), old-looking

sakdambi: (-ka, -pi) to get old, to age

sakdandambi: to near old age

sakdantala: until old, until old age

sakdanumbi: to grow old together

sakdasa: (plural of **sakda**)

sakdatala: ⟶ **sakdantala**

sakidun: a name for the partridge; cf. **jukidun**

saksaha: *Pica pica*: magpie

saksaha damin: a one- to two-year-old eagle

saksahūn: support, prop, rack for piling wood and such things

saksalabumbi: to get stuck (said of an arrow in a tree)

saksalibumbi: (causative or passive of **saksalimbi**)

saksalikū: a frame for setting off fireworks

saksalimbi: to prop up, to make (branches, brush, etc.) into a rack or frame

saksan: **1**. a pole with a hook or branch on the end (used for hanging things up); **2**. a cake used in sacrifices

saksan golbon: a clothing rack

saksan juhe: a number of ice floes frozen together

saksari: onto one's back (said of falling)

saksari kekuhe: the name of a bird that resembles the Asiatic blue magpie but is smaller

saksari tuhembi: to fall on one's back

saksime: ⟶ **ekšeme saksime**

saksin: Chinese juniper — *Juniperus chinensis*

saksu: **1**. a basket made from brambles (for holding grain); **2**. a small bamboo basket for holding tea, paper, etc.

saksulabumbi: (causative of **saksulambi**)

saksulambi: to place in a basket

sakūra: a wooden tripod for hanging a pot over a fire

sala moo: a large Indian tree, *Shorea robusta*

salaba: pineapple

salabumbi: (causative of **salambi**)

salambi: to distribute, to pass out

salame aitubumbi: to relieve, to aid

salambumbi: ⟶ **salabumbi**

salanambi: to go to distribute

salandumbi: to distribute together; also **salanumbi**

salanjimbi: to come to distribute

salanumbi: to distribute together; also **salandumbi**

salgabuha: ⟶ **salgabumbi** (subheading)

salgabuhangge: that which was ordained by heaven, that which was preordained

salgabumbi: to be fixed by fate, to be preordained, to be ordained by heaven

salgabuha abkai banin: nature, inborn quality

salgabuha babi: it is fixed by fate

salgabuha hūturi: preordained happiness

salgabun: fate, decree of heaven, providence

salgabun feten: destiny, fate

salgangga: conscionable, conscientious

salgangga akū: without conscience

salgangga mujilen: conscience

salgatu hoohan: one of the names of the heron; cf. **hoohan**

salhū: **1.** a piece of iron fastened to the end of a plow, the plowshare; **2.** the wooden frame of a comb on a loom

salhūma: pheasant of the north

salibumbi: **1.** to estimate (a price), to set a value, to assess; **2.** to put in charge, to make head of; **3.** causative of **salimbi**

salibume bodombi: to estimate

salifi: ⟶ **salimbi** (subheading)

saligan: **1.** proposal, idea; **2.** autonomy, independence, sense of responsibility; **3.** estimate, calculation; **4.** in small quantity, meagerly, judiciously

saligan akū: lacking a sense of responsibility, lacking initiative

saligan i ba: lands allotted to high officials for revenue

saligan i bumbi: to give meagerly

saligan toose: right of determination

salimbaharakū: not able to undertake responsibility, unable to show initiative

salimbi: **1.** to be worth, to be valued; **2.** to be in charge, to take responsibility, to monopolize, to act arbitrarily; **3.** to inherit

salifi lashalambi: to make an arbitrary decision

salifi yabumbi: to carry out without authority, to act on one's own authority

salirakū: you're welcome (response to being thanked for a favor or gift)

salingga: assertive (person), prone to usurp authority, domineering, peremptory, imperious

salingga ejen: autocrat

salirakū: ⟶ **salimbi** (subheading)

saliyahan: just enough, just barely enough

saliyan: just right, just sufficient

salja: a fork in a road

salja jugūn: a forking road

salmandara: salamander

salu: beard, whiskers

salu fusimbi: to shave (one's whiskers)

salungga: bearded

sama: ⟶ **saman**

samadambi: to perform shamanistic rites

samadi: meditation

samadi baksi: Chan (Zen) master

samadi boo: meditation room

samadi colo: Buddhist religious name

samadi de toktombi: to remain fixed in meditation, to meditate

samadi hūwa: monastery, meditation hall

samadi mama: shamaness, sorceress

samadi tembi: to sit in meditation, to meditate

samadi tere boo: meditation hall (in a monastery)

saman: shaman

saman cecike: *Galerida cristata*: North China crested lark; cf. **wenderhen**

saman hehe: shamaness

saman oktosi: spiritual healer, shamanistic healer

samangga niyalma: shaman, one who practices shamanism

samara: a large wooden bowl

samarabumbi: (causative of **samarambi**)

samarambi: to mix tea or soup by repeatedly ladling out a quantity with a spoon and pouring it back

samaran: the name of an ancient sacrificial vessel (登)

samasa: (plural of **saman**)

samašambi: to perform a shamanistic rite

sambaršambi: ⟶ **sambiršambi**

sambaršame: in a flurry, in a frantic rush

sambi: **(1)** (**-ha**) to know, to understand

saha sahai: at random, at will

sambi: **(2)** (**-ngka, -mpi**) **1.** to stretch, to extend; **2.** to milk; **3.** to be distant, to be far away

sambiršambi: to stretch, to stick out, to extend

samdambi: to perform a shamanistic rite; cf. **samadambi, samašambi**

samdame tarimbi: to plant another type of seed between the furrows of a field

samha: mole or birthmark on the face or body

samina: one ten-sextillionth

sampa: shrimp, prawn

samsibumbi: (causative of **samsimbi**)

samsimbi: to disperse, to scatter, to adjourn

samsu: a kind of fine blue linen

samsulabumbi: (causative of **samsulambi**)

samsulambi: to engrave designs on metal

samuri: one sextillion

sanat: senate (from French)

    sanat yamun: senate (in Russia)

sanca: Jew's ear, wood-ear, the edible fungus *Auricularia auricula-judae*

sanciha: **1**. nose ring or hook for cows and camels; **2**. an iron wire fastening device on a bird trap

sandahūn: distant from, separated from

sandalabumbi: **1**. (causative of **sandalambi**); **2**. to lie in between, to be separated from, to be distant from

    sandalabuha siden: the interval in between

sandalambi: **1**. to have the legs spread apart (when sitting or standing); **2**. to be apart, to have a space in between

    sandalame ilihabi: standing with legs spread

sandaršambi: to walk with the legs spread

sandumbi: to know one another, to know together; also **sanumbi**

sangga: hole, opening

    sangga arambi: to punch a hole

    sangga tucimbi: for a small hole to appear

    sangga tūmbi: to punch a hole

sanggala: river port

sanggata: having holes or openings

sanggatanambi: to form holes or openings

sanggatangga: having holes, riddled with holes

sangguhe: a name for the myna

sangguji: jellyfish

sanggū: something gratifying or satisfying

sanggūšabumbi: (causative or passive of **sanggūšambi**)

sanggūšambi: to take pleasure in, to be pleased with, to rejoice in another person's misfortune

sangka: (perfect participle of **sambi** [**2**]) distant, distantly related

    sangka ahūn deo: great-grandfather's brothers

sangkangga jalahi jui: son of a second or third cousin

sangkangge: very distant

sangsarabumbi: (causative of **sangsarambi**)

sangsarambi: (**-ka**) to fall into disrepair, to fall into ruins, to collapse, to cave in

sangse: **1**. a finger wringer (an instrument of torture); **2**. manacles

    sangse guwangse: manacles

sangselabumbi: (causative of **sangselambi**)

sangselambi: **1**. to press the fingers (as a punishment); **2**. to manacle

saniyabumbi: **1**. (causative of **saniyambi**); **2**. to extend (a deadline or date)

saniyambi: **1**. to stretch out, to extend, to stretch; **2**. to give an extension, to extend a deadline

    saniyame kurbušembi: to stretch (when sleeping)

saniyan: extension, stretching out

saniyangga: extensive

saniyashūn: somewhat extended

sanumbi: to know one another, to know together; also **sandumbi**

sar sar: (onomatopoetic) the sound of grasshoppers flying

sar sar seme: (onomatopoetic) **1**. the sound of insects chirping; **2**. the sound of leaves falling; **3**. the sound of washing rice; **4**. without delay; cf. **sar seme**

sar seme: **1**. pouring out (tears); **2**. without delay, quickly; **3**. (onomatopoetic) the sound of washing

sar sir: (onomatopoetic) the sound of leaves falling

sar sir seme: **1**. (onomatopoetic) the sound of washing rice; **2**. without delay

sara: **1**. umbrella, parasol; **2**. general term for the seven iron pieces fixed to a quiver and bow case

    sara belhere ba: (備傘處) the Imperial umbrella chamber where the ceremonial parasols and umbrellas were kept

    sarai da: person in charge of parasols

sarabumbi: (causative of **sarambi**)

saraca: *Berberis chinensis*: mountain barberry

saraci: magistrate; cf. **hiyan i saraci**

sarahūn: expandable, stretchable, extendable

sarambi: **1**. to open (out), to unfold, to expand, to rub smooth; **2**. to fan, to winnow

sarandumbi: to unfold one after another

sarasu: knowledge

sarašambi: to go on an excursion, to go strolling, to go on an outing, to take pleasure in viewing scenery

sarašan: excursion, outing, pleasure in viewing scenery

sarašanambi: to go on an excursion

sarašanjimbi: to come on an excursion

saratai keire: a sorrel horse with a white crescent-shaped spot on the forehead

sarba: a shuttle or reel used for weaving nets; cf. **sarfu**

sarbacan: **1**. visor on a helmet; **2**. a veil attached to the brim of a woman's summer hat

sarbahūn: **1**. lying spread-eagled on one's back; **2**. sparse, scraggly

sarbašambi: **1**. to keep groping at one another (in wrestling); **2**. to rock back and forth, to writhe, to struggle; **3**. to become agitated when some matter cannot be settled; **4**. to throw a tantrum

sarbatala: writhing, struggling

sarca guwejihe: the third stomach of ruminants

sarcan: ⟶ **sarca**

sarfu: a shuttle used in weaving nets

sarga nimaha: *Stenodus leucichthys*: white salmon, sheefish

sargaji cecike: a name for the titmouse; cf. **jirha cecike**

sargambi: ⟶ **sarašambi**

sargan: wife, woman, female

  sargan gaiha ice niyalma: bridegroom

  sargan gaimbi: to get married (said of men), to take a wife

  sargan jui: girl, daughter

  sargan jui bumbi: to give a daughter in marriage

  sargan juse: girls, daughters

sarganji nimaha: the name of a river fish with a long mouth — white fish; cf. **sarga nimaha**

sargašambi: ⟶ **sarašambi**

sargata: (plural of **sargan**)

sargiya: groin, pubic region, crotch

sargiyakan: rather sparse, rather wide-meshed

sargiyalakū asu: a wide-meshed fish net thrown by hand

sargiyan: sparse, wide-meshed, spare

sarhū: a rack or shelf for dishes

sarhūn moo: the name of a tree with sparse fine branches that grew on the grave of Confucius — *Pistacia chinensis*: Chinese pistache

sarilabumbi: (causative of **sarilambi**)

sarilambi: to feast, to hold a banquet

sarin: **1**. feast, banquet; **2**. skin from which boots are made (from the hind section of a horse, mule, or donkey)

  sarin be dagilara bolgobure fiyenten: (精膳清吏司) Banquet Department, *BH* 376A

  sarin be dagilara yamun: (光禄寺) Court of Banqueting, *BH* 376B, 934

  sarin dagilambi: to hold a banquet, to throw a feast

  sarin gūlha: boots made from skin from the hind part of a quadruped

saringgiyambi: to pour hot and cold tea together

sarki: ⟶ **sarkiyan**

  sarki saliburakū: to do upon one's own initiative, not to take others into account (in handling some matter)

sarkiyabumbi: (causative of **sarkiyambi**)

sarkiyambi: **1**. to copy, to make a clean copy; **2**. to thin out (seedlings); **3**. to make thin, to make sparse

  sarkiyafi selgiyere boo: (報房) Printing Office, *BH* 435C

  sarkiyame arambi: to copy over, to make a clean copy of

  sarkiyame arara ba: office for copying, copy office

  sarkiyame arara falgangga: (謄錄所) office where examination papers were recopied before being read by the examiners

  sarkiyame arara hafan: (謄錄官) an official charged with copying examination papers

  sarkiyame arara niyalma: a copyist

sarkiyan: copy, clean copy

  sarkiyan saliburakū: ⟶ **sarki saliburakū**

sarkiyangga bithe: copies of Imperial edicts kept in the archives of the six ministries

sarkiyanumbi: **1**. to thin out together; **2**. to copy together

sarkū: not to know (contraction of **sara akū**)

sarla: a gray-colored horse

sarluk: yak

  sarluk ihan: yak

sarni boihon: yellow earth, ochre

sarpa: grasshopper

sarpahūn: dragonfly

sarsen doli: the overripe flesh of a melon with a rough, sand-like texture

saršambi: ⟶ **sarašambi**

sarta moro: large wooden or pottery bowl

sartabumbi: **1**. (causative of **sartambi**); **2**. to put at ease, to comfort, to calm (someone) down; **3**. to take up (a person's time), to procrastinate, to postpone, to put off; **4**. to hinder, to impede; **5**. to bungle, to perform some task unsatisfactorily

sartabun: **1**. postponement, delay; **2**. comfort

sartacun: delay, postponement

sartahūn: perilous

sartambi: **1**. to delay, to postpone, to put off; **2**. to act at leisure, to be free and easy, to idle

sartashūn: slow, delayed, postponed

saru: ⟶ **abka saru**

sasa: together

sasambi: **1**. to shuffle (mah-jongg tiles or cards); **2**. to grow up (said of children)

sasari: together

sase: a pastry eaten in summer (made from buckwheat flour, honey, and sesame)

sasukū: mah-jongg tiles, playing cards

sasulin cecike: a name for the oriole; cf. **gūlin cecike**

sasumbi: ⟶ **sasambi**

sasuri: playing cards used in a game popular in the Qing dynasty: *mǎdiào* 馬吊

sata: pine needles

satangga coko: *Tetrastes bonasia*: hazel grouse

sati: male brown bear

saya: a very small cooking pot; cf. **kilakci**

se: **1**. year (said of age), age; **2**. raw silk, unprocessed silk; **3**. the juncture of the stem and root on the ginseng plant; **4**. (plural suffix); cf. **sa**; **5**. ⟶ **se selaha**

se asigan: young, youthful

se baha: aged

se baru ombi: to become old

se be bodome: according to age

se ciksin: mature, grown-up

se de gocimbumbi: to grow decrepit

se de ombi: to age, to get old

se elen telen akū: of almost the same age

se i baru ombi: ⟶ **se baru ombi**

se i onggolo sakdakabi: became old before his time

se jalgan: (length) of life

se jeke: became old, old (said of horses)

se komso: young

se mulan baha: became old

se sakdakabi: has aged

se selaha: content, pleased, happy

se sirge: raw silk, unprocessed silk

se tucike: is above age, superannuated

seb sab: dripping, in scattered drops

seb sab agambi: to rain in scattered drops

sebcelembi: to take the first bite of a newly presented dish, to taste for the first time

sebdembi: (-**ke**) to rust

sebden: rust

sebdenembi: ⟶ **sebdembi**

sebderi: shady, shade

sebderi ba: shady place, shade

sebderi eye: an ice hole used for cold storage

sebderilebumbi: (causative of **sebderilembi**)

sebderilembi: **1**. to take advantage of the shade, to rest in the shade; **2**. to shade, to provide shade

sebe: (the plural suffix **se** and the accusative particle **be**)

sebe saba agambi: to rain in scattered drops

sebederi: ⟶ **seberi**

seberi: a horse or mule with white hooves

seberšembi: to drizzle, to drip, to rain sporadically

sebimbi: to recover, to come around, to feel refreshed after being tired; cf. **sebkimbi**

sebjelebumbi: (causative of **sebjelembi**)

sebjelembi: to rejoice, to be glad

sebjelendumbi: to rejoice together; also **sebjelenumbi**

sebjelenumbi: to rejoice together; also **sebjelendumbi**

sebjen: **1**. joy, gladness; **2**. joyful, happy

sebjengge: joyful, glad

sebjengge baibula: a name for the paradise flycatcher; cf. **baibula**

sebjengge ilha: the name of an exotic purple flower that blooms for long periods without withering

sebjengge yengguhe: another name for the 'phoenix parrot' — **garudangga yengguhe**

sebke saka: just, just now

sebkelembi: to eat at intervals, to eat between meals

sebkembi: to spring (said of tigers, wildcats, and leopards), to pounce

sebken: recently, just, just now, newly, for the first time

sebkesaka: ⟶ **sebke saka**

sebkimbi: to recover, to be refreshed after being fatigued, to regain one's strength

sebsehe: locust, grasshopper

sebsehenembi: to become infested with locusts

sebseheri: locust; cf. **sebsehe**

    sebseheri umiyaha: locust

sebsibumbi: (causative of **sebsimbi**)

sebsihiyen: affable, pleasant

sebsimbi: to shake someone who has passed out

sebsingge: affable, pleasant, friendly

sebtembi: ⟶ **sektembi**

secen: part in the hair

secibumbi: (causative of **secimbi**)

secimbi: **1**. to cut off, to cut away; **2**. to make furrows in a field

secindumbi: **1**. to cut off together; **2**. to make furrows together; also **secinumbi**

secinumbi: **1**. to cut off together; **2**. to make furrows together; also **secindumbi**

secirembi: to stab wildly, to cut at

secu: *Elopichthys bambusa*: yellowcheek

sedehengge: You deserve death!, one who has been killed — an oath

sedeheri: clever, bright child

sedembi: to kill

sedu: bean meal

sedz: dice; cf. **sesuku**

    sedz maktambi: to play dice

sefere: **1**. a handful, a bundle; **2**. twenty strips of meat tied together; **3**. pint: a unit of measure

    sefere yali: meat tied together in strips

seferembi: to take a handful, to grab with the hand, to grasp, to seize

seferešembi: to keep on taking handfuls, to keep on grabbing

seferšembi: ⟶ **seferešembi**

sefu: teacher, master

sefuse: (plural of **sefu**)

sefuta: (plural of **sefu**); cf. **sefuse**

sehehun: standing on end, erect, vertical

sehehun ilihabi: is standing erect (said of someone's hair when angry)

sehehuri: **1**. towering high (said of many mountain peaks), precipitous, sheer; **2**. straight, erect (said of sitting and standing)

    sehehuri den: high and towering (said of many peaks)

    sehehuri hada: towering cliffs, precipitous peaks

    sehehuri ilicahabi: standing tall (said of a group of able-bodied men)

sehercembi: to roll up one's sleeves and get ready to fight

seherembi: **1**. to arch the eyebrows in anger; **2**. to bristle (said of a beard); **3**. to be enraged to the point of violence

seheri: towering, precipitous

    seheri hada: sheer peak, precipitous peak

seheri sahari: **1**. uneven (said of mountain peaks); **2**. uneven or flickering in the distance

    seheri sahari sabumbi: to see one or two things flickering in the distance

seheri seheri: ⟶ **seheri sahari**

seheršembi: to be agitated to the point of violence

sehiyen: ⟶ **sesheri**

sehuji: one tenth to the twentieth power

sehulembi: to step forth, to step to the front

    sehuleme ilimbi: to stand in front (of the ranks)

sei: (**se** plus the genitive particle **i**)

seibeni: formerly, once, in the past

    seibeni fonde: in the past, formerly

seilebumbi: (causative of **seilembi**)

seilembi: to boil meat that has been cut up

seire: **1**. spine; **2**. lumbar vertebra, lower part of the spine

sejeci: wagoner, person in charge of official vehicles, wagon-maker

sejen: wagon, cart, vehicle

    sejen bašambi: to drive a vehicle

    sejen bošombi: ⟶ **sejen bašambi**

    sejen ci ebumbi: to get off a vehicle

    sejen de tafambi: to get on a vehicle

    sejen de tembi: to ride in a vehicle

    sejen i dobton: canopy over a sedan chair

    sejen i faksi: wagon-maker, cartwright

    sejen i yun: cart tracks, wheel rut

    sejen jafambi: to drive a vehicle

sejen kiyoo i fiyenten: (鑾輿司) Carriage Section, *BH* 118

sejen tohoro enggemu: saddle for attaching a cart

sejen turigen: carfare, rent for a vehicle

sejesi: driver, wagoner

sejilembi: to sigh

sejilendumbi: to sigh together; also **sejilenumbi**

sejilenumbi: to sigh together; also **sejilendumbi**

sejulen: wild garlic; cf. **suduli**

sek seme: suddenly, with a start (said of awaking)

seke: **1**. *Martes zibellina*: sable; **2**. sable pelt

seke furdehe: sable jacket

sekejembi: to get worn thin, to become tattered

sekembi: to take the bait (said of fish)

sekimbi: ⟶ **sekiyembi**

sekiyebumbi: (causative of **sekiyembi**)

sekiyeku: a straw hat, a rain hat made of reeds or leaves

sekiyembi: to let drip, to let drip dry, to filter, to strain through

sekiyen: spring (of water), source, origin

sekji: straw laid on the ground (when a woman gives birth), straw spread out for livestock or fowl

sekji funiyehe: hair covering a fetus

sekjingge: not rich but can still manage

sekse saksa: **1**. lacking talent but still employable; **2**. uneven, jagged, of unequal height

sekse saksa teksin akū: jagged and uneven

seksehe: **1**. occipital bone; **2**. a protruding bone located between a horse's ears; **3**. locust; cf. **sebsehe**

seksehun: **1**. wan, sallow, pallid, pale, haggard; **2**. frozen from the cold (the face); **3**. bleak, desolate

sekselibuha: ⟶ **seksen lifabuha**

seksen: ⟶ **seksen i yali**

seksen banjihabi: literally: 'meat frozen in a pitfall has been formed' (used to describe a lucky find or good opportunity)

seksen i yali: meat of an animal that has fallen into a hole and subsequently frozen solid

seksen lifabuha: slipped into a pitfall

sekserembi: (**-ke/-he**) to stand on end (said of hair)

sekseri: firm, fixed (said of an arrow)

sekseršembi: ⟶ **sengseršembi**

seksu: a basket lined with paper treated with oil (used for carrying liquids)

sektebumbi: (causative of **sektembi**)

sektefun: cushion, pad used for sitting

sektefun i jibsigan: a pad of skin or felt spread under a cushion or sitting pad

sektembi: to spread, to make (a bed), to spread out, to cover

sektere moo: boards covering the deck of a ship

sektu: **1**. clever, agile, alert, sharp, quick (said of intelligence); **2**. light (said of sleep)

sektuken: rather clever, rather agile

sektusi: a person who has obtained a post without passing an examination

selabumbi: (causative of **selambi**)

selabun: happiness, contentment

selacuka: happy, content, pleased, cheerful

selacun: joy, happiness, cheer

selambi: to be content, to be pleased, to be happy, to feel cheerful, to be carefree

selame aitubumbi: to provide aid, to bring relief to, to relieve (victims of tragedy)

selbete: *Artemisia lactiflora*: white mugwort

selbi: oar

selbi noho jahūdai: a galley ship

selbibumbi: (causative of **selbimbi**)

selbimbi: **1**. to row; **2**. to tread water

selbin goro: with wide steps (said of trotting horses)

sele: iron

sele faksi: blacksmith, ironworker

sele futa: iron cable

sele futa tabumbi: to bind in fetters

sele garma: an arrow with an iron head surrounded by four barbs (used for hunting pheasants and rabbits)

sele i hosori: iron shavings or splinters

sele i sirge: iron wire

sele ninggiya: an instrument of torture consisting of a pole with barbs on it

sele šoforokū: anchor

sele urebumbi: to smelt iron

selei ejen: magnet

selei holbokū: iron clamp, iron fastener

selei ilhangga moo: veined ironwood

selei jušuru: an iron self-defense weapon shaped like a measuring stick

selei mala: an iron hammer

selei sirge: iron wire, wire

selei taimin: an iron poker

selei yonggan: birdshot

selekje: tapir

selekten: red water found under piles of earth and grass, rusty water

seleme: a dagger somewhat larger than a **dabcilakū** and carried at the belt

selengge moo: ironwood tree — a tree with black trunk and leaves, and a light purple flower that blooms for months without withering

selfen: a slit in clothing

selgiyebukū: an interpreter in ancient times

selgiyebumbi: (causative of **selgiyembi**)

selgiyembi: to promulgate, to announce, to issue, to disseminate, to circulate, to inform, to advertise (for), to make public

    selgiyere hese: Imperial edict, Imperial decree

selgiyen: order, command, announcement, promulgation, advertisement

selgiyere. ⟶ **selgiyembi** (subheading)

selgiyesi: promulgator, announcer, herald

selhe: dewlap, the pendulous fold of skin under a cow's neck

selhen: a cangue

    selhen etubumbi: to have the cangue put on, to cause to wear the cangue

selmin: **1**. a kind of trap placed on animal trails that works like a crossbow; **2**. mechanism, spring

    selmin beri: crossbow, a trap that works like a crossbow

selmiyen: ⟶ **selmin**

sembi: **(1)** (-he) to say, to call, to mean

    sere anggala: instead of, not only (but also)

sembi: **(2)** (-ngke) to melt, to dissolve, to run (said of colors)

sembumbi: (causative of **sembi** [2])

semecen: ⟶ **semejen**

semehuken: rather coarse, rather coarsely woven, rather loose

semehun: coarse, coarsely woven, loose, sparse

    semehun boso: coarsely woven summer cloth

semejen: the fat covering the intestines and inner organs

semembi: to become saturated, to spread and sink in (said of ink on paper), to blot

semeo: (the imperfect converb **seme** plus the interrogative particle **o**, used to form rhetorical questions)

semerhen: a curtain or mat hung over a frame, a cover for a sedan chair, a small tent used for sleeping

    semerhen i yabumbi: to act in earnest, to act with sincerity

semeyen: ⟶ **semehun**

semibumbi: (causative of **semimbi**)

semiku: the end of a thread that has been tapered to pass more easily through the eye of a needle

semimbi: to thread (a needle)

semiyeku: ⟶ **semiku**

semkele: ⟶ **sengkule**

semken: bracelet

semkimbi: to guess, to suspect, to be suspicious, to suspect someone of revealing one's personal affairs to another

semnio: (觜) a constellation, the 20th of the lunar mansions, made up of three stars (λ, ϕ, and ϕ_2) in Orion

    semnio tokdonggo kiru: a banner depicting the constellation **semnio**

semsu: the fat covering of intestines; cf. **semejen**

    semsu nimenggi: ⟶ **semsu**

sen: eye of a needle, small hole (as in ears for earrings), any small opening

    sende genehe: formed a hole, formed a breach

sence: mushroom

    sence jinggeri: a nail shaped like a mushroom (with a large, wide head)

sencehe: **1**. the chin; **2**. a wooden or bamboo hook in the nose of a cow or camel; cf. **sanciha**; **3**. a bamboo hook that is part of a bird trap

    sencehe sibsihūn: the chin is narrow

senceheleku: a part of the bridle that hangs under the chin of a horse

sencetu: a name for the bamboo partridge; cf. **cuse moo i itu**

senci: ⟶ **senji**

sencihe: ⟶ **sencehe**

senciku: leather catches on boots through which the laces are threaded

sende: ⟶ **sen** (subheading)

sendehen: a board on which offerings to deities are placed

sendejembi: to break (said of a levee), to form a breach, to get washed out, to form a hole, to form a notch or gap (in a blade)

    sendejehe angga: a breach

sendelebumbi: (causative of **sendelembi**)

sendelembi: to make a breach (in a levee)

sendembi: ⟶ **sendejembi**

senembi: to be saturated, to spread (said of a wet spot), to leak (said of a brush too saturated with ink)

seng: a reed-pipe musical instrument — *shēng* 笙

sengge: **1**. elder, old; **2**. (Chinese) hedgehog (*Erinaceus europaeus*)

sengge šufatu: a head covering used in ancient times by old men

senggeda: calamus

senggele: **1**. rooster's comb, chicken's comb; **2**. gill (of a fish); **3**. reed (of a musical instrument); **4**. lock spring; **5**. the opening of a bow case

senggele ilha: *Celosia cristata*: cockscomb

senggelengge: having a comb (like a rooster)

senggelengge coko: a name for the gray partridge; cf. **itu**

senggelengge gasha: the name of a black-headed bird with a brown beak and a comb on the top of its head

senggete: **1**. (plural of **sengge**): old men; **2**. Siberian cocklebur (*Xanthium japonica*)

senggi: blood

senggi biljaka: there was a blood bath

senggi cacumbi: **1**. to sprinkle or spill blood; **2**. to smear the blood of a sacrifice on one's mouth as a means of oath taking

senggi duha: blood sausage

senggi fudambi: to spit up blood

senggi hefeliyenere nimeku: typhus

senggi i dalgan: clot of blood

senggi jugūn: blood vessel

senggi jun: artery, blood vessel

senggi kaksimbi: to cough up blood

senggi melmelembi: to form a blood clot

senggi sosombi: to have bloody diarrhea

senggi sudala: ⟶ **senggi jugūn**

senggi tebumbi: to shed blood

senggi tucimbi: to bleed

senggihun: desolate, wretched

senggilembi: to act in a bloody manner

senggileme afambi: to fight a bloody battle

senggime: intimate, friendly, on good terms, devoted

senggime gosimbi: to love tenderly

senggiri hiyan: rue: a kind of incense burned at sacrifices

senggiri ilha: rhododendron

sengguwebumbi: (causative or passive of **sengguwembi**)

sengguwecembi: to be prone to fear, to be fearful

sengguwecuke: dreadful, frightening

sengguwembi: to fear, to dread

sengguwendembi: ⟶ **sengguwembi**

sengguwendumbi: to fear together, to dread together; also **sengguwenumbi**

sengguwenumbi: to fear together, to dread together; also **sengguwendumbi**

sengken: **1**. small loop in which a button is fastened; **2**. a rope or similar object attached to a basket to facilitate carrying; **3**. ring on which a bell is hung; **4**. small knob on the end of a seal

sengkiri hiyan: the name of a plant burned at sacrifices, rue; cf. **senggiri hiyan**

sengkule: *Allium odorum*: a thin-bladed variety of chives, Chinese chives

sengkule i arsun: the yellow sprouts of chives that have been protected from the sun

sengse: a lazy woman

sengsebumbi: (causative of **sengsembi**)

sengsembi: (-**ke**) to dry, to become dry

sengserebumbi: (causative of **sengserembi**)

sengserebume bucembi: to die by drowning

sengserebume wambi: to kill by drowning

sengserembi: (-**ke**) **1**. to drown (intransitive verb); **2**. to choke by getting water in the windpipe

sengseršembi: to like very much, to desire ardently

sengsu: loose rocks on a mountain, scree

senihun: only half cooked (rice, meat), underdone, partially done

seniyehuken: rather underdone

seniyehun: ⟶ **senihun**

senji: back sight on a rifle

sentehe: gap, chip, crack, breach

seo: lacking pupils in the eyes

seolebumbi: (causative of **seolembi**)

seoleku: fussy, overly particular, petty, petty person

seolembi: **1**. to consider, to think over, to reflect; **2**. ⟶ **suwelembi**

seolen: consideration, reflection, thought

seolen be goromilambi: to think far ahead

seoltei: goral; cf. **imahū**

ser seme: small, tiny

    ser seme agambi: to rain lightly

    ser seme ajige: tiny, minute

    ser seme dambi: to blow gently (said of the wind)

    ser sere: tiny

    ser sere ba: detail, small point

serben sarban: **1**. in a swarm, swarming; **2**. in torrents

sere: **1**. fly's eggs, maggots; **2**. at the end of a clause, **sere** indicates hearsay

    sere waliyambi: to lay eggs (said of flies)

serebe: careful, painstaking, meticulous, vigilant, sensitive, watchful

serebumbi: **1**. (causative or passive of **serembi**); **2**. to feel; **3**. to come to light, to become known, to be discovered; **4**. to reveal; **5**. to startle from sleep

serebun: feeling, experience, sense, sensation, perception, discernment

serecun: awareness, consciousness, alertness, vigilance, sensitivity

    serecun akū: unaware, not alert to, lacking awareness

serecungge: **1**. vigilant, alert; **2**. sensitive person, vigilant person

serehun: half-awake, half conscious, easily awakened

serembi: (**-he/-ke**) **1**. to perceive, to be conscious of, to feel; **2**. to be revealed, to be discovered, to come to light

sereme: yellow hair five or six inches long from the tail of a deer (sewn onto shoes and socks as decoration)

seremšebumbi: (causative or passive of **seremšembi**)

seremšembi: **1**. to guard, to defend, to take precautions; **2**. to be vigilant, to be alert

    seremšeme tenembi: to go to do garrison duty

seremšen: defense, prevention

serengge: (from **sembi**) that which is called … (often used as a topic marker)

serge šu ilha: the name of a flower similar to the Tibetan lotus, the filaments of which are like iron wires

serguwen: cool

    serguwen cirku: a pillow used in summertime

    serguwen edun: a cool wind

serguwen seruken: nice and cool, pleasantly cool

serguwešebumbi: (causative of **serguwešembi**)

serguwešembi: to cool off, to take advantage of a cool place or time

seri: sparse, scanty, diluted, infrequent

seriken: rather sparse or thin

serki: scout, spy, a courier who carries military intelligence, a messenger who goes by the post stations

    serki feksibumbi: to dispatch a messenger

serkin: report, intelligence, report sent to the Emperor by the post stations

serkingge temen: a fast camel

serkuwen: ⟶ **serguwen**

sersen sarsan: **1**. shaking, trembling; **2**. as if flying, wafting; **3**. having a dull pain

sersen seme: ⟶ **sersen sarsan**

sertei: harelipped

seruken: **1**. cool; **2**. rather sparse or thin

sese: **1**. gold thread; **2**. a small silver or copper wire that was tied on the tails of falcons; **3**. a die, dice

    sese gecuheri: silk brocade

    sese i moro: cup for dice

    sese tabumbi: to sew with gold thread, to decorate with gold thread

sese sasa: frivolous, shallow, superficial

sesembi: to cover, to cover up

seseme: very little

sesengge bonio: *Pygathrix roxellana*: golden monkey, snub-nose monkey

seseri nenden ilha: *Prunus mume*: a variety of the flowery plum

seshe efen: steamed bread; cf. **feshen efen**

seshebumbi: **1**. (causative of **seshembi**); **2**. to disgust (someone with something)

seshecuke: disgusting, unappetizing (because one has had too much already), loathsome, tiresome, boring

seshembi: **1**. to be tired of, to be disgusted with, to be fed up with, to find loathsome, to be bored with; **2**. to shake, to shiver, to shake out; **3**. to sprinkle (flour, salt, sugar), to scatter, to spread (over)

seshen efen: a kind of steamed bread used in offerings

sesheri: vulgar, common, lacking elegance, tawdry

sesheri gai: disaster, catastrophe
seshetebumbi: (passive of **seshetembi**)
seshetembi: to shake vigorously
seshun: disgusting, loathsome
sesi: a curved deep-fried pastry made from millet and bean meal
sesilembi: to form a herd (said of deer in the summer)
sesiri: one trillionth
sesukiyembi: to shiver from the cold
sesuku: die, dice
    sesuku maktambi: to cast dice
sesulabumbi: (causative of **sesulambi**)
sesulambi: to be surprised, to be startled
sesulembi: ⟶ **sesulambi**
seterinembi: to form holes (in ice at the spring thaw)
seyebumbi: (causative or passive of **seyembi**)
seyecuke: regrettable, vexing, hateful
seyecun: resentment, regret, enmity, hate
seyembi: to regret, to find vexing, to dislike, to hate
seyendumbi: to hate together; also **seyenumbi**
seyenumbi: to hate together; also **seyendumbi**
si: **1**. you (singular); **2**. space, gap, interval; cf.
    siden; **3**. a file of five men; **4**. obstruction, blocking
    si akū: without obstruction, without interruption
    si akū talkiyambi: to lighten without interruption
    si bi seme ilgarakū: without making a distinction between 'you' and 'me'
    si sindame yabumbi: to walk in files of five
si ihan: buffalo, rhinoceros
si yang: the West, Europe
sibak: (Mongolian) artemisia, sagebrush
sibcambi: **1**. to slip down, to slide off; **2**. to come back after finding one is not needed (for some rotating duty)
sibdan: ⟶ **sabdan**
sibe: **1**. equisetum, horsetail, a plant whose stem is used for polishing; **2**. the Sibe (Xibo) nationality, speakers of the most viable Manchu dialect, who reside primarily in the Ili River valley of northwestern Xinjiang and in Liaoning and parts of northeastern China
sibedembi: to scour with stems of the horsetail plant
sibehe: cartilage ribs, costal cartilage

siberebumbi: (causative of **siberembi**)
siberembi: **1**. to knead; **2**. to spin thread in the fingers, to make a small ball (of felt, lint, or thread) by rolling it in the fingers; **3**. to massage
siberhen: **1**. wick; **2**. some substance like paper or hemp that has been rolled into a string between the fingers
siberi: sweat of the hands and feet
    siberi daha: **1**. something held in the hand constantly; **2**. a man who has often been sent on errands; **3**. something left behind by a dead person
sibibumbi: (causative of **sibimbi**)
sibida nasan: *Brassica pekinensis*: the pickled stem of celery cabbage
sibimbi: (-ha) **1**. to grasp in the hand and pull through the fingers (said of various long slender objects), to pull something long and slender; **2**. to pound into a long strip (gold or silver)
sibirgan: a kind of speckled swallow
sibišambi: **1**. to pull through the hand continually; **2**. to look at furtively
sibiya: **1**. wedge; **2**. stopper, plug; **3**. counter, tally stick, tally used in fortune telling, yarrow stalks; **4**. a patch running diagonally downward under the arm of a garment
    sibiya alibumbi: to hand over a tally (said of guards)
    sibiya baimbi: to consult the tallies (a kind of fortune telling)
    sibiya i sihan: a round container for tallies
    sibiya isimbi: to pull out a plug
    sibiya maktambi: to cast tallies (a kind of fortune telling)
    sibiya tatambi: to draw lots, to draw the tallies
sibiyalakū: a clasp or fastener for books and paintings
sibiyalambi: **1**. to cast the tallies, to cast lots; **2**. to split with a wedge; **3**. to fasten or nail with a wooden or bamboo wedge
sibke: a wooden or metal device inserted into an old-style lock to close or open it
    sibke moo: a two-man carrying pole
    sibke sele: iron pin on a spinning wheel
sibkelebumbi: (causative of **sibkelembi**)
sibkelembi: to carry on a pole between two men

sibkelere hūsun: bearer, coolie

sibkibumbi: (causative of **sibkimbi**)

sibkimbi: to ponder deeply, to look into thoroughly, to investigate, to make a thorough enquiry

sibkime fuhašambi: to do research on, to make a careful study

sibkūri: **1**. a hole used as a passage for water at the bottom of a city wall; **2**. gunport, hole in a city wall for a cannon

sibsihūn: **1**. wide at the top and narrow at the bottom; **2**. having a face that is narrow at the bottom, having a narrow chin

sibsihūn furgi: a weir that is pointed at one end

sibsika: a switch, a denuded branch, a branch from a tree (used for beating someone)

sibsikalambi: to beat (hides and rugs)

sibša: suddenly, precipitously, quickly

sibša ebereke: precipitously dropped in price

sibša genehe: suddenly finished

sibša tutaha: suddenly left behind

sibšalambi: to exclude, to shut out, to eliminate

sibumbi: (**-ha/-he**) **1**. (causative or passive of **simbi**); **2**. to be stopped up, to be obstructed

sibushūn: stopped up, obstructed

sicambi: (**-ka**) **1**. to crack, to form a crack (said of porcelain, jade, etc.); **2**. to make an ear-shattering noise

sicing: blue azurite

sidahiyambi: to roll back one's sleeves, to bare one's arms

sidambi: (**-ka**) to begin lactation; ⟶ **huhun sidakabi**

sidambumbi: (causative of **sidambi**)

sidan: **1**. young, immature; **2**. unadorned, unspoiled; **3**. ⟶ **si**

sidan jeku: the scattered grain left behind on the threshing floor

sidan juse: juveniles, youths

sidan moo: a small, immature tree

sidarabumbi: (causative of **sidarambi**)

sidarambi: (**-ka**) **1**. to unfold, to spread out (intransitive verb); **2**. to stretch (said of distance), to become distant; **3**. to be relieved, to overcome anxiety, to become cheerful; **4**. to become long, to lengthen

sidarambumbi: ⟶ **sidarabumbi**

sidehen: ⟶ **sidehun**

sidehulebumbi: (causative of **sidehulembi**)

sidehulembi: **1**. to latch a door, to bar a door; **2**. to leave a space

sidehun: **1**. a horizontal wooden bar for a door; **2**. the horizontal pieces of window frames; **3**. the horizontal supports on the bottom of wagons and sedan chairs; **4**. the steps on a ladder

sidehunjembi: to leave a space, to pause, to do alternately

siden: **1**. space, interval, interstice; **2**. a while; **3**. measure word for rooms; **4**. witness; **5**. official, public

siden bakcin: corroborative evidence

siden de: in between, while

siden i ba: public place

siden i baibungga: official expenditures

siden i baita: official matter, official business

siden i baltalan: official use, official employment

siden i bithe: official document

siden i hacin: public property

siden i haha: extra-quota man

siden i niyalma: **1**. middleman; **2**. witness

siden niru: a company formed from the bannermen of the Imperial household who serve on court duty

siden obumbi: to let serve as a witness

siden temgetu: **1**. official credential or certificate; **2**. witness to an agreement; **3**. evidence

siden waliyambi: to leave a space, to pause

siden yamun: **1**. official office, government office; **2**. court of law, tribunal

sidenderi: in between

sidengge hergen: (隸書) a style of calligraphy — the clerical style

siderebumbi: (causative or passive of **siderembi**)

sidereku: an iron decoration on the side of a horse's bridle

siderembi: to hobble, to tie up, to trip, to encumber

sidereme acilambi: to throw by entangling the feet (in wrestling)

sidereme holbombi: to detain, to control

sidereshun: hobbled, lame, stiff-legged

sideri: **1**. hobbling device, foot fetters, a hobble for animals; **2**. anklet

siderilengge: pertaining to foot fetters

sidu weihe: (human) canine teeth

sidumbi: to scrape, to scrape off; cf. **šudumbi**

sifa maca: wild leek; cf. **sumpa maca**

sifibumbi: (causative of **sifimbi**)

sifikū: a hairpin

    sifikū sifiha se: the age at which a girl began wearing a hairpin (15 years old)

sifimbi: (**-ha**) to wear a hairpin, to stick in one's hair

sifiri ilha: an exotic flower with very thin stems and a blossom resembling a hairpin

sifu fulana ilha: the blossom of a variety of cherry-apple

sifulu: the bladder; cf. **sike fulhū**

sigambi: ⟶ **sihambi**

sigan: **1**. mist, heavy fog; **2**. ⟶ **sihan**

    sigan tembi: a mist settles

sihabukū: funnel; cf. **belei sihabukū**

sihabumbi: (causative of **sihambi**)

sihakū: a short bamboo flute with nine holes

sihali: the area where the buttocks and waist join, either side of the small of the back

sihambi: **1**. to fall (said of leaves), to fall out (said of hair); **2**. to wither; **3**. to give hot pursuit, to follow on the heels of; **4**. to examine in detail, to examine carefully; **5**. to force, to compel, to coerce

    sihame bašambi: to pursue, to persecute

sihan: **1**. tube, pipe; **2**. a cylindrical container, cask, keg, pail; **3**. barrel of a gun, inner barrel of a cannon; **4**. ⟶ **sigan**

    sihan sirabure poo: a 'mother-child' cannon

siharakū moo: a non-deciduous tree

sihe: ⟶ **simbi** (subheading)

sihelebumbi: (causative or passive of **sihelembi**)

sihelembi: to hinder (because of envy or spite), to thwart, to get in the way

siheri ebci: floating rib, short rib near the small of the back

sihešembi: **1**. to cater to, to pander to, to be obsequious, to curry favor; **2**. to shake the head and wag the tail — to assume an air of complacency, to strut, to swagger

sihete: sparse and short (said of a horse's mane or tail)

sihin: **1**. eaves (of a house); **2**. the canopy of a tree, treetop

    sihin den: the top of the tree is high

    sihin i eyebuku: a drain at the junction of two eaves

sihin i kanggiri: a thin piece of metal hung from the eaves that hums when the wind blows

sihin i sele: a piece of iron on a saddle (used for attaching the stirrups)

sihin i ulhun: a board that connects the eaves to the structure of a roof

sihin sele: ⟶ **sihin i sele**

sihingge son: support for eaves

sihiya: roots and other inedible parts of grass left uneaten by cattle, sheep, etc.

sihiyakū: **1**. a hole in the footboard (**cirku moo**) of a door; **2**. a horizontal piece of wood on a pestle

sihiyan: small room or veranda with windows

sija: meat that has been cooked very soft in its own juice; cf. **silja**

sijibumbi: (causative of **sijimbi**)

sijigiyan: a long gown

sijihūn: **1**. straight (not crooked), erect; **2**. frank, straightforward, blunt, candid

    sijihūn ilihabi: is standing erect (and still)

sijilembi: to shoot an arrow with a line attached to it, to throw an object with a line attached

sijimbi: (**-ha**) to sew with very fine stitches

sijin: **1**. line, string, fishline; **2**. line tied to the foot of a falcon; **3**. broken grain from which the chaff has been removed (especially rice and millet)

    sijin bele: broken grain from which the chaff has been removed

sijirahūn: ⟶ **sijirhūn**

sijirambi: to make straight, to be straight

sijirhūn: **1**. straight, not crooked; cf. **sijihūn**; **2**. upright, honest

sika: **1**. an animal's mane or tail hair; **2**. bristle, hair on the back of a hog; **3**. frond of a palm tree; **4**. tassel made for a hat from the mane or tail of a cow

    sika foyo: 'red sand grass' — a kind of red-colored grass that is used for cushioning in shoes and boots

    sika hadahan: a peg on the rim of a wagon to which the load can be attached

    sika moo: *Trachycarpus excelsus*: the windmill palm

    sika sorson: a tassel for a hat (made from a cow's tail hairs)

sikari: a name for the wild pig, the same as **kitari**

sike: urine

> **sike fulhū**: the bladder
>
> **sike onggoho**: 'forgot urine' (said of horses that cannot urinate)
>
> **sike sen**: the opening of the urethra, meatus

sikse: yesterday

> **sikse dobori**: last night

siksergan: a lizard

sikseri: dusk, twilight

siktan: elixir, elixir of immortality

siku: ⟶ **sikū**

sikū: pieces of leather or felt in a quiver (used to hold the arrows in place)

silan: a kind of fine blue cloth

silba: having the same surname

> **silba cilba**: having the same surname and given name

silda yali: neck meat

sile: meat soup, broth

silehen: a name for the crane; cf. **bulehen**

silemi: ⟶ **silemin**

silemidembi: **1**. to act in a lazy, indolent manner; **2**. to be tenacious

silemin: **1**. tough, tenacious, resilient, durable; **2**. lasting, long-winded, untiring; **3**. reluctant to work, sluggish

silenggi: **1**. dew; **2**. saliva, drivel, spit

> **silenggi fuhešembi**: the dew rolls (in abundance)
>
> **silenggi gebkeljembi**: the dew glistens (in the sunlight)
>
> **silenggi sabdan**: dewdrop
>
> **silenggi toktohobi**: the dew has settled
>
> **silenggi wasika**: the dew has fallen

silenggimbi: to envy, to admire

silengginembi: to form dew

silenggišembi: **1**. to drool, to slaver; **2**. to desire someone else's possessions, to covet

> **silenggišeme buyeršembi**: to desire ardently

silgabumbi: (causative of **silgambi**)

silgabun: selection

silgambi: to sort out, to select, to hand-pick

silgasi: (貢生) Senior Licentiate, *BH* 629A

silgimbi: (**-ha**) **1**. to slip through an opening (as a fly through a crack, or a fish through a net); **2**. euphemism for 'to slaughter' in sacrificial language

silgiyabumbi: (causative of **silgiyambi**)

silgiyambi: to rinse, to cleanse

> **silgiyame obombi**: to wash, to rinse and wash

silhambi: ⟶ **silgambi**

silhata: alone, friendless, lone

silhi: **1**. gall bladder; **2**. envy; **3**. courage

> **silhi amba**: courageous, bold
>
> **silhi meijembi**: to lose one's nerve, to lose heart, to lose courage, to be terrified
>
> **silhi sabdambi**: to have one's courage flow away

silhidabumbi: (passive of **silhidambi**)

silhidambi: to envy, to be jealous

silhimbi: (**-ha**) **1**. to penetrate, to slip through, to slip into; cf. **silgimbi**; **2**. to place an arrowhead on a shaft

silhingga: envious, jealous

siliha: ⟶ **silimbi** (subheading)

silihi: a name for the weasel; cf. **solohi**

silimbi: (**-ha**) to select, to pick out; cf. **silgambi**

> **siliha cooha**: crack troops, hand-picked troops

silin: topnotch, elite, crack (troops)

> **silin dacun**: crack (troops), select, topnotch
>
> **silin dacungga kūwaran i siden yamun**: (健銳營衛門) Office of the Light Division, *BH* 733, 738

silja: meat that has been cooked to pieces in its own juices — the same as **sija**

silka: ⟶ **silkan**

silkabumbi: **1**. to act in a crafty or cautious manner, to act in a slippery manner; **2**. to be engrained, to be deep-rooted, to accumulate over a long period

> **silkabuha jemden**: a long-standing debt, accumulated malpractice
>
> **silkabuha tacin**: settled habit, long-standing habit

silkada: crafty, shrewd, slippery, a crafty or shrewd person

silkan: **1**. crafty, cautious, shrewd; **2**. a kind of small oak, the wood of which was used for bow grips and axles

silkari moo: *Quercus sclerophylla*, a kind of oak tree

silmelembi: to dry in the shade, to shade

> **silmelehe yali**: meat that has been dried in the shade

silmen: **1**. shady, sunless; **2**. sparrow hawk (*Accipiter nisus*)

silmen ba: shade, a place in the shade

silmengge sara: a parasol

siltabumbi: (causative of **siltambi**)

siltakū: a shirker

siltambi: **1**. to shirk, to get out of doing something, to refuse responsibility; **2**. to make excuses, to put someone off

siltame anahūnjambi: to decline out of modesty, to defer

siltame anatambi: to shirk, to shift responsibility

siltan: mast, flagpole used in a temple, pole

siltan i hafirakū moo: wooden holder for a mast

siltan i šurdebuku: hoist for a sail (attached to the mast)

siltan moo: a sacred tree erected in the shamanistic shrine of the palace

silun: *Felis lynx*: lynx

simacuka: **1**. lonely; **2**. desolate, mournful; **3**. meager, scant

simacuka acacuka: dreary, desolate

simari cecike: a name for the goatsucker (*Caprimulgus indicus*)

simatun cecike: a name for the goatsucker, the same as **simari cecike**

simbe: (accusative form of **si** 'you')

simbi: (**-he**) **1**. to stop up, to plug up, to fill in; **2**. to stand in for, to substitute for, to replace; **3**. to bribe, to employ as bribery

sihe ba: sluiceway

sime bumbi: to give as a bribe

sime nurhūbumbi: to work two shifts in succession

simebumbi: (causative or passive of **simembi**)

simelembi: to be muddy, to be marsh-like

simelen: marsh, mire

simelen coko: marsh hen

simelen šungkeri ilha: *Arethusa chinensis*: Chinese rose

simeli: **1**. poor and forlorn, miserable, wretched, desolate, bleak; **2**. poverty-stricken

simeli urse: poor orphaned children

simelje: a gull-like bird with a white growth on its black head

simembi: (**-ke/-he**) **1**. to soak, to moisten, to seep into; **2**. to favor

simen: **1**. moisture, juice, secretion; **2**. nutritive fluid, vital fluid; **3**. interest, vitality; **4**. nutrition

simen akū: **1**. uninteresting, dull, unexciting; **2**. lonely, desolate, not prospering

simen arambi: to join in the fun, to keep company, to pass the time, to be friendly with

simen gocimbumbi: the liquids freeze (said to describe an unbearable cold)

simen niyolocuka: saturated with fat, fatty

simen sukdun: vigor, spirit, life force

simen toktombi: to compose oneself

simengge: bustling, exciting, prospering, thriving, animated

simengge kumungge: full of bustle and excitement

simenggi: tung oil

simenggi urangga moo: *Aleurites fordii*: tung tree

simenggilebumbi: (causative of **simenggilembi**)

simenggilembi: to apply (tung) oil, to paint

simenggilehe wadan: an oil cloth

simgan: ⟶ **šumgan**

simhulembi: to play the finger-guessing game

simhulere efin: the finger-guessing game

simhun: **1**. finger, toe; **2**. finger's breadth

simhun buhiyembumbi: ⟶ **simhulembi**

simhun fatame tolombi: to count on the fingers

simhun gidame tolombi: ⟶ **simhun fatame tolombi**

simhun hefeli: palm of the hand, sole of the foot

simhun i faju: the forked area between the fingers

simhun i toron: fingerprint, finger mark

simhun sehei siheri ebci be jafaha: 'saying he would take only a finger, he took a rib' — proverb

simhuri: the name of a wild finger-shaped fruit that ripens in the sixth month

simibumbi: (causative or passive of **simimbi**)

simikte: a cat's-eye (a kind of gemstone)

simimbi: to suck

siminumbi: to suck together, to suck one another

simiyan hoton: Shenyang

simnebumbi: (causative or passive of **simnembi**)

simnehe: ⟶ **simnembi** (subheading)

simnembi: **1**. to examine, to take an examination, to test; **2**. to inspect (troops, horses)

    simnehe cooha: tested soldiers, crack troops

    simnehe silgasi: (拔貢) designation of superior students chosen every twelve years for the court examination, Imperial student by special selection

    simneme dosimbi: to pass an examination

    simnere baitai kunggeri: (學政科) board of affairs relating to examinations in the Board of Rites

    simnere be kadalara kunggeri: (督學科) Examination Office of the Metropolitan Prefecture

    simnere boo: (號房) the place where the examinees were lodged during an examination

    simnere bukdarun: examination paper

    simnere hafan: (考試官) examination officer, examiner

    simnere kūwaran: (貢院) examination hall

    simnere kūwaran i baita be uheri kadalara hafan: (知貢舉) official in charge at the metropolitan examination

simnen: examination, testing

simnendumbi: to take an examination together, to examine together; also **simnenumbi**

simnenembi: to go to take an examination, to go to examine

simnenjimbi: to come to take an examination, to come to examine

simnenumbi: to take an examination together, to examine together; also **simnendumbi**

simnere: ⟶ **simnembi** (subheading)

simnesi: examinee, student — a person who had passed the examination given by the district magistrate

simori: (星) a constellation, the 25th of the lunar mansions, made up of seven stars in Hydra

    simori tokdonggo kiru: a banner depicting the constellation **simori**

simten: taste, tasty

simtu: a large iron cooking pot

sin: a measure equaling one Chinese bushel and eight pecks

    sin i hiyase: ⟶ **sin**

    sin jeku jetere aha: a slave assigned to the Imperial household

sinagalambi: to keep the mourning period, to mourn

sinagan: mourning

    sinagan de acanjimbi: to come to a funeral

    sinagan doro: funeral, funeral rites

    sinagan etumbi: to wear mourning garments

    sinagan i baita: funeral

    sinagan jaluka: the three-year mourning period has ended

sinahalambi: ⟶ **sinagalambi**

sinahi: mourning garment (of sackcloth)

    sinahi etumbi: to wear mourning garments

    sinahi hūwaitambi: to don mourning garments

sinahilambi: to wear mourning clothes

sinci: (ablative form of **si**): from you, than you

sindabumbi: (causative or passive of **sindambi**)

sindakū: a place to lay something; cf. **hiyan dabuku i sindakū**

sindambi: **1**. to put, to place, to set; **2**. to let go, to let out, to release, to liberate; **3**. to dissipate, to be unrestrained; **4**. to play (chess); **5**. to appoint (an official); **6**. to bury; **7**. to fire (a gun); **8**. to give head to (a horse); **9**. to give off (rays of light); **10**. to remit, to forgive

sindaralambi: to free, to release, to let go

sinde: (dative/locative of **si**): to you, for you

sindu ilha: flower of the prickly pear

sindubi: (心) a constellation, the 5th of the lunar mansions, made up of three stars (σ, α, τ) in Scorpio

    sindubi tokdonggo kiru: a banner depicting the constellation **sindubi**

sing sing: an ape; cf. **sirsing**

sing sing jan: ⟶ **singsingjan**

singgebumbi: **1**. (causative or passive of **singgembi**); **2**. to practice graft, to embezzle, to be corrupt; **3**. to digest

    singgebume tebumbi: to sink to the bottom, to fall all the way to the bottom

    singgebume ulhibumbi: to instruct or inform thoroughly

singgeku: the internal organs, viscera

    singgeku baktakū: internal organs, innards

singgembi: **1**. to soak into, to permeate, to saturate, to soak through, to become thoroughly wet; **2**. to be digested; **3**. to suck (into); **4**. to dissolve; **5**. to appropriate, to take for one's own use, to take on the sly

singgeri: **1**. rat, mouse; **2**. the first of the earth's branches (子)

    singgeri biya: the eleventh month

    singgeri erin: the period from 11 PM until 1 AM

    singgeri huhun: (genital) wart

    singgeri šan: cudweed — *Gnaphalum multiceps*

    singgeri yoo: scrofula, growth on the neck

singgeringge: pertaining to the rat

    singgeringge aniya: the year of the rat

singgešu: a name for the large quail (**ihan mušu**)

singgetei: given or taken into permanent possession, securely, permanently

singgirambi: to harm because of envy

singgiyambi: **1**. to ache, to be numb, to be sore; **2**. to stick in the belt (an arrow)

singgiyan: aching, numb

singkeyen: cloudy and cold, cold, frigid

singsilambi: ⟶ **cincilambi**

singsin: physiognomy

singsingjan: red felt

sini: (genitive of **si**): your

    sini cihai: as you wish

    sini cihalahai: ⟶ **sini cihai**

siningge: yours

sioi: foreword, preface (to a book); cf. **šutucin**

siojan: embroiderer

siojuwan: (修撰) a Secretary in the Hanlin Academy

siolembi: to embroider

siowan: an ocarina-like musical instrument with five holes

sir seme: somewhat numb, rather numb, asleep (said of a limb)

    sir seme fungke: gone to sleep (said of the limbs)

sir siyar: (onomatopoetic) **1**. the sound of light rain and wind; **2**. the sound of grass and leaves moving slightly; **3**. palpitating (said of the heart); **4**. the sound of light friction, rustling, pattering

sir šar seme: **1**. walking slowly; **2**. ⟶ **sir siyar**

sira: **1**. yellow; **2**. the bone of the leg below the knee, the tibia

    sira den: long-legged

sira moo: mountain barberry — a vine that grows in thickets and can be woven into walking canes

sirabumbi: **1**. (causative or passive of **sirambi**); **2**. to give assistance, to supply, to provide, to come to someone's aid; **3**. to give up, to relinquish

sirabungga kumun: a kind of beautiful ancient music (韶樂)

siraca: **1**. Chinese boxthorn — *Lycium chinensis*; **2**. a yellow dye made from the rotten bark of the Chinese cork oak (*Quercus bungeana*)

sirakū: false hair

sirambi: **1**. to inherit; **2**. to continue; **3**. to tie, to reattach, to connect

    sirame: in succession, continuing (see separate entry)

    sirame gaimbi: to remarry, to take a second wife

    sirara hafan: hereditary official

    sirara hafan i tacikū: (幼官學) a school for the sons of worthy officials

sirame: **1**. next (in sequence); **2**. step-(father, mother)

    sirame ama: stepfather

    sirame banjibun: continuation (of a work), sequel

    sirame ejen: heir of the owner

    sirame eme: stepmother

    sirame eniye: stepmother

    sirame eshen: a younger first cousin on the father's side

    sirame gaimbi: ⟶ **sirambi** (subheading)

    sirame hafan: (監承) Proctor, *BH* 412A

    sirame hafan i tinggin: (寺丞廳) the name of a hall in the Court of Sacrificial Worship

    sirame inenggi: the next day, the following day

    sirame jalahi jui: the son of a cousin on the father's side

    sirame kadalara amban: (宗正) Controller of the Imperial Clan Court, *BH* 58, 59

    sirame mudan: next time

    sirame sargan: second or third wife, a second wife taken after the death of one's first wife

siramengge: continuing, connecting

siramsi: ⟶ **hiyan i siramsi**

siran: continuation, succession, sequence, order, series

    siran siran i: continually, one after another, in succession

siranduhai: subsequently, in succession, immediately afterward

sirandumbi: to follow one after another, to follow in succession, to connect with, to be attached to; also **siranumbi**

siranuhai: ⟶ **siranduhai**

siranumbi: to follow one after another, to follow in succession, to connect with, to be attached to; also **sirandumbi**

sirara: ⟶ **sirambi** (subheading)

sirasha: an exotic fruit that resembles a clam and tastes like a walnut

sirata saksaha: ⟶ **niyo saksaha**

sirata uksin: net armor; cf. **asu uksin**

sirbašambi: **1**. to wag the tail; **2**. to get agitated, to become flustered

sirbe wehe cinuhūn: a cinnabar mined in the mountains of Yunnan and used both as a medicine and a dye

sirdan: a military arrow with a two-edged iron arrowhead

    sirdan faksi: maker of arrows, fletcher

    sirdan juhe: icicle

    sirdan sele: a piece of iron with two holes that was attached to the top of a sword's scabbard

sirdangga: pertaining to an arrow

sirebumbi: (causative of **sirembi**)

sirebun: the name of a form of ancient Chinese verse (行)

sirecu: an exotic fruit that grows on a vine and resembles small grapes

sirembi: to twist (thread or rope), to spin

siremi: ⟶ **sirembi**

siren: **1**. string, line, thread; **2**. runner, tendril, creeper (all of plants); **3**. fuse; **4**. vein, capillary; **5**. in Chinese medicine, the middle pulse of the wrist; **6**. a paper figure used for exorcisms; **7**. beam (of light)

    siren faitambi: to cut the 'thread of life' on a paper figure used in shamanistic exorcism

    siren fisen: blood vessels, arteries and veins

    siren futa: **1**. pieces of colored paper and cloth attached to a rope on a willow pole and then tied to an altar; **2**. string used to bind books between boards; **3**. rope used to hold a plowshare tight; **4**. fuse

    siren siren: continually, uninterruptedly

    siren sudala: the part of the pulse nearest the wristbone

    siren tatabumbi: to involve, to implicate

    siren tatambi: a rainbow has formed

    siren waliyame asu arambi: to spin a web (said of spiders)

sirendumbi: to collude with, to enter into secret communication with, to ask for a favor secretly; cf. **sirentumbi**

sirenembi: **1**. to be connected, to be joined, to be in rows; **2**. to send out tendrils, to send forth runners; **3**. to keep on sounding, to continue singing (said of birds); **4**. to extend

    sirenehe mailan: *Cuscuta chinensis*: dodder

    sireneme: continually

    sireneme baitalambi: to use continually, to continue to use

    sireneme banjimbi: to grow in rows

    sirenere dalan: a kind of levee longer and narrower than the usual kind

sirenen ilha: *Campsis grandiflora*: Chinese trumpet creeper

sirengge mudan ilha: a flower resembling the peony that grows in shallow water, but with red and pink blossoms that are smaller than the peony

sirentu moo: *Ficus benghalensis*: the banyan tree

sirentumbi: to enter into a secret agreement with, to plot with

sirentusi: secret agent, spy, plotter

siresi: **1**. puller, one who pulls a rope; **2**. agent, middleman

sirga: **1**. reddish brown, bay (said of a horse); **2**. roe deer; cf. **gio**

    sirga kūwaran: a park for keeping wild animals

sirgacin: ⟶ **sirhacin**

sirgahūn: the name of a deep yellow pigment

sirgatu: muntjac, Hydropotes (a variety of deer); cf. **gi buhū**

sirge: **1**. silk thread, silk floss (from a cocoon); **2**. wire, string (of a musical instrument); **3**. a strip (of dried meat); **4**. measure word for a rib

    sirge acabumbi: to tune a stringed instrument

    sirge folonggo: a kind of silk fabric on which the designs resemble carving

sirgelembi: to cut apart the ribs (of a slaughtered animal)

sirgembi: to be anxious, to worry

sirgengge coko: a variety of chicken whose feathers resemble silk threads

sirgeri: spun silk, pongee, silken yarn; cf. **fangse**

    sirgeri fisa: a kind of quail with white feathers on its back

    sirgeri uju: a kind of quail with white feathers on its head

sirgetu gasha: a name for the egret; cf. **guwasihiya**

sirha: ⟶ **sirga**

sirhacin: a female zeren; cf. **jeren**, **onon**

sirhe: ⟶ **sirge**

siri: a young carp

siri fucihi: Mañjuśrī

siribumbi: (causative or passive of **sirimbi**)

sirikū: squeezer

sirimbi: (-ha) **1**. to wring, to squeeze out (a liquid); **2**. to milk; **3**. to blow the nose

sirin: raw copper

    sirin moro: a copper bowl

    sirin saifi: a copper spoon

sirke: long-lasting, protracted, endless, persistent

sirkedembi: to persist, to be persistent, to last a long time

    sirkedeme agambi: to rain for a long time

    sirkedeme narašambi: to linger, to tarry

sirkederi: persisting, endless

sirkembi: ⟶ **sirgembi**

sirsing: an ape

sisa: bean, pea

    sisa do: a filling made of beans

    sisa ufa: bean flour

    sisa wehe: crushed soft stone

sisabumbi: (causative of **sisambi**)

sisalambi: to sprinkle; cf. **sisambi**

sisambi: **1**. to spill (intransitive verb), to be strewn; **2**. to sprinkle, to spray; **3**. to be lost

    sisame sarabumbi: to use wastefully

sisebumbi: (causative of **sisembi**)

sisehen: braid, piping, edging

siseku: a sieve

sisembi: **1**. to sift; **2**. to baste (in sewing); **3**. to do in a rough or unpolished way

    siseme arambi: to make a rough draft

sisetembi: **1**. to write a rough draft, to make a general plan; **2**. to manage in a rough or general manner

    siseteme bodombi: to make a rough estimate

siseteme bodoro falgangga: (料估所) Department of Estimates, *BH* 460A

siseteme gisurembi: to speak in general terms, to speak in outline form

sishe: a mattress

sisi: hazelnut

    sisi jan: an arrow with a hazelnut-shaped head made of horn with three holes in it (used for shooting wild game)

    sisi megu: 'hazelnut mushroom' — a small yellow mushroom found in areas where hazelnuts grow

    sisi niru: an arrow similar to the **sisi jan** except that it has an iron head and is used for shooting deer

    sisi sence: ⟶ **sisi megu**

sisi šaša: shivering (with cold)

sisibumbi: (causative or passive of **sisimbi**)

sisikū: **1**. a vessel filled with ashes or sand in which one can insert incense sticks, candles, etc.; **2**. a vase for flowers

sisimbi: (-ha) **1**. to insert, to stick into; **2**. to shovel food into the mouth

    sisiha gese: 'as if stuck in,' said of someone who eats with gusto

sisin: insertion, sticking in, intake

    sisin amba: 'intake is great' (said of someone who eats a lot)

sisinambi: to stick into (there)

sisingga: having a large intake, glutton

    sisingga huwejehen: a small screen placed in a stand, which may be decorated with a picture or calligraphy

sisiri: pistachio nut

sisku: ⟶ **siseku**

sisuhu: a name for the fish hawk; cf. **suksuhu**

siša: **1**. bells worn on a shaman's belt; **2**. tube on a hat or helmet into which peacock feathers are inserted

    siša arki: a weak distillation, the last of the liquor distilled from koumiss

    siša sele: an ornament with red tassels that hangs from a horse's breast

sišabumbi: (causative of **sišambi**)

sišambi: to worm into (said of maggots)

    sišame waliyame: turning a blind eye to, conniving at

sišanambi: to hang down (said of icicles)

sišantumbi: to offer a small amount of food to a dead person on the eighth day after burial; cf. **boohalambi**

sišargan: a small bird resembling the **fiyabkū** with a blue breast and black markings on the back

sišari: **1**. hemp from which grass linen can be woven (gathered after a frost); **2**. ramie

sišari cecike: a small bird with a pink and yellow beak, pink and yellow tail and wings, and white tufts on the cheeks

sita: **1**. matter, affair; cf. **baita**; **2**. a term used by a spouse to call the other's attention

sitabumbi: **1**. (causative of **sitambi**); **2**. to delay, to cause delay

sitahūn: few, scarce, deficient, sparse

sitahūn niyalma: term used by rulers in antiquity to refer to themselves

sitambi: **1**. to be late (for an appointment); **2**. to fall behind, to lag, to be slow

sitashūn: **1**. behind, lagging behind, late, deficient; **2**. poor, wretched

siteku: a bed-wetter, one who urinates frequently

siteku umiyaha: a winged black bug that bites and causes blisters

sitembi: to urinate

sitere tampin: a chamber pot, night pan

sitenembi: to go to urinate

sithen: box, a box for documents

sithūmbi: to apply oneself, to be diligent, to exert oneself, to concentrate on, to be absorbed in

sithūme kicembi: to work hard, to act in a diligent fashion

sithūn: application, diligence

situhūmbi: **1**. to rinse; **2**. to grind, to whet

situmbi: (-ha) to grow up, to mature

situme genembi: to grow up gradually

siyal: mister, gentleman

siyan: **1**. county; cf. **hiyan**; **2**. one one-hundred-millionth

siyan el: ⟶ **siyal**

siyan fung: vanguard

siyan jang: Daoist abbot

siyan lo gurun: Thailand, Siam

siyan šeng: mister, gentleman, sir

siyanceo: a kind of silk fabric

siyang: European, Western

siyang gung: ⟶ **siyanggung**

siyangci: chess

siyanggung: **1**. your honor, respected sir; **2**. young man of a good family

siyangki: ⟶ **siyangci**

siyanšeng: sir, gentleman

siyoo: **1**. saltpeter; **2**. flute

siyoo jiyei: young lady

siyoo šeng: a young man's role in opera

siyūn an hafan: (巡按) provincial censor (Ming)

siyūn fu: (巡撫) provincial governor

siyūn giyan: (巡檢); ⟶ **giyarimsi**

so: **1**. a bad omen; **2**. vinegar; **3**. dewlap; **4**. (plural suffix; cf. **sa**)

so jorimbi: to point out a bad omen

sobonio: a kind of monkey with long pale yellow hair

sobori: a horse or cow with one hoof that is a different color from the others

soboro: pale yellowish green

soca: rice that is strewn as an offering to a deity

socili niyehe: *Dafila acuta*: pintail duck

soco orho: fodder that is gathered in the mountains or on the steppe

sodz: rice that has turned red from long storage

sofidambi: to mill around, to be jittery (said of livestock)

sofin: restless, jittery (said of livestock)

sofin akū: (of a person) restless, unsettled, unrestrained

soforo: **1**. saddle cushion; **2**. small square pieces of leather covering the upper part of the stirrup straps and placed at both sides of the saddle

soforombi: to take a double handful

sogi: vegetable, edible plant

sogimbi: ⟶ **sohimbi**

sogiya: pock, pustule (especially on a child)

sohimbi: to become dimmed (the eyes, when some foreign object gets in them), to get something in the eye

sohin: a piece of ice in a river in autumn

sohin gūlha: a boot with a round toe

soho: the name of a wild plant with long white leaves, yellow flowers, and a sweet taste

sohoci: the name of a small yellow exotic fruit

sohoco: the name of a variety of sea fish similar to the yellowcheek

sohohori: bright yellow — the same as **sohohūri**

sohohūri: ⟶ **sohohori**

sohokoliyan: deep yellow

sohokon: yellowish, rather yellow

sohon: **1**. deep yellow (the color of a sunflower); **2**. the sixth of the heaven's stems (己)

sohon cecike: a name for the oriole; cf. **gūlin cecike**

sohon hionghioi cecike: a name for the oriole; cf. **gūlin cecike**

sohon hoohan: a name for the heron; cf. **hoohan**

sohon moo: *Buxus sinica*: boxwood

sohon nimeku: jaundice

sohon saksaha damin: a pale yellow young eagle

sohon tashari: a yellow eagle

sohon temgetungge gu: the name of a square jade tablet used at sacrifices to the earth

soiho: the end of a bird's tail

soihon: ⟶ **suihon**

soikara weijun: a name for the stork; cf. **weijun**

soilo: hair of the fetlock of horses, mules, and donkeys

soilombi: **1**. to soar, to fly up; **2**. to fly up after hitting a target, to ricochet (said of an arrow)

soison: squirrel

sokji: aquatic plants, algae, duckweed

soko: the earth god

soksimbi: to sob

sokso saksa: galloping wildly, galloping madly

soksohon: sitting silently, sitting morosely

soksohori: sitting idly, sitting quietly (said of a group)

soksori: suddenly (said of standing up and leaving)

soksorjambi: ⟶ **sosorcombi**

soksorombi: ⟶ **sosorombi**

soktobumbi: (causative of **soktombi**)

soktokū: a good drinker, one who likes to drink, someone addicted to drink, drunkard

soktombi: to be drunk, to get drunk

soktondumbi: to get drunk with one another, to get drunk together

sokū: ⟶ **soko**

solambi: to give one's daughter in marriage

solbibumbi: (causative of **solbimbi**)

solbimbi: **1**. to put an arrow on a bowstring; **2**. to brandish (a weapon)

solbin: estimation, guessing; cf. **tulbin**

solha: a covered vessel for holding solid food or soup

solhi: ⟶ **solohi**

solho: Korea, Korean

solho bing: 'Korean cake' — a cake made of honey, flour, and sesame oil

solho boso: cloth produced in Korea

solho efen: ⟶ **solho bing**

solho gurun: Korea

solho gurun i kuren: the hostel for Korean emissaries

solho hara: *Salvia japonica*: a kind of sage

solho hengke: Korean muskmelon

solho hoošan: a kind of durable paper from Korea

solho leke: flat cakes made of honey, flour, and sesame oil

solho niru: the banner-chief of the Koreans who surrendered to the Manchus at the beginning of the Manchu dynasty

solho yeye handu bele: Korean glutinous rice

solibumbi: (causative or passive of **solimbi**)

solimbi: to invite, to summon, to hire, to engage

solin cecike: a name for the oriole; cf. **gūlin cecike**

solinabumbi: (causative of **solinambi**)

solinambi: to go to invite

solindumbi: to invite together, to invite one another; also **solinumbi**

solinggimbi: to send to invite

solinjimbi: to come to invite

solinumbi: to invite together, to invite one another; also **solindumbi**

solmin: **1**. eyelash; **2**. the end of a hair

solo: the fine hair-like roots of ginseng

solohi: *Mustela sibirica*: weasel

solombi: to go against the current, to go upstream

solon: **1**. Solon (a tribe in northern Manchuria, now referred to as the Ewenk); **2**. the general term for the Evenki

solon jan: an arrow with a narrow steel head used in war and for hunting bears and wild boar

solon majan: a long Solon arrow

sombi: (**-ha**) to strew, to scatter, to scatter in every direction

some gabtambi: to shoot arrows in all directions

some miyoocalambi: to shoot a gun wildly

somibumbi: (causative or passive of **somimbi**)

somihangga niyalma: a recluse, a hermit

somimbi: **1**. to hide, to store away, to conceal; **2**. to bury (a coffin), to inter

   somiha saisa: a hermit, one who has retired from public life to the country

   somime bimbi: to live in seclusion

   somime gisurembi: to speak in a veiled manner, not to speak openly

   somime tembi: to live in retirement, to live as a hermit

somina orho: sedge

somindumbi: to hide together; also **sominumbi**

sominjimbi: to come to hide

sominumbi: to hide together; also **somindumbi**

somishūn: hidden, secret, concealed

   somishūn cooha: concealed troops

   somishūn gisun: veiled speech

   somishūn jalan: 'concealed world' — the grave

   somishūn saisa: recluse, an official who has retired from public service to live in the country

somitambi: to stay hidden, to go into hiding

somo: the votive or spirit pole erected by Manchu families

somoo: ⟶ **somo**

son: rafter, support for a tent's roof

son son i: fragmentary, scattered, in every direction, in disarray

sonambi: to form a callus

soncoho: **1**. pigtail, braid; **2**. a bowstring-holder made from cow's horn and attached to the ends of the bow; **3**. odd numbered; cf. **sonio**

   soncoho biya: an odd-numbered month

   soncoho cecike: a name for the hoopoe; cf. **indahūn cecike**

   soncoho futa: a rope fastened to the middle of a dragnet

   soncoho hūwalambi: **1**. 'to cut the braid' (said of girls who get married); **2**. to deflower a virgin

   soncoho hūwalame holboho: 'parted the braid and made a chignon' — i.e., got married

   soncoho isambi: to plait a braid

   soncoho mutukū: the name of a plant that grows on rocks and roofs (*Cotyledon japonica*)

soncoho šukumbi: to glue on the holders for a bowstring

soncoho sulabumbi: to comb a braid, to plait a pigtail

soncoholombi: **1**. to plait a braid; **2**. to be odd (not even)

sonda: ⟶ **suwanda**

sonduri: a kind of flowered yellow silk

songgiha: **1**. the tip of the nose; **2**. a wooden nose hook for camels and cows; **3**. hook (on a quiver) to which a strap can be attached; **4**. catch on a bird trap

songgin: ⟶ **songgiha**

songgina: wild onion

songgobumbi: (causative of **songgombi**)

songgocombi: to weep together

songgoconombi: to go to weep together

songgombi: **1**. to weep, to cry; **2**. to cry loudly (said of birds before rain)

   songgome fambi: to weep bitterly (when parting)

   songgome fancambi: ⟶ **songgome fambi**

   songgome gasambi: to weep and lament

songgotu: a crybaby, a person who cries frequently

songkiyabumbi: ⟶ **suwangkiyabumbi**

songko: **1**. trace, track, footprint; **2**. ⟶ **songkoi**

   songko akū: without a trace

   songko bargiyambi: to lie low, to cease one's evil deeds for a time, to go into hiding

   songko be burubumbi: to blot out one's tracks, to destroy the traces

   songko benembi: to reveal one's presence to the enemy hoping that they will retreat

   songko de songko: first here then there, changeable

   songko faitambi: to follow the tracks (of a wounded animal)

   songko fulu: good at seeking advantages for oneself

   songko i faitambi: ⟶ **songko faitambi**

   songko waliyambi: to leave tracks (in order to deceive the enemy)

songkoi: (postposition) according to, in accordance with

songkolobumbi: (causative of **songkolombi**)

songkolombi: **1**. to follow the tracks of, to follow in the tracks of; **2**. to imitate, to act in accordance with

songkū: ⟶ **songko**

sonihon: odd (said of numbers)

> **sonihon muduringga suwayan šun dalikū**: a round yellow parasol of the Imperial Escort

soningga: novel, rare, interesting

sonio: **1**. odd (number), single; **2**. odd numbered line of a hexagram of the *Yijing*

> **sonio juru**: odd and even

> **sonio sabu**: a single shoe, an odd shoe

soniohon: ⟶ **sonihon**

sonjobumbi: (causative or passive of **sonjombi**)

sonjoku: vulnerable (because of error), objectionable, criticizable

sonjombi: **1**. to choose, to select; **2**. to select someone for an official post after he has passed the state examination

> **sonjome abalambi**: to select and kill in springtime the animals that have no young

> **sonjome fidembi**: to select and transfer

sonjondumbi: to select together; also **sonjonumbi**

sonjonumbi: to select together; also **sonjondumbi**

sonjosi: (貢士) one who passed the Metropolitan examination

sonokdun: ⟶ **sonokton**

sonokton: tassel on a helmet

sonombi: to protrude the buttocks

sontambi: to fling away

sontu cecike: a small yellow bird with yellow lines over its eyes, a long tail, and yellowish feet

soori: jujube; cf. **soro**

soorilambi: to enthrone

soorin: throne, seat of honor

> **soorin be sirambi**: to inherit the throne

> **soorin de tehe**: ascended to the throne

sor sar seme: in quantity, in profusion

> **sor sar seme nimarambi**: to snow in great quantity

sor seme: **1**. many, in great quantity; **2**. disorderly, confused

sor sir seme: ⟶ **sor sar seme**

sorbo: braid or string on the top of a hat

sori: ⟶ **soro**, **soori**

sori sahambi: to make piles of nine flat round cakes on the altar (during a sacrifice)

sori yali: small pieces of meat used in sacrifices

soriganjambi: to be shaken, to waver (in the face of power or authority)

soriha: strips of cloth tied to a horse's mane and tail during a sacrifice

soriha sirdan: ⟶ **sorimbi**

sorihalambi: to tie strips of cloth to a horse's mane and tail for a religious rite

sorihanjambi: ⟶ **soriganjambi**

sorimbi: **1**. to kick (said of horses), to paw the ground, to jump around; **2**. to be in disorder, to be confused

> **soriha sirdan**: arrows shot wildly

sorin den: running with the chest high (said of horses)

sorindumbi: to be in total disarray, to be criss-crossed

sorko: thimble

soro: *Ziziphus zizyphus*: jujube, Chinese date

sorobumbi: (causative of **sorombi**)

sorocombi: **1**. to be very sensitive and painful (said of the skin and of embarrassing situations); **2**. to be embarrassed

sorocuka: ashamed, shy

soroki: taboo, tabooed

> **soroki amba**: strictly tabooed

> **soroki obumbi**: to avoid as taboo, to treat as taboo

sorokiya: a wasp; cf. **dondoba**

sorokū futa: multicolored strings hung on a child's neck during a shamanistic rite

sorombi: **(1)** (**-ko, -pi**) to turn yellow

> **sorome nimere nimeku**: jaundice; cf. **sohon nimeku**

sorombi: **(2)** (**-ho**) to avoid as taboo, to shun

sorombumbi: (causative of **sorombi**)

sorosu: *Canarium pimela*: Chinese black olive

sorotu: an exotic fruit resembling the sour jujube that is produced at a temple in Gansu

sorson: **1**. tassel on a hat; **2**. the flowers of onions, scallions, and leeks

sorsonggo: pertaining to a tassel

sosambi: to capture (prisoners of war)

sosandumbi: to capture together; also **sosanumbi**

sosanumbi: to capture together; also **sosandumbi**

sose: ⟶ **sodz**

sosombi: to have a case of watery diarrhea

sosorcombi: to back up, to shrink back, to withdraw

sosorobumbi: (causative of **sosorombi**)

sosorombi: (**-ko**) **1**. to back up, to withdraw, to retreat; **2**. to wither, to become senile; **3**. to rake (grass)

sotambi: to strew about, to scatter around, to scatter (grain or rice) wastefully

soti: a name for the parrot

sotki: a sea fish resembling the crucian carp

soyombi: **1**. to tie up livestock to allow them to dry off after having sweated from running; **2**. to draw in, to shrink; **3**. to train a riding horse

soyon: fed to a certain standard, fattened to a certain standard

    soyon acabuha: ⟶ **soyon**

    soyon acabumbi: to fatten to a certain standard, to feed a special diet in preparation for a race

    soyon acaha: ⟶ **soyon**

soyonggū: a sweating horse tied up so that it can dry off

soyori: an exotic fruit about the size of a yellow plum

su: whirlwind

    su edun: whirlwind

    su orho: ⟶ **surho**

subadabumbi: (causative of **subadambi**)

subadambi: to jump about waving the hands and shouting, to throw a tantrum, to make a scene

subargan: ⟶ **subarhan**

subarhan: pagoda; cf. **sumarhan**, **subargan**

subari: a wooden tool for digging up ginseng and other herbs

subcalu: uneven in height (plants)

subdungga: ⟶ **sultungga**

sube: tendon, sinew, nerve, muscle; cf. **ca**

    sube hūsimbi: to wrap with sinew (an arrow)

    sube maktambi: to wrap sinew (around a bow shaft)

subehe: **1**. the end of a branch; **2**. the end of a hair from a beard; **3**. sash, girdle, cord, band, ribbon, mourning sash; **4**. cord for holding pearls or beads (for a ceremonial garment)

subeliyen: silk floss, silk fiber

    subeliyen hūsimbi: to wrap with silk fiber

    subeliyen jurumbi: to produce silk fiber (said of silk worms)

    subeliyen sorson: a tassel of silk floss

    subeliyen umiyaha: silkworm

suberhe: a bird used as bait in catching falcons

suberi: a thin silken fabric with a glossy finish, damask

subetu: sinewy, muscular

subetungge: one who is sinewy, muscular

subkejembi: **1**. to snag, to fray; **2**. (intransitive verb) to unravel, to come unwoven

subkelembi: (transitive verb) to unravel, to take apart (silk cloth)

subkeri: a mourning garment with unsewn hems

subsi: **1**. chronic, persistent (said of an illness); **2**. trifling, insignificant, small

    subsi baita: trivial matter

    subsi keike: harsh and exacting

subsin ilha: the name of a small fragrant exotic flower that grows on thes end of small branches

subuhūn: **1**. sober, not drunk; **2**. slightly intoxicated, just beginning to sober up

subumbi: (**-he/-ha**) **1**. (causative of **sumbi**); **2**. to put off, to remove; **3**. to absolve from guilt or blame; **4**. to explain, to comment on; **5**. to become sober, to recover from a drinking bout; **6**. to abort, to miscarry; **7**. to slake (one's thirst); **8**. to soothe, to calm

subun: explanation, discussion, elucidation

suburi: a sweet-tasting exotic fruit the size of a hen's egg and believed to sober up a person who is drunk

suci: fetus of an animal

    suci sumbi: to miscarry (said of an animal)

sucilembi: **1**. to become pregnant (said of animals); **2**. to form ears (said of grain)

sucin: pregnant (said of animals); cf. **suci**

sucumbi: (**-ha**) **1**. to storm (the enemy's lines), to charge, to attack suddenly; **2**. to soar, to rise upward

sucun weihe: the incisors

sucunambi: **1**. to go to storm; **2**. to fly up, to soar upward

sucungga: the first, initial, beginning

    sucungga aniya: the first year of a reign

    sucungga mudan: the first time

    sucungga nadan: the first seven days after death

sucunjimbi: to come charging in

sucunumbi: to charge together, to storm together

sucutu: a two-year-old horse

sudala: **1**. vein, artery, blood vessel; **2**. the geomantic veins of the earth

    sudala jafambi: to take the pulse; cf. **me jafambi**

    sudala siren: **1**. veins and arteries; **2**. thread of thought, sequence of ideas

sudalabumbi: (causative of **sudalambi**)

sudalambi: to wear short hanging hair

sudamimbi: to remove the bit, to take out the bit (said of livestock)

sudan: **1**. the hair at the temples of a woman; **2**. curly hair

sudara: sutra

suderhen: a kind of rice-colored skylark

sudu: shin, shinbone

    sudu niru: an arrow without holes in its head

suduli: **1**. alpine leek, wild leek (*Allium victorialis*); **2**. wild garlic

    suduli abdaha fukjingga hergen: (薤葉篆) a style of calligraphy

sudunggiyambi: to waste, to spoil, to ravage

suduri: history, chronicle, annal

    suduri amban: annalist, historian

    suduri be aliha amban: (大史) historiographer

    suduri dangse: historical record, historical annal

sufan: elephant

    sufan i weihe: ivory

    sufan i weihe sabka: ivory chopstick

    sufan ileri ilha: an exotic flower from Indochina that blooms at the end of winter and whose leaves resemble the leaves of the jujube tree

sufangga lujen: an Imperial ceremonial coach with a dome decorated with ivory and drawn by eight horses

sufen: Indian rhinoceros

suhai moo: *Tamarix juniperus*: the tamarisk

suharambi: (-ka) **1**. to get drowsy from drinking; **2**. to droop (said of grain)

suhe: **1**. ax, halberd; **2**. gold and silver bars made of paper (used in offerings for the dead)

    suhe argacan i fiyenten: (斧鉞司) Halberd Section, *BH* 121

    suhe hoošan: gold and silver bars made of paper (used as offerings for the dead)

    suhe jurutu: an ancient official garment with axes depicted on it

suhecen: small ax, hatchet

suhelembi: to split with an ax

suhen: commentary on a classic

suhengge: pertaining to an ax, decorated with ax designs

suheri: *Liquidambar orientalis*: oriental sweetgum

    suheri nimenggi: the fragrant resin from the oriental sweetgum

suhešembi: to chop repeatedly with an ax

suhuken: ivory-colored

suhun: very pale yellow, cream-colored

    suhun wenderhen: an ivory-colored skylark

sui: **1**. crime, transgression, sin, guilt; **2**. malevolent influence, evil; **3**. suffering, grief

    sui akū: innocent, without guilt

    sui arambi: to commit a sin or transgression

    sui boco: olive-green

    sui cecike: kingfisher; cf. **ulgiyan cecike**

    sui gung: yearly tribute

    sui i karulan: retribution for evil deeds

    sui isifi ehe de isiname mailakini: an oath with the same meaning as **mailaru**

    sui isika: met with misfortune

    sui isiru: May you meet with misfortune!, Miscreant! (an oath)

    sui mangga: **1**. injustice, wrong, unfairness; **2**. wronged, aggrieved

    sui tuwambi: to suffer

    sui weile: sin, transgression, crime

suibumbi: (causative of **suimbi**)

suifulebumbi: (causative of **suifulembi**)

suifulembi: to bore with an awl, to make a hole with an awl

suifun: awl

    suifun ilire ba: not even enough room to insert an awl — a small piece of land

suiga: ⟶ **suiha**

suiha: **1**. artemisia, moxa, sagewort; **2**. brush, overgrowth

    suiha cecike: 'moxa bird' — the name of a small bird with brown back and sides and a white breast

    suiha fulan: a light gray horse

    suiha sindambi: to treat with moxibustion

    suiha sindambi: to apply moxa, to cauterize with moxa

suihana: resembling artemisia

    suihana wehe: a kind of green stone with spots resembling the artemisia plant

suihana yarha: a leopard with spots resembling the leaves of the artemisia plant

suihe: **1**. an ear of grain; **2**. tassel, crest; **3**. end of a whip; **4**. ribbon, ribbon attached to a seal

suihe ilha: the flower of knotweed (*Fallopia japonica*)

suihen: ⟶ **emu suihen i banjimbi**

suihenembi: to put forth ears (grain)

suihetu: having a tassel or crest

suihetu coko: a name for the turkey; cf. **nanggitu coko**

suihetu fukjingga hergen: (穗書) the name of a style of calligraphy

suihetu gasha: ⟶ **suihetu coko**

suihetu gūwasihiya: a name for the egret; cf. **gūwasihiya**

suihon: a deer-horn awl worn on the belt and used for untying knots

suihon i uncehen: a final stroke in cursive Manchu script

suihumbi: to be rowdy when drunk

suihume laihūdame yabumbi: to behave offensively while intoxicated

suihume omimbi: to drink until drunk, to get soused

suihun: a large earring used by men

suihutu: a rowdy drunk

suilabumbi: (causative of **suilambi**)

suilacuka: distressing, laborious, difficult, agonizing

suilacun: distress, labor, agony, hardship

suilacun be alimbi: to suffer hardship

suilambi: to be in distress, to suffer hardship, to be in agony, to be exhausted

suilan: hornet

suilashūn: **1**. burdensome, onerous, encumbering; **2**. distressed, afflicted

suimangga: ⟶ **sui mangga**

suimbi: (**-he/-ha**) **1**. to grind ink; **2**. to knead (dough), to mix, to blend; **3**. to look for; cf. **suwelembi**

suingga: harmful, grievous, wicked, illegal

suingga jui: **1**. unfilial son; **2**. son of a concubine

suisimbi: (**-ka**) to suffer hardship or distress

suisiru: ⟶ **sui isiru**: Miscreant!

suisirusa: (plural of **suisiru**)

suitabumbi: (causative of **suitambi**)

suitakū: a long vessel used for pouring libations

suitambi: to pour, to water (plants), to spill, to splash, to irrigate

sujabumbi: (causative of **sujambi**)

sujagan: ⟶ **sujahan**

sujahan: supporting pole, prop, support

sujakū: a support, a grip

sujambi: **1**. to prop up, to support; **2**. to push against, to resist, to withstand; **3**. to lean on, to support oneself on; **4**. to be a match for

sujanambi: to push upward (said of sprouts), to sprout while still underground

sujandumbi: to support one another, to resist one another

suje: silk, silk material, satin

suje i namun: (緞疋庫) Silk Store, *BH* 77

sujikde: *Salix gracilistyla*: pussy willow

sujubumbi: (causative of **sujumbi**)

sujumbi: (**-he**) to run, to hasten, to rush

sujunambi: to run there

sujutembi: to run together

suk seme injembi: to laugh while trying to remain serious, to laugh through the nose while trying to hold a straight face, to snigger

sukden moo: *Rhus cotinus*: smoke tree, the leaves of which are used for making a yellow dye

sukduhen: a name for the crane; cf. **bulehen**

sukdun: **1**. breath; **2**. vapor, steam, gas, fume; **3**. air, atmosphere; **4**. the primordial substance from which all things emanate; **5**. vital fluid; **6**. spirit, morale, bearing, airs, manner

sukdun arbun: aspect, manner

sukdun be gidambi: to hold one's breath

sukdun cingkambi: to be breathless, to run out of breath

sukdun cirgabumbi: to hold one's breath

sukdun fiyan: complexion, color

sukdun hūwaliyasun nesuken i mudan: a piece of music played during a banquet given by the Board of War for a new military metropolitan graduate

sukdun niyecebumbi: to nourish the vital vapors (said of the body)

sukdun ton: fate

sukdungga: pertaining to vapor, breath, etc.

sukdunggi: ⟶ **sukdungga**

sukiyabumbi: (causative of **sukiyambi**)

sukiyambi: to drain, to pour out completely

sukiyame omimbi: to drink dry, to drink 'bottoms up'

sukiyangga ilha: a carved or decorated piece of wood suspended in a gate; cf. **bongko sukiyara duka**

sukiyari cecike: *Loriculus*: the green lovebird of Taiwan

sukji: the edible seed pods of the elm tree

sukjibumbi: (causative of **sukjimbi**)

    sukjibure hiyan: a variety of fragrant purple incense

sukjimbi: to receive an offering, to partake of an offering

sukjingge ba: the southwest corner of a house

suksaha: **1**. thigh; **2**. hind leg of livestock

suksalabumbi: (causative of **suksalambi**)

suksalambi: to open up (new land), to open to cultivation, to clear (virgin land)

suksalanambi: to go to open up for cultivation

suksalandumbi: to open to cultivation together; also **suksalanumbi**

suksalanjimbi: to come to open to cultivation

suksalanumbi: to open to cultivation together; also **suksalandumbi**

suksan: newly opened land, land newly opened to cultivation

suksubumbi: (causative of **suksumbi**)

suksuhu: *Pandion haliaetus*: fish hawk, osprey

suksuhun: bristling (mad), enfuriated

suksuku: ⟶ **suksuhu**

suksumbi: (-he) to winnow

suksurebumbi: (causative of **suksurembi**)

suksureku: winnowing fan, winnowing machine, winnower

suksurembi: (-ke) **1**. to be swollen, to become swollen; **2**. to shake out (a bird of its feathers); **3**. to strike prey (said of birds of prey)

suku: **1**. crown daisy chrysanthemum (*Chrysanthemum coronaria*), fleabane; **2**. various invasive opportunistic plants commonly found on abandoned land; **3**. thicket

    suku hamgiya: overgrowth, brush, weeds

    suku suiha: brush, undergrowth

sukū: **1**. skin, hide, pelt, leather; **2**. fruit peel

sukū i jaka weilere hafan: (獸工) an official who was in charge of making leather goods in antiquity

sukū i šošonggo mahala: an ancient-style hat made from deerskin

sukū jahūdai: boat made from animal hides

sukū jumanggi: leather bag

sukū mahala: fur hat, leather hat

sukū soforo: a leather saddle cushion; cf. **soforo**

sukūnambi: to form a skin, to develop a layer of skin

sukūngge lujen: the name of a ceremonial carriage with a leather-covered dome

sula: **1**. loose, slack; **2**. idle, unoccupied, at leisure, free; **3**. incomplete, piecemeal; **4**. not employed in an official capacity

    sula amban: (散秩大臣) Junior Assistant Chamberlain of the Imperial Bodyguard, *BH* 98

    sula ba: empty land, wasteland

    sula baisin: unemployed, at leisure

    sula bithe: novel, storybook, frivolous literature

    sula boihon: loose soil

    sula gisun: idle talk, gossip

    sula hafan i usin: government land

    sula haha: idle laborer, non-quota man

    sula hehe: **1**. wife of a wandering husband; **2**. a household slave girl, female servant

    sula inenggi: a free day

    sula janggin: (散騎郎) the name of an officer in the Palace of a Prince of the Blood

    sula leolecembi: to have a casual conversation, to chit-chat

    sula niyalma: an idle person, man of leisure

    sula saisa: a scholar in private life

    sula sindambi: to put at ease

    sula tembi: to live at ease

    sula umiyesun: a loose belt without a clasp

    sula yafan: uncultivated garden

sulabumbi: **1**. (causative of **sulambi**); **2**. to leave free, to leave a little bit over, to leave remaining; **3**. to let hang; **4**. to let grow (one's hair)

sulahūn: a name for the river gull; cf. **ula kilahūn**

sulaka: ⟶ **sulakan**

sulakan: **1**. rather loose; **2**. rather free; **3**. rather idle; **4**. somewhat better (said of an illness); **5**. relieved, at ease

sulambi: **1**. to be left over, to remain behind, to be handed down; **2**. to be loose, to be free; **3**. to be idle; **4**. to awake from a cat nap

sulaha dursun: traditional character

sulaha tacin: traditional custom

suldargan: a name for the kestrel; cf. **baldargan**

sulfa: **1**. at leisure, free, at ease, without cares; **2**. comfortably off, well off; **3**. spacious, roomy

sulfakan: rather leisurely, rather loose

sulfambi: **1**. to be loose, to be slack; **2**. to be at ease

sulfangga: relaxed, at ease, peaceful, free

sulfangga akū: uncomfortable, uneasy

sulhumbi: to become soft and mushy, to be soft (said of earth or snow)

sulku: a wooden or bamboo flower stand

sultaha: the river gull; cf. **ula kilahūn**

sultei: goral; cf. **imahū**

sultungga: wise, sagacious

sumaga: ⟶ **šumgan**

sumala: a small bag

sumaltu: marsupial

sumambi: (**-ka**) to spread out (said of vapors and mist), to spiral up

suman: vapors, mist

sumarhan: pagoda — the same as **subargan**

sumari alin: ⟶ **sumiri alin**

sumari cecike: the name of the goatsucker in Sichuan; cf. **simari cecike**

sumbi: (**1**) (**-he**) **1**. to take off, to remove; **2**. to shed (horns, said of a deer); **3**. to untie, to unhitch, to unlock; **4**. to abort; **5**. to explain, to annotate; **6**. to cancel; **7**. to expiate, to redeem

sume alambi: to report giving an explanation

sume bodombi: to compute for an expense report

sume bodoro boo: (銷算房) Expenditure Section, *BH* 425

sume efulere kunggeri: (注銷科) Accounting Department of the Court of Colonial Affairs

sume gisurembi: to argue

sumbi: (**2**) (**-ngke, -mpi**) **1**. to freeze, to congeal; **2**. to whirl

sumbuljambi: to be soft (said of wet ground)

sumbur sambar seme: ragged, tattered

sumbur seme: ⟶ **sumbur sambar seme**

sumburšambi: to be in disarray (said of troops)

sume: ⟶ **sumbi** (**1**) (subheading)

sumiri alin: Mount Sumeru (Buddhist)

sumpa: **1**. having gray hair at the temples, graying; **2**. the name of a small plant that resembles artemisia

sumpa maca: wild leek

sumpanambi: to turn gray at the temples

sumu: (Mongolian) lamaist temple

sumusu: rice broth with a few kernels of rice left in it

sun: milk (from domestic animals)

sun i cai: tea mixed with milk

sun nimenggi: butter, cream

sun sambi: to milk

sun sirimbi: to milk

suna: a leather leash for a dog; cf. **sūna**

sunda: garlic; cf. **suwanda**

sundalabumbi: (causative of **sundalambi**)

sundalambi: **1**. to ride two on a horse; **2**. to give hot pursuit, to pursue; **3**. to take up a matter again after it has already passed

sunembi: **1**. to drip down, to fall (said of rain), to condense (said of clouds before the onset of rain); **2**. to drop off, to fall away; **3**. to go to remove, etc.

sung el: the male sparrow hawk; the same as **ajige hiya silmen**

sunggada: *Erythroculter erythropterus*: red-finned culter

sunggali cecike: *Nucifraga caryocatactes*: North China nutcracker

sunggari bira: the Milky Way

sunggari ula: the Sunggari River

sunggartu usiha: the name of a star located south of the Milky Way

sunggeljebumbi: (causative of **sunggeljembi**)

sunggeljembi: **1**. to shake, to tremble, to waver; **2**. to be supple, to bend easily

sunggelson: a red tassel that was attached to certain ancient-style hats

sunggembi: to waste away, to grow skinny and pale

sunggiljambi: ⟶ **sunggeljembi**

sunggimbi: ⟶ **sunggembi**

sunggina: a kind of wild onion that grows in cold spots and on cliffs (perhaps the Altai onion, *Allium altaicum*)

sunggiyen: reasonable, sensible, sagacious

sungguhe: a name for the myna

sungke: congealed, shriveled up; cf. **sumbi** (**2**)

sungniyaha: ⟶ **songgiha**

sunja: five

sunja akjangga kiru: a banner on which five symbols representing thunder appeared

sunja baktakū: the five organs: liver, heart, spleen, lungs, and kidney

sunja biya: the fifth month

sunja ciktan: the five human relationships

sunja colhon: the five sacred mountains of China

sunja dobon: the five offerings that sit on the altar: an incense boat, two candlesticks, and two flower vases

sunja dzang: the five internal organs: heart, liver, spleen, lungs and kidney

sunja enteheme: the five constants: humaneness, loyalty, propriety, knowledge, and trust

sunja feten: the five elements: fire, water, wood, metal, and earth

sunja feten be bodoro hafan: (五官正) Astronomer, *BH* 229

sunja feten be bodoro hafan i tinggin: (五官廳) hall of the astronomers

sunja hacin i jeku: the five grains: rice, glutinous millet, common millet, wheat, and beans

sunja hacin i orobuhangge: a sweet food made from dried pears, dried berries, barberry juice, cream, and honey

sunja hergin: the five ordering principles: year, moon, sun, fixed stars, and planets

sunja iktan: the five aggregations or skandas

sunja irungge mahatun: an ancient-style hat with five ridges on top

sunja jalan genggiyesu: a house slave of the fifth generation

sunja jilgan: the five notes of the Chinese pentatonic scale

sunja tugingge kiru: a triangular shaped banner of the Imperial Escort in five colors embroidered with a cloud design

sunja tuhebuku i mahatu: a crown of ancient times that had five tassels hanging from it

sunja yamun i kunggeri: (五府科) an establishment charged with producing weapons and casting cannon for the provinces

sunjaci: fifth

sunjaci jalan i omolo: a descendant of the fifth generation

sunjangga: pertaining to five

sunjangga faidan: a battle rank in antiquity of five men

sunjangga inenggi: the fifth day of the fifth month — the Dragon Boat Festival

sunjanggeri: five times

sunjari: made up of five elements

sunjari ilha: an exotic flower that resembles the blossom of the pomegranate

sunjari suje: satin woven in strips consisting of five threads

sunjata: five each

sunji: one hundred-thousandth

sunta: **1**. a very small bag; **2**. net bag for meat tied to the waist of falconers (used for feeding)

suntaha: snowshoe, ski

suntalambi: ⟶ **sundalambi**

suntambi: ⟶ **suntembi**

suntanambi: to be stuffed full, to be paunchy, to swell (said of the belly)

suntebumbi: **1**. (causative or passive of **suntembi**); **2**. to annihilate, to wipe out

suntembi: to be annihilated, to be wiped out, to become extinct

sunto: a measure equaling five small pecks

sur sar seme: itching

sur seme: **1**. sharp, fragrant, stimulating to the olfactory nerves; **2**. gently (said of laughing)

sura: ⟶ **suran**

surabumbi: (causative of **surambi**)

surafu: an awl with a round handle

surafun: ⟶ **surafu**

suraha: water in which rice has been rinsed (used as pig feed)

surakū: a pig trough

surambi: **1**. to rinse (rice), to wash (rice); **2**. to hawk goods in a loud voice

suran: **1**. water in which rice has been rinsed; **2**. flea

surbejen: the part of an arrowhead that attaches to the shaft, the part of a knife blade that attaches to the handle

surbu: a cord for holding a hat on

sure: **1**. wise, intelligent; **2**. *prajñā*, wisdom (Buddhism); **3**. chilled (said of fruit); **4**. spirit, soul

sure banin: soul

sure genggiyen: intelligent, bright

sure han: the Tiancong (天聰) reign period (1627–35)

sure hiyan: a variety of light brown incense

sure mama: the goddess of smallpox

sure sektu: smart, clever

sure ulhisu: bright, intelligent

surebumbi: (causative of **surembi** [1])

sureken: rather wise, intelligent

surembi: (1) (-he) to yell, to shout

surembi: (2) (-ke) to be wide awake, to wake up refreshed, to feel refreshed

surembumbi: 1. (causative of **surembi** [2]); 2. to awaken, to arouse

suren: wisdom, mind; cf. **sure**

surendumbi: to yell together

surgi: a smallpox pustule

surgi werihe: left behind smallpox pustules

surgin: damp, humid, warm and humid

surho: goosefoot, pigweed, chenopodium

surhūn: intelligence, understanding, intelligent

surhūn akū: lacking intelligence, lacking understanding, not bright

suri: silk cloth; cf. **cuse**

surimbi: (-ha) to wither, to dry up, to dry out

sursan sursan: intermittent (snow or rain)

sursen orho: *Lysimachia capillipes*: the name of a fragrant plant from South China

surseri: *Citrus medica*; 'Buddha's hand,' a variety of citrus fruit that has the shape of five fingers held together

surtebumbi: (causative of **surtembi**)

surtembi: to race, to run

surtendumbi: 1. to race together, to run a race together; 2. to run in all directions (said of a group); also **surtenumbi**

surtenumbi: 1. to race together, to run a race together; 2. to run in all directions (said of a group); also **surtendumbi**

surtenume baimbi: to ask for without shame, to seek shamelessly

suru: white (said of a horse)

suru morin: a white horse

surudai: the phoenix of the west

suruhūn: ⟶ **surhūn**

suruk: (Mongolian) herd (of livestock)

surumbi: (-ke) to obtain relief, to recover from melancholy

surumbumbi: 1. (causative of **surumbi**); 2. to relieve someone from boredom, to give relief to, to console

susai: fifty

susai nadan gūsa: the fifty-seven Mongolian banners of Outer Mongolia

susaici: fiftieth

susaita: fifty each

susakangge: dead thing! — an oath

susambi: (-ka) to die, to perish

suse: 1. straw, hemp stalks, paper, cord, etc. that is mixed into mortar or adobe; 2. crude, coarse; 3. trash

susedembi: to do crudely, to make coarsely

suseri: 1. *Foeniculum vulgare*: fennel; 2. coarse, worn down

suseri hoošan: coarse paper

suseri jiha: a worn-down copper coin

suseri nenden ilha: the name of a yellow flower with long petals that wave in the wind and resemble butterflies

susu: 1. location of an abandoned campsite, an abandoned village, a ruin; 2. desolate, bleak, overgrown, waste; 3. birthplace, native place, home

susu gašan: 1. an abandoned village; 2. one's native village

susu jafaburakū: not to allow someone to register one's residence

susubumbi: 1. (causative of **susumbi**); 2. to lay waste, to ruin

susukiyembi: to shiver from the cold

susultungga: intelligent, highly gifted, outstanding

susumbi: (-ha) to become desolate, to become bleak

susunggiyabumbi: (causative of **susunggiyambi**)

susunggiyambi: to ruin, to lay waste

sutha: ⟶ **suntaha**

sutuhūn cecike: one of the names of the hoopoe; cf. **indahūn cecike**

suwa: *Cervus nippon*: the North China sika, spotted deer

suwa buhū: ⟶ **suwa**

suwa nasin: *Ursus arctos*: a large brown bear, especially one with a pale yellow tinge

suwabirgan: 'yellow swallow' — the name of a bird

suwafintu cecike: Bohemian waxwing, the same as **taifintu cecike**

suwakidun cecike: the name given by the people of Jiangnan to the crow-tit; cf. **kidun cecike**

suwalin cecike: a name for the oriole; cf. **gūlin cecike**

suwaliya: ⟶ **suwaliyan**

suwaliyabumbi: (causative or passive of **suwaliyambi**)

suwaliyaganjambi: to be mixed up, to mix together

   suwaliyaganjame: mixed up, mixed together, confused

   suwaliyaganjame baitalambi: to use together, to use concurrently

   suwaliyaganjame tembi: to live together in the same area (said of two or more ethnic groups)

suwaliyahanjambi: ⟶ **suwaliyaganjambi**

suwaliyambi: **1**. to mix, to mix up, to blend together; **2**. to implicate, to mix up in an affair; **3**. to confuse, to get mixed up; **4**. to combine, to put together, to connect

   suwaliyame: altogether, together with, jointly, mixed together with something, all at once, including …

suwaliyan: mixing, mixture

   suwaliyan orho: roots of *Coptis chinensis*: the Chinese goldthread (a very bitter herb)

suwaliyasun: seasoning

   suwaliyasun acabumbi: to add seasoning

suwaliyata: mixed, blended, miscellaneous, sundry

suwaliyatambi: to be mixed or blended

suwampan: abacus; cf. **bodokū**

suwan: **1**. the inside of an oven-bed; **2**. *Pholocrocorax carbo*: cormorant

suwanda: garlic

suwandara: a kind of wild cat with a yellow back (which in spite of its small size can catch tigers, cows, and deer)

suwangkiyabumbi: (causative of **suwangkiyambi**)

suwangkiyambi: to graze (said of cattle)

suwangkiyandumbi: to graze together; also **suwangkiyanumbi**

suwangkiyanumbi: to graze together; also **suwangkiyandumbi**

suwanpan: ⟶ **suwampan**

suwasha nimaha: 'siskin fish' — so-called because in the tenth month the siskin is supposed to fly to the sea and there turn into this fish

suwayakan: rather yellow, somewhat yellow

suwayan: **1**. yellow; **2**. the fifth of the heaven's stems (戊)

   suwayan aisin: gold

   suwayan bumbi: to make an offering of 'flour pigs' (a kind of yellow cake)

   suwayan cecike: the siskin

   suwayan cese boo: (黃冊房) Office of Census Records

   suwayan cibirgan: ⟶ **suwabirgan**

   suwayan dangse boo: (黃檔房) Genealogical Record Office of the Imperial Clan Court, *BH* 74

   suwayan engge cecike: *Eophona personata*: hawfinch

   suwayan faitan: a kind of quail with yellow stripes over its eyes

   suwayan faitangga cecike: *Phyllscopus inornatus*: pseudo-goldcrest

   suwayan garudai: a yellow phoenix

   suwayan giyahūn cecike: chicken hawk

   suwayan gūsai falga: (黃旗甲) Bureau of the Yellow Banner

   suwayan gūsai fiyenten: (黃旗司) Section of the Yellow Banner

   suwayan gūsai kunggeri: (黃旗科) Office of the Yellow Banner

   suwayan hošonggo gu: a square jade tablet used during sacrifices to the earth

   suwayan jugūn: the ecliptic

   suwayan jugūn i hetu undu i durungga tetun: (黃道經緯儀) the name of an astronomical instrument in the observatory in Beijing (used for observing the discrepancies in the ecliptics of the sun, moon, and planets)

   suwayan kiltari: a yellow pennant of the Imperial Escort

   suwayan kuringge gasha: a kind of yellow speckled bird

   suwayan meihetu: *Monopterus albus*: yellow eel, swamp eel

   suwayan nasingga kiru: (黃羆旗) a banner of the Imperial Escort embroidered with the figure of a bear

suwayan nenden ilha: *Chimonanthus praecox*: wintersweet

suwayan nothori: *Clausena wampi*: wampee, a kind of tree

suwayan okto: medicine made from the root of *Coptis japonica*: Japanese goldthread

suwayan senggiri ilha: yellow azalea

suwayan sišargan: golden linnet

suwayan solohi: weasel; cf. **solohi**

suwayan šajin: Buddhism

suwayan šeri: 'the yellow springs' — the underworld, Hades

suwayan turi: soybean

suwayan uhumi: yellow winding band used for wrapping the **niowanggiyan uju**

suwayan useri: an exotic yellow fruit that resembles a small pomegranate

suwayan yadana: a yellow swan

suwayan yadanangga kiru: (黃鵠旗) a banner of the escort embroidered with the figure of a yellow swan

suwayan yenggehe: a yellow parrot

suwayan yenggetu: a small green parrot with a yellow neck and breast

suwe: you (plural)

suwelebumbi: (causative of **suwelembi**)

suwelembi: **1**. to search (for), to look for; **2**. ⟶ **seolembi**

suweleme baicara hafan: (搜檢官) an inspection officer, inspector

suwelendumbi: to search together

suwelenembi: to go to search

suwelenjimbi: to come to search

suwembe: (accusative form of **suwe**)

suwenci: (ablative form of **suwe**)

suwende: (dative/locative form of **suwe**)

suweni: (genitive of **suwe**)

suweningge: yours

suya: kindling, small dry branches

suyambi: to kindle, to blow on a small flame to ignite tinder

suyamu: a reed wrapped around the iron needle of a spinning wheel

suyen: **1**. shoe or boot strings; **2**. water that has been filtered through ashes, water that has been filtered through the malt used for making liquor

sūna: ⟶ **suna**

sy: (寺) a Buddhist temple

sycuwan: (四川) Sichuan

Š

For words beginning with **s**, see the section beginning on page 305.

ša: **1**. silk gauze, tulle; cf. **cece**; **2**. a dense forest on the north side of a mountain; cf. **šuwa**; **3**. one billionth; cf. **libu**

ša gecuheri: silk gauze decorated with figures of dragons

ša i fa: (window) screen, a window covered with gauze

ša juwangduwan: gauze material that has gold threads worked into it

ša mi: a Buddhist novice

ša moo: *Cunninghamia lanceolata*: the Chinese fir

ša moo mahala: a gauze hat worn by officials

ša undurakū: silk gauze decorated with figures of prancing dragons

šab šab arambi: to tremble with weakness

šab seme: (onomatopoetic) the sound of an arrow grazing some object

šab sib seme: (onomatopoetic) the sound of many arrows being shot

šaban: a piece of leather with an attached iron cleat (tied to boots or shoes to assist in mountain climbing or walking on ice)

šabargan gidambi: to cure a child's sickness by pressing against his body a container of uncooked rice covered with a handkerchief

šabi: disciple, student

šabinar: (Mongolian) disciples

šabisa: (plural of **šabi**)

šabtun: a protective ear and cheek covering (military)

šabtungga mahala: a hat with ear flaps

šaburambi: **1**. to wait upon, to serve (a guest); **2**. to take care of, to look after, to manage; **3**. to get sleepy, to be on the point of sleep; cf. **amu šaburambi**; **4**. to be numb

šaburu: pale yellow, cream-colored

šaburu aisin: white gold

šacambi: to look in every direction, always to be looking to the side (said of horses and cattle)

šacun niongniyaha: a name for the wild goose

šacungga jahūdai: a flat-bottomed boat

šada ilha: a fragrant flower that resembles the Mandala flower and is usually found in Buddhist monasteries

šadabumbi: (causative of **šadambi**)

šadacuka: tiring, tiresome, tedious

šadali cecike: the name of a small bird — the same as the **wehe yadali cecike** except that this variety has white stripes over its eyes

šadambi: to become tired, to get weary

šadashūn: **1**. somewhat fatigued, languid; **2**. tiring, fatiguing

šadu foyo: *Cyperus rotundus*: a sedge, coco grass

šagu: crabapple

šahasi: a name for the rhinoceros

šahūkan: having a whitish cast

šahūn: **1**. whitish, pale, pallid, dull white; **2**. the eighth of the heaven's stems (辛)

šahūn gūwasihiya: a white crane

šahūn horonggo gu: a round white jade tablet used during sacrifices to the moon

šahūn hurungge alhacan niyehe: a speckled duck with a white back

šahūn saksaha: a white magpie

šahūrabumbi: **1**. (causative of **šahūrambi**); **2**. to catch cold; **3**. to cool, to become cool

šahūrambi: (-ka, -pi) **1**. to become cold; **2**. to catch cold

šahūrukan: somewhat cold, rather cold

šahūrun: cold

šahūrun de goimbi: to catch cold

šahūrun edun: a cold wind

šahūrun halhūn bulukan necin: the four temperatures of traditional medicine: cold, hot, warm, normal

šahūrun injembi: to laugh sarcastically

šahūrun jetere hacin: the three days preceding the Qingming festival when only cold food was eaten

šahūrun jetere inenggi: the days before Qingming in early April when only cold food was eaten

šahūrun silenggi: 'cold dew' — one of the twenty-four divisions of the solar year falling on October eighth or ninth

šahūrun šeri: a cold spring

šahūrungga: cold, frigid

šajilambi: to prohibit, to forbid

šajilan: **1**. birch wood; **2**. the name of a green worm with a horn-like protuberance on its head

šajilan i sirdan: an arrow made from birch wood

šajin: **1**. prohibition, law; **2**. religion, dharma

šajin be dahambi: to follow regulations

šajin de gaimbi: to convert to religion, to become a Buddhist

šajin kooli: laws and regulations

šajin kurdun: the wheel of the law; cf. **šajin i muheren**

šajin i muheren: dharmacakra: the wheel of the Law

šajin yoo: venereal sore, syphilitic sore

šajingga: pertaining to prohibition, religious

šajingga ahūn: brother in a Buddhist or Daoist monastery

šajingga belhesi: ⟶ **belhesi**

šajingga deo: a young brother in a monastery

šajingga gasha: the Buddha bird, so called because its call resembles the word **mito** (Amitābha)

šajingga karan: a platform used for Buddhist and Daoist services

šajintu: another name for the mythical beast **tontu**

šajintu mahatun: an ancient-style hat with the figure of the **šajintu** depicted on it

šajiri gasha: Buddha bird — the same as **šajingga gasha**

šajulan: ⟶ **šajilan**

šak: tall and leafy (trees)

šak seme: tall and rank, towering and dense (trees)

šak sik: **1**. (onomatopoetic) rattling, tingling; **2**. strong, vigorous (said of horses)

šaka: **1**. a fork, a spear with a forked head; **2**. a leftward oblique stroke in writing

šaka belhere ba: (備权處) a place where punting poles, oars, and forked spears were prepared for Imperial use

šaka i tokombi: to stick with a **šaka**

šakalabumbi: (causative or passive of **sakalambi**)

šakalambi: **1**. to fork, to spear with a fork, to stick with a fork; **2**. to cut off (enemy troops); **3**. to interrupt

šakanambi: to crack (said of ice)

šakari: a fork for fruit

šakašabumbi: (causative of **šakašambi**)

šakašambi: **1**. to be crowded; **2**. to be mixed up, to be criss-crossed, to be disorderly; **3**. to bombard a person with questions (said of a group); **4**. to interrupt

šakašame gisurembi: to interrupt someone who is talking

šaksiha: ⟶ **šakšaha**

šakšaha: **1**. the cheek; **2**. gill

šakšaha i giranggi: the cheekbone of a fish

šakšaha maktambi: to lose face, to be embarrassed

šakšaha meyen: wing (of an army)

šakšaha murimbi: to disagree, to be stubborn (about one's own opinion)

šakšaha sele: two pieces of iron on a bridle that cover the cheeks of the animal

šakšahalambi: to attack from the flanks, to outflank

šakšahūn: with one's teeth showing

šakšalambi: ⟶ **šakalambi** and **šakšahalambi**

šakšaljambi: to smile showing one's teeth

šakšan: crafty, cunning, wily

šakšarambi: to expose one's teeth; cf. **šakšaljambi**

šakšari: smiling with one's teeth showing

šakšarjambi: ⟶ **šakšaljambi**

šaktalambi: to cut off the ears (as a punishment)

šala: **1**. edge, end, extremity; **2**. flank, side; **3**. lapel, edge of a lapel; **4**. remnant, scraps; cf. **ujan šala**

šala i niyalma: a man in the wings (of an army)

šalangtu: a fat ox

šalar seme: **1**. in good order, lined up evenly; **2**. (onomatopoetic) rustling (said of bamboo leaves)

šalhūma: the white pheasant of the west

šalibumbi: to become pale

šalu: heated, hot

šambi: (1) to look, to look at

šambi: (2) (-ngka, -mpi) 1. to dry meat or fish by a fire; 2. to rinse hot rice in cold water

šami: young Buddhist monk, Buddhist novice

šampi: breeching on a harness (the part of a harness that runs under the tail), crupper

>**šampi moo**: a horizontal piece of wood that hangs under the tail of a harnessed mule or donkey

>**šampi uše**: a line connected to the breeching of a harness

šampilabumbi: (causative of **sampilambi**)

šampilambi: to put on the breeching of a harness

šamtulambi: to let down the protective ear flaps on a hat; cf. **šabtun**

šan: 1. ear; 2. rowlock; 3. pan of a flintlock or flash-vent of a cannon; 4. handle; 5. shoehorn; 6. brim of a hat

>**šan dabumbi**: to apportion a share

>**šan dasakū**: an ear cleaner consisting of cotton or down on the end of a small stick

>**šan de bahabumbi**: to have come to one's ears, to hear of

>**šan derdehun**: the ears are curved forward

>**šan feteku**: an earpick

>**šan gabtakū**: a support with holes on both sides that is attached to the main beam

>**šan i abdaha**: the outer part of the ear

>**šan i afaha**: ⟶ **san i abdaha**

>**šan i da**: the root of the ear

>**šan i dalikū**: cover for the ears

>**šan i delbi**: the back of the ear

>**šan i fere**: eardrum

>**šan i feteku**: ⟶ **šan feteku**

>**šan i hešen**: the circumference of the ear

>**šan i okto**: gunpowder

>**šan i oktoi kūwaca**: a powderhorn

>**šan i sen**: 1. a hole in the earlobe for an earring; 2. hole for powder on a gun

>**šan i suihe**: earlobe

>**šan i unggala**: the opening of the ear

>**šan kamcime banjihabi**: the ears grow flat against the head

>**šan mila**: sharp-eared

šan sicambi: the ears shake (from hearing a loud noise)

šan sulhumbi: to have an ear infection, to discharge matter from the ear

šan waliyame: listening attentively

šan yasa: ears and eyes — spies

šan yodambi: to perk up the ears

šancilambi: to set up a fort, to fortify, to build a fortress

šancin: fortress, small fortress on a mountain, small town on a mountain

>**šancin fekumbi**: to storm a fortress

>**šancin jafambi**: to set up a fortress

šandumbi: to look at one another

šang: 1. bestowal, reward; 2. ⟶ **šangsin**

>**šang koro**: reward and punishment

šangga: endowed with ears

>**šangga cirku**: a pillow with ear-like projections on the side

šanggabuda: dried cooked rice

šanggabumbi: (causative of **šanggambi**)

šanggambi: 1. to come to an end, to terminate successfully, to finish; 2. to be accomplished

>**šanggaha bithei niyalma**: an accomplished scholar

>**šanggaha doro**: success

>**šanggaha gebu**: honor, well-deserved renown

>**šanggaha gungge**: merit, feats

>**šanggame jabduha**: succeeded, terminated successfully

šanggan: completion, accomplishment, accomplished

>**šanggan i elioi**: one of the six minor pipes (music)

>**šanggan karulan**: karma, retribution

šanggatai: 1. finally, indeed, actually; 2. fully at an end, thoroughly completed

šanggin: the silver pheasant; cf. **šunggin gasha**

šanggiyakan: rather white, somewhat white

šanggiyakū: 1. smoke from a signal fire, smoke signal; 2. ⟶ **šanggiyari**

>**šanggiyakū dabumbi**: 1. to send up signal smoke; 2. to make smoke, to ward off insects

šanggiyambi: to smoke, to emit smoke

šanggiyan: **1**. smoke; **2**. white (in older texts); **3**. the seventh of the heaven's stems (庚); cf. **šanyan**

šanggiyan alan: white birch bark

šanggiyan bulehen: white crane

šanggiyan caise: deep-fried vermicelli made from salt water and flour

šanggiyan faha: the white of the eye

šanggiyan fekšun: alum

šanggiyan fulha: white poplar

šanggiyan fun i fi: chalk (for writing on a slate)

šanggiyan halu i sacima: a deep-fried cake made from sesame oil, fine flour, sugar, and sesame seeds

šanggiyan ija: a variety of small white gnat, sandfly

šanggiyan jiyoo bing: a baked cake made from sugar and flour

šanggiyan mursa: Chinese radish, daikon

šanggiyan niongniyaha: a wild goose that appears white in flight

šanggiyan nisiha: a small whitefish

šanggiyan selbete: *Artemisia lactiflora*: white mugwort

šanggiyan silenggi: 'white dew' — one of the twenty-four divisions of the solar year occurring on about the eighth of September

šanggiyan suiha: white artemisia

šanggiyan teišun: copper nickel alloy, white brass

šanggiyan ulhu: ermine; cf. **šanyan ulhu**

šanggiyari: smoke used for repelling insects

šangguhe: a name for the myna

šangka: **1**. silk gauze flaps on both sides on an ancient-style hat; **2**. halo around the sun; **3**. thinly sliced dried meat; cf. **šangkan**

šangka šombi: to rub vigorously with a copper coin that has been moistened — a method of treating certain diseases

šangka šufatu: an ancient-style hat with gauze flaps on either side

šangkan: dried meat, some dried product

šangkan nimaha: ⟶ **can nimaha**

šangkūra niongniyaha: *Anser anser*: graylag goose

šangnabumbi: (causative or passive of **šangnambi**)

šangnahan: reward, prize

šangnahan koro: rewards and punishments

šangnambi: **1**. to reward, to bestow; **2**. to give (from a superior to an inferior)

šangnan: reward, bestowal

šangsi enduri: the name of a deity sacrificed to in the shamanic shrine

šangsin: one of the notes of the classical pentatonic scale, sounding like *re* (the second note of the scale)

šangšaha: a basket made from willow branches

šangšangdeo: the legendary kalavinka bird

šaniori ilha: an exotic flower that blooms in autumn and resembles a wild goose in flight

šaniri ilha: 'white caltrop flower'

šaniya: hempen floss used for padding

šaniyalambi: to pad (with hempen floss)

šaniyambi: ⟶ **šaniyalambi**

šaniyaha hubtu: a long gown padded with hempen floss

šaniyangga: made from hempen floss, padded

šaniyangga etuku: clothing padded with hempen floss, clothing made from hempen cloth

šaniyangga mahatu: an ancient-style hat made from black grass linen

šanjin: tradesman, merchant

šantu: **1**. heel bone of cows; **2**. zinc; cf. **šanyan teišun**

šantu giranggi: ⟶ **šantu**

šanumbi: to look at one another; cf. **šandumbi**

šanyakan: rather white, somewhat white

šanyan: **1**. white; **2**. the seventh of the heaven's stems (庚); **3**. the hottest times of the summer; **4**. cf. **šanggiyan**

šanyan alan: white birch bark

šanyan bulehen: white crane; cf. **šeyelhen**

šanyan caise: ⟶ **šanggiyan caise**

šanyan dosimbi: to enter the hottest time of summer

šanyan faitan: a quail with a white stripe over its eyes

šanyan fatha: a name for the quail; cf. **mušu**

šanyan gaha: a white raven

šanyan garudai: a white phoenix

šanyan gincihiyan šugin: white lacquer

šanyan gūsai falga: (白旗甲) Bureau of the White Banner in the Board of War

šanyan gūsai fiyenten: (白旗司) Section of the White Banner

šanyan haksangga efen: a baked cake covered with sugar; cf. **šanggiyan jiyoo bing**

šanyan halu i sacima: ⟶ **šanggiyan halu i sacima**

šanyan ija: a small white gnat, a sandfly

šanyan konggolo: a name for the quail

šanyan kuwecihe: a white dove

šanyan meihetu: a white eel

šanyan mursa: Chinese radish, daikon

šanyan nisiha: a small freshwater fish with a white belly whose oil is used in lamps

šanyan samsu: a fine white linen

šanyan selbete: *Artemisia lactiflora*: white mugwort

šanyan sencehe: a name for the quail

šanyan silenggi: ⟶ **šanggiyan silenggi**

šanyan sišargan: the name of a small black bird with white spots

šanyan suiha: white artemisia, wild artemisia

šanyan suksuhu: a white sea swallow

šanyan šahūn: the Milky Way

šanyan šongkon: a white gyrfalcon; cf. **šongkon**

šanyan šošontu: an ancient-style head covering made from white silk

šanyan šungkeri baibula: the name of the paradise flycatcher in Jiangnan

šanyan tasha: a white tiger

šanyan tashangga kiru: a banner of the Imperial Escort, depicting the figure of a white tiger

šanyan teišun: zinc

šanyan ulhu: *Mustela erminea*: ermine, stoat

šanyan ulhūma: a white pheasant

šanyan ulhūmangga kiru: a banner of the Imperial Escort depicting the figure of a white pheasant

šanyan umiyaha: tapeworm, roundworm

šanyan weifutu: a white heron

šanyan yarha: a white panther

šanyangga cece: a kind of white silk gauze

šanyo: yam; cf. **larsenda**

šanyolambi: ⟶ **šayolambi**

šar seme: sympathetic, moved with sympathy, compassionate, moved emotionally, sorrowful, grieving

šar seme gosire mujilen: a sympathetic and loving heart, a compassionate heart

šara: exceedingly

šara fancaha: exceedingly annoyed

šara nimembi: to ache very much

šara yoo: venereal sore, skin lesion, pemphigus

šarambi: (-ka, -pi) to become white

šarhūmbi: to snow while the sun is shining dimly

šari: **1.** sow thistle: a lettuce-like plant with edible leaves and roots, plants of the genus *Sonchus*; **2.** bright, shining

šari gari: bright, snowy white

šari sele: red-hot iron

šari siri: gorgeous, splendid, brilliant (said of blossoms)

šari sogi: sow thistle; cf. **šari**

šari šari: bright, fresh and bright, glowing

šaribudari: Śāriputra

šaribumbi: (causative of **šarimbi**)

šaril: Buddhist relics

šarimbi: to smelt (iron), to refine

šaringga dabtangga loho: a steel sword

šaringgiyabumbi: (causative of **šaringgiyambi**)

šaringgiyambi: **1.** to clean, to scrape clean (an arrow-shaft); **2.** to expiate, to atone, to wipe out (a wrong or shame)

šarinjambi: to squint, to look while rolling the eyeballs, to look at someone while showing the whites of the eyes (as a sign of reproach)

šarišambi: to flash white, to light up, to go belly-up (said of fish)

šarman: śramaṇa, Buddhist monk

šartan: a tall tree with few branches

šaru: strips of dried raw meat

šaruk: the name of the myna in Buddhist scriptures

šasigan: ⟶ **šasihan**

šasigan sogi: a dish of stewed meat and vegetables

šasihalabumbi: (causative or passive of **šasihalambi**)

šasihalambi: **1.** to slap, to clap; **2.** to strike with a whip, to flog; **3.** to attack from the flank

šasihalame dosimbi: to advance from the side, to attack from the side

šasihan: soup, seasoned soup, soup made from meat and vegetables

šasihašambi: to slap repeatedly

šasinjimbi: ⟶ **šašanjambi**

šasišame dambi: to blow from the side (said of the wind), to cut (said of the wind)

šašabumbi: (causative or passive of **šašambi**)

šašajambi: ⟶ **šašanjambi**

šašambi: to be mixed up, to be in a mess

šašan: a sour soup made from bean paste and mixed vegetables

šašanjambi: to be confused, to be criss-crossed, to skirmish

    šašanjame leolembi: to carry on a a verbal skirmish, to debate

šašun: **1**. tinder, small pieces of wood used to start a fire; **2**. shred, piece; **3**. meat or fish paste

    šašun akū: soft, soggy, in shreds, in tatters, in pieces, in a pulp

    šašun akū meijebuhe: shattered to pieces

šašunakū: ⟶ **šašun akū**

šatan: sugar

    šatan ufa cai: tea mixed with sugar and flour

šatubumbi: (causative of **šatumbi**)

šatumbi: **1**. to polish, to scour; **2**. to polish a bow; **2**. to plate metal

    šature okto: a polishing compound

šaturnambi: to form an icy crust (on snow)

šayo: **1**. a vegetarian, a Buddhist, a Daoist; **2**. vegetarian food

    šayo dagilambi: to prepare vegetarian food

šayolambi: to abstain from meat, to keep a vegetarian diet

šayu: ⟶ **šayo**

    šayu buda: vegetarian food

    šayu sogi: a vegetarian dish

še: **1**. amnesty; **2**. the earth god; **3**. a Chinese psaltery, a musical instrument of twenty-five strings; **4**. a name for the black-eared kite; cf. **hiyebele**

šeben: a snare for lynx

šebnio: (參) a constellation, the 21st of the lunar mansions, made up of seven stars in Orion

    šebnio tokdonggo kiru: a banner depicting the constellation Orion

šebtembi: to be soaked through and through, to become soaked, to become drenched with sweat

šehuken: rather barren

šehun: **1**. bright, well-lit, bright and spacious; **2**. barren, forsaken; **3**. vast, extensive, broad; **4**. cf. **gehun šehun**

    šehun šahūn: barren and desolate

    šehun tala: bare steppe

šeji: gods of earth and grain

šejilebumbi: (causative of **šejilembi**)

šejilembi: to recite, to repeat by heart

šekebumbi: (causative or passive of **šekembi**)

šekembi: **1**. to get drenched, to get soaked; **2**. to become stiff

šelbori orho: *Helleborus thibetanus*: hellebore

šelembi: **1**. to part with, to give up; **2**. to give (alms), to distribute

šelen: the continually wet area around a small spring

šelenembi: to go to risk one's life

šeletei: without regard to life, disregarding danger

šempi: green grained leather

šempilebumbi: (causative of **šempilembi**)

šempilembi: to hem with (green) grained leather

šeng: **1**. a Chinese wind instrument consisting of a number of small pipes with metallic reeds; **2**. a Chinese plant (竹); **3**. nephew; cf. **ina**

šengge: **1**. divine, prophetic; **2**. wonderful, magical; **3**. prophet, seer

    šengge hūsun: extraordinary strength

    šengge jui: prodigy, wonder child

    šengge saksaha: prophetic magpie that announces joyful events by its cry beforehand

šenggeci ilha: the name of a beautiful exotic flower that blooms from spring to autumn

šenggehen: a name for the crane; cf. **bulehen**

šenggen moo: a five hundred-year-old tree

šenggetu: the name of a divine beast that foresees the future

šenggetungge kiru: a banner of the Imperial Escort that depicts the figure of a **šenggetu**

šenggi: ⟶ **šenggin**

šenggin: **1**. forehead; **2**. the place where the foot of a mountain and a river meet; **3**. a brick that projects forward above the door of a stove; **4**. eaves of a house

    šenggin gaimbi: to hit lightly on the forehead, to tap on the forehead

    šenggin hiterembi: to knit the brow, to frown

šenggintu: an ancient-style square headband (decorated with lacquer and gold)

šenggiyen boso: undyed cloth

šengkiri: *Achillea millefolium*: yarrow, milfoil

    šengkiri hiyan: rue

šengkitu: one of the names of the fabulous beast called **tontu**

šengsin: geomancy

> **šengsin i siren**: a geomantic vein
>
> **šengsin tuwambi**: to practice geomancy
>
> **šengsin tuwara niyalma**: a geomancer

šentu: a wide cloth belt, a strip of cloth

šentuhen: ⟶ **šetuhen**

šeo ben: a name card presented by inferiors to superiors

šeo giowan: a scroll

šeo seme: (onomatopoetic) the sound of wind blowing, soughing

šeo seme dambi: to blow in sharp gusts

šeo sing enduri: the god of the star of long life

šeo ša: (onomatopoetic) the sound made by the wind blowing

šeo šeo: in gusts

šeo teo: a mask shaped like an animal's head

šeobei: (守備) Second Captain; cf. **tuwakiyara hafan**

šeolebumbi: (causative of **šeolembi**)

šeolehun: ⟶ **šulehen**

šeolembi: **1**. to embroider; **2**. to collect

šeolen: embroidery

> **šeolen bojiri ilha**: the name of a ragged purple chrysanthemum

šeoteo: ⟶ **šeo teo**

šercembi: to feel dizzy at a height, to feel frightened on a high place

šerebumbi: (causative of **šerembi**)

šerembi: (**-ke**) **1**. to glow, to be red-hot; **2**. to be white, to turn pale

šerembumbi: (causative of **šerembi**)

šerentumbi: to suffer labor pains before childbirth, to be on the point of giving birth

šerhe: a dogsled

šeri: spring, source (of water)

> **šeri muke**: spring water
>
> **šeri sen**: the center of the sole of the foot
>
> **šeri uju**: springhead, fountainhead

šeribumbi: (causative or passive of **šerimbi**)

šerikulebumbi: (causative or passive of **šerikulembi**)

šerikulembi: to intimidate, to coerce, to threaten

šerimbi: to extort, to blackmail, to threaten, to coerce

šerin: **1**. a protective piece for the forehead on a helmet; **2**. a golden figure of a Buddha on the front of a Prince's hat

šeringgiyembi: to heat until red-hot

šerinju: a blackmailer, intimidator

šersen inggali: the name of a small bird that has white spots on its tail

šertu: a die made of copper or tin, a copper or tin **gacuha**

šesimbi: ⟶ **šešembi**

šesimpe: ⟶ **šešempe**

šesimpu: ⟶ **šešempe**

šešebumbi: (causative of **šešembi**)

šešembi: to sting (said of insects), to bite (said of a snake)

šešempe: a wasp

šešenembi: to sting, to bite (said of a snake)

šešeri umiyaha: a centipede

šetehuri: dense, solid, thick

šeterembi: (**-ke**) to come to life (said of drooping plants after a rain)

šeteršembi: to reel under a heavy load, to be bent over from carrying a heavy load

šetuhen: a twenty-five-stringed zither-like instrument, a Chinese psaltery; cf. **še**

šetumbi: to swim (said of snakes)

šeyehen ulhūma: silver pheasant; cf. **šunggin gasha**

šeyeke: *Luscina calliope*: female rubythroat

šeyeken: rather white, somewhat white

šeyelhen: a kind of small white crane

šeyen: pure white, spotlessly white, snow-white

> **šeyen gu**: white jade
>
> **šeyen hiyaban**: white coarse linen
>
> **šeyen mederi**: the Milky Way

ši: **1**. a measure equaling one hundred twenty catties; **2**. poem, verse; **3**. army; **4**. examination; **5**. scholar, official

ši cing: azurite

šicing: celadonite

šidu: (侍讀); ⟶ **adaha hūlara hafan**

šidz: **1**. the heir of a feudal lord; **2**. the eldest son of a Manchu Prince of the first rank

šifu: ⟶ **sefu**

šigiyamuni: Sākyamuni

šigiyang: (侍講) a Hanlin official of the fifth rank second class

šilgiyan: (室) a constellation, the 13th of the lunar mansions, made up of two stars (α, β) in Pegasus

> **šilgiyan tokdonggo kiru**: a banner depicting the constellation **šilgiyan**

šilio: pomegranate; cf. **useri**

    šilio moo: pomegranate tree

šo: bureau, office

šo ilha: lotus

šo niyecen: the crotch of trousers

šobin: a baked sesame cake

šobkošombi: **1**. to eat with the hands; **2**. to behave uncouthly, to act meanly or basely

    šobkošome derakū: shameless

    šobkošome jembi: to eat with the fingers

šobumbi: (causative of **šombi**)

šodan ilha: *Paeonia albiflora*: Chinese peony

šodobumbi: (causative of **šodombi**)

šodokū: **1**. a person who likes to stroll; **2**. a small fish net

šodombi: **1**. to stroll, to stroll about at leisure; **2**. to catch fish in a small hand net; **3**. to go at a full gallop; **4**. to pan (gold)

šofor seme: in great haste, flustered, agitated

šoforo: **1**. a pinch of something; **2**. one ten-thousandth of a bushel

    šoforo akū: not sure-footed (said of horses)

    šoforo cecike: a name for the kingfisher; cf. **ulgiyan cecike**

    šoforo sain: sure-footed (said of horses)

šoforobumbi: (causative of **šoforombi**)

šoforokū sele: an anchor

šoforombi: **1**. to pick up with the fingers, to take a pinch of; **2**. to seize in the claws (said of birds); **3**. to scratch

šoforonjimbi: to come to take a pinch of, to come to seize

šoforšombi: to scratch all over, to take random pinches of

šofoyon: narrow-minded, petty-minded, quick-tempered

šoge: ingot of gold or silver

šohadambi: **1**. to hitch an extra horse to a cart or a plow; **2**. to depend on others to do one's work

šohan i morin: a horse or ox added to a team pulling a plow or cart

šoho: the white of an egg, albumin

šohodombi: to drift about, to loaf about

šokin niyehe: a name for the wild duck

šokisilambi: ⟶ **šokšolimbi**

šokšohon: **1**. sharp (said of a mountain peak), prominent (said of a peak); **2**. pursed (the lips, when angry), pouting

šokšolimbi: to heap up, to fill up completely

šokū: a currycomb

    šokū amdun: glue made into squares used for erasing or scraping

šolen: ⟶ **šošon**

šoli: falling short, short of the mark

šolo: **1**. free time, leisure, vacation, leave; **2**. opportunity; **3**. empty space

    šolo akū: without leisure, lacking free time, busy

    šolo amcambi: to take advantage of an opportunity

    šolo bahambi: to find time, to find an opportunity

    šolo baimbi: to ask for leave, to seek free time

    šolo baita: other people's business

    šolo be tuwame: as time permits

    šolo bumbi: to grant leave

    šolo jabdurakū: not to have time

    šolo jalgiyambi: to find time to do something

    šolo jalgiyanjambi: ⟶ **šolo jalgiyambi**

    šolo šolo de: in one's spare time, when unoccupied, at leisure

    šolo tuciburakū: without giving a pause

    šolo yabumbi: to be at leisure

šolobumbi: (causative of **šolombi**)

šolombi: to roast, to cook on a skewer

šolon: **1**. fork; **2**. skewer (for roasting meat); **3**. a sharpened wood or metal object for stabbing or pricking something

šolonggo: **1**. pointed, forked; **2**. point, tip; **3**. adept (at war, hunting, archery), out in front (said of one's competitors at war, hunting, etc.)

    šolonggo mafuta: a two-year-old deer

    šolonggo sacikū: a pickax used for digging in frozen or very hard soil

šolontu: a small-horned dragon

    šolontu cohoro: a spotted horse with pointed ears

šombi: (**-ha**) **1**. to scrape, to scrape off, to level off; **2**. to curry (livestock)

šongge: the phase of the moon on the first day of the lunar month

    šongge biya: synodic month

šongge inenggi: the first day of the month (lunar)

šonggon: ⟶ **šongkon**

šongkon: *Falco peregrinus*: the peregrine falcon

    šongkon gasha: another name of the **šongkon**

    šongkon ija: a thin-waisted insect (somewhat longer than a sandfly) that catches flies

šongkoro: another name for the **šongkon**

šontohojombi: ⟶ **contohojombi**

šonumbi: to scrape together, to curry together

šoo kumun: an eight-strophe piece of music played while the Emperor returned to the palace or went to the throne room

šooboo: (少保) Junior Guardian, *BH* 943

šoofu: (少傅) Junior Tutor (an honorary title bestowed on meritorious officials, *BH* 943)

šooge: hard feathers at the tips of the wings

šooha: heavy rope, hawser; cf. **gūsu**

šooši: (少師) Junior Preceptor — an honorary title bestowed on meritorious officials, *BH* 943

šor seme: briskly, lively, noisily

    šor seme agambi: to rain noisily

šor šar: (onomatopoetic) the sound of a storm, the sound of wind and rain

šor šor seme: (onomatopoetic) rushing, roaring

šordai: the concave side of a **gacuha**

šorgibumbi: (causative or passive of **šorgimbi**)

šorgikū: a drill

šorgimbi: **1**. to urge, to press; **2**. to drill, to bore; **3**. to strike in one place (said of arrows); **4**. to wash out, to wash away

    šorgime gaimbi: to exact payment (of a debt)

šorginambi: to go to urge

šorgindumbi: to urge together; also **šorginumbi**

šorginjimbi: to come to urge

šorginumbi: to urge together; also **šorgindumbi**

šorho: chick

šori: a straw container for holding rice; cf. **šoro**

šorimbi: to oppress (said of heat)

    šorime halhūn: oppressively hot

šoro: a basket made of bamboo or small branches

    šoro sele: a small knife without a scabbard worn at the belt

šoron: the young of pheasants, ducks, and geese

šoronggo dalangga: a dam consisting of rock-filled baskets

šosihi: ⟶ **šosiki**

šosiki: **1**. quick-tempered, irascible; **2**. *Eutamius sibiricus*: chipmunk

šosin: hinge (on a door or a fodder knife), pivot, rotation axis

šositun: the North China mole

šošobumbi: (causative of **šošombi**)

šošohon: **1**. total, sum; **2**. summa, compilation, outline; **3**. result, conclusion; **4**. general principle

    šošohon i ba: a place where roads meet, a hub, a center of operations

    šošohon ton: total number

    šošohon tucibumbi: to come to a conclusion

šošohūn: ⟶ **šošohon**

šošokū: false hair encased in a net (worn by Chinese women)

šošombi: **1**. to compile, to summarize, to add up, to add together; **2**. to wrap one's hair with a net or cloth, to put up one's hair in a bun; **3**. to defecate (said of falcons, eagles, etc.)

šošon: **1**. summary, abstract; **2**. chignon, bun; **3**. falcon or eagle feces

    šošon halgimbi: to put up one's hair in a chignon or bun

    šošon i weren: a hair-ornament made of wire and worn by Manchu women

šošonggo mahala: an ancient-style hat worn to keep a hairdo in place

šošontu: ⟶ **šanyan šošontu**

šošosi: a petty official in charge of keeping account books

šoyobumbi: (causative of **soyombi**)

šoyohūn: shrunken, wrinkled

šoyoljombi: **1**. to curl upward, to spiral upward (said of smoke); **2**. to sway, to swing

šoyombi: to shrink, to wrinkle, to contract, to draw back

šoyoshūn: rather wrinkled, rather shrunken

šu: **1**. refinement, culture, learning; **2**. refined, elegant, educated; **3**. magnificent, well-ordered, beautiful; **4**. office, bureau; **5**. uncle: father's younger brother; **6**. lotus; cf. **šu ilha**; **7**. saltpeter

    šu akū: uncultured, uneducated

    šu be badarambure temgetu: a standard of the Imperial Escort with words **šu be badarambure** written on it

šu bithe: a vow written on yellow paper that was read before a deity and then burned

šu erdemu: education, enlightenment

šu fiyelen: essay, article

šu genggiyen: cultured and enlightened

šu gi ši: (庶吉士); ⟶ **geren giltusi**

šu horonggo: civil and military prowess

šu i belheku: writing materials: paper, brush, and ink

šu i icihiyakū: (署正) President of the Court of Banqueting

šu i suhen: commentary

šu i suihon i bithe icihiyara kuren: (文穎館) an office in charge of compiling literary anthologies

šu i temgetu: a private seal

šu ilha: *Nelumbo nucifera*: lotus

šu ilha fulehe: lotus root

šu ilhai da: edible lotus root

šu ilhai hitha: seed pod of a lotus

šu ilhai omo: lotus pond

šu imiyaha tanggin: (聚奎堂) the name of a two-storied hall in the Examination Halls

šu jamuri ilha: a kind of hedge rose that resembles the lotus

šu tacin: cultured ways or habits, culture, education

šu yangsangga: well-ordered and beautiful

šu yangse: elegant, comely

šu yangse gemun hecen de wesihun ojoro mudan: musical composition played while the Emperor attended a banquet for the Hanlin academy

šu yuwan: academy (of classical learning)

šu žin: (碩人) beautiful woman

šuban: petty clerk, scribe

šubasa: (plural of **šuban**)

šuberembi: ⟶ **siberembi**

šubumbi: (causative of **šumbi**)

šuburembi: (-ke) **1**. to wilt in the sun; **2**. to go bad (said of a horse's hoof)

šuburi: timid, retiring, a timid person

šuburšembi: **1**. to shrink; **2**. to be timid, to fear to put oneself forward, to shrink back; **3**. to be solicitous (about children)

šuceri ilha: an exotic purple flower that blooms in the fourth month

šuci: one who pretends to know what he in fact does not

šucilembi: to pretend to know something that in fact one does not, to feign knowledge

šucileme usucilembi: to pretend to knowledge, to speak nonsense

šudacan yali: pieces of meat and fat roasted together on a skewer

šudangga coko: a name for the chicken

šudehen: ⟶ **sidehun**

šudembi: **1**. to defame, to calumniate; **2**. to give a far-fetched explanation

šudesi: a scribe, a secretary, a clerk

šudesi be baicara kunggeri: (典史科) section of clerks in the Board of Civil Appointments

šudesi be kadalara kunggeri: (都吏科) section in charge of clerks in the Boards of Civil Appointments, Works, and War

šudesi oron i kunggeri: (書缺科) section of clerks in the Board of Works

šudu: **1**. fodder bean; **2**. ⟶ **šudun**

šudu eriku: broom

šudubumbi: (causative or passive of **šudumbi**)

šudukū: a weeding hoe

šudumbi: (-ha) **1**. to shovel, to dredge; **2**. to scrape smooth (a hide), to level off; **3**. to scratch, to abrade; **4**. to weed

šudure jahūdai: a boat used for carrying off sludge from dredging

šudun: scraping, shoveling, dredging

šudun i weihe: the front teeth

šuduran ilha: a small exotic yellow flower that blooms at the end of spring

šudure: ⟶ **šudumbi** (subheading)

šudz: (庶子) Deputy Supervisor of Instruction, *BH* 929

šufa: **1**. handkerchief (sometimes with a fringe on two sides); **2**. in the older language, **šufa** meant head covering, turban; cf. **šufari**, **šufatu**

šufabumbi: (causative or passive of **šufambi**)

šufambi: **1**. to collect, to gather together; **2**. to fold, to pleat, to crease; **3**. to sting, to bite (said of insects); **4**. to take an equal portion or share, to put in an equal share

šufaha hūsihan: pleated skirt

šufan: wrinkle, crease, fold, pleat

šufan jafambi: **1**. to get creased, to get wrinkled; **2**. to pleat, to make pleats

šufanambi: to become creased, to be folded, to be wrinkled

šufangga salu: a full beard

šufari: a head wrapping used by women

šufasu: a hairnet worn under a hat (ancient style)

šufatu: a cloth head covering, a turban

šufin: flour made from lotus root

šufur seme: (onomatopoetic) hissing, whizzing

šufuršembi: ⟶ **fusur seme**

šufuyen: ⟶ **šofoyon**

šugi: **1**. bodily fluid, clear secretion from a wound; **2**. juice (from fruit); **3**. sap from trees; **4**. sweets made from fruit juice

šugi gaimbi: to extract juice or liquid

šugi umgan: bone marrow

šugilebumbi: (causative of **šugilembi**)

šugilembi: to apply lacquer

šugin: **1**. (liquid) lacquer, paint; **2**. hand towel

šugin dosimbuha iletu kiyoo: a gold-lacquered open sedan chair

šugin moo: *Rhus vernicifera*: the lacquer tree

šugingge hasi: a variety of wild persimmon

šugiri: frankincense

šugiri hiyan: **1**. frankincense; **2**. the tree *Pistacia lentisens* from which a kind of pseudo-lacquer is made

šuguri: ⟶ **šuhuri**

šuhi: ⟶ **šugi**

šuhudu: **1**. a variety of pink hawthorn; **2**. a variety of *Dalbergia*

šuhuri: **1**. buckwheat husks; **2**. scab (from smallpox)

šuhuri sihambi: to lose a scab (said of one who has smallpox)

šuhūra: gallnut, oak gall, a growth produced on various kinds of oak

šui gioi cuwan: a flat barge hauling goods

šui jing: crystal

šuijin: crystal

šujin: a name for the peacock; cf. **tojin**

šukdun: ⟶ **siden**

šukibumbi: (causative or passive of **šukimbi**)

šukilabumbi: (causative of **šukilambi**)

šukilambi: to beat with the fist, to strike with the horns (cows, sheep, etc.), to knock against, to butt

šukimbi: (**-ha**) **1**. to put in a dangerous position, to ensnare, to bring harm to; **2**. to put oneself in harm's way

šukišambi: **1**. to strike at random with the fists, to strike one another with the fists; **2**. to butt repeatedly; **3**. to butt one another

šukšuhun: ⟶ **šokšohon**

šukumbi: to sit with the legs outstretched

šukun: the two notches on the end of a bow

šula: **1**. juice (of fruit); **2**. pus, discharge

šulaburu yengguhe: a kind of parrot with a red head and reddish brown shoulders and breast

šulderi tubihe: a fig-like fruit that ripens in the fifth month and tastes like a sweet chestnut

šulebumbi: (causative of **šulembi**)

šulehelembi: to gather, to collect (taxes)

šulehen: **1**. land tax; **2**. collection, taxation

šulehen be eberebumbi: to reduce the land tax

šulembi: **1**. to collect (taxes); **2**. ⟶ **šeolembi**

šuler: ⟶ **šošon**

šulge: ⟶ **šulhe**

šulhe: pear

šulhe i belge: the core of a pear

šulheri: an exotic pear-like yellow fruit having a somewhat sour taste

šulhumbi: to escape from a net

šulhū: wicker or bamboo box

šulihun: **1**. pointed, thick at the base but narrow at the end; **2**. a point

šulihun enggemu: a saddle with a pointed bow

šulihun gūlha: pointed boots

šulihun yoro: an arrow having a five-sided bone and horn head that contains five holes

šulimbi: to twitter

šulin cecike: one of the names of the oriole; cf. **gūlin cecike**

šulmen: strips of dried meat

šulu: hair on the temples, the temples at the side of the head

šulubumbi: **1**. (causative or passive of **šulumbi**); **2**. to suffer hardship or adversity

šulumbi: (**-ha**) to mistreat, to harass (subordinates), to make suffer

šulun: ⟶ **silun**

šuma: ⟶ **šuman**

šumacuka: ⟶ **simacuka**

šuman: the male sexual organs of livestock

šumbi: (**-ngke, -mpi**) to be thoroughly acquainted with, to be well-versed in, to know thoroughly

šumci: sunken, sunken out of sight, underwater, submerged

    šumci dosimbi: to sink out of sight

    šumci genembi: to sink, to fall

šumga: ⟶ **šumgan**

šumgan: **1**. crucible for precious metals; **2**. a container for gunpowder, powder flask

    šumgan gocimbi: to set a small crucible containing fire over a sore spot

šumgiya gasha: a name for the spotted kingfisher; cf. **cunggai**

šumhun: ⟶ **simhun**

šumikan: rather deep, somewhat deep

šumilambi: to do in a profound way, to become deep

    šumilame bodombi: to ponder deeply

    šumilame sibkimbi: to study deeply

šumilembi: ⟶ **šumilambi**

šumin: deep

    šumin boo: boudoir, woman's bedroom

    šumin dobori: in the deep of night

    šumin etuku: clothing for a dead person

    šumin micihiyan: deep and shallow, depth

    šumin seolembi: to ponder deeply

šumpulu: powerless, without support

šun: **1**. sun; **2**. day

    šun be aitubumbi: to pray for deliverance from harm during a solar eclipse (a Chinese rite)

    šun be jembi: there is an eclipse of the sun

    šun be tuwara kemneku: the name of a gnomon in the Beijing observatory

    šun buncuhūn: the sunlight is weak

    šun dabsiha: the sun is on the (western) horizon

    šun dalikū: a (ceremonial) parasol

    šun dalikū i fiyenten: (扇手司) Fan Section (of the Equipage Department)

    šun dekdeke: the sun has risen

    šun dekdere ergi: the east

    šun dosika: the sun has set

    šun dosire ergi: the west

    šun dositala: all day (until the sun sets)

    šun dulimba abka de eldere mudan: a piece of music performed during banquets for meritorious generals and officials

šun halangga: 'of the sun clan' — epithet of the Buddha

šun helmen tuwara tanggin: (暑影堂) hall of the gnomon near the observatory

šun hūcihingga: related to the sun — epithet of the Buddha

šun i foson: sunlight, sunbeam

šun i kemun: a sundial

šun i kiru: a blue banner of the Imperial Escort embroidered with a representation of the sun

šun ibkaka: the days have become shorter (after midsummer)

šun jembi: to have an eclipse of the sun

šun kelfike: the sun has begun to decline

šun kūwaraha: the sun has a ring around it

šun mukdehun: altar to the sun

šun mukdeke: the sun came up

šun niyancambi: the sun shines warmly

šun sangka: the days have lengthened (after midwinter)

šun sidaraka: ⟶ **šun sangka**

šun simen: power or influence of the sun

šun šangga: 'the sun is eared' — i.e., the sun has a rainbow near it

šun šangka: sun prominence (seen on the edge of a solar eclipse)

šun tob: directly opposite the sun — the south

šun tucike: the sun came out

šun tuheke: the sun set

šun tuhere ergi: the west

šun tuhetele: all day — until the sun sets

šun urhuhe: the sun is about to set, the sun is low on the horizon

šunembi: to go wild, to become overgrown (with weeds)

    šunehe ba: an overgrown area

    šunehe orho: weeds

šung šang: (onomatopoetic) the sound of a sleeping person's breathing

šungga hiyan: a fragrance made of osmanthus

šungga ilha: *Osmanthus fragrans*: osmanthus, a fragrant small white flower

šungga moo: **1**. osmanthus tree or bush; **2**. cassia-bark tree (*Cinnamonum aromaticum*)

šunggaci ilha: spring osmanthus — an osmanthus-like flower that blooms in the third month šunggaya: ⟶ šunggayan

šunggayan: tall and slender, lanky, long and slender (said of a hand)

šunggayan beye: slender figure

šungge: **1**. learned, educated, enlightened, wise; **2**. fine-grained

šungge moo: a kind of tree that grows in the mountains and produces a fine-grained, shiny, yellow wood

šungge tubihe: *Xanthoseras sorbifolium*: shiny-leaf yellowthorn

šunggeri: elegant, fine, graceful, in good taste

šunggidei: a name for the golden pheasant; cf. **junggiri coko**

šunggin gasha: a name for the silver pheasant (*Lophura nycthemera*); cf. **be hiyan**

šunggiya: elegant, gracious, in good taste

šunggiyada ilha: narcissus, flowers in the genus *Narcissus*

šunggiyambi: to throw all about

šungke: **1**. perfect participle of **šumbi**; **2**. enlightened, knowledgeable, well-versed; cf. **šungge**

šungkeci ilha: a very fragrant jasmine-like flower of Sichuan

šungken: enlightenment, education, refinement

šungkenembi: to be enlightened, to be well-versed

šungkeri: refined, elegant

šungkeri gūwara: a name for the eared owl; cf. **fu gūwara**

šungkeri hiyan: *Eupatorium Chinense*: hemp agrinomy

šungkeri ilha: *Cymbidium goeringii*: Chinese orchid

šungkon: ⟶ šongkon

šungku: the depression on a man's face just below the lips

šungkubumbi: (causative or passive of **šungkumbi**)

šungkulu: the part of a beard that grows below the lips

šungkumbi: to sink, to subside, to cave in, to sink inward

šungkutu: sunken, depressed, having deep-set eyes, having cavernous eyes

šungsi: ⟶ **bithei šungsi**

šungšun šangšan: speaking through the nose (having a distinct nasal quality in one's speech)

šuntuhule: all day, until sundown

šuntuhuni: ⟶ šuntuhule

šuo: ⟶ šuwe

šurdebuku: windlass, pulley

šurdebumbi: (causative or passive of **šurdembi**)

šurdebure tatakū: a large water wheel used for bringing water from a low place to a higher place

šurdehen: circumference, circuit, circular course

šurdehen cincilan i usiha be acabure durungga tetun: an armillary sphere of the Beijing observatory

šurdejen: ⟶ **abkai šurdejen usiha**

šurdeku: **1**. circumference; **2**. ring, circle; **3**. axle, axis, pivot; **4**. vortex; **5**. a ring attached to the feet of falcons to keep the foot fetters from getting knotted; **6**. ring clasp on a belt

šurdeku muke: a whirlpool, a vortex

šurdembi: **1**. to revolve, to spin; **2**. to go around, to encircle; **3**. to go by turns, to alternate

šurdeme: (postpostion) around

šurdeme afambi: to surround and attack

šurdeme forgošombi: to wind, to circle

šurdeme ukumbi: to surround, to encircle

šurdere dangse i ba: (循還處) control office for coinage in the Board of Finance

šurdere dangse i boo: (循還房) office in charge of making alloys of copper, tin, and zinc in the Board of Works

šurdere nanggin: a winding corridor (in a garden or around a pavilion)

šurdere šusihe: a tally passed on to a relief on some rotating function

šurdere usiha i fukjingga hergen: (轉宿篆) a style of Chinese calligraphy

šurden: **1**. rotation, spinning, swirling; **2**. a ring

šurdenumbi: to encompass one another, to go around one another

šurdere: ⟶ **šurdembi** (subheading)

šurga: **1**. snow blown by the wind; **2**. blowing sand

šurgabumbi: (causative of **šurgambi**)

šurgambi: to blow (said of snow or sand in heavy wind)

šurgan: a three-year-old tiger

šurgan tasha: ⟶ **šurgan**

šurgebumbi: (causative of **šurgembi**)

šurgecembi: to tremble all over, to shiver with cold

šurgembi: to shake, to tremble

> **šurgeme dargimbi**: to shake and tremble

> **šurgeme geleme**: trembling with fright

šurha: a two-year-old wild pig

šurhū: a chick

šurhūn: a name for the chicken, a half-grown chicken

šurteku: copper or tin forks held between the fingers when playing with the **gacuha**; cf. **cohoto**

šurtuku yoo: anal fistula

šuru: **1**. the distance between the thumb and the index finger, a span; **2**. coral; **3**. paper strips tied to the end of a pole that were offered to the gods at the beginning of a child's studies; **4**. heavy (said of a child's weight); **5**. strips of dried meat

> **šuru cecike**: the 'coral bird' that resembles the myna

šurubumbi: (causative of **šurumbi**)

> **šurubuha sele**: twisted iron nailed onto armor

šuruci: boatman, sailor

šurukū: **1**. a punting pole; **2**. a lathe

šurumbi: (-ha) **1**. to spin, to peel off the skin of fruit in a spiral; **2**. to make on a lathe, to drill; **3**. to punt (a boat); **4**. to cut the meat of game into strips

> **šurure faksi**: lathe operator

šurun: a young quail

šurusi: boatman, punter

šusai: **1**. (秀才, 生員) Licentiate — the first literary degree, *BH* 629A; **2**. student, young scholar

šusebuku: **1**. a border or horizontal strip hanging from the top of a curtain, a drapery, or a parasol; **2**. fringe, border, edging; **3**. a bedspread

šusembi: **1**. to slide down, to slip down; **2**. to draw from underneath

> **šuseme tatambi**: to pull out from underneath (an arrow from a quiver), to draw from below

> **šuseme wasibumbi**: to lower from a high place to a lower place

> **šuseme wasimbi**: to slide down, to lower oneself from a high place to a lower place, to shinny down a rope

šusha: a tiger with five claws

šusi ilha: a yellow flower that blooms in the summer, resembling the iris

šusige: ⟶ **šusihe**

šusiha: a whip

> **šusiha guwembumbi**: to make a whip sing

šusihalabumbi: (causative of **šusihalambi**)

šusihalambi: to whip, to flog, to beat with a whip

šusihangga usiha: the name of a constellation (策)

šusihašambi: to beat repeatedly with a whip

šusihe: **1**. a square piece of wood used for writing, a piece of wood with writing on it; **2**. a sign, voucher, attestation, wooden tablet

> **šusihe baicambi**: to check a certificate of merit (certificates given to soldiers for meritorious service)

> **šusihe temgetu bithe**: Imperial patent

šusihiyebumbi: (causative or passive of **šusihiyembi**)

šusihiyembi: to incite, to sow discord, to foment dissension

šusilabumbi: (causative of **šusilambi**)

šusilambi: to whip, to flog

šusilebumbi: (causative of **šusilembi**)

šusilembi: to chisel, to make holes with a chisel

šusin: a chisel

šusiniyambi: to speak in a low voice, to whisper; cf. **šušuniyambi**

šusintu: a kind of ancient chisel

šusu: **1**. provisions for travel; **2**. offerings prepared for a sacrifice or shamanistic ceremony

šusuncambi: to whisper, to hum

šusungga: pertaining to provisions or offerings

šušan: a small hoe-shaped implement for scraping the sides of pots

šušembi: to look everywhere for, to rummage through, to ransack

šušu: **1**. purple; **2**. *Andropogon sorghum*: sorghum, *gāoliáng* 高粱

> **šušu baibula**: the male paradise flycatcher

> **šušu calihūn**: the name of a small red bird — the '*gāoliáng* bird'

> **šušu jilhangga ilha**: the name of an exotic purple flower that grows on a plant with long stalks and pointed leaves

> **šušu orho**: sorghum

> **šušu sogi**: edible seaweed, nori, laver, various edible sea algae in the genus *Porphyra*

šušu sukdungga usiha: (紫氣星) the name of a constellation

šušu šakšaha: a purple-colored quail

šušu ujungga alhacan niyehe: a speckled duck with a purple head

šušu yarukū: a lure for crayfish consisting of a rope with sorghum ears attached to it

šušu šaša: (onomatopoetic) whispering, speaking softly

šušun ilha: *Ipomoea cordatotriloba*: purple bindweed, little purple morning glory

šušungge kiltan: a purple pennant of the Imperial Escort

šušunggiyambi: to whisper, to hum

šušuniyembi: ⟶ **šušunggiyambi**

šušunjambi: to whisper

šušurgan ilha: the blossom of the Chinese redbud (*Cercis chinensis*)

šušuri: the name of a sweet purple fruit

šušuri mašari: meticulous, fussy

šutucin: preface; cf. **sioi**

šutugi ilha: an exotic purple flower with five petals and long pointed leaves

šutuha: ⟶ **šutumbi** (subheading)

šutuhutele: ⟶ **šuntuhule**

šutumbi: (-ha) to grow up gradually; cf. **situmbi**

    šutuha fulhun: one of the six minor pipes

šuwa: dense forest on the north side of a mountain; cf. **ša**

šuwai fu: (帥府) commander

šuwai seme: tall and slender, lank, long and slender

šuwak: (onomatopoetic) the sound of hitting with a whip

    šuwak sik: (onomatopoetic) the sound of several whips striking

šuwang lu: ⟶ **šuwanglu**

šuwangkiyambi: to bite, to eat grass

šuwanglio: ⟶ **šuwanglu**

šuwanglu: 'double six' — a board game at which thirty-two pieces were used

šuwanglulambi: to play the game **šuwanglu**

šuwangšuwangdeo: ⟶ **šangšangdeo**

šuwar: (onomatopoetic) the sound of a sword being drawn from a scabbard, a snake moving rapidly, or an arrow passing through the air

šuwar sir seme: agile (in climbing trees)

šuwarang seme: long and thin

šuwarkiyalabumbi: (causative or passive of **šuwarkiyalambi**)

šuwarkiyalambi: to beat with the heavy staff (an official punishment), the same as **janglambi**

šuwarkiyan: **1.** bramble branches that were used for weaving baskets; **2.** a dried-up branch or twig; **3.** a heavy staff used for flogging

    šuwarkiyan tantambi: to flog with a staff

    šuwarkiyan unumbi: 'to proffer a birch and ask to be flogged' — to offer a humble and sincere apology

šuwarkiyatambi: to flog continuously

šuwaršagiyambi: ⟶ **šuwarkiyalambi**

šuwase: **1.** brush; **2.** fringe

šuwaselabumbi: (causative of **šuwaselambi**)

šuwaselambi: **1.** to print; **2.** to brush

šuwaselembi: to brush

šuwasilembi: ⟶ **šusilembi**

šuwe: **1.** directly, straight, straightaway, totally; **2.** (with negatives) not at all, not in the least; **3.** to a high degree, most

    šuwe hafu: thoroughly versed in, having a comprehensive knowledge of

    šuwe hafumbi: to understand thoroughly, to be well-versed in

    šuwe onggoho: completely forgot

    šuwe uihe beri: a bow made from one horn

šuwefun: thorough realization, clear understanding

    šuwefun hafu: completely versed in something

šuwesin: ⟶ **šusin**

šuyen: **1.** a hole made in the ice of a river or lake for watering livestock and procuring water for household use; **2.** a small hole at the foot of a riverbank

šüngge: ⟶ **šungge**

šürgeku: reel, spool

T ᠊ᡦ ᡦ

For words beginning with **ts**, see the section beginning on page 381.

ta: lamb (in the *Shijing*)

ta seme: **1**. often, continually, uninterruptedly; **2**. (onomatopoetic) the sound of a small bell

ta ti seme: **1**. (onomatopoetic) the sound of a group working energetically; **2**. dripping profusely

tab: upright, regular

tab seme: **1**. (onomatopoetic) the sound of a bowstring hitting the back of the bow; **2**. (onomatopoetic) the sound of water dripping; **3**. (jumped) right over

tab tab: the sound of dripping

tab tib: (onomatopoetic) the sound of dripping water

taba: the smooth side of a **gacuha**

tabarambi: to err, to make an error, to go astray

> **tabarame necimbi**: to affront, to offend unintentionally

tabcilabumbi: **1**. (causative or passive of **tabcilambi**); **2**. to have the bowstring graze the hand or face when shooting

tabcilambi: to plunder, to capture, to seize, to loot

tabcilanambi: to go to plunder or capture

tabcilandumbi: to plunder or capture together; also **tabcilanumbi**

tabcilanjimbi: to come to plunder or capture

tabcilanumbi: to plunder or capture together; also **tabcilandumbi**

tabcin: **1**. robbery; **2**. plunder, booty, loot

> **tabcin hūlha**: thief

tabsitambi: **1**. to talk foolishly, to talk too much, to prattle; **2**. to talk back to; **3**. to talk glibly

tabtašambi: to speak coarsely

tabukū: hook, hanger, hasp, a catch, fastener

> **tabukū umiyesun**: a leather belt with a fastener

tabumbi: **1**. (causative of **tambi**); **2**. to hook, to catch, to engage; **3**. to patch up, to darn; **4**. to attach a string to a bow, to string a bow;

5. to place a rope around something, to tie up (with), to lasso; **6**. to trap, to ensnare; **7**. to trip someone (in wrestling); **8**. to implicate someone, to involve someone in a conversation or lawsuit

> **tabume goholome gisurembi**: to involve someone in one's conversation

tabure asu: ⟶ **eyebuku asu**

tabunang: (Mongolian) son-in-law of the Emperor

taburi: one ten-quintillionth

tabusitambi: ⟶ **tabušambi**

> **tabusitara gisun**: excuse, pretext, subterfuge

tabušambi: **1**. to implicate, to draw someone else into an affair; **2**. to mend, to sew back together

tacibubumbi: (causative of **tacibumbi**)

tacibukū: **1**. teacher, instructor (in the Hanlin Academy); **2**. school, academy

> **tacibukū hafan**: instructional officer

tacibumbi: to teach, to instruct

> **tacibure fungnehen**: a document of enfeoffment for ranks below the sixth degree

> **tacibure hese**: an Imperial decree, an Imperial instruction

taciha: ⟶ **tacimbi** (subheading)

tacihiyabumbi: (causative or passive of **tacihiyambi**)

tacihiyakū: educational institution, school

tacihiyambi: to instruct, to train

tacihiyan: **1**. teaching, training; **2**. religion

> **tacihiyan be ulara urse**: (Christian) missionaries

> **tacihiyan wen**: teaching and culture, culture, civilization

tacikū: **1**. school; **2**. learning, doctrine

tacikū de enggelembi: to go to the Imperial Academy of Learning to lecture on a text (said of the Emperor)

tacikū tacihiyakū: schools, educational institutions

tacikūi baita be kadalara hafan: (提督學政) Superintendent of Provincial Education, *BH* 827A

tacikūi baita be kadalara hafan i yamun: (學政衙門) Office of the Provincial Director of Education, *BH* 827A

tacikūi boo: schoolhouse, school

tacikūi juse: students, pupils

tacikūi yamun: (學院) an office in every province in charge of the examination for the Licentiate

tacimbi: **1**. to learn, to study; **2**. to become accustomed to, to get used to

taciha hafan: (博士) the name of an official in the Hanlin Academy, Bureau of Sacrificial Worship, etc.

taciha hafan i tinggin: the office of the official **taciha hafan**

tacire urse: students

tacimsi: a student of the Imperial Academy of Learning

tacin: **1**. learning, science, skill; **2**. religion; **3**. custom, habit

tacin akū: unfamiliar with, unaccustomed

tacin be badarambure tanggin: (廣業堂) a third hall of the west gallery of the Imperial Academy of Learning

tacin fonjin: learning, scholarship

tacinambi: to go to learn

tacindumbi: to learn together; also **tacinumbi**

tacinjimbi: to come to learn

tacinumbi: to learn together; also **tacindumbi**

tacinun: **1**. custom; **2**. musical air, folk melody

tadumbi: to tear apart, to rip in two

tadurambi: to scuffle, to fight

taduranumbi: to scuffle together

tafabumbi: (causative of **tafambi**)

tafakū: ⟶ **tafukū**

tafambi: (-ka) to ascend, to go up, to climb

tafambumbi: (causative of **tafambi**)

tafanambi: to go to ascend, to go up

tafandumbi: to ascend together; also **tafanumbi**

tafanjimbi: to come to ascend, to come up

tafanumbi: to ascend together; also **tafandumbi**

tafi: ⟶ **tambi** (subheading)

tafitu: a unicorn that is supposed to appear when the world is unified

tafukū: steps, stages, flight of stairs

tafukū i daibihan: the stone ledge on both sides of a flight of stairs

tafulabumbi: (causative or passive of **tafulambi**)

tafulambi: to advise, to counsel

tafulan: advice, counsel

tafumbi: ⟶ **tafambi**

tafuršambi: to act vigorously, to act ferociously or vehemently

tagiri cecike: a name for the goatsucker; cf. **simari cecike**

tahalabumbi: (causative of **tahalambi**)

tahalama: a horseshoe

tahalambi: to nail on a horseshoe, to shoe (a horse)

tahan: **1**. clog, wooden shoe; **2**. horseshoe; **3**. a stepping stone; **4**. a piece of wood attached to the bottom of a shoe, a wooden sole

tahan sabu: clogs

tahi: *Equus przewalski*: a wild horse, Przewalski's horse

tahūra: shellfish, mussel, clam

tahūra efen: a meat-filled pastry shaped like a mussel

tahūra notho: mussel shell, mother-of-pearl

tahūrangga fiyen: a powder made from mussel shells

tai: platform, terrace, stage

tai tebumbi: to erect a (signal) platform

tai giyamun: post station

tai sui enduri: the god of misfortune

tai ši: ⟶ **taiši**

tai tai: lady, mistress

taiboo: (太保) Grand Guardian — an honorary title

taibu: the main beam of a roof or a bridge

taicangsy i yamun: ⟶ **wecen i baita be aliha yamun**

taidz: the Heir Apparent, *BH* 12

taidz šooboo: (太子少保) Junior Guardian of the Heir Apparent — an honorary title

taidz šoofu: (太子少傅) Junior Tutor of the Heir Apparent — an honorary title

taidz šooši: (太子少師) Junior Preceptor of the Heir Apparent — an honorary title

taidz taiboo: (太子太保) Grand Guardian of the Heir Apparent — an honorary title

taidz taifu: (太子太傅) Grand Tutor of the Heir Apparent — an honorary title

taidz taiši: (太子太師) Grand Preceptor of the Heir Apparent — an honorary title

taidz usiha: the first star in Ursa Minor

taifin: peace, tranquility

taifin yendebure calu: a granary of the Board of Finance that was located in the capital

taifingga: pertaining to peace, peaceful

taifingga ilha: a blossom that blooms in autumn, resembling the peach flower

taifintu cecike: the name of a small white bird with a crest on its head, a hooked beak and a black tail that is golden at the end — Bohemian waxwing (*Bombycilla garrulus*)

taifu: (太傅) Grand Tutor — an honorary title

taiga: (Mongolian) forest, taiga, boreal forest

taigiyan: eunuch

taigiyasa: (plural of **taigiyan**)

taiha: a hunting dog with long hair on its ears and tail

taiheo: widow of an Emperor

taihūwa: sea-bream

taiji: (Mongolian) a Mongolian title, Prince

taijingga ilha: the name of a water flower from Guangdong

taili: a saucer for a wine cup

taimin: a stick for stirring a fire

taimiyoo: the Imperial ancestral temple

taimpa: a kind of edible river snail or mussel

taimpari niyehe: a name for the teal; cf. **borboki niyehe**

taipusy yamun: ⟶ **adun be kadalara yamun**

tairan: a slash cut on a tree (used by hunters as a guide or landmark)

tairan gaimbi: to ascend by a winding path

tairan gaime sacimbi: to make a slash on a tree as a landmark

taisui enduri: **1**. the first of the year-gods: the planet Jupiter; **2**. the god of misfortune

taišeo: (太守) governor, prefect

taiši: (太師) Grand Preceptor — an honorary title

taitai: lady, mistress

taiyūn: the name of a sea fish that resembles the bream

taji: naughty, mischievous

tajihūn: ill-bred, naughty

tajirambi: to act naughtily

tak seme: (onomatopoetic) the sound made by hitting something solid

tak tik: (onomatopoetic) **1**. the sound made when chopping wood; **2**. the sound made when moving chessmen

taka: temporarily, provisionally, for the time being, for a short time

taka sidende: for the time being, temporarily

takabumbi: **1**. (causative or passive of **takambi**); **2**. to introduce, to make known

takabun: recognition, familiarity

takambi: **1**. to know (a person), to recognize, to be familiar with; **2**. to physiognomize

takara mangga: good at judging people by their appearance

takan: wild mustard plant

takanambi: to go to recognize

takandumbi: to know or recognize together, to recognize one another; also **takanumbi**

takanjimbi: to come to recognize, to come to know

takanumbi: to know or recognize together, to recognize one another; also **takandumbi**

takara: ⟶ **takambi** (subheading)

takasu: **1**. wait a moment, just a moment; **2**. for the time being

takciha filan: a wooden bow without a horn covering

takdambi: (**-ka/-ha**) to be happy over some success, to be in high spirits, to be elated to the point of haughtiness

takdangga: happy, in a good mood, in high spirits, elated to the point of haughtiness

takdangga be amcambi: to have a happy impulse, to take advantage of a happy feeling

takitu: a protective knee covering made of leather

takiya: an animal's knee

taksibumbi: **1**. (causative or passive of **taksimbi**); **2**. to conceive (a child)

taksiburakū beri: the name of a famous bow of antiquity

taksimbi: **1**. to survive, to remain, to last; **2**. to be there, to exist, to be living; **3**. to preserve; **4**. to be conceived (said of a child)

takta moo: *Taxus cuspidata*: yew

taktan moo: plane tree, sycamore tree

taktu: **1**. storied building, tower; **2**. upstairs

    taktu amban: (武備院卿) Director of the Imperial Armory, *BH* 89

takū: tench (fish)

takūleo: ⟶ **takūlu**

takūlu: wait a moment, just a moment; cf. **takasu**

takūrabumbi: (causative or passive of **takūrambi**)

    takūrabure hafan: (司務) Chancery Chief, *BH* 296

    takūrabure hafan i tinggin: (司務廳) Chancery (in various ministries), *BH* 296

takūrakū: overseer, inspector, etc. — the name of officials in various bureaus of the government

takūrambi: **1**. to send on a mission, to delegate, to commission; **2**. to appoint (to a post); **3**. to employ, to have in one's service

    takūraha hafan: (差官) official for special duty, deputy, *BH* 436, 778 ff.

takūran: commission, duty, mission, task, official post

    takūran be aliha fiyenten: (行人司) a section of the Bureau of Rites concerned with caring for foreign emissaries

    takūran be aliha hafan: (行人) in ancient times, the name of an official who was in charge of caring for foreign emissaries

    takūran de tucimbi: to leave on a mission

takūrandumbi: to send to one another (on a mission)

takūrangge: official summons or invitation

takūrsi: beadle, bailiff, emissary, messenger, attendant, errand boy, footman

takūršabumbi: (passive of **takūršambi**)

takūršakū: servant

takūršambi: to employ as a (personal) servant, to employ as a subordinate

    takūršara dahalji: personal servant, valet

    takūršara hafan: (供用官) an official charged with making preparations for official business, commissions, etc.

    takūršara hūsun: a coolie, a laborer

    takūšara jui: servant boy

    takūršara niyalma: servant, valet

    takūršara sargan jui: servant girl

tala: **1**. plain, steppe; **2**. the space between lines of writing

    talai cooha: field soldiers

talabumbi: (causative or passive of **talambi**)

talambi: **1**. to spread out (wares for sale); **2**. to confiscate, to seize (property as a legal punishment); **3**. to make griddle cakes, to fry flat bread; cf. **jempilembi**

    talame durimbi: to rob in plain daylight

    talame tukiyembi: to lift an opponent by placing one's leg between his thighs (at wrestling)

talbi ihan: a cow that has not been used

talbu: heddle (a tool used in weaving)

talfa: **1**. level land along a stream; **2**. shallow water

talfari: a shallow place where the bottom of a boat may touch bottom

talgan: the surface of a flat, round, or square object

talgari: **1**. surface (of a table); **2**. the outside surface of a memorial or examination paper

talgibumbi: (causative of **talgimbi**)

talgikū: a wooden tool shaped like a fodder knife and used in curing leather

talgimbi: **1**. use a **talgikū** in curing leather; **2**. to deceive someone, to make a fool of, to console with deceitful words

talihūn: undecided, vacillating

talihūnjambi: to vacillate, to be undecided

tališambi: **1**. to flicker, to shimmer; **2**. to blink; **3**. to leer, to roll the eyeballs

talkambi: to cook fish only half-done

talkimbi: to console, to comfort

talkiyambi: to lighten, to flash (said of lightning)

talkiyan: lightning, electricity

    talkiyan fularilambi: to flash in the distance when no clouds are visible (lightning)

    talkiyan mejige: telegram

    talkiyan tališambi: to keep flashing (said of lightning)

talmahan: gossamer — filmy cobwebs floating in the air

talmambi: (-ka) to be foggy

talman: fog, mist

taltan: **1**. serrated edge of a table; **2**. sides of a canoe or boat, gunwale

    taltan tatambi: to make raised decorations on the edge of a table

talu: by chance, accidentally, perchance

    talu de: (see also **talude**) **1**. if by any chance, just in case, supposing, perchance; **2**. sometimes, once in a while

talu jugūn: narrow lane

talude: if perchance, sometimes; cf. **talu de**

tama: sole (a kind of fish), flatfish

tamabumbi: (causative of **tamambi**)

tamalimbi: **1**. to struggle (to keep from falling, etc.); **2**. when afraid, to be unable to get hold of oneself

tamambi: **1**. to collect scattered things into one place; **2**. to fill (a vessel) with; **3**. to tighten up the sagging portion of a battue line

taman: castrated swine, hog

tambi: **1**. to get caught on something, to get entangled and trip over something; **2**. to get caught in a trap or net

tafi tuheke: tripped on something and fell

tame afame yabumbi: to walk dragging the feet

tamin: the end of an animal's hair

tamin acabumbi: to arrange the hairs of a pelt naturally and in the proper direction

tamin acanaha: the hairs (of a pelt) are running in the proper direction

tamišambi: to taste with the lips

tamlimbi: ⟶ **tamalimbi**

tampa: ⟶ **taimpa**

tampin: **1**. vessel, pot, container (for tea or liquor); **2**. water clock, clepsydra

tampin efen: small filled rice cakes

tampin i boo: (壺室) the room where the water clock was kept under the observatory

tamse: a small container, jug, jar

tamsu: ⟶ **tamse**

tamtan: a carp-like sea fish with red fins

tan: **1**. shoal, small island in a river; **2**. altar; **3**. saliva

tana: pearl (especially a precious freshwater pearl from the rivers of eastern Manchuria)

tanangga ilha: the name of an exotic flower with five petals whose filaments resemble tiny pearls

tandambi: ⟶ **tantambi**

tang: **1**. a hall; **2**. a praying mantis

tang seme: **1**. hard, firm; **2**. fluent, with ease (said of speaking)

tang seme gecehe: frozen solid

tang seme gisurembi: to speak fluently

tang tang: (onomatopoetic) the sound of a bell

tang ting: (onomatopoetic) the sound of hitting iron or of chopping a tree

tang u li boo: ⟶ **tanggūli**

tangga: ⟶ **mangga tangga**

tanggambi: to wrap the weak part of a bow with sinew

tanggibumbi: to put something under an object to cushion or support it

tanggikū: a bent piece of wood with cords attached at both ends (used in stringing a bow)

tanggikū i bukdambi: to bend (a bow) with a **tanggikū**

tanggilakū: catapult, sling

tanggilambi: **1**. to fire a catapult or slingshot; **2**. to flick the forehead with a finger

tanggime gisurembi: to correct oneself (in speaking), to cover up an error or faux pas (in speaking)

tanggimeliyan: bent backward, arched, bow-shaped

tanggin: hall, chamber, office of a high official

tanggin i alibun: a matter presented to a superior for consideration by a subordinate, a petition presented to a high ministry official

tanggin i temgetu ejere boo: (堂號房) Registry of the Ministry of Works

tanggingge boo: (堂房) an office of the Board of Finance concerned with draft documents

tanggiri: **1**. a small finger cymbal; **2**. an anvil for making large-headed nails

tanggiri ilha: the name of a colorful flower that blooms in the springtime

tanggiyabumbi: (causative of **tanggiyambi**)

tanggiyambi: to repaint, to relacquer

tanggiyan: repainting, relacquering

tanggū: one hundred

tanggū bethe umiyaha: centipede

tanggū da: ⟶ **tanggūda**

tanggū ging: the last night watch

tanggū hala: the common people

tanggū tumen: one million

tanggūci: hundredth

tanggūda: hereditary head of a hundred families

tanggūha: *Corvus torquatus*: white-necked crow

tanggūli: **1**. the central hall of a house; **2**. the central section of a tent

tanggūnggeri: one hundred times

tanggūri ilha: the name of a red flower that blooms for a hundred days

tanggūt: **1**. Tibet, Tibetan; **2**. Tangut

tanggūt hergenehe suje: silk with Tibetan writing on it

tanggūt tacikū: Tibetan language school

tanggūta: one hundred each

tanggūte: ⟶ **tanggūta**

tangka: ⟶ **tangkan**

tangka akū: without steps or rank

tangka fejile: Your Majesty

tangkambi: to kill small fish with stones in shallow water

tangkan: step, rank, grade, class

tangkan tangkan i: step by step

tangkan tangkan i wesimbi: to ascend step by step

tangki: bump, excrescence

tangse: the Imperial shamanic shrines in Beijing and Mukden

tangsimbi: to drum continually

tangsime gisurembi: to speak fluently

tangsu: 1. darling, dear (children); 2. delicate, tender

tangsulambi: to love, to fondle and hug (children), to dote on (children), to spoil (a child)

tangsulame gosimbi: to cherish, to love dearly

tangsulame ujimbi: to pamper, to spoil

tangsulan: fondling, tender care

tangsun: ⟶ **tangsu**

tani: a measure equaling one hundred-thousandth of a dry quart

tanjambi: to stutter, to stammer, to stumble when speaking

tanji: one ten-quadrillionth

tanjurambi: to pray, to pray for blessings (said of shamans)

tantabumbi: (causative or passive of **tantambi**)

tantalambi: to thrash, to beat

tantambi: to hit, to beat, to strike

tantame bucebumbi: to beat to death

tantame wambi: to kill by beating

tantanumbi: to beat one another, to fight

tantu: a cultivating tool with a forked head

tar seme: startled, suddenly afraid

tar tar seme: timorous, afraid

tara: 1. clabbered milk, curd; 2. children of father's sisters or mother's brothers; 3. relative of a different surname

tara ahūn deo: cousins (see **tara**)

tara eyun non: female cousins (see **tara**)

taracin: farmer, cultivator

tarak: ⟶ **tara (1)**

taran: (heavy) sweat

taran waliyambi: to sweat (profusely)

tarani: a dharani, a magic formula

taranilambi: ⟶ **tarnilambi**

tarbahi: *Marmota bobak*: marmot

tarbalji: one of the general names for the eagle

tarbihi: ⟶ **tarbahi**

tarcan: lead (the metal)

tarcan i irukū: lead weight on a fishing net

tarfu: a name for the tiger; cf. **tasha**

targa: 1. a square piece of cloth worn on the shoulder by children during shamanistic ceremonies; 2. a tuft of straw hung on a door in order to forbid entrance

targa i futa: a rope hung on a door at midsummer to keep evil spirits from entering

targa inenggi: 1. the death day of an Emperor or Empress; 2. the day of a parent's death

targabumbi: 1. (causative or passive of **targambi**); 2. to forbid troops to plunder, to enjoin not to, to admonish

targabun: prohibition, admonition

targacun: 1. admonition, warning, precept; 2. abstinence, avoidance

targacun be tuwakiyambi: to observe the Buddhist precepts

targambi: 1. to abstain from, to avoid, to swear off, to give up; 2. to warn, to admonish; 3. to guard against, to be cautious about

targame sengguweme: on guard, vigilant

targan: small tiger

targangga: 1. religious vows; 2. an oath

targangga be efulembi: to break a vow

targangga be necimbi: to violate an oath or vow

targangga gaimbi: to take monastic vows

targikū umiyaha: a poisonous green caterpillar

targimpa: ⟶ **targikū umiyaha**

targū: fat; ⟶ **tarhūn**

tarhū: ⟶ **tarhūn**

tarhūbumbi: to fatten (livestock)

tarhūdambi: 1. to contradict, to talk back to; 2. to jabber

tarhūkan: rather fat, somewhat fat

tarhūlambi: to make fat, to fatten

tarhūlaha fahūn: deer or sheep liver wrapped in fat and cooked

tarhūmbi: to get fat, to put on weight

tarhūn: **1**. fat; **2**. a mussel

tarhūn efen: small cakes soaked in fat

tarhūn yali: fat meat, fat

taribumbi: (causative of **tarimbi**)

tarimbi: to cultivate, to farm, to plow

tarinambi: to go to cultivate

tarindumbi: to cultivate together; also **tarinumbi**

tarinjimbi: to come to cultivate

tarinumbi: to cultivate together; also **tarindumbi**

tarmin niyehe: mallard; cf. **borjin niyehe**

tarni: dharani, magic formula, charm, spell; cf. **tarani**

tarnilabumbi: (causative or passive of **tarnilambi**)

tarnilambi: to recite a dharani, to recite a spell

tarsi: cousin of a different surname

tarsi niyaman: nephews and nieces: children of father's sisters or of mother's brothers

tarsi omolo: great-nephews and great-nieces: children of father's sister's children and mother's brother's children

tarsilambi: to marry a cousin of a different surname

tarudambi: to chatter, to talk nonsense, to talk back to

tarun: given to talking back, a person who is fond of talking back, a person who talks nonsense

tas seme: (onomatopoetic) the sound of an arrow grazing an object

tas seme tatame gamambi: to jerk from the hand suddenly

tas tis seme: (onomatopoetic) the sound of a number of arrows grazing an object

tasgabumbi: (causative of **tasgambi**)

tasgambi: to stir-fry in a dry skillet (without oil), to pop beans of grain, to fry until dry

tasha: **1**. tiger (the Manchurian sub-species is *Felis tigris amurensis*); **2**. the third of the earth's branches (寅)

tasha biya: the first month

tasha erin: period of the day from 3 AM to 5 AM

tasha gabtara niru: an arrow with a short iron head for shooting lying tigers

tasha gabtara selmin niru: a crossbow arrow with a long iron head for shooting tigers

tasha gabtara yoro: an arrow with a four-holed birch head that was used for rousing recumbent tigers

tasha gida: a spear for hunting tigers

tasha i oron i dogon: the name of a constellation

tasha orho: *Arisaema thunbergii*: 'cobra lily'

tasha ošohonggo fukjingga hergen: (虎爪篆) the name of a style of Chinese calligraphy

tashaci: a tiger skin

tashambi: ⟶ **tasgambi**

tashangga: pertaining to the tiger, tiger-like

tashangga aniya: the year of the tiger

tashangga dobtolon: striped overpants worn by troops of the green banner

tashangga dusihi: a striped skirt worn by troops of the green banner

tashangga etuku: a striped uniform worn by the troops of the green banner

tashangga mahala: a hat was worn by the troops of the green banner and made in the form of a tiger's head

tashari: eagle, vulture

tashū: **1**. a yarn or thread separator used in weaving; **2**. the bottom of the crop of a bird, gizzard

tashūmbi: to go back and forth continually

tashūme yabumbi: ⟶ **tashūmbi**

tasihimbi: to step against one's opponent from the side (in wrestling)

tasima efen: a somewhat larger variety of **toholiyo**

tasma: leather thong made of deer or antelope skin

tašan: **1**. false, spurious; **2**. error, mistake

tašarabumbi: (causative of **tašarambi**)

tašarambi: to err, to make an error, to go astray

tašun: Is it false?, Is it in error?

tatabumbi: **1**. (causative or passive of **tatambi**); **2**. to be too tight (said of clothing); **3**. to act affected, to behave in a ridiculous manner; **4**. to worry, to be concerned

tatakū: **1**. bucket for drawing water; **2**. drawer

tatakū dere: a table with drawers

tatakū i šurgeku: pulley on a well

tatala: many; cf. **tutala**

tatambi: **1**. to pull, to pull at, to pull apart, to tear, to rip, to draw, to pull out, to extract; **2**. to strangle (a criminal as a form of capital punishment); **3**. to stop on a journey, to halt, to lodge, to make camp; **4**. to open wide (the eyes); **5**. to deduct; **6**. to chat informally; **7**. to talk back

tatame niru: an arrow with a short roundish iron head (used for hunting wild beasts)

tatame wambi: to strangle (one of the two forms of capital punishment)

tatame wara weile: a crime punishable by strangulation

tatara boo: inn, hotel; cf. **diyan**

tatara booi niyalma: innkeeper

tatara edun: whirlwind

tatara gurung: a palace used by the Emperor on his travels

tatara yamun: office, public hall

tatan: **1**. a camp, a stopping place, an encampment; **2**. territory of a tribe; **3**. lodging

tatan i boo: residence, abode

tatan i da: chief of a camp

tatan tobo: military tent, command tent

tatanambi: **1**. to go to pull; **2**. to go to stop on a journey

tatandumbi: to stop together on a journey, to rest together; also **tatanumbi**

tatangga hangse: noodles that are pulled by hand

tatanjimbi: **1**. to come to stop on a journey; **2**. to come to pull

tatanumbi: to stop together on a journey, to rest together; also **tatandumbi**

tatara: ⟶ **tatambi** (subheading)

tatarabumbi: (causative of **tatarambi**)

tatarambi: **1**. to cut meat, specifically to slice mutton very finely with two small knives; **2**. to rip to pieces, to rip apart; **3**. to pull at one another (at wrestling)

tatašambi: **1**. to be agitated, to be concerned; **2**. to keep pulling, to pull continually

tathūnjacuka: hesitant, vacillating

tathūnjambi: to hesitate, to vacillate

tathūnjame gūninjambi: to vacillate

tatuhan: the name of a two-stringed musical instrument, a two-stringed fiddle

tayambi: to break out (said of fire)

tayame yabumbi: to suddenly dart across the surface of a pond (said of water striders)

tayungga nimaha: the name of a sea fish that resembles the carp

te: now, at present

te bicibe: at present, presently

te ele oho kai: that's enough now

te i jalan: the present world

tebcimbi: to endure, to suffer

tebeliyebumbi: (causative of **tebeliyembi**)

tebeliyeku: a piece of metal around the middle of a scabbard

tebeliyeku afahari: a piece of yellow paper stuck on the outside of a family genealogy that gives the reasons for obtaining hereditary official positions

tebeliyembi: **1**. to hug, to embrace, to hold in one's arms; **2**. to adopt a child

tebeliyeme acambi: to embrace upon meeting (upon returning from a journey, a junior embraced the legs of his senior, a senior embraced the back of a junior, and equals embraced one another about the shoulders)

tebeliyen: **1**. embrace, hug; **2**. an armload; **3**. (as a measure word) the circumference of the arms wrapped around something

teben moo: a support timber on a ship

tebke: a bone or wooden bridge (or plate) placed under the knots of the bowstring at both ends of a bow

tebke latubumbi: to glue on bridges for a bowstring's knots

tebke tabka: tottering and babbling (said of children learning to walk and speak)

tebkejembi: to catch a shuttlecock that has been thrown up in the air while holding a **gacuha** in the hand, to hold a **gacuha** in the hand

tebkelembi: to cut (meat) into small chunks, to cut meat into cubes

tebku: **1**. placenta; **2**. fetus, embryo; **3**. womb carrying a fetus; **4**. litter (of pigs, dogs, etc.)

tebsehe: a kind of locust that eats crops

tebuku: container, bag; cf. **ilhai tebuku, muke tebuku**

tebubumbi: (causative of **tebumbi** in the senses 'to pour', 'to set out (plants)', 'to fill (a vessel)', 'to distill', 'to fill (a pipe)')

tebumbi: **1**. (causative of **tembi**); **2**. to pour; **3**. to set out, to plant; **4**. to fill a vessel, to fill a pipe; **5**. to pack, to put in; **6**. to install (an official); **7**. to make (liquor), to distill; **8**. to place a corpse in a coffin

tebuhe gūnin: intention

tebuhe mujilen: ⟶ **tebuhe gūnin**

tebun: a small container; cf. **mukei tebun**, **yahai tebun**

tebunebumbi: (causative of **tebunembi**)

tebunembi: to do garrison duty, to be stationed at a border garrison

tebunjimbi: to come to pour, to come to plant, etc.

tebunumbi: to pack together, to plant together, etc.; cf. **tebumbi**

teburelambi: to place in a grave, to inter

tecebumbi: (causative of **tecembi**)

tecembi: to sit together, to sit down together

tecendumbi: to sit in a group, to sit together, to sit facing one another; also **tecenumbi**

tecenumbi: to sit in a group, to sit together, to sit facing one another; also **tecendumbi**

tede: **1**. dative/locative of **tere**; **2**. there, in that place; **3**. up until now

tederi: from there, by there, from that, from him, from her

tefembi: to burn out, to finish burning

tefembumbi: (causative or passive of **tefembi**)

tehe: **1**. frame, framework, rack; **2**. lathe, loom; **3**. *Capra sibirica*: Siberian ibex

tehe uju: a piece of wood that regulates the thread over a loom

tehe wan: scaffold

tehen: **1**. stilts; **2**. ⟶ **tehe**

tehen morin: a stick-horse

teheni tungken: a large drum that sits on a stand

teherebubumbi: (causative of **teherebumbi**)

teherebuku: balance, scales; cf. **pingse**

teherebumbi: **1**. to weigh on a balance; **2**. to make even, to balance out, to make match

teherebure boo: (兌房) the Weighing Office of the Beijing Mint

teherembi: **1**. to be even, to be equal, to be equivalent; **2**. to be worth; **3**. to match; **4**. to counterbalance

teherehe niyalma: a person of the same generation

tehereme yabumbi: to run parallel

tehererakū: not worth ... : **gisureme tehererakū** 'not worth saying'

teherere niyalma: one's match, equal match

teheren: equal, even, matching, balanced

teheren teheren: balanced, in balance

teherendumbi: to counterbalance one another, to be equal to one another

teherešembi: ⟶ **teheršembi**

teheršembi: **1**. to be a match for; **2**. to be the same price, to be equal to; **3**. to correspond to

teifulembi: to use as a staff, to lean on as a staff

teifun: cane, staff

teifun sujambi: to use a cane for support

teifungge: one who walks with a cane — an old man

teifušembi: to walk with a cane or a staff

teike: just now, a moment ago, just

teile: **1**. (postposition) only, just, alone; **2**. (after participles) to the extent of; cf. **muterei teile**, **jabduhai teile**

teile akū: not only

teisu: **1**. (postposition) toward, facing, opposite; **2**. corresponding, matching, suitable, compatible, appropriate; **3**. simultaneous; **4**. one's designated place or status, one's part; **5**. (阀) a subdivision of the Chinese Banner troops

teisu akū: incongruous, not matching, inappropriate

teisu be dabambi: to go too far, to exceed proper limits, to do something out of turn

teisu be dahambi: to follow one's own calling, to be content with one's lot

teisu be tuwakiyambi: to keep one's place, to be content with one's lot

teisu be tuwame: as is appropriate

teisu ci tulgiyen: additional, extra, added on

teisu teisu: separately, individually, one by one, severally, in succession

teisu tembi: to sit opposite

teisulebumbi: **1**. (causative of **teisulembi**); **2**. to adapt, to make fit; **3**. to encounter, to come up against; **4**. to fit, to correspond, to be suited to, to coincide with; **5**. to face, to be relative to; **6**. to inflict the proper punishment

teisulebume bodombi: to settle accounts

teisulebume wecembi: to sacrifice to the earth spirits

teisulembi: **1**. to meet, to encounter, to happen upon; **2**. to correspond, to match, to conform, to coincide

teisulehe dari: in any case, each time that ...

teisulehe oron: a suitable vacancy

teisulen: correspondence, encounter, mode

teisungge: corresponding, fitting, matching, suitable, opposing

teisutu: sergeant of the green banner

teišun: copper, bronze, brass

    teišun faksi: coppersmith

    teišun niowarikū: patina

tejihen: a name for the crane; cf. **bulehen**

tek seme: scoldingly

tek tak seme: (onomatopoetic) the sound of shouting or quarreling

tekdebumbi: **1**. (causative of **tekdembi**); **2**. to burn sacrificial money

    tekdebure hoošan: yellow paper that is burned as an offering before Buddhist images

tekdembi: (**-ke**) **1**. to creep up (said of sleeves); **2**. to ascend, to fly upward; **3**. to die (a euphemism used in shamanic rites)

tekembi: to be soft due to warm moisture (said of leather), to decompose due to excessive moisture or heat

teksi: ⟶ **teksin**

teksiken: rather even

teksilebumbi: (causative of **teksilembi**)

teksilembi: **1**. to put in order, to arrange properly; **2**. to be complete, to be all present

teksilen: ordering, regulation, proper arrangement

teksilgan: the rhythmic shouting of workers at a hard job

teksin: **1**. even, equal, straight (not curved), of equal length or height; **2**. well-proportioned, neatly arranged; **3**. the tamarisk; ⟶ **suhai moo**

    teksin akū: untidy, uneven, not orderly

    teksin jan: a whistling arrow with a bone arrowhead that has a flat point

    teksin niru: an arrow with an arrowhead that has a flat point

    teksin yoro: an arrow with a bone head that has a flat point

teksingga: in a rank, in a row, in an orderly arrangement

teku: **1**. a seat, a place to sit, a perch, a place where one can settle; **2**. measure word for a banquet

    teku undehen: seat in a rowboat

telambi: to give way, to collapse suddenly (said of the hind leg of livestock)

telebumbi: (causative or passive of **telembi**)

telejembi: to be raised, to be embossed

    telejeme jodombi: to weave with an embossed or raised design

telejen: **1**. embossment, raised design, a protuberance; **2**. a courtyard with walls

telembi: to stretch taut, to truss

    teleme wambi: to kill by trussing, to strangle someone

telen: trussing

teleri: a woman's satin ceremonial garment decorated with a design of standing dragons

telgin: belt (for trousers)

telgiyen: ⟶ **telgin**

telimbi: ⟶ **teliyembi**

teliyebumbi: (causative or passive of **teliyembi**)

teliyeku: a steamer — usually made in tiers from bamboo

teliyembi: to steam (a method of cooking)

telšembi: ⟶ **delišembi**

tembi: **1**. to sit; **2**. to reside, to live; **3**. to occupy (a post)

    tehe muke: standing water, stagnant water

    tehei monjiršambi: to move back and forth while sitting

    tere ba: place of residence, address

temciku: a sampan

temege coko: ostrich

temen: **1**. camel; **2**. ⟶ **temun**

    temen cecike: bittern, birds of the genus *Botaurus*

    temen gurgu: wild camel

    temen sele: the pivot of scissors or tongs

temene ulme: a needle with three edges that is used for sewing leather and other thick or dense materials

temenembi: to get insects or worms (grain or leaves), to become insect-infested

temeri: camel-colored, tan, brown

temgetu: **1**. sign, signal, mark, brand, badge, stamp, emblem; **2**. (personal) seal, a seal used by low ranking provincial officials and clerks, *BH* 984; **3**. evidence, proof, verification; **4**. certificate, receipt, written verification; **5**. license, permit, manifest

    temgetu arambi: to sign one's signature, to affix one's seal

    temgetu bithe: license, certificate, receipt, contract, manifest

temgetu bithe icihiyara ba: (辨照處) Office of the Certificate in the Imperial Academy of Learning

temgetu ejehe dangse: a book in which the receipt of documents already acted on by the Emperor was recorded

temgetu etuku: a jacket with the emblem of a military unit on it

temgetu jorin: guide, guidebook

temgetu mahala: a hat with the emblem of a military unit on it

temgetu niru: a signal arrow (used by a commander)

temgetu šusihe: a written order given to a subordinate by a superior

temgetu tuwa šanggiyakū: signal fire, beacon

temgetu wehe: monument, memorial tablet

temgetulebumbi: (causative or passive of **temgetulembi**)

temgetulembi: **1**. to signal, to make a sign; **2**. to confer a mark of distinction on; **3**. to prove, to verify

temgetun: pennon, pennant

temgetun jalasu i fiyenten: (旌節司) Pennons Section, *BH* 120

temgetungge: **1**. exhibiting a sign, mark, or emblem; **2**. distinguished, outstanding

temgetungge gu: a jade object held during ceremonies by rulers in antiquity

temgetungge undehen: a tablet held before the breast by officials during an audience with the Emperor in ancient times

temimbi: to treat with consideration, to treat indulgently, to consider another's reputation out of affection

temnembi: ⟶ **temenembi**

tempin: a flower vase

temšebumbi: (causative of **temšembi**)

temšeku: opponent, competitor

temšembi: to compete, to vie, to contend, to quarrel

temšen: contention, strife

temšendumbi: to vie with one another, to quarrel with one another; also **temšenumbi**

temšenumbi: to vie with one another, to quarrel with one another; also **temšendumbi**

temuhen: **1**. a rod around which pictures or scrolls of calligraphy are wrapped, a spool; **2**. a measure word for scrolls or paintings

temun: **1**. axle, axis; **2**. roller, rod (on which a scroll is rolled)

temun i sibiya: a peg on the axle to keep the wheels from slipping

temurtu kara: an iron-colored horse

ten: **1**. foundation, base; **2**. extreme point, highest point, peak, extreme end; **3**. litter, sedan chair (carried by men, camel, horse, or mule); **4**. small horizontal dragons woven into "dragon satin"; **5**. exalted, lofty, noble

ten gaimbi: to require the facts, to demand evidence from an opponent

ten i: extremely, exceedingly

ten i erun: extreme punishment, death penalty

ten i sebjen: extreme pleasure, bliss

ten i šanyan usiha: the planet Venus

ten i tondo tanggin: (至公堂) the name of a hall in the examination compound

ten i wecen: the suburban sacrifice — made to heaven at the winter solstice and to earth at the summer solstice

tenakū: ⟶ **tengneku**

tenembi: **1**. to go to sit; **2**. to go to reside

teng seme: hard, firm, fast, solid, resolute

teng tang seme: **1**. equally matched; **2**. straightforward

tenggeljeku: marshy ground (which vibrates when one stands on it)

tenggeljembi: to vibrate, to shake (said of earth that is dry on top but still wet underneath)

tenggeri: a three-stringed lute

tenggin: lake, inland sea

tengki tangki: stumbling along, bumping along; cf. **tungki tangki**

tengkibumbi: **1**. (causative or passive of **tengkimbi**); **2**. to collide, to run into

tengkicuke: **1**. apt, suitable, appropriate, feasible, practical; **2**. certain

tengkimbi: to put down into a vessel, to throw down (with force)

tengkime: clearly, really, solidly

tengkime sambi: to know clearly

tengnebumbi: to make equal, to equalize

tengneku: a sedan chair carried by two men and used for traveling in mountains

tengnembi: **1**. to weigh, to balance; **2**. to jump from one horse to another

tengpai: **1**. a rattan shield; **2**. a soldier outfitted with a rattan shield

tengse: **1**. rattan; **2**. vine

    tengse i sirge: **1**. creepers of a vine, branches of a vine; **2**. strands of rattan

tengtembi: to step on stones (in a stream)

    tengteme yabumbi: to go across a stream by stepping on stones

teni: just, then and only then, not until, for the first time

    teni juse: mere children, small children

teniken: just, for the first time, only then

    teniken juse: small children

tenjimbi: **1**. to come to sit; **2**. to come to reside; **3**. to come to occupy a post

tenju: **1**. the imperative of **tenjimbi**; **2**. keel of a ship

tenteke: like that, that kind, such a, the one in question

tentekengge: one like that, such a one as that

tenumbi: to sit together

teo to: mendicant monk

teodebumbi: (causative of **teodembi**)

teodembi: to trade, to exchange, to barter, to transfer

teodenjembi: **1**. to trade with one another; **2**. to move, to transfer

    teodenjeme bošoro niru: (輪管佐領) a banner captain transferred from one company to another

ter seme: in good order, even, splendidly arrayed (said of an army or hunting party)

ter tar seme: ⟶ **ter seme**

terbun: billion

tere: **1**. that; **2**. he, she, it; **3**. (post-position) a certain

    tere anggala: moreover, all the more

    tere ci: ⟶ **tereci**

    tere dade: ⟶ **tere anggala**

    tere onggolo: before that, beforehand

    terei: (genitive of **tere**): of that, his, hers

    terei amala: after that, subsequently

    terei baili de: thanks to him, due to him

    terei dade: moreover, in addition

tereci: **1**. after that, then; **2**. than that, from that, than him

tereingge: his, hers, its

tereni: thereby, like that, with that

terese: (plural of **tere**); cf. **tese**

tergeci: driver, coachman

tergimbi: to insert an arrow shaft snugly into the iron base of the arrowhead

terin tarin: staggering

terken: ⟶ **erken terken**

terki: ⟶ **terkin**

terkimbi: to jump high, to jump over, to jump across

terkin: **1**. steps, staircase; **2**. steps (and terrace) before a palace building or before a government office

    terkin i jergi: steps, staircase

    terkin i jergi wesimbi: to ascend steps, to ascend step by step

terme lorin: a mule purportedly born from a cow

terse: ⟶ **tese**

terten tartan: shivering, trembling (from an illness)

teru: **1**. base of the colon, rectum; **2**. pivot pin on a spindle

    teru yoo: hemorrhoids

tes: (onomatopoetic) the sound of rope, thread, or a leather thong breaking under stress

tese: (plural of **tere**): those, they

teseingge: theirs

teserembi: ⟶ **deserembi**

tesu: **1**. original, local; **2**. one's own, one's native … , the current …

    tesu ba: local area, indigenous place, native place

    tesu ba i cooha: indigenous troops, native troops

    tesu ba i ejeltu: local chief, local ruler

    tesu ba i irgen: local people, native people

    tesu ba i jaka: local products

    tesu ba i niyalma: local person

    tesu ba i niyalmai usin: native-owned land

    tesu baci tucire jaka: products produced locally

    tesu erinde: at the proper time, at a given time

tesubumbi: (causative of **tesumbi**)

tesumbi: to be enough, to suffice

    tesurakū: insufficient, not enough

tesun: sufficient, satisfactory

tete tata: unsettled, unstable, flighty

teteken: rather unsettled, unstable

tetele: up until now

teten: frivolous, unstable

tetendere: (after conditional converb) since, provided that, assuming that, in case that

tetun: **1**. vessel, container; **2**. implement, apparatus; **3**. euphemism for a coffin

tetun agūra: implements, tools, vessels

tetun deijire niyalma: potter

tetun deijire sele weniyere kunggeri: (窑冶科) Bureau of Kilns and Smelting

tetun doolambi: to divide among the relatives the things brought by a new daughter-in-law

tetun jaka i calu: storehouse in the Imperial household for household implements

tetun šušembi: ⟶ **tetun doolambi**

tetušembi: **1**. to use as a utensil; **2**. to employ a person in a position for which he is fitted

teyebumbi: (causative of **teyembi**)

teyehun: rested, fresh (said of troops)

teyehun cooha: fresh troops

teyehun i cukuhe be alimbi: to wait at ease until one's opponent is exhausted

teyembi: to be at ease, to relax, to rest

teyembumbi: ⟶ **teyebumbi**

teyen: rest, pause, relaxation

teyen akū: without rest, ceaselessly

teyenderakū: without resting, without pausing

teyendumbi: to rest together, to relax together; also **teyenumbi**

teyenembi: to go to rest, to go to relax

teyenjimbi: to come to rest, to come to relax

teyenumbi: to rest together, to relax together; also **teyendumbi**

tidu: ⟶ **fideme kadalara amban**

tildargan: a name for the kestrel; cf. **baldargan**

tilhūtan: a name for the pelican; cf. **kūtan**

timu: topic, theme

ting: **1**. pavilion; **2**. office, bureau; cf. **tinggin**

tingdz: pavilion; cf. **tingse**

tinggin: **1**. office, bureau, section; **2**. hall

tinggin i kunggeri boo: (廳科房) a section of the *yámen* of the Provincial Commander-in-Chief

tinggu cecike: a small black bird with white spots on its back and wings

tingguri cecike: a name for the goatsucker; cf. **simari cecike**

tingse: pavilion

tirhūtan: a name for the pelican

titang: (提塘) Superintendent of Military Posts, *BH* 435

tiyan ju: the Catholic term for God

tiyan ju giyoo: Catholicism

tiyan ju tang: a Catholic church

tiyan ju tang miyoo: a Catholic or Russian Orthodox church

tiyan ju gurun: India

tiyelin: a short, sharp-pointed arrow used for bird hunting

tiyoo: cicada; ⟶ **biyangsikū**

to: **1**. a span, the distance between the outstretched thumb and the middle finger; **2**. a grain measure equal to five dry quarts and made from willow branches; **3**. the last bead on rosaries and strings of cash

to gi: ostrich

tob: straight, upright, serious, right, just

tob akū: not upright, not serious, dishonest

tob ambalinggū: imposing, just and honest

tob biya: the first month of the lunar year

tob cira: solemn expression, dour expression

tob doro: justice

tob dulimba: the very middle, right in the middle

tob hošonggo: righteous, upright

tob sembi: to be serious, to be earnest

tob seme: just, exactly, is just so

tob seme tembi: to sit upright, to sit up straight

tob sere niyalma: a serious, upright man

tob sijirhūn: honest, upright

tob tab: honest, forthright

tob tondo: fair, just

tobcilambi: to knot, to knit together, to plait; cf. **gokjimbi**

tobconggo moo: a miraculous tree that grew on the grave of Zhou Gong — the colors of the leaves corresponded to the different seasons, green in spring, red in summer, white in autumn, and black in winter

tobgiya: knee, knee cap, patella

tobgiya dalikū: knee guard, protective covering for the knee

tobgiya hūwaitakū: knee guard

tobgiya murimbi: to fell an opponent in wrestling by twisting the knee

tobgiyalambi: to press together with the knees, to support with the knees

tobo: a simple hut made from willow branches or similar material

toboo: ⟶ **tobo**

tobtelembi: to cut off the knees — a punishment of antiquity

tobtoko: a horse spotted like a panther

 tobtoko yanggali: a speckled water wagtail

todai: ⟶ **todo**

todo: *Otis tarda*: bustard

todolo: omen, portent

todolombi: to be a good omen, to portend well

tofohoci: fifteenth

tofohon: fifteen

tofohonggeri: fifteen times

tofohoto: fifteen each

toforome: around the fifteenth of the month

togiya: a piece of a broken wooden object

tohin: a pointed peg to which ropes holding down the load were attached and which was stuck in the crossboard on the back of a wagon

tohišambi: to beg obtrusively

toho: a half-grown moose

tohobumbi: (causative of **tohombi**)

toholi: ⟶ **toholiyo**

toholiyo: small flat cakes made in the shape of cash (Chinese coins)

toholon: tin

 toholon hoošan: paper pasted to a very thin sheet of tin, tinfoil

 toholon muke: quicksilver

tohoma: saddle skirt: a leather covering that hangs down on both sides of a saddle for the protection of the rider's legs

 tohoma i daldakū: a leather border on the **tohoma** at the place where the stirrups rub against it

tohombi: **1**. to hitch up (a wagon), to saddle (a horse); **2**. to place rope along the edge of a net in order to draw it closed; **3**. to weave rope from bamboo splints or reeds

tohome: ⟶ **tohoma**

tohomimbi: to button, to button up

tohon: a (Chinese-style) button

 tohon hadambi: to sew on a button

 tohon i fesin: eye for a Chinese-style button

 tohon i senciku: loop for a button

tohoro: wagon wheel

 tohoro duha: the small intestine of a pig

tohorobumbi: ⟶ **tohorombumbi**

tohorokū: a stone roller used for leveling cultivated earth

tohorombi: (-ko) to calm down, to set one's mind at ease, to be comforted

tohorombumbi: **1**. (causative of **tohorombi**); **2**. to calm down, to put at ease; **3**. to pacify, to comfort

tohoron: ⟶ **tohoro**

toilokošombi: to gaze around indecisively

toiton: **1**. one name for the cuckoo; cf. **kekuhe**; **2**. a crafty person — so called because, like the cuckoo, he is hard to catch

toitonggo: crafty, wily

tojin: peafowl, peacock; cf. **kundujin**

 tojin funggaha kiru: a light blue banner of the Imperial Escort with the figures of peacock feathers embroidered on it

 tojin funggaha saracan: a tiered parasol with figures of peacock feathers embroidered on it

 tojin gasha: ⟶ **tojin**

 tojin i funggala: peacock feather

 tojin i funggala hadambi: to stick a peacock feather into a hat

 tojin kiru: a banner of the Imperial Escort embroidered with a figure of a peacock

tojingga šun dalikū: a large round silk fan of the Imperial Escort in the form of peacock tail feathers

tok: (onomatopoetic) the sound of striking a hollow wooden object

tok tok: (onomatopoetic) the sound of repeatedly striking a hollow wooden object

tok tok seme: (onomatopoetic) the sound of the heart beating

tokai: the flat side of a **gacuha**; cf. **taba**

tokdon: constellation, lunar mansion

tokdonggo: pertaining to a constellation

tokobumbi: **1**. (causative or passive of **tokombi**); **2**. to have a sharp pain in the belly

tokombi: to stab, to stick, to prick

tokošokū: an implement for pricking or stabbing

tokošombi: to prick, to stab continually

toksibumbi: (causative of **toksimbi**)

toksikū: **1**. a small hammer; **2**. a hollow wooden fish beaten by Buddhist monks

toksimbi: to knock, to strike, to beat

toksin: a wooden percussion instrument shaped like a square peck measure

toksitu: a 'wooden fish' — a hollow wooden fish that is struck rhythmically during Buddhist ceremonies

tokso: village

    tokso be kadalara ba: (管莊房) Office of Village Administration in the Board of Finance in Mukden

    tokso tuli: village

    toksoi bošokū: village chief, one in charge in a village

    toksoi da: village chief

toksorome: toward the village, to the village

    toksorome genembi: to go to the village

tokto: ⟶ **tokton**

toktoba ilha: *Platycodon grandiflorum*: balloon flower

toktobumbi: **1**. (causative or passive of **toktombi**); **2**. to fix, to solidify, to make sure; **3**. to decide; **4**. to inlay; **5**. to pacify, to put down (a revolt), to bring under control

    toktobure gisun: oral agreement

toktofi: (perfect converb of **toktombi**) certainly, surely, without fail

toktoho: ⟶ **toktombi** (subheading)

toktohon: determination, certainty, fixedness

    toktohon akū: uncertain, without certainty, undependable

toktokū: ⟶ **ayan toktokū**

toktombi: **1**. to be fixed, to be established, to be settled; **2**. to be decided, to be determined; **3**. to be pacified

    toktoho doro: an established principle

    toktoho gisun: phrase, idiom, proverb

    toktoho kooli: an established rule

    toktoho leolen: a fixed or definite theory or opinion

tokton: resolution, determination

toktonombi: **1**. to go to fix; **2**. to get backed up (said of water)

toktosi: broker, middleman, agent

tolbotu: a gray horse with circular markings on its side

toldohon: an engraved band or ring on the hilt of a sword or dagger

tolgimbi: (**-ka**) to dream

tolgimbumbi: **1**. (causative of **tolgimbi**); **2**. to appear in a dream

tolgin: dream

tolgin getembi: to awake from a dream

tolgišambi: to dream about crazy things, to have wild dreams

tolhimbi: ⟶ **tolgimbi**

tolhin: ⟶ **tolgin**

tolholombi: to cover with birch bark

tolhon: birchbark

    tolhon i ficakū: a deer lure (a kind of whistle) made of birch bark

    tolhon weihu: a birchbark canoe

toli: **1**. a small mirror used by shamans; **2**. a belt for holding up children's trousers

tolobumbi: (causative of **tolombi**)

tolombi: **1**. to count; **2**. to light a torch

tolon: torch

    tolon tolombi: to light a torch

toltoholombi: to bind with a ring or band; cf. **toldohon**

toltohon: ⟶ **toldohon**

tombi: ⟶ **toombi**

tome: (postposition) every, each

tomgiyambi: ⟶ **tuwamgiyambi**

tomhiyan: ⟶ **tuwancihiyan**

tomhiyatambi: ⟶ **tuwanggiyatambi**

tomika cecike: a name for the wren; cf. **jirha cecike**

tomilabumbi: (causative or passive of **tomilambi**)

tomilambi: to dispatch, to delegate, to assign, to appoint, to give a commission to

    tomilame sonjombi: to select by roll call

    tomilame tucibumbi: to send out on commission, to assign

tomilandumbi: to dispatch together

tomobumbi: (causative of **tomombi**)

tomohonggo: constant, persevering, determined, calm, composed

tomombi: **1**. to nest; **2**. to rest, to stand still

tomon: **1**. nesting, resting; **2**. grave pit, hole in which a coffin is placed

    tomon i ba: a burial vault

    tomon musen: grave

tomonjimbi: **1**. to come to nest; **2**. to come to rest

tomoo: frame used for weaving nets

tomorhan: hood for a falcon

tomorhon: clear, lucid

tomoro: a medium-sized bowl

tomorohon: ⟶ **tomorhon**

tomoron: a bronze sacrificial vessel used for holding soups

tomortai: right in the bull's-eye, right on the mark

tomotu lorin: offspring of a donkey and a cow

tomsobumbi: (causative of **tomsombi**)

tomsombi: **1**. to pick up (something dropped), to collect, to gather up, to recover; **2**. to collect the remains of a cremated corpse on the third or fifth day after the cremation; **3**. to encoffin, to place someone's remains in a coffin

    tomsome yalumbi: to remount after a horse has reared

ton: **1**. number; **2**. counting, reckoning; **3**. fate; **4**. one of the twenty-four divisions of the solar year

    ton akū: **1**. frequently, often, from time to time; **2**. without number, innumerable

    ton arambi: to make up the number, to pass muster, to do perfunctorily, to muddle through

    ton be gaihakū: numberless, innumerable

    ton de daburakū: to hold in contempt, to despise

    ton i: (instrumental of **ton**) in number, in quantity

    ton i kemun: a weight

    ton i sindambi: to set a quota

    ton i songkoi: according to the agreed amount

    ton i sucungga inenggi: the first day of one of the twenty solar divisions of the year

    ton jalukiyambi: to make up the number, to fill the quota

tondo: straight, upright, loyal, fair, accurate

    tondo akdun: loyalty and trust

    tondo akū: inaccurate

    tondo amban: **1**. a loyal subject; **2**. a loyal minister

    tondo baturu: loyal and brave

    tondo hiyoošan: loyal and filial

    tondo hošo: right angle

    tondo sijirhūn: loyal and upright

    tondo unenggi: faithful, staunch

    tondoi hūdašambi: to do business fairly

tondokon: **1**. rather straight; **2**. rather loyal, upright

    tondokon niyalma: an upright man

tondolombi: to go straight, to follow a straight course

tondongge: upright, honest, loyal

tong pan: Second Class Sub-Prefect, *BH* 849A

tong seme: hard, tough

tong tong: (onomatopoetic) the sound of a shaman's drum

tongga: limited, rare, few

    tongga baita: rare event

tonggalu ilha: the common day lily — a plant that deer like to eat

tonggime: brief and to the point

    tonggime alambi: to relate clearly and in detail

tonggo: thread, string, yarn

    tonggo boso: cloth from which an **aktaliyan** is made

    tonggo midaha: a wingless insect resembling a cricket with a large belly

    tonggo suje: satin cloth woven from yarn

    tonggo suri: silk cloth woven from yarn

    tonggo tabumbi: to hang yarn

tonggolibumbi: (causative of **tonggolimbi**)

tonggolikū: somersault

tonggolimbi: to somersault, to tumble

    tonggolime miyoocalambi: to fire salvos

    tonggolime tuhembi: to tumble off a horse

tongki: dot, point

    tongki fuka: dots and circles (of the Manchu alphabet)

    tongki fuka akū hergen: the old Manchu script (before 1641) that lacked dots and circles

    tongki gidambi: to place dots

tongkimbi: **1**. to flip with the finger; **2**. to write a dot, to make a dot

tongkin: a gong used when opening and closing the city gates

    tongkin jungken: hour

tongkišakū: a kind of small cymbal

tongkišambi: **1**. to beat a small cymbal; **2**. to hit, to pound on, to hit repeatedly

tongmo: ⟶ **dongmo**

tongsimbi: **1**. to chirp, to cry (said of the cuckoo); **2**. to recite incantations

tongsirambi: to tell a story

tonikū: chessboard, a board for playing *go*

tonio: **1**. *go*, encirclement chess; **2**. a piece used in playing *go*

    tonio efimbi: to play *go*

    tonio sindambi: to play *go*

tonjimbi: to chase fish in a certain direction by beating the water

tonju: ⟶ **tono jinggeri**

tono: **1**. knob, barb, round head; **2**. barbs on a
garma arrow; **3**. knob on the top of a tent

tono alhūwa: spiral opacity in the eye

tono jinggeri: knob-like decorations on the tops
of palace buildings and on city gates

tontu: a fabulous goat-like beast with only one horn
(said to attack the unjust party in a quarrel)

tontu mahatun: an ancient-style hat

too: **1**. a hand drum; **2**. used in older texts for
Chinese *tuǒ* (庹), a double arm's length, a
fathom (about 5.5 feet)

toobumbi: (causative or passive of **toombi**)

toodabumbi: (causative of **toodambi**)

toodambi: to return (a debt or loan), to repay, to
recompense

toodanjimbi: to bring back, to return to the owner

toodz: pad, support

toohan: small metal ornaments attached to both
sides of a belt

toohanjambi: to vacillate, to be hesitant, to be slow
in deciding

tookabumbi: **1**. (causative of **tookambi**); **2**. to
postpone, to delay, to waste (someone's
time); **3**. to drive away, to banish (sadness,
melancholy); **4**. to miss, to neglect; **5**. to
leave a place

tookambi: to procrastinate, to delay, to postpone, to
waste (time)

tookan akū: **1**. without procrastination, without
delay; **2**. unrestrained

tookanjambi: to procrastinate, to drag out, to delay,
to be delayed

tookanjame ilinjame: lingering about, pacing
back and forth

toombi: to scold, to rail at, to abuse, to curse

toome: ⟶ **tome**

toonumbi: to quarrel, to abuse one another

tooro: peach; cf. **toro**

toose: **1**. weight (for a balance); **2**. power, authority,
right; **3**. spindle

toose akū: lacking authority, without power

toose arga: flexible tactics

toose be jafara amban: plenipotentiary

toose horon: power and influence

toose hūsun: power, authority

toose salibumbi: to monopolize power

tooselambi: **1**. to weigh on a balance; **2**. to wind on
a spindle; **3**. to exercise authority, to

exercise one's power; **4**. to ponder, to
discuss

toosengge: powerful, mighty

tor seme: winding, whirling, spinning

torgibumbi: (causative of **torgimbi**)

torgikū: a top

torgikū tungken: a drum, narrow at the top and
bottom, which is beaten on horseback

torgimbi: **1**. to spin, to circle; **2**. to write a circle of
the Manchu script, to make a circle

torhikū mahala: a hat with a straight fur-trimmed
brim

torho cecike: a name for the wren; cf. **jirha cecike**

torho moo: long poles at both ends of a dragnet
used for fishing in a river

torhombi: **1**. to encircle, to surround; **2**. to revolve,
to rotate

torhome: ın a cırcle, around

torhome tembi: to sit around in a circle

torhon: a name for the woodpecker; cf. **fiyorhon**

torhonombi: to form circles, to form rings

toribumbi: to wander, to roam, to have no fixed
abode

toribuhangge: wanderer, one without a fixed
home, a bad name applied to women who
have had more than one husband, or to a
slave who has served more than one master

torimbi: to wander around homeless, to live as a
vagabond

toro: peach

toro efen: peach cake — a symbol of longevity

toro moo: peach tree

toroci: the name of a sour peach-like fruit from
Anhui that is eaten salted

torombi: (-ko) to calm down, to settle down, to put
one's mind at ease

torombumbi: **1**. (causative of **torombi**); **2**. to put at
ease, to comfort, to console

toron: **1**. flying dust, a dust storm; **2**. footprint, trail,
trace; **3**. scar, blemish; **4**. brand (on cattle)

tos seme: (onomatopoetic) the sound made by an
arrow or similar implement piercing an
object cleanly

tos seme tucike: came right through (an arrow)

tose: ⟶ **toose**

tosi: white spot on the forehead of an animal

tosingga: having a white spot on the forehead

tosobumbi: (causative of **tosombi**)

tosombi: **1**. to guard against, to prepare for in advance, to take precautions against; **2**. to intercept, to cut off, to ambush on the way, to lie in wait for

 tosome bodombi: to plan in advance

totan: a name for the pelican; cf. **kūtan**

totorombi: to be mischievous, to fool around

toyon: aim, accuracy (in archery)

 toyon baha: hit the target, aim was accurate

toyonggo: accurate (especially of clocks)

tu: **1**. a large military standard; **2**. banner cavalry, banner guard

 tu elkimbi: to wave a banner

 tu i janggin: (護軍統領) Captain-General, *BH* 734

 tu i janggin i siden yamun: (護軍統領衙門) headquarters of a **tu i janggin**

 tu kiru: standards and banners

 tu wecembi: to make a sacrifice to the standard

tu mei ilha: *Rubus rosifolius*: roseleaf raspberry

tub: esteemed, earnest

tuba: there, that place

 tubaci: thence, from there

 tubade: there, at that place

tubaingge: that which is there

tubehe: *Hemibarbus labeo*: Amur barbell

tubet: Tibet, Tibetan

 tubet abuha ilha: Tibetan sunflower

 tubet kiongguhe: Tibetan myna

 tubet mooi hasi: Tibetan persimmon

 tubet šu ilha: dahlia

tubi: **1**. half of a half, one fourth, piece, fragment; **2**. a basket that is placed upside down on chickens; **3**. a weir basket for fish, a weel; **4**. basket or cage for catching crickets

tubihe: fruit

 tubihe belhere falgari: (掌醢署) section in charge of fruit in the Court of Banqueting

tubihenembi: to form fruit, to bear fruit

tubilembi: to catch in a weir basket, to place a basket over chickens

tubingga moo: a tall tree of Jiangxi with thick, red, bitter bark and a chestnut-like fruit

tubišembi: to conjecture, to guess, to surmise, to infer

tubitu: another name for the **tontu**

tucibubumbi: (causative of **tucibumbi**)

tucibumbi: **1**. (causative of **tucimbi**); **2**. to take out, to bring out, to remove (from inside something); **3**. to take a coffin to the place of burial; **4**. to recommend; **5**. to reveal, to discover; **6**. to appoint, to delegate, to send out (on a mission); **7**. to publish; **8**. to save, to rescue

 tucibure bithe: copy of a memorial sent from the provinces

tucibun: **1**. promotion, recommendation; **2**. postface (of a book)

tucibunjimbi: to come to take out, etc.

tucibunumbi: to take out together, etc.

tucibure: ⟶ **tucibumbi** (subheading)

tucibusi: publisher

tucimbi: (-ke) **1**. to come out, to come forth, to appear; **2**. to exit, to go out, to leave; **3**. to rise (said of the sun); **4**. to sprout, to spring forth, to originate from; **5**. to come about, to happen

 tucire de selgiyebure kiru: a yellow banner of the escort embroidered with the words **tucire de selgiyebure** 'announcing when going out'

tucin: reason, cause, origin

tucine: red center of a target, bull's-eye

tucinderakū: to be nothing other than

tucinembi: **1**. to go out (there); **2**. to appear

tucinjimbi: to come forth, to appear

tucinumbi: to come out together, to exit together

tucire: ⟶ **tucimbi** (subheading)

tudi enduri: the earth god; cf. **boihoju**

tufulembi: to put one's foot in a stirrup

 tufuleme dabali fiyelembi: to vault over a horse after putting one's foot in the stirrup

tufun: stirrup

 tufun de gaifi niyamniyambi: to shoot at close range from a horse

 tufun fesheleme kurbume fiyelembi: to turn around by kicking in a stirrup

 tufun i fatan: the bottom or footrest of the stirrup

 tufun i sengken: hole on a stirrup through which the thong that connects the stirrup to a saddle is passed

 tufun i tura: the iron (or bronze) support for the base of a stirrup

tufun jafafi kurbume fiyelembi: to turn around by taking the line that holds up the stirrup in the hand

tufun tatame cashūn fiyelembi: to lean backward by pulling back on the stirrups

tufun temšembi: to quarrel over the stirrup — i.e., the horse tries to prevent the rider from mounting

tugi: **1**. cloud; **2**. a cloud-shaped ornament

tugi aga: sexual intercourse

tugi alhata: with scattered clouds

tugi hetehe: the clouds dispersed

tugi neigen: clouds cover the sky

tugi noho suje: satin covered with cloud designs

tugi sunggari: Milky Way

tugi wan: a ladder used for scaling walls

tugi yur sembi: clouds billow upward

tugidei: a name for the golden pheasant; cf. **junggiri coko**

tugingga omolo: a descendant of the eighth generation

tugingge: cloud-like, cloud-shaped

tugingge fan: a tablet for Imperial edicts of favor

tugiri: *Canavalia gladiata*: sword bean

tugitu: a small sparrow-like bird that nests in the sand

tugitu ilha: the name of a tall lotus-like flower

tugitun: a gong that was beaten at Tianan gate when Imperial edicts of favor were issued

tuhan: **1**. a tree that has fallen over, roots and all; **2**. a single tree used as a bridge across a stream; **3**. a long pole

tuhašambi: **1**. to go across a bridge made from a single tree; **2**. to go step by step, to climb step by step

tuhe: **1**. lid for a pot; **2**. a trap for weasels made from willow branches and shaped like a pot lid

tuhe efen: a flat thin cake made of wheat flour and oil and fried on a skillet smeared with fat

tuhebuku: **1**. curtain; **2**. watergate, sluice; **3**. portcullis; **4**. a tassel of coral or gems hanging from a ceremonial hat; **5**. pendant (on a saddle, hat, or fan)

tuhebuku doohan: suspension bridge, drawbridge

tuhebuku eye: pitfall, trap

tuhebuku horho: a bird trap with a falling door

tuhebumbi: **1**. (causative of **tuhembi**); **2**. to bring to ruin, to drag into a crime, to implicate in a crime; **3**. to sentence; **4**. to lower (taxes); **5**. to let flow (tears), to shed (tears); **6**. to let one's hair hang freely; **7**. to bring to an end, to bring to completion

tuhembi: (-ke) **1**. to fall, to collapse, to fall down; **2**. to sink, to set (said of the sun)

tuheme afambi: to fall into poverty

tuhere fere: a kind of edible wild plant with yellow flowers

tuhen: conclusion, outcome, destination, final place of settlement

tuhenembi: to fall in, to fall behind, to go to fall, to fall (to the ground)

tuhenjimbi: to fall down from above, to fall toward the speaker, to come to fall

tuhenumbi: to fall together

tuhere: ⟶ **tuhembi** (subheading)

tuheri ebci: the short ribs of the chest cavity

tuhete: hanging down, dangling

tuhi: ⟶ **tugi**

tuhū: butcher, slaughterer

tui janggin: ⟶ **tu i janggin**

tui tui: from mouth to mouth, from hand to hand

tuibalabumbi: (causative of **tuibalambi**)

tuibalakū: carpenter's plane

tuibalambi: **1**. to plane; **2**. to scrape hair from a hide

tuiban: ⟶ **tuibalakū**

tuibumbi: to blow out the lamp and once again sacrifice to the gods after a shamanistic rite in the home

tuihūlu: short-lived

tuikūlu: ⟶ **tuihūlu**

tuilambi: to stampede, to run wildly, to be spooked (said of cattle)

tuilebumbi: (causative of **tuilembi**)

tuilembi: to scrape the hair of a slaughtered animal after scalding it

tuilendumbi: to scrape together the hair from a slaughtered beast; also **tuilenumbi**

tuilenumbi: to scrape together the hair from a slaughtered beast; also **tuilendumbi**

tuipan: ⟶ **tuibalakū**

tuk tuk seme: **1**. (onomatopoetic) pounding (said of the heart); **2**. filled with apprehension; **3**. to and fro, back and forth

tukda: sticks laid crosswise in a pot for steaming bread and things made with glutinous rice and millet, grate for steaming

tukden moo: *Calligonum mongolicum*, a tree similar to the **fiyatarakū**

tukiya da: a variety of wild onion

tukiyebumbi: **1**. (causative or passive of **tukiyembi**); **2**. to be elegantly attired, to have a striking appearance (after having made up)

tukiyeceku: boastful, proud, arrogant, having a feeling of superiority

tukiyecembi: **1**. to lift or raise together; **2**. to praise, to extol; **3**. to boast, to be conceited, to be self-satisfied; **4**. to take boiling water off the fire, to cool hot water by pouring it from one vessel to another

tukiyecenumbi: to extol one another

tukiyecun: hymn of praise, panegyric

tukiyehe: ⟶ **tukiyembi** (subheading)

tukiyeku: **1**. boastful, proud, arrogant, having a feeling of superiority; **2**. rack; cf. **mahala tukiyeku**

tukiyelembi: **1**. to have trembling shoulders (when a sick person has trouble breathing); **2**. to pout one's lips, to purse one's lips as a signal

tukiyembi: **1**. to lift, to raise, to hold up, to hold high, to carry; **2**. to offer, to offer in both hands; **3**. to hoist; **4**. to recommend, to praise, to laud; **5**. to promote, to advance; **6**. to call (honorific)

tukiyehe afaha: resumé of a memorial on a slip of paper

tukiyehe gebu: honorary name, courtesy name, style

tukiyehe gisun: memorandum, synopsis

tukiyehe silgasi: (優貢) Senior Licentiate of the second class, *BH* 522A, 631

tukiyehe šošohon: a summary of the important points of a memorial attached to the original with a yellow strip of paper

tukiyehe šošohonggo kunggeri: (貼黃科) an office in the Board of Civil Appointments

concerned with preparing summaries of memorials

tukiyeme gaiha hehe: midwife

tukiyeme gaimbi: to assist at a birth, to act as midwife

tukiyen: **1**. praise, form of address; **2**. offering

tukiyenjimbi: to come to lift, etc.

tukiyenumbi: to lift together, etc.

tukiyeri cecike: *Emberiza godlewski*: meadow bunting

tukiyeshun: looking up, facing upward

tukiyeshūn: written for **tukiyeshun**

tukiyesi: (舉人) Provincial Graduate, *BH* 629B

tuksa boo: a house made of birch bark — the same as **jeofi**

tuksaka: bastard, son of a whore; cf. **lehele**

tuksicuke: **1**. dangerous, in danger; **2**. frightful, startling

tuksimbi: (-ke) **1**. to pound, to throb (said of the heart); **2**. to be alarmed, to be anxious, to be afraid; **3**. to be exhausted (said of livestock)

tuksin: throbbing, alarm, anxiety

tuksitebumbi: (causative of **tuksitembi**)

tuksitembi: to be alarmed, to be very anxious

tukšan: calf

tuktan: **1**. beginning; **2**. originally, at first, for the first time

tuktan de: in the beginning

tuktan moo: a tree resembling the **fiyatarakū**, but redder; cf. **tukden moo**

tuktarhan: a ladder made from a single tree

tuktuma: armor used by cavalry

tuku: **1**. the outside surface, the outside; **2**. the outside part of a garment, facing

tuku jodon: grass linen with designs of wax on it

tukulembi: to put an outside part on something, to surface (transitive verb), to add an outer covering

tulbimbi: to estimate, to surmise, to ponder, to plan beforehand, to guess

tulbin: estimation, guessing

tule: outside

tule benjire kunggeri: (外解科) a section of the Board of Works

tule genembi: to go to relieve oneself

tule genere ba: privy, toilet

tule genere boo: privy, outdoor toilet

tule genere horho: ⟶ **tule genere ba**

tule genere hunio: commode, slop bucket, portable toilet

tulebumbi: (causative of **tulembi**)

tulejembi: to put on weight, to become portly

tulembi: **1.** to set (a snare); **2.** to cast (a net), to spread a net; **3.** to attach (a handle or frame)

tulergi: **1.** outside; **2.** outer, foreign

tulergi amsu i boo: (外膳房) foreign kitchen in the palace

tulergi ba: the area north of Kalgan (Zhāngjiākǒu 張家口)

tulergi efen i boo: (外餑餑房) foreign bakery in the palace

tulergi golo be dasara jurgan: (理藩院) Court of Colonial Affairs, *BH* 491

tulergi goloi bolori beidembi: to review in autumn the death sentences from the provinces

tulergi goloi hafan i kunggeri: (外官科) office in charge of enfeoffments and honorary titles for provincial officials

tulergi gurun: foreign country

tulergi hergen: the letters of the Manchu alphabet used for transcribing foreign sounds

tulergi jijuhan: the three upper lines of a hexagram

tulergi kūwaran i simnere baita be baicara hafan: (外簾監試官) the Examination Inspector of the outer hall

tulergi simnengge kunggeri: (外考科) an office in charge of successful examination candidates from the outer provinces

tulergi tanggingge boo: (外堂科) the name of an office in the Board of Civil Appointments

tuleri: the outside, the outer edge, outside

tulesi: outward, toward the outside

tulesi etumbi: to wear inside out

tulfambi: **1.** to ricochet, to bounce off; **2.** to fail

tulgiri niyehe: the name of a variety of duck — the same as **aka niyehe**

tulgiyen: **1.** outside, external; **2.** besides, otherwise, other (the word preceding is followed by the ablative suffix **-ci**)

tulgiyen arambi: **1.** to treat as an outsider; **2.** to act differently

tulgiyen be buyembi: to have an extramarital affair

tulgiyen gūnimbi: to consider an outsider

tulgiyen obumbi: to consider an outsider, to consider a special case

tulgiyen sargan: concubine

tulgun: ⟶ **tulhun**

tulhu: lambskin

tulhun: cloudy, dark

tulhušembi: to become cloudy

tuli: ⟶ **tokso tuli**

tulibumbi: (causative of **tulimbi**)

tulimbi: (**-ke**) to run over a deadline, to be overdue, to expire, to run out

tulimbumbi: ⟶ **tulibumbi**

tulin cecike: the name of the oriole in Shandong; cf. **gūlin cecike**

tuljembi: ⟶ **tulejembi**

tulu: the breast of livestock

tululambi: to promote, to advance, to push forward

tulum: a cowhide or sheepskin filled with air that is used to support the body across a river

tulume: a belt made of lacquered rattan and filled with air to aid a person crossing a river

tumbi: to hunt, to pursue

tumehe ilha: a white flower whose petals resemble butterfly wings

tumen: ten thousand, a myriad

tumen arbun bolgo niktongga mudan: the name of a piece of music played at a palace banquet while food was brought in

tumen de: in case, should it be that …

tumen de emgeri: in case, should it happen that …

tumen gurun: the myriad nations, all nations

tumen jaka: the myriad things, everything on earth

tumen jalafun dengjan: a lantern placed on a stand in the inner court at the New Year

tumen jalafun jecen akū: a myriad lives without limit — a birthday wish

tumen mukei tampin: the fourth vessel of the observatory's clepsydra (water clock)

tumen se: ten thousand years — long live … !

tumen se okini: long live … !

tumen tumen: one hundred million

tumenci: ten-thousandth

tumene ilha: the name of a flower whose leaves resemble birds' wings (of the two varieties, one is red with purple spots, the other is green with brown spots)

tumengge moo: *Ligustrum sinense*: Chinese privet

tumenggeri: ten thousand times

tumenleme: forming a myriad

tumete: ten thousand each

tumgetu: a certificate given to an official leaving on a new assignment

tumiha: teat

tumikan: rather thick, rather viscous, rather deep (colored)

tumin: **1**. thick (said of soup, paste, etc.), viscous; **2**. close, dense, concentrated; **3**. on close terms, intimate; **4**. deep (said of colors); **5**. strong (said of tea)

tumin lamun gu: lapis lazuli

tumin lamun suje de aisin dambuha ajige kiru: a blue banner of the Imperial Escort depicting a golden dragon

tumin lamun suje de aisin dambuha muduringga turun: a blue standard of the Imperial Escort depicting a golden dragon

tumin niowanggiyan: deep green

tumin soboro: olive green

tumin šušu: deep purple

tumin temeri: dark brown

tumpanambi: to have a large face, to have a pudgy face

tumpinambi: ⟶ **tumpanambi**

tumsoro: a variety of jujube from Sumatra

tun: island

tun giowan: ⟶ **mangga ceceri**

tung io: tung oil

tung jeng sy yamun: Transmission Office, *BH* 928; cf. **dasan be hafumbure yamun**

tung moo: *Vernicia fordii*: the tung oil tree

tung seme: (onomatopoetic) the sound of a drum

tung šeng: (童生); ⟶ **simnesi**

tung tang: (onomatopoetic) the sound of bells and drums

tung tung: (onomatopoetic) the sound of a drum

tungdz: lad, boy

tunggalabumbi: to run into unexpectedly

tunggalambi: **1**. to run into, to encounter; **2**. to experience

tunggalanambi: to go to encounter

tunggel: young boy

tunggen: breast, chest, bosom

tunggen bokšon: breastbone of cattle

tunggen de nikebumbi: to take to heart, to treat respectfully

tunggen jaka: breast, chest

tunggen neimbi: to be happy, to feel at ease, to feel unrestrained

tunggen nekeliyen: smart, bright

tunggi: **1**. bent over, curved, crooked; **2**. too taut (said of a bow when the string is too short)

tunggimbi: ⟶ **tunggiyembi**

tunggiowan: ⟶ **mangga ceceri**

tunggiyebumbi: (causative of **tunggiyembi**)

tunggiyembi: **1**. to pick up, to gather up; **2**. to collect the remains after a cremation

tunggu: a deep pool, deep part of a river, lake, or pond, the depths of the sea

tunggulembi: to treat a wound or bite with fluid obtained from burning willow branches

tungio: ⟶ **tung io**

tungjeo i calu: a granary in Tongzhou near Beijing

tungjy: ⟶ **uhei saraci**

tungken: **1**. drum; **2**. archery target

tungken can: drums and small cymbals

tungken can i kiru: a yellow banner of the Imperial Escort with the words **tungken can** woven into it in gold thread

tungken dumbi: to beat a drum

tungken i kemun: the round hole in the middle of a target

tungken lakiyara kemun: a hanging archery target made of felt

tungken tinggin i yamun: (鼓廳衙門) Complaint Section of the Transmission Office; cf. *BH* 928

tungken yoro: a small bone-headed arrow used for target shooting

tungkesi: drummer

tungki tangki: staggering, reeling

tungku: a small dragnet used for fishing under ice

tungkutembi: to fish with a harpoon through a hole in the ice

tunglu: patina, verdigris

tungnibumbi: (causative of **tungnimbi**)

tungnimbi: to treat a wound or bite with the fluid obtained from burning willow branches

tungse: translator, interpreter; cf. **hafumbukū**

tungse kamcimbi: to bring along an interpreter

tungserebumbi: (causative of **turgserembi**)

tungserembi: to translate, to interpret

tungsika gurgu: jackal

tungši: translator; cf. **tungse**

tungtung tangtang: (onomatopoetic) the sound of bells and drums together

tuniyeltu cecike: another name of the bird **niyengniyeltu cecike**

tuniyeme fekumbi: to jump with the aid of a pole, to pole-vault

tunuhū: *Chrysanthemum coronarium*: crown daisy

tur: **1**. (onomatopoetic) the sound of a horse clearing its nose; **2**. at a gallop

tur seme: at a gallop, fast, the sound of guns firing

tur tar: **1**. (onomatopoetic) the sound of muskets firing; **2**. anxious, frightened; **3**. (onomatopoetic) crackling (like frying beans)

tur tar seme: **1**. crackling, sputtering; **2**. anxious, fearful

tura: pillar, supporting pole in a tent

tura i ten: the base of a pillar, pedestal

turabumbi: (causative of **turambi**)

turaki: *Corvus dauricus*: jackdaw

turakū: waterfall, cascade

turambi: **1**. to pour, to pour off, to pour the water off rice or meat; **2**. to stand firm (like a pillar)

turame agambi: to rain heavily

turame ilimbi: to stand firmly

turbelji: a name for the eagle; cf. **tashari**

ture: the leg of a boot

turemimbi: to attach the leg of a boot or a shoe

turga: **1**. thin, skinny, lean; **2**. a round piece of cloth over the tassel of a hat

turga efen: round cakes made of bean meal without any oil

turgalambi: to become skinny, to slim down

turgatu: a skinny person

turgen: **1**. fast, swift; **2**. urgent, acute, serious (illness)

turgimbi: to clear the nose (said of horses), to snort

turgun: reason, motive, circumstances

turgun akū de: for no reason, without cause

turgun arbun: circumstances, situation

turgun be anambi: to put forth as a reason

turgun hacin: circumstances, plot (of a story)

turgunde: (after a participle) because, since

turgūt: Torgot, Oirat

turha: **1**. a round piece of cloth on the tassel of a cap; **2**. a dab (of rouge); **3**. ⟶ **turga**

turhun: ⟶ **turgun**

turi: bean, pea

turi arsun: bean sprout

turi cai: *Camellia japonica*: camellia

turi cecike: *Euphonia personata*: hawfinch

turi hoho: pea pod, bean pod

turi miyehu: bean curd

turibumbi: (**-he**) **1**. (causative or passive of **turimbi**); **2**. to come loose, to come untied; **3**. to let go, to lose; **4**. to emit (semen), to ejaculate; **5**. to catch fire

turibuhe ejen: loser, one who has lost something

turigen: **1**. rent; **2**. wages

turimbi: (**-he**) to rent, to lease, to hire

turihe hūsun: hired worker

turihe irgen: hired man, farm laborer

turihe niyalma: hired man

turihe ula: hired porter or servant

turitu: fermented soy beans, fermented bean paste

turšul: scout, spy

turšun: ⟶ **turšul**

turtun: a kind of thin silk yarn

turtun cece: a very light silk gauze

turu: **1**. a belt for carrying a sword; **2**. sayings of holy or wise men, traditional methods handed down by the disciples of a wise man; **3**. head, leader

turulabumbi: (causative of **turulambi**)

turulambi: to be first, to be at the head of, to be the leader

turun: a large standard

turun i cooha: Chinese troops of the Green Banner

turun i wecen: sacrifice to the standard (performed before battle)

turun wecembi: to sacrifice to the standard

turungge jungken: a musical instrument consisting of twelve bells on a frame, each one of which corresponds to one of the twelve earth's branches

tus seme ukcambi: to come loose (said of something tied)

tusa: profit, gain, benefit, advantage

tusa acabumbi: to have the desired effect

tusa akū: of no benefit, profitless

tusa arambi: to do something profitable, to do something to benefit someone

tusa ombi: to be of use, to be beneficial

tusalambi: to be advantageous, to be profitable

tusangga: beneficial, profitable

tusangga calu: a government granary in which surplus grain was stored to be sold to the people in years of famine

tusergen: a tall table on which cups and plates were placed at banquets

tushū: a cup given at the door to guests to drink from

tusihiya: a net for catching falcons

tusihiyalambi: **1**. to catch falcons with a net; **2**. to catch in the claws (said of panthers, tigers)

tusu biya: a month propitious for marriage

tusulambi: ⟶ **teisulembi**

tusumbi: (-he) **1**. to give away a girl in marriage; **2**. to be married (said of a woman)

tusy: chieftain of a native tribe

tusy irgen: subjects of a native chieftain

tušabumbi: (causative of **tušambi**)

tušahū: a name for the owl; cf. **hūšahū**

tušambi: **1**. to encounter, to meet with (something undesirable); **2**. to experience, to undergo; **3**. to commission, to charge with

tušan: **1**. duty; **2**. office, official post; **3**. commission

tušan be akūmbumbi: to fulfill a duty to the best of one's ability

tušan be alime gaimbi: to accept a post or commission

tušan be funtuhulembi: to neglect one's duty

tušan be gūtubumbi: to neglect one's duty

tušan be mutebumbi: to be fit for one's job, to fill a post successfully

tušan ci aljambi: to leave a post

tušan de afaha hafan: (登仕佐郎) honorary title for officials of the ninth rank second degree, *BH* 945

tušan de akūmbuha hafan: (儒林郎) honorary title for officials of the sixth rank second degree, *BH* 945

tušan de baitalabuha daifan: (奉直大夫) honorary title given to officials of the fifth rank second degree, *BH* 945

tušan de baitalabuha hafan: (修職佐郎) honorary title given to officials of the eighth rank second degree, *BH* 945

tušan de dosika hafan: (登佐郎) honorary title given to officials of the ninth rank first degree, *BH* 945

tušan de faššaha daifan: (朝議大夫) honorary title given to officials of the fourth rank second degree, *BH* 945

tušan de faššaha hafan: (微仕郎) honorary title given to officials of the seventh rank second degree, *BH* 945

tušan de ginggulehe daifan: (奉政大夫) honorary title given to officials of the fifth rank first degree, *BH* 945

tušan de ginggulehe hafan: (修職郎) honorary title given to officials of the eighth rank first degree, *BH* 945

tušan de kicehe daifan: (中憲大夫) honorary title given to officials of the fourth rank first degree, *BH* 945

tušan de kicehe hafan: (文林郎) honorary title given to officials of the seventh rank first degree, *BH* 945

tušan de mutebuhe hafan: (承德郎) honorary title given to officials of the sixth rank first degree, *BH* 945

tušan jergi: official rank

tušan ufarambi: to lose an official position

tušanambi: to happen upon something, to go to meet

tušangga mahatun: a hat worn by officials in ancient times

tušanjimbi: to come to meet

tušu: a private seal

tutabumbi: **1**. (causative of **tutambi**); **2**. to leave behind

tutala: as many (as that), those several

tutambi: **1**. to fall behind, to lag behind; **2**. to remain behind; **3**. to survive (from antiquity); **4**. to be overdue, to expire (said of a deadline)

tuttu: like that, thus, so

tuttu akū oci: otherwise

tuttu bime: nevertheless, however, yet

tuttu oci: if like that, if so, in that case

tuttu ofi: therefore, so

tuttu oso: so be it

tuttu otolo: even so, even to the point of being like that

tuttu seme: but, however, yet, although it is so

tuttusi: in that direction, thither, to there

tuttusi oso: a little more in that direction

tuwa: fire

tuwa agūra: firearm

tuwa buleku: convex lens, burning lens

tuwa dabumbi: to start a fire, to kindle a fire

tuwa fileku: brazier

tuwa i agūra: firearms

tuwa i fithen: sparks that fly out from a fire

tuwa i okto: gunpowder

tuwa ibere sabka: fire tongs

tuwa latubumbi: to set a fire

tuwa sindambi: to set a fire

tuwa turibumbi: to catch fire

tuwa usiha: the planet Mars

tuwa yaha: charcoal

tuwai agūra: firearm

tuwai agūrai kūwaran i siden yamun: (火器營衛門) Headquarters of the Artillery and Musket Division, *BH* 733

tuwai bujan usihai doohan i mudan: a piece of music played at court on New Year's evening when the lanterns were hung

tuwai buleku: burning glass, lens

tuwai efin: fireworks

tuwai eye: a fire pit

tuwai gūrgin: flame

tuwai okto: gunpowder

tuwai okto i namun: (火藥庫) ammunition-store of the palace

tuwai poo: a cannon

tuwai siberhen: fuse

tuwai siren: fuse

tuwabgiya: ⟶ **tobgiya**

tuwabumbi: **1**. (causative or passive of **tuwambi**); **2**. to introduce into an audience; **3**. to divine; **4**. to show, to exhibit

tuwabure afaha: a slip of paper on which appeared the names of those attending an audience

tuwabun: **1**. survey, review; **2**. view, prospect, situation

tuwabunambi: to go to be seen, to go to be examined, to go to show or exhibit

tuwabungga: the published list of names of successful candidates in an examination

tuwabungga hoošan: the paper on which examination results were written

tuwabunjimbi: to come to show or exhibit

tuwabure: ⟶ **tuwabumbi** (subheading)

tuwaci: ⟶ **tuwambi** (subheading)

tuwai: ⟶ **tuwa** (subheading)

tuwakiyabumbi: (causative of **tuwakiyambi**)

tuwakiyakū: guard, watchman

tuwakiyambi: to watch, to guard, to watch over, to observe

tuwakiyame tembi: to garrison, to defend

tuwakiyara cooha: garrison troops, guard troops

tuwakiyara hafan: (守備) Second Captain, *BH* 752D

tuwakiyan: discretion in conduct, watchfulness

tuwakiyanambi: to go to watch

tuwakiyandumbi: to watch together, to watch one another

tuwakiyangga: inspecting, supervising

tuwakiyanjimbi: to come to watch

tuwakiyantu enduri: the guardian deity of city walls

tuwakiyasi: guard, watchman

tuwakiyasi da: (守吏尉) chief of the watch

tuwakū: **1**. aspect, appearance; **2**. exemplary behavior; **3**. model, example

tuwakūn: **1**. appearance, sight, spectacle; **2**. the twentieth hexagram of the *Yijing*

tuwambi: **1**. to look, to look at; **2**. to observe, to examine, to oversee; **3**. to consult (the yarrow stalks), to divine; **4**. to visit; **5**. to treat in a certain way; **6**. (as an auxiliary) to try, to attempt

tuwaci: it looks as if … , it seems …

tuwame: (postposition with the accusative) in accordance with, depending on

tuwame kadalara hafan: (監督) supervisor, director, superintendent

tuwame weilebure uheri tuwara hafan: (監修總裁官) director-general

tuwara ba akū: extremely bad, hard to endure

tuwara gisun: reference to a case in the statutes

tuwara niyalma: a fortune teller

tuwamcin: circumspect, prudent (used in posthumous names)

tuwamehangga: nice to look at, attractive

tuwamgiyabumbi: (causative of **tuwamgiyambi**)

tuwamgiyambi: to straighten out, to correct (an error), to correct (something one has said)

tuwamgiyatambi: to correct, to make straight

tuwanabumbi: (causative of **tuwanambi**)

tuwanambi: to go and look, to go to visit

tuwancihiyabumbi: (causative of **tuwancihiyambi**)

tuwancihiyabun: cultivation, rectification

tuwancihiyakū: **1**. corrector; **2**. (庶子) Supervisor of Instruction in the Supervisorate of Imperial Instruction; **3**. rudder, helm

tuwancihiyakū be gidara moo: a piece of wood holding the rudder on the stern of a ship

tuwancihiyambi: **1**. to set upright, to straighten, to set aright; **2**. to correct, to rectify, to redress; **3**. to cultivate (virtue); **4**. to guide (a horse); **5**. to instruct, to train, to admonish

tuwancihiyara yamun: (春坊) a subsection of the Supervisorate of Imperial Instruction

tuwancihiyara yamun de baitalambi: to be promoted to the Supervisorate of Imperial Instruction from the Hanlin Academy

tuwancihiyan: correction, ordering, putting into order

tuwancihiyan dailan: a punitive war, a just war against an unrighteous enemy

tuwancihiyangga: rectifying, cultivating, admonitory

tuwanggibumbi: (causative of **tuwanggimbi**)

tuwanggimbi: to send to look, to send to examine

tuwanggiyakū: inspector

tuwanggiyambi: to inspect, to look over

tuwanjimbi: to come to look, to come to visit

tuwanumbi: to look together, to observe together, to look at one another

tuwara: ⟶ **tuwambi** (subheading)

tuwaran: Daoist temple

tuwašabumbi: (causative of **tuwašambi**)

tuwašambi: **1**. to watch, to guard; **2**. to keep close watch on, to supervise, to take care of, to watch over

tuwašara hafan: (雲騎尉) an honorary title of the eighth degree

tuwašara hafan i jergi janggin: (防禦) Captain, *BH* 97E, 746, 748

tuwašatabumbi: (causative of **tuwašatambi**)

tuwašatambi: **1**. to take care of, to supervise, to look after; **2**. to look at, to gaze upon; **3**. to be concerned, to worry

tuwekiyembi: to lift up (the hem of a skirt); cf. **tukiyembi**

tuwelebumbi: (causative of **tuwelembi**)

tuwelembi: **1**. to buy at one place and sell in another, to deal in, to trade in, to peddle; **2**. to hand back and forth

tuwelesi: peddler, small tradesman

tuweri: winter

tuweri be bodoro hafan: (冬官正) Astronomer for the Winter, *BH* 229

tuweri dosimbi: **1**. winter comes; **2**. one of the twenty-four divisions of the solar year, falling on November seventh or eighth

tuweri hetumbi: to pass the winter, to spend the winter

tuweri hetumbumbi: ⟶ **tuweri hetumbi**

tuweri ten: the winter solstice

tuweri wecen: the winter ancestral sacrifice

tuwerikten: the winter sacrifice to the ancestors

tuwerimu ilha: the name of a fragrant red flower with long thorny stems and a yellow center

tuweturi cecike: another name for the **turi cecike**

tuyabumbi: **1**. (causative or passive of **tuyambi**); **2**. to be sprained (said of the hands or feet), to be twisted

tuyambi: **1**. to bend, to curve, to make crooked; **2**. to bend backward (in wrestling)

tuyebumbi: (causative or passive of **tuyembi**)

tuyekte: *Vaccinium vitis-idaea*: red whortleberry

tuyeku: instrument for punching holes in metal

tuyeku yonggan: impure ammonia salts

tuyembi: **1**. to punch a hole in metal, to pierce (armor); **2**. to make a concentrated attack against one point

tuyembubumbi: (causative of **tuyembumbi**)

tuyembumbi: **1**. to appear, to be revealed, to be exposed; **2**. to have one's poverty or difficult circumstances become known at large

tūbumbi: (causative of **tūmbi**)

tūku: **1**. a wooden mallet; **2**. a pestle for pounding grain; **3**. flail

tūmbi: to hit, to beat, to pound; cf. **dumbi**

tūme efen: a kind of steamed millet cake

TS ⚹

For words beginning with **t**, see the section beginning on page 355.

tsai fung: tailor

tsai šen enduri: the god of wealth

tsaidz: festoon of colored thread or paper

tsaifung: ⟶ **tsai fung**

tsandzan: (參贊) advisor, consultant

tsang: **1.** granary; **2.** cabin on a boat

tsanjeng. (參政) councillor to a provincial treasurer; ⟶ **aliha hafan**

tsanjiyang: (參將) Lieutenant Colonel; cf. **adaha kadalara da**

tsoo ba dalan: dam made of grass

tsu: vinegar

tsui cecike: kingfisher; cf. **ulgiyan cecike**

tsui gasha: ⟶ **ulgiyari cecike**

tsui ilga: an ornament made of kingfisher feathers

tsun: a Chinese inch; cf. **jurhun**

U ᡩ᠊ ᡪ᠊

u: **1**. thorn, splinter; **2**. (onomatopoetic) noise made by ghosts and demons; **3**. elder; cf. **ungga**

u da: elders, the senior generation

u dzo: coroner

u seme: wailing, howling

u tung moo: *Firmiana simplex*: Chinese parasol tree; cf. **urangga moo**

u u: (onomatopoetic) the sound of weeping

uba: **1**. here, this place; **2**. this (thing)

    uba adarame: What is this all about?, What is going on here?

    ubaci: hence, from here

    ubade: at this place, here

    ubade ainambi: what is wrong here?

uba taba gisurembi: to talk randomly

ubaingge: that which belongs here, one who is from here

ubaka tubaka: hemming and hawing

    ubaka tubaka seme: evasively

ubaliyambi: (-ka) **1**. to turn over (intransitive verb); **2**. to be inside out; **3**. to change, to have a change of heart, to turn against, to revolt; **4**. to turn into, to change into, to be transformed into

    ubaliyame etumbi: to wear inside out

    ubaliyame fahambi: to overturn (at wrestling)

ubaliyambubumbi: (causative of **ubaliyambumbi**)

ubaliyambumbi: **1**. (causative of **ubaliyambi**); **2**. to translate; **3**. to turn over (transitive verb)

    ubaliyambure hafan: official translator

ubaliyan: change, alteration, turning back

ubambi: (-ka) to go bad, to get moldy, to decompose

    ubame niyambi: to become discolored and start to go bad (of stored food)

ubasitambi: ⟶ **ubašatambi**

ubašabumbi: (causative of **ubašambi**)

ubašakū: **1**. changeable, fickle (person), volatile; **2**. fried dough twist

ubašambi: **1**. to turn over, to turn up (soil); **2**. to revolt, to rebel

    ubašaha hūlha: rebel

    ubašame forimbi: to strike repeatedly

ubašatambi: **1**. to turn over and over; **2**. to be devious, to be fickle; **3**. to do repeatedly

ubihiya yali: the meat from the cavities of an animal's shoulder bone

ubise: gallnut: excretions caused by insects on certain trees (used in Chinese medicine)

ubiyabumbi: (causative or passive of **ubiyambi**)

ubiyaburu: monster, horrid creature — an oath

ubiyacuka: detestable, hateful, disgusting

ubiyacun: disgust, abomination, loathing

ubiyada: detestable, hateful, execrable

ubiyambi: to detest, to loathe

ubiyoo: **1**. a kind of edible seaweed, agar-agar; **2**. a kind of shellfish

ubu: **1**. part, portion, share; **2**. fraction; **3**. responsibility; **4**. times, -fold; **5**. fate, destiny

    ubu akū: lacking a share

    ubu banjibumbi: to apportion duties

    ubu be suwaliyambi: to join parts, to amalgamate

    ubu goibumbi: to divide into portions, to allot shares

    ubu sibiya: portions and shares, shares

    ubui fulu: several times better, several times more

    ubui nonggimbi: to redouble

    ubui ubu: many times more, manifold

ubungge: pertaining to portions or shares

uca: hindquarters (of a cow, sheep, or deer, frequently cooked whole), butt portion of an animal

ucalambi: to dry meat in the open air

    ucalaha yali: meat dried in the air

ucarabumbi: (causative or passive of **ucarambi**)

ucarabun: encounter, experience, fate

ucarambi: to meet, to encounter

ucaran: meeting, encounter, chance, opportunity

uce: door

> **uce be cobalame neimbi**: to force a door open
>
> **uce gunireke**: the door is warped

ucika: **1**. waterproof case for a bow; **2**. the front fin of a fish; cf. **fethe**

ucikalambi: to put a bow in a case

ucilen: *Corylus heterophylla*: Asiatic hazel

ucubumbi: (-ha) **1**. (causative of **ucumbi**); **2**. to smear, to plaster

ucubun: mixing

ucudambi: to keep on mixing, to mix steadily

uculebumbi: (causative of **uculembi**)

uculembi: **1**. to sing; **2**. to mix

> **uculeme hūlambi**: 'to sing and shout' (said of troops after a victorious battle when one person sings a line and is then joined by all the troops in chorus)
>
> **uculere hehe**: female singer

uculen: **1**. song; **2**. *cí* (詞), a genre of Chinese poetry; **3**. ⟶ **ucilen**

uculenjimbi: to come to sing

uculere: ⟶ **uculembi** (subheading)

uculesi: a singer, a boy singer

ucumbi: (-he) to mix, to mix together, to blend, to mix plaster

ucun: song, ballad

ucuri: **1**. time, opportunity; **2**. ⟶ **ere ucuri**

> **ucuri nashūn**: opportunity, chance

ucusi: singer

uda: ⟶ **uta**

udabumbi: (causative of **udambi**)

udala: bridle bit

udambi: to buy, to purchase

> **udame icihiyara ba**: (買辦處) purchasing section of the Board of Banqueting

udanabumbi: (causative of **udanambi**)

udanambi: to go to buy

udanjimbi: to come to buy

udanumbi: to buy together, for each one to buy

udelembi: to take a midday rest

uden: rest at midday (especially on a journey)

udu: **1**. How many?, How much?; **2**. several; **3**. although

> **udu goro**: How far?
>
> **udu juwan**: several tens

udu tuttu seme: although it is like this

udu udu: several, a number of

udu ursu: several layers

uduci: what … ordinal place?, **si uduci de bi?** 'What rank are you (among your brothers)?', **bi jakūci de bi** 'I am the eighth.'

uducingge: pertaining to which number in a series

ududu: several, a number of, many

udumbara: fig

udunggeri: how many times, several times

udursu: several layers

udute: How many each?

uduwen: *Euarctos thibetanus*: male Tibetan black bear; cf. **jaira**

ufa: flour, meal, powder

> **ufa cai**: tea with flour mixed in it
>
> **ufa i da**: (wheat) bran
>
> **ufa i šugi**: wheat gluten
>
> **ufa moselambi**: to mill flour

ufabumbi: (causative of **ufambi**)

ufambi: to mill flour

ufarabumbi: **1**. (causative of **ufarambi**); **2**. to be missing; **3**. to lose; **4**. to die

ufaracun: loss, failure, error

ufaraki: a slight error

ufarambi: **1**. to err, to make a mistake about something, to fail, to miss, to lose (interest); **2**. to perish, to die

ufaran: fault, error, failure

ufaršambi: to make continuous errors

ufibumbi: (causative of **ufimbi**)

ufihi: ⟶ **ufuhi**

ufimbi: to sew; cf. **ifimbi**

> **ufire tabure sain**: talented at sewing

ufin: seam; cf. **ifin**

ufuhi: part, share, portion

ufuhu: lung

> **ufuhu efen**: small deep-fried pastries made of honey, egg, and flour
>
> **ufuhu fahūn**: inner being, inner thought
>
> **ufuhu i abdaha**: lobe of a lung
>
> **ufuhu niyaman i gucu**: trusted friend, bosom friend
>
> **ufuhu wehe**: pumice: a very porous stone found in streams and that can be used for dressing sable hides

ufuhunembi: **1**. to form a soft, porous core; **2**. to form a red, porous appearance on the face

ugingge coko: a name for the chicken; cf. **ikiri coko**

ugung: centipede

uhala: testicles, scrotum

uhe: **1**. common, general, united, uniform, of one kind; **2**. joined together, joint; **3**. communality, generality, unity

uhe acambi: to join together

uhe dakū: **1**. harmonious, concordant; **2**. common assent, mutual agreement

uhe hūwaliyan: **1**. harmonious, compatible, concordant; **2**. mutual harmony

uhe hūwaliyasun: compatible, amicable

uhe kooli: general code (of law)

uhe obumbi: to unite

uhei: united, together, mutual, cooperative, by common agreement

uhei saraci: (同知) Subprefect

uheci: controller; cf. **dabsun juwere uheci**

uhelembi: **1**. to act together, to be together, to act cooperatively; **2**. to unite, to make general; **3**. to share

uhelenjimbi: to come to unite

uhen: sister-in-law: younger brother's wife

uhereme: altogether, *in toto*

uheri: **1**. altogether, jointly, in common, in general, taken as a whole; **2**. chief, main, head; **3**. general, outline, summary

uheri ba: headquarters

uheri be baicara yamun: (都察院) the Censorate, *BH* 206

uheri be baicara yamun i ejeku: (都事) Official of the Censorate Chancery, *BH* 211

uheri da: (總管) director, superintendent, commandant, controller-general, etc., *BH* 87A, 97E, 570, etc.

uheri da yamun: (總管衙門) Office of the Director, etc.

uheri dangse asarara kunggeri: (櫃總科) the Central Chancery of the Board of War

uheri dangse boo: (總檔房) Archives at the western and eastern Imperial tombs

uheri gebu: general term

uheri hešen: general principle, general program

uheri iktambure calu: the name of a granary in the city of Mergen (now Nènjiāng 嫩江) in Heilongjiang

uheri kadalara amban: (總督) Governor-General, *BH* 820

uheri kadalara da: (總兵) Brigade General, *BH* 751

uheri kooli: (會典) the assembled statutes of a dynasty

uheri kooli bithei kuren: (會典館) office charged with compilation of the **uheri kooli bithe** (會典)

uheri kunggeri: (總科) central chancellery

uheri saraci: Subprefect

uheri ton: total, sum total

uheri tukiyen: general name, general designation

uheri tusangga calu: the name of granaries of the Board of Finance in Mukden and Canton

uheri tuwame simnere hafan: examination proctor

uheri tuwara amban: (掌衞事大臣) Superintendent of the Imperial Equipage Department

uherilembi: to unite, to compile, to put together, to do in a general way

uherileme ejehe bithe: (一統志) the general dynastic geographical gazetteer

uherileme ejehe bithei kuren: (一統志館) office charged with the compilation of the general dynastic geographical gazetteer

uheritei: altogether, as a whole

uhesu: learned, highly educated

uhete: (plural of **uhen**)

uhetun: harmony

uhubumbi: (causative or passive of **uhumbi**)

uhukedembi: to act from weakness, to appease, to indulge

uhukeliyan: rather weak, soft

uhuken: **1**. soft, weak; **2**. gentle

uhuken niyeniyehun: weak, cowardly

uhuken niyere: feeble, weak

uhuken nomhon: docile, gentle

uhuken tuwabungga hoošan: white announcement paper

uhuken yadalinggū: weak, feeble

uhumbi: to wrap, to roll, to roll up

uhume: aunt: father's younger brother's wife

uhumete: (plural of **uhume**)

uhun: bundle, package

uhun buheliyen: a bundle made of grass or reeds

uhun i hūsun: packer, bundler: a man who puts rice into bundles at a granary

uhungge hoošan: wrapping paper

uhuri: ⟶ **okjiha uhuri**

uhutu: a scroll

uhūbumbi: (causative of **uhūmbi**)

uhūkū: a knife used for gouging or scooping — especially the knife used for making holes in bone and horn arrowheads

uhūlja: *Ovis ammon*: wild sheep, argali, Darwin's sheep

uhūlji: ⟶ **uhūlja**

uhūma niru: an arrow with a head curved on the end like a crescent moon (used for hunting)

uhūmbi: to gouge, to scoop out

uhūyan: a gouged out hole

ui nimaha: flying fish

uihe: horn; cf. **weihe**

uihe hadambi: to nail on the horn facing of a bow

uihengge: horned, having horns

uiherin: rhinoceros

uiheton: a fabulous pig-like beast with a horn on its nose (said to be able to walk ten thousand miles in one day and to understand the language of the barbarians)

uihetongge kiru: a banner of the Imperial Escort depicting a horn

uile: ⟶ **weile**

uilebumbi: (causative of **uilembi**)

uilembi: to serve, to wait on, to attend

uilen: service, attendance

ujan: **1**. boundary of a field; **2**. the end point, the end, extremity; **3**. minor details, nonessentials

ujan i boo: a building built near the side wings of a large house

ujan jecen: border, boundary

ujan šala: **1**. minor details or matters; **2**. odds and ends, patches, remnants, trifles

ujan šala de: secretly, behind one's back

ujan yalu: paths between cultivated fields

ujan yalu akū: boundless, limitless

ujeken: rather heavy

ujelebumbi: (causative or passive of **ujelembi**)

ujelembi: **1**. to be heavy; **2**. to act respectfully, to treat respectfully; **3**. to be serious, to act in a serious manner; **4**. to act generously; **5**. to value greatly

ujeleme baitalambi: to employ in an important position

ujeleme olhošombi: to be cautious

ujeleme tuwambi: to attach importance to, to consider important, to pay great attention to

ujen: **1**. heavy; **2**. serious; **3**. valuable; **4**. worthy of respect

ujen aciha: heavy load

ujen be etere morin: a horse that can carry heavy loads

ujen cooha: Chinese Banner troops

ujen coohai gūsa: (漢軍都統) a banner general of the Chinese banner troops

ujen erun: severe punishment

ujen etembi: to be able to bear a heavy load

ujen fafun: heavy penalty

ujen jingji: steady going, sedate, serious, grave

ujen jiramin: grave but magnanimous

ujen madagan: high interest

ujen weile: serious crime, felony

ujibumbi: (causative or passive of **ujimbi**)

ujibure tacihiyan i mudan: a piece of music played during the wine-drinking ceremony of the Metropolitan Prefecture

ujibun: nurture, upbringing

ujima: livestock, domestic animal

ujima eriku: a broom made from old wild broomstraw

ujima i horigan: a corral for livestock

ujimbi: (**-he**) **1**. to raise, to nurture, to nourish; **2**. to give birth to; **3**. to let live

ujihe ama: foster father

ujihe eme: foster mother

ujihe eniye: ⟶ **ujihe eme**

ujihe jui: foster son

ujire eme: nurse, wet nurse

ujire hafan: (牧夫) an official title of the Zhou dynasty

ujire kūwaran: a shelter or asylum for the destitute

ujime: ⟶ **ujima**

ujin: **1**. child of a household slave; **2**. colt of a family horse

ujin dahan: colt born of a family mare

ujin jui: child of a household slave

ujinambi: to go to raise, to go to nourish

ujindumbi: to raise together, to nurture together; also **ujinumbi**

ujingga niongniyaha: a name for the goose; cf. **niongniyaha**

ujingga niyehe: a name for the duck

ujinumbi: to raise together, to nurture together; also **ujindumbi**

ujirhi: *Felis manul*: manul, cat of the steppes

uju: **1**. head; **2**. first; **3**. the first month of one of the four seasons; **4**. a large bead at the beginning of a rosary; **5**. beginning; **6**. one of the twelve Manchu syllabic headings

uju ci aname uncehen de isitala: from head to tail

uju de acamjafi bahambi: to make it on the first try

uju de tebumbi: to seat in the place of honor

uju eterakū: without being able to lift the head

uju fusimbi: to shave the head (a sign of submission to Manchu rule)

uju gehešembi: to nod the head

uju gidambi: to bow the head

uju haihambi: to incline the head

uju henggenembi: to have disheveled hair

uju ilhi: first, first in rank

uju jai: first and second

uju jergi: first class, first rank

uju jergi hiya: attendant of the first class

uju jergi unenggi hehe: the wife of an official of the first rank

uju langtanahabi: has a big head

uju liyeliyembi: 'the head is dizzy' — to be dizzy

uju liyeliyešembi: to feel giddy, to feel light-headed

uju marimbi: to turn one's head

uju nimembi: one's head aches, to have a headache

uju sencehe: the chin of edible animals

uju šarambi: for the hair to turn white

uju šenggin fucihiyambi: to be badly battered, to be in a sorry plight

uju tengkibumbi: to let one's head hang, to be unable to lift one's head (said of someone ill)

uju tuwancihiyakū: a rudder at the bow of a boat used for turning the boat around

uju wašambi: to scratch one's head

ujuci: first, from the beginning

ujude: at the beginning, first

ujui bayan: richest

ujui coko: first, of the first rank

ujui funiyehe: hair on the head

ujui gebu: first place, champion

ujui jergi sain: best

ujui miyamigan: jewelry for the head

ujui mudan: the first time

ujui uju: first of all, paramount, the very best

ujulabumbi: (causative of **ujulambi**)

ujulambi: to head, to head up, to be in charge, to be head

ujulaha amban: (首輔大臣) Chief Minister

ujungga: first, leading

ujungga dangga: leader, headman

ujungga jui: first son

ujungge: ⟶ **ujungga**

ukabumbi: (causative of **ukambi**)

ukacambi: to steal away, to sneak off, to run away together

ukada: grassy mound in a swamp or bog

ukadambi: to run away

ukambi: (**-ka, -ra/-ndara**) to flee, to run away, to desert

ukaka hūlha: escaped criminal, fugitive from justice

ukambumbi: **1**. (causative of **ukambi**); **2**. to bury (a coffin)

ukan cecike: the name of a small black-headed bird that resembles the sparrow

ukandumbi: to flee together; also **ukanumbi**

ukanju: fugitive

ukanju be kadalame jafara bolgobure fiyenten: (督捕清吏司) section of the Board of Punishments concerned with deserters from the banner troops

ukanumbi: to flee together; also **ukandumbi**

ukaralambi: to be in flight

ukatan: a name for the pelican; cf. **kūtan**

ukcabumbi: (causative of **ukcambi**)

ukcambi: **1**. to come loose, to fall apart; **2**. to get free, to escape from, to elude

ukdu: ⟶ **ukdun**

ukdun: **1**. a hole in the earth in which people live; **2**. kiln

    ukdun boo: a cave dwelling, hole dwelling

ukeci: a kind of monkey resembling a black dog without a tail

uki: a female otter; cf. **hailun**

ukiyaka cecike: a name for the common snipe; cf. **karka cecike**

ukiyebumbi: (causative of **ukiyembi**)

ukiyembi: to eat gruel or some other thin substance, to sip, to slurp

uksa: unexpectedly, suddenly

    uksa faksa: totally unexpected

uksajambi: to come loose, to slacken, to become disengaged

uksalabumbi: (causative of **uksalambi**)

uksalambi: **1**. to loosen, to detach, to release, to disengage, to take apart, to dismantle, to untie; **2**. to leave, to depart from; **3**. to push away, to separate from; **4**. to extricate oneself from; **5**. to release an arrow after having taken aim

uksan: ⟶ **uksa**

uksen: a small woven belt or band

uksilebumbi: (causative of **uksilembi**)

uksilembi: to put on armor

uksilendumbi: to put on armor together; also **uksilenumbi**

uksilenumbi: to put on armor together; also **uksilendumbi**

uksin: **1**. armor; **2**. a soldier wearing armor

    uksin sumbi: to take off one's armor, to leave the army

uksingga: wearing armor, armored

uksun: **1**. clan, family, kin; **2**. members of the Imperial family descended from Nurgaci, the Imperial clan

    uksun be kadalara yamun: (宗人府) the Imperial Clan Court, *BH* 56

    uksun i hergen: the rank or position of a member of the Imperial clan

    uksun i tacikū: (宗室學) Imperial Clan School

    uksun mukūn: patriarchal clan

uksungga: consisting of many kin, having many relatives

uksura: **1**. branch of a clan; **2**. a people, a tribe

uktu: plaintive, sad

uktun: quiet, possessing character, able to hold one's temper

uku: **1**. a falcon trap made of a net and cage and containing a live bird as bait; **2**. a fish weir, a cage used for catching fish, a weel

ukuhe: ⟶ **ukumbi** (subheading)

ukuhu: *Physalis alkekengi*: Chinese lantern plant

    ukuhu yoo: ⟶ **ukuhe yoo**

ukulebumbi: (causative of **ukulembi**)

ukulembi: **1**. to turn down the brim (or ear flaps) of a hat; **2**. to surround

ukumbi: **1**. to surround, to form around (someone), to form a circle, to crowd around; **2**. to form the retinue of an official

    ukuhe yoo: small pustules on a horse's body

ukundumbi: to form a circle together, to form around together

ukunjimbi: **1**. to come to form a circle, to come to surround; **2**. to come with a retinue to pay homage at court; **3**. to turn toward; **4**. to surround

ukunu: a surrounding crowd or retinue

ukuri: *Oncorchynchus gorbuscha*: hump-backed salmon

ukūda: ⟶ **ukada**

ula: **1**. a (large) river; **2**. relay post, post station; **3**. *yámen* runner, porter, servant

    ula jafambi: to dispatch an official emissary

    ula kilahūn: the Yangtze gull

    ula kunesun: provisions provided at post stations, provisions provided by the government for a trip

    ula morin: post horse

    ula šusu: provisions taken by relay posts for a trip

    ula turimbi: to hire a porter or servant

    ula yalumbi: to ride a post horse

    ula yalure šusu jetere: post mount and provisions

ulabumbi: (causative of **ulambi**)

ulabun: **1**. tradition, what is handed down; **2**. biography

ulaci: post rider, relay rider

uladambi: to be lame because of a damaged hoof

ulahūn: another name for the Yangtze gull

ulambi: to hand down, to pass on, to hand on, to pass to, to transmit

    ulame afabumbi: to pass on to someone

ulame alambi: to pass on a message

ulame benere kunggeri: (遞送科) Transmission Office of the Board of War

ulame sarkiyaha bithe: copy of a document issued by a board for distribution outside

ulambumbi: (causative of **ulambi**)

ulan: **1**. traditional teaching, something handed down; **2**. ditch, moat, ravine, gorge; **3**. furrow, groove; **4**. (Mongolian) red

ulan hat: ⟶ **eikte**: Manchurian red currant

ulan ulan i: **1**. by tradition, in unbroken tradition; **2**. from mouth to mouth, from hand to hand; **3**. by stages

ulan yohoron: ditches and canals

ulana: *Prunus humilis*: Chinese dwarf cherry

ulanambi: to go to pass on to someone

ulandumbi: to hand down from one person to another, to pass on from one person to another

ulandume juwere falgangga: (遞軍所) freight transfer point on a river or canal

ulandusi: (提塘) Superintendent of a Military Post, *BH* 435

ulandusi tinggin: (塘務廳) Office of an **ulandusi**

ulangga kiru: a banner of the Imperial Escort with waves of the Yangtze depicted on it

ulbimbi: to jump from branch to branch (said of squirrels, sable, etc.)

ulcen: ⟶ **ulcin**

ulcilembi: to string (cash)

ulcin: string (of cash), strand (of jewels, pearls, etc.)

uldefun: large wooden winnowing shovel, winnowing fork

uldembi: (-ke) to become light, to dawn

ulden: light, light at dawn, the sun's rays, first light

uldengge: shining, lit up

uldengge usiha: a bright star of good foreboding

ulderhen: a name for the lark; cf. **wenderhen**

ule: *Atriplex sibirica*: mountain spinach, orache

ule umiyaha: a long yellowish insect with narrow wings that is used as fish bait

ulebubumbi: (causative of **ulebumbi**)

ulebumbi: **1**. (causative of **ulembi**); **2**. to feed, to raise (domestic animals); **3**. to dip a writing brush in ink, to saturate a brush with ink; **4**. to bestow favor

ulebusi: a man who fed animals destined for sacrifice

ulejebumbi: (causative of **ulejembi**)

ulejeku: collapse, landslide

ulejembi: to collapse, to fall down, to cave in, to tumble down

ulembi: to sew (a straight seam), to sew with long stitches

ulen: irrigation ditch, small ditch between fields

ulenggu: **1**. navel; **2**. large bead at the end of a rosary

ulenggu i siren: umbilical cord

uleri: ⟶ **uluri**

ulga: ⟶ **ulha**

ulgabumbi: (causative of **ulgambi**)

ulgakū: inkwell, well for ink on an inkstone

ulgambi: to wet, to dampen, to dip into a liquid

ulgan: pliant, flexible (bows that hold the bowstring well)

ulgimbi: ⟶ **ulhimbi**

ulgitun: ⟶ **ulhitun**

ulgiyaci: pigskin

ulgiyada nisiha: the name of a speckled river fish

ulgiyan: **1**. swine, pig; **2**. the twelfth of the earth's branches (亥)

ulgiyan biya: the tenth month

ulgiyan cecike: *Alcedo atthis*: kingfisher

ulgiyan erin: period of the day from 9 PM to 11 PM

ulgiyan manggisu: a name for the badger; cf. **dorgon**

ulgiyan orho: 'pig grass' — the name of a plant with fine stems, green leaves, and many branches

ulgiyan tūmbi: to hunt pigs in winter

ulgiyan umiyaha: woodlouse, sow bug

ulgiyangga: pertaining to the twelfth cyclical sign, pertaining to the pig

ulgiyangga aniya: the year of the pig

ulgiyari cecike: a name for the kingfisher; cf. **ulgiyan cecike**

ulgū: ⟶ **ulhū**

ulha: livestock, domestic animal

ulha tuwakiyara niyalma: someone hired to watch livestock, herdsman

ulha wara niyalma: butcher, slaughterer

ulhai oktosi: veterinarian

ulhambi: ⟶ **ulgambi**

ulhi: sleeve

ulhi asu: a net with sleeve-like appendages for catching fish

ulhi be lakcaha nimeku: homosexual tendencies

ulhi fisihiyembi: to shake one's sleeves as a sign of anger

ulhi hetembi: to roll back one's sleeves

ulhibukū: in antiquity, an interpreter for the eastern languages

ulhibumbi: **1**. (causative of **ulhimbi**); **2**. to explain to, to make clear to, to publicize

ulhibume selgiyere bithe: proclamation, announcement

ulhibure fungnehen: a letter of appointment for an official position of the fifth rank and above

ulhibure hese: ⟶ **ulhibun**

ulhibun: proclamation, notification, notice, bulletin

ulhicuke: understandable

ulhicun: understanding, insight, knowledge

ulhicun akū: without understanding or insight, ignorant

ulhicungga: possessing understanding or insight

ulhilembi: to put something in the sleeve

ulhimbi: (**-he**) to understand, to comprehend

ulhingge: understanding, comprehending

ulhingge akū: lacking in understanding

ulhinjembi: to begin to understand, to have a slight understanding

ulhisu: **1**. quick to grasp, sensitive, keen, clever; **2**. in one's right mind (not crazy)

ulhisungge: clever, intelligent

ulhitun: a protective sleeve, oversleeve

ulhiyembi: ⟶ **ulhimbi**

ulhiyen: gradual

ulhiyen ulhiyen i: gradually

ulhu: **1**. squirrel, ermine; **2**. ermine pelt

ulhu alban: tax on ermine pelts

ulhun: **1**. dewlap; **2**. hand guard on a knife or sword; **3**. band of cloth or a border on the neck of a garment or at the top of a quilt

ulhungge: made of squirrel skin

ulhū: reed

ulhū i hašahan: a reed basket for grain

ulhū i hida: a curtain of reeds

ulhūi hali: a swamp overgrown with reeds

ulhūma: *Phasianus colchicus*: pheasant — in particular the ring-necked pheasant

ulhūma algan: a large net for catching pheasants

ulhūma kūthuri: the name of a plant whose fine stems were used to make baskets and bird traps

ulhūma uncehengge šun dalikū: a parasol of the Imperial Escort decorated with pheasant tail feathers

ulhūmangga: decorated with pheasant designs

ulhūri gūwara: a name for the eared owl

uli: **1**. bowstring; **2**. fruit of *Prunus japonica*: the oriental bush cherry

uli acabumbi: to attach a bowstring

uli ilgin: thong of tawed (alum-tanned) leather

uli moo: the bush cherry

ulibumbi: (causative of **ulimbi**)

ulikū: a hole used for stringing (like the hole in a cash)

ulimbi: (**-ha**) **1**. to run a string or rope through a hole, to string (cash); **2**. to thread a needle; **3**. to put meat on a skewer; **4**. to make an offering to a deity

ulin: **1**. goods, property, possessions, riches, wealth; **2**. bribe

ulin banjibumbi: to create riches

ulin bayan: riches, wealth

ulin benembi: to give a bribe

ulin boigon: property, belongings

ulin de dosimbi: to be covetous

ulin dosimbi: to get rich

ulin fusembumbi: to become rich

ulin gaimbi: to take a bribe, to accept a bribe

ulin gidambi: to offer riches (silk, cows, horses, etc.) to a deity and after kowtowing, to sell them and offer the money

ulin i da: (司庫) Treasurer, Inspector, *BH* 77, 298, 384A, etc.

ulin i niyalma: (庫使) Inspector, Treasury Overseer, *BH* 77, 298, 384A, etc.

ulin kokirabumbi: to lose money

ulin madambi: to grow rich, to prosper

ulin nadan: riches, goods, possessions

ulin simbi: to bribe

ulin tebumbi: to plant stolen goods

ulin turire fusi: worthless creature (said of girls)

ulintumbi: (**-ha**) to bribe
    ulintume yabumbi: to practice bribery
uliyen: a container made from birch bark
ulkidun: a name for the partridge; cf. **jukidun**
ulku giranggi: collarbone, clavicle
ulkume: breast strap of a harness
ulme: needle
    ulme hūlhatu: dragonfly
    ulme i sen: eye of a needle
    ulme jibci: cushion for needles (especially one made of nuts and seeds)
    ulme tonggo: needlework
    ulme tonggo i weile: sewing, work of a seamstress
ulu: **1**. lacking a seed (pinenut, hazelnut, etc.); **2**. infertile (said of eggs); **3**. incapable of producing descendants, sterile; **4**. unclear; ⟶ **ulu wala**; **5**. a black horse with white markings
    ulu morin: ⟶ **ulu** (**5**)
    ulu umgan: unfertilized egg
    ulu wala: unclear, muddled (said of speech), muttering, murmuring
uluken: soft, spongy, fluffy
ulumbi: to collapse, to fall down; cf. **ulejembi**
ulume: roach (kind of fish: *Rutilus rutilus*)
    ulume butara se sirge asu: a small-meshed net made of silk used for catching roach (fish) in a swift current
ulun gidambi: in summer, to hunt wild animals that are lying in high grass to escape insects, to go on the summer hunt
uluncu: a wild plant from which a sour drink is made (possibly sorrel)
ulunembi: **1**. to wither on the stalk (said of grain); **2**. to become black and wither, to suffer blight (said of kernels of grain)
uluri: **1**. Chinese gooseberry, carambola (*Averrhoa carambola*); **2**. a kind of soft jujube
ulusu: entire, whole
    ulusu gurun: the entire country
ulusun: olive (apparently refers to the *Olea europaea*)
    ulusun moo: olive tree
umai: **1**. (not) at all, totally, entirely; **2**. (with negative verbs) nothing
    umai akū: not at all, there is nothing

umai banjinarakū ba: an area where nothing grows
umai sabuhakū: saw nothing
umai sarkū: knows nothing at all
umai seme henduhekū: said nothing
umai serakū: silent, without words
umainambi: there is not, nothing
    umainaci ojorakū: there is no way out, there is no other choice, unavoidable, inevitable
    umainaha ba akū: nothing happened, nothing can be done
    umainahakū: it is no harm, it was nothing, it did not amount to anything, nothing happened, it was of no consequence
    umainame muterakū: there is nothing that can be done (about it)
    umainarakū: it is nothing, it does not matter
    umaiserakū: say (said) nothing
uman: **1**. gums; **2**. the soft inner part of a hoof
    uman dabambi: to have a sore hoof (said of camels)
    uman sindambi: to thaw out frozen ground by building a fire on it
umbubumbi: (**-ha**) causative or passive of **umbumbi**
umbuci cumbuci: ⟶ **umburi cumburi**
umbumbi: (**-ha**) to bury, to inter
umburi cumburi: uneven, of uneven height (said of plants)
ume: verb used for negating imperatives (stands before the imperfect participle): **ume genere** 'Do not go'
umehen: the bone of the upper part of the front leg of animals
umerlembi: to become fat without conceiving (sows)
umesi: very, to a high degree
    umesi fakcambi: to pass away, to die
    umesi gajimbi: to bring more
    umesi teki: Let it be so
umesihun: ⟶ **umusihun**
umesilebumbi: (causative of **umesilembi**)
umesilembi: **1**. to put into effect, to carry out; **2**. to be to a high degree, to do to a high degree
    umesileme: truly, really
umga: ⟶ **umgan**
umgan: **1**. marrow; **2**. egg; cf. **umhan**
    umgan banjimbi: to lay eggs

umgan giranggi: thigh bone, femur

umgan šugi: the innermost marrow, quintessence

umhan: **1**. egg; **2**. ⟶ **umgan**

umhan banjimbi: to lay eggs

umhan bilembi: to lay eggs

umhan durun: cake (made with eggs)

umhan haksangga efen: baked cakes made from wheat flour, eggs, and sugar

umhanambi: to lay eggs, to form eggs

umhangga tubihe: egg fruit — a plant that grows wild, blooms in the second month, and has mature fruit in the eighth

umiyaha: insect, bug, worm; cf. **imiyaha**

umiyaha aššambi: one of the divisions of the solar year that occurs on the fifth or sixth of March

umiyaha yerhuwe: insects

umiyahalambi: to plait with colored thread

umiyahanambi: to get worms (said of fruit), to become wormy

umiyahangga fukjingga hergen: (蟲篆) the name of a style of Chinese calligraphy

umiyelebumbi: (causative of **umiyelembi**)

umiyelembi: to tie (a belt), to gird oneself

umiyesu ilha: the name of an exotic red bloom with supple stems

umiyesulembi: to put on a girth (saddle belly-strap), girdle, or sash

umiyesun: girdle, girth (saddle belly-strap), belt, sash

umpu: *Crataegus cuneata*: hawthorn

umpu debse: hawthorn jelly

umpu erhe: a red-bellied small black frog that lives in very cold springs

umriha: membrane, inner bark of a tree, membrane in an egg, thin skin of nuts

umudu: orphan

umuhun: the upper surface of the foot, the instep

umuhun be fehume murimbi: in wrestling, to throw one's opponent by stepping on his instep

umuhun tuheke: to be paralyzed by fear

umuri: a string for pulling closed the opening of a bag, drawstring

umursu: ⟶ **emursu**

umusihun: ⟶ **umušuhun**

umušuhun: lying on the stomach, prone, prostrate

un: a place for pigs to sleep, pigsty

una: *Lycium chinense*: Chinese wolfberry

unagan: ⟶ **unahan**

unahan: colt, foal

unahan sumbi: to foal, to give birth to a colt

uncabumbi: (causative of **uncambi**)

uncambi: to sell

uncanambi: to go to sell

uncanjimbi: to come to sell

uncanumbi: to sell together

uncehen: **1**. tail, tail end, tail (in Manchu writing); **2**. rear end (of a vehicle); **3**. the rear (of troops)

uncehen bošoro aga: a sudden brief shower

uncehen giranggi: tail bone, coccyx

uncehen golmin buhū: *Elaphurus davidianus*: Père David's deer, *mílù* 麋鹿

uncehen hetembi: **1**. to bring to a close, to conclude; **2**. to surround and attack suddenly from the rear

uncehen i da: the base of the tail

uncehen sarbašambi: to wag the tail

uncehen sirabumbi: to follow, to tail, to shadow

uncehen sirandumbi: ⟶ **uncehen sirabumbi**

uncehen šolonggo alhacan niyehe: the name of a speckled duck with a pointed tail

uncehen tuwancihiyakū: rudder

uncehen tuwancihiyakū jafambi: to steer the rudder

uncihen: ⟶ **uncehen**

unda: (see below)

unda sube: sinew of the spine

unda yali: tenderloin, meat on both sides of the backbone

undan: spring snow that has frozen on the surface and for which snowshoes are required

undanambi: to freeze on the surface (said of spring snow)

undarambi: (**-ka**) to creep, to spread, to get worse (said of an illness)

undašambi: to hunt on frozen spring snow

unde: not yet (particle used after the imperfect participle)

undeci: underling, bailiff (who administered floggings), *yámen* runner

undehelembi: to beat with a bamboo rod

undehen: **1**. board, plank; **2**. rod for flogging; **3**. wooden printing block

    undehen falan: **1**. floor board; **2**. a low legless wooden frame on which the throne sat

    undehen šusihe: boards and bamboo strips used for writing on

undeo: not yet?

undesi: lictor, policeman; cf. **undeci**

undu: vertical, upright

undufun: ⟶ **undehen**

undurakū: satin with a design of large standing dragons and without smaller horizontal dragon designs interspersed

undurambi: ⟶ **undarambi**

unduri: on the way, along (the road)

undustan: Hindustan, India

    undustan suje: a kind of red Indian silk with golden designs brought as tribute from Hami

unenggi: **1**. truly, really, honestly; **2**. true, honest, genuine; **3**. pious

    unenggi gūnin: sincerity, honesty

    unenggi hehe: title of the wife of an official of the second rank

    unenggi mujilen: honesty, probity

    unenggi tondo: loyal, faithful

    unenggi yalanggi: true and genuine

    unenggi yargiyan: honest, truthful, sincere, conscientious

unenggilembi: **1**. to deem true, to treat as genuine; **2**. to be true, to be genuine; **3**. to act sincerely, to behave honestly

    unenggileme yabumbi: to act conscientiously

unenggingge: that which is true, genuine

unesi: family objects handed down for several generations, heirlooms

ung: (onomatopoetic) the sound of a bell

ung ang: (onomatopoetic) sound made by deer and cattle

ung wang: (onomatopoetic) a nasal sound

ungga: older generation, elders

    ungga da: elder, person of an older generation

    ungga dangga: elders, the older generation

    ungga jalan: the older generation

unggala: **1**. cavity, hollow, empty space; **2**. muzzle of a gun; **3**. orifice

    unggala i ulenggu: the part of a musket that holds gunpowder, flash vent

unggalambi: to respect (one's elders), treat as an elder

unggalangga moo: a wooden clapper

unggan: ⟶ **ungga**

ungganumbi: to treat as an elder, to respect (as an elder)

unggašambi: to revere (one's elders)

unggata: (plural of **ungga**)

ungge: a kind of very fine, small wild onion

unggibumbi: (causative of **unggimbi**)

unggilakū: the covering of a pig's kidney, renal capsule

unggiljembi: to wag

unggimbi: (**-he**) to send, to dispatch, to send off

unggin: the hole in a spade, hammer, or ax used for attaching its handle

unggindumbi: to send together, to dispatch together

unggu: **1**. first, original; **2**. the first player at the **gacuha** game

    unggu amji: uncle father's elder brother

    unggu ging: the first watch (of the night)

    unggu mafa: great-grandfather (paternal)

    unggu mama: great-grandmother (paternal)

ungkan: frozen snow on the top of grass

ungkebumbi: (causative of **ungkembi**)

ungkembi: **1**. to turn over, to tip over; **2**. to cover with something inverted; **3**. to turn one's cup upside down to show that one has drained it completely

ungken ilha: the name of a flower that resembles an overturned cup

ungkeshūn: tipped over, awry, bent forward

uni nimaha: a spotted white sea fish that reaches a length of four spans

unika: a young locust

uniyehe: a name for the duck

uniyele: the yellow hair that grows at the base of a deer's tail

uniyen: female of certain animals, a milk cow

    uniyen honin: ewe: a female sheep

    uniyen ihasi: a female rhinoceros

uniyeri: strings of raw silk

untuhuken: empty, vacant

untuhukesaka: empty, seemingly empty

untuhulebumbi: (causative of **untuhulembi**)

untuhulembi: **1**. to be empty, to leave empty, to become vacant; **2**. to be idle

    untuhuleme dasimbi: to leave unlocked

untuhun: 1. empty, vacant; 2. hollow; 3. idle, vain; 4. emptiness, space

    untuhun acilambi: to grasp an opponent by the shoulders and fling him from side to side (in wrestling)

    untuhun anggai niyalma: idle prattler

    untuhun buda: vegetarian food

    untuhun de: in the air, in midair, in space

    untuhun doro: insincere courtesy

    untuhun durun: empty form, form without substance

    untuhun fiyelembi: to leap through the air and mount a horse from behind

    untuhun forgošome fiyelembi: in trick riding, to do a somersault on the horse

    untuhun gala: empty handed

    untuhun gebu: false reputation

    untuhun gisun: grammatical elements in a sentence, affixes and particles

    untuhun hergen: grammatical function word

    untuhun jergi: a sinecure

    untuhun simengge: vanity

untuhuri: in vain, for nothing

    untuhuri dasimbi: to be unlocked, to leave unlocked

untuhurilambi: to act in vain

untun: a small drum used by female shamans during rites in the home

untušembi: to beat a small drum (said of female shamans)

unubumbi: (-ha) 1. (causative of unumbi); 2. to put the blame on someone else

unucun: a child born after the death of its father

unujun: a name for the stork; cf. weijun

unumbi: (-ha) to carry (on one's back), to shoulder, to put (the hands) behind one's back

unun: a load (that can be carried on one's back), burden

    unun damjan: burdens, load

    unun fiyana: a frame used for carrying things on one's back, a pack frame

    unun uše: a strap used for carrying a gun on one's back

unurtu: opossum

upi jahūdai: a warship with sides painted black

ura: buttocks, rear end, rump

    ura fajukū: anus

    ura fulcin: the cheeks of the buttocks

    ura tebumbi: 1. to pursue an animal from the rear (after its escape route has been cut off); 2. to render someone speechless by saying something blunt

    ura tembi: to plump down on one's rump, to be unwilling to go forward

    ura tūmbi: to whip (the buttocks)

urahilabumbi: (causative of urahilambi)

urahilambi: to make inquiries, to seek information

    urahilame donjimbi: to learn from hearsay

urambi: (1) (-ha) to echo, to resound

urambi: (2) (-ka) to be bruised (with extravasated blood under the skin), to be bloodshot

uran: echo, resonance, peal

urandambi: to reverberate, to re-echo, to peal

urangga: sonorous, resonant

urangga moo: *Firmiana simplex*: Chinese parasol tree

urdebumbi: (causative of urdembi)

urdembi: to race a horse; cf. uruldembi

urebukū: 1. a home school; 2. driller, reviewer

urebumbi: 1. to practice, to review, to drill, to rehearse; 2. to cure (boil) silk floss or other fiber; 3. to refine (metal)

    urebume gūnimbi: to ponder deeply

    urebume hebešembi: to discuss at length

    urebume tacibumbi: to train, to coach

    urebure kūwaran: military training ground

urecuke: sad, lamentable, pathetic

urembi: 1. to be sad, to become sad; 2. to get ripe, to be ripe, to be done (said of food); 3. to be acquainted with, to be familiar with; 4. ⟶ urumbi

    urehe banjiha: alike by nature

    urehe usin: a ripe field, a field ripe for harvest

ureshūn: familiar, acquainted with, skilled, proficient, practiced

    ureshūn niyalma: acquaintance

urgalabumbi: (causative of urgalambi)

urgalambi: to lasso (a horse), to catch in a noose

urgan: a lasso (either a rope or a noose on the end of a pole)

urge: a paper figure of a person (used by shamans against baleful spirits)

    urge faitambi: to cut out a paper figure for use in a shamanistic ceremony

urgedembi: to turn one's back on, to be ungrateful for, to fail to live up to, to be unworthy of, to let someone down

urgen: **1**. length, extension, measurement, dimension; **2**. tone of one's speech

urgešen: a year-old deer

urgetu: a wooden funerary figure

urgumbi: ⟶ **urhumbi**

urgun: **1**. joy, felicity, happiness; **2**. auspicious sign, good portent; **3**. congratulations; **4**. half an inch; cf. **urhun**

    urgun arambi: to congratulate, to wish well

    urgun i baita: joyous event, pregnancy

    urgun i doro: congratulations

    urgun i doroi hengkilembi: to congratulate (by kowtowing)

    urgun i jiha: money given on festive occasions

    urgun i sarin: wedding feast

    urgun jobolon: joy and sorrow

    urgun sebjen: joy and pleasure

    urgun šanggaha dengjan: lanterns used at court to celebrate the New Year

urgungga: blessed, fortunate, auspicious

urgungge: joyous

    urgungge abka: Tuṣita heaven, one of the Buddhist heavens

    urgungge derengtu: a portrait

urgunjebumbi: (causative of **urgunjembi**)

urgunjembi: to rejoice, to be glad

urgunjen: one of the eight trigrams of the *Yijing*, consisting of one broken line and two solid lines

urgunjendumbi: to rejoice together; also **urgunjenumbi**

urgunjenumbi: to rejoice together; also **urgunjendumbi**

urguntu: joyful, happy

urguri: ⟶ **urhuri**

urgutu: ⟶ **urhutu**

urgūmbi: ⟶ **urhūmbi**

urhalambi: ⟶ **urgalambi**

urhu: tilting, one-sided, prejudiced, partial

    urhu akū: impartial, unprejudiced

    urhu amuran: partial to, having a special liking for

    urhu haiha: ⟶ **urhu haihū**

    urhu haihū: leaning to one side (said of walking), staggering

urhu haršakū: partial to one side

urhubumbi: (causative of **urhumbi**)

urhufi: ⟶ **urhumbi** (subheading)

urhuhe: ⟶ **urhumbi** (subheading)

urhulambi: to stagger, to stumble

urhumbi: **1**. to lean to one side, to be lopsided, to be partial; **2**. to be prejudiced to one side, to show prejudice

    urhufi gosimbi: to have a special liking for, to be partial to

    urhuhe ba: prejudice

urhun: the width of a finger, half an inch

urhuri: leaning, bent, not straight

    urhuri haihari: **1**. leaning to one side, staggering, poking along, weaving, fluttering to and fro; **2**. whirling (when dancing)

    urhuri niokan: a small arrow used in a game in which the arrow is thrown into a pot

urhušembi: to tilt toward one side, to stagger, to incline sharply to one side, to be very partial

urhutu: leaning to one side, having one leg shorter than the other

urhūmbi: to shy: to start in fright (said of livestock)

urhūn: shyness (said of livestock)

urhūtū: easily frightened (said of horses and other livestock)

uri: **1**. a round straw container used for storing grain; **2**. ⟶ **urui**

uribumbi: (causative of **urimbi**)

uriha: the tender (inner) bark of trees or the thin skin of nuts

urilembi: **1**. to get so fat that motion becomes difficult (pheasants), to be packed full (said of rat's nests); **2**. to store grass in a hole (said of mice)

urimbi: (**-he**) **1**. to collapse (said of a mountain or hill); **2**. to die (said of the Emperor)

urka cecike: common snipe, the same as **karka cecike**

urki: a horizontal support for a sail on a small boat

urkilambi: **1**. to make a big noise deliberately, to cause a commotion; **2**. to follow the lead of one horse in shying or urinating (said of other horses)

urkin: **1**. big noise, commotion, tumult; **2**. momentum, trend of events

urkin be dahambi: to drift with the stream, to follow the herd

urkingga: ⟶ **urkingge**

urkingge: noisy, tumultuous, mighty

    urkingge teišun: a kind of brass from which gongs were made

urkuji: often, continuously, steadily, uninterruptedly

urkulji: ⟶ **urkuji**

urlembi: ⟶ **urilembi**

urlu morin: a black horse with white spots; cf. **ulu morin**

ursan: new shoots that sprout from old roots, new branches that appear on a tree that has been cut back, shoots sprouting from grain dropped accidentally

    ursan sindambi: to leave something unsaid, to leave a sentence half finished, to pause in speaking

    ursan sursan: sprouts, new shoots

ursanambi: to sprout from grain that has fallen on the ground, to sprout from old roots or an old stock

urse: **1**. people, men, persons (plural of **niyalma**); **2**. others, other people

urseingge: someone else's

ursu: layer, level, -fold

ursungga: consisting of layers

    ursungga hoseri: five or ten boxes, one smaller than the next, placed one inside another

    ursungga hūntahan: cups, one smaller than the next, placed one inside another

    ursungga polori: baskets, one smaller than the next, placed one inside another

uru: right, correct

    uru waka: right and wrong

urubumbi: (causative of **urumbi**)

urui: **1**. steadily, constantly, always, usually; **2**. just, only

uruldebumbi: (causative of **uruldembi**)

uruldembi: to race a horse, to test a horse for speed

urulembi: **1**. to deem right, to consider correct, to approve, to agree with; **2**. ⟶ **urilembi**

urumbi: (**-ke, -ndere**) to get hungry, to be hungry

urun: **1**. daughter-in-law; **2**. wife

    urun gaijambi: to get married (said of a man)

    urun hengkilembi: to get engaged

urunakū: certainly, surely, for sure, necessarily, must, under all circumstances

urundumbi: to be constantly hungry

urunembi: to go about hungry

urusa: (plural of **urun**)

urušambi: to fulfill the duties of a daughter-in-law

urušembi: to deem right, to consider correct, to approve, to agree with

usa: exclamation used to get someone's attention

usabumbi: (causative of **usambi**)

usacuka: **1**. regrettable, deplorable, too bad; **2**. pitiful, sad

usacumbi: (**-ka**) to grieve or be distressed

usacun: sorrow, grief, sadness

usacungga: sorrowful, afflicted

usambi: (**-ka**) to be without hope, to be disappointed, to feel broken-hearted

    usame gasambi: to grieve, to be sad

usambumbi: (causative of **usambi**)

usandumbi: to be without hope together, to give up hope together; also **usanumbi**

usanumbi: to be without hope together, to give up hope together; also **usandumbi**

usari cecike: a name for the goatsucker, the same as **simari cecike**

usata: milt, soft roe

use: **1**. seed; **2**. insect egg

    use faha: grain, seed

    use faha cifun: grain tax

    use tarimbi: to sow seed

    use usembi: to plant seed

    use waliyambi: to lay eggs (said of insects)

    usei hithen: a large box for holding seed

usebumbi: (causative of **usembi**)

useku: a seeder, an implement for planting seed

uselembi: ⟶ **usembi**

usembi: to plant, to seed

    useme tarimbi: to plant, to seed

usen: ⟶ **juwen usen**

usene ilha: the name of a species of ranunculus

usenembi: **1**. to go to plant seeds, to go to plant; **2**. to form seeds, to run to seed

usengge: seed-like, grain-like

usenumbi: to seed together, to plant together

userci: a sour pomegranate-like fruit

userembi: ⟶ **usuršembi**

useri: pomegranate; cf. **šilio**

useri cuse moo: a bamboo-like plant that forms red seed pods

ushabumbi: **1**. (causative or passive of **ushambi**); **2**. to be blamed or rejected (by spirits or demons)

ushacun: anger, resentment, disappointment

ushambi: **1**. to be annoyed, to resent, to complain, to feel aggrieved; **2**. to be disappointed; cf. **usambi**

ushandumbi: to be angry together, to resent together; also **ushanumbi**

ushanumbi: to be angry together, to resent together; also **ushandumbi**

ushatambi: to sulk, to pout, to be resentful

ushe: semen, seminal fluid

usi umiyaha: intestinal worm

usiha: **1**. star; **2**. acorn; **3**. front sight of a gun

usiha be aliha hafan: court astronomer in ancient times

usiha fajambi: to glow in passing (said of stars)

usiha geri gari: stars are dim (at dawn when they begin to disappear from sight)

usiha kemun: sight of a cannon

usiha moo: oak tree

usiha oron: stars, starry sphere, constellation

usiha oron be cincilara karan: (觀察台) the observatory in Beijing

usiha tuwara hafan: (監侯) astronomer of the Beijing observatory

usiha yoo: scrofula

usihangga: **1**. pertaining to a star; **2**. clairvoyant, prophet, sensitive (in a psychic way)

usihangga gurgu: sensitive animals — tigers and wolves

usihangga maitu: a staff of the Imperial Escort topped by a carved wooden star

usihibumbi: **1**. (causative or passive of **usihimbi**); **2**. to moisten, to make wet

usihiken: rather wet

usihimbi: (**-he**) to become moist, to become wet, to become damp

usihin: wet, damp, moist

usihitembi: to continue to become moist

usihiyebumbi: (causative of **usihiyembi**)

usihiyembi: to slurp (gruel or a liquid)

usihiyen: ⟶ **usihin**

usilembi: to release (the bowstring)

usima: thick padded cotton armor

usimangga: **1**. skilled astrologer; **2**. under favorable astrological signs

usin: field (for cultivation)

usin bošokū: a kind of gray grasshopper

usin buta: cultivated field

usin dehen: farmland, cropland

usin enduri: god of agriculture

usin hethe: land property, estate

usin i fiyenten: (農田司) an office of the Board of Finance in charge of agricultural affairs

usin i hafan: the name of an official of antiquity who was in charge of cultivation and animal husbandry

usin i haha: tenant farmer

usin i jalin abalambi: to hunt animals detrimental to crops in summer

usin i narhūn cese: register of land boundaries, land register

usin i niyalma: farmer

usin i ujan: boundary of a field

usin suksalambi: to open up new land for cultivation

usin wecembi: to make offerings of cakes and small paper flags when crops were threatened by insects or drought

usin weilembi: to work in the fields

usin weilere agūra: farm tools

usin yalu: fields (collectively)

usingga: alone, forlorn, orphaned

usisi: farmer, cultivator of the land

usitambi: ⟶ **ušatambi**

usiten hailan: linden tree; cf. **nunggele**

usnika: a fleshy outgrowth on the head of the Buddha

usucilembi: to be fussy, to be bothersome

usukan: rather fussy

usumbi: to go downstream, to go with the current

usun: **1**. hateful, annoying; **2**. pedantic, stuck in old ways; **3**. smelling of fish, rank, smelly

usuršebumbi: (causative of **usuršembi**)

usuršecuke: **1**. hateful, unpleasant; **2**. unsavory, not good to eat

usuršembi: to detest, to find unpleasant

ušabumbi: (causative or passive of **ušambi**)

ušabun: implication (in a crime or plot)

ušakū: hard to control, hard to rein in (said of horses)

ušambi: **1**. to pull, to drag, to haul; **2**. to scratch; cf. **wašambi**; **3**. to implicate, to hold back, to burden with

ušan fašan: confused, entangled, muddled, without conclusion

ušarki: *Crataegus pinnatifida*: hawthorn

    ušarki moo: hawthorn

ušatabumbi: (causative of **ušatambi**)

ušatambi: **1**. to pull with force, to yank at; **2**. to vex, to plague, to afflict, to distress, to harass

uše: cord, band, belt, thong, strap, tape

    uše šaban: a strong cord (with four knots tied in it) attached to the bottom of boots or shoes to prevent slipping

    uše tatakū sele: a small iron fastener on a quiver strap

    uše umiyaha: tapeworm

ušebumbi: (causative of **ušembi**)

ušembi: to stitch the soles of cloth shoes

ušengge: tough, stringy

uta: a dessert made from milk, sugar, and oil

    uta bele: a cake consisting of rice fried with oil and sugar

utala: as many (much) as this, many, a certain number of

utan: a name for the pelican; cf. **kūtan**

utbala ilha: (from Sanskrit utpala 'kind of lotus') a red lotus-like bloom

uthai: **1**. then, thereupon, at once, and then, immediately; **2**. ordinary, common; **3**. (used with the verb form **-kini**) even though

    uthai niyalma: ordinary person

    uthai sakini: even if he knows

uttu: thus, like this, so

    uttu akū oci: otherwise

    uttu be dahame: therefore

    uttu bicibe: although it is like this, although this is the case

    uttu bime: however, moreover

    uttu dabala: only like this

    uttu oci: if it is like this, if so

    uttu ofi: therefore

    uttu ohode: if it is so

    uttu otolo: even like this

    uttu seme: although it is like this, nevertheless

    uttu tuttu seme: now like this now like that

uttumbara ilha: (from Sanskrit uḍumbara) flower of the cluster fig (*Ficus racemosa*)

uttusi: in this direction, over here

    uttusi oso: so it is like this!

utu: a name for the tiger; cf. **tasha**

utulimbi: to pay attention, to notice, to be conscious of

utun weijun: a name for the stork; cf. **weijun**

utung: ⟶ **urangga moo**

uturi: the end of a battue line

    uturi acambi: to join both ends of the battue line to form a circle

    uturi feksimbi: to run from both ends of the battue line to form a circle

uya: *Antilope cervicapra*: a male Indian antelope

uyakan: rather thin, rather diluted

uyaljambi: **1**. to move winding like a snake, to slither; **2**. to be sinuous; **3**. to move in a graceful manner (said of women)

uyan: **1**. thin, diluted, weak; **2**. feeble, delicate; **3**. weak (said of a domesticated animal's back); **4**. the meeting point of the two halves of a canoe, keel

    uyan buda: gruel, rice broth

    uyan i aligan: keel retainer

    uyan lala: rice gruel eaten on the eighth day of the twelfth month

    uyan matan šatan: thin sugar cakes

uyanjambi: ⟶ **uyaljambi**

uyašambi: to chew the cud

uyašan: **1**. loach (fish), fish of the family *Copitidae*; **2**. tendons of the hands and feet

    uyašan dekdembi: ⟶ **uyašanambi**

uyašanambi: to have a pain in the ligaments of the hands or feet

uyašangga jahūdai: the name of a small, long boat used on the Yangtze that was thought to resemble the loach

uye: the name of a white sea fish

uyebumbi: (causative of **uyembi**)

uyembi: **1**. to soften; **2**. to knead; **3**. to cure, to tan (leather); **4**. to break in (a horse)

    uyere faksi: a tanner

    uyere šu: saltpeter used in the curing of leather

uyu: **1**. the name of a sea fish; **2**. turquoise

uyuci: ninth

uyulembi: **1**. to punish an offense by a fine of nine head of cattle (a Mongolian punishment); **2**. to climb to a high place on the ninth day of the ninth month

uyun: nine

uyun biya: the ninth month

uyun dabkūri: the Imperial Palace

uyun eyen: the nine philosophical schools

uyun garudai mudangga fesin i suwayan suje sara: an Imperial Escort's yellow parasol with a crooked handle and nine phoenixes depicted on the cover

uyun garudangga tumin lamun suje sara: a blue parasol of the Imperial Escort with nine phoenixes depicted on it

uyun hengkin: nine kowtows (three genuflections with three kowtows per genuflection)

uyun jafambi: to make small offerings on the two days before a big sacrifice

uyun jubki: deep place in a body of water

uyun mudangga jijun: (九叠文) the name of a style of seal writing (in Chinese calligraphy)

uyun muduri duin garudai mahatun: the name of a hat (worn by Emperors in antiquity) with nine dragons, four phoenixes, and a string of pearls attached to it

uyun muduri mudangga fesin i suwayan sara: the name of a yellow parasol of the Imperial Escort with a crooked handle and nine dragons depicted on it

uyun muduringga suwayan sara: a yellow parasol of the Imperial Escort with nine dragons depicted on it

uyun saitu: the nine ministers (the heads of the six Boards plus the heads of the Censorate, the Court of Judicature and Revision, and the Transmission Office)

uyun sen: the nine bodily orifices

uyun sihangga sunta: a pouch for nine cartridges

uyun šeri: 'The Nine Springs' — the underworld, the world of the dead

uyun tuhebuku i mahatu: an ancient ceremonial hat with nine tassels

uyun uncehengge dobi: a nine-tailed fox

uyungge: pertaining to the ninth day of the ninth month (a festival)

uyungge efen: the name of cakes baked on the ninth day of the ninth month

uyungge inenggi: the ninth day of the ninth month

uyunggeri: nine times

uyunju: ninety

uyunju dulefun i durungga tetun: an armillary sphere of the Beijing observatory

uyunjuci: ninetieth

uyunjute: ninety each

uyuri: **1**. a name for the cat; cf. **ninuri**; **2**. female slave

uyursu: ninefold, consisting of nine layers

uyursu muheren: a toy consisting of a piece of brass with nine brass rings attached to it — a puzzle ring

uyuršembi: to laugh pleasantly, to laugh prettily

uyute: nine each

uyutu jofohori: an orange containing nine sections

uyutungge gasha: a name for the owl; cf. **yabula**

ūlen: house

ūlet: Oirat, Elut (a western Mongolian tribe)

ūn cecike: bullfinch, birds of the genus *Pyrrhula*

ūren: **1**. an image, a doll, a Buddhist image, a religious image; **2**. tablet of a deceased person

ūren i pai: tablet of a deceased person

ūren tuibumbi: to burn at the grave the clothes and hat of a deceased person together with a paper image

W ᴧ

wa: odor, smell

    wa akū: **1**. odorless; **2**. lacking prospects, without promise

    wa ehe: having a foul odor

    wa sain: having a pleasant odor, fragrant

    wa su: odor, smell

    wa tucike yadarangge: in dire need (like a polecat that passes foul smelling gas when it is in distress)

    wa usun: having an obnoxious odor, smelly

wabumbi: (causative or passive of **wambi**)

waburu: deserving of death! — a curse

wacan: a protective covering on armor for the armpits

wacihiyabumbi: (causative of **wacihiyambi**)

wacihiyambi: to complete, to conclude, to finish

    wacihiyame: completely, totally

    wacihiyame omi: bottoms up!

    wacihiyame omimbi: to drink up

wacihiyan: completion, conclusion

wacihiyašambi: to take care of, to manage

wacir: thunderbolt of Indra (sacred instrument used in Lamaist rites as a symbol of the 'indestructible'), Sanskrit vajra

wada: knife for dismembering

wadabumbi: to put a dog on a scent

wadambi: to sniff, to follow a scent (said of dogs)

wadan: **1**. unpadded cloth wrapper, a width of cloth used for wrapping things; **2**. unpadded bed covering; **3**. curtain around a sedan chair; **4**. cloth of a flag or banner; **5**. small bag; **6**. cloth bag used to entrap birds; **7**. cloth used in Manchu rites (the same color as that of one's banner)

    wadan managan: swaddling clothes

wadanambi: to become distended (said of livestock's bellies when they have overeaten)

wahai: extremely, very, to a great degree

wahan: **1**. hoof; **2**. end of the sleeve of a gown in the form of a hoof

    wahan dabambi: to stumble (said of hoofed animals)

wahiyabumbi: (causative of **wahiyambi**)

wahiyambi: to support by holding under the arms, to help up in this way

wahūn: stinking, smelly, malodorous

    wahūn jalgangga moo: *Ailanthus glandulosa*: tree of heaven

    wahūn jalgasu moo: ⟶ **wahūn jalgangga moo**

    wahūn nišargan: diphtheria eruption in the throat, tonsil infection

    wahūn umiyaha: bedbug

    wahūn urangga moo: *Clerodendron trichotomum*: glorybower, bleeding-heart

    wahūn yasa: bare spot on the front leg of a horse

wahūnda: a foul-smelling wild plant that resembles garlic

wahūtu cecike: a name for the myna

wai: askew, tilted, crooked, curved

    wai seme: exhausted, tired out

waidabumbi: (causative of **waidambi**)

waidakū: a dipper

waidambi: to scoop out, to dip out (with a ladle or large spoon), to draw water from a well

    waidara hoto: gourd used as a dipper

waidanambi: to go to scoop out, to go to draw water

waidanjimbi: to come to scoop out, to come to draw water

waidanumbi: to scoop out together

waidara: ⟶ **waidambi** (subheading)

waihū: **1**. askew, tilted, off-center; cf. **waiku**; **2**. unreasonable

waihūdambi: to act unreasonably

waihūngga: a person who acts unreasonably

waikiyambi: ⟶ **wangkiyambi**

waiku: askew, tilted, not straight

    waiku daikū: crooked, curved

waikurabumbi: (causative of **waikurambi**)

waikurambi: to be askew, to be tilted, to be crooked

waikuršambi: to walk leaning to one side

wailan: **1**. in antiquity, an official who was in charge of a city; **2**. a petty official, a minor official

    wailan hafan: (魏吏) a minor official in charge of revenue and grain

    wailan šudesi: (吏典) Secretary in a prefecture

wainambi: to be crooked (said of part of a battle line)

waitukū: bucket with a handle (used for drawing water); cf. **waidakū**

wajibumbi: (causative of **wajimbi**)

wajima: end, termination

    wajima dube: end, conclusion

    wajima nadan: the seventh of the seven-day periods after death

wajimbi: **1**. to finish, to end; **2**. to be done completely; **3**. to die

wajin: the finish, the end

    wajin mohon akū: without end, endless

waka: **1**. (sentence particle that negates nominal predicates) is not, are not; **2**. mistake, error, guilt, blame; **3**. wrong, mistaken

    waka alimbi: to accept blame, to apologize

    waka bahambi: to offend, to displease, to do something wrong

    waka sabubumbi: to commit an offense, to offend

    waka wakai: **1**. muddled, fouled up, confused; **2**. carelessly, recklessly

    wakai erun: unlawful punishment

    wakai gisurembi: to make a mistake in speech, to speak erroneously

wakalabumbi: (causative or passive of **wakalambi**)

wakalambi: **1**. to blame, to fault, to accuse, to impeach, to deem wrong; **2**. to upbraid, to bawl out

wakalan: error, transgression

wakan: *Nycticorax nycticorax*: night heron

wakangge: wrong, mistaken, something that is wrong or mistaken

wakao: (contraction of **waka + o**) "Isn't it?", "*N'est-ce pas?*"

wakašabumbi: (causative of **wakašambi**)

wakašambi: **1**. to blame, to accuse; **2**. to deem wrong, to consider an error, to impeach, to disagree with

wakiyambi: ⟶ **wangkiyambi**

wakjahūn: having a big belly, having a distended belly (said of livestock that have overeaten)

wakjanambi: to form a big belly, to have a distended belly

wakšan: toad, frog

    wakšan burga: toad willow — a variety of willow tree

wala: **1**. underneath, under, low; **2**. the west side of a Manchu house — the place of honor; **3**. the lower position at a banquet

    wala ergi: the place below

    wala tembi: to take a lower seat (at a banquet)

walda: base, vile — a term of contempt

walgiyabumbi: (causative of **walgiyambi**)

walgiyambi: **1**. to sun, to expose to the sun, to dry in the sun; **2**. to heat

wali: trick, illusion, magic, conjuring, sleight of hand

    wali deribumbi: to perform magic tricks, to create an illusion

    wali efimbi: to play magic tricks, to juggle

    wali efiyen: conjuring, juggling, magic tricks

    wali fadagan: magic tricks, magical arts, conjuring

    wali mama: a goddess represented by a piece of cloth hung on the back of the door to which all food brought into the house must be presented for inspection

walingga: a device used for playing tricks, magical, illusional

waliyabumbi: **1**. (causative or passive of **waliyambi**); **2**. to be lost, to get lost, to be left behind, to be abandoned

waliyambi: **1**. to throw away, to abandon, to get rid of; **2**. to remit, to exempt; **3**. to spit out water after washing the mouth, to gargle; **4**. to make an offering at a grave; **5**. to lay eggs (said of insects); **6**. to produce silk (said of silkworms); **7**. to be disheartened

    waliyaha: **1**. (interjection) Alas!, Woe is me!; **2**. Now we're in trouble!, Now we've had it!

    waliyaha jaka: **1**. something abandoned, refuse; **2**. a person without promise or prospects

    waliyaha jui: orphan

waliyaha usin: abandoned land, land unfit for cultivation

waliyame gamambi: to treat leniently, to excuse, to forgive

waliyame gamarao: please excuse me

waliyan: abandonment

waliyan gemin: wastefully

waliyanambi: to go to make an offering at a grave

waliyatai: to the death, without regard for one's own safety, risking one's life

waliyatambi: **1.** to fling about, to throw around; **2.** to lose (face)

walu: boil, furuncle, ulcer, carbuncle

wambi: to kill, to slay

waha inenggi: day of execution

waha sedehe: You deserve death!

wame: resolutely, severely

wame abalambi: to go on the autumn hunt

wame mukiyebumbi: to annihilate, to exterminate

wame šusihašambi: to flog severely

wame tantambi: to administer a severe beating

wara ba: execution ground

wara tai: scaffold (for executions)

wara weile: capital crime

wan: ladder

wancarambi: to ridicule, to make fun of someone behind his back

wanci: an area on a pond that does not freeze in the winter

wandumbi: to kill together, to kill one another; also **wanumbi**

wandure sukdun: violent aspect, venomous appearance or mood

wandz: pill, small ball

wang: **1.** Prince; **2.** (in antiquity) king, monarch

wang ni dukai hiya: (護衛) Officer of a Prince's Bodyguard, *BH* 45

wang sai baitai kunggeri: (王府科) office in the Board of Rites concerned with the affairs of Princes

wang gin: a hair net

wangga: **1.** fragrant; **2.** pond heron, pond egret; **3.** pertaining to the new moon

wangga giyancihiyan hoošan: perfumed letter paper

wangga inenggi: the fifteenth day of a lunar month

wangga jalgasu moo: *Cedrela sinensis*: Chinese toon tree

wangga muke: perfume

wangga singgeri: muskrat

wangga sogi: coriander, Chinese parsley

wangga šangga: unconscious, in a coma

wangga šulhe: *Pyrus sinensis*: Chinese pear

wanggari: *Citrus medica*: citron

wanggiyanambi: to have a runny nose, to have a head cold

wanggiyanahabi: has a head cold

wangkiyabumbi: (causative of **wangkiyambi**)

wangkiyambi: to smell (transitive verb)

wangnambi: to embroider (designs on shoes)

wangnaha sabu: embroidered shoes

wanse: pill, small ball

wantaha: *Cryptomeria japonica*: Japanese cedar

wanumbi: to kill together, to kill one another; also **wandumbi**

war: (onomatopoetic) the sound made by toads and frogs

war ir: (onomatopoetic) the sound of toads and frogs croaking together

warabumbi: (causative of **warambi**)

warambi: to fish out, to remove from a pot (things that have been cooked)

wardabumbi: (causative of **wardambi**)

wardambi: **1.** to tread water; **2.** to dig up (dirt)

wardašambi: to work with the hands and feet, to exert great effort

wargi: **1.** west, western; **2.** right (side); **3.** under, underneath

wargi ashan: (西廂) an office of the Imperial Academy of Learning

wargi ashan i baita hacin i boo: (西廂案房) Archives in the Imperial Academy of Learning

wargi ba: the Western Regions — Xinjiang

wargi dzang: Tibet

wargi ergi munggan: the Imperial tombs of Mukden

wargi ergi simnere bithei kūwaran: (西文場) the rooms for examinees (just to the right of the Mingyuan tower in the Examination Compound)

wargi fiyenten: (西司) an office in the Imperial Equipage Department

wargi hetu boo: western wing of a house

wargi nahan: the oven-bed on the western wall

wargi namu: the West

wargingge: western, pertaining to the west

waru: ⟶ **waburu**

warumbi: (**-ka**) to have a bad odor, to stink, to give off a foul odor

wase: **1**. tile; **2**. pottery, earthenware; **3**. socks, stockings

wase boo: house with a tile roof

wase fengse: earthenware pot

wase tetun: earthenware vessel, pottery vessel

wasei faksi: a tile-maker, roofer

wasei holbokū: a piece of timber that holds the tiles on the roof

wasei jaida: mason's trowel

waselabumbi: (causative of **waselambi**)

waselambi: to tile (a roof)

waseri weijun: stork; cf. **weijun**

washa cecike: a name for the sparrow

wasibumbi: **1**. (causative of **wasimbi**); **2**. to degrade, to demote

wasifi: ⟶ **wasimbi** (subheading)

wasiha: claw, talon; cf. **ošoho**

wasihalabumbi: (causative of **wasihalambi**)

wasihalambi: to grasp in the claws, to snatch, to scratch, to claw

wasihašambi: **1**. to scratch repeatedly; **2**. to dig in the earth (said of domestic animals)

wasihi: awkward, clumsy, sluggish

wasihi calgari: dilatory, sluggish

wasihūn: **1**. downward, down; **2**. westward, to the west; **3**. downstream

wasihūn bethe gaiha: slipped down, fell down, encountered bad luck, met with misfortune

wasihūn i hontoho: the last quarter of the moon

wasihūn yabumbi: to travel downstream

wasihūrame: **1**. in the last ten days of the month; **2**. downstream

wasika: ⟶ **wasimbi** (subheading)

wasimbi: (**-ka**) **1**. to descend, to go down, to sink; **2**. to fall (said of rulers); **3**. to decline (said of value); **4**. to become skinny, to become pale, to become wan; **5**. to die (said of birds)

wasifi genggehun ombi: to become thin and pale

wasika jalan: a decadent age

wasimbumbi: **1**. (causative of **wasimbi**); **2**. to issue (an order), to send down (an edict); **3**. to demote, to degrade; cf. **wasibumbi**

wasinambi: to go down (there)

wasingga mudan: the departing tone of classical Chinese phonology

wasinjimbi: to come down

wasuri monio: a name for the monkey

wašakta burga: a kind of red willow whose leaves are wider and longer than those of the common willow

wašakū: an iron ladle-shaped instrument used for scraping hides

wašambi: to scratch, to scrape; cf. **ušambi**

watai: **1**. to the death, fiercely; **2**. exceedingly

watai amuran: terribly fond of

watai tantambi: to beat severely

watan: a fishhook with barbs

watangga: barbed

watangga gida: a spear with barbs

we: who?

we ya: anyone

webe: whom?

wecebumbi: (causative of **wecembi**)

weceku: household god

weceku i sendehen: altar to the household god, a board on which offerings were made to the household god

weceku soko: household god and earth god, the gods in general

wecembi: **1**. to make an offering to a deity, to sacrifice; **2**. to shamanize

wecere bithe: book containing the rites of certain sacrifices

wecere jaka: sacrificial vessel or object

wecere juktere bolgobure fiyenten: (祠祝清吏司) the name of an office in the Board of Rites concerned with sacrifice

wecere juktere kunggeri: (祭祀科) section on sacrifice in the Board of Rites and the Court of Sacrificial Worship

wecere usin: a field set aside for growing grain used in sacrifices

wecen: offering, sacrifice, shamanistic rite

wecen bithe: book containing the rites of certain sacrifices

wecen i baita be aliha falgari: (祠祭署) the name of various offices concerned with sacrifices

wecen i baita be aliha yamun: (太常寺) Court of Sacrificial Worship, *BH* 933

wecen i kumun urebure falgari: (神樂署) Office of Sacred Music, *BH* 390

wecen i ulha ujire falgangga: (犧牲所) Office of Sacrificial Animals in the Court of Sacrificial Worship

wecen jukten: offerings and sacrifices

wecenembi: to go to sacrifice

wecenjimbi: to come to sacrifice

wecere: ⟶ **wecembi** (subheading)

wecesi: official in charge of sacrifices, presider at a sacrifice

weci: **1**. (ablative form of **we**): from whom, than whom; **2**. who (plural), (plural of **we**)

wecu ilha: *Dianthus chinensis*: rainbow pink

wede: (dative of **we**): to whom, for whom

wehe: stone, rock

wehe alikū: the lower millstone

wehe bei: a stele

wehe biyangsiri ilha: the name of a purple flower with five petals that resembles a cicada

wehe cinuhūn: cinnabar

wehe dabsun: rock salt

wehe dalan: a stone dam

wehe fiyelen: *Portulaca oleracea*: purslane

wehe fungkū: a stone roller

wehe giyen: smalt (cobalt) blue

wehe hengke: 'stone melon' — the name of a very hard melon-like fruit that grows on a tree in the vicinity of Mt. Emei in Sichuan

wehe hūwaise: a kind of pagoda tree; cf. **hūwaise**

wehe hūwangse: realgar, red orpiment

wehe i king: a musical stone hanging from a frame

wehe lamun: cobalt blue

wehe lefu: the name of a medium-sized bear with a white spot on its neck that hibernates in a cave in the winter, the same as **mojihiyan**

wehe muhaliyan: a stone ball

wehe selmin: **1**. a stone drill; **2**. a crossbow for shooting stones

wehe šu ilha: cotyledon (a kind of flower)

wehe tuyeku yonggan: impure ammonia salt

wehe yadali cecike: 'stone thrush'

wehe yaha: coal

wehe yaha i nemuri: coal mine

wehei fungkū: stone drum, stone cylinder

wehei nikebuku: a stone used for holding a door open

wehengge: stone, made of stone

wehengge usiha: 'stone chestnut' — a nut tasting like a walnut and grown in the mountains of Tonkin

wehetu coko: the name of a chicken from Southeast Asia that is supposed to cackle when the tide comes in

wehiyebumbi: (causative of **wehiyembi**)

wehiyembi: to support, to aid, to watch after

wehiyen: **1**. assistance; **2**. protective spirit

wehiyendumbi: to support together, to support one another; also **wehiyenumbi**

wehiyenumbi: to support together, to support one another; also **wehiyendumbi**

wehiyetembi: to support continually

wei: **1**. whose? — genitive of **we**; **2**. minute, very small; **3**. kind of fish

wei ping: a screen

weibin: (危) a constellation, the 12th of the lunar mansions, made up of three stars; α in Aquarius and η and ε in Pegasus

weibin tokdonggo kiru: a banner depicting the constellation **weibin**

weifutu: ⟶ **kuri weifutu**

weihe: **1**. tooth; **2**. horn; cf. **uihe**

weihe dasakū: toothpick

weihe hadambi: to attach a horn facing to a new bow

weihe ilha: gums

weihe jaka: space between the teeth

weihe juyembi: to clench one's teeth

weihe niombi: to sneer at, to ridicule

weihe niome basumbi: to sneer at, to make fun of

weihe saimbi: to gnash one's teeth, to grit one's teeth, to grind one's teeth (in sleep)

weihe silgiyakū: toothbrush

weihe šakšarambi: to bare one's teeth

weihe tokošokū: instrument for cleaning one's teeth

weihede: leftover pieces of brick or tile

weihen: a name for the donkey

weihengge: having teeth

    weihengge ulgiyan: another name for the wild boar; cf. **aidagan**

weihu: boat made from a single tree, a hollowed-out canoe

    weihu huju: dugout canoe

weihukelebumbi: (causative or passive of **weihukelembi**)

weihukelembi: to treat disrespectfully, to slight, to treat lightly

    weihukeleme gisurembi: to speak carelessly

    weihukeleme yabumbi: to act in an offhanded manner

weihuken: **1**. light (in weight); **2**. not serious, frivolous, unimportant

    weihuken balama: frivolous, flighty

    weihuken furdehe: a light fur coat

weihun: alive, living

    weihun jafambi: to capture alive

    weihun ningge: a living creature

weihungge: living thing, sentient being

weijubumbi: **1**. (causative of **weijumbi**); **2**. to revive, to bring back to life

weijuhen: a name for the stork; cf. **weijun**

weijumbi: to be alive, to live, to revive

weijun: **1**. pliers, pincers, nippers, fire tongs; **2**. stork (*Ciconia ciconia*)

    weijun gasha: stork; cf. **weijun**

weile: **1**. crime, offense, guilt; **2**. punishment, sentence; **3**. matter, affair, work, deed (especially in early texts); cf. **baita**; cf. **weilen**

    weile alimbi: to take the guilt upon oneself, to admit guilt, to admit an error, to apologize, to plead guilty

    weile arambi: to bring to justice, to punish (for a crime), to take disciplinary action

    weile bahambi: to offend, to commit an offense, to admit guilt, to violate a prohibition

    weile be aliha hafan: Minister of Works (in Zhou China)

    weile be fonjimbi: to denounce, to condemn

    weile be nikebumbi: to undergo punishment

    weile be sumbi: to expiate an offense

    weile beidembi: to judge a case

weile beidere bolgobure fiyenten: (理刑清吏司) Judicial Department, *BH* 495

weile beidere kunggeri: (理刑科) judicial section of the headquarters of a Provincial Commander-in-Chief

weile beidere tinggin: (理事廳) a court dealing with matters between Manchu garrison troops and local Mongolians in Mongolia

weile daksa: misdeeds, crimes, sins

weile de taha: fell into crime

weile de tambi: to offend, to trespass, to fall into crime

weile de tanaha: ⟶ **weile de taha**

weile de tuhenehe: ⟶ **weile de taha**

weile endebuku: crime, evil, misdeeds

weile jolimbi: to atone for a misdeed, to expiate an offense

weile necimbi: to commit a crime

weile tambi: to be involved in a crime

weile tuhebumbi: to sentence (for a crime), to bring to justice, to condemn, to convict, to punish

weile wakalan: blame for an offense

weile waliyambi: to exempt from punishment, to forgive

weilebumbi: **1**. (causative of **weilembi**); **2**. to sentence to forced labor

    weilebure weile: a crime carrying a penalty of forced labor

weilembi: **1**. to work; **2**. to make, to construct; **3**. to serve; cf. **uilembi**

    weileme arambi: to labor, to work

    weilere aha: serf

    weilere arara ba: (造辦處) Workshop of the Imperial Household, *BH* 86

    weilere arara fiyenten: (營造司) Department of Works, *BH* 82

    weilere arara kunggeri: (營造科) construction section of the Board of Works

    weilere arara namun: (制造庫) warehouse in the Board of Works for building materials

    weilere boo: (工房) a department of the Court of Colonial Affairs

    weilere dasara bolgobure fiyenten: (營繕清吏司) Building Department, *BH* 345

    weilere falga: workshop, place of work

weilere fiyenten: (工司) the office concerned with construction matters in the headquarters of the Manchu General-in-Chief in Mukden

weilere jakai boo: (材料房) storage room for materials in the palace printing shop

weilere jurgan: (工部) the Board of Works, *BH* 460

weilere jurgan i kungge yamun: (工科) an office of the Board of Works in the Grand Secretariat

weilen: **1**. work, construction, construction project; **2**. deed; cf. **weile**

weilen be aliha amban: (司空) Minister of Works (in Zhou China)

weilen i šanggan: karma, recompense for one's deeds

weilendumbi: to work together; also **weilenumbi**

weilenembi: to go to work

weilengge: **1**. guilty, criminal; **2**. a criminal

weilengge niyalma: criminal, guilty man

weilengge niyalma be kadalara tinggin: (司獄廳) Office of the Jail Warden

weilengge niyalma kadalara hafan: (司獄) Jail Warden, *BH* 850A

weilenjimbi: to come to work

weilenumbi: to work together; also **weilendumbi**

weilumbi: **1**. to do secretly, to act deceptively, to hide the truth from someone; **2**. to desert, to turn away from

weingge: whose

weiping: a screen; cf. **huwejehen**

weisha: (尾) a constellation, the 6th of the lunar mansions, made up of nine stars in Scorpio

weisha tokdonggo kiru: a banner depicting the constellation **weisha**

weji: (dense) forest

weji ba: a (densely) forested area

weji una: the fruit of a wild plant that has small yellow leaves and stems resembling artemisia

wekce: weaver's beam

weke: hey you! (word used for calling someone whose name is unknown or forgotten)

wekji: bran, grain husks

wekji ara: husks and chaff

wekjibumbi: (causative of **wekjimbi**)

wekjimbi: **1**. to move the shuttle across horizontally, to weave in the woof threads; **2**. to manage, to operate

wekjime dasambi: to plan and manage

wekjime dasara amban: (經略) a high officer in charge of military affairs in border regions

wekjire sirge: woof threads

wekjin: woof, weft

welderhen: a name for the Eastern house swallow (*Hirundo rustica*)

welhūme: (胃) a constellation, the 17th of the lunar mansions, made up of three stars (*935, 39, 41*) in Aries

welhūme tokdonggo kiru: a banner depicting the constellation **welhūme**

welmiyebumbi: (causative of **welmiyembi**)

welmiyeku: fishing pole

welmiyeku sirge: fishing line

welmiyembi: to fish (with line and hook)

welmiyere cooha: decoy troops

wembi: (**-ngke, -re/-ndere, -mpi**) **1**. to melt (intransitive verb); **2**. to be transformed, to be converted, to become cultured or civilized, to be reformed, to be influenced

wembumbi: **1**. (causative of **wembi**); **2**. to make cultured, to transform (to something better), to convert, to educate, to civilize, to improve, to reform, to influence

wemburi: *Crataegus pinnatifida*: a species of edible hawthorn, Chinese hawthorn

wempi: (perfect converb of **wembi**) improved, converted, reformed

wen: **1**. influence, reform, education; **2**. culture, civilization, cultural pursuits; **3**. notch (for the string on an arrow)

wen fetembi: to make a notch

wen jang: essay — the same as **šu fiyelen**

wen šu: essay, document

wen tebumbi: to put the notch of an arrow to the bowstring

wence: *Acer ginnala*: Amur maple, the name of a tree whose leaves are used to make dye; cf. **buduhu**

wence moo: ⟶ **wence**

wencen: ⟶ **wence**

wenceo: a cloth made partly of silk and partly of coarse grass linen — the same as **jurhu suri**

wendeden: a name for the lark; cf. **wenderhen**

wendergen: ⟶ **wenderhen**

wenderhen: *Galerida cristata*: North China crested lark

wendumbi: to melt together, to become civilized simultaneously

wenembi: to melt away, to go to be reformed

wengge: highly educated, cultured

weniyebumbi: (causative or passive of **weniyembi**)

weniyembi: to melt, to fuse, to smelt, to refine

wenje: *Callistephus chinensis*: Chinese aster

    wenje nimeku: consumption, tuberculosis

wenjebumbi: (causative of **wenjembi**)

wenjehu: ⟶ **wenjehun**

wenjehun: **1**. warm; **2**. prosperous, flourishing, thriving, exciting, lively, full of activity

    wenjehun simengge: exciting, bustling, lively

wenjembi: **1**. to warm up, to heat; **2**. to be warm, to have a fever; **3**. to be tipsy

    wenjeme bahabumbi: to become very intoxicated

wenjen doholon: expression used to describe a horse or other beast of burden that limps when one first begins to ride it and then becomes normal after it has gone a little way

wenjendumbi: to become tipsy together; also **wenjenumbi**

wenjengge: heated

    wenjengge giyalakū: heated part of a house

    wenjengge kiyoo: a heated sedan chair

    wenjengge yuwan: an inkstone heated with charcoal in the winter

wenjenumbi: to become tipsy together; also **wenjendumbi**

wenšu: document

wer wer: (the sound used to call a dog)

werdembi: to climb hand over hand on a rope, to shinny up a rope

were: ⟶ **banjire were**

werebumbi: (causative of **werembi**)

werembi: **1**. to wash (rice), to rinse; **2**. to pan (gold or other mineral); **3**. to preserve on ice in the summer, to chill food or drink with ice

weren: **1**. ripples on water; **2**. hoop (on a barrel, tub, etc.), a wire circle inside a hat

werenebumbi: (causative or passive of **werenembi**)

werenembi: to eat, to bore (said of insects in the tender bark of trees)

werešebumbi: (causative of **werešembi**)

werešembi: **1**. to investigate thoroughly, to get to the bottom of; **2**. to be careful, to show care

weri: another, other, someone else

    weri niyalma: someone else

weribumbi: (causative of **werimbi**)

werimbi: **1**. to leave behind, to leave (transitive verb); **2**. to retain in one's possession; **3**. to collapse; cf. **urimbi**

    werire bithe: last will and testament

weringge: someone else's

werinjembi: ⟶ **werešembi**

werire: ⟶ **werimbi** (subheading)

werišembi: ⟶ **werešembi**

weriyangge: belonging to someone else

werumbi: (-ke) to melt (intransitive verb), to thaw out (said of frozen meat)

wesibumbi: **1**. (causative of **wesimbi**); **2**. to lift, to raise; **3**. to promote, to advance; **4**. ⟶ **wesimbumbi**

    wesibume fungnembi: to give a higher title

wesibun: advancement, lifting up

wesihulebumbi: (causative of **wesihulembi**)

wesihulembi: to honor, to revere

wesihulen: posthumous respect paid to one's parents

wesihun: **1**. upward, up; **2**. eastward, east; **3**. honorable, revered, respected, superior; **4**. your (honorific)

    wesihun beye: you (honorific)

    wesihun colo: Imperial honorific title

    wesihun erdemungge: the Chongde (崇德) reign period, 1636–43

    wesihun fusihūn: high or low (in status)

    wesihun hūwašan: eminent monk

    wesihun i hontoho: first quarter of the moon — the eighth and ninth days of the lunar month

    wesihun jalan: a brilliant age

    wesihun mukdembure poo: the name of a large iron cannon

    wesihun niyalma: superior person

    wesihun se: how old are you? (honorific)

    wesihun šabi: brilliant student

    wesihun tembi: to sit in the place of honor

wesiku: steps (provided with a railing) used to ascend an Imperial sedan chair or coach

wesimbi: (**-ke**) **1**. to ascend, to go up, to rise; **2**. to advance (in rank), to be promoted

wesire forgošoro kunggeri: (陞調科) Bureau of Promotions and Transfers in the Board of War

wesimbumbi: **1**. (causative of **wesimbi**); **2**. to raise, to lift; **3**. to advance, to promote; cf. **wesimbi**; **4**. to submit, to present (to the Emperor), to report to the throne, to memorialize

wesimbu seme arambi: to write '**wesimbu**' — i.e., to write on a document or memorial that it should be presented for the personal attention of the Emperor

wesimbure afaha: a memorial presented without a cover to the throne

wesimbure bithe: a memorial presented to the throne

wesimbure bithe arara ba: (本房) Copying Office, *BH* 138

wesimbure bithe icihiyara boo: (本房) an office charged with copying Chinese memorials

wesimbure bithe pilere ba: (批本處) Office for copying the Emperor's endorsements of documents, *BH* 138

wesimbure bithei benesi: (奉差) a messenger for memorials

wesimbure bithei jise icihiyara boo: (題稿房) an office of the Board of Civil Appointments in charge of drafting documents

wesimbure bithei tebeliyeku: a strip of paper on the outside of a memorial that keeps it from coming apart

wesimbure bithei ton: a list of the memorials to be presented to the throne

wesimbure bukdari: a folded memorial

wesimbure kunggeri: (啟奏科) memorial office

wesincmbi: to go up

wesingge ilha: *Tecoma grandiflora*: Chinese trumpet-creeper

wesire: ⟶ **wesimbi** (subheading)

wešelembi: to catch with a **wešen**

wešen: a net for catching deer, roe, rabbits. etc.

Y ᠶ

ya: **1**. which?, what?; **2**. (a sentence particle expressing mild assertion); **3**. evening vapors that arise right after sunset

ya ba: What place?, What kind of place?

ya de: Where?, Whither?

ya emken: Which one?

ya emu inenggi: Which day?

ya gese: How much?, How many? (Sibe)

ya hacin: What sort of … ?, What kind of … ?

ya ici: Which direction?

ya jaka: What sort of thing?

ya niyalma: Which person?, Who?

ya kumun: court music

ya me li giya: America

ya me li giya jeo: the American continent(s)

ya si ya: Asia

ya si ya jeo: the Asian continent

ya si ya jeo i alin i honin: the Asian goat

yaba: where?

yabe: (ya plus the accusative particle be)

yabi: boards or reeds laid on rafters before tiles are put on a roof

yabihan: ceiling; cf. ilhangga yabihan

yabilabumbi: (causative of yabilambi)

yabilambi: to lay the boards or reeds (yabi) on which the tiles rest

yabsa: *Coregonus pidschian*: Siberian whitefish

yabsi: how very …

yabsi balai yabuha: how very carelessly he acted

yabšahū: *Bubo bubo*: eagle owl

yabubumbi: **1**. (causative of yabumbi); **2**. to put into effect, to carry out; **3**. to approve; **4**. to dispatch (a document)

yabubufi bure kunggeri: (準支科) an office of the Board of Works in charge of supplies

yabubume afabure kunggeri: (承發科) Transmission Office, *BH* 212B

yabubure bithe: an official communication between organs of equal rank

yabuha: ⟶ yabumbi (subheading)

yabulan: a kind of owl

yabumbi: **1**. to go, to walk, to leave; **2**. to travel, to go about, to live (in a certain way); **3**. to act, to perform, to be put into effect; **4**. to serve at a post; **5**. to betroth

yabuha ba: a *curriculum vitae*

yabuha baita: deed, achievement, something that has occurred

yabuha songko: track, trace

yabure feliyere: Imperial tours away from the capital

yabure kūwaran: field camp, military unit on the march

yabure niyalma: traveler, pedestrian

yabure on: route, itinerary

yabun: act, action, performance

yabun be dasambi: to practice a religious discipline

yabun facuhūn: actions are in a confused state, in a confused condition

yabun halai fudasi: perverse and rebellious in his actions

yabun tuwakiyan: behavior, conduct, morality, moral conduct

yabundumbi: to go together, to have comings and goings with one another; also yabunumbi

yabunumbi: to go together, to have comings and goings with one another; also yabundumbi

yabure: ⟶ yabumbi (subheading)

yaburelame: **1**. on the way; **2**. walking a while, resting a while

yaci: (ya plus the ablative particle ci): From where?

yaci jaka: Where did all these things come from?

yaciha: the name of a black fruit (about the size of a finger) that comes from Annam which when dried can be made into a kind of liquor

yacihiyabumbi: (causative of **yacihiyambi**)

yacihiyambi: to sneeze

yacikan: blackish, rather black

yacike: a small sparrow-sized bird with black cheeks

yacin: black, dark; cf. **sahaliyan**

    yacin bosoi mahatun: an ancient-style hat made from black cloth

    yacin bulehen: a dark gray crane

    yacin dobi: a black fox

    yacin fekšun: a dye concocted from the leaves and stems of the Amur maple; ⟶ **wence moo**, **hoifan**

    yacin garudai: a black phoenix

    yacin garunggū: a legendary dark bird considered to be a divine messenger

    yacin garunggū ilha: a deep blue exotic flower the buds of which resemble the **garunggū** bird

    yacin hontohonggo gu: a dark blue gem used in ancient times during sacrifices

    yacin samsu: a kind of fine dark blue cloth

    yacin šempi: black grained leather

    yacin šošontu: an ancient-style black cloth scarf for the hair

    yacin ulhu: a dark gray squirrel

    yacin ūn cecike: *Euphona migratoria*: black hawfinch

    yacin weijun: a pure black stork

    yacin yarha: a black panther

yacingga: dark, somber

    yacingga cuse moo: a kind of ornamental bamboo

yacisu: a name for the cormorant; cf. **suwan**

yadahalambi: to become disabled

yadahūn: **1**. poor, wretched; **2**. sparse (said of pocks)

    yadahūn fusihūn: poor and humble

yadahūšambi: to be hungry

yadali cecike: *Garrulax canorus*: song thrush

yadalingge: weak, feeble

yadalinggū: weak, soft, feeble

yadambi: **1**. to be poor, to be wretched, to suffer want; **2**. to be lacking; **3**. to be pale (said of the face); **4**. to grow tired, to become exhausted; **5**. to die; **6**. to be weak (said of one end of a bow)

    yadara aniya: intercalary year

yadan: sapped of enthusiasm, lacking in confidence

    yadan cecike: a kind of thrush; cf. **fiyabkū**

    yadan oliha: shy and retiring

yadana: *Cygnus cygnus*: whooper swan

    yadana ilha: the name of a flower that blooms at the beginning of spring and resembles a swan

    yadana ujungga fukjingga hergen: (鵠頭書) a style of Chinese calligraphy

yadara: ⟶ **yadambi** (subheading)

yadarakū: undetermined, unforeseeable, hard to foresee

yade: Where?, Whither?, To whom?

yafagalambi: ⟶ **yafahalambi**

yafagan: ⟶ **yafahan**

yafaha: ⟶ **yafahan**

yafahalabumbi: (causative of **yafahalambi**)

yafahalambi: to walk, to go by foot

yafahan: pedestrian, on foot

    yafahan cooha: infantry

    yafahan coohai uheri da: (步軍統領) General Commandant of the Gendarmerie, *BH* 797

    yafahan genembi: to go by foot

    yafahan gūsai da: (步軍參領) Commander of the Banner Infantry

    yafahan hūsun: porter

    yafahan isibure hūsun: an errand boy at a post station

    yafahan isibure kunggeri: (腳力科) a section of the Board of War

    yafahan kūwaran i fiyenten: (步營司) Office of Police Affairs at the headquarters of the Manchu General-in-Chief at Mukden

    yafahan uksin: armed foot soldiers, police on foot

yafan: garden, orchard

    yafan i da: chief gardener

    yafan i niyalma: gardener

yafasi: gardener

yagi: ⟶ **yahi**

yaha: **1**. charcoal, coal; **2**. smoldering embers, charcoal fire

    yaha filembi: to warm oneself by a charcoal fire

    yahai tebun: an iron container that can be hung from a chain (for burning charcoal)

yahana: sorghum ears that turn black and fail to develop grains

    yahana coko: turkey; cf. **hogi**

    yahana moo: a wood from the South Seas that leaves no ash when it burns

yahanambi: **1**. to become coal, to become charcoal; **2**. to turn black and not develop grain (said of ears of grain)

yahari: 'charcoal fruit' — the name of an exotic fruit

yahi: something earned dishonestly, profit gained on the sly

yahilambi: to swindle, to embezzle, to earn in a dishonest way, to earn on the sly

yai: one one hundred-billionth

yak: (onomatopoetic) the sound made by a whip

yak seme: **1**. hard, painful (said of falling or tripping); **2**. choked off (said of the voice); **3**. hard, heavy (said of things striking)

    yak seme sibuha: choked up (said of the voice)

    yak seme šusihalaha: beat hard with a whip

yaka: someone, who?, anyone

yakajambi: to eat gritty food

yakca: **1**. demon, yaksha; **2**. ugly person

yaki: a sack-like cover placed over arrows sticking out from a quiver

yakilambi: to put a case or cover on a quiver

yaksa: a place on a riverbank where the earth has caved in

    yaksa hoton: Nerchinsk

yaksargan: *Scopolax rusticola*: woodcock

yaksibumbi: (causative of **yaksimbi**)

yaksigan: a thin board that is placed vertically on the main beam of a roof

yaksikū: bolt of a door, linchpin

yaksimbi: to close, to shut, to bolt

yaksitai: bluntly, decisively, definitely

yakūngga: **1**. peculiar, bizarre, out of the ordinary; **2**. graceful, charming, seductive

    yakūngga mudan: **1**. graceful bearing, charm; **2**. graceful, charming; **3**. peculiar sound, strange intonation

yakūnggalambi: **1**. to act in a peculiar or unusual manner; **2**. to sing; cf. **yangkūnggalambi**

yala: truly, indeed

yalake: truly, indeed, in fact

yalanggi: true, genuine

yaldargan: a name for the kestrel; cf. **baldargan**

yalga: ⟶ **yalgan**

yalgan: a kind of crow with speckled wings that nests in wild areas

yalhū: a large wooden tub with four handles and four legs

yali: **1**. meat, flesh; **2**. fat (said of livestock)

    yali be targambi: to abstain from meat

    yali belhere falgari: (大官署) meat department of the Court of Banqueting

    yali gūwacihiyašambi: to tremble with fear, to fear that something bad is going to happen

    yali gūwaššambi: ⟶ **yali gūwacihiyašambi**

    yali hafirakū: the flexible part of an elephant's trunk

    yali i boo: (肉房) meat section of the palace kitchen

    yali i erun: bodily or corporal punishment

    yali jokson: (of livestock) thin, skinny

    yali jun narhūn: the wood fiber is fine

    yali misun: meat paste, meat condiment

    yali monggon: gullet, esophagus, food pipe

    yali sain: (of livestock) well-fleshed, sturdy

    yali wasika: (of livestock) has lost fat

yalihangga: fleshy, fat, adipose

yalinambi: to form flesh

    yalinaha doli: the pulp of a melon

yalingga: fleshy, fat

yalitu: a fat person, 'fatso'

yalmanggi: soot, especially soot that forms in a stove

yalu: the boundary between two fields

yalubumbi: (causative of **yalumbi**)

yalucambi: to mount or ride together

yalukū: **1**. rider; **2**. an animal for riding, a mount; **3**. a boundary

yalumbi: to ride (an animal), to mount

    yalume etembi: to overcome the resistance of a horse by riding, to break (a horse)

yalunabumbi: (causative of **yalunambi**)

yalunambi: to go to ride

yalundumbi: to ride together; also **yalunumbi**

yalunjimbi: to come to ride

yalunumbi: to ride together; also **yalundumbi**

yamaka: **1**. seemingly, apparently, probably; cf. **aimaka**; **2**. some, any

    yamaka bade: in some place or other

    yamaka niyalma: some person or other

yamakambio: is someone there?

yamari gaha: a name for the raven

yambi: to rise (said of the evening vapors that come during the still period right after sunset)

yamburakū: **1**. does not fit; cf. **yumburakū**; **2**. unclear, vague

yamdun: enmity, rancor, bad feelings (due to an injustice)

yamerigiya: America

yamji: evening

 yamji buda: supper, the evening meal

 yamji idu: night shift

 yamji tome: every evening

yamjidari: every evening

yamjimbi: to become evening

yamjishūn: late in the day, late, toward twilight

yamjitala: until late, until evening

yamka: **1**. probably, seemingly; cf. **yamaka**; **2**. some

 yamka inenggi: some day or other

yamtari: the name of an exotic quadruped with very tasty flesh

yamtun: a respiratory ailment, asthma

 yamtun nimeku: ⟶ **yamtun**

yamtungga: afflicted with a respiratory ailment

yamulabumbi: (causative of **yamulambi**)

yamulambi: **1**. to go to a *yámen*, to go to a government office; **2**. to go to court

yamulanjimbi: **1**. to come to a *yámen*; **2**. to come to court

yamun: **1**. a government office, *yámen* 衙門, headquarters; **2**. the court, palace

 yamun i wailan: *yámen* attendant

yan: (Chinese) ounce, tael

 yan i ton: weight

yan ho: fireworks

yan siyoo: saltpeter

yandaci: a young badger; cf. **dorgon**

yandubumbi: (causative of **yandumbi**)

yandugan: request, entreaty

yandumbi: to request, to trouble someone to do something, to beg

yandunjimbi: to come to request

yang: *yáng*, the male or positive principle

yang ing: (onomatopoetic) the sound of insects flying

yang seme: ⟶ **yang ing**

yang yang: (onomatopoetic) the sound of bells ringing

yangduwan: foreign satin

yangga: **1**. pine pitch; **2**. a torch made with pine pitch

 yangga tolon: a torch made with pine pitch

yanggaha: carrion crow

yanggali: a kind of dark wagtail

yanggar seme: sounding for a long time, re-echoing, resonant

yanggidei: a name for the golden pheasant; cf. **junggiri coko**

yanggilabumbi: (causative of **yanggilambi**)

yanggilambi: to tease, to incite, to flirt with, to dally with

yanggilandumbi: to tease one another

yanggir iman: a wild sheep of Shaanxi that resembles the female argali

yanggon: bells attached to a horse's forehead

yanggūha: ⟩ **yanggaha**

yanggūwan: sand; cf. **yonggan**

 yanggūwan aisin: alluvial gold, gold dust

yangkambi: to throw to the ground (in wrestling)

yangkūnggalambi: to sing; cf. **yakūnggalambi**

yangmei: **1**. fruit of the plant *Myrica rubra*: Chinese bayberry; **2**. a small red sore on the skin

yangsabumbi: (causative of **yangsambi**)

yangsambi: to weed, to chop weeds

yangsanambi: to go to weed

yangsangga: **1**. comely, beautiful, gorgeous; **2**. possessing literary elegance, refined

yangsanumbi: to weed together

yangse: **1**. form, kind, appearance, model, style; **2**. beauty, comeliness; **3**. beautiful, splendid, comely, ornate; **4**. yoke for an ox

yangselabumbi: (causative of **yangselambi**)

yangselambi: to make up, to decorate

yangsembi: ⟶ **yangselambi**

yangsimu niyehe: sheldrake (*Tadorna tadorna*, a kind of duck)

yangšan: **1**. (minor) sickness, ailment; **2**. noisy, talkative; **3**. dispute, dissension

yangšangga: **1**. noisy, overtalkative, troublesome; **2**. grating on the ears

yangšarabumbi: **1**. (causative of **yangšarambi**); **2**. to make someone impatient, to vex someone

yangšarambi: **1**. to be vexed and impatient (especially of a sick child); **2**. to grate on the ears; **3**. to chatter on and on

yangturi: *Spondias dulcis*: ambarella

yar seme: **1**. flowing in a fine line, trickling; **2**. talking on and on; **3**. long and delicate (said of eyebrows or hair)

yardu: a name for the bustard; cf. **humudu**

yarfun: rein, a long leather cord attached to the headstall or bridle, tether

    yarfun tembi: the reins hang down (said of a horse that cannot remain still)

yarga: ⟶ **yarha**

yargican niyehe: the name of a variety of duck

yargiyakan: rather true, really

yargiyalabumbi: **1**. (causative or passive of **yargiyalambi**); **2**. to be wounded in battle

yargiyalambi: **1**. to ascertain the truth, to verify; **2**. to be wounded in battle

yargiyan: **1**. true, real, genuine, factual; **2**. truth, reality

    yargiyan baita: fact

    yargiyan i: truly, really

    yargiyan kooli: veritable record

    yargiyan mujilen: sincerity, true intention

    yargiyan tašan: the real and imaginary, the true and false, the full and empty

    yargiyan turgun: true situation, facts

yargiyangga: true, honest, factual

yargiyūn: is it true?

yargū: panther; cf. **yarha**

yarha: *Felis pardus*: leopard

    yarha uncehengge girdan: a pennant made from a leopard's tail

yarhūdabumbi: (causative of **yarhūdambi**)

yarhūdai: guide, leader

yarhūdambi: **1**. to lead, to guide; **2**. to entice, to lure

yarhūdan: introduction, guidance

yaribumbi: to have the face and ears freeze

yarju cecike: a name for the hawfinch, the same as **yacin ūn cecike**

yarkiyabumbi: (causative or passive of **yarkiyambi**)

yarkiyambi: **1**. to entice, to lure, to dally with, to decoy; **2**. to tempt

    yarkiyame wambi: to lure someone to his death

    yarkiyame yanggilambi: to dally with, to make unwelcome advances to a woman

    yarkiyara cooha: decoy troops

yarkiyan: **1**. luring, enticement, dalliance; **2**. temptation

yarkiyandumbi: to entice one another

yarsi dambagu: opium; cf. **afiun**

yartan ilha: the name of a blue flower that faces the sun when it blooms — Chinese larkspur (*Delphinium grandiflorum*)

yaru: **1**. a soup made with a kind of frog found in Jilin; **2**. brook char; **3**. ⟶ **yarun**

yarubumbi: (causative or passive of **yarumbi**)

yarudai: 'jade phoenix' — the phoenix of the center

yarugan: **1**. leading; **2**. an added ingredient to an herbal medicine (used to increase its efficacy)

    yarugan i fangse: a banner (at the head of a funeral procession) on which the name and rank of a deceased official was written

    yarugan sejen: the vehicle of a deceased official (used to lead a funeral procession)

yarukū asu: a large-meshed fish net that one lets flow with the current

yarumbi: **1**. to lead, to guide; **2**. to be connected together, to be close together in a row; **3**. to quote, to cite

    yarume: continually, next to one another, successively

    yarume bargiyara edun: the name of the wind that blows from the west after the vernal equinox

    yarume jurume: continually

    yarume okdoro kumun: a piece of music of two strophes that was played during the Emperor's return to the palace after a sacrifice

    yarume yabumbi: to walk in a row

    yarume yarume: one after another, in a row

    yarure morin: a leading horse

    yarure okdoro kumun: ⟶ **yarume okdoro kumun**

    yarure okto: an ingredient added to enhance the efficacy of a medicine; cf. **yarugan**

yarun: **1**. introduction (to a book); **2**. citation; **3**. leading, guiding; **4**. a measure equaling one hundred Chinese feet

yarungga mukšan: a gold-lacquered staff of the Imperial Escort

yarure: ⟶ **yarumbi** (subheading)

yasa: **1**. eye; **2**. a round hole, mesh of a net

    yasa arambi: to wink, to signal with the eye

    yasa bohon: the pupil of the eye is clouded over

yasa darambi: to glare, to look at intently, to scrutinize

yasa durahūn: with eyes staring

yasa dushun: having blurred vision

yasa efebumbi: to lose one's sight

yasa faha: eyeball

yasa faitan: eyebrow

yasa fetembi: to make a round hole in an arrowhead

yasa fulahūn: envious, covetous

yasa gadahūn neimbi: to open the eyes very wide, to bulge the eyes

yasa gedehun neimbi: to open the eyes wide, to gape

yasa gehun holtombi: to lie blatantly

yasa gehun ombi: **1**. to open the eyes wide; **2**. to be reduced to dire need

yasa habtašara sidende: in a wink, in the twinkling of an eye

yasa hadahai tuwambi: to stare at intently

yasa hirandumbi: to have a falling out (said of husband and wife), to become mutually hostile

yasa hošo: corner of the eye

yasa ilhanambi: to have blurred vision

yasa jerkišembi: for eyes to be dazzled

yasa monjirambi: to wipe one's eyes upon awakening

yasa morohon tuwambi: to look with gaping eyes

yasa morombi: to have the eyes wide open

yasa nicumbi: to close the eyes

yasa niowanggiyan: having covetous eyes

yasa sele: pieces of iron attached to the three holes at the bottom of a quiver

yasa silenggi: tears, teardrops

yasa sohimbi: to get something in the eye

yasa šahūn golombi: to be frightened until the eyes turn white

yasa tatambi: **1**. to open the eyes wide; **2**. to act in a proud manner

yasa tuwahai: in an instant, right before one's eyes

yasa wajimbi: to be covetous

yasai buleku: eyeglasses, spectacles

yasai faha: eyeball

yasai hošo: the corner of the eye

yasai humsun: eyelid

yasai hūntahan: the eye socket

yasai jerin: the edge of the eye, the corner of the eye

yasai juleri: before one's very eyes, right now, at present

yasai muke: tear

yasai muke hafirambi: to have tears in one's eyes

yasai muke tuhebumbi: to shed tears, to weep

yasai siden: between the eyes

yasai silenggi: tears caused by wind or some other irritation

yasahangge: provided with small holes or openings

yasalabumbi: (causative or passive of **yasalambi**)

yasalambi: to glance at, to look at, to peer at

yasatabumbi: **1**. to be unable to get any sleep; **2**. to keep a hawk from closing its eyes all night

yasatu hafan: an ancient designation for censors

yasatu hiyan: a kind of incense

yase: middleman, agent

yasha: **1**. netting, screen, grating; **2**. a net woven from the hair of a horse's tail (for catching small birds and animals); **3**. a screen placed on the eaves of the palace to keep birds from nesting there

yasha fa: a window covered with a criss-crossed net-like screen

yashalabumbi: (causative of **yashalambi**)

yashalambi: **1**. to make netting or a screen; **2**. to make lanterns; **3**. to place in a net bag

yashalaha dalangga: a dam with filters

yashalaha huwejen: a kind of delicate screen used in antiquity

yashangga: provided with grillwork

yashangga giyalakū: a grillwork partition

yashangga loho: a sword with grillwork designs on the blade

yashangga uce: a grillwork door

yasuka: an eagle resembling the **isuka** that is found in Liaodong

yatarabumbi: (causative of **yatarambi**)

yatarakū: an instrument for striking a fire, a flint

yatarakū fadu: a bag for flint

yatarakū miyoocan: a flintlock

yatarambi: to strike a fire (with a flint)

yato: ⟶ **yatu**

yatu: female servant, girl slave

yatugan: ⟶ **yatuhan**

yatuhan: zither (a musical instrument with fourteen strings)

yaya: every, each, any

    yaya demun: in every way

    yaya demun i oci okini: let it be as it may

    yaya emu: each one, every one

    yaya ere gese: things like this, such things

    yaya hacin: every kind, every sort

    yaya niyalma: anyone

    yaya we: anyone, any person

    yaya we sehe seme: no matter who

yayadambi: to lisp, to speak unclearly

yayambi: to mumble (an incantation)

ye: the secondary beams of a roof, a small beam

ye ca: demon, yaksha

yebcuke: ⟶ **yebcungge**

yebcun moo: a tree found in the Emei Shan region of Sichuan

yebcungge: pretty, likable, attractive, cute

    yebcungge baita: affair of the heart

    yebcungge hojo: very pretty, attractive

    yebcungge ildamu: romantic, free-spirited

yebe: better, improved (said of an illness)

yebecungge: one who has gotten better, convalescent

yebelembi: to find amusing, to find pleasure in, to esteem (generally used in the negative)

    yebelerakū: not pleased, unhappy with

yebendembi: ⟶ **yebelembi**

yebešembi: ⟶ **yebelembi**

yebešeo: bailiff, constable

yebihen: a ceiling cover made from paper

yebkelembi: to be capable

yebken: **1**. handsome, pretty, beautiful, alluring; **2**. capable, efficient; **3**. fine (said of horses)

    yebken haha: a capable man

    yebken kangkiyan: having outstanding talent, heroic

    yebken morin: a fine horse

    yebken sain: pretty, attractive

    yebken saikan: graceful, elegant, beautiful

yebkengge: talented, heroic

yebkesi: an attractive person, a talented person

yeca: ⟶ **yakca**

yece: a ghost with white hair and bloody wounds, an ogre

    yece hutu: ⟶ **yece**

yecuhe: **1**. the name of a small black fly; **2**. flying ant; **3**. midge

yedun: a deer-head mask worn by deer hunters

yehe: **1**. a tube on the top of a helmet used for attaching a tassel; **2**. the surface of an arrowhead; **3**. white hemp that has been treated in lime water, bleached hemp

yehengge: made of bleached hemp

    yehengge etuku: a mourning garment

    yehengge mahala: a mourning hat

yehere: **1**. porcelain, chinaware; **2**. shell of a snail

    yehere buren: conch, sea snail

    yehere fengse: porcelain basin

    yehere moro: porcelain bowl

    yehere tetun: porcelain vessel

yeherengge: made of porcelain

yehetun: a kiln (for making porcelain)

yeise: coconut

yekembi: to sing erotic songs

yeken akū: lacking talent, lowly, worthless

yekengge: of noble character, commanding respect, noble, grand

    yekengge haha: a man of fortitude and courage, an outstanding man, a noble man

yekerakū: not upright, ignoble

yekeršebumbi: (causative or passive of **yekeršembi**)

yekeršembi: to tease, to make sport of, to mock, to deride

yekse: a shaman's cap

yeksehe: ⟶ **yekse**

yekserhen: house lizard, gecko

yelmen: a name for the sparrowhawk; cf. **silmen**

yelu: boar, male pig

    yelu baimbi: to seek a boar (said of a sow)

yemcen: **1**. ⟶ **imcin**; **2**. ⟶ **yemji**

yemji: **1**. apparition, ghost; **2**. a deity of lakes and rivers — it takes the form of a three-year-old child with long ears, red eyes, and beautiful hair

yemjiri gasha: a name for the owl

yemjitu dobi: the name of a mythical reptile on the Yangtze River

yen: **1**. a mountain path, an animal trail, a winding road in the mountains; **2**. yin — the female principle; cf. **e**

yen hing moo: ginkgo tree

yendebumbi: (causative of **yendembi**)

yendebun: (*xìng* 與) a kind of verse in which natural objects are used to represent feelings

yendembi: to rise, to flourish, to be prosperous

yendehe: flourishing, prosperous

yenden: **1**. ascent, rise; **2**. passion or desire to do something, interest, excitement, ardor

yendengge mudan: the rising tone of classical Chinese phonology

yengge: *Prunus padus*: bird-cherry

yenggehe: small parrot

yenggeheri: bright green, parrot-green

yengguhe: large parrot

yenggūhe: ⟶ **yengguhe**

yenghuhe: a female parrot

yengke menggun: small silver bars of about five ounces in weight

yengsi: a banquet, a bridal banquet

yenju: a mountain path

yenmanggi: soot on the bottom of a pot

yentaha: an ancient bronze vessel for liquor

yentu: **1**. narrow woven belt; **2**. new feathers that grow next to the large wing feathers on a bird; **3**. clothes iron

yentu cecike: the name of a small bird with brown eyes, blackish beak, white stripes over its eyes, speckled feathers, and yellow legs

yerguwe: ⟶ **yerhuwe**

yerhuwe: ant

yertebumbi: (causative or passive of **yertembi**)

yertecuke: shameful, embarrassing

yertecun: shame, embarrassment

yertecun girucun: shame and disgrace

yertembi: to be ashamed, to be embarrassed

yertešembi: to be mortified with shame

yeru: hole, pit, den (said of tigers, panthers, leopards, wildcats, etc.)

yerutu: a stone house used by various aboriginal peoples of South China

yerutu boo: stone house found among the aborigines in South China

yesoro: an exotic apricot-like fruit

yeye: **1**. maggot; **2**. glutinous, sticky; **3**. sticky mud; **4**. annoying, obtrusive; **5**. (paternal) grandfather

yeye bele: glutinous rice

yeye boihon: sticky mud, slush, mire

yeye gisun: annoying talk, importunate speech

yeye handu: ⟶ **yeye bele**

yeye ira: glutinous millet

yeye seshun: annoying and loathsome

yeye šušu: glutinous sorghum

yeyedembi: to speak in a long-winded, annoying manner

yo: **1**. a handful; cf. **sefere**; **2**. one hundredth of a dry quart (**moro**); **3**. ⟶ **yoo**

yobo: **1**. fun, play, game, joking; **2**. cheerful, fun-loving, merry; **3**. merrymaker, mischievous person

yobo arambi: to joke around, to make merry, to make a joke

yobo faksi: witty, clever

yobo gisun: a joke

yobo maktambi: to make someone laugh by amusing talk, to joke

yobo niyalma: a mischievous person, a practical joker

yobodobumbi: (causative or passive of **yobodombi**)

yobodombi: to have fun, to joke, to make sport of

yocambi: to itch, to be bitten by bugs

yodambi: to carry suspended, to carry at one's side (e.g., a basket)

yodan: raincoat, rain cape

yodombi: ⟶ **yodambi**

yodzana: Sanskrit yojana: a measure of distance (from forty to eighty *lĭ*)

yogan: ⟶ **yohan**

yoge: a food offering (in the following expressions)

yoge sindambi: to perform a service for the dead, to perform the ullambana service during which a miniature pagoda made of fruit is scattered by monks

yoge sindara isan: a gathering for the ullambana service

yoge sindara karan: miniature pagoda made from cakes (a kind of offering)

yoge sindara mandal: the place where the ullambana service was performed (a service for the dead)

yohan: silk floss, silk wadding

yohan suri: cloth made from silk floss waste

yohan uksin: padded armor

yohi: **1**. complete, intact, without gaps; **2**. a (complete) set

yohibun: an abbreviated account of something, summary, brief account

yohimbi: (**-ka, -ra/-ndara**) **1**. to form a scab; **2**. to pay heed to, to mind, to pay attention to
  yohindarakū: to look down upon, not to respect
yohingga: whole, entire, made up of sets
yoho: yolk
yohon: water ditch in a field
yohoron: **1**. a waterway in the mountains; **2**. small stream or canal, ditch, channel
  yohoron gocimbi: to expand like a dammed stream (said of fattening horses)
yohoronombi: to form a groove or furrow, to form a channel or waterway
yojin: a name for the peacock; cf. **tojin**
yojoho: itching
yojohošombi: to itch to the point where one cannot bear it any longer
yojombi: to itch; cf. **yocambi**
yokcin: nice appearance, impressive appearance
  yokcin akū: short in stature, unprepossessing, unattractive
  yokcin bakcin akū: ugly, unbecoming
yokcingga: having a good appearance, impressive
yokidun: the (Cantonese) partridge; cf. **jukidun**
yoktakū: ⟶ **yokto akū**
yokto: **1**. proper, suitable, meet; **2**. interest, meaningfulness; **3**. ⟶ **ai yokto**
  yokto akū: **1**. embarrassing, awkward; **2**. embarrassed, feeling put out; **3**. meaningless, uninteresting
  yokto bi: possesses meaning or interest
yoktokū: ⟶ **yokto akū**
yolo: **1**. cinereous vulture (*Vultur monachus*); **2**. a breed of Tibetan dog; **3**. ⟶ **yolo yokto akū**
  yolo indahūn: the name of a dog with a thick head and tail, hanging lips, and big ears
  yolo jahūdai: the name of a boat propelled by a scull at the stern
  yolo yokto akū: very embarrassing, very awkward
yoloju: ⟶ **yolo indahūn**
yolokto: *Dryobates cabanisi*: pied woodpecker
yolonggi: sparks or cinders that fly out from a fire
yolonggo jahūdai: ⟶ **yolo jahūdai**
yombi: (**-ha**) to go, to walk, to leave
yombumbi: ⟶ **yumbumbi**
yon: walking, going

yonambi: **1**. to go there; **2**. to accommodate, to contain, to fit (said of clothing); cf. **yondombi**
yondombi: to hold (said of containers), to contain, to fit, to accommodate
yong seme: stupid, foolish
yonggadun hoošan: sandpaper
yonggaji niyehe: a kind of small gray wild duck
yonggan: sand
  yonggan aisin: low-grade gold, gold dust mixed with sand
  yonggan cibin: *Riparia riparia*: sand martin
  yonggan feteku: the name of a small fish that burrows into the sand
  yonggan mucen: earthenware pot
yonggari: *Malus prunifolia*: Chinese crabapple
yonggor seme: continually, ceaselessly
yongguci: the Yao nationality
yonggūwan: ⟶ **yonggan**
yongkiri coko: a name for the peewit; cf. **niyo coko**
yongkiri inggali: a name for the peewit; cf. **niyo coko**
yongkiyabumbi: (causative of **yongkiyambi**)
yongkiyambi: to be complete, to do completely, to complete
  yongkiyaha niyalma: perfect man
yongkiyan: **1**. completion, perfection; **2**. complete, perfect
  yongkiyan unde: still incomplete
yongkiyangga: complete, perfect
yongsikū: a person who talks foolishly
yongsombi: to lose (at gambling), to be wiped out (at gambling)
yongsu: ceremony, rite, custom, usage
yoni: ⟶ **yooni**
yoo: **1**. sore, skin ulcer; **2**. a kiln; **3**. name of a South Chinese aboriginal people, Yao; **4**. the ace face of dice
  yoo tuhenehe: threw an ace (at dice)
yoohan: ⟶ **yohan**
yoombi: ⟶ **yombi**
yoonambi: to form a sore or skin ulcer
yooni: complete, entire, all together, all
  yooni beye: the entire body
  yooni obumbi: to make whole, to protect
  yooni šošobume acabumbi: to bring together in a single compilation
yooningga: complete, perfect

yooningga dasan: the Tongzhi (同治) reign period, 1862–1874

yoose: lock

yooselabumbi: (causative of **yooselambi**)

yooselambi: to lock, to lock up

yooselarakū umiyesun: a leather belt with a lock

yor seme: in a row, in a file

yordobumbi: (causative or passive of **yordombi**)

yordombi: to shoot a horn or bone-tipped arrow; cf. **yoro**

yoro: **1**. arrow (tipped with horn, bone, or wood) that makes a sound when shot; **2**. rumor, wild talk

yoro baita: useless matter

yoro gisun: rumor, gossip

~~**yoso**: ⟶ **yoose**~~

yoso: principle, rule, doctrine, the accepted way; cf. **doro**

yoson: ⟶ **yoso**

yosu: ⟶ **yoso**

yoto: **1**. foolish, stupid, dull-witted; **2**. fool, moron, idiot, imbecile

yotombi: to go back and forth continually

yoyo: an interjection of derision

yoyombi: (**-ho/-ko**) to be in dire need, to suffer dire poverty

yuburšembi: to crawl (said of worms and insects), to crawl away, to sneak off; cf. **iburšambi**

yukūmbi: ⟶ **ikūmbi**

yumbi: (**-ngke, -mpi**) **1**. to be absorbed, to soak into; **2**. to have a preference for, to have an inclination to; **3**. to become addicted to, to become entranced; **4**. to contain; cf. **yondombi**

yumpi banjinambi: to become addicted

yumpi buyembi: to have an inordinate liking for, to be addicted

yumbu seme: peacefully flowing

yumbu yumbu seme: swarming

yumbumbi: **1**. (causative or passive of **yumbi**); **2**. to soak, to moisten; **3**. to convert to proper behavior, to give guidance

yumk'a: one of the five notes of the classical pentatonic scale sounding like **la**

yumpi: ⟶ **yumbi** (subheading)

yun: rut, track

yunggan: ⟶ **yonggon**

yungge: harmonious, peaceful

yunggioi gasha: the emu

yungturu: fearless, dauntless

yungturu jangkū: a very sharp large sword with a thick back

yur seme: flowing ceaselessly, billowing (said of clouds)

yurudai: the phoenix of the center; cf. **yarudai**

yurun: ⟶ **irun**

yutu: one quadrillionth

yuwamboo: a large bar of silver weighing fifty taels

yuwan: **1**. an inkstone; **2**. an ape; **3**. a kind of large turtle

yuwan aihūma: a kind of large turtle

yuwan boo: ⟶ **yuwamboo**

yuwan pan: (院判) an official in the Board of Colonial Affairs

yuwan siyoo: the lantern festival

yuwanšuwai: commander, marshal

yuwei: battle-ax used in ancient China

yuwei tai: a platform; cf. **celheri**

yuyumbi: (**-he**) to starve, to go hungry

yuyuhe irgen: starving people

yuyure aniya: year of famine

yuyure beyere: hunger and cold, starving and freezing

yuyun: **1**. hunger, starvation; **2**. poor harvest

yuyun omin: famine, starvation

yūn ban: a kind of a cymbal or gong

yūn fu: (運副) Deputy Assistant Salt Controller, *BH* 835A

yūn hiyang: rue

yūn pan: (運判) Sub-Assistant Salt Controller, *BH* 835A

yūn sy yamun i yūn ši: (鹽運司運使) Salt Controller, *BH* 835

yūn tung: (運同) Assistant Salt Controller, *BH* 835A

Ž ㅜ

žan: black gibbon; cf. **sahaldai**

ži ben gurun: Japan

žu lai: Tathāgata, epithet of Buddha used by Buddha when speaking of himself